'Any Australian high school that lacks a copy of this book in its library has ceased to teach Australian history.'

Peter Ryan, *The Weekend Australian*

'They are the custodians of the Australian Digger legend, typified by mateship, compassion and selflessness, forged at Gallipoli . . . Triumphant is the Australian soldier to whom this book is dedicated.'

Christopher Bantick, *The Canberra Times*

'With the skill of a great storyteller, Brune blends these high-level strategic command issues with riveting accounts of combat and its aftermath, often letting soldiers speak for themselves . . . Brune's book is a timely reminder that, despite the warmest alliances, nations sometimes have to stand up and save themselves.'

Geoffrey Barker, *The Weekend Australian Financial Review*

'. . . *A Bastard of a Place* undeniably ranks as the best book ever written about the Aussie battles in Papua . . . Very highly recommended, and certainly one of the best books of the year.'

Bill Stone, Stone & Stone Second World War Books website

'Few are better qualified to write of the Papuan campaign than Brune.'

Chris Brice, *The Advertiser* (Adelaide)

For: Ralph, Harry, Max, Hugh, Bill, Theo and Andy . . . all sadly gone now, but all of such critical help. And to Cedric and Bert, who picked up their baton, and inspired me to keep running with it.

PETER BRUNE

A BASTARD

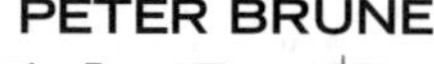

OF A PLACE

THE AUSTRALIANS IN PAPUA

KOKODA

MILNE BAY

GONA

BUNA

SANANANDA

First edition published in 2003
This edition published in 2004

Allen & Unwin
83 Alexander Street
Crows Nest NSW 2065
Australia
Phone: (61 2) 8425 0100
Fax: (61 2) 9906 2218
Email: info@allenandunwin.com
Web: www.allenandunwin.com

National Library of Australia
Cataloguing-in-Publication entry:

ISBN 1 74114 403 5

A catalogue record for this book is available from the National Library

Maps by MAPgraphics
Set in 11.5/13pt Bembo by Midland Typesetters, Victoria
Printed by South Wind Productions, Singapore
10 9 8 7 6 5 4 3 2 1

CONTENTS

ACKNOWLEDGMENTS

This book is the culmination of fourteen years' work, five previous books, the material from a PhD thesis, and much previously unused research concerning the Papuan Campaigns. It is also the valued chance to reflect upon those previous works and material for a book that attempts to cover the whole Papuan Campaign. Along that lengthy journey many veterans and colleagues have given tireless help and great encouragement.

The late Lieutenant-Colonel Ralph Honner's contribution to this book is enormous: he proofread much of the Kokoda and Gona material during the late 1980s and early 1990s, offered great encouragement and vital interviews and, above all, would have greatly supported the concept of a work on the whole Papuan Campaign. Although this book arrives some nine years after his passing, his influence has been both ongoing, and inspirational.

Similar Kokoda and Gona guidance and inspiration also came from the late Harry Katekar, the late Hugh Dalby, the late Max Bidstrup, the late Geoff Cooper, the late Ken Murdoch, the late Keith Goldsmith, the late John Hearman and Stan Bisset.

The Milne Bay and Buna–Sanananda material owes much of its substance to the late Bill Spencer, the late Theo Schmedje, the late John 'Andy' Andrews and the late Allan Kumnick. All of these veterans offered detailed interviews, astute proofreading, and great advice and encouragement. Their influence upon this work, even in their absence, has been monumental.

Throughout the many years of travelling and interviewing, I have received great assistance and support from

Battalion secretaries, presidents and other officials who have gathered their comrades together, and continually liaised with them on my behalf. Their influence, goodwill and inspiration are greatly appreciated: Noel and Erica Hall, 39th Battalion; John Stirling, 2/14th Battalion; Glen Williss, 2/27th Battalion; the late Ken Murdoch, 2/16th Battalion; the late Fred Cranston, 49th Battalion; the late Frank Budden, 53rd Battalion; Keith Irwin, 53rd and 36th Battalions; Noel Worton, 61st Battalion; Ernie Bain, 25th Battalion; Frank McCosker and David Radford, 9th Battalion; the late Allan Kumnick, 2/10th Battalion; Norm Foster, 2/10th Battalion; Bruce Martin, 2/9th Battalion; Angus Suthers and Roy Rodgers, 2/12th Battalion; and Cec Ganderton, 2/6th Armoured Regiment.

Sadly, the great majority of the oral history presented in this book has been provided by veterans who have since passed on. I am proud to record that their voices have not. Over 250 hours of their Papuan recollections are now in the capable hands of George Imashev, Curator of Sound and Film at the Australian War Memorial. I thank George for his help and assistance on numerous occasions.

To Professor David Horner I owe a great debt: his groundbreaking work and writing on the Australian High Command, and Australian military history generally, has been of enormous assistance to me. His astute advice and willing assistance are most gratefully acknowledged and appreciated. I also greatly appreciate David's permission for me to quote from his many works and his discussion of many of the subjects contained within them.

To Neil McDonald I owe an enormous debt: we have collaborated on *200 Shots: Damien Parer, George Silk and the Australians at war in New Guinea*; Neil's tireless support, our not infrequent exchanges of material and his friendship are greatly acknowledged and appreciated. I also thank Neil for permission to quote from his *War Cameraman: The story of Damien Parer.*

I also thank Bill Edgar for his ongoing assistance and friendship through our mutual interest in the Kokoda Campaign and great admiration for Brigadier Arnold Potts. Bill's permission to quote from his *Warrior of Kokoda* is also appreciated. Clive Baker has provided great encouragement and offered material for the Milne Bay section of the work. I also thank him for permission to quote from his *Milne Bay 1942*.

I thank Dr Peter Stanley, of the Australian War Memorial, for his kind permission to quote from the Official Histories, and to the Australian War Memorial for permission to use their photographs throughout this work; Associate Professor Brian Dickey of the Flinders University of South Australia, for his enthusiasm, encouragement and expert supervision of my PhD thesis; David Lewis for our chance meeting at Buna, for his advice concerning pre-war Papua, and for his book *The Plantation Dream*; I acknowledge Dudley McCarthy, the Official Historian; Raymond Paull, and his *Retreat from Kokoda* as being substantial previous works that have made the task of more recent historians much easier; and, I wish to thank Professor Hank Nelson for his tolerance of my harassment of him by phone.

To Lieutenant-Colonel Cedric Issachsen, 2/27th and 36th Battalions, and Private Bert Ward, 2/27th Battalion, I owe a debt I shall never be able to repay. Their astute advice, their rigorous proofreading, their constant encouragement, and their cheerfulness and enthusiasm for this project have inspired the author.

I owe Frank Taylor, of Kokoda Treks and Tours, an enormous debt. In July 2002, Frank organised a trek of the Kokoda Trail that I shall never forget. My every wish was facilitated, including a visit to Myola, and extra time at Brigade Hill, Isurava and Kokoda. Helicopters, village elders and his personal staff were always on hand when needed and his own considerable knowledge always available. In October 2002, Frank organised my Beachhead tour. Four-wheel drive vehicles, accommodation, expert guides and my complete timetable and wish list were magnificently accommodated. I hope and trust that a multitude of Australians will see the extreme benefit and joy of Milne Bay and Gona–Buna–Sanananda tours as being every bit as much a tour through our history as Kokoda already is. I sincerely thank Shane Scanlan, Mark Ryan, Carl Kitchen, Louise Fitzgerald, Rys Jenkins, Christina (Josephine) Kruger and Tony Onley for their wonderful company and friendship on the Kokoda Trail—friends always. I thank Sue Field of Kokoda Treks and Tours for her assistance at Myola and Brigade Hill; and last, but by no means least, I thank Adrian Koe of Kokoda Treks and Tours ('Don't call me Sir, Adrian, call me Peter.' 'Yes Sir!') for his work as a guide on the Kokoda Trail and particularly his expert assistance and company at the Beachhead. Thanks also to Tim, Mathias and all the wonderful carriers of Kokoda Treks and Tours.

I should like to record my appreciation to Vicki Neville of Milne Bay Magic Tours for her kind hospitality and wonderful guided tour of the Milne Bay battlefields.

To my publisher, Ian Bowring, I hope and trust that the following pages will do justice to the confidence and trust and hard work that he has given the project; to Alex Nahlous of Allen & Unwin I owe a great debt for her professionalism and patience and encouragement; and, to their colleagues at Allen & Unwin who have helped the cause, I say a sincere thankyou.

I am greatly indebted to my partner Meredith for her patience and encouragement; my daughter Kylie who remains the inspiration for all that I do; and to my mother Bea Brune (1921–2003) whose support and encouragement I will miss always.

It should be appreciated that despite all of the help and encouragement of others, the conclusions reached in *A Bastard of a Place* are not necessarily those of other persons. I gladly stand by what I have written.

Last, I would thank the Australian soldier who fought in Papua during 1942–43. I hope this book will be seen as some fair and accurate assessment of his greatness.

Peter Brune
Adelaide
September 2003

MAPS

Brotherhood never was like it;
Friendship is not the word;
But deep in that body of marching men
The soul of a nation stirred.

Australia Today 1916

A.B. 'Banjo' Paterson, 1916

PART ONE

KOKODA

The soul of a nation stirred . . .

SPREADING THE OIL

1

The Australian digger moved in for the final fight. He looked at his mates. During torrential tropical downpours, they'd worn their rubberised ground sheets as capes and looked like gaunt, shining grey ghosts as they slowly waded through waist-high swamps. The lethargic flow of the brackish water had also borne the incomplete, maggot-infested Japanese corpses to softly nudge them or float slowly past. If you needed a shit here, you didn't have toilet paper, so you wiped your arse with your hand or sand or leaves and then washed it in the swamp. You took your socks off only when clean socks arrived—they'd had only one change. And hungry! Just one feed a day. To all who fought here, this was a bastard of a place.

Their otherwise silent passage out of the swamp was accompanied by the unmusical yet rhythmic sound of weary, almost unwilling, booted feet being withdrawn from oozing mire.

This area seemed to be a base hospital. Only the sick and the dying appeared to await them. They came to a timber-framed square hut, with thick earthwork up to about waist height, and an Australian .303 rifle pointing out on each side. Moving cautiously inside, they saw four emaciated Japanese huddled together. Etched in the digger's mind was the fear that whatever the condition of any enemy soldier, it was probable that he had a concealed bayonet or grenade and that he expected to die, wanted to die, and would use any ruse to take an Australian with him—death was preferable to surrender. Three of the Japanese had maggots in their mouths and eyes, while the fourth just lay with his eyes shut. The digger belted that fourth soldier on the head, his eyes opened with a start, and one of the digger's mates shot him.

The Australians then moved off to a half-finished dugout paradoxically raised above ground level. Another enemy lay across it. The digger lent over and took hold of the man's watch. His wrist moved and so the Australian's mate shot him too. They rolled the enemy soldier over and found an unexploded grenade. On to the next hut. This one was only partly built—a timber frame with ground sheets over it. Inside was a Japanese naked from the waist up, with his helmet on his lap and a grenade held to his sternum. For a moment that seemed an eternity, the two men stared into each other's eyes. As the grenade exploded and the enemy's chest caved in, the digger instinctively turned around and searched the remaining huts for movement. A few heads bobbed up and one man sat bolt upright. He was in full uniform with helmet, rifle and bayonet. In a flash the heads disappeared from view. The diggers moved methodically forward and fired shots into them. Kill all of the bastards, trust not one of them and get this nightmare over with.

Later that day the Australian was wounded and evacuated. The date was 22 January 1943. The last bastion had fallen and, with its capture, the Japanese invasion of Papua which had been halted at Milne Bay and along the Kokoda Trail, and all but smashed on the northern beachheads of Gona and Buna, was brought to its final and irretrievable conclusion here at nearby Sananda.

One of the wounded digger's mates went to a church parade a day or so later. He knelt down and quietly observed the ritual. But after a while he stood up. The priest looked up with a disapproving stare, but the soldier merely shook his head and walked away. During that split second, the digger had lost his faith, and had come to believe that there was no one out there to help him and care for him but himself.[1]

When Australians talk of the men who saved Australia in 1942–43, of that time in their history when they also had to stand alone and help themselves, who fought not for the birth of a nation, but for its very rites of passage, it has become fashionable to visualise a wounded Australian being carried over a famous trail by Papuan carriers with fuzzy wuzzy hair. But Kokoda's glory constitutes but one-fifth of the Australian legend of Papua during 1942. It is an integral part of that legend, but not its whole. This is the story of Milne Bay, Gona, Buna and Sananandaa as well. But also, it is the sad saga of a nation still ignorant of this great Australian legend, still largely unaware of the feats of some of its most deserving military commanders and the soldiers they served. In some measure, regrettably, it is the story of others who have been accorded undue praise.

First impressions are often misleading. As you fly closer to the airport, you notice the brown, bare hills. Your attention is drawn to a number of small, swirling spot fires dotted around the width of your vision. The locals are playing with matches or lighters again. You will get used to this. No real rhyme or reason to it. On many a Port Moresby street corner the same phenomenon is in progress. Litter, and there's an abundance of it, is piled and set alight. Perhaps it's ingrained in them: clear the land, leave it to dry, burn, plant, reap, and move on. But even if you're not going to perform this ancient cycle, you light a spot fire anyway. Ingrained. Your first impression of Port Moresby, the capital of Papua New Guinea.

And then you see the forbidding monster in the background. Not mere hills these, but a towering, mist-peaked, purple-blue mountainous wall: the Owen Stanley Range. Many Australians are not familiar with this name, but most will have at least a vague concept of the trail that winds its way over it to a distant outpost called Kokoda.

You land. Wait awhile. There's a vine on the Kokoda Trail called lawyer vine (wait awhile). Get caught up in lawyer vine and its associated prickles, and you do indeed wait awhile. This botanical marvel seems to have woven its way throughout the entire population. Wait awhile—so they do. The most menial task is accomplished at a pedestrian pace. Check in or out at the airport and you're at the mercy of a tired computer system prone to break down with monotonous regularity. The staff are used to it. Looks of resignation. Never mind, wait awhile. Days later, and in different surroundings, you will learn to love this Papuan pace of existence.

The motel bus picks you up or, if the driver forgets, you take a cab. This vehicle, and many others in line, would immediately cop a defect notice in any city or town in Australia. Severely cracked headlight, evidence of numerous accidents, suspension in name only and a boot that only just surrenders on the fourth attempt to a bent key. As the barefooted driver explains that it's his first day on the job, you're already missing his Turkish counterpart in Sydney.

A few hundred yards out of Jackson's Airport, you spot the first billboard: on it a warning in pidgin followed by the third-world reaper in bold type, 'AIDS'. A few more hundred yards and another billboard: 'Corruption Is Killing Papua New Guinea'. Not spot fires these, but raging infernos. AIDS and corruption.

Ahead trucks, small buses, utes and wagons abound. You get the impression that one would not make a living selling family or business sedans here. People travel en masse and every conceivable space is occupied as their vehicles disappear behind palls of smoke that would have done a naval smokescreen proud. The motel. You pay the driver and stand at the boot for your luggage. But the bent key has been bent once too often. As the unlocking ritual continues, you notice the betel nut (*buai*) sales across the road. The nuts are arranged on a small mat on the ground. They are about the size of a squash ball and yellow and green in colour. Hands reach through the fence, money changes hands, and the nut, mustard or pepper stick (*daka*) and small container of lime (*kambang*) are passed back. The lime is derived from crushed coral or shells. Bite the outer casing off the nut, combine the ingredients, chew well, and enjoy. The effect of betel nut chewing on a Papuan is rather like a *dim dim* (a Caucasian) having a few beers. The nut produces a red, pasty lining around the chewer's gums and on their teeth. After further chewing, a casual spit to the road or footpath (the end result of many passers-by is rather like a modern art canvas), and the social drug has been consumed.

Back to your luggage. Wait awhile. The driver's an adaptable creature. He's lying inside the taxi with a screwdriver and pulls the back seat out and retrieves your bags from the boot, across the dismembered seat, out of the rear door and into your grateful hands. You pass through the now opened gate and notice the razor wire around a high, graffitied fence. Nothing new about this you will soon discover; the sale of razor wire and high fences and the career opportunities for security guards are booming in Port Moresby. The people of that city do not have the safety net of social security. Many of them will have left their regional villages and therefore much of their family structure and mutual support systems. In Port Moresby they must survive on whatever they can earn from menial, spasmodic jobs—or perhaps, for some of them, from other less legitimate pursuits. To many of these people, their lives are a complex meeting of the traditional and the modern. This is 'new Port Moresby'. 'Old Port Moresby' is down around the extensive harbour and constitutes the prewar and early postwar dimensions of the city. It is an impressive and relatively picturesque area: there are homes, apartments and places of business that would do many Australian cities proud. The Australians and Europeans—and some Papuans—live there. On the edge of the harbour sits the yacht club, which is a magnificent mooring for long lines of plush vessels and an equally plush clubhouse. No spot fires, extensive litter, graffiti or betel nut sales here. Two understandably different worlds and, arguably, a poor introduction to a land and a people of such breathtaking beauty and charm.[2]

The tourist town of Alotau, at Milne Bay, is about forty minutes by plane east of Port Moresby. As you descend through the cloud cover, you sit enthralled by a vivid, green, tropical paradise: row after orderly row of thick palm trees which appear as though nature's gardener has taken to them with a giant hedge clipper and made a systematic, dense and manicured garden. This runs right up to the tarmac and virtually surrounds it. As you check in there are two now inevitable signs: 'No Smoking' and 'No Betel Nut Chewing'. You drive to your motel along a picturesque narrow road, enclosed at most places by a wall of jungle or palms. The locals wave, smile and sing 'oooohhh' in chorus. Their local language does not contain the word 'goodbye', and so 'oooohhh' suffices. To the near north lies the rugged but attractive Stirling Range, while to the most immediate south is the stunning Milne Bay, bordered by a continuous, narrow, black-sanded beach with its vivid vegetation running right up to it. The bay's stark mountains are shrouded in a swirling mist and cloud cover. Alotau is built on the rise of a hill and is in three parts: High Town, Middle Town and Low Town. Prior to 1942 there was no town, but as that fateful year approached, Milne Bay, like Port Moresby, was to assume monumental significance to the defence of Australia.[3]

Papua New Guinea lies a mere 150 miles from mainland Australia. It is positioned just south of the equator with its main island constituting over four-fifths of its land mass and the remainder being made up of a further six hundred islands of varying size. The main island is dominated by a rugged east–west central mountain spine with peaks at times reaching more than 13 000 feet. Intersecting this dominant feature are numerous rushing rivers and creeks which have produced, along with volcanic action, areas of rich soil inland and along parts of the coastal lowlands. The vegetation in the highlands is dominated by thick tropical rainforest, jungle and man-made grasslands. These are the by-product of centuries of burning, clearing and planting and the resultant regrowth of vegetation. Along parts of the coastline the ground is dominated by grassland and swamps. From the air the terrain appears to be rugged, impenetrable, and inhospitable.

The climate of Papua is hot and humid and dominated by high rainfall all year long. The wet season is usually between October and May and, apart from Port Moresby, which is in a rain shadow, the rainfall is very high indeed—especially by Australian standards. (Milne Bay, for example, has an annual rainfall of some 200 inches.) The temperature and humidity in the highlands is high during the day, but can plunge during the nights, while the coastal lowlands remain hot and humid all year round.

The fact that there were at least seven hundred different languages in the country prior to the onset of the Second World War demonstrates both the isolation and therefore the diversity of the people—a direct consequence of the nature of its geography.[4] In hundreds of isolated little parts of the country small clans or tribes of people existed and were based on 'kinship through blood, marriage, or adoption'.[5] The term 'village' is misleading in its Papuan context: such groups lived in as small a group as three or four families, while others might be a part of a hundred or more family units. All clans had access to their land on which subsistence crops were grown: taro, yam, sago, sweet potato, bananas and the various leaves of numerous vegetables. Meat was procured from the hunting or catching of marsupials, reptiles, fish and pigs. The land was used through an almost ageless cycle: clear, allow to dry, burn, plant, reap and move on within the bounds of your land; allow the soil to rest and repeat the cycle.

The system that bound the people of a clan or tribe together was—and still is—*wantok*, which is the pidgin word for 'one talk'. Thus, language and the kinship derived from it provided the Papuans with their welfare system. Wantoks provided food, goods, hospitality and additional security, and functioned on the basis of unqualified reciprocity. A critical component of the wantok system was—and still is—'payback'. Payback is the retribution exacted from other clans for a perceived wrong. It may have to do with disputes over such issues as land, women or goods. In the case of women the conflict might be concerned with the non-payment of 'bride price', the agreed price payable in goods for the marriage between a man of one clan or tribe and a woman from another. Payback was also the cause of continual warfare between clans. Wars and even skirmishes would continue until equality of suffering or of material loss was agreed upon. Sometimes formal compensation was paid. In some regions, war was as much a test of manhood as it was a means of resolving disputes, or in other cases, it was as a means for supporting allied clans who had grievances. On occasions, cannibalism was practised (often for no other reason than the need for protein). Women might be taken during such confrontations and forced to marry into the victor's clan, or they might be used in intermarriage to strengthen the relationship between clans in a given region. Accompanying the use of war as a means of payback, was the use of sorcery as a commonly employed tool of revenge. Until the advent of white influence in Papua New Guinea, trading took the form of travel and exchange by sea for coastal and island dwellers and, inland, the interchange of goods between clans in the same or nearby regions. The stone axe, bamboo knife, bow and arrow, the spear, the sling and the gardening stick were the most common implements of war and/or agriculture.

By early November 1884, New Guinea had been divided into three areas of European rule: on 3 November of that year the north-eastern section was proclaimed a German protectorate; three days later the south-eastern section became a British protectorate; and the western half of the island remained under Dutch control as part of the Dutch East Indies. In 1906 the British dependency became an Australian territory and was duly named Papua. With the advent of the Great War, Australia seized from the Germans the northern portion of the eastern half of the mainland and New Britain and the islands from Bougainville to the Admiralties. The Australian Prime Minister William Morris Hughes, using the great sacrifice of his countrymen during the First World War as a strong bargaining tool at the Peace Conference at Versailles, managed to secure an Australian mandate over the former German possessions. The mandate began in 1920, and during the following year, the Australians established a civil administration over it. To claim land and send administrators to Papua and the mandated territory was one thing; to subdue the people and nurture the dream of wealth and prestige for Australia had already been shown in Papua to be no small task.

The period of Papuan history from 1906 to the onset of the Second World War was dominated by its Lieutenant-Governor Sir Hubert Murray. Murray was born into an Irish Catholic family in the Sydney suburb of Manly on 29 December 1861. A law graduate from Oxford University, he journeyed to Papua as the administration's Chief Judicial Officer in 1904.[6] When Australia took control over Papua in 1906, a Royal Commission was established to examine the administration of its new protectorate and the feasibility of expanding its economic development. The commission saw two seemingly impressive opportunities: to compete for a share of the world market in such tropical commodities as rubber, copra, hemp and tobacco; and, secondly, to exploit available mining resources. The two key issues confronting the Royal

Commission were how best to deal with white land tenure and how to utilise the indigenous people as a cheap labour supply.[7]

Murray chose to allow whites the opportunity to lease land for the purpose of mining or for plantation production. His conditions of lease were most liberal: no payments were required for the first ten years if the lease was taken over a period of thirty years or more. Speculation on land leases was made difficult by relatively strict development time frames with some leeway granted in cases where difficulty could be demonstrated. The only organisation that could actually purchase land was the Government, and in so doing, its officials had to satisfy themselves that the natives were both prepared to sell the land and that it was 'not required or likely to be required by the native owners themselves'.[8] In this generous policy—generous mainly to the whites—Murray understood that attractive incentives must be available to attract European settlers who might otherwise see equal opportunity in Australia without the hardship of life in Papua.[9] His policy had the desired effect: within four short years of the Royal Commission and within two years of his governorship, there were around 360 000 acres under lease and by 1910 around 140 plantations in Papua.[10] Mining in Papua centred mainly around gold and copper. It was often the story of fruitful but brief finds in such places as Yodda (near Kokoda), Misima in the Trobriand Islands and at the Lukekamu River.

Mines and plantation development in any colonial setting required cheap, indigenous labour. In Papua, Murray presided over a system whereby the natives signed on as indentured labourers for a period of usually eighteen months or three years. The indenture usually involved up to a 50-hour week with Sundays off; the plantation owner was required to provide adequate shelter and food; the pay was usually ten shillings a month; discipline was maintained in the long term by the planter's ability to bring the labourer to the district magistrate, who might inflict a gaol sentence or, in the short term, the plantation manager or one of his assistants might administer an on the spot retribution—a kick in the posterior or a 'box in the ears'; and at the conclusion of the indenture, the labourer had to be paid his wage in full in front of a district magistrate. John Dademo Waiko notes:

> The work was hard, the diet uninteresting, and there was little justice. But there is much evidence that labourers went back to their villages much bigger and physically healthier than when they left. They brought back with them knives, axes, tin dishes, tin whistles, pieces of cloth, kerosene lamps, and many other things which had a significant effect on the lives of the villagers.[11]

Just prior to and during the 1920s, as the majority of the young Australian soldiers who were destined to fight in this land called Papua were being born, Murray was busily engaged in both exploring that land and subduing its people, and also encouraging what the author David Lewis has called 'The Plantation Dream'.[12]

The early years of Murray's administration were marked by the technique of deploying small patrols to pierce and pacify the interior. Such patrols crisscrossed the geography of their division and were small by design: usually one European officer, anywhere between six and a dozen Papuan police officers and their associated carriers. These men were instructed to fire on local tribesmen only when attacked first, and were further required to compile a report after each patrol. Murray likened his policy to the 'oil-stain' policy in use in Indo-China: 'A post or station was like a spot of oil which slowly expanded up to a certain point when dropped upon a surface; if enough drops fell, then the whole area would be covered by their slowly widening to merge with each other.'[13]

By the onset of the war, there were nine divisions of administration in Papua, with each staffed by a resident magistrate, an assistant magistrate and a patrol officer under him. In an attempt to provide a more permanent government influence in the villages, Murray employed the use of a village constable and/or councillors to adjudicate between opposing individuals or groups. This measure met with mixed results: at Milne Bay and in the Trobriand Islands the results were encouraging, while in a number of other areas such personnel tended to usurp the influence of the tribal or regional 'big man' or chief.[14]

By the onset of the Second World War, Murray's 'oil' had spread if not 'merged': large areas of the mandated territory were still 'under influence', while most of Papua was loosely considered to be 'under control'.

Prior to Murray's 'oil-stain' the Christian Missions had been busily engaged in creating their own influence in Papua. At a conference in Port Moresby in 1890, the then administrator of Papua, in cooperation with a number of the missions, created regions of influence: the London Missionary Society took the southern coast; the Anglican Mission took the north coast; the Methodists the eastern islands; and although they were not represented at the conference, the Catholics later acquired Yule Island and the mainland region opposite (approximately 60 miles north-west of Port Moresby); and the Seventh-Day Adventists eventually became established along the Kokoda Trail. During the early 1930s this system of areas of influence began to break down, but the earlier agreement had given the participants ample time to strongly establish their chosen areas.

While Murray had been grappling with the administration of Papua and the Mandated Territory and encouraging its economic development, the white plantation owners and managers had been immersed in the practical application of his and their dream. Papua was not like India or Malaya:

> . . . comfortable hotels, cars, trains in which one could travel in comfort, instead of the long journeys—per boot—that had been the usual method of travel in Papua . . . every district had its little club, with its billiard table, tennis courts, reading room, etc . . . How different the lot of the Papuan planter! Not his blocks of ice, the daily paper, mails and cold storage goods delivered each morning; nor when his day's work was done could he get into his car, and spend his evening with others of his kind.[15]

The Papuan prewar white planter was essentially an adventurer seeking his or her fortune in one of the last frontiers: isolated, vulnerable, and without an infrastructure of modern transport and technology and creature comforts. They were men like Herbert Kienzle, who had arrived in Papua in 1927 as an assistant manager and, when joined by his brother

Wallace and his father in 1936, had settled at Yodda near Kokoda as a planter and miner.[16] Or men like Doctor Geoffrey Vernon, who had served on Gallipoli during the Great War, had suffered acute deafness as a result of a shell burst, and had, postwar, sought his fortune as a doctor and planter at Daru in western Papua. Such planters toiled long and hard and in great isolation for little reward. Although they had odd years of good prices and modest profits, the ambition of viable Papuan rubber, copra and sugar industries remained an elusive aspiration. The white planter struggled between the wars against declining world markets and competition against other tropical producers who were closer to the markets and often operating with imported labour—and more modern and accessible transport systems. In essential terms their 'plantation dream' had not in any real measure been realised. But even tougher times lay ahead.

Murray died barely two years before the Pacific War came to Papua. When that war came, it came with a rapidity of defeat and brutality that was to shock the western world and its associated notions of white supremacy.

From a Papuan perspective, it mattered little whether the war intruded into the village setting, or upon the indentured labourer conscripted into the carrier lines, or the policeman who had joined the Papuan Infantry Battalion or, for that matter, upon the press-ganged carrier with the Japanese, because this conflict would be fought on their land, with all the associated by-products of twentieth-century warfare. These people were to suffer the destruction of non-combatant human life, war atrocities, the loss of property and, tragically, the frequent ruination of their gardens and therefore their very existence. The Papuans would become immortalised, if vaguely, as the fuzzy wuzzy angels.

For the white planter, miner, district magistrate, or patrol officer—and sometimes the missionary—their local knowledge of the terrain and the indigenous people was to prove invaluable. Together with the natives, these white adventurers were to become an intriguing substitute for the modern infrastructure of war.

But before the war there was no real Australian interest in Papua. There was a lack of economic endeavour and consequent poor financial gain caused by a paucity of funding and protective legislation. There was the ruggedness of the land itself. And there was deep cultural ignorance and an unawareness of Papua's strategic significance. Australian policy and Australians themselves were looking elsewhere.

THE DEEP THINKERS

2

The recruit stepped forward to be allotted his role in the battalion. As the officer looked the man up and down, it was his physical appearance that determined his fate. Above-average height and a powerful build were the necessary physical attributes of a member of an infantry battalion's mortar platoon, as the base plate, bipod, barrel and the mortar bombs themselves were heavy and cumbersome. When the officer asked whether he would like to be a mortar man, the recruit replied, 'Mortar, brick laying, anything you like boss.'[1]

Private George 'Babe' Luscombe had come from Port Pirie to enlist in the 2/27th Battalion, Second AIF. He came to fight this bloke called Hitler whose army had stopped the 'phoney war' in Europe by invading the Low Countries. The game was up and something had to be done. Luscombe could not have contemplated that he was destined to mortar Frenchmen and not Germans, and that he would later give his life only a few hundred miles from mainland Australia near an Anglican Mission on the north coast of Papua New Guinea called Gona—on Australian soil.

The Australian society that nurtured the young men who fought in Papua New Guinea during the period July 1942 to January 1943 bears little resemblance to the Australia of the new millennium. But the changes wrought by the Pacific War in which they fought were so monumental, so pivotal and so dramatic that they changed the nation forever.

Most of them were born in an Australia which had been a federated nation for only a handful of years. If 1 January 1901 was the official date of the creation of the Australian nation, then 25 April 1915 was the occasion of its spiritual birth. The landing at Anzac Cove in Gallipoli was seen as that critical moment when six states and a territory really became a nation. The subsequent sacrifice of the flower of Australia's youth on the Western Front in France during the remainder of the First World War gave the nation a solemn sense of loss, but a surge of nationalistic pride, and there was scarcely a child who would not grow up 'in sight of a war memorial or honour board in town, or school or church'.[2] These young Australians were also taught that the Great War had been the war to end all wars.

The onset of the 1920s saw a postwar rush of patriotism, pride and confidence that was expressed in many ways: the expansion of the nation's iron and steel industry; an impressive capital works program of harbour development; bridge building and road construction; and ambitious programs of land settlement, migration and the development of the nation's resources. In short, the theory—pursued by the Bruce Government during the period 1923–29—was that increased capital works programs would facilitate a modern and efficient transport network and therefore lower production costs, which would make exports more competitively priced. By developing the nation's resources, enlarging its industries, providing the necessary labour force through a migration policy, and aggressively seeking larger markets through lower costs, the economy, protected by tariffs, would expand.[3] The migration policy and the funding for such programs was primarily imperial by nature.[4] In the economic sense, the 1920s were essentially the years of borrow, build, protect and prosper, and were a reflection of a supreme Australian optimism.

Amongst the heroes of the 1920s were the aviators, who seemed to somehow shorten the vast distances between Australia and the rest of the world: on 28 February 1928 Bert Hinkler smashed the previous time of just under 30 days for a flight from England to Australia, while Kingsford Smith and Charles Ulm became the first aviators to cross the Pacific when they landed the *Southern Cross* at Brisbane on 9 June

1928, after an epic flight of three days, ten hours and forty-two minutes.

The 1920s were also characterised by a rapidly increasing materialism and social progress. When Holden's Motor Body Builders Ltd gained the exclusive rights to build their car bodies on imported chassis from the United States in 1924, the days of the horse and cart were numbered. The following year the Melbourne Cup was broadcast on radio for the first time, with the winner appropriately named Windbag, while a wide range of other household appliances gradually found their way into an increasing number of homes. And sound found its way into full-length motion pictures with Al Jolson's *The Jazz Singer* in 1928. So popular was this new medium that Hoyts in Melbourne converted twenty suburban theatres so that audiences could experience the magic of the 'talkies'.

When, in 1927, the Duke and Duchess of York opened the first session of the Commonwealth Parliament in Australia's new capital of Canberra, it was as if the world was coming to Australia. As for the rest of the globe, Australians took little interest in world affairs because they 'knew in their hearts that Australia, by tradition and sentiment, and by necessity or expediency, was bound to Britain'.[5] And this notion was taught and instilled into young Australians, who were soon unwittingly destined to fight in defence of their own soil.

When you examine atlases used by these young students in school in the 1920s or 1930s, it is as if the world was sharply divided, with few exceptions, between the pivotal nations of Europe and the vast, far-flung territories they had discovered, conquered or settled.[6] The Australian in school during these times saw not Indonesia but the Dutch East Indies; not Malaysia but Malaya and Singapore; not Thailand but Siam; the Philippine Islands had '(United States)' written beneath them; there was French Indo-China, with Vietnam labelled as Annam; and, critically, they proudly noted that stretching from Australia westwards to India—the shining jewel of the British Empire—quite a significant portion of this part of the world was coloured in red—it was British.[7]

It is not surprising that they knew little and cared less about the region that their children and grandchildren now call South-East Asia. And their history lessons, be they in primary school, or central school,[8] or high school, taught them about 'mother' and about how 'mother' had acquired these large and small red 'blobs' around the globe. It was all 'terribly' British. The South Australian primary school syllabus of the time—many of these future soldiers only attended primary school—covered the following topics: The Romans in Britain; The Coming of the English; Alfred and the Saxon Kingdom; The Norman Conquest; The Crusades; The Magna Carta; Growth of Parliament; The Hundred Years War; The Early Tudors; The Elizabethan Period—Shakespeare, Drake, Raleigh, Grenville; The Struggle Between King and Parliament—Pym, Hampton, Cromwell; Expansion of The British Empire—Wolfe, Clive; The Struggle for World Power—Wellington, Nelson, Napoleon; The British Dominions and Their Heroes, India: Havelock, Lawrence, Roberts, South Africa: Cecil Rhodes, Egypt: General Gordon, Kitchener; The Empire and The Great War. And after they had finally struggled through The League of Nations and a table of sovereigns and some important events, they concluded with Historical Novels for Supplementary Reading.[9]

In the last years of his life, one of those schoolboys, Bill Spencer, would remember that: 'Britain was our ideal, if it was British it was best: the substantial red shadings on any world map seemed ample proof of this and gave us great confidence.'[10]

If the pride and patriotism of the Great War had provided the impetus for the boom years and confidence of the 1920s, then the Great Depression of 1929–33 attacked the fundamental assumptions of Australian society: that personal security could be assured by 'hard work, self-reliance, independence, mateship, family solidarity and compassion for your fellows'.[11] The Depression in some cases destroyed those beliefs, in others it severely challenged them. It was as if your future was not in your hands any more, and that there were international forces of doom operating that were too powerful for you to control. At the height of the Great Depression, one in every three Australian workers was unemployed—this simple ratio becomes more stark when the figure of one million unemployed Australians is contemplated out of a total population of little more than 6.5 million.

By Australian social welfare standards of the new millennium, the safety net seemed virtually non-existent. The immediate enemy was the employer, who either sacked you, cut your wages and conditions, or looked as though he could or would at any time; the bank manager or landlord became the uncompromising collector of your housing loan repayment or rent that you suddenly didn't have. Barricade yourself inside your castle and the police or debt collectors would simply end your siege and cast you onto the street. You might be able to stay with relatives, or move regularly from boarding house to boarding house as temporary work came and went or, if all else failed, you could live on the urban fringe in your city's shanty town. If you were on the land, what you could earn for your produce was probably insufficient to satisfy your creditors or bank manager.

But there was a basic if humiliating form of help. If you could show that you had been unemployed for at least a fortnight and that you had absolutely no means of your own to fall back on, sustenance coupons were available. Phillip Knightley:

> Being a 'susso' was a demeaning experience for an Australian man. First he had to admit to himself that he could no longer support his family. Then he had to queue at the Government Labour Exchange to register as unemployed . . . there to be mocked by public servants. Then there was the humiliation of using the special shops and thus revealing to your neighbours that your family was on sustenance. Many would do anything to avoid this.[12]

While the man in the street was having problems enough paying his way, the nation's hefty 1920s borrowing cycle certainly didn't help the problem: in the period 1919–29 Australia's overseas debt—chiefly owed to Britain—amounted to some £225 million, while the prices gained from exports fell by 50 per cent during the period 1928–31.

Although the great majority of the future soldiers bound for Papua were more than likely either young boys or young adolescents during these harrowing times, many entered the work force during the Depression, or just as it was showing signs of abating. High among their list of heroes were aviators, a cricketer and a horse: aviators such as Kingsford Smith ('Smithy'), and Don Bradman and Phar Lap. When Bradman became a run-making machine, the Poms invented 'bodyline' to combat him, and in so doing, they were judged to have lowered their own sense of fair play and propriety, long used by them as a measuring stick of both their game and their honour; and, when Australia had a seemingly unbeatable horse and took him to the United States to prove it, Phar Lap mysteriously died. As was said in those days, 'You couldn't take a trick.'

These soldiers of ours often grew up around, or with, characters like 'the fowl man', 'the pie man' and 'the trapper', who sold their wares at the local pub or wherever the elusive market might be found; or with a man like 'Lazarus', who was as honest as they come, as hard working as they come, but whose lean and hungry look adequately portrayed his poverty.[13] If they were single, much of the money they earnt would be turned over to their mothers to assist in the survival of the family unit. There wasn't much left for spending. Perhaps Bill Spencer best sums up his peers:

> As I look back on the Depression's child and the society that nurtured him I have come to realise that the soldier is a by-product of the society into which he is born. That great economic disaster was actually the making of us.
>
> . . . out of our relative hardship came the realisation of initiative; of the value of social groups; family, friends, sporting and club organisations, and perhaps the belief that the group was more important than the individual. When adults around us were down and nearly out during those troubled times . . . we too learned that there were only you and your mates to drag you forward.[14]

Out of the Depression also came a brand of fatalism and a certain physical and emotional resilience: you took what life or circumstances dealt you and pressed on. Such a view of life and living during the Depression would stand them in good stead in Papua.

Amidst the material wealth amassed from the rapid technological and communications explosion of the 1920s came the idealistic crusade amongst western nations for world pacifism and, as a consequence, disarmament. The result was a massive dilution of the military strength of the western powers and a consequent closing of the armament gap between them and their would-be antagonists. Prime Minister Hughes put nearly half of the ships in the Australian Navy out of commission, reduced the CMF (Citizen Military Forces) to approximately 25 per cent of its former strength and, tragically, diminished the permanent army by discharging 72 officers. To so reduce the trained and professional core of an already small army was an act of extreme folly.

Reflecting the contemporary empire emphasis upon sea and air power in the period 1923–29, Australia devoted its already meagre defence budget more towards its navy and air force than its army. From 1924 until the onset of the Great Depression the ailing army relied upon a small but devoted core of officers whose experience and knowledge were enhanced by very effective exchange duty with the British Army in England and India. This period also saw the CMF grow to some 45 000 men through compulsory training—training by committed regular and CMF officers and staff imbued with a high sense of public duty and service.

If the preoccupation of Britain and its dominions with air and naval power as the keystone of their defence was ill advised during the interwar period, then their Pacific strategy during that time was a calamitous blunder that would result in the biggest British capitulation in history. On account of a massive 40 per cent cut in military funding in the 1920s, a marked diminution of British naval power in the Pacific, a vulnerability to a main attack from its landward side and a population who were neither trained nor adequately skilled to furnish a prime base, Singapore became a focal point for disaster.

As German expansionism threatened security in Europe and Japanese ambitions for a wider empire escalated in Asia during the 1930s, successive Australian governments continued to place their faith in naval and air power and the hope that the British diplomacy of appeasement would at least prolong a tenuous European peace. Yet the warnings of impending disaster were many and unmistakably clear. Most Australians took comfort in the belief that future forces committed in a European conflict could be recovered, in time, behind the security screen of the Singapore fortress. Japan's undeclared war upon China, the merciless rape of Nanking and the incredible breaking of the Japanese naval code through which the Allies were given stark evidence of Japanese intentions, all served to vividly convey both the tactics and the ruthlessness of the Japanese. By September 1939, the proverbial chickens incubated by two decades of politico-military ineptitude were coming home to roost—and they looked ominously like vultures.

'It is my melancholy duty to inform you officially that in consequence of a persistence by Germany in her invasion of Poland, Great Britain has declared war upon her, and that as a result, Australia is also at war . . .' With these words, on 3 September 1939, Prime Minister Robert Menzies declared Australia to be at war with Nazi Germany.

As was the case prior to the Great War, there were three types of armies to be found in the world in September 1939. The first was the longstanding volunteer army which was usually very efficient, as it had the advantages of being staffed and trained by full-time soldiers and of having a large proportion of trained troops who provided a long-term stability to its ranks. The British Army at this time was an excellent example of such an army.

The second type of army was the large conscript army of which Germany provided a classic example. When given conscripts for a period of two to three years, such an army was able to quickly raise, in time of need, a very formidable force.

The last of the three alternatives was a militia army, which was considered inferior to the first two options because it was raised out of a need, or desire, for an economical army which was trained for an initial period to enable its troops to receive a very basic training, and then be given once weekly sessions and an annual camp of seven to sixteen days' duration. The two primary criticisms of the militia army were related to the fragmentary nature of its training and to the insufficiency of the time for that training. Thus, the Australian Army in the period leading up to Prime Minister Menzies' declaration of war was essentially a threadbare defensive force, rather than a highly trained army capable of either overseas service or offensive action at home.

While the majority of the Australian electorate favoured an empire defence entailing possible service by Australian forces anywhere in the world, a significant number of those electors had an abhorrence of conscription as a means of raising forces for 'unrestricted service'. This had been amply demonstrated during the Great War when two referendums on the conscription issue were defeated by an electorate that was pro-war but anti-conscription. The relatively recent political memories of a divided, passionate debate during that period were still too vivid for the Government to contemplate such a course of action. The resulting decision to raise a Second Australian Imperial Force (AIF) was therefore taken for political expediency rather than the best interests of the army itself—'a decision which was to bedevil the Army until the end of the war with its division of the service into what was, in effect two armies'.[15]

For young men like George 'Babe' Luscombe, there were a number of ways of getting involved in the Second World War.

Many of the initial volunteers for the Second AIF were, no doubt, imbued with a sense of duty towards the British Empire (the large expanses of red on their school atlas), but they were also prompted by the belief in the duty of a citizen, the attraction of travel and adventure as part of a large, overseas force and, to a degree, a desire to emulate the deeds of the First AIF, who were not, after all, faceless figures from history books, but fathers or uncles or other contacts in their society from recent living and breathing—and a proud—history.

However, there is evidence to suggest that some of the volunteers for the AIF joined because of far less romantic ideals. The Labor politician Eddie Ward is credited with being one of the first people to coin the term 'economic conscripts' when describing many of these initial recruits. By joining the Second AIF, an unemployed man could receive five shillings a day and his food and lodgings instead of his dole payment of eight shillings and sixpence a week. It should also be stated that others joined the AIF and took a pay cut in doing so.

Just as there were a multitude of reasons for the enlistment of many young men into the AIF, so too were there a number of reasons why others chose not to join that force, or were prohibited from doing so.

While the bitterness, frustration and despair born of the Depression years caused some young men to join, these very same reasons caused others to reject enlistment in that force. There was also the political view that the defence of Australia was a matter for Australian troops defending their own shores, and that they should not be involved in another bloodbath such as had been experienced in the Great War—and some of those veterans would have advised their sons or nephews or friends not to enlist, at least not as infantrymen. Still others were engaged in occupations that became known as 'reserved occupations', that is, they could do more on the home front because of the importance of their vocation than they could accomplish by joining.

Thus, while nearly all of Australia's young men of military age were quite prepared to defend their nation, there remained some very strong and conflicting opinions as to the most effective means of doing so.

The division between the AIF and the militia was expressed in a number of uncomplimentary ways. The AIF referred to the militia as either 'chocos' or 'koalas'. The term 'chocos' was used because some of the AIF volunteers believed them to be 'chocolate soldiers' (the term 'choco' is believed to have come from a comic operetta called *The Chocolate Soldier* by Franz Lehar), who would 'melt' if action ever came, and who, because of the conscription law of service for the militia in Australia, could fight only on Australian soil. This, the AIF reasoned, would be unlikely to ever happen. The term 'koala' was particularly cutting: 'not to be exported or shot at'. The AIF also wore two unmistakable metal shoulder badges, each made up of the word 'Australia'. 'Get a bit of weight on your shoulders' was another common expression to a militiaman.

For their part, some of the militia saw the AIF as arrogant in their dealings with them, and might join more cynical members of society in using the term 'five-bob-a-day murderers' or 'five-bob-a-day tourists' when referring to the AIF. All of this was derisive and counterproductive. It would take the Papuan campaign to draw a divided army together.

During the Great War, the First AIF was comprised of five divisions that encompassed fifteen brigades. Accordingly, at the outbreak of the Second World War, the 6th Division was the first volunteer AIF division that was raised. The men of the 7th Division—who are, along with a number of militia units, the main characters of our story—were formed up in May 1940 and were dubbed 'the deep thinkers' by the originals of the 6th Division because of their eight-month delay in joining the AIF.

An infantry battalion becomes a soldier's home. When George 'Babe' Luscombe journeyed to Adelaide to volunteer for the Second AIF, he was accepted into a very structured and formal organisation. In Luscombe's case he was volunteering to join the South Australian 2/27th Battalion AIF. Quite soon after joining, he was made aware of the heritage of his unit, as there had been a 27th Battalion in the First AIF during the Great War. The '2/' simply identified the same battalion (27th), but as part of the Second AIF. He would wear the same identifying colour patch as his predecessors in the 27th Battalion First AIF; a small brown over blue diamond proudly sewn onto his upper sleeves. To distinguish his AIF battalion from its militia counterpart, his colour patch had a thin grey border around its perimeter. The critical point was that the pride in the First AIF meant that there was a legend to emulate.

To bring an infantry battalion up to strength required the recruitment of about 850 men, officially aged between eighteen and 35. But the edicts of officialdom and the practicalities of the real world meant that some men were well past the upper limit—some small number of men were over 60[16]—while some 'lads' had employed all manners of deception (perhaps by forging their parent's signature of consent), and were as young as fifteen.[17] However, the vast majority of recruits were in their mid-twenties.[18]

After their medical examination and the necessary form filling, recruits were allotted their tasks in the battalion: a clerk who wrote clearly and legibly might find his way into the signals; Luscombe for reasons earlier given found his way into the mortars; but the majority found their way into a rifle company. A battalion consisted of four rifle companies (A, B, C, and D), each of 129 soldiers and commanded by a captain or, in some cases, a major. A rifle company was made up of three platoons each of 38 soldiers commanded by a lieutenant. A platoon consisted of three sections each of ten men and each commanded by a corporal—three sections each of eleven soldiers. The remaining few of the 129 soldiers in a company constituted Company HQ.

In essential terms, the soldier became a member of an extended family: the other ten men in his section usually became his close mates, as they lived together, complained about the food together, marched together, dug in together, and above all fought together, and became, in many cases, 'mum, dad, and God' for each other. The next stage of the 'extended family' was the soldier's platoon. Not unlike a child in a classroom, he would know the remaining members of his platoon (the other two sections each of eleven men) quite well. His company consisted of two more platoons, whose members of which he was highly likely to know at least by sight and, in many cases, reasonably well. There was usually a very healthy and competitive rivalry between the four rifle companies.

The Battalion Headquarters and Headquarter Company of an infantry battalion were, in basic terms, its nerve centre and bureaucracy. Battalion Headquarters contained the commanding officer (a lieutenant-colonel), who was a tactician, trainer and disciplinarian (his power was almost absolute in terms of docking pay, handing out confinement to barracks and various other means of discipline); his second-in-command; the adjutant (an administrative assistant to the CO); the Intelligence Section (the gatherers of information, maps etc.); the Regimental Aid Post (the battalion doctor and his assistants and stretcher-bearers, who were usually members of the battalion band); and the padre, who was present for the soldiers' spiritual needs. Headquarter Company consisted of six platoons: number one was the signals, two anti-aircraft, three were the mortars, four the armoured carriers, five the pioneers (tradesmen); and six were the transport and quartermaster's staff (responsible for issuing of supplies of food, equipment etc.).

Battalions initially embarked upon weapons training, physical fitness and marching, followed by platoon training, then company training; and finally the men learnt to operate at battalion level. This process usually—and preferably—took some consistent, concentrated work over a number of months. By the time a proficient soldier went to war, he had the structure, training and a growing confidence in himself and those around him. The recruit therefore quickly developed a strong esprit de corps at this level: ask any veteran his section, company and battalion, and the response is automatic (e.g. number one section, 7 Platoon, A Company, 2/27th Battalion).

The pertinent point is that for a nation that prides itself on its egalitarian outlook, the army was, perhaps, the ultimate model of equality. In action, a soldier's civilian vocation, his pay, his social standing, his religion and his standard of education—all came to nought. When the enemy attacked you, or you attacked him, no such distinctions were made or were relevant.

The army then made a number of further distinctions of structure. Three battalions composed a brigade which was commanded by a brigadier; and three brigades formed a division commanded by a major-general. The soldier was aware of his brigade and division and was proud of them, but, in all this, he operated on a more personal level within his battalion structure. And three or two divisions constituted a corps under a lieutenant-general—a structure which meant little or nothing to the private soldier in his day-to-day existence.

As a result of a restructuring of the Australian Army early in 1940 to the model described above, the 7th Division was composed of the 18th Brigade consisting of the 2/9th Battalion (Queensland), the 2/10th Battalion (South Australia), and the 2/12th Battalion (Tasmania/Queensland); the 21st Brigade consisting of the 2/14th Battalion (Victoria), the 2/16th Battalion (Western Australia), and the 2/27th Battalion (South Australia); and the 25th Brigade consisting of the 2/25th Battalion (Queensland) and the 2/31st and the 2/33rd Battalions. The 18th Brigade had been originally raised as part of the 6th Division, and the 25th was formed from elements of the army while in England during early 1940.

This 7th Division would later become known as 'The Silent Seventh'—silent, because its incredibly distinguished campaigning would receive little recognition and even less publicity.

DOG RIVER

3

A significant proportion of Australia's early military history took place in the Middle East during the Great War and in the early years of the Second World War.

During early 1941, the Second AIF's first committed division to the Middle East, the 6th Division, added fresh laurels to Australia's proud record of Middle Eastern service. First committed to action at Bardia on the North African coast, the 6th Division served with great distinction in the advance to Benghazi. Replaced by the newly formed 9th Division in Cyrenaica (now a part of Libya), the 6th was subsequently involved in the ill-fated campaigns in Greece and Crete during April–May of that same year. And out of those early and varied campaigns, a number of senior officers rose to great heights, tried and tested and, in most cases, not found wanting. It has been claimed that there was enough real or potential talent in the original 6th Division to command a future force five times its size.[1] The great significance to our story is the fact that a number of those original 6th Division senior officers would play, within eighteen short months, both critical and controversial roles in the Papuan campaign. General Sir Thomas Blamey was the first.

Blamey had had a most distinguished military career. Born at Lake Albert near Wagga Wagga in New South Wales on 24 January 1884, he had won a commission in the Commonwealth Cadet Forces in 1906; he had joined the Australian Military Forces in 1910 and had subsequently furthered his professional training at Quetta in what was then British India; he had been attached to the British Army in

England; and, at the outbreak of the Great War, he was working in the War Office in London.

During the early stage of that war, a colleague described Blamey thus: 'Short of stature, rugged in appearance, it took some little time to discover that behind that broad forehead there was well seated an unusual brain, and that the square jaw denoted not obstinancy and lack of tact, but quiet resolution and a calm and definite power of expression.'[2]

After a number of staff appointments during the war, Blamey's unsurpassed abilities and performance came strongly to the fore as General Monash's chief of staff. The fact that this period saw such stunning Australian successes, and that General Monash rose to such prominence both in and outside his own force, is also in part a reflection of Blamey's ability and performance as his chief staff officer. And Monash freely acknowledged Blamey's contribution:

> No reference to the staff work of the Australian Corps during the period of my command would be complete without a tribute to the work and personality of Brigadier T.A. Blamey, my Chief of Staff. He possessed a mind cultured far above the average, widely informed, alert and prehensile. He had an infinite capacity for taking pains. A Staff College graduate, but not on that account a pedant, he was thoroughly versed in the technique of staff work, and in the minutiae of all procedure . . .
>
> Some day the orders which he drafted for the long series of history-making military operations upon which we collaborated will become a model for Staff Colleges and Schools for military instruction . . .
>
> He worked late and early, and set a high standard for the remainder of the large Corps Staff of which he was the head. The personal support which he accorded to me was of a nature which I could always feel the real substance. I was able to lean on him in times of trouble, stress and difficulty, to a degree which was an inexpressible comfort to me.[3]

David Horner has rightly concluded that:

> At the beginning of the war Blamey had been a newly promoted major. But for four years he had been near or at the centre of the main operations conducted by the Australian forces. While not experiencing the challenges of command obtained by some of his colleagues, he had been given an unrivalled opportunity to observe the new developments in warfare and to learn how to manage the vast resources involved in modern war. Still only 34 years of age, he had much to offer the Australian Army and expected further advancement in an already brilliant career.[4]

But this was not to be. After a number of further prestigious army appointments during the early postwar years, Blamey was offered the position of Chief Commissioner of the Victoria Police Force in September 1925. The offer was too good to refuse.

Blamey's eleven-year reign as Chief Commissioner (1925–36) was marked by his already demonstrated flair for progressive, strong, astute administration and his single-minded ability to push through his agenda despite often influential opposition. His tenure of office saw the force transformed from the divisiveness that had resulted in a mutiny and a resulting Royal Commission to a state in which there were far improved recruit training procedures, an ongoing battle for better pay and conditions, the increased use of radio communication, changes to the promotion system, the decentralisation of the criminal branch and the plain-clothes branch and, last but not least, improved welfare schemes and facilities for members of the police force.[5]

But this period also amply demonstrated his not inconsiderable personal and professional flaws. Two incidents illustrate the point. The first was the notorious 'Badge 80 affair'.

When, late on the night of 21 October 1925, three plain-clothes police from the licensing squad raided a brothel in Fitzroy, a policeman was found with a woman in a bedroom on the premises. The officer in question produced a police badge, claiming it as his own—it was Blamey's badge. Controversy has since raged as to the circumstances surrounding this incident. Was Blamey the man caught? If not, how did the policeman in question get his badge? The three policemen who raided the brothel, and the madam of that establishment, all denied that Blamey was the officer in question. An army officer friend of Blamey's testified that he (Blamey) had been home that night. Amidst calls for a public inquiry, Blamey was allowed to appoint an internal inquiry. This 'inquiry' absolved him from any wrongdoing. It has been claimed that Blamey acted to protect an acquaintance to whom he had lent his badge. The story went that he had given the man in question his key ring with his badge attached, so that the man could borrow some alcohol from his locker. Further, it was claimed that the man, an old army friend, was a family man with three young children.[6] This incident amply illustrates a prominent Blamey flaw, which was simply that out of a fierce loyalty to a friend or colleague he was prepared to use his office and his powers to manipulate a situation, at the expense of a greater loyalty and propriety owed to his public responsibilities and the public image of his office.

The second incident ultimately cost Blamey his job. On the night of 22 May 1936, Superintendent Brophy, who was chief of the Criminal Investigation Branch, was parked in a street in Royal Park in Melbourne awaiting an appointment with an informer. With him in the vehicle were two women and a driver. David Horner: 'Suddenly two masked and armed men attempted to hold up the occupants of the car. Brophy drew his pistol and fired two shots but was himself shot in three places. The other occupants of the car were unharmed, the bandits escaped and Brophy was taken to St Vincent's Hospital.'[7] After Blamey had visited Brophy in hospital, information was later released to the press that Brophy had accidentally shot himself[8]—a remarkable accident given that Brophy had been shot three times. Nor was the presence of the two women in the car stated. A Royal Commission into the incident found Brophy had lied about the presence of the women in the car to protect their good names, but that Blamey had given the press 'replies that were not in accordance with the truth'.[9] His letter of resignation was handed to a Cabinet meeting, called to deliberate on the findings of the Royal Commission, on 9 July 1936.

Blamey's period as Chief Commissioner of the Victoria Police Force was thus marked by great controversy at both the beginning and the end of his service. However, his dealings with the press (with whom he conducted ongoing battles), his almost unique ability to alienate governments—particularly of the Labor variety—during the period, and even his ability to antagonise the police union, all conspired to turn those groups and individuals he should have carefully cultivated into powerful enemies. And a significant section of the public were added to this already formidable list—Blamey was regularly seen flouting the admittedly restrictive licensing laws of the time, which prompted those in his company to feel a certain sense of security while also breaking the law.[10] Allied to his liberal drinking habits was a similar appetite for women. Moral judgments aside, the point is not necessarily that he excessively indulged in either pursuits; it was that he was so indiscreet, often to the detriment of his standing amongst his peers and, most certainly, amongst those whom he served.

During the early 1930s, Blamey was also involved in the clandestine organisation known variously as the League of National Security (LNS) or, in some circles, the White Army. This extreme, right-wing organisation was a response to the supposed threat of communism, particularly during the Depression years. The organisation operated within small, localised groups or cells, had a strong ex-servicemen component, and was seemingly prepared to gather at militia depots for the acquisition of arms and ammunition during a perceived time of crisis. Blamey was by no means the only prominent high-ranking soldier in its ranks.[11] Speculation has risen as to whether his was the senior position, but his involvement at a relatively high level seems beyond doubt.[12]

During his time as Chief Commissioner, Blamey lost his eldest son in an aircraft accident in 1932 and his wife to a debilitating illness in 1935.

Cast into the wilderness in 1936 at 52 years of age, Blamey remained in the militia as General Officer Commanding the 3rd Division until his tenure expired in 1937. He was then placed on the unattached list with the rank of major-general. All seemed over—both in terms of a future public life and a military one.

As the Second World War approached, Blamey's considerable military experience and acumen were rediscovered. In 1938 he was appointed chairman of the Commonwealth's Manpower Committee and Controller-General of Recruiting; and, in a move surrounded by some controversy, when war broke out he was given command of the first division raised for overseas service: the 6th Division. In this selection, Blamey had influential supporters such as Prime Minister Menzies, the Federal Treasurer Richard Casey, the Minister for External Affairs, Sir Henry Gullett, and not least in influence, the then Secretary of the Department of Defence, Frederick Shedden. The decision caused some friction within the Staff Corps, as it was felt that the appointment should have gone to a permanent soldier, and also with people such as General Gordon Bennett, who was, after all, senior to Blamey. On 13 October 1939, Blamey was officially promoted to lieutenant-general and began working with his newly selected senior officers. His raising of the Second AIF and his selection of its senior staff and structure displayed his wide knowledge and experience. On the whole, the brigade commanders chosen—Allen, Morshead and Savige—and the key staff appointments were sound.

Perhaps one of the main reasons Blamey was appointed to this position was the fact that a sound politico-military aptitude was required. One of the great lessons to come out of the Great War was the manner in which the British were able to disperse AIF fighting formations which, of course, made them very easy to control. Blamey astutely sought, and was granted, very specific conditions embodied in a charter as to the operation of the Second AIF while serving with the British.[13] In essence, the charter proclaimed the AIF commander's obligation and, more importantly, his right, to direct communication with his government on any given issue; it forbade the removal of any part of the AIF force from its whole without the express permission of the AIF commander (Blamey); and stipulated that the administration of the AIF with regards to internal matters was a matter for its Australian commander (for example, matters of discipline). To Blamey's great credit, this charter was enforced by him on a number of occasions, and often in the face of considerable British intimidation.[14]

The second key character in the 6th Division—which was to play a prominent and controversial role in the Papuan campaign—was Colonel (later Lieutenant-General) Sydney Rowell. A graduate of the first class from Duntroon, Rowell was born on 15 December 1894 at Lockleys, in Adelaide. According to the Official Historian, Rowell was 'clear and incisive in thought, sensitive in feeling, frank and outspoken in his approach to men and to problems'.[15] He served at Gallipoli as a troop and squadron commander before a brief period as adjutant of the 3rd Light Horse Regiment. In a turn for the worse for his career, he was invalided out of Gallipoli and eventually returned to Australia in early 1916. As there was a rather strange regulation that permanent officers were prohibited from a return overseas once sent back to Australia, Rowell missed the opportunity to advance his career in France during the remainder of the Great War.

During the interwar period, Rowell's career was enhanced by study at the Staff College at Camberley in England during the period 1925–26. After a number of postings in Western Australia, Rowell was posted to Army Headquarters in 1932, followed in 1935 by another posting to England on exchange, and a period as a student at the Imperial Defence College. Known almost universally within the Australian Army as 'Syd', Rowell was regarded as one of its most capable, hardworking and professional staff officers. It was hardly surprising, therefore, that Blamey chose him as his chief of staff upon the raising of the Second AIF. When the 7th Division was raised, causing the formation of a corps command, Blamey further recognised Rowell's previous performance and ability by promoting him to the position of Brigadier General Staff.

The third 6th Division officer to play a critical role in the Papuan campaign was Colonel (later Lieutenant-General) Edmund Herring. Known among his peers as 'Ned', Herring was born at Maryborough in Victoria on 2 September 1892. He became a Rhodes Scholar in 1912 and served in the Officers' Training Corps while at Oxford University. Herring was subsequently commissioned into the Royal Field Artillery (RFA) and served during the Great War in France and Macedonia, where he was awarded the DSO and MC. After qualifying in law at Oxford after the war, he returned to

Australia where he gradually built up a successful law practice, culminating in his becoming a King's Counsel in 1936.

Between the wars, Herring maintained a keen interest and participation in soldiering through militia service which saw him acting as a legal officer with a cavalry division in 1922; as commander of an artillery battery in 1923; and, as the Second World War was declared, as Commander, Royal Artillery of the 3rd Division, Citizen Military Forces (CMF). Like Blamey, Herring was a member of the White Army, being responsible for a 'cell' of the organisation on the Mornington peninsula.

Herring was known for his ability to maintain cordial relations with almost everybody in both army and civilian circles, and particularly with Blamey, with whom he had relatively frequent contact. Their militia service between the wars, their mutual involvement in the White Army, similar political views, and various social contacts in Melbourne all conspired to make Herring a rather strong Blamey supporter. When Blamey secured the position of commanding officer of the 6th Division, he appointed Herring as its Commander Royal Artillery (CRA). In August 1941, Herring was appointed by Blamey as MacKay's successor to command the 6th Division.

The fourth officer was Major-General Arthur Allen. Born at Hurstville in Sydney on 10 March 1894, Allen was, prior to the outbreak of the Second World War, a chartered accountant. Short in height and stocky in build, he was known throughout the army as 'Tubby', and had had a magnificent record as a civilian soldier. In the Great War he had been a platoon commander with the 13th Battalion; a captain and major with the 45th Battalion; and by war's end, had commanded the 45th, 48th and 13th Battalions.

In the interwar period Allen had furthered his experience as a battalion and then brigade commander. When Blamey selected his three original brigade commanders for the 6th Division, Allen was given command of the 16th Brigade. The Official Historian described Allen as: 'Blunt in speech, honest as the day, choleric yet kindly, completely without affectation or pomposity, he was a leader of a kind that appeals immediately to Australians. His military lore was drawn from experience rather than study, and was based on a wide and sympathetic knowledge of men in battle.'[16]

When the 6th Division went into its first battle at Bardia on 3 January 1941, it was Allen's 16th Brigade which spearheaded the operation. From Bardia to Benghazi, the brigade, and its commander, developed a tremendous reputation. Allen's star continued to shine during the ill-fated Greek campaign[17] to the point where Blamey promoted him to major-general and gave him command of the 7th Division on 18 June 1941 during the fighting in Syria. When the 7th Division returned to Australia in March 1942, few officers in the Australian Army could claim to have commanded in action (collectively during both world wars) from platoon level through to company, battalion, brigade and, finally, on through to divisional level.

The fifth Australian officer to participate in both the drama and controversy of the Papuan campaign was Brigadier, later Major-General, Cyril Clowes. Born at Warwick in Queensland on 11 March 1892, Clowes was a professional soldier who, like Rowell, had graduated from the first Duntroon class. Sent straight after graduation to the newly formed First AIF and posted to the 1st Artillery Brigade, he had landed at Gallipoli on 25 April 1915 and was wounded on that first day while directing naval gunfire support. Awarded the Military Cross (MC) during action in France as a divisional mortar officer in 1916, he was in addition twice mentioned in dispatches. Perhaps the highlight of Clowes' Great War career was his DSO awarded for service with the artillery at Villers-Bretonneux in 1918. During the period 1920–25, Clowes was an instructor at Duntroon before being posted to various training and staff appointments in Brisbane, Sydney and Darwin. After graduating from the staff course in gunnery at Larkhill in Britain in 1938, his last posting before the onset of the Second World War was to Tasmania as commander of the 6th Military District.

Clowes was a man of few words to those he knew and less to those he did not. His quiet, calm disposition merely masked a professional, highly trained and courageous officer who was at his best in a crisis. When the I Australian Corps was formed early in 1940, he was chosen as its artillery commander.

The sixth and last officer to play a critical role in the Papuan campaign was Lieutenant-Colonel (later Major-

General) George Vasey. Born in Malvern, Melbourne on 29 March 1895, Vasey was a professional soldier who had graduated from Duntroon in 1915. His Great War service consisted primarily of a posting as adjutant of the 22nd Field Artillery in France in 1915, and as brigade major of the 11th Infantry Brigade, 3rd Division during the period 1917–19. For a short time during the latter part of 1919 Vasey worked as a staff officer involved in the demobilisation of the First AIF. In common with most Staff Corps officers during the interwar period, Vasey had to contend with a diminished army where conditions and pay were poor and advancement for professional soldiers was hard to come by.

Various staff and training appointments were interrupted in the period by a posting to the Staff College in Quetta (1928–29) and to the British Army in India on exchange (1934–37). When the Second World War broke out, Vasey undertook two critical staff appointments in succession with the 6th Division: that of Assistant-Adjutant and Quartermaster-General (the prime administrative officer at Headquarters) and General Staff Officer 1 (the principal staff officer for operations). This high-level staff work was of enormous benefit to Vasey before he undertook a field command as commanding officer of the 19th Brigade in March 1941. What followed was critical operational experience in the Greek and Crete campaigns during the period April–May 1941.

Vasey was known throughout the Australian Army as 'Bloody George'. The Official Historian: 'Highly strung, thrustful, hard-working, Vasey concealed a deeply emotional even sentimental nature behind a mask of laconic and blunt speech.'[18] He was, perhaps, a generation ahead of his time in his ability to be seen with his troops, communicate with them, and develop a strong rapport with them. An illuminating incident which occurred during the both exhausting and testing fighting withdrawal in Greece best illustrates the Vasey persona. Making it crystal clear that a particular position had to be held, Vasey told his commanders: 'Here you bloody well are and here you bloody well stay. And if any bloody German gets between your post and the next, turn your bloody Bren around and shoot him up the arse.'[19]

The relationship between Blamey and some of his officers began to deteriorate in the Middle East and became increasingly tense in Greece. Although much of Blamey's decision making during the AIF's early months in the Middle East had been astute, there had been some worrying incidents.

The first was Blamey's ability to unnecessarily antagonise both the public at home and, more importantly, his peers in the Middle East. In December 1940, after intense lobbying by Blamey to Menzies and Spender, a passport was issued for Mrs Olga Blamey (Blamey had married the 35-year-old Olga Farnsworth, a fashion artist, in April 1939) to join her husband in the Middle East, ostensibly to work with the Red Cross. It should be mentioned that a passport was also issued to Major-General Mackay's wife. When the Cabinet reacted to adverse comment in Australia concerning the incident and asked Blamey to send the women home, Blamey replied that he was seeking legal opinion on the matter. He won the confrontation. Menzies later observed that Lady Blamey's presence might 'do much to keep him fit and well . . .'[20] The point is, surely, that there existed no shortage of high-ranking Australian officers—or fighting soldiers—in the Middle East whose wives may have positively affected their sense of fitness and well-being also. If this was not enough, Blamey further flouted his position by tactless sojourns to nightclubs in Cairo where his partners and activities were on public display.[21] The consequences were obvious—his standing amongst some of his senior subordinates and, most certainly, the troops themselves, fell substantially.[22] Such behaviour had another outcome: Blamey's physical fitness. In February 1941, he was castigated by Burston (his Assistant Director of Medical Services) and later Rowell, for a succession of medical problems: obesity, leg ulcers, kidney stones and gout.

But it was during the campaign in Greece that the controversy became critical. On 11 February 1941, British Prime Minister Winston Churchill and his Chiefs of Staff decided that General O'Connor's advance in the Western Desert was to be halted and a force sent to Greece in an attempt to resist the imminent German invasion, and thereby perhaps to encourage Yugoslavia and Turkey to enter the war.[23]

Whether or not General O'Connor's startling success in the Western Desert would have culminated in the capture of Tripoli before the arrival of General Rommel and his Afrika Korps in North Africa is debatable. The Greek campaign was to provide perhaps the most striking example of Churchillian strategy at its worst: it severely debilitated the Western Desert Force and offered far too small a force for Greece.

On 17 February 1941, General Wavell, Commander-in-Chief Middle East Command, ordered General Blamey to Cairo. Two days later Blamey was informed that a force (codenamed Lustre Force) was to go to Greece and would comprise the New Zealand Division, the Australian 6th and 7th Divisions, I Australian Corps Headquarters and a Polish Brigade group. Wavell planned to leave the 6th Division in Cyrenaica, send the New Zealand Division to Greece first, then the 7th Division AIF. Blamey—to his great credit again—would have none of it. He insisted that the 6th was his only fully trained and equipped division, and should therefore be the first Australian formation to go to Greece.[24] Wavell eventually yielded.

The British effort during the Greek campaign was to operate under some major handicaps. The first was air power. The German Air Force was to outnumber the RAF by 490 planes to about 80,[25] with the consequence that the Germans were at liberty to attack Greek ports, shipping and the transport network, knowing that the resistance they faced was only token.

The second problem was the state of the Greek Army. Although it had successfully defeated the Italian invasion of Greece from 28 October 1940, it was to prove no match for the Germans. It lacked decent equipment and its transport was outdated.

The third problem lay in the Greek rail and road network. The area in which the Australians were to fight was served south to north by only one railway line, which ran from Athens to Plati before moving east to Salonika, west to Florina, and then to Yugoslavia. This railway, antiquated and vulnerable to air attack, was at the time of the arrival of Lustre Force already being overtaxed by the Greeks. The Greek road network was also primitive and often so narrow that two vehicles could not pass, 'particularly on hills and side cuttings'.[26]

The last major problem was more one of strategy. If the Germans overran Yugoslavia quickly, advanced from Monastir through Florina and then to the Aliakmon Valley, and finally onwards towards the River Pinios and the Plain of Thessaly, they would effectively drive a wedge between the Greek forces and Lustre Force. This later transpired.

It was during the period 15–18 April 1941 that Blamey and Rowell had a major falling out. When the fighting withdrawal of the Anzac Corps ran into severe trouble near the Pinios Gorge—the Germans were threatening to stage a breakthrough that might have resulted in a large segment of Lustre Force being cut off—Rowell suggested to Blamey that Clowes should go to the New Zealand 21st Battalion area and both assess the situation and take any required remedial action. Blamey refused, stating that a New Zealand officer attached to their HQ should perform this role. When Rowell pointed out to Blamey that the New Zealand officer in question was too old and not up to the task, Blamey 'agreed with very ill grace'.[27] Rowell's decision proved to be an astute one, as Clowes (not for the first or last time in his career) journeyed down to the position (leaving at 1.00 a.m. on 16 April), calmly summed up the situation, and ordered the New Zealand commander to immediately halt his withdrawal and hold the gorge[28] 'even to the point of extinction'[29] and that 'reinforcements would arrive within twenty-four hours'.[30] Further, he gave the commander assistance as to how and where he might improve his dispositions. The position was temporarily restored.

But more pressure was to follow. In the early hours of that same morning, while Clowes was making his way forward to remedy the situation at the Pinios Gorge, a further German breakthrough seemed imminent. Rowell was woken and informed of the situation. With Blamey still asleep, he immediately made a change in the role of Allen's 16th Brigade. When he told Blamey of the move, he (Blamey) 'was furious but wrong',[31] according to a senior staff officer who was present. Blamey then 'reluctantly agreed and diverted the remainder of the 16th Brigade'.[32] Rowell's action was the only sensible and obvious one to take, which is precisely why he took it without waking

Blamey. The pressure continued to mount. When, on 18 April, the withdrawal again was being jeopardised by a strong German tank attack in the Pinios Gorge and German aircraft were delaying the withdrawal along the main road, Rowell suggested that either Blamey or he (Rowell) should go forward to visit the forward commanders, MacKay and Freyberg, to assess and, possibly, assist the situation. Blamey refused and also denied Rowell the opportunity to go. When Rowell insisted after lunch again that one of them should go, Blamey finally allowed Rowell to perform the task.

The issue is clear cut. Blamey and Rowell would later each offer their versions of events in Greece. Did Blamey crack under pressure or was Rowell lying? In the end the matter comes down to who one is to believe. Rowell, and a number of senior officers present, maintain that Blamey lost his nerve, his 'grip' of the situation, and others had to respond to the pressure that he (Blamey) was duty bound to accommodate.[33] Blamey's supporters were, on the whole, not directly present other than Carlyon, his ADC, and, possibly, Mander-Jones, the air liaison officer.[34]

On the basis of the evidence, Rowell should be believed, as there is no instance in his public life of his code of conduct and resultant behaviour being anything other than exemplary. David Horner: 'Proud, very austere and sensitive, he was high principled to the degree that one senior officer remarked 'the trouble with Syd is that he expects everyone to act like a saint'.[35] General Blamey's public record tells a different story.

If all this was not enough, Blamey gave his detractors further reason to doubt both his morality and his behaviour—and therefore his suitability for operational command. When, late on the night of 23 April 1941, Blamey was ordered to fly out from Greece by flying boat, he made the serious mistake of allotting one of the very limited number of seats available to his son, Major Thomas Blamey, who was a liaison officer from HQ. This was surely the act of a father who had lost one son in tragic circumstances in 1932 and desperately wanted to avoid losing his second son—an understandable human emotion. But Blamey was the GOC of a corps in battle and could have—and should have—set the example. He did not. The fact that Blamey has received criticism for being on the plane himself (when Freyberg, the New Zealand commander, refused to go) is not valid, since he was *ordered* to leave by his superior officer.[36]

These then were the key Australian senior officers in the war in Papua: Blamey, Rowell, Herring, Allen, Clowes and Vasey. This campaign will vividly demonstrate how pressure, both in the military and politico-military sense, increases dramatically when an army, for the first time in its brief but proud history, fights on its own soil. The stakes are therefore incredibly high, and there is the added pressure of establishing a working relationship with a new and more powerful ally who is not a part of the old imperial—and largely redundant—order. As a result, the pressures, friction and controversy already identified in Greece would multiply drastically in Papua for these officers.

The soldiers who fight battles usually have little or no idea whatsoever of the manner in which decisions are taken by those above them—or of the intrigue sometimes involved. Ignorance can sometimes be a blessing.

Having identified and briefly described a number of the prominent commanders of the future Papuan campaign, and the background from which they emerged, a brief description of the 7th Division's Middle Eastern campaigning is both warranted and illuminating in view of subsequent events in the jungles of New Guinea.

The 7th Division's first brigade, the 18th, fought in the famed siege of Tobruk. As Private Bill Spencer journeyed from Kantara in Palestine to join his 2/9th Battalion of the 18th Brigade, he was conscious of his military heritage:

> In the afternoon we were loaded into cattle trucks, without doubt the same trucks used by our Light Horsemen in the Great War. As the train jerked and bumped through the Sinai Desert, I felt a close affinity with those ghosts I felt certain were sharing our experience. The clink of harness and the snorting of horses, the sounds of laughter and ribaldry, the smell of dressed leather and the acrid cigarette smoke—they were all there in my imagination. The sons of Anzacs were following in the footsteps left years ago. Most of all, I felt that those glorious ghosts were carrying us along those tracks

> towards their fateful footsteps. I hoped that we would emulate their successes and know that others felt the same during that journey in the cold, unlit confines of the cattle trucks . . . [37]

Spencer and his mates' ambitions were to be fulfilled in no uncertain terms.

It will be remembered that by the middle of March 1941, British forces had driven the Italian Army out of Egypt and taken the coastal towns of Bardia, Tobruk, Derna, Benghazi and El Agheila. The 6th Australian Division had played no small part in these stirring victories. The newly arrived 9th Australian Division was subsequently deployed at Benghazi to relieve the 6th for action in Greece. But when Hitler determined that he would come to the aid of his Italian allies, General Erwin Rommel and his famed Afrika Korps were sent to restore the Axis position on the North African coast. In what was later to become known as the 'Benghazi Handicap', Rommel pushed the British forces back to the town of Tobruk during a most chaotic and rushed British Commonwealth withdrawal.

From a British perspective, Tobruk simply had to be held, and held for at least two months, so as to facilitate a build-up of forces for a counteroffensive. By holding Tobruk, not only would a critical port be denied to Rommel's ever lengthening line of communication, but he would further be forced to commit a substantial part of his force to at best capture its garrison or, at worst, continue its siege.

During the period April–September 1941, Major-General Leslie Morshead and his 9th Division—and various other attached forces—conducted a masterly defence of Tobruk. In essence, Morshead's defence relied upon a strong outer perimeter (the Red Line) and two further lines (the Blue and Green). However, his defence was also based on the tactic developed by the Australians on the Western Front in 1918: constant, aggressive patrolling of no-man's-land, which was in fact regarded by the Australians as their property. This was designed to keep the Germans off balance and unable to clearly reconnoitre the defensive perimeter. The one limited German gain occurred in an area known as 'the Salient', with its dominant feature, Hill 209. After making modest progress, the Germans took heavy casualties in the Salient attempting to hold their ground, while the Australians suffered proportionally attempting to retake it.

When General Blamey later sought the relief of the Australian garrison in Tobruk—their heavy casualties and poor physical condition being the main reasons—the British Government and the British commander in the Middle East, General Auchinleck, attempted to reverse the decision. Blamey, employing the conditions of his charter and the ultimate responsibility to preserve the integrity of his force, won out, once again to his great credit.

During the approximately four-month-long siege of Tobruk, the 7th Division's attached 18th Brigade performed a key role in the siege. Its 2/9th Battalion served longer than any other unit in the Salient. Some concept of that contribution might be realised by a letter Morshead sent to Blamey when he learnt that the 18th Brigade was to be the first unit to be relieved:

> . . . I had planned that it should be the last to go because it is the best brigade here as it should be seeing that it was formed nearly two years ago. During the process of relief the defence will be affected by the force being a mixed one and the new units being unfamiliar with the ground and the situation generally. Consequently I feel very strongly that the 18 Bde should be retained until the last and I trust that you will approve of this.[38]

Blamey rightly pressed ahead with his decision to bring the 18th Brigade out first.

The other two brigades of the 7th Division—the 21st and 25th Brigades—fought their first fights in the Syrian campaign during a five-week period in June–July 1941. A year before the fighting broke out the British Government had stated that it would not allow either Syria or Lebanon to be occupied by the enemy. After the fall of Greece and Crete, the possibility that the Germans could advance on the Suez Canal by landing and attacking through Lebanon—then part of Syria—and southward through Palestine was greatly increased.

In the end, it was enough that Germany might invade Syria that caused the British to invade it—and the perception that Syria might be easy pickings, as the admittedly large and well-equipped Vichy French would be likely to capitulate. Nothing could have been further from the truth, as the Vichy French depised both the Free French and de Gaulle.

Rowell would later write that:

> I could not see that there was any reason in the world for the Vichy French to surrender without a fight. They had long resisted overtures to hand over their territory—the armed forces were regulars (and very good ones too) whose professional code required them to obey the orders of their political leaders; they had all the advantages of ground and had practised frequently the defence of their territory in tactical exercises with and without troops.[39]

The British plan involved an advance on three fronts: the 5th Indian Brigade and the Free French were to compose the inland attack on the right flank with the objective of Damascus; the 7th Australian Division's 25th Brigade was to form the centre of the attack with its objective being Rayak; and the left flank or coastal thrust was to be undertaken by the 7th Division's 21st Brigade with its objective being Beirut.

The fighting in Syria was conducted on tough terrain which was 'much after the Gallipoli Peninsula style',[40] and was therefore ideal defensive ground: rocky, steep ridges and vegetation that easily concealed the multitude of enemy guns and their positions. The Australians and British did have considerable naval fire support; more numerous and effective artillery and, as the campaign progressed, improving air support, while the French employed the ground well, generally put up stubborn resistance and employed their tanks (as old as they were) and mortars effectively. After five weeks of bitter fighting the French asked for an armistice on 12 July 1941.

From a 7th Australian Division perspective the Syrian campaign gave its 21st and 25th Brigades priceless experience in mountain fighting and its associated lessons:

> . . . the need in such country of securing the ridges, the danger of defiles [the narrow valley or gorge approaches], and the necessity for attacking defiles from a flank; the use of cover on rocky slopes; the value of mortars in tangled, steep-sided hills where field artillery was unable to operate with full effect.
>
> . . .The frequent possibility of ambush in mountain passes was seen and practised.[41]

And the fighting was exhausting to the point where those soldiers—and officers—who were not physically or mentally robust were found out.

Who allocates the lofty mantle of fame upon an individual or a group? Politicians often do, through their manipulation of the press or their surplanting of it by an unreasonable censor—and we will see later, in graphic terms, that some generals often do. In the case of the Syrian campaign the British censor operated under political as well as military guidelines. The Australian Official Historian: 'The first communique issued at Cairo stated that "only slight and often no resistance" had been met; the censors were instructed from Wavell's headquarters that they must delete references to fighting.'[42]

How does one cover a war, where the troops faithfully and honourably commit themselves to action and many pay the ultimate sacrifice, without reporting the fighting? But where the enemy includes Frenchmen of the famed Foreign Legion (tough troops indeed), and where the fact that the French must be seen *only* as a gallant ally under the heel of Nazi Germany, the truth in Syria becomes the first casualty. The only difference between being a famed 'Rat of Tobruk' and some poor bastard who fights and sometimes dies in Syria—or for that matter, in Greece or Crete—is political expediency. The tag the 'Silent Seventh' begins in Syria.

The Syrian campaign affects our Papuan story in two more ways. The first is the introduction of a further critical character.

Some men's lives are merely a series of seemingly unrelated rehearsals for one great event. It is as if fate has preordained the range of their experiences, carefully teaching them, and thus preparing them. But fate can also be a cruel master. The preparation is done, the great event occurs, the subject passes his critical test with flying colours only to be unrecognised, or even criticised and removed, and then cast into the shadow of history by the actions of more powerful but lesser men.

Born on the Isle of Man on 16 September 1896, Arnold Potts migrated with his parents to Western Australia in 1904. Potts' father was a schoolteacher who, after working in comfortable circumstances in Cottesloe, journeyed as a deputy headmaster to Kalgoorlie before being promoted to headmaster at neighbouring Boulder. As a young boy, Potts was exposed to a tough, uncompromising environment and people of the same ilk. At fourteen, he became a boarder at the prestigious Guilford Grammar School in Perth. Potts joined the cadet unit in 1910 and subsequently served with the 86th Infantry Regiment at Pinjarra in Western Australia.[43]

When the Great War broke out, he joined the 16th Battalion and arrived as a reinforcement at Gallipoli on 28 July 1915 with the rank of acting sergeant. After the 16th Battalion was evacuated from Gallipoli in December 1915 and sent to Egypt to recuperate, Potts was commissioned and then served on the Western Front with distinction, being promoted to captain and winning an MC. On 6 July 1918 he was seriously wounded at Vaire Wood, when a sniper's shot pierced his chest, just missing his spine. After a month in hospital in France on the critical list, he spent two months in hospital in London.[44]

Classified as 20 per cent disabled and awarded a 25 shillings a fortnight pension, Potts, after working on a farm to gain experience, purchased a property at Kojonup through the soldier settlement scheme.

After serving with the CMF between the wars, Potts' posting to the 25th Light Horse (Machine Gun) Regiment based in the Great Southern farming area of Western Australia was interrupted by the onset of the Second World War.

Potts joined the 2/16th Battalion upon its formation in May 1940 as its second-in-command. His ability as a trainer and a judge of men was exceptional—it needed to be as the 2/16th had an element of fierce individuals from places such as the Kalgoorlie goldfields and the Great Southern farming area. Bruce MacKenzie was one of Potts' soldiers:

> The city-based men didn't realise what he (Pottsy) was on about, but we country fellows who had been through some pretty tough times could pick what he was about straight away. He would push us to see if he could break us. It was perfect pre-battle training. The Potts credo was that every single soldier was an individual fighting machine who should use his initiative and know-how when the time came. It was to pay off later, especially at Litani River [in Syria] when things went badly at the start.[45]

During the fighting in Syria Potts displayed outstanding leadership and was rewarded with command of the battalion in August 1941 and awarded a DSO. His ability to relate to, command and inspire soldiers during the campaign was legendary, both within his battalion and the 21st Brigade. Not unlike Allen or Vasey, Potts was very much a soldier's soldier. Potts' biographer, Bill Edgar: 'At the river crossing outside Damour one digger remembered Potts, with the bullets flying thick and fast all round, urging his hesitant men on, calling to them, "Come on boys, this is for free; you'd pay for something like this at home and it wouldn't be half the fun!"'[46] Back in Australia in July 1942, Potts was promoted to brigadier and given command of his brigade.

The second noteworthy point concerning this Syrian campaign is a further problem between General Blamey and his senior officers—chiefly Rowell and Lavarack. It will be remembered that Blamey's charter had, as one of its keynote considerations, the desire to avoid the splitting of Australian formations and, where possible, the maintainance of operational control over its forces. And in this regard Blamey had been single-minded and successful within the bounds of common sense and the practical considerations at hand. Just prior to the Syrian campaign, however, Rowell went to Blamey to point out to him that as the majority of the invading force would be Australian, and as the British commander's HQ was to be in the King David Hotel in Jerusalem—hundreds of miles from the front line—an *Australian* HQ should be interposed between the far-distant British HQ and the front to conduct the operation. Rowell:

> To my amazement I found him dead against it, an attitude which ran counter to his whole philosophy of the command of national forces. To his comment that we had no corps commander I replied that he himself could remedy that defect with a stroke of the pen, but it was clear that he did not want Lavarack as corps commander unless forced to appoint him.[47]

Blamey was soon forced to appoint him. When on 18 June 1941 the command structure had indeed proved to be faulty and impaired by the severe distance between HQ and the front, and when progress had become slowed, Blamey belatedly promoted Lavarack. Brigadier 'Tubby' Allen became the new commander (major-general) of the 7th Division.

Here is another example of a man and a soldier who is full of contradictions. We have seen Blamey's qualifications and performance in staff work; his tremendous ability to select senior commanders and then raise a highly successful volunteer army; his foresight in framing and enforcing a charter for the administration of the AIF in operation with the British; and his strategic grasp of operations in the Middle East. But we have also seen his range of extreme personality flaws that affect his decision making and his standing—under operational pressure or in a crisis (in Greece), he is found wanting; he is reluctant to acknowledge high performance in others (Clowes for example); in Syria he is prepared to flout his charter as well as enforce it, if the promotion or enhancement of a peer (Lavarack) is at stake. Then, when the situation in Syria deteriorates, he moves with purpose and speed to rectify his error and insist on Lavarack's elevation to a temporary corps command and Australians in action being commanded by an Australian where they are in the majority.

But perhaps his greatest flaw is his poor judgment. That Blamey has moral flaws is secondary to the critical point that he makes no attempt to conceal them: he is tactless. He brings his wife to the Middle East and flouts and then fights a government request that he send her home; he engages in sleazy relationships and excessive drinking in nightclubs in Cairo despite the knowledge that his peers and troops will know and will not be impressed; and he takes his son out of Greece on a plane when he must surely know what the reaction will be.

The Syrians call this place Nahr-El-Kelb, which means 'River the Dog'. The eternal soldier has walked this land, has passed this way. Through centuries of war his generals have been forced to attack this position where the hills climb high above the river as it finds its way to the sea. This obstacle favours the defender no matter in which century the battle is fought or with what weapons—warfare is relative to time, place and weaponry. Here the Egyptian pharaohs came and conquered, the Assyrians came, the Babylonians, the Romans, and the French. Every army and nation perpetuates its military prowess, its moments of glory. The inscriptions of the eternal soldier and his nations are carved into the rock here. In early 1942 a fresh inscription was cut on General Blamey's orders to commemorate the capture of Damour by the Second AIF—chiefly the 7th Division.

The Australian war correspondent and poet Kenneth Slessor wrote the following poem, which above all reveals his deep contempt for Blamey:

An Inscription for Dog River

Our general was the greatest and bravest of generals.
For his deeds, look around you on this coast—
Here is his name cut next to Ashur-Bani-Pal's,
Nebuchadnezzar's and the Roman host;
And we, though our identities have been lost,
Lacking the validity of stone or metal,
We, too, are part of his memorial,
Having been put in for the cost,

Having bestowed on him all we had to give
In battles few can recollect,
Our strength, obedience and endurance,
Our wits, our bodies, our existence,
Even our descendants' right to live—
Having given him everything, in fact,
Except respect.[48]

THEATRE OF WAR

4

Immense political and military changes occurred in Australia during 1941 as both the Government and the army were forced to ponder the Japanese potential to bring them to war in the Pacific. In February, the Chiefs of Staff provided their political masters with an appreciation of possible Japanese ambitions and military options and how Australia might best react to the apprehended threats.

Firstly, it was perceived that an invading force would be likely to attack an area essential to Australia's economic ability to wage war: the region Newcastle–Sydney–Port Kembla. Secondly, Melbourne, Brisbane, Fremantle, Albany and Adelaide were identified as additional defensive focal points. The Northern Territory and Papua and New Guinea, although strategically important, were seen as areas that could deplete and therefore dilute the army's ability to protect the more important centres. It was believed that the Japanese would be forced to conquer the Malayan peninsula and the Dutch East Indies and neutralise the American Pacific Fleet as a prerequisite to an invasion of Australia.

To react to the needs of a South-East Asian and home defence, the forces in Australia at this time consisted of the AIF 8th Division and the militia: the 1st and 2nd Cavalry Divisions, four infantry divisions and components of a fifth division and corps troops. On paper, this seemed a formidable force. However, severe deficiencies in strength, training, equipment and, above all, leadership, due to the priority given to the AIF 6th, 7th and 9th Divisions in the Middle East, caused this paper assessment to represent not much more than a military paper tiger.

In short, the cupboard was almost bare. Australia had made an enormous contribution of sailors, airmen, soldiers and equipment to the Middle East and Britain, believing that the British base at Singapore and the American Pacific Fleet at Pearl Harbor would hold a Japanese thrust in the Pacific or, at worst, that Australia would at least have time to recover her forces behind the security screen of these bases.

To compound an already disastrous state of affairs, the 8th AIF Division was dispersed in token gestures to the threatened north: a battalion to Rabaul to hold airfields; another portion of the division to Timor and Ambon and the remainder to participate in the not-too-distant disaster of Singapore.

As a result of the preliminary appreciation, it was decided to raise a militia battalion to garrison Port Moresby. The role was allotted to the 49th Battalion from Queensland. Its personnel were volunteers for tropical service and, after a commendable degree of enthusiasm towards embarkation, the battalion left Brisbane on 15 March 1941, on the SS *Katoomba* and the SS *Zealandia*.

The staff work, dealing with the logistics for the arrival and care of this battalion in Port Moresby, was abysmal. It might be justifiably claimed that such a state of affairs would never have been tolerated had an AIF battalion been involved. 'They had no mess tins, plates, pannikins or mosquito nets (all of which had to be purchased locally) and a number had no waterproof sheets.'[1]

Until the outbreak of war with Japan, in December 1941, the degree of effort given to the training, equipping and morale of the 49th Battalion was a disgrace which was to place it at a severe disadvantage when the time later came to commit it to battle. It was given the laborious tasks of building roads, unloading ships and constructing buildings, as well as the expected duties of siting and preparing defensive positions. All such tasks were necessary but the battalion was essentially intended for a defensive role and the emphasis should have been upon ensuring more advanced training than the minimum platoon-level instruction it received. When the Chief of the General Staff, Lieutenant-General Sturdee, visited Port Moresby on 11 July 1941, he described the 49th Battalion as 'quite the worst battalion in Australia'.[2]

If all this was not poor enough, on 26 May 1941 Brigadier, later Major-General, Basil Morris had assumed command of the 8th Military District (Papua and New Guinea). Morris had hardly had an impressive Second World War record. When Blamey had first arrived in the Middle East, he had discovered that the Australian Overseas Base, commanded by Morris, was 'living in Jerusalem largely by taking in its own washing',[3] and that he was reluctant to use Morris further because he didn't 'get down deep enough into things'.[4] Blamey later transferred Morris to Bombay as the Australian liaison officer. His appointment to Port Moresby therefore reflects the fact that in mid-1941 Port Moresby was considered nothing more than a backwater garrison.

Towards the latter part of 1941, as war clouds loomed larger on the South-East Asian horizon, it was decided to increase the Port Moresby garrison to brigade strength: the 53rd Battalion from New South Wales and the 39th Battalion from Victoria were chosen to implement that decision.

In the long, proud history of Australia at arms, there can be no more tragic and damning story than that of the raising, deployment, equipment and training of the 53rd Battalion. Originally raised for service in Darwin, the battalion came into being around 1 November 1941, after eighteen militia battalions were each ordered to supply a quota of 62 men for the new unit. To bring the battalion up to full strength, an additional 100 personnel were recruited in a manner that reflects the appalling staff work of the time. Sergeant Keith Irwin, 53rd Battalion:

> Even at this stage we received a draft of soldiers, mostly eighteen years of age. These poor devils had no idea what was happening to them. They had not been told where they were going, what unit they were destined for, or any information at all. They had received no final leave, were given no chance to let their families know what was happening to them. They were just taken down to the *Aquitania* and put on board. Most of them had never seen or handled a rifle. This was a disgrace because many of these youngsters, who had literally been shanghaied, later paid the supreme sacrifice during

> the battles in the mountains [the Kokoda campaign] and at Sananada. Once the *Aquitania* put to sea, we were told that we would be heading for Port Moresby, not Darwin. A training programme was implemented so that we NCOs could give the new recruits some elementary training in the use and handling of the .303 rifle.[5]

We have identified the manner of the raising of a Second AIF battalion during the early stages of the war, and have seen its structure, its growing training and confidence before embarkation and, then, its training in the Middle East, before being committed to battle: time, expertise and motivation in formation and training and, most usually, by carefully selected and capable officers. The 53rd Battalion was denied all of this, and in its place was to develop a bitterness and anger within its ranks that would work directly against the very qualities needed for success. This sorry story did not end with the battalion's raising.

After making the journey from Sydney in company with the 39th Battalion on the *Aquitania*, the 53rd arrived in Port Moresby on 3 January 1942, to be confronted with a logistical nightmare. The Barry Commission Report:

> Making every allowance for the state of affairs existing in Australia at the time of the outbreak of the Japanese war, the condition which manifested itself immediately after the arrival of [the *Aquitania*] convoy calls for severe censure of the persons responsible for the loading of the troops' camp equipment. The troops were of the average age of eighteen and a half years, and had received no proper training. They were in the charge of inexperienced officers who appear to have had no control over them. They were inadequately equipped in every way; in particular, they were without much of the equipment necessary to give them any reasonable prospect of maintaining health in an area such as Port Moresby. In [the] general state of unpreparedness, that may have been inevitable, but no excuse is apparent . . . for the gross carelessness and incompetence which resulted in the stowing of camp equipment at the

> bottom of the holds, so that when the troops were disembarked, there were no facilities to enable them to be fed and encamped.[6]

The 39th Battalion was raised in Victoria in October 1941 from elements of the 3rd and 4th Infantry Divisions (Militia), and the 2nd Cavalry Division. The circumstances of its raising were far less trying than those of the 53rd Battalion. Its original commander was Lieutenant-Colonel Conran, a veteran of the First AIF. Although 52 years of age, and later destined to suffer a decline in health from the demands of tropical service, Conran, and some of his officers, deserve high praise indeed for the esprit de corps that they instilled in their battalion.

The Japanese attacked the American Pacific Fleet at Pearl Harbor and landed on the Malayan peninsula during the period 7–8 December 1941. If Pearl Harbor deeply shocked Australia, then the events of the following six weeks shook it to its very foundations. A roller-coaster ride of disaster saw the British capital ships HMS *Prince of Wales* and HMS *Repulse* sunk only two days later; Hong Kong fell on 26 December; the Japanese attacked Rabaul on 23 January 1942; Ambon was attacked a week later; and, on the last day of 1941, British and Commonwealth forces withdrew from the Malayan peninsula into the bastion of Singapore.

If these events seemed like a nightmare, then the fall of Singapore on 15 February 1942 was like waking up in a cold sweat and realising that the nightmare was in fact the real world. The biggest capitulation in British military history saw over 130 000 soldiers (14 972 of them Australians)[7] captured by the inferior yellow hordes. The atlas studied for generations in school with its impressive Far Eastern 'red blobs' was now suddenly a humiliating relic of another time.

With Singapore gone, little stood between the Japanese and the shores of Australia. If the first air raid on Port Moresby on 3 February was also sobering enough, when war came to the Australian mainland on 19 February in the form of the

Japanese bombing of Darwin—and a landing on Timor on the same day—all seemed lost. Java was attacked nine days later.

In the second half of 1941, the Australian Government and the Australian Army had begun to consider how best to strengthen the nation's defence and provide the home army with more experienced commanders. To this end, it began to send home some of its more successful officers—and others who had shown themselves to be too old or inefficient for modern warfare, but whose services could be used constructively at home. Three of those promoted on high merit (and critical to our story) were Brigadier Rowell, who returned in September as a major-general and became Deputy Chief of the General Staff; Brigadier Vasey, who became Chief of Staff to the GOC of Home Forces; and Brigadier Cyril Clowes, who also became a major-general and assumed command of the 1st Division. Brigadier, now Major-General, Morris, the former Overseas Base Commander and Liaison Officer in Bombay, had been an example of the latter category.

On 3 January 1942 the British requested that two of the three AIF divisions in the Middle East be dispatched to the Far East. Blamey chose the 6th and 7th Divisions. The 7th began boarding ships in Suez during January and the process of their departure continued until early March. But the Japanese interfered with these arrangements—their rapid subjugation of South-East Asia threatened to envelop the destination points of the soon-to-arrive AIF. During February 1942, a most extraordinary cable confrontation occurred between 'mother' and one of her dominions. David Horner:

> On 17 February Curtin asked Churchill to divert the following convoys to Australia [the first one had just docked in Java] rather than to Burma. In his unpublished memoirs Blamey wrote that he 'whole heartedly' agreed that the 7th Division should go to Australia. Its troops were on passenger ships, its equipment was on cargo ships and had not been loaded tactically, not all the ships were travelling at the same speed, and the division would have been of little use in Burma.[8]

A part of Churchill's reply to Curtin on 20 February stated that:

> I suppose you realise that your leading division, the head of which is sailing south of Colombo to the Netherlands East Indies at this moment . . . is the only force that can reach Rangoon in time to prevent its loss and the severance of communication with China. It can begin to disembark at Rangoon about the 26th or 27th. There is nothing else in the world that can fill the gap . . .
>
> I am quite sure that if you refuse to allow your troops which are actually passing to stop this gap, and if, in consequence, the above evils, affecting the whole course of the war, follow, a very grave effect will be produced upon the President and the Washington circle, on whom you are so largely dependent . . .
>
> We must have an answer immediately, as the leading ships of the convoy will soon be steaming in the opposite direction from Rangoon and every day is a day lost. I trust therefore that for the sake of all interests, and above all your own interests, you will give most careful consideration to the case I have set before you.[9]

Churchill also cabled President Roosevelt seeking his support. This was forthcoming in the form of a cable to Curtin on 20 February, which in part proclaimed that: 'While I realise the Japs are moving rapidly, I cannot believe that, in view of your geographical position and the forces on their way to you or operating in your neighbourhood, your vital centres are in immediate danger.'[10] These were easy words to compose from Washington. Roosevelt was probably referring to the 41st American Division of National Guardsmen when he talked of 'forces on their way to you'. We shall see the quality of this force when the battle for Buna unfolds. Secondly, the forces 'operating in your neighbourhood' were threadbare and rapidly dwindling through capitulation and withdrawal. The 'neighbourhood' was, in fact, rapidly becoming the backyard. Curtin replied to Churchill on 22 February:

> I have received your rather strongly worded request at this late stage, though our wishes in regard to the disposition of the A.I.F. in the Pacific theatre have long been known to you . . .
>
> Malaya, Singapore, and Timor have been lost, and the whole of the Netherlands East Indies will apparently be occupied shortly by the Japanese.
>
> . . . having regard to what has gone on before, and its adverse results would have the gravest consequences on the morale of the Australian people. The Government therefore must adhere to its decision.
>
> . . . We feel therefore, in view of the foregoing and the services the A.I.F. have rendered in the Middle East, that we have every right to expect them to be returned as soon as possible, with adequate escorts to ensure their safe arrival.[11]

Churchill then had the temerity to divert the Australian convoy to Rangoon 'assuming a favourable response'[12] from the Australian Government after reading his latest cable sent on 22 February 1942:

> We could not contemplate that you would refuse our request, and that of the President of the United States, for the diversion of the leading Australian division to save the situation in Burma. We knew that if our ships proceeded on their course to Australia while we were waiting for your formal approval they would either arrive too late at Rangoon or even be without enough fuel to go there at all. We therefore decided that the convoy should be temporarily diverted to the northward.[13]

Churchill then went on to say that the convoy was now too far north to reach Australia without refuelling. But his cable to General Wavell on the same day smacked of even further arrogance and failure to recognise Australia's independent rights. He pointed out to Wavell that his decision to point the convoy northwards gave the Australian Government 'three or four days' to think the matter over, 'with its majority of one'.[14]

Not only was the size of the Australian Government's majority not Churchill's concern, he had absolutely no fair grounds to adopt this high-handed attitude. His was a failure to acknowledge the splendid AIF recent record along the North African coast and its sacrifice in Greece, Crete, Syria and Tobruk. To this should be added the ongoing commitment of the Australian Navy in the Mediterranean and the sterling service of its air force personnel in both Fighter and Bomber Commands in Britain. In addition, the fact was that Australia, as he wrote these lines, was still engaged in sending additional personnel to Canada for the Empire Training Scheme—to say nothing of the loss of her soldiers during the Singapore debacle.

In what might almost be seen as a declaration of independence, Curtin replied to Churchill on 23 February:

> In your telegram of February 20 it was clearly implied that the convoy was not proceeding to the northwards. From your telegram of February 22 it appears that you have diverted the convoy towards Rangoon and had treated our approval to this vital diversion as merely a matter of form. By doing so you have established a physical situation which adds to the dangers of the convoy, and the responsibility for the consequences of such diversion rests with you . . .
>
> We feel a primary obligation to save Australia not only for itself, but to preserve it as a base for the development of the war against Japan. In the circumstances it is quite impossible to reverse a decision which we made with the utmost care, and which we have affirmed and reaffirmed.[15]

Curtin won his battle. The convoys carrying the 7th Division AIF—the division that was to shoulder the chief burden of the Papuan campaign—arrived back in Australia during March 1942.

In July 1941, the Japanese negotiated with the Germans to force the Vichy French to allow their presence in French

Indo-China. From naval and air bases in that region, Japan could strike southwards from a firm base. In response, President Roosevelt had almost immediately placed a total oil embargo upon her. This forced Japan's military hand. Given that she would run out of oil for her navy by about the middle of the following year, it was decided to neutralise the American Pacific Fleet at Pearl Harbor and, with the Americans disabled for at least the immediate future, and the British standing alone on the continent, to strike rapidly to secure oil supplies in the Dutch East Indies.

The Japanese also knew that the Philippines would have to be captured. The commander of the American forces in the Philippines was General Douglas MacArthur, who would play a critical role in the rapidly approaching Papuan campaign.

MacArthur was born on 26 January 1880 at Little Rock Barracks, Arkansas. The son of a professional soldier, he was born during the last days of the taming of the American frontier. His father, Arthur, had fought in the American Civil War and had subsequently been posted to a number of frontier outposts followed by service and promotion in Washington. When the Spanish–American War broke out in early 1888, his father, now a brigadier-general, was posted to the Philippines. His career progressed rapidly to the point where he became a major-general and then the Military Governor of that country. While these events were in train, Douglas MacArthur entered West Point on 13 June 1899. His mother was a monumental influence upon his character and his career. With her husband serving in the Philippines, 'Pinky' MacArthur travelled to West Point to be close to her son. MacArthur's record during his four years as a cadet was exceptional: he regularly topped his class in his academic study as well as drill.[16]

A number of Douglas MacArthur's early postings gave him some experience in, and an understanding and love for, the Far East. However, his father's professional demise as a result of a conflict with the US Government over the transition of the Philippines to civilian rule gave his son an early insight and a lasting unease as to the dangers of politicians to a professional soldier. Despite the fact that Arthur MacArthur returned to the United States as the highest ranking soldier in the army, he subsequently missed the post of chief of staff and soon retired.

He died in 1912. Douglas MacArthur resolved to not only emulate his proud father's achievements, but to surpass them.

His chance to build a legend and begin to realise his father's ambitions came during the Great War. He became chief of staff of the 42nd Division, which would become known as the famed 'Rainbow Division'. It was during his service on the Western Front in 1918 that much of the MacArthur persona was developed. He was haughty, brave and utterly inspiring as a leader of men. The chief of staff of the Rainbow Division stands out in battle, not only because of his courage, but equally as a result of his appearance. You have to notice this man: '. . . his smashed-down cap instead of a steel helmet . . . a four-foot muffler [scarf] knitted by his mother, a turtleneck sweater, immaculate riding breeches, and cavalry boots with a mirror finish. From his mouth a cigarette holder jutted at a jaunty angle. His only weapon was a riding crop.'[17] The important characteristic of MacArthur as a Great War leader is not the actual combat itself, but the fearless, charismatic and inspirational leading of his comrades in battle. His career blossomed. As a staff officer with the rank of brigadier-general serving under General 'Black Jack' Pershing, and not therefore in any circumstances expected to serve in action, MacArthur became America's highest decorated soldier during the Great War. He was recommended for the Medal of Honour but this was turned down by Pershing. Not surprisingly, MacArthur developed a deep mistrust of politicians and his military superiors that was later to approach paranoia.

After the war MacArthur landed one of the United States Army's finest jobs when he became the superintendent of West Point. He was given a brief to radically change the army's training of its young future officer graduates. With characteristic energy he revolutionised its curricula, broke down some of its outdated customs and dragged it towards a realisation that future warfare in the twentieth century was going to be won or lost by large intakes of civilians into the army and not fought, as was believed at the time, by small, professional armies involved in small-scale conflict. The modern army, MacArthur reasoned, needed officers who were far more broadly educated and were therefore much more worldly, and who could, as a consequence, understand and relate to the civilian conscript or volunteer.[18]

During his period as superintendent of West Point MacArthur married a wealthy socialite by the name of Louise Brooks, who had had an affair with General Pershing in Paris during the war (and with a Pershing aide just after it). In November 1921, Pershing ended MacArthur's position at West Point (to conclude on June 1922) and promptly posted him to the Philippines. There was no real job there for a soldier of his rank.

MacArthur's period in the Philippines was noteworthy only for his training of the limited American and Filipino personnel in his new command. When the Filipino and American components of the army were merged into the new Philippine Division (far under strength), MacArthur took to the task of its administration and training with great ability and enthusiasm. When two glowing efficiency reports were received in Washington MacArthur was promoted to major-general and posted home. When he returned in early 1925 Major-General Douglas MacArthur was the youngest of the 21 soldiers holding that rank in the United States Army.[19]

MacArthur's seven-year marriage failed in 1927 after his wife, who had increasingly detested the life of a soldier's spouse, failed to talk him out of his army career for a highly paid position with her step-father's firm of J.P. Morgan. However, his love of soldiering was dramatically rewarded when he was promoted to the army's highest position by President Hoover in August 1930. Thus Douglas MacArthur gained the position that his father had coveted but had failed to achieve.

MacArthur's period as chief of staff was a tough time marked by a number of problems. The first was the infamous Washington Bonus March of 1932. In 1924 Congress had passed a law allowing for three and a half million Great War veterans to be paid a $1000 bonus either upon death, or in the year 1945. As the Great Depression worsened during 1932, many of those veterans were unemployed and destitute through no fault of their own, and they wanted their bonus payments immediately. Thousands of bonus marchers arrived in

Washington and set up rough camps and occupied derelict buildings. President Hoover decided to buy time in anticipation of the successful passage of a bill through Congress which would allow the bonus payments. However, while Congress passed the legislation, the Senate subsequently rejected it. The numbers of Bonus Marchers now steadily increased to the point where the police were incapable of controlling the situation. When the marchers reoccupied a number of the derelict buildings, the police attempted to evict them. During the resulting confrontation, a number of police and marchers were seriously injured, which forced the police to request army assistance.

MacArthur made a number of serious errors of judgment during the crisis. Against his aide's advice (Major Dwight D. Eisenhower), MacArthur not only personally went down to the scene of the problem, but sent Eisenhower home to change into army uniform and sent for his own. There would be no unobtrusive informality here. He took over full command of the situation rather than work hand in hand with the police, and then proceeded to apply a heavy hand using tear gas, the blunt side of swords and fixed bayonets. The marchers were driven back. Some controversy has since raged as to whether MacArthur then actually received President Hoover's order to *not* cross the Anacostia Bridge and enter the marchers' shanty camp, which was occupied by the veterans' women and children. In the event the troops did, and the camp was burnt to the ground. It was an ugly scene made worse by MacArthur's claim to the press that the demonstrators were communists, or at least communist led, and that had Hoover waited another week the very survival of the US Government and law and order would have been seriously threatened.

The fact remains that the overwhelming majority of the marchers were veterans who wanted nothing more than to exercise their democratic right to procure their bonus. In the eyes of many Americans the whole sad episode remained a stain on MacArthur's reputation for the rest of his life—and remains so. However, since MacArthur's politics were to the extreme right of the Republican Party, the incident merely enhanced his reputation among a considerable number of like-minded Americans.[20]

MacArthur's second problem during his tenure as chief of staff was one shared by all military free-world commanders of the time: poor funding. It was not fashionable to be a professional soldier in the 1930s in the United States, as Americans were predominantly anti-military and isolationist. The Hoover administration had drastically cut defence spending and the Roosevelt administration at first sought to slash it even further. Roosevelt had been elected to implement his 'New Deal' and saw further military cuts as a means of finding some of the funding. His decision caused a caustic scene between the president and his chief of staff. When MacArthur demanded an interview with Roosevelt, he later told him that during the next war when 'an American boy, lying in the mud with an enemy bayonet through his belly and an enemy foot on his dying throat, spat out his last curse, I wanted the name not to be MacArthur but Roosevelt'.[21] After this outburst, MacArthur offered his resignation on the spot and left.[22]

Given that the two men were absolutely poles apart in their politics, and that the President of the United States was/is both the political leader of the nation *and* the Commander-in-Chief of the armed forces, and was destined, therefore, to be MacArthur's political and military superior for almost the duration of the coming war, MacArthur's outburst did little to foster a good relationship. Although Roosevelt backed down on his further cut to spending, the damage had already been done. But Roosevelt was a cunning politician. He kept MacArthur on where he could essentially control him, rather than accept his resignation and see him develop into a potential political opponent. In succeeding years MacArthur again passionately argued for greater funding. Eventually in 1935 when the Nazis and the Japanese were demonstrating their potential for aggression, he actually received more than he requested.

MacArthur's destiny now swung back again to the Philippines via two attractive offers. The country was to become a republic in 1946, with Manuel Quezon as the first president of a transitional Commonwealth. He was initially to work with an American high commissioner. When Quezon came to the United States in mid-1935, he approached

MacArthur for advice as to how best prepare the defence of his country. MacArthur's advice was simple: a plan, time and, above all, money. Quezon offered MacArthur the job of building and training his country's future army. At virtually the same time, Roosevelt approached MacArthur to become the inaugural high commissioner of the Philippines. When MacArthur found out that Roosevelt's offer entailed his resigning from the US Army's active list, while Quezon's allowed him to collect two salaries and remain on that list, he naturally chose Quezon's proposal. It was destined to make him a wealthy man. He took Eisenhower with him as his principal aide.

While sailing to the Philippines in late 1935 MacArthur met Jean Faircloth, a 37-year-old from Tennessee whom he married within eighteen months of their meeting on board ship. The marriage was to prove a long and happy one and would produce a son, Arthur MacArthur, on 21 February 1938.

MacArthur's task of preparing the Philippine Army for war with Japan was a daunting one indeed. It was almost an unreal military world into which MacArthur arrived: he was made Field Marshal of a Philippine Army that was virtually non-existent. His ten-year plan envisaged an eventual purchase of 50 PT boats, about 250 aircraft and an army of some 400 000 conscripts.[23] The thinking was that Japan would have to be prepared to fight a protracted war in the jungles and rainforests of the numerous Philippine islands against a guerrilla army, and that a mobile, hard-hitting PT torpedo boat fleet would force the enemy to attack with small naval forces. MacArthur was simply relying on the theory that the time, energy and funding necessary for an enemy attack might make it prohibitive. It was a pipedream. When Eisenhower costed the plan at $25 million he was told by MacArthur and Quezon to make do with a third of that amount. In fact, in 1940, the budget was actually $1 million.[24]

In 1937 Roosevelt cancelled MacArthur's assignment as military adviser to the Philippine Army and indicated that he intended to post him back to the United States. MacArthur resigned from the United States Army. With severe budget cuts from Quezon and a cooler relationship between them leading up to the war, MacArthur's Philippine Army was poorly funded and therefore poorly equipped and motivated. Eisenhower became increasingly frustrated and left during late 1939.

When Roosevelt cut US oil supplies to Japan in July 1941, he also placed MacArthur back on the active list and put him in command of all US forces in the Far East. This was nothing more than a splendid title and a prestigious posting, but an empty one. If the British bastion at Singapore and its troops on the Malayan peninsula were threadbare and lacking in support, then the Americans were no better placed in their colonial outpost in the Philippines. Years of appeasement by the British and, in America's case, of rampant isolationism and—in both cases—the neglect of their armed services by a generation of poor funding and training were not made good by last minute oil embargos and stopgap defensive measures.

The final plan for the defence of the Philippines in 1941 was merely a forlorn hope. When Japan struck, the American and Philippine forces on the principal island of Luzon would withdraw to the Bataan peninsula and the island of Corregidor, which lies in Manila Bay. This, it was believed, would not only deny the enemy one of the finest harbours in the Pacific, but allow the Americans to await reinforcement.

Disaster struck in the Philippines within 24 hours of the heavy mauling of the US Pacific fleet at Pearl Harbor. When Brereton, the air force commander at Clark Field, requested permission at 7.15 a.m. on the morning of 8 December to send his B-17 Bombers to hit the Japanese, MacArthur told him to wait for orders. When he rang again about 90 minutes later, although he could not identify specific targets for MacArthur, he again asked permission to attack.[25] MacArthur, understandably, was waiting to clarify the events of the past hours before ordering any action, let alone offensive action. And then the Japanese struck. Brereton had bungled. When the news reached the Philippines that the Japanese had bombed Pearl Harbor and that the Japanese could be expected to attack the Philippines at any time, Brereton had scrambled all but three of his B-17s. He had then requested permission to attack the enemy. By the time Macarthur had authorised either attacks or reconnaissance flights, Brereton had been forced to land his planes for refuelling. He made the mistake of landing the lot at the same time. The Japanese appeared and destroyed his force on the ground.

Even had the B-17s not been caught out at Clark Field, the Americans knew only too well their chances of survival. Edwin Ramsey, US Army: 'I went to the officers club and had a drink with the Chief of Intelligence for General Wainwright . . . "Lieutenant, are you religious?" And I said, "No Sir, not particularly". "Well" he said, "I think you'd better give your soul to God, because your arse belongs to the Japanese!" '[26]

The enemy landed on 20 December 1942 and shattered the Philippine Army within 48 hours. MacArthur could do little else but pull back through the Bataan peninsula and direct the fighting from the island of Corregidor. The problem was that not only did the American and Philippine soldiers withdraw to Bataan, but around 20 000 civilians followed them. The main long-term problem was obvious: food.

General Marshall cabled MacArthur to hold the enemy back as air and ground reinforcements would be sent, but it was an empty undertaking since the Chiefs of Staff knew that the relief of the Philippines was beyond them. The nation was reeling from the disaster of Pearl Harbor; any potential drive towards the Philippines was fraught with tremendous danger because of the Japanese naval superiority in the Pacific; and the allies had decided to adopt the 'beat Hitler first' strategy that would see an overwhelming preponderance of men and material heading for the European theatre of operations. And, further, the resources of the nation were at a premium and could not be squandered on a forlorn hope.

As the situation on Bataan and Corregidor worsened through January 1942, MacArthur's fate came under serious discussion back in Washington. There were grave propaganda issues at stake as well as the obvious loss of a senior soldier. Marshall could not sanction MacArthur's capture by the Japanese, either for the damage it might cause American morale, or the disgrace it would bring to the United States Army. Overtures began in early February for MacArthur to leave. He would have none of it, nor the proposed evacuation of his wife and child. When Quezon left by submarine on 20 February he left MacArthur with the tidy sum of $500 000, which was part of a deal he had struck with him when his appointment had originally been negotiated. In other words, MacArthur would have earnt that sum as a bonus over his ten-year appointment, had it been fulfilled. The payment might have been generous in the circumstances, but it was entirely legal.[27]

Two days after Quezon's departure, Roosevelt ordered MacArthur to leave his post and assume command of all United States troops in Australia. At first MacArthur seemed disinclined to obey even the Commander-in-Chief of the American Armed Forces, but his staff convinced him to leave. On the night of 11 March 1942, MacArthur, his wife and son, and a number of his staff left Corregidor on four PT boats for Mindanao where they would rendezvous with two B-17s for the flight to Australia.

When MacArthur boarded his plane, he carried little baggage in the literal sense, but enormous emotional and psychological baggage. Within him burned a fierce desire for military redemption: to return to his army, many of whom were now calling him 'Dug-out Doug' and accusing him of deserting them. This land was also the country that his father had fought in, that he had lived and served in for a large portion of his career and which he regarded as his second home. But there was also a strong politico-military dimension to his torment. He must answer his critics in Washington, from the president with whom he had argued during the tough budget days during the depression, to General Marshall, Admiral King and even Eisenhower, whom he thought to be against him.

Some of his enemies were real, while others were mere phantoms. But above all, when MacArthur arrived in Australia in March 1942, he knew his stocks were low and that those in high places would not tolerate defeats and withdrawals forever.

Faubion Bowers was an aide to MacArthur: 'He was like old Grecian statues, larger than life, and such absolute self-confidence. He had such dignity, such presence. He was a tremendously great man with tremendously great weaknesses. He was a paranoid: everything was an arrow in his heart, and yet he was a magnetic person, who could charm anyone.'[28] Edward H. Simmons, an historian: 'Wherever MacArthur was, he was the centre of attention. All eyes were always riveted by MacArthur. He was a great actor. When you speak of theatre of war, he was the producer, the director, the star actor in that theatre, and he played it to the limit.'[29]

On 18 March 1942, one day after MacArthur arrived in Darwin, it was announced that he had been appointed Supreme Commander of the newly designated South West Pacific Area. When General MacArthur's train subsequently arrived at Terowie, north of Adelaide, two days later, he delivered his now famous line, 'I shall return', referring to his pledge to return to the Philippines. Arriving at the Spencer Street Station in Melbourne on 21 March, he was received more as a conquering hero than a defeated general. In Canberra for a welcoming dinner on 26 March, MacArthur was awarded the Medal of Honour. The medal was, of course, given for nothing more than political and propaganda reasons. America, ravaged by Pearl Harbor and the events in the Philippines, needed a hero, and the Roosevelt administration and General Marshall (neither of whom were fond of MacArthur) reluctantly decided that their right-wing Republican general had to be that icon. Both the American and Australian people adopted their new hero with considerable enthusiasm. During the course of his speech in Canberra, MacArthur said:

> I have come as a soldier in a great crusade of personal liberty as opposed to perpetual slavery. My faith in our ultimate victory is invincible, and I bring to you tonight the unbreakable spirit of the free man's code in support of our joint cause . . . There can be no compromise. We shall win or we shall die, and to this end I pledge you the full resources of all the mighty power of my country and the blood of my countrymen.[30]

The problem was that MacArthur, as Supreme Commander South West Pacific Area, had only a modest deposit of American blood: two divisions of raw, poorly led young conscripts whose build-up in Australia was not going to be completed until 14 May. The Australians could look to the

The Pacific Theatre

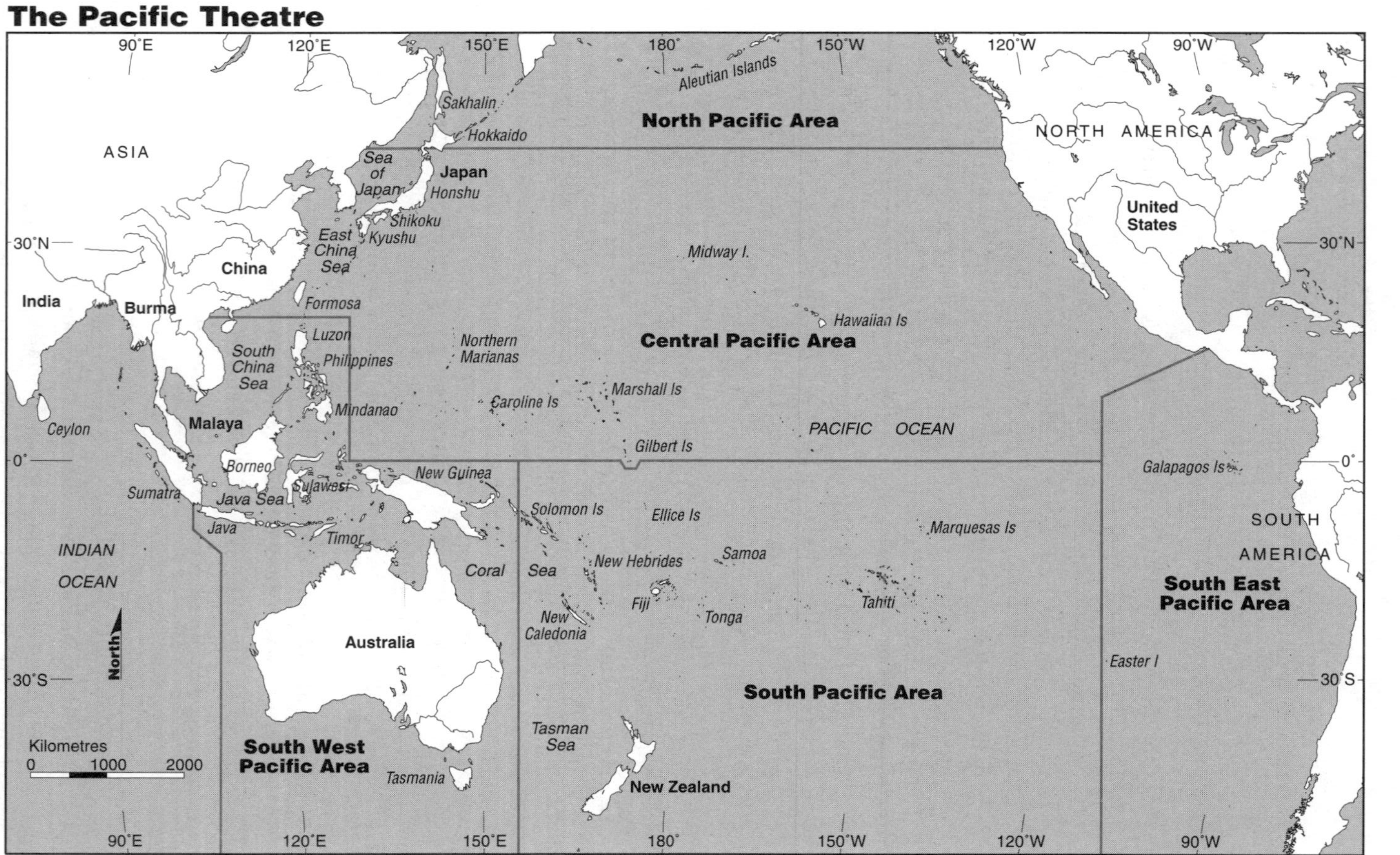

trained, battle-hardened and recently returned 7th Division and a brigade of the 6th Division, in addition to five divisions of militia (admittedly poorly trained). In short, until the long-awaited accumulation of US supplies and personnel in Australia could be accomplished, it would be the Australian Army which would have to provide most of MacArthur's 'blood'. And we will see that this stark truth would always be played down—and even criticised—by MacArthur, and later merely passed over by a long line of American historians engaged more in the making of false legends than the reporting of real ones.

It was during the following month that the Australian Government made a horrendous error of judgment. On 3 April, Prime Minister Curtin received a copy of a directive sent to General MacArthur by the Joint Chiefs of Staff, defining MacArthur's orders and powers. It was confirmed on 15 April. Part nine of the charter stated that: 'Your staff will include officers assigned by the respective Governments concerned, based upon requests made directly to national commanders of the various forces in your area.'[31] However, when MacArthur announced his staff on 19 April 1942, it contained not one Australian soldier's name. This decision was to cause unnecessary friction between the Australians and the Americans and would prove detrimental to the conduct of the Papuan campaign.

When General Blamey had taken his 6th Division to the Middle East in 1940 he had astutely demanded and had received a carefully worded charter which protected the independence and integrity of the Second AIF. We have seen that Blamey used that charter with great wisdom and commendable stoicism in his dealings with the British. But when a new master came to a new theatre of war on Australia's doorstep, the offer of an inside voice in the day-to-day administration of a war in which Australia's sacrifice was to be pivotal to the successful conduct of operations was not taken up by the Curtin Government. This mistake should be seen both as an indication of the widespread panic of the time in Canberra, and the inexperience of the Curtin Government in the portfolio of foreign affairs. And the lesson is simple: when a minor ally in war is granted a concession or a privilege by a greater power, that concession should be grasped wholeheartedly, as they are rarely given. The tragedy is that eight of the eleven nominated staff who were brought out from the Philippines by MacArthur—known as the 'Bataan Gang'—were vastly less experienced than the available Australian staff officers at the time. In addition, as the early battles were to be fought chiefly by Australian troops, and quite possibly on Australian soil in the near future, a strong representation of staff officers who were familiar with their troops, geography and resources would have been desirable.

General Blamey arrived back in Australia at Fremantle on 23 March 1941 to be informed that he had been appointed Commander-in-Chief of the Australian Military Forces. There was no brass band, no swarm of reporters, and no thronging crowd, yet the appointment was a most significant one. This position made Blamey the undisputed master of his army both at home and abroad, and had, on the whole, been earnt despite some friction and mistakes in the Middle East.

However, there was one effort to 'dethrone' Blamey. During the evening of 18 March in Melbourne, in what has become known as 'the revolt of the generals', Major-General Herring, Brigadier Clive Steel and Major-General Vasey saw the Minister for the Army, Frank Forde, and proposed to him that all officers in the Australian Army be retired at 50 years of age. They further advocated the appointment of Major-General Horace 'Red Robbie' Robertson as the new Commander-in-Chief of the Army. This was a preposterous proposal. It is worth mentioning that on the international scene General Montgomery, the future hero of Alamein, was 54 years of age in 1942; MacArthur was 62; General Patton was 56; and in the Australian Army this poor idea would have seen, amongst others, Lavarack, Morshead, Northcott and Sturdee retired. What Forde did not tell his three guests was that Blamey had in fact been appointed Commander-in-Chief by the Cabinet a week earlier. The motive of Forde's three visitors was more an effort to make certain that neither Blamey nor Bennett, who had recently escaped from Singapore under circumstances that were being questioned, would be placed to secure this prime posting. And as David

Horner has pointed out,

> Most of the younger senior commanders had been absent from Australia for about two years . . . They found some of the officers filling divisional commands were too old for war, while others . . . had been promoted rapidly in Australia but had no recent operational experience. It was galling for the officers returning from the Middle East to find that they had been overtaken in the promotion stakes by officers who had stayed behind.[32]

It is also worth mentioning that in a further demonstration of Major-General Rowell's absolute integrity, when Vasey visited him and asked for his support, Rowell told him that 'if he weren't so bloody big, he'd toss him out of the room'.[33] If anyone had had just cause to conspire for Blamey's removal it would have been Rowell, but his loyalty to his commander—however much he loathed him—and to the army itself forbade such behaviour.

On 8 April, to further strengthen his position after having already formed a solely American staff, MacArthur made it abundantly clear that he desired a direct two-way communication between himself and Curtin regarding the higher direction of the war. Thus, while Curtin informed his Commander-in-Chief, Australian Military Forces, General Blamey, that a direct access still lay open between them, MacArthur had now become the key military adviser to the Australian Government concerning strategy.

During early 1942, General Sturdee, at that time Chief of the General Staff, had been working towards a restructuring of the Australian Army. When General Blamey was appointed Commander-in-Chief most of Sturdee's proposals were incorporated in the restructuring, which was announced on 9 April. David Horner again:

> The state-based geographic command structure was disbanded and the Army was divided into the First Army, responsible for the defence of New South Wales and Queensland, the Second Army (Victoria, South

> Australia and Tasmania), the 3rd Corps (Western Australia), Northern Territory Force, the forces in New Guinea and LHQ [Land Headquarters] units.[34]

A number of our chief Papuan campaign commanders were affected. Major-General Rowell was promoted to lieutenant-general and assumed command of the I Corps of the First Army; Brigadier George Vasey was promoted to major-general and took Rowell's position as Deputy Chief of the General Staff; Major-General Herring was posted to Commander Northern Territory Force; and Major-General Cyril Clowes was posted as Commander 1st Division, Second Army.

By April 1942, there seemed no end in sight to the dark days of the Pacific War. The Japanese continued their successful offensive in Burma, the capitulation of the Americans on Corregidor was imminent, air raids against the Solomons were intensifying and the Japanese Navy could sail southward with the advantage of land-based aircraft support from Rabaul.

The rapid enemy advances and their resultant access to the multitude of much-needed raw materials in South-East Asia had been gained at a relatively low cost. After Pearl Harbor, the Imperial Japanese Navy stood unscathed, while the American Navy had been savagely mauled. Given this superiority, the Japanese now sought to cut, or at least weaken, the Allied line of communication from the United States to Australia—the obvious future base for projected Allied counteroffensives.

The Japanese Imperial Headquarters now ordered the capture of Port Moresby, Fiji, Samoa and New Caledonia. Port Moresby was identified as the first objective; its capture would facilitate the acquisition of the other locations. But on 1 May 1942, the American Navy played its tactical trump card.

Prior to the Japanese attack on Pearl Harbor the Americans had three signal intelligence centres: at Washington, Hawaii and in the Philippines. After the rapid enemy advance through the Pacific, orthodox intelligence gathering was made extremely difficult as a consequence of the massive area of ocean that the Japanese now dominated. Much of the Allied special intelligence—codenamed ULTRA after 1944—was obtained through monitoring, intercepting and decoding Japanese radio traffic. By the beginning of the Battle of the Coral Sea, the Americans and their allies were decoding a significant amount of the Japanese Fleet code, known as J25b.

By deploying the aircraft carriers *Lexington* and *Yorktown* to the eastern side of the Coral Sea, the Americans were able to intercept the Japanese Fleet bound for Port Moresby. The battle was inconclusive—the Americans lost more shipping than the Japanese—but the really telling outcome from an Allied perspective was that the invasion transports shadowing the carriers were turned back. Port Moresby had had a critical reprieve.

The Japanese were now forced to alter their plan. Two new objectives—Midway and the Aleutians—were identified as a strategy to draw the American carriers (missed by the Japanese at Pearl Harbor) into a final and, it was believed, crushing confrontation in the Pacific. The Japanese believed that the rapid capture of New Caledonia and Port Moresby would follow their Midway victory.

On 14 May in anticipation of the American 32nd and 41st Divisions arriving in Australia, General Blamey strengthened his positions in North Queensland and Port Moresby by sending the 7th Militia Brigade to Townsville and the 14th Militia Brigade to Port Moresby.

During three action-packed days from 4 to 6 June 1942, the Americans gained a sweet revenge for their massive defeat at Pearl Harbor only six short months before. Using additional information gathered prior to Coral Sea and continuing their splendid work through May and early June, the Allied cryptanalysts were able to predict Midway as the next Japanese target. As a result of ULTRA, the American Navy was able to concentrate its carrier force in good time and achieve total tactical surprise. The very four Japanese carriers that had wrought such utter destruction at Pearl Harbor were either sunk or crippled by the US carriers *Yorktown*, *Enterprise* and *Hornet*. If ever the Australian nation has owed a great debt to its American ally before or after Coral Sea and Midway, it is to those brilliant cryptanalysts and to the magnificent heroism and self-sacrifice of the pilots of those American aircraft carriers.

Following the dramatic naval victory at Midway, the Allied high command's focus turned towards offensive action. On 8 June, General MacArthur sought the necessary amphibious troops and shipping to capture Rabaul. He considered the Australian 7th Division to be a critical component of this operation. On 2 July the Joint Chiefs of Staff belatedly responded to the Midway victory.

There was, not for the first or last time, intense argument between the American Navy and Army over priority of the limited resources for the Pacific War. The Chief of the Navy, Admiral King, considered the Pacific War to be a navy-dominated theatre, and therefore considered that Admiral Chester Nimitz's South Pacific Theatre of Operations should have priority of those resources—that is, that the US Navy and its Marine Corps should prevail. General Marshall, however, maintained that MacArthur and his South West Pacific Area should have at least equal consideration. The Joint Chiefs of Staff identified three objectives. The first was an invasion of the Santa Cruz Islands, Tulagi and adjacent areas, and the Solomon Islands (Nimitz); the second was an invasion of Lae, Salamaua and the north coast of New Guinea (MacArthur); and the third was an invasion of Rabaul and adjacent areas in the New Britain–New Ireland area (MacArthur also).

It is at this point that we see a major flaw in the MacArthur character. On 18 May, naval intelligence in Melbourne predicted that the Japanese had suspended plans for a seaborne invasion of Port Moresby and had instead hastened preparations for an overland attack on that objective; and, on the same day, naval intelligence in Hawaii identified the forthcoming Midway enemy operation and also concurred with their colleagues in Melbourne—that the Japanese were going to mount an overland assault upon Port Moresby. If Coral Sea had not yet established ULTRA's credibility in General MacArthur's eyes, then the uncanny accuracy and impending result at Midway should have. Edward J. Drea:

New Guinea and Papua

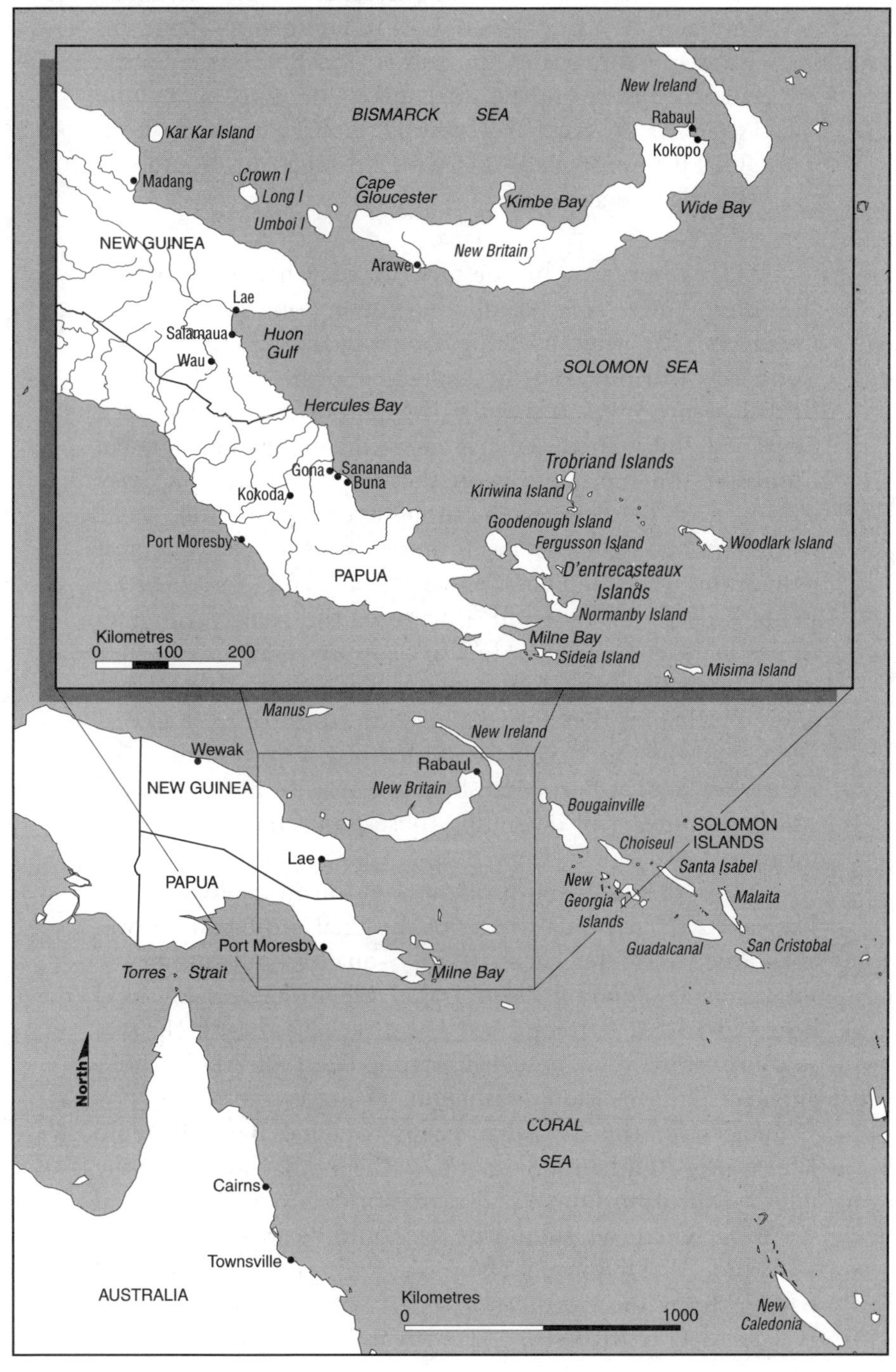

BISMARCK SEA
New Ireland
Rabaul
Kokopo
Kar Kar Island
Madang
Crown I
Long I
Umboi I
Cape Gloucester
Kimbe Bay
Wide Bay
New Britain
Arawe
NEW GUINEA
Lae
Salamaua
Huon Gulf
Wau
SOLOMON SEA
Hercules Bay
Trobriand Islands
Gona
Sananada
Buna
Kiriwina Island
Kokoda
Goodenough Island
Fergusson Island
Woodlark Island
Port Moresby
D'entrecasteaux Islands
PAPUA
Normanby Island
Kilometres
0 100 200
Milne Bay
Sideia Island
Misima Island
Manus
New Ireland
Wewak
Rabaul
NEW GUINEA
New Britain
Bougainville
SOLOMON ISLANDS
Choiseul
Lae
Santa Isabel
New Georgia Islands
PAPUA
Malaita
Port Moresby
Guadalcanal
San Cristobal
Torres Strait
Milne Bay
North
CORAL SEA
Cairns
Townsville
AUSTRALIA
Kilometres
0 1000
New Caledonia

> What remains is a striking impression that MacArthur did not rely heavily on ULTRA either to frame his strategic concept of the war in the Southwest Pacific or to devise operational plans to implement the strategy. A sense of destiny, not revelations from ULTRA, propelled MacArthur through his Southwest Pacific operations.[35]

MacArthur saw his destiny in two haunting words: the Philippines. Any conflicting operation, or piece of intelligence, or army in the field, or officer or politician who stood between him and the realisation of his sacred mission ('I shall return') was to be either ignored or destroyed. Liddell Hart best sums up the character of the impending Papuan campaign and the controversy that would ensue: 'The way that the wish has fathered the thought throughout the course of warfare, and led to endless futilities, is apt to seem the most extraordinary of military phenomena.'[36] Nor can General Blamey escape fair criticism concerning the events leading up to the Papuan campaign. He also discounted the intelligence that the Japanese might attempt an overland crossing to Port Moresby. Blamey therefore deployed the 14th Brigade to that venue and the 7th Brigade to Milne Bay, believing that two militia brigades at Port Moresby and one at Milne Bay would suffice as a means of defending those positions from seaward invasion.

Thus, the early and prudent decision to deploy the 7th Division AIF in Papua to secure the vital ground there was abandoned—in the face of high-quality and privileged intelligence—pending its proposed use in a foolhardy and doomed-to-fail attempt to invade Rabaul, which was nothing more than a selfish, vain pursuit of MacArthur's agenda. This decision was soon to have appalling consequences for the Australian Army. General Rowell would later write: 'And I am on record, on the Sunday following the fall of Tobruk in June 1942, as saying to my officers that, if we were where we should be, it would be in New Guinea with the 7th Division.'[37] There was only one vital overland passage from the northern ramparts of the Owen Stanley Range to Port Moresby. Any such military route would be dominated by the desire to secure the only viable airstrip in the immediate area: Kokoda. After the capture of that small village and airstrip, its precipitous trail led overland to Port Moresby.

BERT AND DOC

5

The betel nut sales continue across the road. It is early afternoon and your world has changed almost completely, because you're on the other side of the motel fence and its graffiti and razor wire. Here you have a comfortable room, a beautiful garden and a swimming pool. A just-returned trekking group arrives. You naturally ask the bloke who has collapsed in the chair by the pool alongside you what the experience was like. 'Christ, that bloody trail cuts you no slack!' He looks thoroughly worn. Hardly encouraging. And then the preparations start.

Your group consists of two public relations men from Melbourne, both in their early forties; a female occupational, health and safety worker in her early twenties, and a young male 31-year-old Army Reserve sergeant, both also from Melbourne; a business executive from Sydney who was once one of Paul Keating's advisers and who accompanied him to Kokoda in 1992 for the fiftieth anniversary celebrations; and, finally, a young couple in their twenties from Brisbane who, like others in your group, have done their fair share of travelling and trekking.

Why do they come here? Amongst the just returned is a woman in her late fifties who just 'wanted to follow in their footsteps'; a man in his early sixties who wanted to follow in his father's footsteps, and when I asked him which battalion his deceased father had served in, he gave me the name of a battalion which had been at Milne Bay and Buna and Sanananda! A father who had served his country well but had not been on the trail. Such is the mystique of this Kokoda Trail, but also the ignorance of the Papuan campaign as a whole.

Frank Taylor of Kokoda Treks and Tours maintains that during his twenty years of conducting treks, his parties have comprised nearly 50 per cent of people between 35 and 55 years of age; that the oldest person taken over was 74; and, although some small number come specifically for the physical test of the trail, all will be touched by the history and the thought that *they* have followed in the footsteps of the Australians of 1942.

Time to pack. Frank gathers you around the pool. Standing in a line are eight Papuan carriers, who like their 1942 ancestors on the Kokoda Trail are from many different regions. A couple are from Buna on the north coast; one is from Dobodura, the site of an old airstrip which will become known to us; another is from Oro Bay not far from Buna; three are from Sogeri near the beginning of the trail; and one is from Efogi, on the Kokoda Trail. These Papuans are not unlike their indentured counterparts from the 1940s, in the sense that a trek earns them good money which will be taken home and converted to rice supplies, kerosene for lamps, soap (which has to be bought because it cannot be locally made), clothing and funds for their children's basic education. There is also the matter of the prestige to be had from gaining extra money from outside the normal village activities.

These men are not mere porters, but very proudly known as *carriers* in the best traditions of their ancestors, and whose stories are proudly known to them. For a minimal cost by Australian standards—but an impressive sum in Papuan Kina—a carrier can be hired to carry the intrepid trekker's pack. It is a wise decision. Food supplies are packed, patrol boxes are also packed to be flown in ahead of the party, and tents and first aid kits are checked. Your first aid kit contains antiseptic solutions, bandages and one priceless item: malaria tablets. All is ready for the big adventure.

Two four-wheel-drive vehicles take you to the first, and one of the most moving, stops: the Bomana War Cemetery. It is as if these sleeping Australians are now performing their last guard duty before the final gateway to Port Moresby. But even Bomana can be deceiving to the uneducated eye—along this long, green, manicured incline lie the soldiers who gave their lives not only along the Kokoda Trail, but also at Milne Bay, Gona, Buna and Sanananda. The name of the soldier's battalion and the date of his sacrifice are the only two clues on his headstone as to the location of his final fight.

After passing the towering Rouna Falls, followed by the Sogeri turn-off and MacDonald's Corner, Ower's Corner is reached and the trek begins.

In 1942, take the best of the youth of Australia and take them at their physical peak; burden them with equipment weighing anywhere between 50 and 70 pounds (22 to 31 kg). Dress them in a khaki uniform designed for the desert, not the jungle; expose them to a claustrophobic environment that will test their alert minds; and send them across terrain that will exhaust the fittest of them. Feed them so sparingly that they will lose two to three stone in weight (13 to 19 kg) over a period of six to eight weeks; expose them to humid, sweating days and cold, wet nights, blessed only with half a blanket or a ground sheet; put them in a weapon pit half full of water. Isolate them, by creating a situation where they can be resupplied only by air or by overtaxed Papuan carriers, and never to a degree whereby they can gain sufficient strength to perform at their optimum level.

These young soldiers are not naïve: they know that the further they struggle forward, the further they slip away from their supplies—bullets and tucker—and in every man's mind is the daunting thought of a wound. Will there be enough stretchers, enough carriers to take them out, and critically, if they can't crawl out or stagger out, what price falling into the enemy's hands?

In 1942, you had to be there to understand this campaign. The commanders at home, and some closer, just did not comprehend this totally unique environment. This is the Kokoda Trail: the ultimate military obstacle course.

Prior to the outbreak of the war in Papua in 1942, travellers from Port Moresby to the north coast could either sail around to it or fly to an inland outpost 1200 feet up in the northern foothills of the Owen Stanley Range. This was Kokoda, a Papuan administration post with a magistrate's house, an assistant magistrate's house, police houses, a native hospital, a rubber plantation and the only airfield in the region.

The Papuans had their own routes including the hazardous one over the Owen Stanley Range: a primitive foot track, often three to four feet wide, restricting movement in most places to single file. Only scant knowledge of that track had reached the outside world through occasional reports of patrol officers, plantation owners, miners and missionaries.

The 25-mile journey from Port Moresby to Illolo and then to Ower's Corner had given the young soldier facing the great mountain crossing little insight into what he was to experience; but he received his first inkling as he slithered, out of control, down steep muddy slopes on his way to the village of Uberi, the first on the Kokoda Trail. From Uberi lay an extremely hard day's march to Ioribaiwa. Distance, so he would quickly learn, was not to be measured in miles on a non-existent map, but in hours of gruelling marching. Most soldiers quickly acquired a trademark body-length stick to become their 'third leg' on the trail. This first day's march across the mountains began with a daunting climb up a razorback spur on the Imita Ridge. The soldier was confronted by the first, but by no means the last, excruciating ascent on the trail: the Golden Stairs.

The Golden Stairs consisted of several thousand pieces of wood pushed into the ascent and held in place by wooden pegs. Filthy, putrid mud constituted the rest of the 'step'. At some points the exposed roots of trees formed the steps, thereby making them irregular in distance and shape and often harder to climb, especially for shorter soldiers. The stairs became permanently sodden and slippery because of the daily rains that soaked and saturated the jungle. Men fell, banged knees, shins and ankles on the exposed steps, gave vent to their anger and struggled agonisingly to their feet; and orderly progress became impossible. Lieutenant Hugh Dalby, 39th Battalion:

> They were so steep . . . We soon had it worked out that instead of trying to walk over the mountain range in sections as we started off doing, and nearly killed

The Kokoda Trail

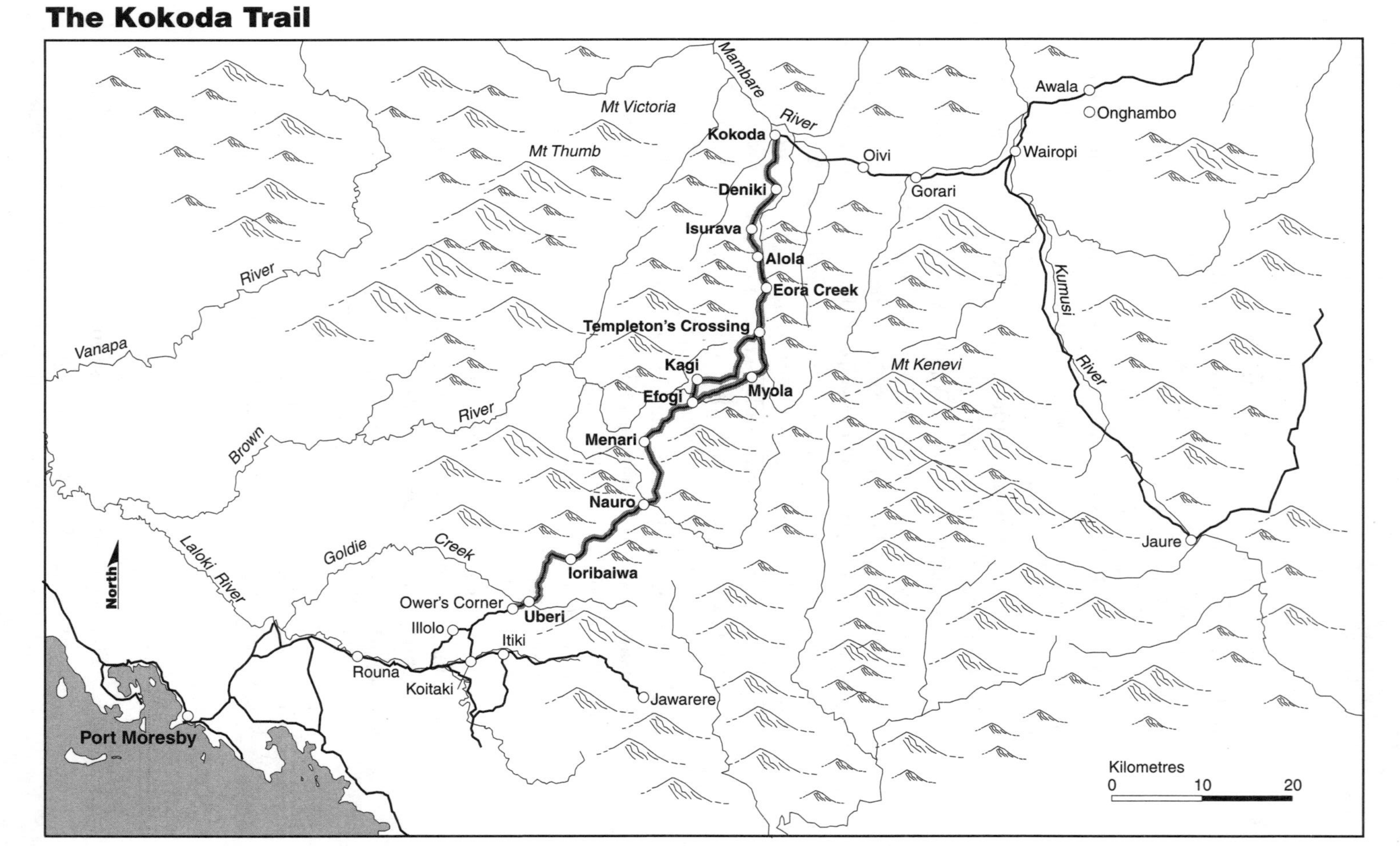

> ourselves, the next day we set off at intervals . . . So you might be five minutes getting rid of your men. But instead of getting to the next staging place at five o'clock at night when it was dark and have people out looking for you, you'd get there at two in the afternoon because you weren't hampered by this stop start, stop start.[1]

Periodically the soldier would catch and clutch at a glimmer of hope through the foliage: it was the sky. The top of the ascent was near; extra strength was summoned; the ultimate exhausting effort was put forth; the Golden Stairs were beaten. But the beguiling point of success was repeatedly found to be a false crest, and the daunting reality that there were many hundreds of steps still to climb became evident. When the summit was eventually reached, to reveal that the distant horizon bounded a succession of ridges and valleys, all of which appeared as formidable as the one just conquered, the true proportion of the torture of the Kokoda Trail began to appal even the toughest soldier.

From Imita Ridge the trail swung steeply down through dense forest to a fast-flowing stream, whose course it followed for a few miles before climbing up to traverse a stretch of kunai grass and continue the long and ever-steeper ascent to Ioribaiwa Ridge and its village. Little distinguished one village on the trail from another save its location. Each consisted basically of a collection of native huts built to accommodate small native groups, and never able to cope with a daily influx or occupation of soldiers in at least company strength. Some of these villages were to be found clustered below abrupt excruciating descents, while others were seemingly precariously perched upon knolls above steep and depressingly gloomy, thick jungle ascents. However, whether the overburdened soldier travelled up or down, he experienced the unending aching of strained knees and a suffering back never designed to carry a heavy load over the Owen Stanley Range.

After his last sporadic spurts of desperate, joint-wrenching, lung-bursting scaling of the Golden Stairs, many a sweat-sodden campaigner reached Ioribaiwa utterly worn out. Accustomed to a more open countryside, he was hopelessly disoriented as the strange pitch-black darkness of the enveloping jungle closed in with the descending evening; and huddled in the chill of the night nearly 3000 feet above sea level, he was hardly warmed by his issue of half a blanket or comforted by the prospect of another 100 miles of clawing up and catapulting down mountains two or three times as high as Ioribaiwa.

The second day in the mountains began with a series of descents and ascents until the village of Ioribaiwa could be seen again from the direction of Nauro. This village was situated at the end of a slippery slope down to a pleasant valley on the edge of the Brown River. This river had a fast-flowing current and afforded the soldier a refreshing stop before he headed on to Menari. He was then faced with about half a day's journey consisting of a march through a river valley, followed by a very steep and exhausting climb over a high mountain and an equally sheer descent to an open area where Menari lay at the junction of two creeks with precipitous banks. The trail negotiated one of these by means of a long, large log—the standard creek crossing. Yet another steep and tiresome ascent saw the soldier on the summit of what became known as Brigade Hill, just forward of Mission Ridge—a derelict Seventh-Day Adventist hut on this spur would give the ridge its name—later the scene of some very savage fighting and subsequent bitter controversy.

Just out of Brigade Hill, the trail left the jungle and overlooked a small kunai patch and then a staggering and yet depressing view of numerous summits and spurs—seemingly an endless characteristic of the Owen Stanley Range. This scene was dominated by Mount Victoria, some 13 000 feet high, its summit wreathed by swirling cloud. The kunai patch was yet another feature that the soldier would frequently encounter. Private Bert Ward, 2/27th Battalion:

> Kunai grass . . . grows six, seven, eight feet high and the track at times would go through this . . . and you wouldn't have the faintest clue what was twelve inches off into the kunai grass. Those were the areas I used to find stifling; and for some reason or other, we always seemed to strike the kunai patches at the hottest time of the day—early afternoon.[2]

From the kunai, the trail swung down approximately 1700 feet into a valley where yet another fast-flowing river with a log crossing awaited the weary men. Many veterans today regard Efogi as the most soul-destroying segment of the trail. The day's exertions to reach Efogi culminated in the final scaling of a lofty height, towering up some 700 feet, whose sharp gradient had to be renegotiated next morning as a descent. An extremely steep climb of 1800 feet was then to be faced which led to a ridge where the village of Kagi, seemingly perched on the hillside, awaited the soldier. From Kagi the track ran east, rising some 3000 feet in about five miles before turning sharply north to the watershed at 9000 feet that formed the western rampart of the deep seven-mile-wide Eora Creek Valley.

'The Gap' was the name sometimes given to the upper reaches of that valley but more specifically to the lowest point—below 6900 feet—in the summit line of the Owen Stanley Range over which aircraft entered the top of the valley. It was fancied in high places that a few well-trained troops, with explosives, could defend or demolish this 'Gap' to deny passage to a vastly superior enemy force.

But the soldier on the Kokoda Trail did not see the Gap—away to the south-east—as he marched north along the summit at close to 9000 feet for almost another five miles before swinging east for the steep descent of 3000 feet in a few miles down the side of the valley. The track plunged so dramatically to the raging torrent below that the hapless soldier was forced to cling to saplings and vines to minimise the frequency and severity of falls before slithering over the log crossing of Eora Creek, which became known as Templeton's Crossing. Some three hours later, after a difficult zigzagging scramble north above the eastern bank, he was confronted by the now familiar cluster of huts; he had arrived at Eora Creek village on a steep, timbered height some 200 feet above the rushing waters.

From that crossing the trail was constricted by the very thick jungle to its narrowest form until near Alola, where it emerged into clearings with cultivated native gardens. Alola stood about 500 feet above Eora Creek on an open spur on the western side of the valley. Some two hours ahead, along a track hugging the hillside between overgrown slopes, on the east falling away to Eora Creek and on the west rising to dominating heights, lay Isurava, where one of the most epic battles in Australian history would later be fought.

From Isurava the trail, while running generally downhill, taxed the soldier with a series of rises over substantial spurs lifting its path, to be followed in turn by slippery descents down their farther slopes. The rough hillside going also offered a variety of huge rocks, swift creeks, sudden waterfalls and tangled roots as additional obstacles to progress on the winding way to the village of Deniki, where the Yodda Valley lay exposed below with the Kokoda airstrip clearly visible.

The trail quickly descended into the green Yodda Valley and, after some three hours' walking, the soldier had journeyed out of the mountains and into the oppressive heat of Kokoda.

Leaving Kokoda, the track wound its way much more gently down to the coast for three full and extremely tiring and hot days' marching. The soldier still faced the crossing of numerous streams and had to pass through the villages of Oivi and Gorari before arriving at the Kumusi River. This presented him with a raging torrent that rushed between widely separated, steep banks. There a bridge suspended by wire cables and aptly known as *Wairopi*, the pidgin for 'wire rope', allowed him safe passage across the river.

Further on the village of Awala was the starting point of many hot steamy tracks that led through lowlands and swamps in the vicinity of Sangara Mission and Popondetta to eventually reach the coast and the settlements of Buna and Gona. Buna was the administrative centre for the district, while Gona was an Anglican mission. They were only small outposts, but they were later to become the scenes of some of the most bitter and controversial fighting—and therefore the least publicised—fighting of the Pacific War. Private Bert Ward, 2/27th Battalion:

> Once you got on that trail there was for most people that sense of personal pride or ego, call it what you like, to keep battling, to go a bit further, a bit further, and not realising a bit further was getting you more and more into trouble and to the stage where it didn't matter how

> severe things had been up to that point, the next day was going to be worse, and the following day was going to be worse again.[3]

The next day was nearly always worse again, because the soldier was slipping farther and farther away from his headquarters' ability to supply and therefore sustain him. Wireless sets were unreliable in those days, particularly in mountainous terrain, and consequently communication with the outside world consisted for most of the campaign of a single telephone line back along the trail to Port Moresby.

Papuan carriers, despite superhuman efforts, could not cope with the demands of brigade-strength forces fighting in such conditions. When supplies were dropped by air they were often either lost due to the nature of the terrain or to defective dropping techniques, or destroyed totally or partially upon impact.

Many medical problems were the result of living in an environment in which a change of clothing, a hot meal and a reasonable period of sleep were impossible dreams rather than regular occurrences. Thrust into this green nightmare, the young soldier was thus faced with a titanic struggle against an environment that would impose upon him a very great physical penalty for every ignorant, thoughtless mistake that a totally inexperienced staff in Port Moresby could make.

While the sweeping political and military events previously described were in train in the Middle East, Australia and the Philippines, the garrison of Port Moresby—chiefly the 30th Brigade's 39th, 49th and 53rd Battalions—had been primarily involved in labouring duties rather than the training they both needed and deserved. There were ships to unload, roads to construct, defensive positions to be dug and wired, and the constant, losing battle against malaria, dengue fever and dysentery.

In early April 1942, Major-General Vasey wrote to subordinate army commanders requesting monthly reports concerning the combat efficiency of brigades in the army. He gave six guidelines, or ratings:

- A Efficient and experienced for mobile offensive operations.
- B Efficient as a formation for mobile offensive operations but not experienced.
- C Individual brigades are efficient for mobile operations, but higher training has not been completed.
- D Individual brigades are efficient in a static role. Additional brigade and higher training is required.
- E Units have completed training. A considerable amount of brigade and higher training is required.
- F Unit training is not yet complete.[4]

Barely five weeks before the 30th Brigade was committed to action on the Kokoda Trail, its grading was given as 'F': unit training incomplete. The garrison of Port Moresby was thus given the lowest possible rating while being deployed in the most threatened area. The 7th Division, which was stationed in Queensland at this time, was graded A.[5]

With the commencement of the Japanese bombing of Port Moresby on 3 February 1942, followed on the 5th by a far greater bombardment, the natives fled, desertions from coastal ships became high and general chaos reigned in Port Moresby itself. After Zero fighter planes had sunk three Catalina flying boats off the coast on 28 February, there remained just two Catalinas and a Hudson bomber for the defence of the garrison. The only reinforcement for a period of some three weeks was the eventual arrival of the promised Kittyhawk squadron, which because of the endless delaying of the planes' arrival had been dubbed, amongst other things, 'Tomorrow Hawks' and 'Neverhawks'.

As the situation deteriorated further in the South West Pacific Area during early April, the army had decided to act in a more positive way. On 17 April, it sent Brigadier Selwyn Porter to assume command of the 30th Brigade. As the former commanding officer of the 2/31st Battalion in Syria, Porter brought with him a distinguished Middle Eastern record and a youthful and driving personality to the garrison. Upon arrival, Porter soon realised that he faced four critical problems. The first was the quality of the defences: easily identifiable from the sea, far too dispersed, static and, therefore, restrictive in their potential for mobility. The garrison's very poor overall standard of leadership was the second, while the standard of training and the brigade's outdated equipment were the third and fourth problems. While not in much of a position to remedy the equipment problem, an injection of young, trained and experienced officers from the 7th Division as reinforcement officers to his brigade would assist in the leadership and training. The age and health standards of the older, mostly Great War officers in Port Moresby were used as excuses to send them back to Australia. However, we shall notice that some of these older officers escaped the net.

On 21 June 1942, 36 AIF officers from the 7th Division were posted to the 30th Brigade. Sixteen were taken by the 39th, eight by the 53rd and twelve by the 49th.[6] How each battalion decided to use these young officers was critical to later performances. The 39th posted one lieutenant-colonel (Owen) as the new battalion commander; one major; six captains, of whom three were given company commands and three second-in-command postings; and eight lieutenants who went straight to platoon commands. It is at platoon level particularly where basic training is successfully implemented; and it is usually supervised by a capable officer commanding a company. In the 39th Battalion's case these officers—and the young, capable and enthusiastic militia officers who had been retained—performed magnificently under the pressure of little time. But the arrival of the AIF officers was rarely well received. Lieutenant Hugh Dalby arrived on 22 June from the 2/27th Battalion and was posted to the 39th:

> Of course it was so. All you have to do ever is put yourself in the other fellow's situation. Number one; we monitored [censored] their correspondence. So one of the words I was cutting out mostly was AIF. In other words, 'We've got some new AIF officers, they're

> bastards!' I left 'they're bastards' in. I can take this a step further. When we went there these men were unshaven, they wore dirty clothes; they were hang-dog if you like. We started in on training. They had to get rifle drill; rifle practice . . . But after a few weeks, they started to feel like soldiers . . . They became good troops. Although they resented us their resentment was understandable. Me, I could understand it. I knew what they were telling me in their correspondence. They knew I was going to get the message from them. There was a very deep distrust when I went to New Guinea between the AIF and the militia. It was something that had to be broken down. The officers had to make the effort.[7]

Apart from the obvious culture shock for some of these young soldiers, there was a grievance against some of these AIF officers that was entirely fair. On 7 July 1942, Jock Reid of the 39th Battalion noted in his diary: 'the AIF officers have settled in and the fangs are going into the militiamen now trying to get them to sign over to AIF, but not going about it the right way.'[8] The AIF officers were unaware that many of the young militiamen had, months before, applied to join the AIF but were refused 'membership' because at that time the AIF had all the recruits it needed. This had caused resentment. Further, the manner of some of the AIF officers with their troops was far from subtle. Many of the militiamen in the 30th Brigade refused outright to join the AIF under any circumstances for the remainder of the war.

Thus the 39th Battalion, manned by volunteers for tropical service and led in June 1942 by a very capable leavening of AIF and enthusiastic young militia officers, was a battalion in change. This did not apply to the 53rd Battalion, as the majority of the militia company commanders were in their forties and, although some were proficient, a number of company commanders were 'slow in carrying out his [Lieutenant-Colonel Ward's] orders and lacked the ability to do so'.[9]

When General MacArthur was given his directive by the Chiefs of Staff in America to capture Rabaul (which he had strongly advocated before their decision was taken), he had ordered a small party of American and Australian officers to the north coast of Papua to reconnoitre a suitable site for an advanced air base from which he might carry the war forward into Japanese-held territory. This patrol suggested that an area north-east of Dobodura might be suitable.

As a consequence of such thinking, Blamey instructed Major-General Morris, on 29 June, to secure Kokoda, north of the range, envisaging that the occupying force could later protect the proposed Allied air base planned for Dobodura.

Brigadier Porter was ordered to send a rifle company over the Kokoda Trail to fulfil this order. Captain Sam Templeton's B Company of the 39th Battalion was selected. Templeton was ordered to march his company over the Kokoda Trail and meet the lugger *Gili Gili* at Buna. The lugger's supplies were then to be unloaded and the construction of the airfield would begin. Templeton did not fit the conventional description of a company commander in the Australian Army. Known as 'Uncle Sam' to his mostly adolescent soldiers, he had been refused service with the AIF because of flat feet and his age (at least 50 years). Lieutenant A.G. 'Judy' Garland was one of his platoon commanders:

> He'd fought in the Irish Rebellion, the First War and this was to be his last fling. He set an example to the whole company, in other words, I think he realised that we were a lot of young blokes . . . A man that you couldn't get to know very well, but he always said that if he went into action against the Japs, he wouldn't come back and that's exactly what happened, he told me that.[10]

It is extraordinary to contemplate that the first Australian contact against the best jungle fighters in the world at that time was to be undertaken by a company of raw young militiamen graded at fighting proficiency 'F', and led by a commander who was over 50 and had flat feet. Yet Templeton would prove an inspiration to his young soldiers.

Morris had no transport aircraft based in Port Moresby. His only means of supply for Templeton's party would be the traditional one: native carriers. It is at this point, right from the start of the Kokoda campaign, that the priceless use of the indentured natives and the employment of the whites who were engaged in their 'plantation dream' came critically into play. On 21 March 1942 Morris had formed the Australian New Guinea Administrative Unit (ANGAU) to:

> . . . function as a military administrative unit for both Territories. At that time Angau was divided into a headquarters and two branches: District services—to police the Territories and maintain law and order, regard the welfare of the native people, and to provide and control native labour; Production Services—to provide the food required by the natives, transport for the men of the District Services and those working the plantations, and technical direction for production.[11]

To administer the area on the far side of the Owen Stanley Range, Morris had Captain Grahamslaw at Awala as the officer in command of the northern district, and operating under him at Kokoda was Lieutenant Peter Brewer; at Tufi (south-east of Buna) was Lieutenant Anderson; and at Buna was Lieutenant Champion. Brewer, Anderson and Champion were assistant magistrates under the old civilian administration.

But there was one 'old hand'—an ANGAU officer—who was to outshine them all. Lieutenant Herbert Kienzle was a plantation owner and miner from Yodda, a small outpost about six miles north-west of Kokoda. He was a mountain of a man who stood at about six feet two inches in height and weighed about eighteen stone (115 kg).[12] Lieutenant 'Bert' Kienzle:

> About midnight on the 31st of March, 1942, I was awakened by a loud knocking to be confronted by a native constable of police, who handed me an important message from Kokoda. It was a message from H.Q. Port Moresby to the effect, I was to 'close down mines and plantations, and report to H.Q. immediately' . . . I reported to Kokoda, where Lieutenant Brewer instructed me to take a number of 'deserters'; these were natives who had deserted their employ, during the

> earlier air raids on Port Moresby, back to their villages, and I was to escort them back to Port Moresby. It was my first crossing of the now famous 'Kokoda Trail', and it took me 7 days to reach Koitaki with my line of about 64 'deserters' . . .
>
> On the 29th of June, 1942, I received an urgent message to report to H.Q. Port Moresby immediately. I was instructed that I was to take charge of approximately one thousand native labourers on a line of communication to Kokoda, being established between Illolo (McDonald's Corner) and Kokoda immediately.[13]

There have been some unbelievable orders given to unsuspecting—and innocent—subordinates through the annals of history, but the edict given to Lieutenant Kienzle just prior to his departure with Templeton's B Company must surely rank as one of the most ludicrous. 'C.O. Angau to make arrangements to fulfil requirements up to a maximum of one thousand native labourers. Construction of road to Kokoda to commence not later than 29th June. Road to be completed by 26th August, 1942.'[14] Kienzle's reaction to the author in 1986 was a masterly piece of understatement: 'It is asking too much to organise (a) a line of communication with suitable stages/depots/camps en route, all equipped and manned with sufficient carriers and (b) to build a road over this mountainous terrain within a time limit. I have heard of superman but have yet to see him in action!'[15] Right from the start of the Kokoda campaign, Kienzle and his comrades in ANGAU became the indispensable 'engineers' along a human highway that was to supply, sustain and, if necessary, evacuate the Australian soldier on the trail. And all of that vital expertise depended on their unique knowledge of the geography of Papua and the natives who lived there.

Kienzle quickly realised that the carriers would be far better suited to working in set sections of the trail only. This decision meant a virtual relay system where successive ANGAU personnel and their assigned carriers would operate continuously in a given area. In other words, to begin with, Kienzle would administer the section as far as Kagi, and Lieutenant Peter Brewer would handle the section Kagi to

Kokoda. At this early juncture, Kienzle was thinking in terms of *one* company:

> I found that to have carriers based at each stage and to carry only between two stages, was the best method, making the carrier line feel more settled and contented, with a reduction in 'desertions'. The trail from Uberi to Kagi is a series of steep ascents and descents, crossing six ridges en route. It is indeed a test of endurance. A steady stream of urgent rations, supplies, medical, ammunition had to be planned and put into operation immediately and maintained on the Line of Communication from Illolo or Ower's Corner to Kokoda, to help provision a company of men. Little did I know or was advised at this stage, that this was to be my responsibility for a full battalion, then a brigade and later a division.[16]

When, on 15 July 1942, Templeton's B Company, 39th Battalion reached Kokoda, Kienzle ventured back to his plantation at Yodda and gathered further food supplies for them. He then marched back over the trail to further assess the supply situation and, in so doing, came to a far-reaching decision:

> A carrier carrying foodstuffs consumes his load in thirteen days and if he carries food supplies for a soldier, it means six and a half days supply for both soldier and carrier. This does not allow for the porterage of arms, ammunition, equipment, medical stores, ordnance, mail and dozens of other items needed to wage war, on the backs of men. The track takes eight days, so the maintenance of supplies is a physical impossibility without large-scale co-operation of plane droppings.[17]

Kienzle came to these critical conclusions on about 19 July. Two days later, the Japanese interrupted everyone's already rushed timetable.

On 14 June, Lieutenant-General Hyakutake, the commander of the Japanese 17th Army, was ordered to prepare a plan for an overland attack upon Port Moresby. Some measure of the widespread lack of knowledge of the geography of Papua, even by the Japanese, was the fact that the initial force for the proposed invasion would constitute only 1500 soldiers—this initial operation was merely a reconnaissance in force. The combat component of the force was built around Lieutenant-Colonel Tsukomoto's 1st Battalion, 144th Regiment and a company of the crack 5th Sasebo Naval Landing Force. This later unit was destined to spearhead not only the Kokoda Trail campaign but the landing at Milne Bay, and, in so doing, engaged in horrendous war atrocities. Its insignia was composed of two crossing anchors and a chrysanthemum. The men of the unit were also recognisable by an anchor on their belt buckles. And many of them were tall and thick-boned and, consequently on sight, instantly dispelled the stereotype of the Japanese soldier: short, thick glasses, and no physical match for an Australian.[18] This combat component of the force was to engage any enemy troops between Gona–Buna and Kokoda. The combat part of the invading force could also look to invaluable support from elements of the 55th Mountain Artillery. The logistic component of the initial force were elements of the 15th Independent Engineer Regiment and one company of Formosans of the 15th Naval Pioneer Unit.

For the later assault across the Owen Stanley Range, overall command would pass to Major-General Tomitaro Horii, whose South Seas Force was built strongly round the 144th Regiment. Horii had served with distinction in China and was: '. . . a small, plump and bespectacled figure, he campaigned with his troops, and directed operations from headquarters never far behind the most forward outposts. His troops saw him occasionally astride a carefully groomed white thoroughbred, a remote, powerful and dignified being.'[19] The eventual Japanese build-up if the thrust was to be given the all clear would comprise some 13 500 troops; 10 000 of these were seasoned combat troops, veterans of victories in China, Guam, Rabaul and Salamaua.

At approximately 2.40 p.m. on 21 July the Japanese seized

the initiative by a float-plane machine-gunning of the Buna station followed by the appearance of a convoy off the coast near Gona. Despite some spirited defence by Allied aircraft, the Japanese began landing troops late in the afternoon; under the cover of darkness the disembarkation was completed unchallenged during the night.

ANGAU had seven observation posts along the Papuan north coast as an early warning radio system. When the Japanese machine-gunned Buna and appeared off Gona, Sergeant Alan Champion and Sergeant Harper radioed their information to Port Moresby. There was no immediate reply.

In response to the Japanese landing on 21 July, Major-General Morris was ordered to concentrate one battalion at Kokoda forthwith. He ordered Lieutenant-Colonel Owen of the 39th Battalion to leave by air for Kokoda on 23 July to command all troops on the northern ramparts of the trail. There were, in addition to Templeton's force, some members of the Papuan Infantry Battalion, later to be designated 'Maroubra Force'.

When the Japanese landed, Templeton had pushed two of his three platoons forward to stage delaying actions, while his third occupied Kokoda. The Japanese were easily able to push the Australians back: their numbers were far superior, as was their drill.

They would often send a scout forward and be prepared to lose him, which would be followed by an almost immediate strong frontal attack, in which quick casualties were often accepted. But the speed with which they then outflanked and encircled and destroyed the enemy reflected their light equipment, their excellent camouflage and, above all, their tremendous and almost silent deployment. To the inexperienced Australians, the enemy's preoccupation with his frontal attack merely ensured a rapid envelopment. And even the enemy's food supplies were lightweight—the Japanese soldier could survive for 24 hours on a little rice ball, some seaweed and perhaps some dried fish. He travelled light and fast and was practised in most matters of jungle warfare.

In a series of brave engagements between Gorari and Kokoda the two platoons of B Company 39th Battalion were engaged in almost constant contact and withdrawal. It was during one of these forays that Templeton, who insisted on fulfilling tasks that he should have delegated to others, disappeared while heading back to guide a party who had landed at Kokoda. His body was never recovered. The party Templeton had moved back to meet included the CO, Owen and a platoon of D Company which had been flown in.

During another brief but sharp action at Oivi, the Japanese were able to concentrate much of their force and firepower to the rear of the defenders, who answered with grenades and rifle fire before a degree of panic broke out just prior to abandoning a position they could no longer hope to hold. Some pushed forward to their less threatened original front, while others moved towards their rear and certain annihilation. It was the bushcraft of Sanopa, a Papuan policeman serving with the PIB (Papuan Infantry Battalion), that saved a number of the forward moving men, and those they were able to cut off from heading to their rear where a strong enemy force lay in wait for them. Amongst brave actions that day there was also much understandable confusion and bewilderment, which was to cause an unfair assessment of some of these young militiamen by a soon-to-arrive officer.

With these events in train, Owen considered that the trail would be easier to defend than Kokoda village, and to this end he set fire to some of the buildings and stores and fell back to Deniki. To his later amazement he was told that the Japanese had not yet occupied Kokoda.

Owen reasoned that time might yet afford him the chance to be reinforced by air. He therefore decided to leave a small force at Deniki and hurry back to Kokoda. It was a long shot but worth the risk; if his small force of around 80 soldiers could hold the Kokoda airstrip long enough, substantial reinforcements might be landed.

It is at this juncture that one of the most extraordinary characters of the Kokoda campaign enters our story. Doctor Geoffrey Vernon, in addition to his vocation as a doctor, was a planter from Daru in western Papua. When the Pacific War broke out, Vernon knew that his advanced age—he was almost 60—and his acute hearing disability would prevent his service in the current war. Despite being ordered to evacuate Papua in December 1941, Vernon had not only refused to leave, but had actively sought a role in the coming war. When Kienzle and Templeton set off on their journey in late June 1942, Vernon became responsible for the physical well-being of the carriers.

Tall, thin and with a drawn, lined face that bore testimony to his tough life, Vernon's appearance and age disguised a hard constitution that was entirely at home climbing ranges and therefore walking tremendous distances. When Owen decided to re-occupy Kokoda, Vernon had reached Deniki while in the process of checking the carriers' condition along the trail. The temptation, and his sense of duty, proved too great. As the medical officer of the 39th was still busily engaged in walking over the trail, Vernon took it upon himself to follow B Company back to Kokoda. The young soldiers would need a doctor. At this point their only medical assistance had been provided by Warrant Officer 2 John Wilkinson of ANGAU, who had been a shift boss and miner from Misima, about a hundred miles east of Milne Bay (not to be confused with Missima on the Kokoda Trail). His reaction to Vernon's arrival at Kokoda is illuminating:

> Captain Vernon arrived out of the fog. Very pleased to see him. He had some instruments and dressings in two triangular bandages. He nearly got shot when first seen owing to his unregimental dress. Captain Vernon had shorts, which were really strides rolled up; a blue pullover with the arms tied around his neck and hanging down his back; a felt army hat, worn as no hat ever should be worn, and a long newspaper cigarette in his mouth. A small dillybag and some army biscuits and tobacco in it. He saw me and spoke, 'Jack, I heard there was some action up here and thought you may need some assistance. Where do I start?' What a man![20]

The 'action up here' was not long in coming. Shortly after Owen had deployed his small force, two droning Douglas transport aircraft circled the airstrip, while some of his men cleared the barricades from the drome. On board this aircraft were the battalion's adjutant, Lieutenant Keith Lovett, Captain Bidstrup and a second platoon of his D Company. Bidstrup could see the Australians below removing the obstacles, but despite a severe verbal exchange between the American pilot and the officer the plane flew back to Port Moresby. Consequently, the opportunity for a critical if only partial reinforcement of Owen's force at Kokoda was lost.[21] The remaining A, C, D (less one platoon having already landed with Owen) and E Companies of the 39th were now faced with the laborious march over the trail. It should be noted that militia battalions had an 'E' or machine-gun company that AIF battalions did not have.

In the early hours of 29 July 1942 the Japanese launched an all-out attack against the 39th up the steep slope at the northern end of its perimeter. Lieutenant Gough 'Judy' Garland was one of the platoon commanders occupying the Kokoda plateau:

> He [Owen] was another one similar to Sam Templeton, that wanted to show his leadership, and he walked around the top of the perimeter where we were all lying down; naturally you would . . . And I said to him, 'Sir, I think you're taking an unnecessary risk walking around among the troops like that'. 'Well', he said, 'I've got to do it'. I suppose half an hour later he got shot right through the forehead.[22]

It was not long before the Kokoda plateau became a confused mass of defenders and attackers who, at times, became unaware of who was friend and who was foe. But one realisation came to the Australians quite quickly: the enemy were breaking through their perimeter and a withdrawal was required. Doctor Vernon has left an extremely vivid account of the events of that night, when the bravery of those few soldiers of B Company helped to start the legend of the 39th Battalion:

> On arrival, I reported to the 39th Battalion and then inspected and arranged the police house, which had been converted to the R.A.P. . . . dusk fell early, a grey, misty, cheerless evening though the moon was at the full. Jap scouts had already been reported, and about 7.30, cat-calls and a stray mortar shot or two came

ringing across the Mambare [river]. Thereafter, there was increasing noise and salvoes of firing, mostly I think, from the Japs, who had a big mortar with them, at shorter and shorter intervals. By midnight, the firing on both sides had become almost continuous . . . About one o'clock . . . a hand touched my shoulder. It was Brewer, with news that Colonel Owen had been wounded. The moon was now in full strength, and shone brightly through the white mountain mist as I hurried with Brewer past the old magistrate's house, now the H.Q., where we picked up a stretcher and several bearers . . . Major Watson came in to see him, and then we had four or five casualties in rapid succession who, when dressed, were told to go back to Deniki as soon as they could. Wilkinson held the lantern for me, and every time he raised it, a salvo of machine-gun bullets was fired at the building. This particular enemy machine-gun was as yet a little below the edge of the escarpment, probably just behind Graham's back premises, so its range was bound to be too high, and while the roof was riddled, those working below could feel reasonably safe . . .

We had now evacuated our walking wounded, and there was a lull in our work. Presently, Wilkinson came bursting into the R.A.P. during which we fixed up Colonel Owen, who was now dying as comfortably as possible—moistening his mouth and cleaning him up. Then I stuffed our operating instruments and a few dressings into my pocket, seized the lantern, and went out towards the rubber. Outside, the mist had grown very dense, but the moonlight allowed me to see where I was going. Thick white streams of vapour stole between the rubber trees, and changed the whole scene into a weird combination of light and shadow. The mist was greatly to our advantage; our own lines of retreat remained perfectly plain, but it must have slowed down the enemy's advance considerably, another chance factor that helped save the Kokoda force . . .

I thought on reflection that I should remain for a while, at least till I had met some responsible officer,

Kokoda—the first battle

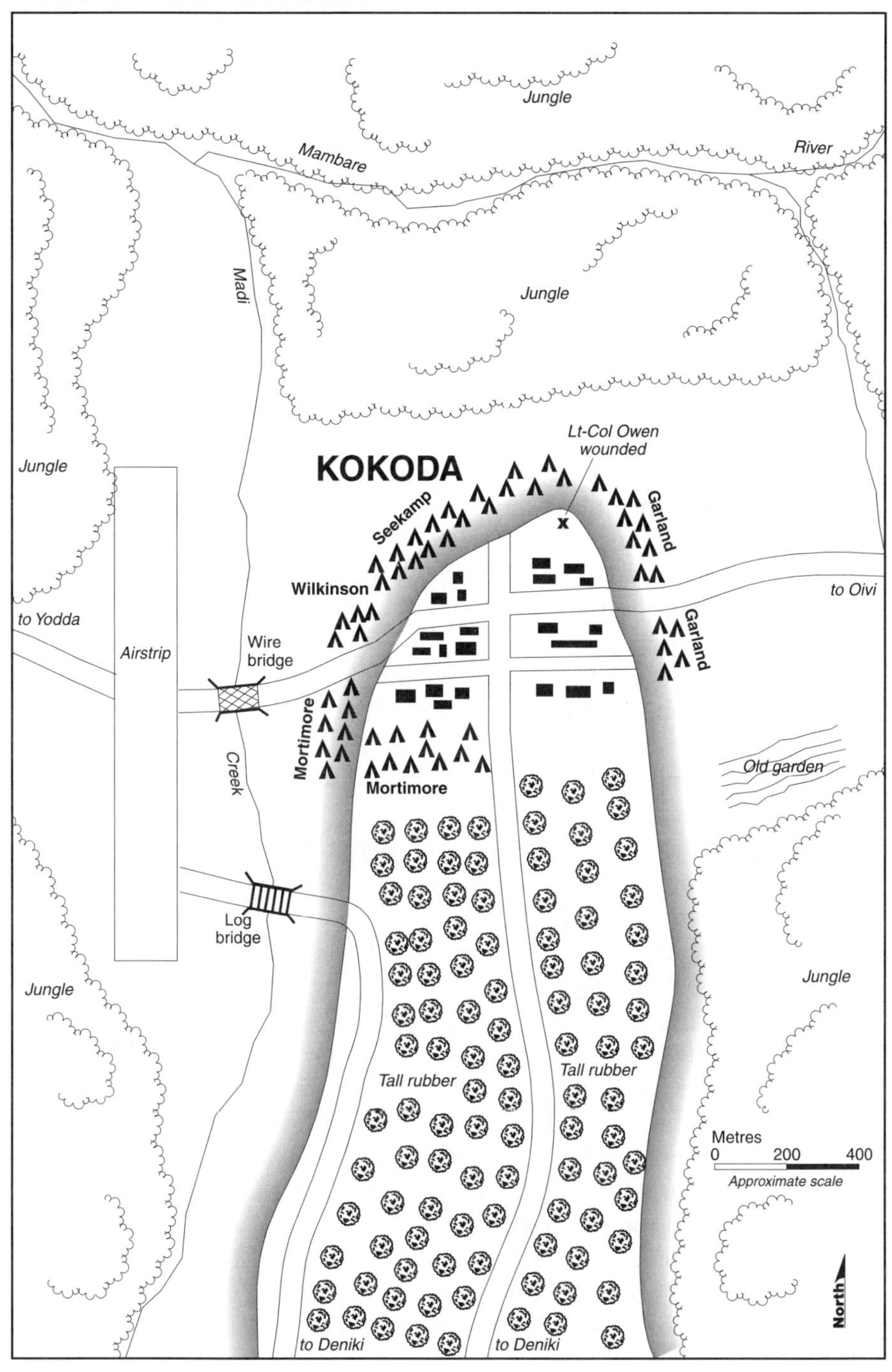

Jungle
Mambare
River
Jungle
Madi
Jungle
Lt-Col Owen wounded
KOKODA
Seekamp
Garland
Wilkinson
to Yodda
to Oivi
Airstrip
Wire bridge
Garland
Mortimore
Creek
Mortimore
Old garden
Log bridge
Jungle
Jungle
Tall rubber
Tall rubber
Metres
0
200
400
Approximate scale
North
to Deniki
to Deniki

> and so I called to several withdrawing parties to ask if there were any officers amongst them. The men seemed neither to know, or greatly care; their orders to leave had been definite enough, and they were carrying them out. By now, I had gone nearly half a mile through the rubber, and I turned back and hid behind the trunk of a tree just [near] the edge of the Kokoda clearing, in sight of the R.A.P. and the station garden. The firing had almost died down, and the parties making for the hills were smaller and came less frequently. Finally, after a long period, during which no-one passed and I was beginning to think I had better leave, Major Watson, in company with Lieutenant Brewer and a couple of officers of the 39th Battalion passed along the track. I felt considerably relieved, and leaving my hiding place, called to Watson, who said, 'come on, we are the last out.' Actually, two men followed us a little later. I heard afterwards that the station was then full of Japs, but in the mist, I recognised none, nor was I molested in any way . . .
>
> . . . It was an experience I would not have cared to miss, and among the impressions of that exciting night, none stands out more clearly than the weirdness of the natural conditions—the thick white mist dimming the moonlight, the mysterious veiling of trees, the almost complete silence, as if the rubber groves of Kokoda were sleeping as usual in the depths of the night, and the men had not brought disturbance.[23]

Unable to hold Kokoda, B Company again withdrew to Deniki. The remaining companies of the 39th Battalion concentrated at Deniki between 1 and 5 August 1942. Major Allan Cameron, the brigade major of the 30th Brigade, arrived at that village on 4 August to assume temporary command of Maroubra Force. His arrival was recorded in Warrant Officer John Wilkinson's diary: '4/8/42. Changed to A Company. Major Cameron arrived later and took charge of all troops. Very bitter towards men. Says they are cowards. Must have met up with the few who shot through.'[24] The soldiers referred to were some of the youngsters of B Company who had 'gone bush' during that company's baptism of fire at Oivi and Kokoda. Cameron refused to acknowledge these soldiers and considered that the company had lost its good name; he thought it fit for no more than a reserve role in the future. These young men had suffered the full brunt of the Japanese advance to Kokoda and had lost Templeton and Owen in the process. Sleepless, wet and ill fed, they had encountered the best jungle fighters in the world at that time, and in far superior strength. Further, Cameron's slur did not fairly apply to the whole company but merely to a small number who had become horribly disoriented in that jungle environment.

Upon his arrival at Deniki, Cameron decided to mount a three-pronged attack to retake Kokoda. The decision was fraught with tremendous risks. The aim of the mission was the recapture of the key airstrip at Kokoda to facilitate rapid reinforcement and supply. However, the chance existed that should his force be dispersed and out of his direct control, a virtual open path to Port Moresby would be provided for the enemy. Further, one of his available companies, B Company, was physically spent and, out of favour, was sent back to Isurava. This left him with a three-company force for the offensive and one company available to hold Deniki as a base for his operation.

Reconnaissance patrols discovered that an alternative track to Kokoda, which appeared to be not in use, might allow his A Company 39th Battalion an uncontested passage into Kokoda. To inhibit the enemy's ability to send reinforcements from his base area to Kokoda, Cameron planned to have Captain Bidstrup's D Company set up an ambush to the east near Oivi to disrupt the critical enemy potential to reinforce Kokoda. Meanwhile, Captain Dean's C Company would advance along the main track towards Kokoda.

The battle to retake Kokoda contained some interesting outcomes: Captain Symington and his A Company, surprisingly, not only entered Kokoda but found it held by a weak force. He set his dispositions, dug in and awaited his reinforcement by air. Bidstrup's ambush on the eastern flank was highly successful—estimated enemy casualties were 46 killed and roughly the same number wounded—but his continued presence in the area was untenable, as the enemy had the potential to quickly reinforce its ambushed remnant, while Bidstrup was isolated from his base. Forced into a close perimeter, D Company withdrew just before dark, carrying their wounded with them. Wilkinson had accompanied them:

> 9/8/42. Left for Deniki 0800 hours. Sat up all night putting hot stones round stretcher case. Sucking chest wound of back. Holding Rosary and Crucifix all the time. Very bad wound. No rations at all. Made Deniki 1700 hours very wet and tired. Completely buggered but felt better after a meal. Cameron chewing his whiskers. Deniki was fired on today.[25]

Major Cameron had good cause for 'chewing his whiskers'. When Captain Dean's C Company had moved down the main track towards Kokoda, they were met by the main enemy force. In the ensuing firefight, Dean was killed and the company took casualties. C Company was doomed to turn back before it ever left Deniki.

Symington's A Company had left for Kokoda with each soldier carrying about a hundred rounds of ammunition, two grenades and two days' dry rations. Knowing nothing of the trials and tribulations of Bidstrup's D Company and Dean's C Company, he deployed one of his platoons around the plateau overlooking the airstrip; another covered the likely approach of any enemy force from the direction of Oivi—from where Japanese reinforcements were most likely to come—and the third platoon he placed in the rubber plantation to the south.

When the Japanese reacted to their 'visitors' at Kokoda, it was with considerable force and fury: late on the morning of 9 August, and in the early afternoon, two attacks were launched with about two hundred troops. At 5.30 p.m. the Japanese launched a force of three hundred against Symington. His immediate problem was ammunition. When a plane circled the village and airstrip during mid-morning the following day and dropped nothing, and worse, reported to Port Moresby that the enemy were in close proximity to Kokoda, any hope Symington had of the 49th Battalion reinforcing him from that centre was dashed.

Major Cameron's attack on Kokoda, 8–10 August 1942

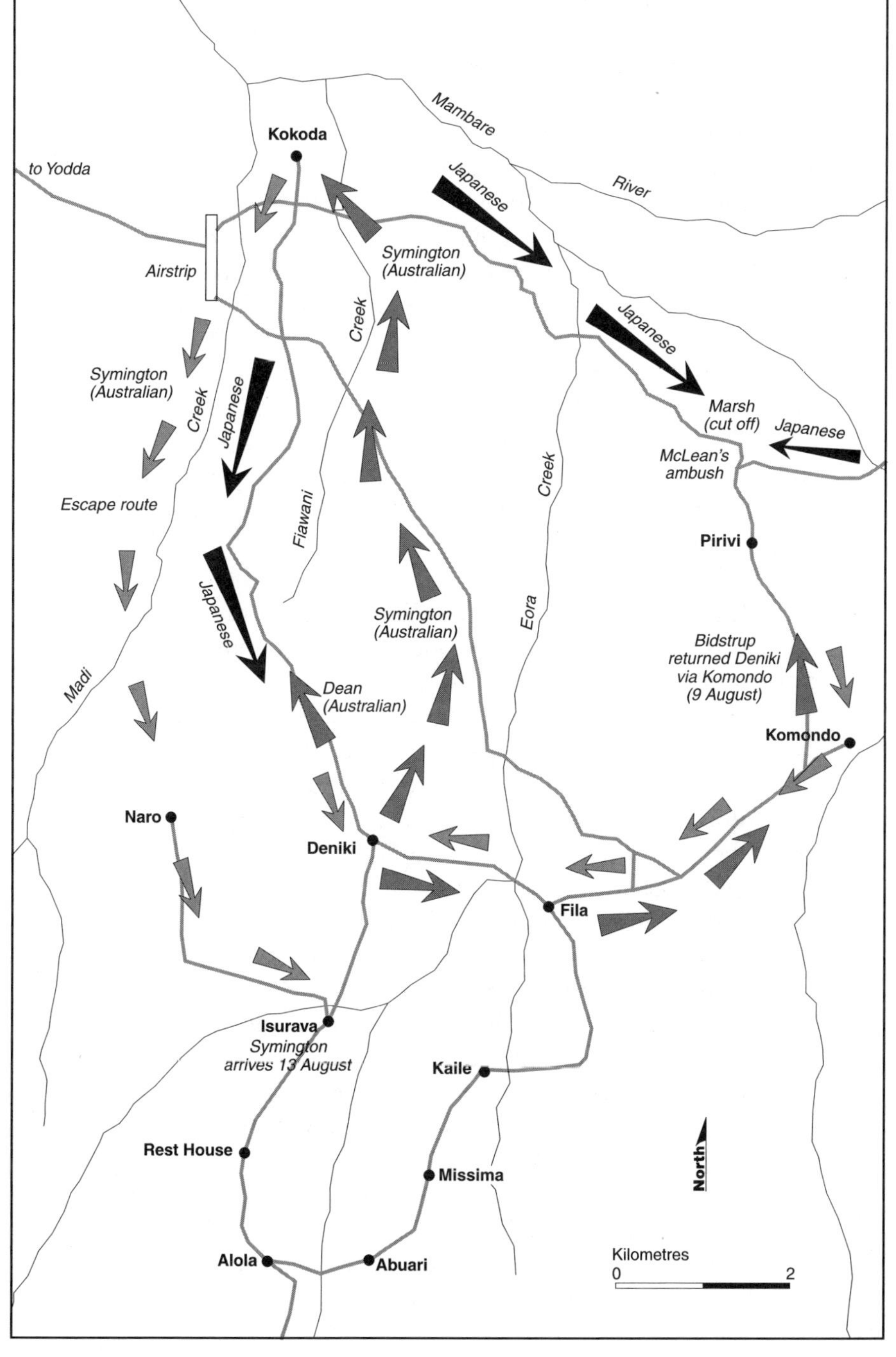

Perhaps Corporal Larry Downes best summed up A company's predicament:

> The closest they'd got to us until then was about 5 yards—the distance to the next row of rubber trees. That was pretty close. Then one of them would blow a whistle and they'd all go back again. They couldn't get through and that's why they were so frustrated. They never would have got through if we'd had enough ammunition. They would have had to kill every one of us—but you can't fight without ammunition.[26]

For not the first time during this remarkable chain of early events, it was an old hand who steadied the young soldiers of the 39th and blazed a trail to safety. In doing so he also helped create a battalion legend. J.D. McKay has left us with a vivid account of some of A Company's soldiers' escape from Kokoda:

> Just on dusk there was a nice little shower of rain and the first assault wave came in and we stopped 'em. My Bren gun group, Bill Drummond and Bill Spriggs, were firing and I can see the gun firing now—no kidding, you could see the bullets going up the barrel and it ran red-hot. Vern Scattergood had a Bren too and he was firing wildly. We stopped 'em again. Then there was a bit of a pause before the next wave came in and overran us. So we said, 'We'd better get out because they've gone past us.' Well old Scattergood (or should I say young Scattergood?—he was younger than me) he got excited. He was standing up firing the Bren from the hip and that was the last I saw of young Scattergood. He must have been hit. We couldn't find him in the dark and we moved back. After we came out of the rubber, we found Johnnie Stormont in the Company Headquarters dug-out. We tried to put a shell dressing on him but the wound was too big and he was dying. We had to leave him. We only moved a few yards and we were challenged! It was old Jim Cowey [52 years of age, First World War 46th Battalion][27] the coolest, bravest man I have ever known. There he was, in the kneeling position,

> with his rifle pointing at us. Jim's motto was if you were a 'digger' he had to get you out. The rest of the company had gone, but he's stayed to get us out because he knew we'd been left behind.
>
> Old Jim had picked up about three or four of us by now and he said, 'Just stay quietly', and then he dispersed us a bit. And then he got Roy Neal and Larry Downes, and I think that was about all of us. You know most were dead then. There was no wounded in our group. Then Jim said, 'Good, we'll walk out.' I was all for running out but there were Japs everywhere. They were throwing grenades into weapon-pits, they were searching under huts, and Jim said, 'We'll walk out, they don't know who we are.' And, if you don't mind, casually got up, put us into single file and walked us out over the bloody bridge!' We walked across the airstrip into the dense scrub and then Jim said, 'Good! We'll rest here till daylight.' So he puts us down and then 'clunk', being a youth and mentally and physically exhausted, I fell straight asleep. But I suppose old Jim Cowey, being the amazing soldier that he was, stayed awake all night.[28]

Cowey not only 'stayed awake all night', but made a thorough search for more of Kokoda's forgotten 'rubber men'. As he led his small party to safety, he added to his group's size and, in the process of reaching Symington's main A Company group at Naro, killed a Japanese machine-gun crew along the way.[29]

Late on the following day, the 12th, a native from Naro arrived at Deniki with a message from Symington reporting that A Company was moving back but needed help with its wounded. Warrant Officer Wilkinson volunteered again:

> . . . Deniki expecting attack when I left. Japs on track to A Company but we sneaked through long grass. Held my breath for nearly half an hour, or seemed like it. Worst trip I have ever made. Jap coughed about ten feet away . . .
>
> Too black to see six feet. Could see Naro Village outline on top of hill. Was told troops were there. Five of us fell into deep ravine from a log we were crawling

> across. Heard voice from top of hill and got scared that troops would fire on us and I would lose carriers. Swore loudly and long to let them know it was an Australian there. Also because I had fallen on top of one native but three more had fallen on top of me. Heard someone say faintly, 'That's Wilkinson down there. I recognise the way he swears.' Reached NARO Village by 2320 hours. A bit buggered. No food. Several wounded. Peter Brewer very weak with dysentery, but still able to smile . . .
>
> 13/8/42. Left 0600 hours. Arrived W.T. station 1200 hours. Still no food. Peter Brewer still able to move feet but unable to stand. Most troops tired but still a fighting force. Very little ammo. Fr Earl [Padre 39th Battalion] had long stick in one hand and Rosary in other. He shivered every time a mortar went off in the hills. Then he said to carriers 'Come on, they won't hit us', and the carriers followed him. We raided line and shared a tin of salmon with every two men. Cut my tongue licking tin. Hell, I was hungry. Reached Isurava 1700 hours absolutely done in. Only one big building. Rain all night. Mud everywhere . . .[30]

The 39th Battalion expended much energy and resources (both material and human) on a mission that was based more on wishful thinking than on military prudence. After a series of attacks on its positions at Deniki, the battalion was forced to stage another withdrawal to Isurava, the next village back along the Kokoda Trail.

While these climactic events were in train, Lieutenant Bert Kienzle and Doctor Geoffrey Vernon were being confronted with pressing problems. The logistic and medical contingencies confronting them had now been increased eightfold—they were dealing with not one company but at least eight, as the 53rd Battalion was marching forward to increase the size of Maroubra Force.

We have noted Kienzle's early realisation that native carriers would not be alone able to maintain the flow of supplies; that airdropping must occur. To this end, he remembered that he had seen 'Dry Lakes' from the air during his prewar travel. On 2 August, therefore, in the company of four carriers, Kienzle left Eora Creek and headed east:

> August 3, 1942. We broke camp at 0700 hours and arrived at first 'dry lake' at 0725 hours. Only 20 minutes walk from where we camped the previous evening. It presented a magnificent sight—a large patch of open country right on top of the main range of the Owen Stanleys. It was just the very thing I had been looking for . . . open ground measuring roughly about one and a quarter miles long by one-third of a mile wide, a creek running through the middle . . . each side covered with a sharp reed and the higher ground with short tufts of grass. [Kienzle named this dry lake bed 'Myola'] . . .
>
> August 4, 1942. I left Myola at 0800 hours for Eora Creek, and blazed a new trail north-west over the 'Gap' by following a ridge. The junction of this new trail with the Kagi Eora Creek track is where I established another camp and named it 'Templeton's Crossing' in memory of Captain Templeton.[31]

The first experimental drop at Myola was made on 5 August and, although the techniques used were to prove rather crude—items were encased in two sacks, so that when the inner burst on impact, the outer retained the goods—Kienzle's Myola discovery was the logistical turning point of the campaign. He then set up staging posts at Templeton's Crossing, Eora Creek, Alola and Isurava.

While Kienzle had been thus employed, Vernon had immediate problems of his own. Although Myola might well alleviate some of the pressure upon the carrier line, supplies still needed to be carried forward of Myola, and in ever increasing amounts as the build-up of Maroubra Force continued. Vernon recognised that the treatment of the carriers had not always been ideal:

> The native carrier starts with a physique and constitution considerably inferior to that of the white soldier, nor is he anything like so carefully selected medically for service. The medical examination on

> entrance, even in the best of hands, does not aim at a very high standard, and only obvious disabilities debar service. A standard similar to that adopted for the A.I.F. or A.M.F. would almost deplete the force. In addition, the native resisting powers to disease is inferior to the white man's and both physically and mentally he is more likely to succumb to sickness. The sole advantage is that he is more used to the country and to the hardships (inferior diet, exposure to rain and cold, excessive walking, climbing etc.) it imposes on all who are working along the Main Range route . . .
>
> During this period . . . conditions were but little improved on account of the pressing need for the Australian troops who were given preference in portable goods. Thus at that time many carriers were without a single blanket, rice was practically the only food issue, meat was withheld for two or three weeks and tobacco scarce; the regulation governing the reduction of loads to 40 lbs (18 kg), was often ignored and excessive weights and distances imposed on the carriers as if they were merely pack animals. No day of rest could be given for weeks.[32]

If events on the Kokoda Trail had occurred with a frightening rapidity to this juncture, then the village now occupied by the 39th Battalion would see a build-up of the opposing forces that was to turn this place into one of the most desperate confrontations in Australian history: the battle of Isurava.

COURAGE FEEDS ON HOPE

6

After the collapse of Singapore, the Australian Army examined the daunting task of defending the extensive Australian coastline with the meagre forces at its disposal. It realised that the eastern seaboard was the vital ground to defend, and as a consequence the infamous 'Brisbane Line' strategy was formulated. The Brisbane Line marked the northernmost extremity of territory that the army considered itself capable of defending at that time. In line with this assessment, the 7th Division was deployed on the Brisbane Line prior to the Battle of the Coral Sea to defend this ground. Much of the division's time and energy was spent constructing defensive positions and roads in this area.

After the naval battles of Coral Sea and Midway, after which General MacArthur's mind swung to the offensive, the 7th Division was given much hard training in anticipation of operations against the Japanese.

Many changes had occurred in the 7th Division's 21st Brigade in the period just before, and after, its return to Australia. While still in Palestine, the 2/14th and 2/27th Battalions had been allotted new commanders. Lieutenant-Colonel Arthur Key had served in Greece and Crete with great distinction and was posted to command the 2/14th Battalion. Sergeant John Gwillim, 2/14th Battalion:

> I was rather disappointed when Lieutenant-Colonel Key was introduced to us as our new C.O. when Lt-Col Cannon was transferred in January 1942, as he had a rather fragile appearance and did not fit my picture of an infantry commander . . .

> It was therefore quite a shock to find that he was indeed of very tough moral fibre and had obviously learned how to handle hard types during his service with the 6th Australian Division . . .
>
> He was a very sound soldier who spared himself in no way, and was in evidence to the forward fighting troops to inspire their performance.[1]

The new commander of the 2/27th was Lieutenant-Colonel Geoff Cooper. Cooper was a member of the well-known Adelaide family who brewed beer of the same name. Captain Harry Katekar was his newly promoted adjutant: 'He was first of all courageous, no question of that. He was competent; he'd been well trained and he'd already shown his ability with the 2/10th Battalion over in the Middle East. He was compassionate; he had a great feeling for his troops, although he didn't show it.'[2]

Not long after the 21st Brigade arrived home Lieutenant-Colonel Arnold Potts was promoted to brigadier and given command of the 21st Brigade. It was a fitting reward for his tremendous performance during the Syrian campaign. In his place, Major Albert Caro of the 2/16th was promoted to lieutenant-colonel, and given command of that unit. Captain F. H. Sublet, 2/16th Battalion: 'Lieutenant-Colonel Albert Caro was a courageous officer who displayed plenty of military knowledge. To me he seemed a little too forgiving and his compassion was pronounced. I held him in the highest esteem as a commanding officer, and as a man of great goodness.'[3]

When Potts took command of his brigade in Queensland, it therefore had received a new brigadier and three new battalion commanders. All four would play key and controversial roles in the Papuan campaign. In a letter to his wife Potts stated:

> I'm not blaming Tubby [Major-General Allen]. I've got a new Brigade and that includes responsibility for the whole group. I'm new, the Brigade has been torn to ribbons to help the AMF and I'm building it up again and it is my job and no one else's. If I make a success that's my pigeon. If it's a flop the crack Brigade in the AIF (that is not a joke) has slipped . . .[4]

When Potts talked of his brigade being 'torn to ribbons' he was referring to the young officers within its ranks who had been posted to Port Moresby in June to bolster the quality of experienced leadership in the militia battalions in Port Moresby. In the period before its deployment to Port Moresby the 21st Brigade did not 'slip'. Although its three battalion commanders were new, their credentials were first class—and they were young, experienced and promoted on very recent merit. As for the junior leadership within the ranks of the 21st Brigade, proven performers were promoted from within its ranks to fill the void left by recent promotions and departures.

As a means of both physically conditioning his brigade and attempting to simulate conditions for a drastic change in geographical conditions, Potts soon turned his mind to 'jungle' training. In this, he had absolutely no previous framework to draw upon, as the Australian Army was modelled on British lines in terms of structure, equipment, communication, supply, intelligence gathering and even uniform. In short, the army's very existence was established upon the precept that its fighting would occur where it had always occurred: in Europe or the Middle East.

Potts' brigade was not anywhere near the jungle of Far North Queensland, and there was no jungle training school such as Canungra at that time. The 2/14th Battalion was stationed at Yandina, the 2/27th at Coloundra and the 2/16th was at Maroochydore. The 7th Division—and the militia units then in New Guinea—was in the unenviable position of having to create a future training course, an ethos and a track record of service and expertise *as it went.* And it was up against the best jungle fighters in the world at that point in history. Some of the veterans of Papua were destined to be amongst the first instructors at Canungra and the instigators of a reputation in jungle fighting that sees Australia at the forefront of such campaigning to this day.

In July 1942, therefore, Potts attempted to expose his brigade to the most realistic training possible. After examining the surrounding country, he chose the eastward Blackall Range with its expansive area of dense scrub and rough inclines as a suitable test of his soldiers' fitness and ability to learn. Potts wrote to his wife:

> The 2/16th did over 65 miles in two days and a 2/14th platoon did 120 miles in 4 days, 9 hours—not too dusty. A 2/27th party did 80 miles across country—rivers and all and no boats allowed—in 3 and a half days and a whole Coy [company] will swim a river 150 yards wide—weapons, ammo, and everything in 20 minutes . . . [5]

But when Potts sent an 'enemy' force of company strength into the range to both harass and engage in guerrilla warfare against each of his pursuing battalions in turn, he and the brigade proceeded to gain quite an insight into future problems. Major Cedric Isaachsen, second-in-command of the 2/27th, commanded the 'enemy' force. His three platoons operated on his strict guidelines: rapid movement in platoon strength; ambush and then melt away through the scrub behind the next platoon for action; constant movement of dispositions to restrict the enemy's ability to locate and engage him; and constant sniping and disruption of the attackers' force around the clock by alternating his three platoons. His later report stated in part: '. . . our long range patrols had constantly harassed the attackers and destroyed several more vehicles and quite a large number of personnel—it is estimated that at the end of the exercise at least 40% of the attackers were casualties.'[6] From the attackers' perspective, a telling discovery was the fact that communications broke down and evacuation of the wounded proved most difficult.

While the 7th Division was thus occupied in Queensland during this period, the Japanese advance upon, and the securing of, Kokoda made little real impact upon MacArthur. He was still quite convinced that this 'incursion' was nothing more than an enemy determination to secure his beachhead and airfields in the region. With the American marines due to land on Guadalcanal on 7 August, he considered that the enemy might well withdraw troops from the north coast of New Guinea to that theatre.

It is highly likely that two events finally influenced MacArthur to belatedly reinforce New Guinea. The first was Blamey's ultimate acceptance of the intelligence from Colonel Wills, GSO I (General Staff Officer Intelligence) with the Australian First Army, who was in fact predicting the build-up of the Japanese force and a subsequent offensive over the Owen Stanley Range.[7] Blamey therefore began to emphasise this assessment to MacArthur. The second event was an enquiry from Washington, apparently driven by Admiral King, which questioned whether the use of air power and limited ground forces would prevent the enemy from mounting an assault upon Port Moresby.[8]

On 1 August 1942, Lieutenant-General Sydney Rowell was ordered to Port Moresby with his I Corps Headquarters to assume command of New Guinea Force. His task would be to secure the defence of Port Moresby and then destroy the enemy in Papua. The following day Rowell met with Major-General 'Tubby' Allen to inform him that his 21st Brigade was to go to Port Moresby, while the 18th Brigade was to sail to Milne Bay. The last brigade of the 7th Division, the 25th, would be held in Queensland pending events. The two 7th Division brigades set sail from Brisbane on 6 August. When HQ realised that Morris in Port Moresby had not been told of these important arrivals, Vasey sent a simple message: 'Syd is coming'.

Brigadier Potts arrived at Port Moresby by air on 8 August, and chose the Itiki–Koitaki area as a staging camp for his brigade. He had two reasons for this choice. First, its high altitude minimised the risk of malaria, and second, this venue was close to the end of the motorised transport section leading to the start of the Kokoda Trail at Ower's Corner. Three days later Rowell and Allen arrived in Port Moresby.

As a result of the arrival of Rowell, Morris was now transferred to command ANGAU. On 13 August, Allen and Potts held a conference with Morris. Their newly issued orders were quite brief, if ambitious: 21st Brigade was required to recapture Kokoda as a supply base for further operations against Gona and Buna. The outcomes of this conference were twofold. Morris pledged that at least two planeloads of rations, wrapped in blankets, would be dropped at Myola each day, pending the arrival there of the 21st Brigade, to provide a 40 000 ration dump for its offensive. However, Morris was astounded to hear Allen and Potts inform him that the troops would carry their own supplies to Myola. Morris believed this to be a physical impossibility. He warned that the terrain would limit the weight of the troops' equipment to fifteen pounds. For their part, Potts and Allen knew that existing carrier capabilities were grossly inadequate to provision 21st Brigade's movement over the Owen Stanley Range. They therefore determined that the troops would indeed carry their rations to enable them to reach Myola.

The troops spent much time preparing their weapons and equipment. While bayonets were sharpened to a razor's edge, deciding the essential contents of, and their arrangement in, a standard haversack became a major task prior to departure.

On the very night preceding the departure of the 2/14th Battalion, intelligence reported that a further 4000 Japanese had landed at Gona, of which some 1800 were identified as combat troops. Potts was undeterred. He believed that, provided the 2/27th was sent to him immediately (it was, for the time being, to be kept in Port Moresby pending events at Milne Bay), and the promised supplies were awaiting him at Myola, all would be well. He had fair cause for his confidence. He could look to his command of Maroubra Force consisting of five battalions: the 39th, 53rd, 2/14th, 2/16th and 2/27th Battalions. He had an advanced airdrop zone at Myola for his supplies and, in addition, native carriers. On information available to him, the Japanese would be of comparable numerical strength.

The 2/14th commenced its journey to Myola on 16 August. The 2/16th followed the next day. Sergeant R.O. Clemens, 2/14th Battalion: 'How can one describe the monotony of following a trail over mountains, and climbing endless steps which had been cut up the slopes and then finishing the day's march physically exhausted, and then after a respite, move out at first light for a repetition.'[9] Captain R.N. Thompson, 2/14th Battalion: 'I was one of the fittest members, but on the second day, climbing the Golden Stairs I was extremely fatigued. A small dixie of tea caused me to vomit and I could not eat. Next morning I and others had a great craving for salt which surprisingly was given to us . . .'[10]

During all this, Potts was doing what Potts was well known for within his brigade. Lieutenant John Blythe, 2/16th Battalion:

> He was everywhere. On one occasion I crawled to the top of a ridge, trembling with exhaustion and covered in

> mud. I looked up to the figure standing before me. It was Pottsy . . .
>
> He looked at me and said, 'You haven't shaved. Go and clean yourself up. You're filthy!' It was one of the worst things anybody could have said to me at that moment, but it was the best thing. I felt wonderful after I'd hopped in a stream for a while.[11]

These occurrences are the quoted words of a few, but the harrowing experiences of the many. It is worth recording that these soldiers had in June–July 1941 endured the Syrian campaign, where the country was extremely rugged, and had not long before further experienced a gruelling period of training in the Blackall Range in Queensland.

Even sixty years later with a personal carrier carrying your pack, the false crests, the slippery moss rocks and tree roots, all force a level of concentration upon you that is emotionally draining, apart from the physical strain of seemingly unending steep, slippery ascents. To let the mind wander, to gaze at the stunning scenery for just a second, often causes a fall, and in one case a trekker fell off the three-foot track and thirty feet down a steep slope, before grasping at vegetation and coming to an anxious stop. Your party numbers less than two sections, while in August 1942 this narrow path to war carried at various times anywhere in the region of 4500 soldiers and carriers until it became nothing more than 'a great boot-sucking porridge'.

Unbeknown to his battalions, struggling so laboriously over the trail, two disasters struck which would drastically inhibit the implementation of Potts' ambitious plans. At approximately ten o'clock on the morning of 17 August 1942, the Japanese bombed the Seven-Mile airfield outside of Port Moresby and destroyed two Dakota transport planes, damaged five others, and also destroyed three Flying Fortress bombers. The Dakota transports were the soon-to-become famous 'biscuit bombers' upon which Bert Kienzle's planned airdrops were reliant. This misadventure was a carbon copy of the disaster at Clark Field in the Philippines all over again: priceless aircraft wingtip to wingtip to enable the enemy's frequent raids upon Port Moresby to bear maximum fruit for minimum effort. The biscuit bombers were also fully fuelled and laden with supplies. Rowell had warned the Americans of the potential danger only the day before, but the Japanese had struck before American orders had been executed for the planes' dispersal.

But the second disaster remains one of the great mysteries of the Papuan campaign. When Potts, travelling ahead of his troops with characteristic energy and enthusiasm, arrived at Menari, he witnessed the abominable lack of preparation of the supply personnel at staging camps. He also came to realise that the promised dumps of supplies were simply not there. The tragic conclusion to his journey came at Myola when he discovered that the promised 40 000 rations in fact numbered only 5000. In the later *Report Into Operations 21st Brigade*, there is this stinging rebuke:

> It is considered that from the outset a senior experienced officer . . . should have been forward to coordinate the following:—
>
> 1 L of C [Line of Communication] to Base to forward troops.
> 2 Control of staff and stocks at intermediate stations en route.
> 3 Arrange priority of droppings at Myola and creation of reserves based on anticipated and actual demands.
>
> Maintain accurate up-to-date stock figures so that correct information as to supplies and ammunition position could be obtainable on demand by any senior officer who may be ordered to take a force into that country.
>
> To co-ordinate the work of different branches of the service such as A.A.S.C. [supplies], A.A.O.C [ordnance and ammunition], A.N.G.A.U [carrier line].
>
> To maintain close liaison with Base and be in a position to obtain early information as to large scale troop movements in area.[12]

The report then mentions the fact that had these basic and crucial considerations been put in place, the 21st Brigade would not have had to carry five days' rations on each soldier.

Some debate has since raged as to what became of the 35 000 missing rations. Captain Ken Murdoch maintained that he was sent to the supply people in Port Moresby before 21st Brigade left for Myola and was *refused* the figures of the advanced airdrops at Myola as the staff were 'sworn to secrecy'.[13] This is abnormal procedure. The Official Historian claimed that the supplies were 'never dropped at all and the explanation lay in faulty staff work by an inexperienced staff'.[14] Rowell, writing in his autobiography fifteen years later (1974), called McCarthy's statement 'preposterous'[15] and claimed that the closest scrutiny revealed that they (the rations) 'fell outside the target area of the Myola Lake'.[16] Further, Rowell pointed out that some of the biscuit bomber pilots were untrained civilian personnel who did not possess the 'sense of duty and urgency that could be expected from enlisted and trained personnel'.[17]

Rowell's statement concerning the pilots is taken as entirely fair, but the claim that the rations fell outside the Myola target area is hard to believe. When you fly by helicopter from Efogi to Myola, the rolling green jungle below essentially hides the trail, and orientation, especially to the untrained eye, is terribly difficult. But when Myola comes into view it is like a massive yellow-brown 'oasis' in a green 'desert'. Further, in stark contrast to Kagi and later Nauro, where only small drop zones were available, Myola is a vast, wide, dry lake bed with reeds and tufts of grass as its only vegetation. From the air, you just could not miss it. The only excuse for such a massive mistake is the extreme possibility that the pilots flew so far from the area in question that Myola, even allowing for its great open expanse, was not visible. In that case, the supplies should not have been dropped at all.

Although conjecture, it would seem that the Official Historian has some basis to his argument: if the supplies *had been dropped*, why were the staff in Port Moresby sworn to secrecy to the point where the soldiers about to go to war were denied accurate figures? And why did Potts, therefore, insist that his already severely burdened soldiers carry five days' rations? It would seem that Potts suspected that all was not well before he departed, and that subsequent events only confirmed his suspicions. It should be remembered that the supposed 40 000-ration dump was claimed to be in existence at Myola before the loss of the transport planes at Port Moresby on 17 August. The loss of a number of the biscuit bombers placed extra strain on the administration's task of replenishing the Myola dump.

When Rowell pressed Blamey for more transport aircraft, MacArthur told Blamey that he had assigned further but limited numbers of aircraft to Port Moresby:

> There are available in Australia only thirty transport planes at the present time. Of these an average of not more than 50 per cent are available at any one time. Air supply must necessarily be considered an emergency rather than a normal means of supply. Consequently every effort should be made by the GOC, NGF, to develop other means of supply.[18]

What other modes of transport did MacArthur have in mind? The above is a contemptible statement made by an ignorant general who was totally divorced from the reality of Potts' position.

Potts and his 2/14th and 2/16th Battalions were now forced to wait at Myola for some critical days pending the dropping of enough supplies to allow them to go forward and execute their orders. During this passage of time the Japanese were concentrating their force near Isurava.

The exhausted young soldiers of the 39th Battalion dug in at Isurava on 15 August 1942 using bully beef tins, helmets and bayonets. The 21st Brigade was, on this day, in final preparation for its departure across the Owen Stanley Range.

At 1.30 p.m. on 16 August, the adjutant of the 39th Battalion, Lieutenant Keith Lovett, was 'standing around' at Isurava with a group of fellow officers when:

> This person . . . walked up to a group of us . . . I saw he was an officer, and I said, 'Can I help you in any way?' He said, 'Yes, I'm Colonel Honner, I'm your new CO.' And he said, 'Who are you?' And I told him who I was.

> He said, 'Well, I'd like you to take me around and introduce me to the company commanders and we'll settle down and start our business.' He looked a very fit specimen . . .
>
> He told me briefly about his history and what he's done, and I thought, 'Well, that's good enough for me, let's go!'[19]

Lieutenant-Colonel Ralph Honner was an original member of the 2/11th Battalion, 19th Brigade, 6th Division. He brought to Isurava a varied knowledge of war that was to prove invaluable in two of the five Papuan battles: Kokoda and Gona. He had practised the fluid advance in Libya, the fighting withdrawal in Greece and the set-piece defence at Retimo in Crete. But when he arrived at Isurava the condition of his new command shocked him:

> Physically the pathetically young warriors of the 39th were in poor shape. Worn out by strenuous fighting and exhausting movement, and weakened by lack of food and sleep and shelter, many of them had literally come to a standstill. Practically every day torrential rains fell through the afternoon and night, cascading into their cheerless weapon-pits and soaking the only clothes they wore—the only ones they had. In these they shivered through the long chill vigil of the lonely nights when they were required to stand awake and alert but still and silent. Only the morning brought a gleam of comfort—a turn at sleeping and forgetting, a chance perhaps, to lie and dry in the warmth of the glowing day.[20]

They were, according to Honner, 'just growing boys'.[21] Honner's analogy is misleading and, in line with the Official Historian's comment that one platoon in Templeton's B Company had an average age of eighteen and a half years,[22] it has become fashionable to label the 39th and 53rd Battalions as having an average age of eighteen and a half years.[23] Honner was looking through the eyes of an original member of the 6th Division, where the average age of recruits was in the mid-twenties. A significant number of his soldiers were therefore in their late twenties and early thirties. His statement is therefore relative to what he had seen in his soldiering up to that time. The average age of the 39th was probably more around the early twenties[24]—a noticeable difference to someone like Honner and the range of his relatively recent experiences.

Captain 'Blue' Steward, RMO (battalion doctor) 2/16th Battalion, saw the 39th near Isurava: '. . . gaunt spectres with gaping boots and rotting tatters of uniform hanging around them like scarecrows. Their faces had no expression, their eyes sunk back in their sockets. They were drained by malaria, dysentery and near starvation . . .'[25] But a fifth of these 'growing boys' carried the ultimate military stigma. Cameron had branded B Company as cowards after their far distant Oivi fighting, and had suggested to Honner that they be broken up and scattered within the remaining companies of the battalion. Honner would have none of it. In a moral as well as military decision he decided to give B Company the post of honour, the ground where he expected the Japanese most likely to attack. Such a decision inspires not only the 'victims' but those around them. Sergeant Jack Sim, Signals 39th Battalion:

> I think the battalion's spirit may have been inspired, it was certainly exemplified, by Ralph Honner the leader. That decision . . . that rather than wreck them completely, he'd let them stay with the unit that they'd helped to make . . . it was a wonderful decision, and that spirit was shown again and again by B Company.[26]

If Honner was a well-practised soldier, he was also a highly educated scholar and romantic. He was well versed in English literature, had an intimate knowledge of Shakespeare, had read many of the great epics, and he spoke French, Spanish, German and Italian fluently. From the moment Ralph Honner arrived at Isurava, he was engaged in the creation of the Kokoda legend—not a fable, or mere story, but the making of an Australian legend. When Honner cast his experienced military eye over his new command, he most definitely did not see defeatism, exhaustion and hopelessness but the lofty, ageless nobility of the eternal soldier. He would later write: 'That glory is not of the exultation of war but the exaltation of man, the nobility of man sublimated in the fiery crucible of war, shining faithfulness and fortitude and gentleness and compassion elevated from all dross.'[27] In Honner's epic view of life and war, Isurava was not merely a battle on the Kokoda Trail but Australia's Agincourt. Given his knowledge of Shakespeare, it is little wonder that he saw Isurava in those terms: at Agincourt King Harry and his liegemen were also outnumbered by about five to one; the driving rain and mud and savage marching to Agincourt had its parallel at Isurava; and the slaughter of the English boys by the French would also have its parallel at Isurava, and at numerous other places along the Kokoda Trail. Thus, a commander does not brand a group of young boys as cowards to be sent back in disgrace. Such a decision was anathema to everything he believed in—you did the opposite by deploying them in the post of honour.

After a thorough tour of his lines, and a resulting appreciation on his first day at Isurava, Honner made adjustments to his company dispositions. He found Isurava to be a reasonably good delaying position. Its northern and southern extremities allowed for some observation over the eastward-flowing creeks, which provided obstacles, if narrow ones, for the enemy. Although thick scrub ran virtually up to both the front and rear creeks, there were cleared patches of ground on each side of the track in the central area. The village of Isurava was on a flat clearing to the east of the track and south of the front creek. Through the village an extremely steep, descending track ran eastwards to Asigari, situated on the other side of the Eora Creek Valley—not far as the crow flies but a very steep, exhausting descent and an equally tough ascent to that village. The western flank was dominated by timber and very thick jungle beyond. Just over the front creek, and through a native garden, a track ran westwards to the Naro Ridge.

Its track command and its tactical advantages made Isurava an acceptable defensive proposition, but it was far from impregnable, and the fact that it was now being held by a weakened, exhausted force at less than battalion strength made its defences thin indeed.

Honner perceived that the Japanese had three alternatives for their capture of Isurava. The first was an attack along the eastern side of the Eora Creek Valley through Missima–Asigari and through to Alola. By using this route, the enemy could bypass the 39th and cut their line of communication. Honner rightly discounted this approach because he had deployed the incoming 53rd Battalion at the junction of the 'loop' at Alola and he judged that the Japanese were more likely to want to deal with the 39th Battalion at Isurava first. The second alternative was a movement along the higher ground from Naro to Alola. He also discounted this approach because of the extremely thick jungle and scrub between the Naro Ridge track and Alola. The enemy's third alternative was a direct assault upon Isurava.

Honner deployed his companies to meet the expected attacks. The area bounded by his B, D and E Companies and the main track contained open, overgrown gardens, with some high grass and a sugar cane plantation. The only real killing ground—low grass with excellent fields of fire—lay west of B Company's main positions towards the edge of the timber. While the enemy should avoid this Australian killing ground, they might be tempted to use it because they could swing from the main track to the Naro track and come across the creek to approach from the high ground, through sparse jungle and fairly open woodland opposite B Company, and then concentrate in such numbers that a fast movement across the killing ground would have them in amongst the B Company defenders.

Honner's appreciation, done within hours of his arrival at Isurava, was spot on. The Japanese were indeed destined to use the very approach he had identified. B Company was ordered to dig in, in deep, narrow pits, with forward posts in the timber edge in front of them and reserve positions behind them for their support—or their retirement in the event of a limited withdrawal. During his tour of the area the previous day, Honner noticed that these key pits were far too shallow, and therefore ordered them to be dug far deeper to enhance the chances of their prolonged use.

But Honner was not one for just static defensive positions. He quickly decided that:

> There wasn't much I could do in the way of an attack except hold the enemy at arm's length as long as possible

> to prevent them from finding out how weak we were and how small indeed was our garrison. Had they known how small we were they should have gone around us and cut us off from our supplies and annihilated us. We had to buy time and buy distance as long as possible and as far as possible.[28]

From the time of the withdrawal of the 39th to Isurava, its D Company had manned a standing patrol about 45 minutes down the track towards Deniki. When Honner inspected this position on his first day at Isurava, he decided to reduce its size from two platoons to one, and change its personnel daily. The 39th Battalion Unit Diary best sums up this audacious policy:

> Patrols lightly equipped for 24 hrs tour of duty were now changed during the first hour of light when morning mist made visibility bad and the enemy, owing to difficulty of night movement, were unlikely to attack so far forward of Deniki base. Role of the patrols was to deny the enemy use of the track and thus delay enemy reconnaissance of our main positions at Isurava. To give defence in depth and a ready reserve at the time when an enemy attack was most likely (mid-morning), each patrol, when relieved, moved back to the next delaying position about 200 yards to the rear and remained there until 1130 hrs, then returned to Isurava. The platoon next for duty stood ready equipped for instant action for 24 hrs before taking over the standing patrol, ready to move to the support of the forward patrol if needed.[29]

Within 36 hours, Lieutenant-Colonel Ralph Honner had stamped himself on events at Isurava. His adjutant, Lieutenant Keith Lovett:

> First of all he was always a perfect gentleman, no matter what the situation. He didn't lose his temper, he didn't show disgust . . . He had a strong personality about him . . . A very easy man to work with . . . He went to give

Isurava before the attack, 27 August

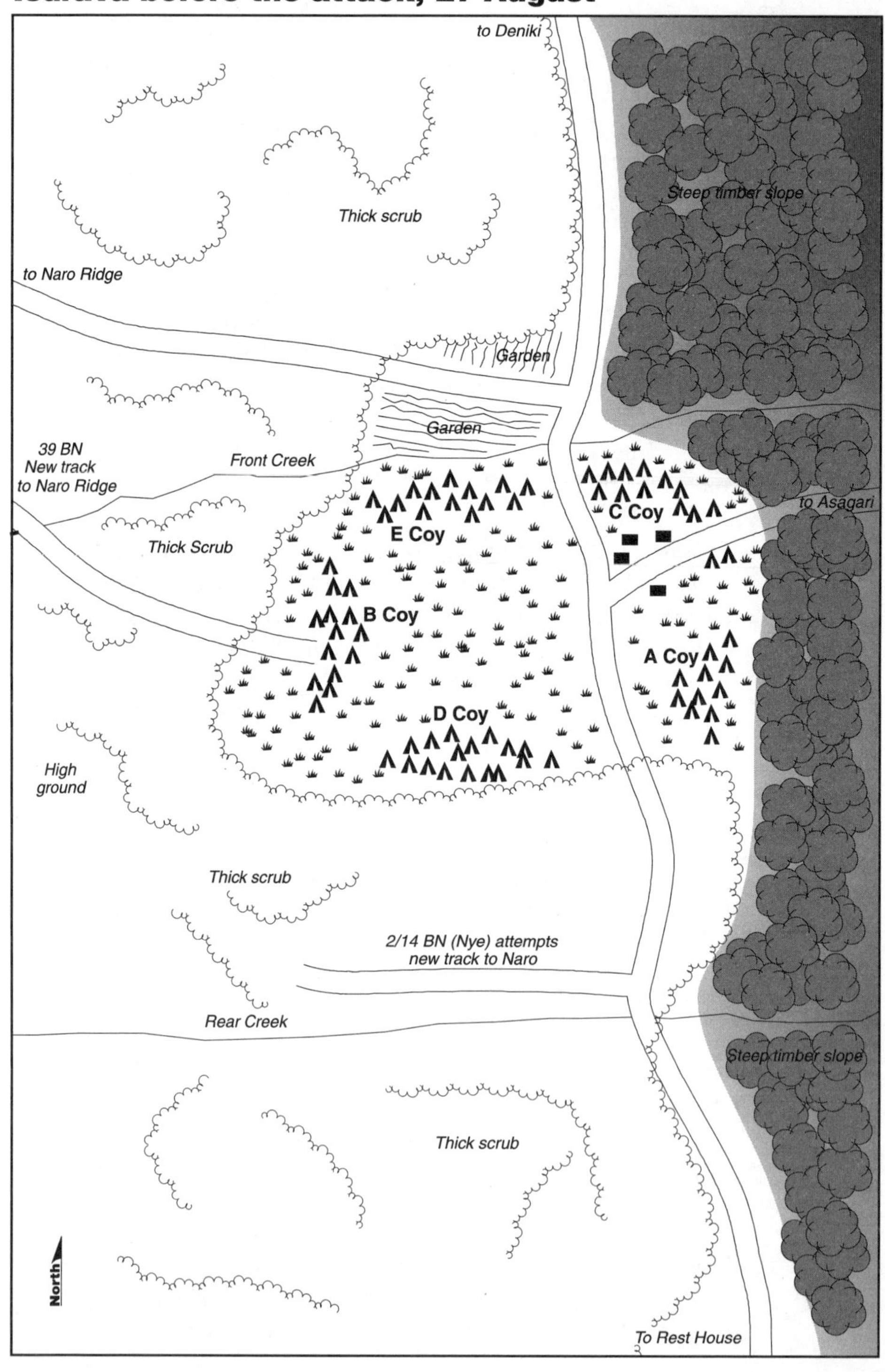

> himself a bit of time to work everything out, instead of just taking over what was there. He made the war his war.[30]

On 21 August came the news that the 39th Battalion could expect relief. Honner would later write that 'all the news seemed good news, and courage feeds on hope'.[31]

The following days were spent by the 39th Battalion patrolling and preparing for the inevitable Japanese offensive. But if there seemed to be a distinct lull in proceedings, it was because the Japanese were landing and bringing forward their main force under Major-General Horii, which included five battalions of his South Seas Force: all three battalions of the 144th Regiment and the first two (the third to arrive on 2 September) of the 41st Regiment. With these were deployed a formidable array of ancillary and support units, including the 55th Mountain Artillery and the 15th Independent Engineer Regiment equipped to double as infantry troops.

The scene is set. The battle for Isurava will rage for four critical days, from 26 to 29 August 1942. The Japanese have wreaked utter havoc along a path of victory through South-East Asia. The strategic jewel of Port Moresby will be seized by a thrust over the Owen Stanley Range which will rely on speed of movement, the capture of Australian food, medical supplies and stores—all this in ten days. General MacArthur, meanwhile, considers the Japanese actions thus far as nothing more than an incursion to Kokoda to secure their air bases at Buna.

To face the initial brunt of this fresh, confident Japanese force is deployed at Isurava an exhausted, almost spent and depleted militia battalion commanded by a new officer who has had about 36 hours to prepare his defences. Behind him at Alola is another militia unit, the 53rd Battalion, whose manner of raising, equipping, training and leadership is open to severe questioning. Back still further at Myola are two battalions of a crack AIF brigade who have been forced to halt their advance because of a supply bungle of monumental proportions. The Australian ability to hold this place will depend upon the initial fighting qualities of the 39th Battalion and the speed of the 21st Brigade's arrival. Finally, it will be decided in an all-in battle that will have an enormous influence upon the long-term battle for Port Moresby.

General MacArthur's 'enemy incursion' is about to develop into a major battle that will send shock waves through Supreme Allied Headquarters.

GOD, KING AND COUNTRY

7

Brigadier Arnold Potts assumed command of Maroubra Force on 23 August 1942 when he relieved Brigadier Porter at Alola. This village was an ideal location for a Brigade HQ as it stood at the southern base of one of the only two loops on the Kokoda Trail. To the north-east lay the track through Abuari–Missima–Kaile which wound its way to Kokoda. The main track through Alola passed on through Isurava, to Deniki and then to Kokoda. Alola is about a 45-minute march from Isurava.

When Potts assumed command, the 39th Battalion was forward at Isurava, patrolling the eastward track to Asigari and the westward approach from Naro. Most important was the maintenance of the forward standing patrol 45 minutes down the main track towards Deniki. The 53rd Battalion, after being held at that village by Honner and then Porter, was then assigned the role of patrolling the right flank track through Abuari–Missima–Kaile. It also pushed out through the forward standing patrol of the 39th on the main track.

It will be remembered that Potts' orders were to recapture Kokoda. He had three courses of action open to him. The first, and the most desirable, was to leave his two militia battalions where they were and build up his supply dumps at Myola while retaining his 2/14th and 2/16th Battalions at that venue. This would place less strain on his carriers taking supplies to the front and, most significantly, mask the presence of his two battalions near the front at Myola. It might also allow him time to concentrate his third 21st Brigade battalion, the 2/27th, at Myola (the 2/27th was being held in Port Moresby as the divisional reserve). This first option was rather quickly discounted when he saw the condition of the 39th at Isurava. On 26 August Potts signalled Major-General 'Tubby' Allen in Port Moresby: 'Condition of 39th Battalion weak due to continuous work lack warm clothing blankets shelters curtailed rations and wet every night monotonous diet combined with comparative static role last fortnight.'[1]

The second option involved deploying his 2/14th to the high ground near Naro to the west and his 2/16th on the high ground to the east, while leaving his two militia battalions where they were. Again, hoping that the 2/27th would soon join him, he would then be in a position to have a solid defence of Isurava against the potential Japanese ambition of outflanking him from the high ground, and a reserve at Alola to embark upon offensive action. His supply problems, the condition of the 39th and the absence of the 2/27th precluded this option.

Potts' least desirable course of action was the very one that he reluctantly adopted: relieve the exhausted 39th with his fresh 2/14th at Isurava and hold his 2/16th at Alola, to be used either in a defensive or offensive role. Unfortunately for the Australians, General Horii was operating to his own timetable. Having concentrated his fresh force, he unleashed it on 26 August at Isurava.

It should be clearly grasped that Horii's vastly superior force did not mean that 10 000 Japanese attacked a depleted, debilitated 39th Battalion, soon to be reinforced by one AIF battalion. One of the prime principles of war is 'concentration of force'. In that terrain, the decided advantage Horii did have was the ability to alternate his battalions in action and maintain pressure upon the Australians at will—in other words, the same small force of Australians had to maintain the defensive, while fresh Japanese in far greater numbers could be brought in to maintain the offensive. And at this early stage the Japanese were operating from a firm and nearby base, while the Australians were operating from a far-distant base over a long, tenuous mountain track. Horii's forward combat force outnumbered the Australians by about four or five to one.

Around midday on the 26th, Lieutenant Simonson's forward patrol was heavily attacked in unison with a prolonged shelling of Isurava by an enemy mountain gun which had been manhandled up the track. This gun had a range of about two thousand yards and outranged the future deployment of Australian mortars. The repeated use of this weapon was to give the Japanese a decided advantage for some weeks. The enemy also began to infiltrate around the dense jungle adjoining the Naro track to form up in the native garden across the Isurava front creek.

Simonson's position was quite quickly reinforced by Lieutenant Sword's platoon, which was the next-for-duty standing patrol. Together the Australians drove the probing enemy back some two hundred yards and tried to locate the troublesome mountain gun. Unable to locate it, they returned to their original position. At around 3.30 p.m., the Japanese resumed their bombardment of Isurava for a further 90 minutes and deployed additional infantry through the dense jungle adjoining the Naro track. Lieutenant-Colonel Honner would later write:

> A hundred yards forward of our front line the sentry of a listening post, beside the Deniki track, ambushed the leading bunched patrol. He emptied his Tommy-gun magazine into them at a range of two or three yards, then seeing a larger force swarming down through the garden, jumped across the track and crashed recklessly over the steep hillside, hurtling and slithering to the rocky creek-bed below, there to begin the long laborious climb back to regain C Company's lines next morning. The other two members of the listening post, stationed some distance farther south—to keep him in sight and to keep themselves in view from our forward posts—seeing that he no longer needed their protection, raced back along the track and over the creek already coming under fire.[2]

With Simonson and Sword thus occupied, Lieutenant Clarke, whose C Company platoon were due to relieve Simonson and Sword the next day, had earlier journeyed down the track to Deniki to reconnoitre the forward positions. His party was small, consisting of his section leaders and seconds-in-command only. As he was making his way back towards the front creek garden at around 5.00 p.m., Clarke found that area alive with infiltrating enemy. This small group did not avoid a fight but actively sought one. Clarke's 'force' not only drove the Japanese out of the garden and into the rearward wooded area, but then Clark and one of his soldiers stalked the enemy remnant through the high grass in the old garden area. They killed eight.

When Lieutenant Clarke returned across the front creek with his small party they were greeted by new and fresh faces. Captain Dickenson and his C Company 2/14th Battalion had arrived at Isurava and taken over C Company 39th Battalion's positions. The meeting would have given Clarke much pleasure as well as relief—he was greeting old comrades, as he was an AIF reinforcement officer from the 2/14th Battalion who had been posted to the 39th in June.

That night the Japanese again attempted to eliminate Simonson's standing patrol on the Deniki track. Norm Downey was among the defenders:

> . . . two Japs broke through our perimeter and in the shooting that followed Lieutenant Simonson and two men from Lieutenant Sword's platoon were wounded besides Norm Whitehead who got a bayonet through the shoulder. One of the Japs managed to get away, but the other one copped a bullet 'up the Kyber' and lay moaning in the jungle all night.[3]

Simonson and his two wounded comrades decided to risk a return back down the main track to Isurava. On that pitch-black, rain-soaked night they saw no one, but heard close movement and enemy voices on a number of occasions.[4] Sword's platoon were not so lucky. Norm Downey:

> Lieutenant Sword was now in command, and he and the two platoon sergeants decided we should withdraw to the next delaying position . . . When we got there we tried to contact BHQ by phone but the line was dead. Albert Grace was sent to report to Battalion but he never got there and was never seen again. Soon after

> Albert left, Jimmy Woods was given permission to return to Isurava (he was shaking with fever) but he had only been gone a little while when we heard gunfire and Jimmy came pelting back to our perimeter.[5]

Cut off from the main track, Sword and his men were forced to climb to the ridge above and make their way back to Isurava.

On the morning of 27 August 1942, with Sword and his patrol out of contact and Simonson's soldiers having returned to the perimeter, Potts ordered Honner to post a standing patrol at Naro to block any enemy outflanking movement along the western Naro track to Alola. Lieutenant Pentland and the fittest of C Company were given the role. But Pentland could not use the track through the front garden to Naro as it was now reoccupied by the enemy, so he was forced to slash a new path west of the B Company positions for that purpose. Pentland and his patrol reached Naro unharmed.

That day, 27 August, saw the Battle of Isurava erupt in an intensity that had not been seen previously during the campaign. The Japanese had now virtually eliminated all posts and standing patrols forward of the Isurava perimeter. There could be no further attempts at holding the enemy at arm's length, or trying to mask the strength of the defences. The battle from now on was to be a pure and simple set piece defence of a perimeter against an enemy who outnumbered the Australians and could use his artillery to constantly bombard their positions. Further, Horii now deployed a battalion around his left flank to attempt to outflank the Australians and sever their supply line.

Having moved through the garden on the far side of the front creek and having also penetrated the thick jungle on the Naro flank, the Japanese were soon probing Lieutenant French's B Company and Captain Merritt's E Company positions.

Potts envisaged a complete relief of the 39th on 28 August; he therefore required the recovery of Pentland's Naro patrol to allow Honner's battalion to withdraw intact, and he ordered Honner to replace that patrol with a platoon from C Company, 2/14th Battalion. Dickenson assigned the task to Lieutenant Arthur Davis and his platoon.

When Davis and his patrol, guided by the intelligence sergeant of the 39th, Buchecker, set out to follow Pentland's route they found, upon crossing the front creek, the jungle alive with Japanese. In the ensuing action Davis lost a soldier killed and was then seriously wounded himself. Despite his wound, he fought a single-handed rearguard action, sacrificing his own life to enable the successful withdrawal of his platoon. Buchecker was wounded in the leg, suffering a shattered thigh. Chaplain Nobby Earl and the battalion doctor, Captain Shera, moved out to the sound of the action, located Buchecker and carried him in. The patrol followed them back to Isurava pressed closely by the enemy. With Pentland now cut off—in addition to Sword—the 39th Battalion was without the fittest men of three of its five companies. To replace E Company's missing men Sergeant Kerslake, with the remainder of C Company after Pentland's Naro patrol had gone, was posted in a reserve platoon position with a counterattack role. At the same time Sergeant Murray's platoon of A Company became the battalion reserve, ready to rush wherever it might be needed.

Honner has left his nation with a vivid account of the remaining events of that action-packed day:

> With the situation apparently well under control I went to the rear creek—outside the perimeter but our only water supply—for a wash and a shave. There were about a dozen of us there, including Merritt. A breathless runner brought me a message that the enemy had broken through into 'E' Company's position. I looked over at the unsuspecting Merritt. It seemed a pity to disturb him. 'Captain Merritt,' I said, 'when you've finished your shave will you go to your company. The Japs have broken through your perimeter.' Merritt didn't appreciate the Drake touch. An astonished look hung for an instant on his half-shaved face; then it lifted like a starter's barrier and he was off like a racehorse.
>
> Odd parties of the enemy were already bursting through the thinly-held timber to be shot down in the open ... Then, in the middle of the afternoon, the intermittent bombardment was suddenly intensified. As

the precise Japanese diarist of No. 3 Battalion records it: 'At 1538 our guns all join in together and the attack and advance begins along the whole front.'

And while the bombs and bullets crashed and rattled in an unceasing clamour that re-echoed from the affrighted hills, the enveloping forest erupted into violent action as Nippon's screaming warriors streamed out of its shadows to the assault.

Across the creek they swept in a swift thrust that sliced through E Company's thin front line . . . The attacks on E Company were repulsed mainly by Merritt's own men, but with a quick counter-attack by Kerslake's counter-penetration platoon driving out the enemy breaking through one gap and with Murray's mobile reserve also racing up to the rescue. For the rest of the day B Company bore the brunt of the enemy's attacks.

Its forward platoons had occupied advanced positions near the timber edge to obtain some cover from it and to force the infiltrating Japanese deeper into the denser forest; but the violence of the enemy onset pressed them back to a better line prepared slightly to the rear to give them more open killing space on an occasion such as this. There they held, fighting magnificently, while the enemy came on in reckless waves, regardless of the casualties that soon cluttered that short stretch of open ground.

These incessant assaults were slowly sapping B Company's strength—and at the end of the day, when the heaviest attack of all rolled in over French's men their endurance was stretched almost to breaking point. Lieutenant Garland, their second-in-command, reported that they were unlikely to hold much longer unless reinforced. I gave him a message for French that he would have to hold—there was only battalion headquarters behind him. But in the light of the enemy's obviously superior strength I recognised that it would be only a matter of time before our small garrison was overrun—in the evening, the night, or next morning. There was only one source of quick reinforcement to forestall disaster.

In the middle of the afternoon Captain Nye had arrived with 'B' Company of the 2/14th not to strengthen the defenders but with orders to push through to relieve Pentland on the Naro Track. Davis had already found Pentland's route through French's lines impassable, so Nye's company started to cut its way west through the jungle bordering the creek to the rear of our perimeter. It was with considerable misgiving that I watched this formidable force march out of our lines just as the big offensive was commencing. When 'B' Company was so sorely pressed at sunset I resolved to recall Nye if he could still be reached. Fortunately the jungle was so thick that two hours of laborious slashing had not taken the head of the column more than a couple of hundred yards—his rear troops were hardly off the track. They quickly returned to take part in the fight and I do not remember anything more heartening than the sight of their confident deployment. Their splendid physique and bearing, and their cool automatic efficiency—even the assembly-line touch as two platoon mortar-men stepped one on either side of the track to pluck bombs from the haversacks of the riflemen filing past them without checking their pace—made a lasting impression on me. And they were to prove even better than they looked.

I sent their first platoon to strengthen 'E' Company's left, and the second to 'D' Company's right to close the pincers from either flank on the enemy still endangering 'B' Company; and the pressure had already eased when the third platoon was placed under French's command. It was dark by the time the three strengthened companies had consolidated their positions, and the firing died away to a silence that seemed strangely eerie after the twelve-hour tumult. And the peace of the night was broken only by an occasional stealthy foray—as when one of Dickenson's men was bayoneted without seeing his assailant.[6]

On the morning of 28 August 1942, Captain Cameron and his D Company, 2/14th Battalion, took over the positions of E Company, 39th Battalion which in turn allowed Nye's three platoons to congregate under his command and assume control of his opposite number's 39th Battalion dispositions. Captain Merritt's two E Company platoons and Lieutenant French's men now occupied gaps in the lines to the rear which had been created by Sword's and Pentland's missing patrols.

Captain Max Bidstrup, an AIF reinforcement officer to the 39th from the 18th Brigade's 2/10th Battalion, was well positioned to watch the sudden and magnificent birth of a battalion—and against formidable odds. From the moment of its first action near Oivi, to Kokoda—twice—through to Deniki and Isurava, the 39th had found itself out on a limb and on its own. When it had had every reason and excuse to fail, it had alternatively drawn on the experience of AIF reinforcement officers, or the tremendous spirit and determination of its militia officers; at other critical times it had drawn on an old hand, an old soldier like Templeton or Cowey, and somehow, out of that unique blending of youth, experience and sheer guts and fortitude, it had triumphed. Captain Bidstrup, in the last years of his life, still stood in awe of the young warriors of the 39th, a battalion of which he was intensely proud to be a member:

> The 2/14th and 2/16th came up the track just as we were on our last bloody legs. We couldn't have lasted another day. We were gone for all money. Despite the fact that the blokes were down to the last human resource, they were still prepared to fight, to carry on. I have never ceased to marvel at the way those boys did carry on.[7]

While these events had been unfolding at Isurava, a gradual build-up of enemy activity had been witnessed by elements of the 53rd Battalion through the right flank along the Abuari–Missima–Kaile track. It began on 25 August.

The 53rd had been maintaining a standing patrol at Kaile and radio communication between Missima and Alola. On that day, Lieutenant Alan Isaachsen and twenty men of his platoon left Alola to occupy Kaile as the standing patrol.

Approaching Kaile, Isaachsen's patrol was ambushed by a two-platoon strength Japanese force which attacked from the high ground, with the support of a mortar and a machine-gun. In the ensuing action Lieutenant Isaachsen was killed (not to be confused with Major Cedric Isaachsen, 2/27th Battalion, Alan's older brother). Captain Ahern, who had accompanied the patrol, abandoned Kaile after having inflicted heavy casualties upon the enemy. Upon his return towards Missima, Ahern found that village to be occupied by the Japanese. Forced into a withdrawal via Eora Creek, the patrol finally reached its own lines on the evening of 28 August, having been three days without rations.

During 26–27 August, when the Japanese had began their concentrated assaults upon the 39th at Isurava, it was also pressing along the Abuari–Missima–Kaile track. At 8.00 a.m. on 27 August Potts, growing increasingly concerned about events on this flank, ordered Lieutenant-Colonel Ward, 53rd Battalion, to retake Missima.[8] Ward ordered D Company to move through B Company and secure this objective. The problem was that D Company did not begin its movement until 10.00 a.m.[9] In other words, the order to move was given at 8.00 a.m. and its execution did not occur for two hours. At around 2.00 p.m. D Company was moving out through B Company's perimeter towards the high ground, where enemy fire was holding up B Company.[10] The Official Historian:

> At 3.30 Ward reported to Potts that the two companies were moving on to Missima and, believing this to be correct, himself set out along the track with Lieutenant Logan. But the two forward companies had failed in their tasks because (the battalion diarist records) of:
>
> (1) Nature of the country (2) Heavy MMG [Medium Machine Gun] fire by enemy which could not be located (3) Lack of offensive spirit and general physical condition of troops.[11]

When Ward moved up the track towards his forward two companies, he and Logan were ambushed and killed. *Report Into Operations 21 Brigade*:

> As far as could be ascertained later, B Company did no more than make contact with the enemy but broke and

> scattered, while it is doubtful if D Company did any more than make contact with the enemy. At 1620 hours a runner from the 53rd Battalion informed Brigade that the Japs had come around the waterfall and were making towards the river crossing and Alola. 53rd Battalion were ordered to hold Abuari Village, waterfall and river crossing with the remaining companies pending the arrival of 2/16th Battalion. At nightfall the position on the right flank was as follows:—B and D Companies, 53rd Battalion, out of contact with Brigade and reported to have pressed on to Missima. Jap patrols thought to be in occupation of Abuari Village. In addition seventy of 53rd Battalion on patrols NOT reported in and subsequently found to have taken to the bush.[12]

It would be 8.00 a.m. on the following morning before approximately 70 missing men from B and D Companies of the 53rd were able to regain contact with their HQ. Another small group returned via the waterfall at about 2.00 p.m. The remainder had scattered.

By nightfall on the 27th, the position on his shattered right flank around Abuari was one of deep concern for Potts. A major part of the 53rd Battalion was out of contact with his HQ and the leaderless and aimless remainder were close to the Eora Creek crossing below Alola. Forward on the left flank Honner was being reinforced by a third company of the 2/14th and was holding Isurava but against a great enemy strength that would still require the commitment there of the rest of the 2/14th.

The 2/16th Battalion, Potts' original unit, had been in the process of moving Captain McGee's A Company and Captain Sublet's B Company forward to spearhead the Australians' right flank advance from a firm base at Alola to Missima. The failure of the 53rd to carry out its orders and to provide any semblance of coordination or order on that crucial flank forced Potts to commit his prized 2/16th Battalion company by company, upon arrival at Alola, to the rescue of the defence and dashed any hopes he held for an offensive operation.

However, 27 August was also an important day for the Japanese. If ever Horii was to have a chance to wreak utter havoc and defeat upon the Australians, then this would have been his golden opportunity. He had them pinned down at Isurava and had, at minimal cost, extended his left flank towards Alola. His only opposition between Missima and Alola was a militia battalion which had failed dismally to contest his advance.

The next day was unaccountably quiet on the right flank. This was a rare piece of good fortune for Potts as he moved his A and B Companies, 2/16th Battalion across Eora Creek to close on Abuari by nightfall after the Japanese had been seen from Alola moving towards that village. But the 28th had been a busier day at Isurava. At daybreak Captain Cameron's D Company, 2/14th Battalion, which had reached Isurava the previous evening, took over the creek and the forward native garden covering positions of Merritt's E Company, 39th Battalion. Dickenson's C Company established itself beyond the main track to the right and Nye's reunited B Company took over French's 'killing-ground' front to its left rear. The 39th Battalion now moved to the less threatened south and east sectors of the Isurava perimeter.

Dawn was shattered by a menacing roar of Japanese mountain gun, mortar and heavy machine-gun fire, which was to continue uninterrupted until approximately eight o'clock that morning. Through the still echoing shock waves of the subsiding bombardment stormed the Japanese, who initially attacked in company strength upon Dickenson's positions. The seemingly insane, fanatical frontal assaults had begun. Bodies began to litter the approaches as the attackers were met with concentrated machine-gun and rifle fire and grenades and, as that relatively small killing ground was gradually traversed by the sheer weight of Japanese numbers, the enemy were met with the bayonet. Such a set piece defence of a perimeter takes enormous discipline, coordination and nervous energy, particularly when the enemy has the numbers to repeat such attacks and, critically, is fully prepared to take high casualties in the process.

Employing what was to become standard procedure, the Japanese turned their attention towards Cameron's company in the centre positions, and upon Nye's company on the left flank. It will be remembered that Nye had taken over the high ground on the western flank, on what Honner had called 'the post of honour'. It was a tough climb to this high ground, and there were pits along the steep gradient down to Isurava's rear. Although a signal line did run up to the position, it would be very hard not to feel a sense of extreme isolation on this westward left flank. As Honner had noted, there was a substantial killing ground present here for the defenders, but there were also ample assembly points for the Japanese.

Having spent adequate time in reconnaissance of this sector, the Japanese now began to devote much of their attention upon Lieutenant Moore's 11 Platoon positions. Before the fighting eased on the 28th Lieutenant Moore had made the supreme sacrifice and a number of his men had been wounded. Ralph Honner:

> There were already four times as many men holding our front and flanks as there had been the previous day; and when A Company and part of Headquarters Company of the 2/14th arrived it was possible for the first time to provide a powerful reserve. So Isurava seemed secure when Lieutenant-Colonel Key of the 2/14th marched in at midday and took command, relieving the 39th which was due to leave for Port Moresby. But I told Key I considered the holding of Isurava against the strength the enemy had shown the previous day would need more than one battalion, and I would not leave him in the lurch.[13]

It is highly likely that Honner and Key would have known each other, as both had served in Vasey's 19th Brigade—Key with the 2/8th and Honner with the 2/11th—through the fighting withdrawal in Greece and the subsequent fighting in Crete. Both were cool-headed, quiet and efficient soldiers and both now advised Potts to leave the exhausted 39th with Key at Isurava.

The Japanese sustained their attacks upon Dickenson and Nye until mid-afternoon. Having attempted to pierce the Australian positions at a number of points, they again turned their attention to Cameron's D Company later in the day. They had good reason to do so. First, they knew by then that the 39th had been reinforced. Second, their attacks over cleared killing grounds had proved most costly. Cameron's positions were now seen as the best possibility of a breakthrough. While two of his three platoon positions offered some reasonable view of the enemy approaches, the third, commanded by Lieutenant Pearce, was sited in thick jungle that allowed far less observation of the front, and less opportunities for communication and support.

The plan worked. A part of Pearce's perimeter was overrun and the position was only restored after a platoon from the reserve A Company counterattacked. With critical hours slipping away from him by 29 August, the fourth day of his offensive, and despite appalling losses in earlier wholesale attacks, Horii decided to commit his considerable reserves to a final massive assault upon the Australians at Isurava. Potts, meanwhile, was engaged in reinforcing his right flank with his 2/16th Battalion; he repeatedly requested the dispatch of his much needed 2/27th Battalion from Itiki (near the beginning of the Kokoda Trail), as without that strengthening of his force he was reduced to conducting his unequal battle with grossly inadequate forces.

On 29 August, the 2/16th was committed to the right flank along the Alola–Abuari–Missima axis. Its role was to stabilise the right flank, and if possible push on to Missima. In order to execute Potts' orders, the CO of the 2/16th, Lieutenant-Colonel Albert Caro, dispatched his A Company under the command of Captain McGee and his B Company under Captain Sublet, who recalls:

> All was quiet around Abuari when I reached there and almost immediately I made a reconnaissance with a couple of men along the track to Missima. About one hundred metres down this track we came across the bodies of Lieutenant-Colonel Ward, C.O. of the 53rd Battalion and his Adjutant or Intelligence officer. I concluded they had been ambushed, and firing on my right rear told me that A Company had contacted the enemy. Soon afterwards I received orders to take command of both A and B Companies, and I did so. When A Coy scouts discovered the enemy in position above Abuari Village, the Company Commander

> ordered 7th and 9th Platoons to attack, and they went in with gusto and continued to press the Japanese all afternoon. 9th Platoon killed about fifty of the enemy and captured several light machine guns while 7th Platoon continued their assault. In accordance with Colonel Caro's wishes, I had handed over B Coy to Captain George Wright when I assumed command of the two-company force and I decided that B Coy should move and attack the enemy's right flank while A Coy continued their frontal attack. I judged that at least one hundred Japanese were holding well prepared positions covering the partially cleared area of the village and the Missima track where it emerged from the cover provided by a thirty foot cliff at the top of a sliding track up which we had travelled from the deep gorge below Alola. In view of the threat of Japanese reinforcements from Missima, B Coy was to post a strong standing patrol to secure their left flank.[14]

By mid-afternoon it was clear to Sublet that if he was to push on to Missima, he must mount an attack using his A Company in a frontal assault, his B Company on his left flank, and a third force along his right flank to fall upon the Japanese rear. He requested that a company from the 53rd Battalion come forward to accomplish this task. This plan was to be executed the next day.

While the situation on the right flank was thus poised, the battle at Isurava was becoming a titanic struggle. From daylight until dusk on 29 August, the Japanese mounted further furious frontal assaults upon the 2/14th's positions. B Company's 10 Platoon, commanded by Lieutenant Harold 'Butch' Bisset, had relieved 11 Platoon towards the previous evening. The Japanese mounted eleven determined attacks upon Bisset's men, each of company strength. During these attacks the enemy penetrated 10 Platoon's perimeter, with the result that any movement during such close-quarter fighting brought down a concentrated wall of small arms fire. This caused the treatment and evacuation of the wounded to be undertaken at great peril. By dusk the 10 Platoon perimeter had become a splintered graveyard for no fewer than 200 Japanese soldiers. This area was 'splintered' because 10 Platoon's ground was behind a sugar cane patch about the size of a 'normal street block'[15] which had been ravaged by constant automatic and small arms fire.

When you fly by helicopter over this Isurava high ground you are struck by its isolation. It was part of an organised perimeter, but in this type of close fighting the individual soldier, as the enemy gains ground under attack, fights an exceedingly personal war and is out of touch with the rest of his platoon, let alone the current standing of his company and much less his battalion. The high ground and its cane field had to be held—lose it and lose Isurava.

This isolation in terms of intelligence and communication and supply were the very three factors that cost Bisset (and many others) his life. While distributing grenades and ammunition to his men he was mortally wounded by a burst of machine-gun fire. As the enemy pressure mounted and their consequent gains in this vital area slowly increased, Bisset's men were forced to withdraw. This movement became a nightmare for the survivors of 10 Platoon as, burdened with their wounded, they struggled over uneven ground in the encroaching darkness, turning repeatedly to inflict delaying casualties on the enclosing enemy hotly pressing the pursuit. But amidst all this they carried the dying Bisset out with them.

Undoubtedly, 11 Platoon also fought under intense pressure and strain on that fateful afternoon. Lieutenant 'Mocca' Treacy, having assumed command of the platoon after Moore's death, provided sound leadership and inspiration to his men as he calmly held back the enemy and personally attended to the recovery of the wounded and the making of stretchers while the withdrawal was in progress.

While 10 and 11 Platoons of B Company, 2/14th Battalion had been thus occupied, 12 Platoon had experienced a quiet morning. It bore no resemblance to the confrontation that was to follow—particularly in the case of Corporal Charlie McCallum. After successfully repelling four attacks during the afternoon, this platoon was finally subjected to a fifth, which contained such venom and continual reinforcement of its numbers that 12 Platoon also had no choice but to withdraw.

McCallum provided covering fire with his Bren gun blazing and a wounded comrade's Tommy gun used from his left shoulder. When his Bren magazine ran out the Japanese stormed his position, only to be met by a torrent of fire from his Tommy gun while he changed magazines with his right hand. His brave action was fought at such close quarters that one of his enemy actually managed to pull his utility pouches off as McCallum pulled away from him. Apart from saving many of his comrades' lives, McCallum inflicted no fewer than 40 casualties upon the Japanese.[16] And this gallant action had been performed after McCallum had been wounded three times.

Dogged resistance was also being offered by Dickenson's C Company. Having been repulsed on a number of occasions, the Japanese mounted a determined attack upon his company which resulted in numerous C Company casualties. In order to stem the Japanese attacks, Key sent Lieutenant Cox and his 9 Platoon from A Company to thicken the C Company lines. When Cox was killed upon reaching the perimeter, Corporal Bear assumed command and, despite sustaining two wounds, temporarily stemmed the Japanese advance with his Bren gun. Despite heavy casualties, the Japanese were methodically gaining ground through the C Company and A Company perimeter.

Sergeant Bob Thompson had not long arrived at Isurava with some of his signals personnel. As the position on C Company's front deteriorated further during the afternoon Thompson was ordered to take his signallers and help bolster the right flank of the C Company perimeter. Sergeant Bob Thompson:

> I came across this little mob of fellows. There was Teddy Bear, Alan Avery, Bruce Kingsbury and Jimmy Truscott . . . they were part of 9 Platoon. There was also a dead Jap there and a slit trench . . . then Jack Clements, the Platoon commander, he came along . . . Teddy Bear was wounded, he had one in the leg and also in the hand . . . Teddy said, 'I'll come with you!' And I said, 'You'll go straight back to headquarters!' . . . And he [Bear] gave his Bren gun to Bruce Kingsbury . . . And we were going down this very narrow track . . . and I came to a part where there was a slit trench . . . and there was

> growth all around it, and I just parted that and as I did that a Japanese did exactly the same thing. We were closer than you and I [about five feet] . . . after a second, he yelled out and dived back. And Jack Clements had followed me along the track, and he grabbed a couple of grenades and threw them over . . . and then we came out through the scrub and into open ground . . . looking right across this open ground in front, about a hundred yards away, was a belt of timber . . .[17]

Thompson then ordered his 'section' of about eleven or twelve men to fix bayonets and storm forward. What followed is best described by Bruce Kingsbury's citation, which Thompson and Avery and Clements later wrote and witnessed:

> [Kingsbury] rushed forward firing his Bren-gun from his hip through terrific machine-gun fire and succeeded in clearing a path through the enemy. Continuing to sweep enemy positions with his fire and inflicting an extremely high number of casualties on them, Kingsbury was then seen to fall to the ground shot dead by a bullet from a sniper hiding in the wood.[18]

Kingsbury was shot just as Thompson's men paused to confer with two C Company soldiers who were sited on a small plateau and had been briefly cut off. This point is marked by a large rock, which has become known at Isurava as 'Kingsbury's Rock'.[19] The startling revelation when you visit Kingsbury's Rock is the closeness of it to the Battalion HQ area, and out of that realisation comes the desperate nature of both C Company's fighting and its attached A Company, 9 Platoon. Had the position not been as heavily contested as it was, an enemy breakthrough at this location would have seen HQ overrun and the entire 2/14th perimeter, especially on the high ground to the west, either cut off or eliminated.

Private Bruce Kingsbury was the first Australian to win the Victoria Cross in the South West Pacific Area and the first Australian to win the British Commonwealth's highest award for bravery upon Australian soil.

By nightfall on 29 August 1942, the situation at Isurava was desperate. Although the 2/14th Battalion had inflicted over five hundred casualties upon its enemy and had held its ground against monumental odds, the Japanese had nonetheless penetrated the battalion perimeter and still held the high ground to the west. Key needed further reinforcement. Responding to Key's request, Potts ordered C Company, 53rd Battalion to move from Alola to Isurava. That company was to be of little use then or later. It simply camped by the track at the Isurava Rest House while others performed its task.

But Key was indeed destined to gain a reserve that day. Later events were to prove that this reinforcement was by no means large enough or fit enough, but its origins add further substance to the stirring Isurava story. In its support of the 2/14th at Isurava, the 39th had still been committed to battle after declining to leave. There can surely be no more inspirational examples of the dramatic transformation of this previously untried and untested battalion into the remarkable unit that it had quickly become, than that of its invalid contingent sent out of battle but defiantly coming back to it, and that of its returned patrols led by Lieutenants Pentland and Sword.

Ralph Honner:

> When, on the 27th, the complete relief of the 39th was ordered for the following day, I had sent back, under Lt Johnson [a reinforcement officer from the 2/16th Battalion], the weakest of the battalion's sick to have them one stage ahead on the long march to Moresby—they were too feeble for the fast moving fighting expected at the front.[20]

Two days later with his band of wounded and wasted comrades, Johnson learnt of the plight of the 2/14th and 39th Battalions back at Isurava. He then proceeded to lead the fittest of the unfit back to the battle. 'J.W.B.' in the book *We Were There* has left a moving account of the incident: 'The battalion was in trouble, so twenty-seven out of thirty went back. The three who didn't were minus a foot; had a bullet in the throat, and a forearm blown off. We never did it for God,

King and Country—forget that. We did it because the 39th expected it of us.'[21] And there were others in the 39th who marched to the beat of the same drum. It will be remembered that, when the battle of Isurava had begun, Lieutenant Sword's standing patrol north of Isurava had been cut off and, not long after, Lieutenant Pentland's standing patrol on the high ground out to the west of Isurava near the Naro track had also been cut off. After four days of tough walking through the jungle—always well away from the enemy and the tracks they were using—this now combined force staggered out onto the Kokoda Trail between Isurava and Alola. Ralph Honner:

> A corporal of the 2/16th told me afterwards, 'It was enough to make a man weep to see those poor skinny bastards hobble in on their bleeding feet.' They were greeted with the news that the 39th and 2/14th were fighting for their lives. Without a word, or a thought for the food their stomachs craved, they turned and hurried off to Isurava as fast as their crippled feet could carry them.[22]

Such inspiring stories are the stuff of legends, but in the hard, cold reality of war they did not stem the tide of superior numbers, firepower and support. Isurava's fall was imminent. Back at Alola, Potts was faced with three options but had to make an immediate decision. First, he could deal with the threat to his right flank and then seek to stabilise his Isurava front, possibly by committing the remainder of his 2/16th Battalion. Second, he could, as with his first option, deal with the right flank, and then commit his 2/16th Battalion to the left flank and come in on the Japanese rear. Lastly, he could withdraw his 39th and 2/14th Battalions and seek to stabilise his position at a rearward venue. But events at Isurava made his decision for him. Key requested an immediate withdrawal to the Isurava Rest House as his perimeter had been severely penetrated. Potts gave immediate permission. A 'rest house' in 1942 Papua was a locally constructed facility for white patrol officers or magistrates or missionaries who desired a degree of increased creature comfort away from the noise and activity of the traditional village setting. The fact that the Isurava Rest House was about six hundred yards from the village demonstrates the point.

The withdrawal from Isurava of the 2/14th and 39th Battalions was completed during the late hours of 29 August 1942. It was a grim, deathly quiet and backbreaking experience, as the sleepless and worn troops held on to the bayonet scabbard of the soldier in front, or picked up a piece of bark or fungi with its dim, phosphorescent glow and groped, stumbled and at times fell along that pitch-black route to the Isurava Rest House.[23] Some carriers assisted the removal of the wounded, while others were carried by their mates. And others again confirmed the validity of the term 'walking wounded' by making their own way out.[24] By 2.00 a.m. on the 30th both battalions had occupied their new positions and awaited the next enemy onslaught.

With the two battalions thus disposed at the Isurava Rest House on 30 August, Captain Sublet prepared to attack the Japanese on the right flank. He had, on the previous day, requested a company from the 53rd Battalion to attack along his right flank. This role was given to D Company. As Sublet's two 2/16th companies would be quite out of touch and therefore control, it was agreed that the attack by the 2/16th component would commence as soon as the first 53rd Battalion shots were heard. Captain Sublet:

> On the next morning—30th August—A and B Coys prepared for their roles in the attack and we waited for the sound of firing on the enemy's left flank, which was to be the signal for our assault. However no sound came from where I hoped the 53rd Company would be, so I decided that A and B Companies would attack as planned. Earlier at my request, the C.O. had directed H.Q. Coy to take up positions on the track between A and B Companies and Alola to secure my Line of Communication, and this they did, during the afternoon of the 29th of August. I had eliminated the 53rd Company from calculation and timed the attack by A and B Companies to commence at 1100 hours.[25]

Captain Wright's B Company was to move around the Japanese positions, while A Company had the task of a frontal assault along the track. Captain McGee's A Company took heavy casualties in this direct thrust on to the enemy positions but also managed to inflict many Japanese losses.

B Company was confronted by a large, well-positioned Japanese force and in the resulting action its 10 Platoon, commanded by Lieutenant Gerke, was ambushed and cut off. This company also inflicted heavy losses upon the enemy. It would be some days before Gerke and his men could regain their lines. The role of this 2/16th attack transpired to be a critical one, as it frustrated the Japanese attempt to cut the Kokoda Trail at Alola, thereby isolating the 2/14th and 39th Battalions. Gerke:

> My platoon found a number of the 53rd in and around Abuari, in the jungle, they were not aware of what was going on, had little or no food or ammunition and some were without weapons. As I had a mission to fulfil at the time, they were instructed to keep behind us and out of sight. They appeared most grateful and relieved to see us. At no time did I use them during the four days that they were with me, and they were not a problem, other than we had to ration out our food as we had been cut off . . . At the waterfall near Abuari we located a large 53rd Battalion patrol that had walked into an ambush, and all had been killed. Their bodies had been dragged off the track and into the jungle, out of sight . . .
>
> A similar fate could have happened to us, but one of the forward scouts in the platoon noticed fallen branches and damaged trees from bullets passing through them, which resulted in our locating a Jap machine-gun post further down the track which we disposed of before we could advance to carry out the task allotted to us. I took the particulars from the dead bodies, removed any food or ammunition and some personal items that they had, marked the spot and proceeded with the task ahead. This delayed us . . . which eventually resulted in our being cut off, although

> when I received my orders and instructions . . . I, with 11 Platoon, was to take the high ground covering the track to Abuari at the same time that a company of the 53rd Bn was to attack the Japanese positions below. I believe this never eventuated, and it was some of these troops that we picked up and took with us.[26]

While Sublet's force was thus engaged on the right flank, Potts was forced to react to a very rapid deterioration of the position at the rest house. Key had insufficient men to attempt to cover the high ground to the west, where a platoon of the 2/16th had been posted. When that patrol was driven back into Key's defensive perimeter in the late morning of 30 August, the Japanese began to bypass the front positions and prepared to fall upon his rear. Potts now ordered Sublet to fall back. Captain Frank Sublet:

> We were still attacking when news was received that the battle on the other side of the gorge [the Rest House] was going badly for our forces, and that a withdrawal was likely. I was told to withdraw my companies to a position covering the track as it passed behind the waterfall—thus forming a narrow defile—and which would prevent or severely impede any attempt by the Japanese to outflank Alola from Abuari ridge.[27]

While Sublet was engaged in repositioning his force to the rear of the waterfall, a further deterioration took place at the Isurava Rest House. The Japanese were bypassing Key by moving around the high ground to the east. At 3.00 p.m. on 30 August, Potts ordered a full Maroubra Force withdrawal to Eora Creek.

The decision to withdraw came just in time. To enable the bulk of his force to escape the rapidly closing enemy net, Key now ordered his C and D Companies to remove the Japanese from the heavily timbered high ground above his positions. It was a tall order. But at the same time, the Japanese put in an attack against the lower ground at the rear of his perimeter. In the ensuing hail of fire from both quarters, Key and his headquarter's personnel—assembled on the track at that very time—were driven over the steep edge of the track down towards Eora Creek. Corporal Fielding was amongst them:

> I was cut off with Lieutenant-Colonel Key, the Adjutant Captain Hall, and fifteen others at the Rest House when the Japs attacked our rear. We tried to make it around the enemy lines and link up with the 2/14th and 2/16th battalions. On the following morning Lt-Colonel Key advised us to break up into two parties each of nine men.[28]

Fate played a cruel hand with these unfortunate soldiers. Bisset and a handful of companions regained the 2/14th lines five days later; a small contingent was cut off for some weeks; and, tragically, Key and his small party were captured. At some later stage, Key was probably executed as an unwelcome encumbrance, after having already escaped once. This was a tragic end for a soldier who had fought a magnificent fight and had, at all times at Isurava, maintained a clear, precise grasp of his unequal battle.

Over an hour passed before A and B Companies repulsed the threat to their rear, but even that action had its price. While fighting a savage rearguard action to allow their battalion to escape the perimeter and form up south of Alola, Captain Buckler and parts of both A and B Companies were cut off when the Japanese managed to cut the track between them and the rest of Maroubra Force south of Alola. An attempt to clear the enemy off the track by Sergeant Gwillim and a small fighting patrol failed. Sergeant Gwillim: 'Personally I was knocked about a bit, as a result of a gunshot wound in my left shoulder which smashed the collarbone and shoulder blade before exiting from a couple of holes in the back. We were subsequently cut off from the main body and did not rejoin the main body for almost seven weeks.'[29]

If events had moved rapidly at the rest house, then Captain Sublet also found his passage to Alola in great jeopardy. Captain Sublet:

> It was late in the day when we took up our positions round the edges of a cleared area and I waited anxiously

Isurava to Alola, 29–30 August

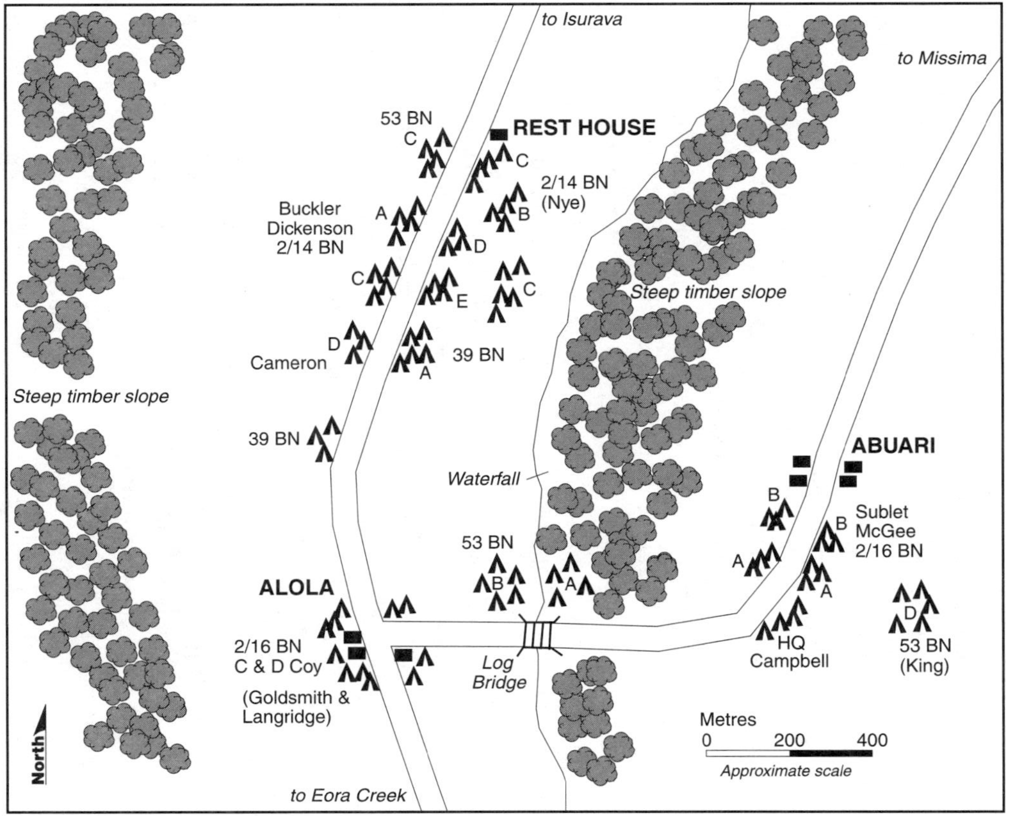

to be joined by B Coy HQ, 11 Platoon, and other elements of B Coy to whom I had apparently not been able to convey my order to withdraw. I felt frustrated at the lack of telephone contact with 2/16th Bn HQ, but eventually a signaller found a break in the line, repaired it, and was able to bring me a message confirming the Brigade withdrawal and warning me NOT to attempt to bring my troops through Alola after 1900 hours. I was left to guess where the Brigade was withdrawing to, but I knew it would be somewhere down the single track. It was pitch dark when we reached the fallen tree crossing the fast-running creek swollen by the regular afternoon rain, and there was no prospect of getting the straggling line of men through Alola in time. As it seemed the Japanese were not on our heels, I directed the troops some hundreds of yards upstream and rejoined them to remain quiet in the thick undergrowth on the left bank of the stream. I then clawed my way up the steep track to Alola to try and judge whether our people were still holding the village. When I reached the top of the track I found all was dark and silent. Forced to make a judgement, I decided that, rather than risk taking my party consisting of A Coy, HQ Coy and about half of B coy, up the track and through Alola, I would wait about four hours to moonrise, when the rain should have ceased, then move upstream until we located the remainder of the 2/16th Battalion. Soon after the morning mists rose, Australian troops were spotted on a kunai spur to our right front and I reported my force back to Colonel Caro before midday. The afternoon was unusually clear and sunny and I watched with chagrin a parade and apparently some sort of celebration by Japanese troops in the hilltop village of Alola which seemed so secure when I first arrived there.[30]

8 BOTH SIDES OF THE VALLEY

You are ready to go at sun up. With you are your carrier, Mathias, and Frank Taylor's assistant. By having a head start on the rest of the group extra time will be afforded you at Isurava. We leave the Alola guest hut and journey for five minutes down to the creek, cross it, and after a ten-minute climb arrive at a large, level, almost bare patch of earth. This is 1942 Alola. No village, just a cleared site.

It is not hard to imagine the tremendous strain Potts was under here. Retake Kokoda. Fat chance. This is where Potts originally envisaged the relief of the 39th by the 2/14th and pondered the deployment of his 2/16th Battalion—literally his 2/16th. This is the unit he has virtually raised and trained and taken to war in Syria. It has excelled. Kalgoorlie goldminers, farmers from the Great Southern (like himself) and the numerous city boys who have also done their bit in a very good battalion. Potts desperately wants to employ the 2/16th on the right flank. But rapidly unfolding events on this right flank—and the course of the battle at Isurava itself—will force him to abandon his plan.

Despite the fact that the supply debacle has seen his two AIF battalions brought in company by company to be committed straight to battle on two worrying fronts, he is still confident. He prays his 2/27th Battalion will be with him soon—another unit with a sound Syrian reputation. His force is therefore committed piecemeal on both flanks as he is forced to react to Horii's complete possession of the initiative.

The climb to Isurava is not too difficult by Kokoda Trail standards. Your sense of anticipation mounts as you come to the back creek. Fresh, cold running stream water. It is not hard to picture Honner here, silently shaving and then calmly receiving the runner who tells him Merritt's front is being penetrated. 'Captain Merritt, when you've finished your shave . . .' Vintage Honner. The man was still understated and calm and considered even when you saw him for the last time in his 90th year.

You walk into the village site. Papuans are working down on a slope before you. The monument is taking impressive shape.

This place does have an atmosphere. When you stand near the monument, you are struck by the reality of a jungle perimeter. It is small. The high ground to the west and its cane field site where French and his B Company of the 39th were given the post of honour by Ralph, and where Moore and Bisset and a host of the 2/14th gave their lives, appropriately looks down over the top of two flying flags at the actual village site, one Papuan and the other Australian.

To the perceptive eye Isurava is a symbolic meeting place. Here, in August 1942, two armies were forced to stand together: on the one hand, you are struck by your presence at a village where a crack, professionally trained AIF battalion stood its ground against monumental odds and did not flinch or fail, but set the seal of conduct for the entire Kokoda campaign. The price paid by the 2/14th was enormous: its CO and adjutant killed, horrific casualties and missing soldiers. Lieutenant-Colonel Arthur Key and his 2/14th Battalion therefore form the very core of the Isurava legend.

And there are other ghosts here also. Who could forget the return to Isurava of Pentland and Sword and their almost crippled soldiers and the return of Johnson and his wounded contingent? In simple terms, the saga of the 39th Australian Infantry Battalion's Kokoda campaigning is a classic illustration of what egalitarian Australia has always celebrated and commemorated: the seemingly impossible triumph of the underdog against all conceivable odds.

If the Battle of Isurava constituted his battalion's toughest test, then history should also record that it may well have been Ralph Honner's defining moment. Here was the culmination of the painstaking acquisition of, and the interplay between, what Liddell Hart called the 'moral courage' and the 'creative intellect' of the competent commander.

The critical fusion of the 2/14th and 39th Battalions at this village destroyed the myth of 'chocos' and 'koalas', and therefore the absurdity of a two-army system. This is the stuff of legitimate and stirring legends that Australians should all proudly embrace. Isurava is sacred ground.

There are other focal points of interest. Kingsbury's Rock is nearby. You gaze down the track towards the front creek and imagine Lieutenant Clarke and his small contingent sweeping the garden on the other side of that creek for Japanese who threaten their perimeter.

When you look over the eastern edge of the village it is obvious why the enemy chose not to try an approach from that side. It is an incredibly long and steep and savage climb. And then you look further.

Across the other side of the valley the vegetation obscures the Abuari–Missima–Kaile track, which also leads to Kokoda. Along that path lies the other portion of the Isurava story, a chain of events which Australia should also recognise and should never forget—and never allow to happen again.

This work has chronicled the unhappy plight of the 53rd Battalion's Kokoda campaigning. Natural justice and balanced history poses the obvious question: Why did the 53rd fail?

The first reason is concerned with the nature of its formation. The story of the hundred shanghaied young men on the docks of Woolloomooloo is relatively well known. Denied pre-embarkation leave, virtually press-ganged and taken on board the *Aquitania*, we note that some of these hundred young men are being taught on that ship how to fire a .303 rifle for the first time. But there is yet another disgruntled, negative collection of men on this ship. Keith Irwin, 53rd Battalion:

> Sometime during December [1941], the battalion received a draft of men from my old 1st Battalion . . . these men were fine soldiers . . . I asked them how they came to be sent to the 53rd . . . they replied that they had no option . . . I do know that other battalions made the most of the opportunity to off-load their

> misfits and undesirables, these people did have a chip on their shoulder.[1]

The point is that not every one of the shanghaied young men or every one of these 'off-loaded' soldiers sent to the 53rd Battalion were poor soldiers, but rather that there were a significant number of disgruntled and bitter men who would work against its chances of success.[2] For these soldiers, as distinct from what happened in most Australian units, the ideals of efficiency, teamwork and a resulting high esprit de corps were almost completely foreign to them—in both thought and understanding.

Another factor is the nature of the treatment given these men from the time of their arrival in Port Moresby until their commitment to battle on the Kokoda Trail. Corporal Clarry Meredith, 53rd Battalion:

> The conditions were appalling . . . no mosquito nets, no proper cooking, very little fresh water . . . This was the beginning of the breakdown of morale in the early stages. We were forced to light fires at night and cover them with green leaves and try and keep in the smoke to keep the mosquitos at bay, but of course this was against orders but ignored quite often . . .
>
> The company was moved . . . we erected our tents and even whilst trying to get settled in we were on work parties at the dock and on barges plus night picquet guard duty on Naval fuel dumps, erecting wire entanglements, digging slit trenches on the hills around Port Moresby . . . rations [were still] in short supply and fresh water rationed . . .
>
> All of this had personnel wondering what we were—soldiers or labourers and morale was poor . . . The company moved [again] . . . air raids were prevalent and the placing of this camp was in line with the flight path of the bombers attempting to silence the A/A 3-7 batteries on Mt Tuaguba . . . No lights were allowed at night naturally, but I remember on some occasions when the officers' lines used lanterns, this caused dissention amongst the troops. On one occasion a threat

> was made to shoot a light out when an alert was on. Morale was not good at this time.[3]

Padre Roy Wotton, 53rd Battalion: 'I took one church parade which was the only time the 53rd got together, there were no athletics, no social events to give them esprit de corps . . . The 53rd was nothing more than a collection of companies scattered around the town and they developed a "garrison mentality".'[4] Wotton is referring to the total time between the battalion's arrival in Port Moresby from January 1942 until its movement along the Kokoda Trail in August of that year.

The standard of training and the performance of the battalion's officers is the next and, arguably, the most critical issue. Once again, generalisations are both unfair and misleading. There were a number of the officers of the 53rd Battalion who were both capable and enthusiastic. Captain Fred Ahern is a case in point. This officer, after the death of Lieutenant Alan Isaachsen near Missima, took charge of his soldiers and led them back to safety. Ahern's later service with the 36th Battalion was also exemplary.[5] Lieutenant McDonald also performed well on patrolling forward of the 39th Battalion at Isurava. Captain Henderson was greatly respected and admired by his troops, and would give his life bravely at Sananandа later during the Papuan War. These are but examples of a number of officers who performed admirably.

The point is that no small number of the battalion's senior commanders and a number of its platoon commanders failed on the Kokoda Trail during August 1942. To the trained eye, the deficiencies were immediately obvious. Lieutenant Stan Bisset, 2/14th Battalion:

> Key directed me to move back from the original position at Isurava to select an area a short distance to the rear as a new defence position to which the Battalion would withdraw [this was the Isurava Rest House area]. This was on the night of 29 August and on selecting a suitable position I discovered a number of troops in the area lying around with packs on their backs resting or sleeping. I was unable to locate an officer. These were men of the 53 Battalion.[6]

Bisset is referring to C Company of the 53rd, which had been ordered to reinforce the 2/14th and 39th at Isurava. They did not arrive and went to ground near the rest house. Yet many of these soldiers did not know the role they were being asked to play. And the fact that Bisset was unable to find an officer is significant. Officers were hard to find on a number of other occasions. Sergeant John Gwillim, 2/14th Battalion: 'The officers were very easy to distinguish from their troops, and were as one of my troops put it, "dressed up like Christmas trees" . . . their appearance filled me with a degree of apprehension as they looked far from business like.'[7]

This story has in part chronicled the impressive contribution of Warrant Officer John Wilkinson of ANGAU and his early work with the 39th Battalion at and near Kokoda. Wilkinson's diary:

> 25/8/42. Went on recce on Deniki Ridge. Found crashed Jap plane but no tracks. Puzzling country. Had two 53 Bn men with me. Appear to be good chaps but very green and untrained. One carried a Tommy-gun but did not have a magazine loaded as he said it weakened the spring. I gave them some training on the spot, and showed them how to get along the road with the least noise and danger.[8]

These soldiers were more than likely members of A Company, 53rd Battalion. It is a great pity indeed that there were not senior officers in Port Moresby who had taken the opportunity for a substantial amount of 'training on the spot'.

But the critical 53rd actions during the Battle of Isurava were on the right flank along the Abuari–Missima–Kaile track. Captain Frank Sublet was in command of the 2/16th fighting on that right flank: 'It seemed to me that the 53 Battalion was not properly prepared physically or psychologically for battle. The one or two officers I saw did not appear to be dynamic, and I was disappointed that the company detailed to assist the Abuari operations seemed so easily deterred.'[9] Sublet is referring to D Company of the 53rd. The Official Historian notes that this company was ordered to make its move to the right flank at 8.00 a.m.[10] He has also noted that the move did not commence until 10.00 a.m.[11] Two hours is a long time to make a move out to action. The truth is that there was an element in the company who were malingering.[12] Further, the reason that Lieutenant-Colonel Ward and Lieutenant Logan and the two or perhaps three soldiers accompanying them were ambushed and killed that day was that neither B or D Companies were where they had been ordered to deploy themselves. But the substance of questionnaires and letters from the members of these companies indicates that the soldiers in neither were aware of their roles. Private Bob Jones, D Company:

> I was with Captain ____ when Col. Ward, Lieutenant Logan . . . were ambushed and killed. From there on it was total confusion. A few of our officers failed us and we didn't have anyone to give orders. What I remember of that was some troops were withdrawing and said they were told to get out, every man for himself. So more confusion.[13]

The story of the 53rd Battalion's fighting on that right flank is therefore one of confusion and a lack of control and drive by some of its officers. But some of its patrolling was carried out successfully, and the fact that a number of those patrols were subsequently cut off as the enemy simply moved around them is hardly an unusual Kokoda scenario.

There is another critical issue concerning the officers of the 53rd. On 22 June 1942, 36 reinforcement officers from the AIF were posted to the 30th Militia Brigade. How were these soldiers posted? Captain Max Bidstrup, 39th Battalion, was one of them, posted from the 2/10th Battalion, 18th Brigade (of Tobruk fame), and was a company commander on the Kokoda Trail with the 39th Battalion:

> I think this was the way it happened. He [Porter] was told to, or asked for [this *was* Porter's initiative] a certain number of experienced officers, which he got. Now he would have said to the CO's 'How many do you want?' Because when we were allocated to the 39th, I remember a bloke who was acting in command, Finlay;

> he personally posted these officers. So I think it was up to the CO's. 'You want so many officers? You post them!'[14]

The 53rd Battalion received eight of the 36, two captains and six lieutenants. Captain Joe Gilmore, ex-2/12th Battalion, was posted to one of the 53rd Battalion companies as its second-in-command. The officer commanding that company was 'hard to find' on the Kokoda Trail, and would later be removed from his command at Sananada. Further, Gilmore secured a transfer to the 39th after the Kokoda campaign and would later lead a company of that battalion to stunning success during the capture of Gona. In short, even when offered trained, experienced and therefore valuable reinforcement officers in June 1942, the soldiers of the 53rd Battalion were again sold short. Too much is often made of 'AIF' and 'Militia'. Take the two words out of the equation and recompose the sentence and the statement becomes compelling: 'In June 1942, three inexperienced Australian battalions were given the opportunity to receive a trained injection of 36 young, experienced and proven officers. The 39th received 16, the 49th received 12 and the 53rd 8.'

In summary, it should be said that the formation of the 53rd Battalion, its deployment in Port Moresby, its subsequent treatment during its garrison days and, critically, the quality of its leadership in the collective sense—all of it is a national disgrace. And a further point should be noted. The notion that an Australian citizen need only enlist in his armed forces and almost immediately become the stuff of a new legend is quite simply nonsense. That citizen requires, and deserves, trained, dynamic leadership; he should have adequate equipment and the time to train and learn how to engender esprit de corps. The legends come later. In August 1942, all this was denied the young men of the 53rd Battalion.

The 53rd Battalion's tragic story did not end with its less than proud return to Port Moresby. The 53rd Battalion Unit Diary, 15 September 1942:

> . . . the following work parties ordered to report by New Guinea Force.

> 5 officers 120 other ranks wharf unloading.
> 1 officer 40 other ranks town cleaning party.
> 35 drivers to drivers' pool.
> 1 N.C.O., 25 other ranks to unload canteen stores.
>
> These men to report for duty immediately. This made the task of reorganising and training impossible and general morale of the troops was not improved. These working parties with other operational roles such as guards on wireless stations, powerhouse, oil tank and coastal watching posts, leaves strengths of coys very depleted.[15]

On 26 October 1942, the battalion in Port Moresby which had been denied so much by so many faded quietly into history. The Unit Diarist was very perceptive with his closing comments:

> Today the 26 October ushers the breakup of the good old 53rd after exactly one year of service in World War II. What a tragedy to terminate the glorious old record of the unit without the proper opportunity of it adding further honours to its already famous scroll [its Great War record] . . . Although many factors and circumstances add shadow to the unit's activities in action which will never be known in the true perspective, the future development of New Guinea both during the war and in the future years of peace, will always bear monument to the boys who did the work during the early days of troop concentrations at Port Moresby.[16]

The reader could be forgiven for thinking that this sad and sorry tale ends with the disbandment of the 53rd Battalion. It does not. Its personnel were sent to a number of other formations: about 100 to the 39th Battalion; about 40 to the 36th Battalion and the majority to the 14th Brigade's 55th Militia Battalion in Port Moresby—to therefore comprise part of the new 55/53rd Battalion. The soldiers of these three battalions, including former members of the 53rd Battalion, will serve in some of the toughest fighting of the Pacific War on the Papuan coast at Gona and Sananananda. Finally, given their fundamental right to sound leadership, these soldiers will serve their country well. But as these events unfold, there will be further instances of triumph, tragedy and more controversy.

. . . THE DEVOTION OF A MOTHER

9

Ken Harley, 2/16th Battalion:

> . . . there was no panic. Despite the fact we could see the Japs beginning to outflank us on the ridge above, everything remained well organised. We knew it was alright, Pottsy was there. All of us understood what was happening and understood what we had to do. We still had our tails up even though we had to go back for the moment.[1]

The fighting withdrawal. Few soldiers would dispute the maxim that this military tactic is the hardest one to employ in battle. It is normally executed because the enemy has a vastly superior force, usually more firepower and support, and often possesses a shorter line of communication. He therefore has the initiative.

Given this unpalatable state of affairs, an army can retreat: withdraw without much intent on contesting ground and redeploy at an already established firm base and continue the war. But if a high military premium is placed on the intervening ground then the fighting withdrawal is employed.

Brigadier Arnold Potts faced such a dilemma. At all costs he had to keep his weary and rapidly diminishing force between the Japanese and Port Moresby. The critical element of war he attempted to control was time. Time to inflict as many casualties upon the Japanese as possible. Time to allow the enemy's line of communication to slowly lengthen, knowing that as the Japanese line became appreciably longer, the supply of ammunition and food and the evacuation of the wounded would gradually become more difficult for them than for Maroubra Force. Eventually he hoped to exhaust the enemy to a standstill. Somewhere along that jungle trail, a position would be reached where the enemy's possession of the initiative would weaken to the point where a fresh Australian force operating with the very same advantages that Horii had had at Isurava would see the tables turned from withdrawal to attack.

In hindsight, or with the advantage of a well-written textbook, the proposition seems logical enough, but its execution is terribly difficult because it relies upon the hard-won qualities of astute command, thorough training, tremendous discipline and, last but not least, remarkable reserves of energy. Competent command stands above all other considerations because the commander must determine where to stand and fight, for how long, and at what cost. To withdraw too quickly is to surrender ground and therefore run the risk of failing to delay your enemy long enough to achieve your overriding aim: the denial of the enemy's objective. Stay too long and you risk casualties that you may not be able to afford, or encirclement and annihilation, or the risk that you are simply bypassed, lose the trail, and become a redundant relic of the battlefield rather than an active participant in the war. Russ Rosengren, 39th Battalion:

> The only clothes I had after we dropped our pack before Deniki were a pair of shorts; a pair of boots and an army jumper; that's all . . . No blanket, no groundsheet. In fact anyone lucky enough to have a blanket, maybe a half dozen of us would share it. If someone had a cup or a dixie, maybe a dozen of us would use the same implement and share out what food we had.[2]

Lieutenant Hugh Dalby, 39th Battalion:

> My condition feet wise had deteriorated because my boots had worn out. I had pulpy feet; like crevices; ridges a quarter of an inch thick. You were soaking wet

> all the time. White puffy skin just started to peel off. Your clothes stank. My sergeant cut my hair with a safety razor blade and then I cut his hair with the same blade. It was all matted with dirt; you couldn't wash it properly because you had no soap, so with long hair you would grab handfuls of it, slash it with a razor blade and thereby get some of the muck out of your hair.[3]

Laurie Howson, 39th Battalion:

> The days go on. You are trying to survive, shirt torn, arse out of your pants, whiskers a mile long, hungry . . . Some days you carry your boots because there's no skin on your feet. But when you look around at some of the others—hell! They look crook! Then I have seen the time when you dig a number of holes in the ground and bury your dead. Nothing would be said, but you think 'maybe it will be my turn next'.[4]

When you walk this trail perhaps one of its most moving revelations will be the repeated discovery of what might be called 'the anonymous sacrifice'. It is one thing for the historian or the trekker—or the reader—to contemplate the large, dramatic and crucial set-piece battles such as Isurava. They are, after all, the stuff of high drama, the more prolonged engagements that give a campaign its seeming substance.

But scattered along the trail, as you struggle over its tough terrain, are the numerous Australian pits. Each is always sited on a small rise, tucked away anywhere from three to twenty feet from that narrow, slippery, root-ridden lifeline. You tend to walk past them or, if you are the enemy, almost onto them, before their significance is realised. Each will have at least a forty-yard line of vision along the trail, protected in some small measure by the sudden and extreme drop in height over the eastern side; and to protect the right inland and vulnerable flank, each will usually have a support pit(s) diagonally behind and around fifteen yards back to allow you covering fire when your job is done and you hurriedly move back to your next position. These brief, brave actions will occur along a succession of similar delaying positions, which will slow the enemy, cost him casualties and, hopefully, wear him down. Surely the Official Historian, when describing this campaign, is referring to such pits and places when he says:

> . . . it is the story of small groups of men, infinitesimally small against the mountains in which they fought, who killed one another in stealthy and isolated encounters beside the tracks which were life to all of them; of warfare in which men first conquered the country and then allied themselves with it and then killed or died in the midst of a great loneliness.[5]

When some individuals laid down their lives on the Kokoda Trail, therefore, they did not have the fame of 'Isurava' or 'Brigade Hill' or 'Imita Ridge' to add immediate substance to their action but, in all this, they may have died in a most furious fight at an isolated place that has no real name.

Of the four battalions engaged forward of Alola, the Victorian 2/14th was the one that bore the brunt of the heaviest fighting. The battalion gave far in excess of what could reasonably have been expected of it, and paid so very dearly in terms of casualties and hardship. The main body of the battalion withdrew from Isurava Rest House between 5.00 p.m. and 6.00 p.m. on 30 August. It was to be around 11.30 p.m. before all its men who had not been cut off were back and in position.

Its diminished strength bore stark testimony to its role in the actions at Isurava and Isurava Rest House. It had completed its concentration at Isurava on 28 August with 542 troops. Early on the morning of the 31st it mustered 160, 30 in HQ and A Company, 54 in B Company, 42 in C Company and 34 in D Company—little more than a company at full strength. On the 30th alone—the first day of the withdrawal—48 men lost their lives and, in addition to those, 44 had been cut off, including the CO, adjutant, intelligence officer and nearly half of A Company with its commander. The command of the battalion now passed to Captain Rhoden, who was destined the following year to be promoted and command the battalion until the end of the war.

By early morning of 31 August, the 2/14th Battalion was deployed about a mile south of Alola, Brigade HQ was set up halfway between Alola and Eora Creek, the 39th Battalion was occupying defensive positions at Eora Creek and the 53rd Battalion was being sent out of battle. Goldsmith's and Langridge's companies and the headquarters of the 2/16th Battalion had withdrawn through the 2/14th dispositions and were astride the track near Brigade HQ, to be joined later in the morning by Sublet with HQ Company, A Company and about half of B Company of the 2/16th, which had moved back through the moonlight and the morning mist beside the creek, well east of the track.

Meanwhile, the Japanese were busily engaged in widening tracks using Formosan, Korean and native labourers. And with fresh reinforcements coming forward after the capture of Alola, Horii was able to use the Abuari track to shorten his line of communication. Although in total command of the initiative and enjoying the enormous advantages of superior numbers and weaponry, he was still faced with worrying problems. A Japanese report:

> When the Australians are forced to retire, they show a tendency to first destroy their establishments. They must be attacked, captured, and any fires extinguished . . .
>
> Because the quantity of arms and ammunition within the detachment is limited, the method of using captured arms and ammunition should be studied . . .
>
> The progress of the operation must be swift, brave and resolute, and much practical use can be made of captured supplies.[6]

Such was the air of confidence displayed by the Japanese command in Rabaul before Horii's force landed at Gona–Buna between 21 July and 22 August. Their combat troops were supplied with about eleven days' rations. At the outset of the Kokoda campaign it was hoped that these light rations and captured Australian supplies would see them through to the capture of Port Moresby.

Major-General Horii's advance to Efogi would now increase his supply difficulties to a critical level. And the disciplined, defiant and resolute Australians of Maroubra Force were not obliging in their surrender of the very few supply dumps that they were forced, during September, to abandon. Supplies that could not be carried out from Myola, for example, were destroyed. Bully beef tins were punctured, the contents contaminated and rice scattered in the mud—and the more cold-hearted amongst the Australians added urine to the recipe.

Desperate, weary and starving soldiers are not discerning gourmets. The fouled food jettisoned by the Australians was to be the cause of widespread dysentery amongst the Japanese. And those soldiers were not hygiene-conscious troops. Excrement and rotting corpses breed horrific consequences for men already hungry and debilitated.

While Brigadier Arnold Potts and his Maroubra Force had been immersed in their struggle at Isurava, two Australian reporters and a cameraman had arrived at Eora Creek. The reporters were Chester Wilmot (ABC) and Osmar White (Melbourne *Sun* and *Daily Telegraph*), and the cameraman was Damien Parer (Australian Department of Information). Neil McDonald is the biographer of both Damien Parer and Chester Wilmot:

> Damien Parer was a filmmaker. Before the war he'd been part of the floating crew Charles Chauvel used for films like *Uncivilised*, *Heritage* and *40,000 Horsemen*. Parer had also worked as a photographer with Max Dupain . . .
>
> Parer persuaded his bosses [at the Department of Information] to let him accompany 6th Division to the Middle East. It was here that Parer made his reputation covering bombing raids, action in Syria and Greece and naval engagements. It was here too, that he met Chester Wilmot in a traffic jam during the Australians' attack on Tobruk . . .
>
> Chester was a graduate from Melbourne University, had worked briefly as a lawyer and had been a formidable debater. Argumentative, dogmatic, but never personal, Wilmot was exactly the kind of tough, competent professional Parer had always been drawn to. In the Middle East Wilmot had won a reputation for

> broadcasts explaining the underlining strategy of the battles they were reporting. When they were together, Parer would use Wilmot's insights in his decisions about what he should film.
>
> Osmar White made a fascinating contrast to the heavy-set Wilmot and exuberant Parer. Slim, lantern-jawed, quiet, Osmar's years knocking around what was then known as the Far East as a freelance writer and journalist had given him an encyclopaedic knowledge of tropical conditions.[7]

The interesting thing about all three of these Australians during the Kokoda campaign was the fact that their roles transcended mere reporting—especially in the case of Wilmot.

Chester Wilmot had grave doubts about the wisdom of the Menzies Government's decision to even appoint Blamey to command the Second AIF,[8] let alone approve of his subsequent performances across the Middle East, Greece, Crete and Syria. We also know that Blamey knew of Wilmot's antipathy towards him *before* the AIF sailed for the Middle East.[9] In short, each was aware of the other's dislike and mistrust. The Papuan campaign would see a final and almost inevitable confrontation between Blamey and Wilmot. It should also be realised that both Wilmot and Parer were great admirers of Vasey, Allen, Potts and especially Rowell, as they had witnessed their campaign performances.

Rowell also claims that he arranged for the three men to journey along the Kokoda Trail and, in Parer's case, he actually assisted him escaping the Department of Information's instruction to return to Australia to make a 'stunt film'.[10]

The three men's descriptions of what they saw and experienced are arguably amongst the best accounts of the Maroubra Force fighting withdrawal. Along the Kokoda Trail during September 1942, Parer captured some of the most dramatic film footage of the Second World War. When White, Wilmot and Parer arrived at Eora Creek, Osmar White described the scene:

> Hundreds of men were standing about in mud up to their shins. The whole village built of pandanas and grass

> looked as if it were about to flounder in the sea of mud. The huts leaned drunkenly. There were piles of broken-out ration boxes half submerged. The men were slimed from head to foot, for weeks unshaven, their skin bloodless under their filth.
>
> Lines of exhausted carriers were squatting on the fringes of this congregation eating muddy rice off muddy banana leaves, their woolly hair was plastered with rain and muck. Their eyes were rolling and bloodshot with the strain of long carrying. Some of them were still panting.[11]

Damien Parer's Eora Creek film is the only footage shot on the Kokoda Trail that comprehensively depicts the scale and magnitude of Maroubra Force's fighting withdrawal—the congestion in villages that were built to house and supply small groups of Papuans, not battalions of modern-day soldiers; the severe gradients and jungle conditions, of which the average Australian had no concept; and the general debilitation of the troops. While Wilmot and White went forward and encountered the early stages of the withdrawal, Parer kept filming at Eora Creek.

With Kokoda now clearly lost and news that Milne Bay had been attacked by the Japanese, Wilmot and White made the decision to return with their stories to Port Moresby. Neil McDonald, in *War Cameraman: The Story of Damien Parer*:

> Parer's position was now desperate. He was too sick and tired to carry the tripod and cameras as well as the cans of exposed film stock that he was trying to protect from the mould and damp. In a weak moment at Eora Creek he had asked 'Smokey' Howson of the 39th Battalion if he might give him a hand with the camera gear. 'You can go and get fucked, I have enough of my own to carry,' Howson told him.[12]

This was a completely understandable if blunt reply. Not long after, Captain Max Bidstrup saw Parer throwing some of his cans of film into Eora Creek. When he offered assistance Parer refused it—he had another solution. Rather than impose on the

Kokoda Trail—Kokoda to Eora Creek

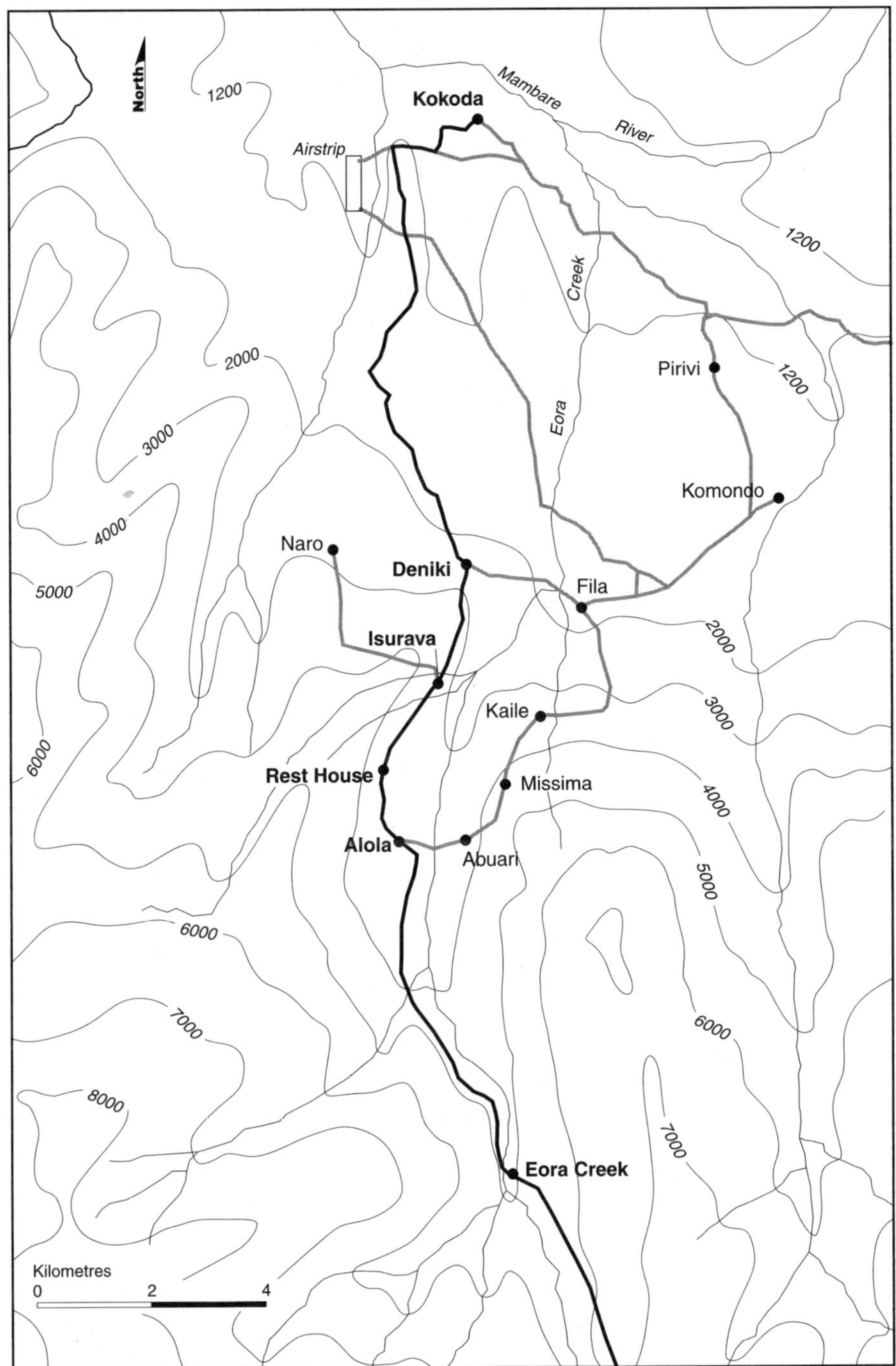

soldiers, he began to discard his 'excess' weight. All his personal gear went first, including his socks, next went 'the leather case and accessories for the Newman Camera',[13] then he jettisoned his tripod and, finally and painfully, his Graflex still camera that he had won as a prize in Melbourne.

When Parer learnt that 1500 feet of film awaited him at Myola, he decided that he would stay on the trail. The last Wilmot and White saw of Parer, 'he was standing in the rain, clutching his Newman in one hand and his tins of exposed film in the other'.[14] Parer's determination to capture the elements of the extraordinary withdrawal occurring before his very eyes enabled Australians to later see it before theirs. Even bouts of malaria and dysentery—Parer had inserted into his anus a tube which ran down his trouser leg and into a container which he had shoved into his sock[15]—couldn't prevent him from fulfilling his brief.

During their climb up the trail, their time spent forward of Parer and, finally, during their journey back, the two reporters also made detailed observations. Wilmot:

> They must be going through hell on this track—specially those with leg wounds. Some have been hit in the foot and they can't even get a boot on, but they're walking back over root and rock and through mud in bare feet, protected only by their bandages. Here's a steep pinch and a wounded digger's trying to climb it. You need both hands and both feet, but he's been hit in the arm and thigh.
>
> Two of his cobbers are helping him along. One goes ahead, hauling himself up by root and branch. The wounded digger clings to the belt of the man in front with his sound hand, while the other cobber gets underneath and pushes him up. I say to this fellow he ought to be a stretcher case, but he replies 'I can get along. There's blokes here lots worse than me and if we don't walk they'll never get out'.[16]

White:

> I was grateful for the blanket of dark. Walking wounded. Wounded walking. There's a difference. They're going

> out to prepare the new positions. Stretchers, each with bearers juggling them up vertical banks as slippery as ice, edging them inch by inch over log crossings with rapids twenty feet below, all in the pitch dark.
>
> A line of men, whole and wounded, form up behind me, snail's pace. Faces stare up from beds in the bush. 'Going to——?' 'Yes'. 'Tell them to send a lantern down and a blanket will you?' Never a call for a stretcher. Never. Not once. Mortars still going behind, rain is falling gently, steadily. There can be no more fortitude than I saw on that Track.
>
> Fortitude is not a thing to pity or be sad over. I wish by some magic words I could make all the mothers, the sweethearts—even the shirkers and the place-seekers and cowards at home, feel what I feel so passionately now. That's what men suffer in their minds and bodies for a good cause. Not suffering to be pitied or wept over. It's a suffering for which to be grateful and proud with a calm heart.[17]

On 6 September 1942 at the village of Menari, the 39th Battalion had just been relieved. Lieutenant-Colonel Ralph Honner issued an order to his adjutant:

> I want you to put the battalion on parade for me, I want to talk to them. I haven't met a lot of them, I don't know them by name. They should be very proud of their performance and I'd like them to know that I think they're some of the best soldiers that I've had anything to do with and they've got no fears about being able to hold their heads up.[18]

This was a unique gathering. Few battalion parades in Australian history could have consisted of about fifty unregimentally dressed, exhausted young men, waxen-faced and many carrying not rifles but the common Kokoda Trail stick. As the soldiers lined up and then snapped to attention, Parer began to move along the lines of men, his 'eye fixed to the eyepiece of the box-like Newman camera'.[19]

Honner passed on Potts' commendation: Potts later

wrote, 'their efforts represented gallantry, courage and fortitude of the highest order, and their fighting prowess was an inspiration to all who saw it'.[20] Parer also captured Honner's proud and dignified bearing. Immersed in the moment, Honner, like most of his men, was unaware that Parer was filming. Sergeant Jack Sim was at the parade:

> He stood in front of those men and he gave us in Australianese that great Henry the Fifth oration, and he paid us that compliment of telling us we were heroes, in his own way. I think I knew that it was a moment when history was in the making or had been made. I did know that here was a man that knew it . . . [21]

Honner made a further remarkable reference at the Menari parade. Jack Sim:

> I can't remember his exact words; I can't quote him verbatim, but I'll always remember what he meant and what he implied when he said: 'You're all Australians and some of the things you've been through you must forget. Some of the men that were with you, you feel have let you down [Honner would have been referring to the 53rd Battalion]. But they didn't. Given different circumstances they'd be just the same as you. The fact that their leaders may have failed them, and yours didn't, doesn't mean they're any worse than you.[22]

Damien Parer's historical perspective, unlike Honner's, did not perceive an Australian Agincourt, but in his diary he referred to the Menari parade as 'almost like a roll call on Anzac'.[23]

Both Honner and Parer saw not only the historical significance of the campaign but the nobility of the young soldiers who participated in it—and both made such perceptions through Catholic eyes. Honner would later write:

> But Kokoda came to signify much more than an outpost and its airstrip. The Kokoda Track, up from the northern beaches and over the Owen Stanley range, was chosen by the Japanese South Seas Force for its push to Port

General Sir Thomas Blamey. AWM 107532

General A.S. 'Tubby' Allen. AWM 023271

General S.F. 'Syd' Rowell. AWM 26299

General Sir Edmund 'Ned' Herring. AWM 20401

General Cyril Clowes. AWM 013337

General George Vasey. AWM 52620

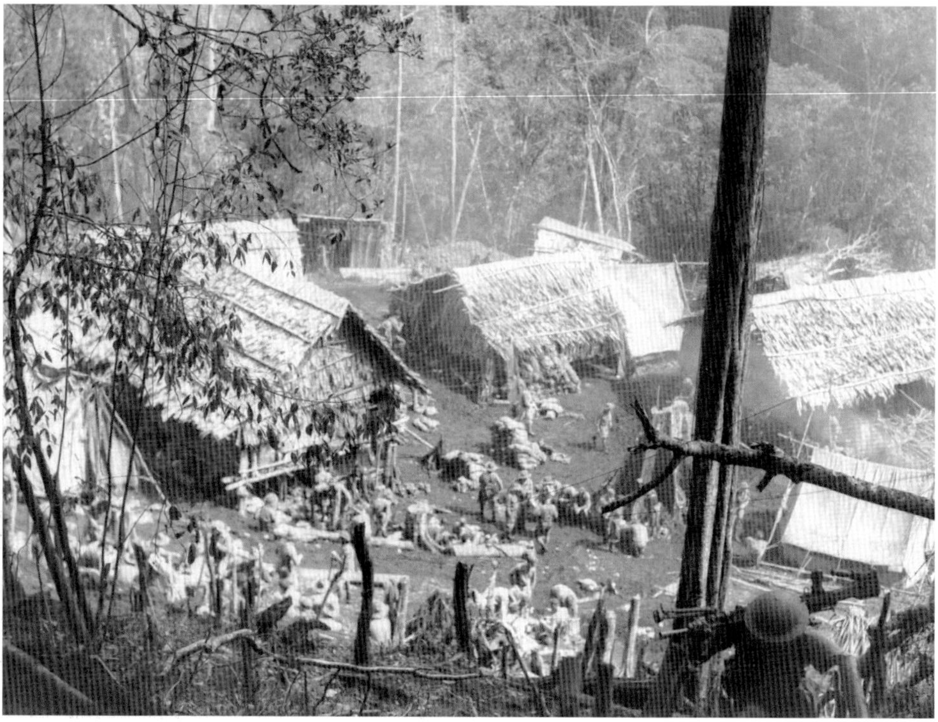

A typical Kokoda Trail village—Eora Creek. AWM 013257

Congestion on the Trail, Eora Creek. AWM 013260

The long way home—a seven to ten day ordeal. AWM 013286

Owen Stanley Range, New Guinea. Wounded Australians being carried on stretchers out of forward battle areas through a mountain stream by native bearers (Fuzzy Wuzzy Angels). AWM 013262

A biscuit bomber drops supplies at Myola. Note the exploding flour sack, bottom right-hand corner. AWM F01212

Wounded Australians being carried out of forward areas by native bearers. AWM 013282

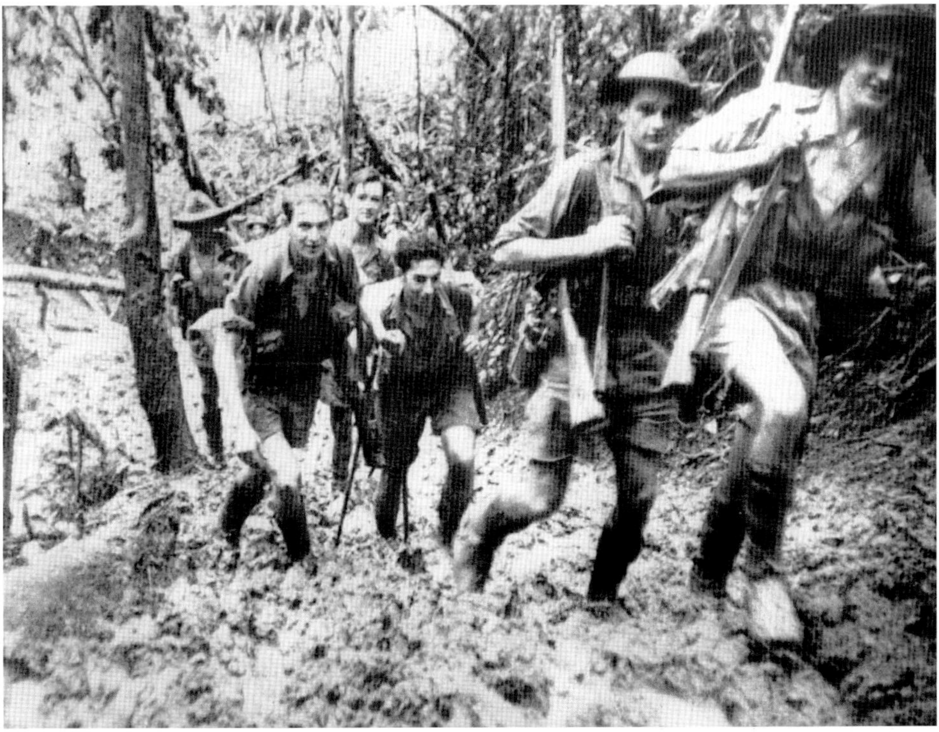

The Kokoda Trail—the great boot-sucking porridge. Members of D Company, 39th Battalion, during the withdrawal. AWM 013288

The 2/27th Battalion after having been cut off for 13 days, have just reached Itiki. AWM 027017

AWM 013289

Ralph Honner addresses his 'Ragged Bloody Heroes' (also at top of page) of the 39th Battalion at the Menari Parade. AWM FO1212

Brigadier Arnold Potts (far left) and some of his officers, September 1942. AWM 026716

Owen Stanley Ranges, New Guinea. Private H.R. Nash, a Western Australian typical of the tough infantrymen recruited from this state. Wounded during a jungle clash with the Japanese in the Kokoda area, Nash made his way back to the base on foot, taking seven days to cover the distance. (Photographer Damien Parer) AWM 013259

Kalikodobu, New Guinea. Three members of the party of the 2/14th Infantry Battalion which was cut off from the main body of troops near Myola during the withdrawal across the Owen Stanley Ranges. In the final stage of the withdrawal in August the party used rafts made by friendly natives, to move down the Kemp-Welch River to safety after being in the jungle for 42 days. AWM 069243

MacArthur and Blamey outside Port Moresby. AWM 013424

> Moresby, the final stepping-stone for the invasion of Australia. That primitive path was to become a soldier's Calvary . . . [24]

Neil McDonald, in *War Cameraman: The Story of Damien Parer*:

> Ron Williams believes that Parer was portraying redemption emerging out of suffering in these sequences [Parer's shots of the stretcher-bearers]. While Damien's notes give no indication of any such intention, one particular shot does have a religious undertone. It shows Salvation Army Major Albert Moore on the far right of the frame lighting a cigarette for a wounded soldier. This is carefully balanced by a group of soldiers on the other side. Parer's composition is similar to a mediaeval or Renaissance painting showing as its centrepiece Christ being taken down from the cross. The religious analogy is strengthened by the fact that the soldier is naked, covered from the waist down by an army blanket.[25]

The 39th now continued its journey through Nauro, Ioribaiwa, Uberi, Ower's Corner and then five miles to Koitaki camp—about twenty miles from Port Moresby. The battalion lost 54 men killed in action, four died of wounds and 125 were wounded during its Kokoda Trail fighting.

When you climb the Kokoda Trail ample time is accorded you to observe the descendants of the fuzzy wuzzy angels. The first observation is their sure-footedness. When you fall, they stroll behind or turn around to inspect the damage. Times change. Many carriers now wear quality trekking boots, although a number are bare footed. Their judgment of a step or a slippery tree root or a narrow, slippery log river crossing is uncanny. Your relative clumsiness does amuse them to a degree, particularly when they note the Caucasian's multitude of gear, both in terms of its variety and sophistication.

Their reserves of energy seem endless. No ascent or

corresponding descent appears to unduly trouble them. 'Forward is good' becomes a quiet, subconscious and recurring theme for each day's climbing. Brief and welcome interludes occur when a difficult rise or fall is encountered. And with those geographical obstacles comes the obvious question: How in God's name does one—and the other three people carrying this imaginary stretcher—keep it horizontal? How does one negotiate the really rough spots with a portion of a man's dead weight on your shoulders and still synchronise one's movement over this terrain with three other carriers? How did they cross a stream with the encumbrance of a stretcher when you are slowly and painstakingly inching your way across hanging on to a rope-rail that is being held by a carrier from either side of the river?

These Papuans are also expert tradesman. Their stock-in-trade tool is the machete (one hears stories that this implement is also, on occasions, a stock-in-trade weapon). When the trek starts the carrier looks you up and down, disappears into the vegetation and returns with a mentally measured stick that suits your height and becomes your third leg. It has been cut to a point at the bottom for easy contact with the ground as you walk. On one occasion, at a jungle camp, you might see a table constructed almost instantly before your eyes, made from small saplings and bamboo.

Fires with wet wood are a difficult task, but the machete is quickly used to trim timber until the dry inside portions are reached and a blazing fire occurs within minutes.

But it is during the nights that some of the most informative and enjoyable observations and meetings occur. You might be a smoker. You might have decided to give this anti-social and obnoxious habit away. Smoke your last packet at Ower's Corner because, after all, how can you obtain more out in the middle of the Owen Stanley Range? Day one and you've got this habit beaten. Darkness day two. The bloody wind's blowing the wrong way and a crude, almost overpowering aroma scales the 40-yard rise to your tent and the torment begins. *Mutrus*, the legendary 'newspaper' cigarette. I comfort myself with the 'fact' that Doc Vernon smoked a 1942 variety of these rough smokes. This journey down to the carriers is therefore strictly research. Gone again. Papuan Kina changes hands and each night becomes a wonderful session of interrogation—sometimes known as interviewing—and provides some of the most rewarding and stimulating moments of the whole trek.

These carriers have been repeatedly offered tents, sleeping bags and western food. No thanks. To sit with them under their tarpaulin, near their fire and witness their cooking, usually rice and a variety of locally grown vegetables, to listen to their conversations, to talk about which of them had relatives involved in the war and in what capacity is fascinating. They are tremendously proud of their part in winning the war. You notice their blankets in a neat line and wonder how many of their ancestors during the Kokoda campaign must have laid in the mud or perhaps under a hut desperately wishing they had one blanket even between two or three.

By the time of the Pacific War, the medical procedure for the evacuation and treatment of the wounded had become quite sophisticated.

A wounded soldier's recovery from the battlefield was usually undertaken by his battalion's stretcher-bearers, who often had a secondary role as members of a battalion band. Such stretcher-bearers displayed great personal bravery in that they often recovered their comrades under enemy fire. With the assistance of a stretcher-bearer or a mate or, if left to his own devices, the soldier's first friend was his field dressing. The casualty was then carried, or walked or crawled to the Regimental Aid Post (RAP), where basic but vital first aid was administered by the Regimental Medical Officer (RMO) or, put simply, the battalion doctor.

From the RAP the casualty was passed to the Field Ambulance for emergency surgery or further dressing of his wound(s). If his condition warranted additional treatment, or if he required an operation, he was then conveyed by motor transport back to the Casualty Clearing Station and then to a hospital. This process from stretcher-bearer to hospital was efficient and speedy and gave the soldier an optimum chance of survival.

The Kokoda Trail negated this proven and efficient system of medical evacuation. The medical staff in the Owen Stanley Range created their own system under enormous pressure and with minimum time. The senior medical officer in the 7th Division was Colonel Norris.

Norris had the 2/6th Field Ambulance available for use in the Kokoda campaign. This team were not strangers to the 7th Division, as they had served it with distinction during the Syrian campaign. Norris knew that the terrain, difficulties of supply and the type of fighting would limit the use of all of the 2/6th Field Ambulance. He therefore decided to appoint a senior medical officer and limit the number of his staff by the criterion of age and fitness as well as competency. The post of senior medical officer was given by Norris to Captain Rupert Magarey, who was promoted to major. Magarey was ordered to select his team and to design and implement a strategy for the treatment and evacuation of the wounded.

He struck out from Uberi on 17 August 1942 with Captain Oldham and 31 other ranks. He assigned five pairs of orderlies to the villages of Uberi, Ioribaiwa, Nauro, Menari and Efogi. He then left the rest of his team at Myola, where he could expect the balance of his supplies to be dropped by aircraft.

Magarey's plan for the evacuation of the wounded was most unorthodox. Sir Rupert Magarey:

> As this plan never came into operation, it will not be given in detail; but it should be mentioned that it embodied the unusual feature of a medical evacuation forward, ie to Kokoda for evacuation by air. Hence the general policy was to push medical posts forward and hold all patients as far forward as possible, to avoid the waste of labour—and labour was always the biggest problem—of a carry two ways over the same track.[26]

When the Maroubra Force fighting withdrawal began after the battle of Isurava, Magarey was therefore faced with the immediate problem of evacuating his wounded all the way back to Uberi. It is at this point that the sterling efforts of the medical staff, the carriers and ANGAU came into play in the most appalling conditions imaginable.

For the medical staff the problems were many and instant. If a soldier crossing the trail took seven days to reach Isurava, then an outgoing stretcher case from Isurava took ten, and that was provided the carriers put in a twelve-hour day in transit.[27] And each stretcher case consumed the labour of eight carriers working in two shifts of four on regular rotation.

As the number of troops rapidly increased during late August and the fighting became more fluid, standards of hygiene were not only more difficult to follow, but also harder to enforce. Even allowing for the normal absence of flies at such high altitudes, human foulings and spent ration tins attracted flies to the point where a number of blankets on stretchers reaching Myola were flyblown.[28]

The problem of transportation of medical supplies also caused concern, as airdrops damaged equipment. The rugged terrain also demanded stronger carrying equipment. The restrictive nature of transportation inhibited the amounts and types of medicines and gear sent to the front—there was, for example, a shortage of plaster.

One of the critical problems facing Magarey and his staff was the lack of any facilities that even faintly resembled a clearing station, let alone hospital conditions. The task in village locations was simple and immediate: stabilise, classify the wound, give immediate treatment, but always move the patient on. If that meant that there was even a remote chance of a normally allocated stretcher case being coaxed into walking, then the patient was pushed on. Magarey:

> It was necessary to be quite ruthless in this respect. Every man who could possibly walk had to, and over and over again men arriving at medical posts could be given only short rests and then had to be pushed on again. The fortitude and cheerfulness shown by the majority of these men was beyond praise, and the feats of endurance performed by some of the wounded, particularly those with wounds of the lower limbs, were almost incredible.[29]

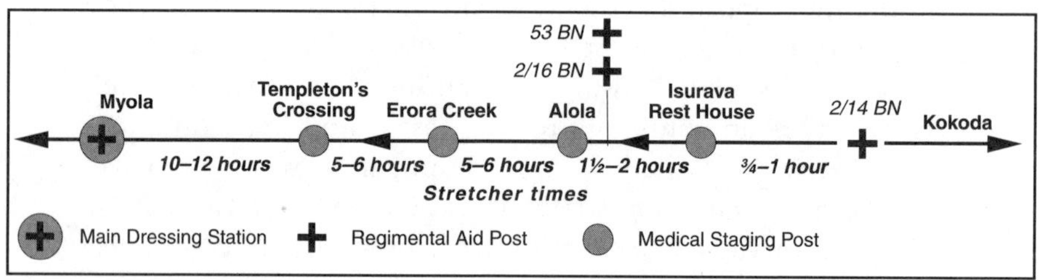

While the Japanese high-velocity, small-calibre bullet did have one advantageous attribute in that it often did not cause bone fragmentation, its penetration of the stomach or chest was often a tragic death penalty caused not by a lack of medical know-how, but by the remoteness of the battleground and the time taken to reach a hospital. Magarey: 'If you got an abdominal wound on the Kokoda Trail you might as well have given up. You never told the troops that, but you knew bloody well that that was what would happen . . . So you gave them a shot of morphine . . .'[30] But there were exceptions. Bill Edgar describes the fate of John Blythe, 2/16th Battalion:

> Johnny Blythe was hit in the chest, the chin, the back, the right hand and the leg. A very busy Blue Steward [2/16th doctor] treated him as best he could and said, 'I've bandaged you up and you've got no chance of reaching Moresby. Goodbye.' Blue was always 'straight'. 'Thanks very much,' said Johnny, as he was carried away. The journey took twelve days. There was no treatment. He wasted from 12 stone 4 pounds to 6 stone 6 pounds in that time.[31]

Perhaps one of the most critical concerns for the medical personnel was the widespread outbreak of dysentery. Magarey: 'A large majority of sick were bowel disorders varying from mild diarrhoea to true bacillary dysentery with the passage of blood and mucus. These began to appear in serious numbers about the 1st and 2nd September and from then on steadily increased.'[32] The condition could be remedied quite quickly with rest and sleep, dry clothes and adequate food, but such luxuries were just not available on the Kokoda Trail. The consequence was a significant number of soldiers with the backside cut out of their shorts or trousers, carrying themselves exhaustingly over the trail while in great pain and discomfort.

The infrastructure for this remarkable evacuation was totally reliant upon the ability of the ANGAU personnel and their carrier lines. We have seen the enormous contribution of Bert Kienzle. It is all too easy to isolate his efforts in one chapter of this story. His contribution was ongoing and insistent; his file sent to the author contained old, wrinkled pieces of 1942 paper with indelible pencil figures of approaching numbers of carriers and approximate times of their arrival, and signed 'Peter' (Brewer) or 'Ned' (there was a 'Kelly' in ANGAU). It was a crude telegraph but a vital one and, in the end, a successful one. Warrant Officers Preece and Davies are but two further examples of ANGAU soldiers and local hands who were able to muster carriers almost on the spot for a critical evacuation of the wounded, or the need for improved facilities at a clearing station.

The ANGAU carrier organisation of supplies and evacuation of the wounded was not unlike looking down upon a multitude of ants carrying weights out of all proportion to their size over a tough path. Look at any one and the performance seems minuscule, look at the lot and the caravan is both unrelenting and irresistible.

No one knew the trials and tribulations of travel, survival and the organisation of the human lifeline like the white 'locals' of ANGAU. They led patrols for intelligence purposes; patrols for the rescue of cut-off soldiers marooned in the jungle; they ensured the arrival of supplies into villages and staging camps; they built and supervised the huts as staging camps and for medical treatment; and most of all, they selected, supervised and 'grouped' the carriers according to the always pressing needs of the war. And 'grouped' the carriers was an expression that transcended mere numerical calculations: 'The problem of dialects [language] was difficult among the boys; bearers were sometimes assembled in groups who could not talk to each other.

The ANGAU representatives were very helpful here and were able to group together boys with a common tongue.'[33]

Imagine carrying supplies—and sometimes being excessively overloaded—which consist in part of tinned meat for the soldiers (however limited), while the reward for your labours will be limited amounts of rice. Malaria, diarrhoeal disorders and respiratory complaints will inevitably impact upon you. But when Isurava falls and the casualties cannot be evacuated forward, a steady stream of stretcher cases will require you to carry them back. You therefore carry both ways, often with fellow carriers who might not be able to communicate with you. If you are from the northern coast or other lowland areas, the cold nights will affect you rapidly. You won't even have a blanket. And yet desertions from the carrier line during the critical month of September 1942 were only slightly above 3 per cent.[34] And could you blame the 3 per cent, who might be from Buna, or Gona, or for that matter from villages near Kokoda and therefore under Japanese occupation? Are your family and wantoks safe and are their gardens being rifled by the Japanese? Sir Frank Kingsley Norris:

> If night finds the stretcher still on the track, they will find a level spot and build a shelter over the patient. They will make him as comfortable as possible, fetch him water and feed him if food is available—regardless of their own needs. They sleep four each side of the stretcher and if the patient moves or requires any attention during the night, this is given instantly.[35]

Neil McDonald has recorded that Damien Parer was more blunt:

> As Parer came up behind a stretcher party, he would see the natives yell and gesticulate. The men would dig in with their big toes and inch their way up a hill. 'This is a war of walking and hill climbing', Damien wrote in his notebook. 'No field guns, no petrol. If a stretcher case wants anything—a drink, a shit—the natives will fix it.'[36]

'Blue' Steward, the 2/16th Battalion doctor:

> The men on the stretchers they tended with the devotion of a mother and the care of a nurse. A quick word . . . that the doctor needed a shelter for his wounded . . . and a rough but almost rainproof lean-to rose before your eyes. When a stretcher went 'bugger-up finish' they lashed a new one together in a matter of moments.[37]

After Isurava, Maroubra Force's fighting withdrawal became quite fluid. But Brigadier Arnold Potts found one more location for a major set-piece defence of his ground, and he could look forward to the arrival of the third battalion of his 21st Brigade, namely the 2/27th Battalion.

The fighting at Brigade Hill would produce some of the toughest, most controversial fighting of the Papuan campaign and would see Maroubra Force approach extinction.

. . . CALMLY BRAVE

10

During the first days of September 1942, Brigadier Arnold Potts was seeking another suitable position to hold the enemy for another more protracted set-piece defence of the Kokoda Trail. A position between Myola and Efogi was initially chosen. To have to pull so far back was a bitter pill for Potts to swallow. Myola was his main supply dump; its dry lake bed had been the focal point of his 'biscuit bomber' supply drops. The tragedy was that just as supplies had been forthcoming in a regular pattern for some days, he was forced to abandon Myola. The whole supply debacle was quite simply a tragic case of far too little when it mattered most, and almost too much when all seemed lost between Myola and Kokoda.

The key factor in Potts' decision to abandon Myola was the terrain. While Myola was an ideal drop zone it was an extremely poor defensive position against a large enemy force. In addition, it lay quite near to one of two tactical 'loops' in the track. Away to the west of Myola stood the village of Kagi; on the other loop was the Kokoda Trail, which the Japanese could readily use to outflank the Australians and thus cut them off from their line of communication near Efogi. Potts therefore decided that a stand would be made between Myola and Efogi with the Kagi track junction held to protect his left flank.

At dawn on 2 September 1942, the move from Eora Creek began. By 8.00 a.m. the 2/16th, strengthened by the return of a platoon cut off on the last night of August, had passed through the 2/14th and halted an hour's march north of Templeton's Crossing. Rhoden led the 2/14th through the 2/16th at about 10.00 a.m. and an hour later a standing patrol from Sublet's left forward company shot ten of the advancing enemy. The Japanese pushed into closer contact with the main positions and moved around the left flank to threaten the route to the south. Caro decided to leave the track, moving out to follow the ridges to the east. His soldiers, leaving their secure positions as the day waned, were rushed by the alert enemy and some close fighting followed with the Japanese sustaining heavier losses.

The next day, hungry and thirsty, the men of the 2/16th struggled across rough country, tearing their way through thick bush and drinking the moisture oozing from the moss-covered trees. In the late afternoon they emerged where the 2/14th were waiting, between Templeton's Crossing and Myola, and they settled there while the 2/14th continued its journey to Myola. With them went a welcome reinforcement; Lieutenant Stan Bisset, Warrant Officer Tipton and eleven others who had been cut off with Lieutenant-Colonel Arthur Key near the Isurava Rest House had returned in the wake of the 2/16th.

Even by day the track to Myola was an abomination of a thousand pitfalls: a steeply ascending and descending, slippery, muddy bog; in the dark the invisible obstacle course became a disorientating, shattering nightmare. The 2/14th reached Myola late in the night of 3 September and early in the morning of the 4th, most so tired that they dropped to sleep in their sodden cold clothes. But they were to awake in a 'promised land' which provided luxuries so long denied them.

Clothes were removed and cast away and fresh, clean uniforms acquired. Boots and socks were cut away and, in many cases, away too came the rotten skin with them. Corporal Clark, the unit chiropodist, set about the task of paring away the rotten tissue and smoothing out the wrinkles. Men bathed and washed, and slept the sleep of the reprieved. Most welcome of all was the hot food; the first they had had since they had left this very venue before journeying to Isurava. The cooks at Myola worked with the most humble of ingredients and recipes. There was a stew composed of bully beef, dehydrated tinned vegetables and rice, which formed the main course, and which was followed by a rice and raisin dessert and hot tea. Ammunition was also on the 'menu', confirming the old infantryman's adage 'bullets and tucker'.

While the 2/14th was enjoying its first and thoroughly deserved respite, the 2/16th was busily withdrawing towards it under increasing pressure. It was slowed by the burden of its stretcher cases and by exhaustion. At approximately 2.00 p.m. on 4 September, Lieutenant Hicks, who had led a patrol out to the west, reported to Captain Sublet (Caro was at a conference with Potts at this time) that the Japanese were rounding the left flank in considerable force. Not long afterwards McGee's company was attacked in the forward battalion positions. Sublet wisely chose to withdraw to the high ground to his rear. What then happened is an excellent illustration of the spirit and elan of the 2/16th Battalion. Captain Frank Sublet:

> When Hicks reported to me . . . that a large party of Japs had passed our left flank, I luckily guessed they were making for exactly the higher position behind us to which we then withdrew. The Japs put in a strong frontal attack as we were thinning out. When I arrived back at the previously selected holding position Sgt Morris very irately told me that I had mistakenly allocated his Company to a position that was already occupied. However a quick inspection disclosed that the position (a key one) WAS occupied, but by the Japanese! The dynamic Morris reacted like a flash and waded in with his men, evicting the Japanese in short order. Morris' determined and full blooded action no doubt saved the battalion from a difficult situation.[1]

There was good and bad news in a signal from 'Tubby' Allen to Potts on 3 September:

> Expect to have Ken here for dinner approximately 6 September . . . Supply situation demands vital necessity for holding Myola as dropping area . . . We cannot allow enemy to use Myola. Therefore we must establish firm base forward of Myola as soon as possible. Is it possible to revert to offensive action now?

The good news was obvious to Potts. 'Ken' was Brigadier Ken Eather, the commanding officer of the 7th Division's

25th Brigade. His arrival would signal a critical influx of fresh, trained and experienced troops into the campaign. But Allen's reference to a 'firm base forward of Myola', and his enquiry about reverting 'to offensive action now' only bring discredit upon him and Rowell. As Potts' divisional commander, it was Allen's responsibility to know what the nature of Potts' battle was. His was the task of understanding the terrain, the difficulties of supply, the size of the enemy force and, critically, of remembering the standard of the commander of the 21st Brigade and the quality of his troops, which had so recently been proven during the Syrian campaign. The obvious answer to both Allen and Rowell's ignorance lies in the remoteness of the terrain, the difficulty of intelligence gathering and the added complication of signal communication when one has to rely purely upon a rather tenuous single signal cable from the front to base. Major-General 'Tubby' Allen would later write:

> Either the G1 [the 7th Division's Colonel Spry] or myself would have gone forward before if I had not the added responsibility of the defence of Moresby area from a sea attack. The first I [intelligence] report received was an even greater menace (if possible) than the attack over the mountains . . . When given the dual roles I expressed doubt to [Rowell] but at the time there appeared no alternative.[2]

Colonel Spry did in fact offer the suggestion that he could personally go forward to give 'moral support to Potts and to report to Allen'.[3]

The point is surely that if permission and encouragement had been given for two journalists and a cameraman to climb the Kokoda Trail and report to Australia concerning the nature of the Kokoda campaign, it might have been prudent for either Spry, or another selected officer, to do precisely the same thing for the sake of an accurate military appreciation. A signal cable, however precariously operated in such a terrain does, after all, operate both ways. It would take the deteriorating position all the way back to Menari before a liaison officer finally made his way forward.

The plain and simple—and undeniable—truth is that on 4 September 1942, Arnold Potts could muster no more than 400 exhausted soldiers with whom to defend Myola. And all this while the Japanese were thrusting battalion after battalion against him. At 6.00 p.m. Potts sent a succinct signal to Allen:

> Strong enemy attack driven in 2/16th Battalion one and a half hours Myola. Am supporting defence with 2/14th Battalion, but country entirely unsuitable for defended localities. Regret necessity abandon Myola. Intend withdrawing Efogi. No reserves for counter-attack. Men full of fight but utterly weary . . . will keep you informed.

Potts' initial decision to establish a position between Myola and Efogi had been based on his inaccurate maps which showed the two Kokoda tracks: the old through Kagi, and the new, passing near Myola, joining north of the village. The junction of those two tracks appeared to be the logical place to hold the enemy advance, regardless of which of the two tracks the Japanese might choose to advance upon. However, Potts' reconnaissance showed that this junction was no place to contest the enemy advance—from the Mission Ridge spur rising southward above the village the junction was below in an open valley; it could be bypassed on either side to seize that very same commanding spur in its rear, cutting off withdrawal. There was no realistic hope of effectively holding any ground in the junction area or of escaping from the very likely enemy trap. The heights of Mission Ridge offered the only local hope, hence Potts' change of plan from a point between Myola and Efogi (the tracks' junction) to Mission Ridge.

If General Allen or a competent intelligence officer had been with Potts at this time they would have noted his still-aggressive intent.

Prior to his enforced abandonment of Myola, Potts had intended to use his fresh 2/27th to achieve two aims. His first objective was to deploy a company to approach Templeton's Crossing along the track via Kagi, and then fall upon the Japanese rear. That role was given by Lieutenant-Colonel Cooper to Captain Lee's B Company. Potts' second aim was to reinforce the undermanned and exhausted 2/16th on the new track between Myola and Templeton's Crossing. Captain Sims and his A Company, 2/27th Battalion were dispatched on that mission. The last two companies of the 2/27th, C and D, were earmarked for the reinforcement of Myola.

The fluid nature of the battle now manifested itself very quickly indeed. Having dispatched his A and B Companies in compliance with Potts' orders, Cooper was forced to retrieve them after receiving the news that the Japanese had forced the 2/16th back to Myola, and that Maroubra Force was to withdraw to Efogi. Captain Lee's B Company was contacted and turned back. However, Captain Sims and his A Company, who had set themselves a gruelling pace over very rough country between Kagi and the Myola track, could not be contacted by a Papuan policeman who had been sent after them. These events were recorded by Sims in his diary:

> 4 September:
>
> . . . Brigade Commander ordered Coy to leave Kagi and make Myola by night fall, as a result Coy left Kagi at 1730 hours for Myola taking cross country track for the first one and a half miles to the main Myola track. The going was very treacherous owing to the rain and two men had to be left behind because of injuries sustained whilst crossing a creek. Coy reached main track and continued on towards Myola travelling until 2100 hours that night. They lay either side of that track in the undergrowth and spent a most uncomfortable night in the rain. It was found out afterwards that native police had been sent out to order our return to Kagi . . .
>
> 5 September:
>
> Early morning A Coy moved off towards Myola. One hour distant they contacted Bde HQ withdrawing to Efogi. Brigade Major put the Company in the picture and Coy about turned and moved back to Efogi . . . [4]

The position chosen by Potts dominated the ground overlooking Efogi, which lay just to the north, and the village of Menari to the south. From Efogi the ground fell away to a creek just south of the village and then climbed steeply to

The Withdrawal—Alola to Efogi

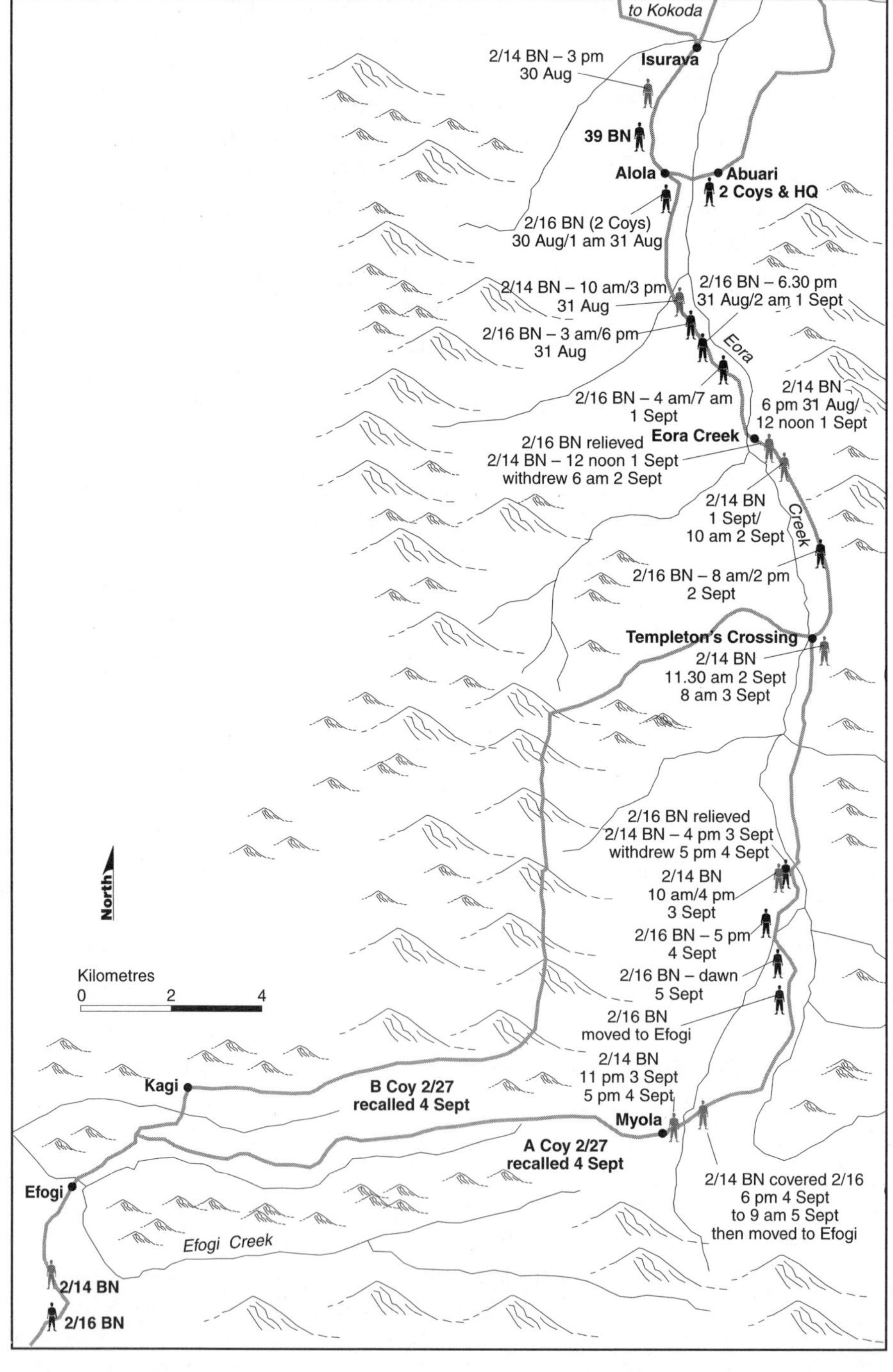

to Kokoda
Isurava
2/14 BN – 3 pm
30 Aug
39 BN
Alola
Abuari
2 Coys & HQ
2/16 BN (2 Coys)
30 Aug/1 am 31 Aug
2/14 BN – 10 am/3 pm
31 Aug
2/16 BN – 6.30 pm
31 Aug/2 am 1 Sept
2/16 BN – 3 am/6 pm
31 Aug
Eora
2/16 BN – 4 am/7 am
1 Sept
2/14 BN
6 pm 31 Aug/
12 noon 1 Sept
Eora Creek
2/16 BN relieved
2/14 BN – 12 noon 1 Sept
withdrew 6 am 2 Sept
2/14 BN
1 Sept/
10 am 2 Sept
Creek
2/16 BN – 8 am/2 pm
2 Sept
Templeton's Crossing
2/14 BN
11.30 am 2 Sept
8 am 3 Sept
North
2/16 BN relieved
2/14 BN – 4 pm 3 Sept
withdrew 5 pm 4 Sept
2/14 BN
10 am/4 pm
3 Sept
2/16 BN – 5 pm
4 Sept
2/16 BN – dawn
5 Sept
2/16 BN
moved to Efogi
Kilometres
0
2
4
2/14 BN
11 pm 3 Sept
5 pm 4 Sept
Kagi
B Coy 2/27
recalled 4 Sept
Myola
A Coy 2/27
recalled 4 Sept
2/14 BN covered 2/16
6 pm 4 Sept
to 9 am 5 Sept
then moved to Efogi
Efogi
Efogi Creek
2/14 BN
2/16 BN

a spur which ran southward to another steep hill. The spur was a mixture of timber and patches of kunai grass varying in height from six to eight feet. The only artificial feature on the spur was a derelict, roofless, Seventh-Day Adventist mission hut which was on the highest point of the spur. This spur, soon to be the scene of desperate fighting, became known as Mission Ridge. The hill dominating the rear of Mission Ridge became known as Brigade Hill and was also very heavily timbered. To the east and west of the Mission Ridge–Brigade Hill feature the terrain fell away very steeply into dense, heavily timbered jungle. South from Brigade Hill the terrain ran down an extremely precipitous decline to the village of Menari.

On the night of 4 September 1942, Potts ordered Cooper and Honner to evacuate Kagi the next morning and establish defensive positions on Mission Ridge. Honner was the first away; he reconnoitred defensive localities for both battalions and had his men in position before midday and partially dug in by the time the 2/27th arrived around 2.00 p.m. With Cooper's last companies marching in from the south that afternoon, Potts was able to effect the long-awaited relief of the 39th. Its War Diary records: 'At about 1530 hours, 2/27th Bn commenced taking over 39th Bn positions with all 39th Bn's automatic weapons, grenades, rations, blankets, signal stores and medical supplies. In the afternoon 39th Bn marched to Menari.' It will be recalled that it was at Menari where Honner held the famous 39th Battalion parade, during which time he passed on Potts' congratulations while Parer filmed the proceedings.

The afternoon rains of 5 September poured down on the four rifle companies of the 2/27th Battalion as they dug in within a well-linked but isolated perimeter on the northern end of Mission Ridge. The previous afternoon the 2/16th Battalion's skilful and savage withdrawal to defeat encirclement by the Japanese II Battalion of the 41st Regiment had precipitated Potts' decision to abandon Myola. On 5 September, at 7.00 a.m., Horii changed the composition of his pursuit force to include the II and III Battalions of the 144th Regiment with elements of the Mountain Artillery and a Pioneer Company. After the 2/16th, with its wounded, had passed through the holding position of the 2/14th north-west of Myola—to which the hungry Japanese, hot on the scent of rations, were temporarily diverted—the unhurried Victorian rearguard left for Efogi at about 9.30 a.m., arriving there seven hours later. The 2/16th had stopped at the creek crossing below Efogi village to cut the rotted socks from their pulpy, swollen feet, oblivious to the soaking rain. Both battalions sheltered at the village for the night.

On the morning of 6 September, Caro and Rhoden led their weary men through the fresh 2/27th Battalion to occupy positions to the rear. Bill Edgar, Potts' biographer:

> 'Better late than never' or 'You'd be late for yer (sic) own bloody funerals' was tossed at them but there were weary grins as they threw the banter at the Croweaters [South Australians]. It was good to have them up at last; it was good to know someone else would take the initial shock when the Nips showed up again.[5]

Some insight into Potts' professionalism, his resilience and his confident relationship with his men is gained by Cooper's impression of his brigade commander upon his arrival at Mission Ridge:

> When we met Arnold Potts at Efogi he didn't show the strain or pressure he'd been under. He was quiet and gentlemanly and had a sort of gruff farmer's approach to people. He was quietly ebullient, if that's not a contradiction . . . a little bubbling up all the time; never depressed, always pleasant to people. I never heard him, ever, dress anyone down; I never heard him make any aggressive comments about anyone in his own force. He was not an aggressive man, but he had a great deal of drive. He tended to jolly people along, to help them. He might make a suggestion, 'Well, have you thought of doing it this other way? . . . What about this proposition? . . . Never overbearing. There was, however, never any question that he was the boss.
>
> He was a strong man but never had the attitude, 'I'm at the top; I'm leading . . . this will be a big deal for me'—which a lot of commanders (then) did have. He

> was one of the commanders who was never looking for his own professional future. He was just doing his job with the brigade . . . he knew all his company commanders; he got around, he was always there in the thick of it . . . a very competent commander and a pleasure to be under . . .
>
> He certainly was a good planner . . . He didn't take a risk at Brigade Hill. He had to sit down and shoot it out at every point usable for that purpose.[6]

This is strong praise indeed from a soldier who had himself served under officers of the calibre of Morshead during the siege of Tobruk.

During the late afternoon of 6 September, Potts re-examined the 2/27th Battalion positions and concluded that a tightening of the brigade perimeter was imperative in order to reduce the length of exposed flanks. Accordingly the battalion was moved back on Mission Ridge to a higher position overlooking the earlier Brigade HQ at the old mission hut.

That move reduced the length of the brigade's track-holding by approximately 800 yards. As the late afternoon passed, the 2/27th had its B Company in the left forward position, its A Company in the right forward position, and its C and D Companies deployed in the left and right rear positions respectively. And just as their fellow soldiers of the 2/14th, 2/16th and 39th Battalions had done throughout the Kokoda campaign, the 2/27th dug in without entrenching tools.

Potts sited his 21st Brigade HQ on the rearward Brigade Hill with D Company (Captain Langridge) and a C Company platoon (both from the 2/16th) approximately two hundred yards north of his HQ.

While Potts and his soldiers were thus engaged, General Horii was executing his own well-constructed plans. He had been forced to lose four days from his timetable at Isurava and had lost another six before deploying his force near Mission Ridge. In short, by the rather ambitious timetable he had employed, he was at that very date supposed to be in Port Moresby. Further, there is no evidence that at any time did he employ either the Kokoda airstrip or Myola as a means of landing or dropping supplies. But he had been reinforced with about 1500 freshly landed troops. Therefore, he had at the Efogi front two complete regimental (brigade) groups with their own supporting arms such as quick-firing mountain gun detachments and strong support units of engineers and dismounted cavalry. This gave him a superior concentration of force in the order of four or five to one.

At Isurava he had been overconfident. His left flank operation along the Kaile–Missima–Abuari track had been more of a probing exercise than a full-blooded attempt to outflank the Australians. The fact that an ill-disciplined, unsuccessful two-company force of the 53rd and only a two-company commitment by Potts of the 2/16th had been able to substantially delay his force demonstrates the point. The resulting crippling casualties sustained at Isurava at the hands of the 2/14th and 39th Battalions had made a deep impression upon him. He determined that another Isurava would not occur. This time there would be a highly synchronised attack on the Australians' forward positions, in unison with an audacious scaling of the high, steep ground to the west. Horii was employing that age-old key principle of war: surprise.

When you stand on this precipitous left Australian flank, Private Bert Ward's observation of that western ground becomes so easy to understand:

> I must admit I had some degree of amazement as to how active they were, to be able to keep going. We were flat out! Physically exhausted! And so they must have been! Still, when they encircled us at Efogi in an area like that . . . Well, you'd have to be a qualified mountain goat to be able to do physically what they did—to be able to get right around the Battalion [the 2/27th]; around Brigade Hill.[7]

Arnold Potts had covered almost every contingency: he had ordered patrols out on both flanks of his new perimeter; he had planned an escape route should the enemy fall upon his rear; further, he ordered that the route be covered by a small force; he had wisely sited his full, fresh battalion to the front; and he had further deployed a company and a further platoon (four platoons) on the higher ground and near his HQ. Potts' patrols did encounter and did attack probing enemy patrols out to the east, but did not encounter such patrols or an enemy build-up to the west.

Just on darkness and during the night of 6–7 September 1942, the Australians on Mission Ridge and a number on Brigade Hill were spellbound witnesses to what many veterans have called the 'lantern parade', which wound its way down the precipitous slope opposite them. The 'lantern parade' was in fact collected and cut pieces of Australian rubber-coated signal wire which were lit and used as 'lanterns'.[8] Private 'Slim' Little, 2/27th Battalion:

> The night that we dug in at Efogi. I'll never forget that night as long as I live! We dug in, in a bit of open Kunai grass and we dug a hole with a bayonet and tin hat, and that's where we slept that night. And coming down the other hill towards the river were Japs, hordes of Japs with lanterns, and you could hear them jabbering and carrying on. And no noise! I mean there was us, no lighting a cigarette, no making any noise. We had to sit there watching them come up. It was pretty nerve-racking![9]

The point is that if the Australians had been equipped with Vickers machine-guns, many of the lights might have been 'put out'. As it was, the soldiers on Mission Ridge did note with some humour the odd 'lantern' that suddenly swung, dropped, was raised, and began again to move down the opposite slope. Even with a light the most sure-footed of soldiers had many a fall on the Kokoda Trail.

Arnold Potts also watched the steady and seemingly endless lantern procession with great chagrin. He took the only offensive course of action open to him: he signalled Port Moresby requesting a bombing and strafing operation from the air force at dawn. Captain Sims, deployed with his men on the right front Mission Ridge perimeter, watched the attack: 'The first one was good. That gave us great heart, everyone. This'll fix the little so-and-so's! It came fairly close. They blasted down over the river and up the track.'[10] Horii was probably inconvenienced by this strafing and bombing attack, but it did not stop him from painstakingly moving a substantial portion of his force in a wide encircling movement around his right or the Australians' steep left flank. He must have spent some considerable time in organising a forming up position in slow, quiet movement and, above all, in a covered position where his force could scale that steep obstacle before attacking the Australians.

The fact that Arnold Potts was only too well aware of the tactical options available to Horii is amply demonstrated by the succinct signal he sent Allen at 9.05 a.m. on 7 September:

> Will not give ground if you guarantee my line of communication . . .
> . . . full of fight, but physically below par, mainly feet and dysentery, naturally affects most. Every endeavour being made to contain enemy on line approach but nothing to prevent him bypassing, hence line of communication problem . . . Respectfully consider offensive ops require more than one Bde task. Air action this morning most successful and heartening.[11]

Horii was ready during the last cold but peaceful moments of moonlight before the dawn of 8 September. At around 4.30 a.m. a three-company assault attempted to shatter Sims' company front in fighting which was reminiscent in its volume, deafening noise and slaughter of recent events at Isurava.

By daybreak the Japanese were raking the whole 2/27th front with concentrated and relentless mountain gun, machine-gun and mortar fire. Sims' A Company had had a very trying time the previous day as it was positioned in kunai patches exposed to the morning and early afternoon intensity of the sun and then the heavy afternoon rains. It relied on water, ration and ammunition replenishment from its rear but its supply operations had been continually disrupted by accurate Japanese fire. As the enemy attacks mounted in both intensity and frequency the disruption became continuous, and conservation of ammunition became critical.

Training, experience and fortitude answered the challenge and in repelling some eight attacks during the morning,

A Company wrought utter carnage upon their attackers. As wave upon wave of the Japanese attacked they were met with a concerted hail of small arms fire and a liberal supply of grenades either thrown or rolled down the hill at them. During this action the intensity of the fighting was such that A Company's total supply of 1200 grenades and 100 rounds of ammunition per man were expended in addition to the battalion's reserve supplies and the reserve companies' stocks.

An attack upon B Company's front at approximately 7.30 a.m. was met with the same resolute defiance; at no time during 8 September were the Japanese able to penetrate the 2/27th A and B Company positions. However, the price paid was high. Sims had six of his Bren guns knocked out and suffered numerous casualties from both the Japanese infantry and the artillery shelling of his perimeter. In a duplicate of the fighting at Isurava, the ground in front of A and B Companies became a macabre scene of slaughter and splintered vegetation.

Arnold Potts could hear the distant firing on Cooper's front as he was walking down to the latrine with Private Gill of the guard platoon. There was no panic; he'd spoken to Cooper and the situation was under control. Potts had just returned to the HQ hut when a shot rang out—Gill had been killed by a sniper. That single shot was followed by an eerie respite. Lieutenant Cairns, who was one of Potts' liaison officers, and Corporal Beveridge had reacted to Gill's death by moving to the edge of the western incline. The enemy soldier saw Beveridge at almost precisely the same instant that the Australian saw him. Beveridge got a grenade away but the enemy soldier had also been quick to react with a machine-gun burst. Both men would soon die.

Cairns slithered across and had only just managed to grab the dying Beveridge when he in turn was confronted by a rushing enemy soldier coming straight for him. The Australian's desperate rise and run was interrupted by a piercing rifle shot fired by Burnham Fraser, another of the brigade's liaison officers.

These sudden and dramatic moments heralded the intense battle for Brigade Hill. A Brigade HQ almost always consists of a motley collection of personnel who comprise the nerve centre of the administration of a brigade. And they are often a curious blend of ages, ranging from older men who were members of the guard platoon, or cooks, storemen, or perhaps signallers, or medical 'orderlies' through to the young liaison officer or intelligence gatherers. Such soldiers did not under normal circumstances see action—especially the older variety as they'd often seen it in the Great War or in earlier campaigns. But on Brigade Hill on 8 September 1942, these men, known affectionately as the 'old and bold' or the 'toothless and the ruthless', fought for their lives.

On a number of occasions the Japanese were able to press very close to Brigade HQ—about fifteen yards from the edge of the perimeter once—before being thrown back. The only thing that saved Potts and his HQ was the fact that Horii, or the officer in charge of this part of the operation, chose to attack 21st Brigade's front and rear and then tried to annihilate the three battalions, instead of attacking and eliminating Potts himself and his small force and then pushing onwards to Menari. And the attitude is understandable. No commander relishes a relatively intact force in his rear which, although cut off from his line of communication, is still capable of some sort of offensive endeavour.

By 10.00 a.m. the 2/27th was under heavy mortar and machine-gun fire, and its A and B Companies were still under close attack. In addition, its water, ration and ammunition supplies, already having been spasmodic for over 24 hours, were being further restricted. The 2/16th Battalion HQ, also without water and under intense attack, was in grave danger and Potts and his brigade HQ were besieged on Brigade Hill. As a consequence of the invasion of the track by the Japanese and of their digging in, in force, between Caro and Potts, the telephone cable had been cut, and the less reliable wireless communication between Potts and his battalions was only intermittent.

Report Into Operations 21 Brigade—Owen Stanley Campaign:

> Communications with the units was now a matter of great difficulty but, 2/14th Bn was contacted by W. T. [wireless transmitter] during two periods from 0830 hrs to 1600 hrs. Apart from this no communication was

> possible. In view of the probability that Brigade HQ would be wiped out Brigade Commander at 1000 hrs sent a message to commander 2/16th Battalion that in such an eventuality he was to take control of the Brigade and move back to Menari.[12]

The contingency plan was thus in place. But both Potts and his battalion commanders sought one more concerted effort to break the deadlock. Two decisions were made. The first was to shorten the brigade perimeter, by a withdrawal by the 2/27th and 2/14th Battalions further back to and along the high ground. This was a move fraught with great risk of casualties, as it was to be accomplished as the battle was still raging. Although encumbered by a number of stretcher cases, the two battalions pulled off the move with minimum casualties.

The second part of the plan involved an attempt to clear the rearward track and thus open it for the movement of ammunition, water, rations, the evacuation of the wounded and, most importantly, open a route for the inevitable withdrawal. It was planned that Caro's 2/16th would mount an attack back towards Arnold Potts along the eastern side of the track, while the 2/14th was to attack along its western side. The problem was that the Japanese had taken the opportunity to dig in strongly along their portion of the track, and using their ground along the western slope they could push telling numbers into a reinforcement of their hard won gains. The Australians faced a tough task. The attack began at 2.15 p.m. Jack Scott was amongst the 2/16th attackers:

> The Japs had set up machine-gun nests between HQ and the rest of the brigade. The order came through for us to break through if we could. Hec Hodge, our company commander, was as game as Ned Kelly. He stood up and called, 'Alright C Company, each man for his bloody self!'
>
> Jack Harris and I were on the bottom end of the line of C Company on the left, a fair way down the slope from the pathway on top of the saddle. The fellow above me on my right was a married man with children. As soon as we stood up to go, he copped a

> couple in the chest. As he fell he said, 'I don't want to die.'
>
> We could see the others on the higher ground above us getting belted. We got through eventually, climbing up to the top through the undergrowth via a re-entrant or sort of gully. As we hauled ourselves over the edge, Brigadier Potts looked straight over at us. I can still see those blue eyes flashing to this day. 'How did you fellas get here?' he asked. We explained. 'Could you make it back?' Jack and I looked at each other, none too keen. 'If it's necessary,' I mumbled.
>
> 'No you don't,' Ken Murdoch interjected, 'we need you here!' We breathed a sigh of relief.[13]

As the usual afternoon Owen Stanley rains set in, the 2/16th Battalion's component of the attack had failed. Its A and B Companies, attacking along the track, had suffered greatly from heavy machine-gun fire, while C Company's effort, running on the eastern side of the track and partly down its slope, had also taken heavy casualties. Jack Scott was one of only a dozen or so men who had gained Potts' perimeter.

On the western side of the track the gallant Isurava veterans of B Company, who had shed so much blood in the infamous cane field, went in with characteristic drive. At their head was the brave and inspirational Captain Claude Nye. In the ensuing carnage on this Brigade Hill site, Nye and his soldiers of 11 and 12 Platoons savagely mauled their enemy. When the almost constant attacks upon the Japanese had ended—the last before a Japanese bugle call sounded, which had rallied and reinforced the enemy positions—the day was lost. Warrant Officer Noble and only eight soldiers broke through to Potts. Behind them lay the brave Nye and seventeen of his comrades. To an already stricken company after Isurava these losses were most keenly felt.

In a last desperate effort to force a pathway through to Potts, Caro requested that his brigadier send a force towards the 2/16th lines. Captain 'Lefty' Langridge was allotted the task. Sited about two hundred yards north of Potts, Langridge went in with one of his own D Company platoons and another from C Company. After passing his paybook and discs to a comrade, Langridge, without a word of dissent or obvious emotion, weighed in with his determined few. This attack also failed, and in its wake lay the dead Langridge, Lieutenant 'Bluey' Lambert and about twenty of their men.

The Battle for Brigade Hill typified the spirit of Maroubra Force—trained, disciplined soldiers who had an enormous spirit and an unshakeable confidence in their leaders, from Potts down to the last section leader. These soldiers were not just blindly reckless but calmly brave, and throughout this uneven battle they had faithfully and calmly accepted their duty which often meant death.

The 21st Brigade contingency plan was now immediately executed. The race was on for Menari. If the Japanese could get there first, all three Maroubra Force battalions would be cut off and finished as a fighting force. But if the Australians won that unequal race, then the fighting withdrawal could continue.

Two critical occurrences helped Potts in his race for Menari. The first was the venom of the 2/16th and 2/14th attempts to clear the track between HQ and the battalions. Those attacks failed, but they did buy time for Potts and assist in his effort to extricate himself from the battlefield, while the second factor was the timely arrival of the Brigade Major, Major Hugh Challen, with 40 soldiers of the Brigade Composite Company, who added valuable strength and therefore further resolution to Potts' withdrawal. Walking out in the fading light of that crucial day Potts knew that his three battalion commanders would rapidly execute the contingency withdrawal plan.

Caro, Rhoden and Cooper were confronted with three immediate problems. The first was time. The second problem was the terrain. The narrow alternative track to Menari confined by surrounding dense jungle was, even by Kokoda Trail standards, a desperately taxing route. It would have been a very severe test for fit troops, let alone those in the condition that these men were in. The last problem was the wounded. Each battalion had a number of stretcher cases to carry. If this battle had been fought in the desert against the Germans or the Italians, the stretcher cases could have been left to the enemy's care. This option was not for a moment considered by the three battalion commanders. To leave the wounded to the Japanese was quite simply unthinkable. Potts and his soldiers had learnt this at Isurava. Years later, Arnold Potts would recall that: 'We had to sit in the jungle listening to the screams of comrades tortured by the Japanese in an attempt to provoke an attack.'[14] The fact is, therefore, that to leave any man to the enemy invited torture and a savage execution.

Menari seemed almost an impossible goal as the 2/16th left its positions on Brigade Hill at 4.32 p.m. on 8 September. The Official Historian: 'Progress was painfully slow in that terrible country. The men cut and slashed at the scrub. Their hearts seemed to be bursting as they struggled to help their wounded, hoisting, lowering, pulling and pushing the clumsy stretchers on which the worst cases had to be carried.'[15] The 2/16th and 2/14th struggled on until nightfall when further movement on this track became an impossibility, given its very narrow nature, its enveloping vegetation and the necessity of carrying the wounded. The two battalions now dropped and slept where they were, somewhat strung out along their perilous path.

The same problems had confronted the 2/27th. As the battalion last out and therefore responsible for the rearguard, Cooper's soldiers had a greater distance to cover and were additionally burdened by fifteen stretcher cases, some of whom were from their sister battalions.

In perhaps one of the most audacious rearguard actions of the campaign, Captain Mert Lee's B Company did not content itself with merely fighting the rearguard, but decided on a more bold form of battle. The adjutant of the 2/27th, Captain Harry Katekar:

> They [B Company] had to buy time some way or other and the way they did it, they counter-attacked down towards the Japs. The Japs were so shocked that they broke contact. We didn't see them again that day. They had the impetus and they were hot on our heels. We were withdrawing with our wounded; they would have known that because they were in contact with us . . . And then B Company was given this job to stop them.

> Instead of just standing there and firing at them they counter-attacked and that must have shocked them considerably.[16]

The remarkable aspect of this final counterattack was that it was performed by Lee and only a handful of his men, who had gathered Bren guns and Thompson sub-machine guns for maximum firepower and also to create the illusion that the counterattack was delivered in considerable force. It was not.

The 2/27th did precisely what its brigade comrades further along the escape route had done: as soon as it became dark, the withdrawal ground to a halt and the men slept where they could find a suitable position. It was not unusual for many soldiers to sleep with their feet against a tree or sapling, or put a bayonet in the ground and then place their heels against it, to avoid slipping down a slope during the night. That they had a chance to sleep at all may well have been due to Captain Lee's superb counterattack, which marked the conclusion of the action of the 2/27th in the Efogi area with a fitting end to its splendid achievement. It had not yielded one inch of its embattled territory and had, under appalling conditions of heat, lack of water and rations and precarious ammunition supply, upheld its own proud reputation and that of its brigade. Its historian would later write:

> In the two-day battle at the Efogi position, the battalion had lost 39 other ranks killed in action and 2 men missing believed killed. In addition, 3 officers and 43 other ranks had been wounded. This was approximately 1 man in 6 and was a high price for such a relatively short action. It is an indication of the intensity of the action fought, particularly by A and B Companies. The enemy dead later counted in the battalion area by the 25th Brigade exceeded 200, so that he was forced to pay a heavy price.[17]

At dawn on 9 September the weary troops of the 21st Brigade set forth, resuming their tortuous journey through the thick jungle towards Menari:

Report Into Operations 21 Brigade:

> At 1115 hrs enemy mortar, QF [quick-firing mountain gun] and L.M.G. [light machine-gun] fire began to fall on the village from North and NW and almost simultaneously the leading troops of 2/16th Bn began to arrive in the village . . .
>
> The posn at midday was, the Bde Comd had to decide at what time to evacuate Menari in view of the possibility of the 2/27th Bn coming in. The village itself was extremely vulnerable and could not be held. The time given for the evacuation was 1430 hrs . . . [18]

The 2/14th and 2/16th had pushed their fit men forward with all possible speed to reach Menari, bolster Potts' force there, and hopefully hold that village until the whole brigade could be recovered at that venue. The 2/27th acted with similar judgment. Cooper sent Captain Sims with his A Company and Lieutenant Sandison with two platoons of C Company forward to Menari without the encumbrance of the stretcher cases. It was hoped that these soldiers would find Menari still in Potts' possession.

Cooper could not send forward any more troops than he did. He had to retain a sufficient number of men to carry the stretchers to safety and, in order to keep them moving at a maximum speed, there had to be an equal number of replacements to relieve those actually carrying. In addition, he had to retain enough men to be an effective fighting force as a rearguard. At any time he had to expect that the enemy could easily catch up with his slow-moving column and try to destroy it. The Japanese failure to press the pursuit is surprising. Perhaps this failure should be understood in terms of Horii's already lagging timetable, the rapidly deteriorating condition of his troops and, therefore, his desire to reach his objective with all possible speed.

Circumstances beyond Cooper's control denied him access to Menari. First, his was the last formation out from the Brigade Hill feature. As a consequence of covering less ground before dark on 8 September, he had further to travel than the 2/14th and 2/16th Battalions but less time with which to

Brigade Hill, 6–9 September

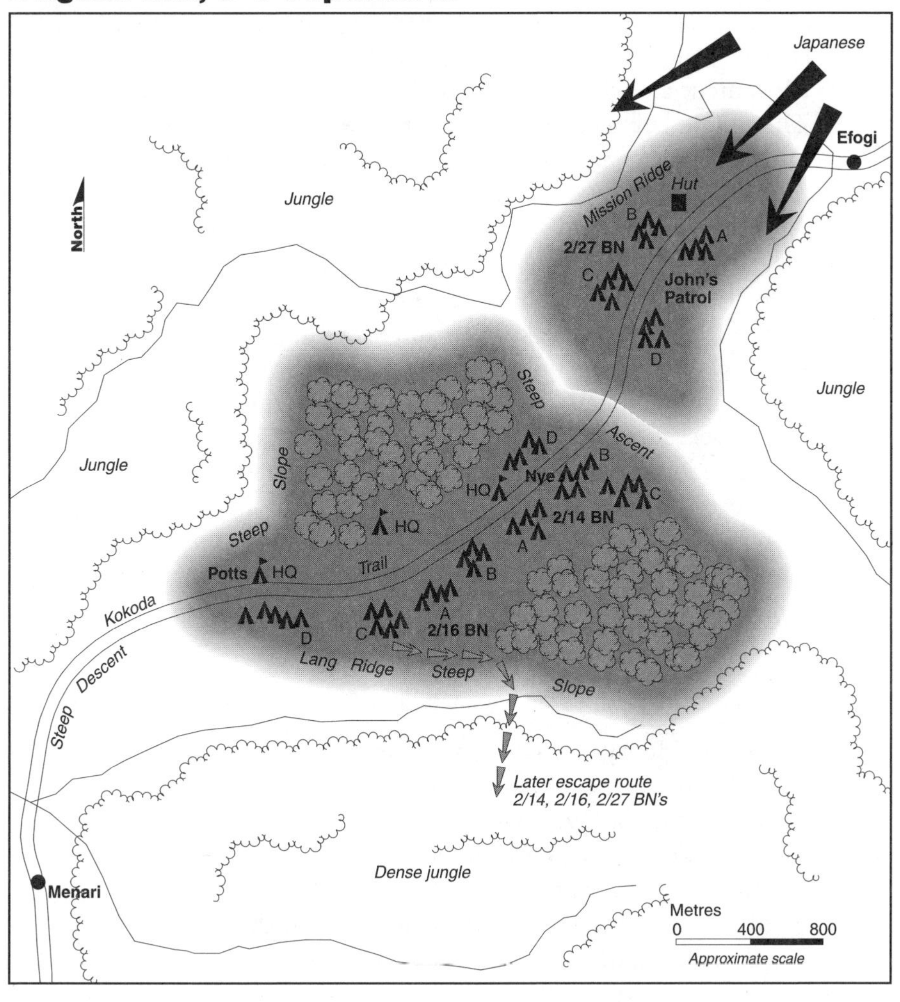

traverse the ground into Menari before the withdrawal deadline. Second, the stretcher cases, comprising men from all three units, made his progress unbelievably slow. During the action on Mission Ridge and Brigade Hill no native stretcher-bearers were available, as they were not expected to endanger their lives. Thus, the stretcher cases carried by the 2/27th required 120 soldiers to carry them and an equal number to act as relief carriers. The third factor was the terrain. Movement along the Kokoda Trail itself was arduous enough. The jungle between Efogi and Ioribaiwa made progress more difficult. The geographical position of Menari itself was the fourth factor.

When you stand at the final approach to Brigade Hill and look back and down on the very steep and taxing climb you have just made from your overnight stay at Menari, you realise what a set of sitting ducks Potts and his returned and returning soldiers were. Not only was Menari well within Japanese mountain gun range, but that village lay beautifully exposed to easy observation. When Potts decided that 2.30 p.m. was the last possible time for him to stay at that vulnerable location he was, even then, exposing himself to prolonged shelling. Cooper and his 2/27th Battalion quite simply did not, and could not, arrive at Menari in time, and Potts could stay no longer.

Brigadier Henry Rourke was on Rowell's staff in Port Moresby. On 1 September 1942, he wrote a letter to Vasey back in Australia: 'We have had some shocks but things seem to be in hand and all here are enjoying themselves. The closer one gets to the war the less "worse" it seems.'[19] Prophetic words. Rourke is referring to events both on the Kokoda Trail and at Milne Bay.

The nature of the fighting on the Kokoda Trail, the tremendous difficulties of intelligence gathering, the acute problems of the concentration and distribution of supplies, the lack of artillery support (while the enemy was busily using a mountain gun to hammer the Australians), the severe testing of the communication system on the trail and back to Port

Moresby, and the trying challenge of the evacuation of the wounded were all largely hidden beneath that rolling green carpet called the Owen Stanley Range.

Rowell and Allen and their staffs had some concept of a number of these factors, but not all, and not a clear concept of their cumulative nature. As the pressure upon Potts and his soldiers mounts, so too does the pressure upon their immediate superiors in Port Moresby. We have noted the signal sent to Potts to hold Myola with 400 exhausted soldiers, and the enquiry as to when he proposes to establish a firm base from which to begin offensive patrolling. But as the situation deteriorates to and at Brigade Hill, 'less worse' becomes 'more worse'.

This is demonstrated by the final if far-too-late arrival of some eyes and ears from Port Moresby to accurately assess Potts' plight. Captain Geoff Lyon was the liaison officer belatedly sent up the trail by 'Tubby' Allen. But his arrival only coincided with the battle for Brigade Hill. As Potts was immersed in this fight, Lyon communicated with him by signal line for the first time. His resulting message to Allen was alarming to say the least:

> Jap in strength between ABOG [Brigade HQ], two platoons 2/16 Battalion and remainder. At worst, can hold feature as fortress two days, destroy Menari and withdraw line of communication troops. At best, can hold as fortress four days, as not water on position, forward supplies short. Alternatively, withdraw and establish eight days fortress vicinity Nauro. We have not sufficient troops to prevent outflanking. Following troops from Moresby would have to fight in to us. Please instruct urgently.[20]

Potts' biographer, Bill Edgar:

> Tubby Allen, taken aback, wanted clarification from Potts: 'Has [Lyon's] message been sent with your approval? Is situation stated correct? Advise immediately.' At that point Arnold was busy. Only metres away the Japanese were readying themselves to pounce on Brigade HQ. Lyon was

> out from Menari and could not be contacted for any clarification. Potts' reply was brusque: 'Message confirmed.'[21]

Rowell to Vasey (Deputy Chief of the General Staff), 8 September 1942:

> Potts is at this hour in serious trouble between Efogi and Menari, as a result of enemy penetration. Porter is being sent forward . . . to relieve Potts and take charge of all elements in the forward area. I trust you appreciate [the] gravity of immediate situation, and will produce additional troops asked for particularly infantry, with minimum delay.[22]

Rowell had decided to relieve Potts. David Horner has written that the decision was taken to 'obtain a first hand account of the conditions',[23] but also Rowell was 'angry with what he saw as Potts's mishandling of his brigade'.[24]

It would appear that the second given reason for Rowell's assessment might well have been the overriding one. Rowell did not consult Allen but merely informed him of his decision. Allen raised no objection.

Two events saved Potts. The first was an interview between Rowell and Potts on 12 September which was instigated by Allen.[25] This interview did much to placate Rowell and Allen as to the position at the front. The second event was the arrival of the reporter Chester Wilmot back in Port Moresby and his subsequent briefing of Rowell.[26] The pertinent point is surely that, Potts' interview aside, a war correspondent was briefing a general when in fact a competent liaison officer like Lyon should have been given the task at the start of the campaign, and not after it had ran into trouble at Brigade Hill.

'Less worse' prior and even during Isurava therefore became 'more worse' in Port Moresby during and briefly after the battle of Brigade Hill. But further away still, in the hallowed corridors of high command at MacArthur's HQ, there is a different perspective again.

The first issue is MacArthur's standing at the political level in Washington, coupled with his politico-military standing with his Chief of the Joint Chiefs of Staff, General Marshall. This work has identified MacArthur's dislike for and mistrust of President Roosevelt; it has also identified the mistrust MacArthur feels towards Marshall.[27]

MacArthur therefore does two things to consolidate his position. The first is a conscious decision to heighten the alarm in Washington over events in his South West Pacific Area, while also denigrating the Australian performance in New Guinea. In so doing, he maximises his chances of procuring more men and material for his theatre of war. MacArthur to the Joint Chiefs of Staff, 30 August 1942:

> Unless the strategic situation is constantly reviewed in the light of current enemy possibilities in the Pacific and unless moves are made to meet the changing conditions, a disastrous outcome is bound to result shortly; it is no longer a question here of preparing a projected offensive; without additional naval forces, either British or American, and unless steps are taken to match the heavy air and ground forces the enemy is assembling, I predict the development shortly of a situation similar to those that have successfully overwhelmed our forces in the Pacific since the beginning of the war.[28]

MacArthur to Marshall, 6 September 1942: ' . . . the Australians have proven themselves unable to match the enemy in jungle fighting. Aggressive leadership is lacking.'[29] Vasey to Rowell, 7 September 1942:

> . . . I convey to you General MacArthur's grave fear that present situation may develop into one in which we shall be denied use of Moresby airfields . . . He feels that present is wrong policy and I know it is against your instructions. He urges greater offensive action against Japs whose difficulties now considerable.[30]

11 MODERN DAY DISCIPLES

From the very beginning of the Kokoda campaign, groups of men varying in number from a few soldiers through to platoons, companies and, eventually, a battalion were cut off from their one and only secure lifeline: the Kokoda Trail. Such episodes occurred as a direct consequence of the fighting withdrawal.

Had this tactic not been employed by Brigadier Arnold Potts and his Maroubra Force, then the whole course of the campaign may have been decisively altered. Stand, fight, withdraw, and repeat the process. The inevitable by-product of this form of fighting is that some groups of soldiers will be denied their line of communication.

Three examples of the suffering and privations of such groups during this Kokoda campaign are now described. They are part of the paradox of war. Sometimes during, but often after, the heat of battle come heart-rending examples of the best of the human being: compassion and selflessness and willing sacrifice.

During the desperate fighting at the Isurava Rest House on 30 August 1942, parts of the 2/14th Battalion's A and B Companies had acted as the rearguard, holding the enemy back so that the main body could escape. An hour after the designated time for the withdrawal, Captain Claude Nye and a portion of B Company made their way back along the track to safety.

But a further hour passed while Lieutenant 'Mocca' Treacy and a devoted party of six soldiers constructed stretchers, under sniper fire, for the wounded. That fighting did not abate until a further hour had elapsed. When Captain Buckler's group tried to extricate themselves from the position, they found the track ahead occupied by the enemy. Buckler now assumed command of this collection of soldiers: Treacy, Lieutenant Butler of 7 Platoon, 42 soldiers from A, B and C Companies and the stretcher cases.[1] The move out occurred around dusk.

Here begins one of the most inspirational stories of the Kokoda campaign. When the movement off the track began, Corporal John Metson, a young lad from Sale in Victoria, refused outright to be carried out, despite being unable to walk because of a bullet wound to an ankle. Knowing the cost in manpower to his comrades should he be carried, he defiantly wrapped his hands and knees in bandages and began to crawl out. W.B. Russell: '. . . for three weeks, chilled, rain-soaked, mud-caked, starved, exhausted—never complaining, always encouraging. With two stretcher cases, three walking wounded, and one crawling, the party struck into the jungle in the darkness, reaching a point on the Eora Creek just before dawn.'[2] Along their perilous path to safety Buckler's party found Private Mayne who, after being carried away from the Japanese, had crawled into the jungle rather than be an encumbrance on his comrades. A stretcher was constructed for him and he thereby joined this desperate party.

But the going was tough and the pace of their progress far too slow. Hampered by almost constant rain and the varying levels of stamina and endurance of the group, the line began to stagger out to the point where Buckler was forced to split the group. After making the same distance in three days that they might have made in one on the trail, Buckler now sent forth an advanced group to contact base and help.

He ordered Lieutenant 'Mocca' Treacy to go ahead with two 'fit' men and proceed with all possible haste for Myola, pick up medical supplies, food and carriers, and return for the main group. He further informed Treacy that if he had not returned within four days, he would leave the wounded under care and strike for the north-east coast via the Kokoda Valley.

Desperate men

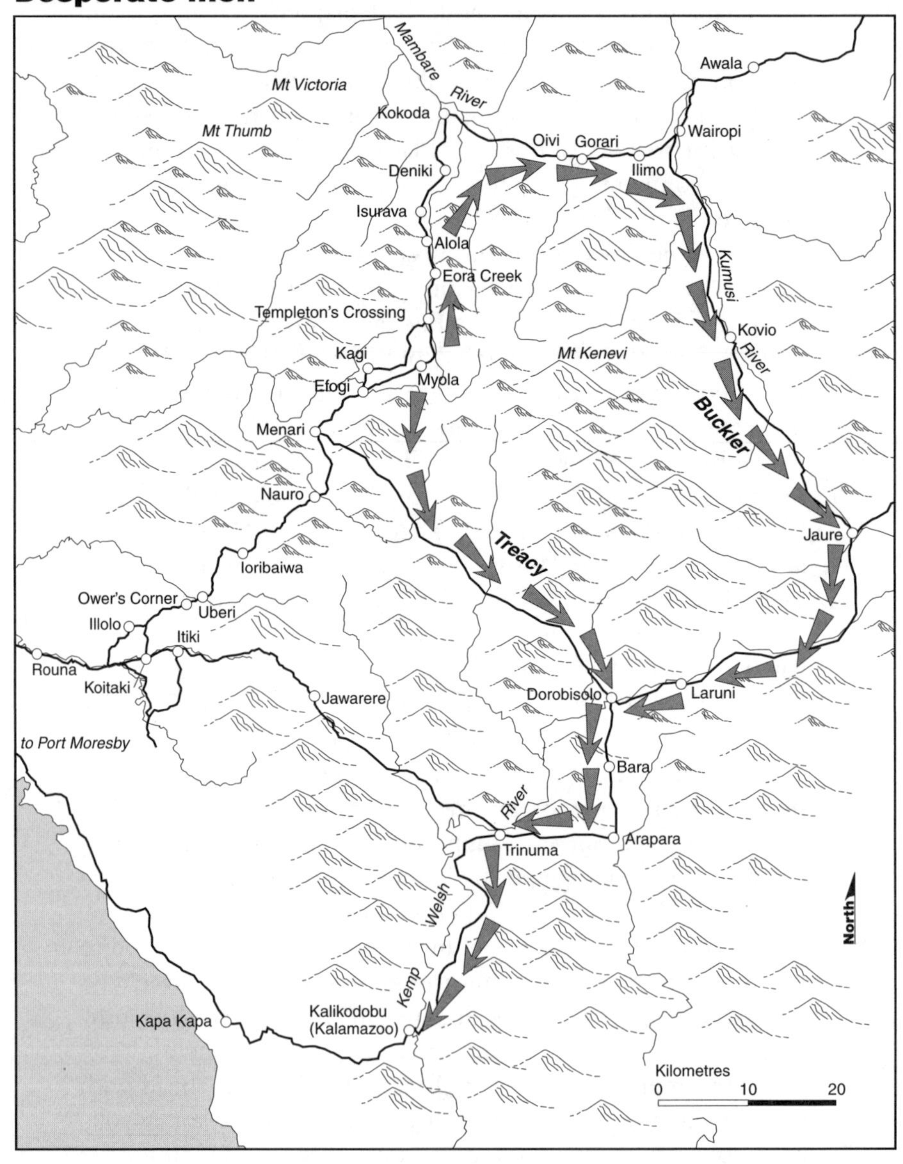

Treacy's group of three basically lived for the first few days by ambushing small Japanese parties and taking their meagre food supplies. But moving too closely parallel with the trail was always going to be fraught with great danger. On 10 September the three men '. . . met a party of eight Japs face to face. The Tommy gun failed to fire, the rifle fired only one round, a grenade thrown failed to explode. Lieut. Treacy's pistol then rose to the occasion, killing three and putting the rest to flight.' Now striking far off the trail due to the enormous risk of further enemy contact—that they were by now too weak and poorly armed to deal with—Treacy's three struck the village of Dorobisolo, about parallel to Owers Corner after a twelve-day trek.

While Treacy's party were thus occupied Buckler had set out, after waiting for four days, following the plan described. After moving in the general direction of Kokoda for about ten days, Buckler's group—with Metson still crawling—arrived at the village of Sangai 2, south-east of Kokoda. Here they left the wounded with Private Tom Fletcher, who was the medical orderly for B Company. Fletcher had five wounded and two men suffering from severe fever whom he volunteered to care for.

As Buckler's party left the wounded and Fletcher, they paid them the only tribute that they were able to offer. The bedraggled, almost spent and ragged main party lined up, stood stiffly to attention, and proceeded to 'Present Arms' to the wounded and Fletcher. As Fletcher and his heroes watched Buckler's men disappear into the jungle, they knew that their chances of survival now lay exclusively with them and their ability to press on through some of the toughest terrain in the world.

After an extraordinary journey of some 42 days, the group reached help. They were now confident that they could get help for the wounded, rejoin their 2/14th Battalion, and carry on the war. Supplies were duly dropped by air to the isolated little group at Sangai 2, but it was all in vain, as a Japanese patrol had found Fletcher's brave few and executed the entire party. Metson and the other stretcher cases were slaughtered where they lay. For his sheer bravery and selflessness, Corporal John Metson was awarded the British Empire Medal.

When Lieutenant-Colonel Geoff Cooper and his 2/27th were cut off after their fighting on Mission Ridge, Cooper had pushed Captain Sims, his A Company, and two platoons of C Company forward towards Menari, to either assist in its occupation by Maroubra Force or, at worst, confirm whether that village was in enemy hands. Sims and his soldiers discovered the latter. Having lost contact with the main body of the battalion, Sims and his force divided into small tactical groups and pushed on to the base area.

Cooper, meanwhile, was now faced with the monumental task of carrying and caring for his own wounded—plus a number of 2/14th and 2/16th stretcher cases—and regaining his line of communication.

What follows is an account of that horrendous journey told through the eyes of the battalion adjutant, Captain Harry Katekar, and Sergeant Clive Edwards from D Company. Katekar's account was written in hospital in Queensland during May 1943 and Edwards' description was written very shortly after the experience. Perhaps one of the most interesting aspects of the two accounts rests in the realisation that an officer and a private soldier will often have different perspectives of the same experience. Interspersed with their accounts are interviews with a number of other participants. Wednesday, 9 September 1942, Katekar:

> In the meantime the rest of the Unit, Bn HQ, HQ Coy, B and D Coys with 14 stretcher cases (300 men) and 60 carriers heard the bad news about the fall of Menari where we had hoped to pick up rations and ammunition.
>
> The only course was to continue to cut a separate track through the rough stuff, approximately 1 mile from and parallel to the main track. We hoped to reach the next village Nauro, ahead of the Japs.
>
> . . . On that night we dossed down wet and miserable in the undergrowth near Menari. Again we had to remain particularly alert and silent as we were so close to the Japs. Our stretchers were the limiting factor.

On this day Captain Peter Smith, brigade staff captain, met the column with 79 native carriers, who took over the main burden of the carrying. Most of these natives stayed with the column for only two days before vanishing into the wilderness at night because of the lack of food. Thursday, 10 September, Edwards:

> We didn't get a very early start despite being up at first light and we chafed with impatience as the day wore on, and a tortuous track had to be carved down toward a fairly large stream . . . and as the pangs of hunger began to hit us in earnest we chafed even more at the inactivity . . .
>
> Dysentery in a mild form has hit the lads and some of them, particularly Dave Sheppard, are in a bad way . . . we finally had to halt for the night at a place where I had to use my string to tie my gear to a bush to prevent it sliding down hill. I had only the tiniest of hip-holes in which to sleep.

Katekar:

> After struggling all day, we only covered a couple of miles. We had passed through a native garden of sugar cane and sweet potatoes, but at that time the C.O. would not let us forage, as the garden was possibly under enemy observation . . . I finished my rations that day, and faced the future foodless.

Friday, 11 September, Edwards:

> . . . commenced a long and stern climb—we are getting weaker and the effort to be expended on such a climb is growing greater and thus we found the spells ever more welcome . . .
>
> We lay down tonight with a light head apiece.

Katekar:

> The men were feeling the strain and the natives were starting to complain about lack of food.

Saturday, 12 September, Katekar:

> It was very disheartening to have to move so slowly; the stretchers limited our pace to almost a crawl. By the afternoon the men were too exhausted to go on, so the C.O. sent back D Coy, along the trail to the native garden we had passed two days before . . .
>
> . . . we could not light a fire until after dark when the mist settled down to cloak us. Then we cooked yams and had some sort of meal.

Edwards:

> Certainly when the issue came back of 3 cooked and about 4 uncooked vegetables per man we had a reasonable feed and felt a little more secure as regards the future . . .

Sunday, 13 September, Katekar:

> The wounded, God only knows, were going through purgatory, hungry and in great pain. Some of our natives began to desert, meaning that our men had to replace them as bearers [understandably, the natives would soon all be gone]. 'Doc' Viner-Smith allowed the maggots to remain on the wounds in order to eat the rotting flesh and so prevent gangrene . . . I found it a great mental strain and so did the C.O. and other officers, with that great responsibility of not only saving our wounded but of saving ourselves from starvation.

Doug Keane, 2/27th Signals:

> One chap from the 2/14th Battalion had one straight through the throat and kept asking for water and as you kept giving him the water much of it ran straight out again. He didn't last. One day I thought, 'He looks better today'—and then he was gone . . . [3]

Monday, 14 September, Katekar:

> The 14th of September brought us to the outskirts of Nauro . . .

> We could hear no firing; we did not know if the village was ours or the Japs. So we moved down a long spur and by nightfall, when we halted, we guessed that Nauro was only a mile or two away.

Tuesday, 15 September, Katekar:

> . . . we hurried down the spur to the river—it took us some time to ford this deep swift flowing stream with the stretchers . . .
>
> The men were absolutely exhausted and ravenous. Nauro was our hope . . .
>
> Imagine our intense anguish and disappointment when the report came back that the Japs were occupying the village.
>
> We considered the wisdom of attacking the village, in the hope of capturing food; but our better judgement prevailed, as we still had to consider our wounded and we didn't want to be encumbered with more . . .
>
> By this time the men were desperately exhausted and it was a cruel blow to them to be told to about-turn. A couple of providential incidents occurred that day; it seemed as if God was taking a hand in the matter. While we were waiting outside Nauro it suddenly occurred to me that a lot of the food which had been dropped by our planes would be scattered far and wide in the undergrowth around the village . . .
>
> I wandered off into the jungle in search of food. Something must have led me to the spot, for after a while I noticed that a branch of a tree had been broken off, as if by a fallen object, and so looking down I saw a bag-covered bundle. Almost tenderly I went down on my knees to tear away some of the bag. And lo and behold inside was a perfectly good tin of Arnott's Army biscuits. Some of the starving men were watching me, and it was as much as I could do to stop them from struggling to get a share. I managed to salvage some of the biscuits which were distributed amongst our wounded. In the meantime a flank guard patrol of B Coy had stumbled over a 25 lb tin of Crowe & Newcombe's dried apricots . . .

Doug Keane:

> Carrying those stretchers! That really taxed us to the limit. You'd just stand up and hold yourself with your stick against a tree and stand there till your head stopped spinning enough to go pick up the stretchers again![4]

Katekar:

> . . . the C.O. decided to leave D Coy to look after the stretcher cases and to push on unencumbered with the rest of the column with the idea of finding food and sending back sustenance to D Coy and the wounded. In this event the plan was for the main body to wait in that garden until D Company had carried them forward—then the stretchers would be left in the garden and the rest move back rapidly to Base for help.

Corporal Glen Williss:

> Absolute murder! Now I carried one every day. There were eight of us to a stretcher, and I being a corporal was in charge of it. And it was almost agony to get those fellas, particularly older members of the section to take their turn. It was the thought of getting nowhere that got at me. I mean, I was only a corporal, but I knew that while we were carrying them . . . I didn't want to just dump them and leave them, but I knew that while we had them we had no hope of getting out . . .[5]

Lieutenant-Colonel Cooper, CO, 2/27th Battalion:

> Now in this case the problem was this; the speed at which we were travelling with those wounded was so slow that we'd never get anywhere. The whole battalion would (a) be collapsing through lack of food; not just the wounded but the whole battalion, (b) we would never intercept the Japanese at the lower parts of the Trail or get into the Moresby area fast enough to be of any use to delay them. So really the question was, which

> was the greater method, keeping the battalion together, making it, getting it on to do its job, or having it just be dispersed and destroyed virtually through being bound down in the jungle looking after its wounded.
>
> When we felt we were a fair way from the Japanese and they were not following us beyond where we were going, we had to find a quiet place back in the jungle a bit, and put them in there with a few volunteers . . . who were prepared to look after them until we could get down to wherever we would end up and send men back to look after them.[6]

Thursday, 17 September, Katekar:

> Sgt. Raftery and a small party had been despatched with a message stating our circumstances and to move to Base with all haste. That party got through three days ahead of us and as a result search parties were sent out with food and native bearers, but unfortunately we missed them. The thing that played on our minds a lot these days was the deathly silence of the jungle; no firing could be heard and we didn't know how far the Japs had advanced.
>
> About midday that day we found succour in the shape of hundreds of yams and green paw-paw in a couple of native huts. We put out protective patrols and lit fires, cooking a stomach full of yams and roast paw-paw for each man. We sent back a message with a patrol of 3 men to Tom Gill O.C. D Coy, telling of our find, and after they had had their meal we despatched a party with food asking them to reach D Coy that night. The message carrying patrol was waylaid by a Jap patrol, and one of their men was killed. The food party also bore a message instructing D Coy to move the stretchers to this village, to leave them with attendants, and push on for base.

Saturday, 19 September, Edwards (D Company):

> Well about 8 a.m. we set off minus the encumbrance of stretchers and full of hope . . .

> At 11 a.m. we commenced climbing the long ridge and when we settled down at nearly dusk tonight we were still climbing but had made great progress though at the cost of absolutely tired out bodies. A highlight of our trudge was the rifling of a native garden which was lousy with sweet spuds.

Sunday, 20 September, Katekar:

> We struggled on that day across many steep waterfalls. In the afternoon we crawled on top of a high range . . . we heard what seemed to be a tractor or bulldozer working in the distance.

Edwards, one to two days behind Katekar and the main group:

> The climb continued this morning until we judged we had drawn level at least with Ioribaiwa though 'tis hard to judge. Our track then lay along the top of a ridge which narrowed to a mere foothold in parts and towards evening began to descend sharply in places and ascend in others—a muddy and rough track which nearly jarred us out of our senses.

Monday, 21 September, Katekar:

> . . . seemed endless, just plodding on wearily and seemingly getting nowhere . . .
>
> I felt very baffled and forlorn. I wondered if our troops were still at Itiki or even Moresby.

Edwards:

> One of the hardest days we have yet put in for the track led us down many hills, across creeks, up steep and rugged hills and tested our every muscle and every ounce of our endurance. We had no clue as to whether the track was leading us back to civilisation or not and again we find ourselves cheering each other up.

Tuesday, 22 September, Katekar:

> . . . we set out early and when our hopes seemed lowest, at about 1200 hrs a ray of hope beamed, for there at a point where 2 tracks met was a stick on which a piece of paper was fastened saying '92 this way'—that meant that Brigade HQ was along that track, somewhere. An hour later we got the thrill of our lives when we suddenly met a patrol of the 2/14th Bn . . .

Edwards, upon his arrival at the base area:

> We were only allowed 4 biscuits and jam for lunch plus a chocolate but it was a glorious taste. After lunch they supplied towels and soap and we all had a bath in the creek and I've never seen such a mob of wrecks in my life. I look so skinny that I frightened myself and my legs are in a shocking state with these sores.

These are the last paragraphs from both diaries.
Edwards:

> I can't possibly describe the hopes and fears, achievements, and disappointments, the sheer determination and will to survive which was all that kept us going during some of the harder stages. The longing for food was such that one would dream about it at night . . .
>
> Each night I used to think of the mob at home and pray for them and myself, how I used to long for the old home comforts. And now we're safe—a feeling of security pervades my veins and I'm truly happy, thoroughly relaxed but above all, thankful to my Maker for His care.

Katekar:

> Search parties, natives and food were sent out to bring in the wounded. In the meantime D Coy had left them in the garden with food and with Cpl (corporal] Johnny Burns and a small party to attend to them. No words of mine will ever be able to express the wonderful, unselfish, the tender way in which Johnny and Alf [Zanker] looked after those suffering men . . .

Kokoda Trail—2/27th Battalion

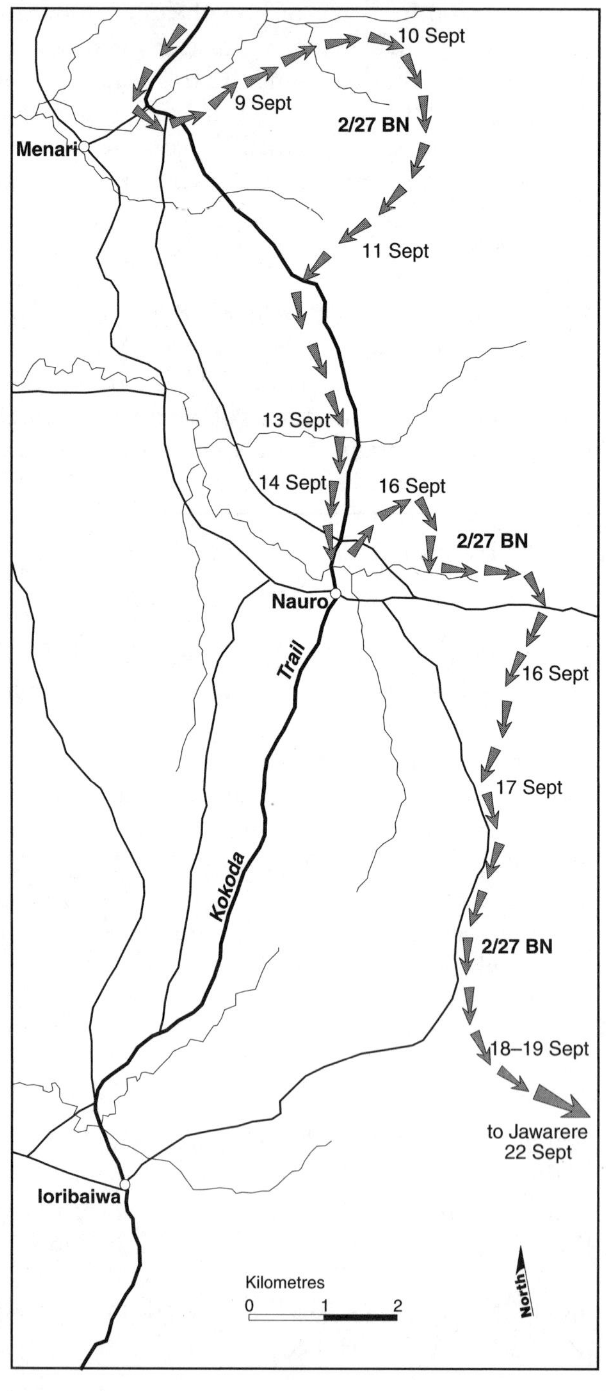

While Cooper and his main body were making their way back, Burns and Zanker had volunteered to stay behind with the wounded. Burns would later write a report of that experience.

> 0810 hours on September 19th, 1942, found Private Zanker and myself in charge of the wounded, seven stretchers and nine walking cases, our sole supplies being ten shell dressings, bottle of morphia and syringe and a garden of yams. The garden was several miles east of Nauro and right on the northern bank of Nauro Creek. When D Company moved off Zanker and I set to and built shelters to help protect the lads from the terrific heat and rain which was to come later in the day. At approx. 1000 hours an American bomber appeared overhead and circled several times. I tried hard to attract his attention but he made off . . .
>
> It was a great disappointment to us all but our prayers and thoughts went to better luck on the morrow. We experienced very heavy rains all afternoon and by the time it ceased at 1700 hours we were all looking like half-drowned rats. At 1800 hours I lit a small fire and boiled enough yams for us all. We then baked enough on the coals to last us the following day.
>
> Sunday arrived after a night which seemed more like an eternity. The lads had a very bad night. Zanker and I spent no more than 2 hours on a bunk . . . We gave the wounded a spongeover during the morning; it was the first they had had since they were wounded some thirteen days previously and it brightened them up no end. We tried hard to erect a more substantial shelter for them but when the rains came in the afternoon a party of drowned rats would have been a more apt title than human beings. A party of bush natives visited us during the afternoon and I tried to get them to bring some food, but I'm afraid my 'pidgin' was bad . . . They departed very hurriedly when Nippon fired a rifle on the other side of the creek.
>
> Monday arrived after a terrifically cold night. The boys were very restless all night, especially Corporal Williams, and I sat with him for the best part of the night.

The heat and flies were so bad that they nearly drove us to the first stages of insanity . . . The lads all received a wash and shave this morning, my shaving gear, fresh water and toothbrush serving everyone. Corporal Williams and Private Bourke felt the going very hard from this stage on. We had to be with them day and night . . .

Corporal Arthur brought his New Testament to light during the afternoon and it used to help fill in many of our long, hungry hours. At 1510 a mortar landed very close to our place of abode and it gave the lads a terrible fright. We did our best to cheer them up but a couple of them appeared to lose all nerve . . .

The 22nd finds our Air Force over us again at dawn and bombed and strafed right opposite us on the southern side of the creek . . . The flies were around in millions again by lunch time, or should I say midday, and several of the lads' wounds were badly blown [fly blown] at this stage . . . Heavy rains during the afternoon spoilt all our wood for the evening fire and we could only boil a very limited quantity.

Wednesday 23rd was one of our hardest days. The sun was fiercer than ever and it took a lot out of the lads. Corporal Williams spent a terrible night and when Zanker and I had washed the lads we decided to put him on a new stretcher and put the first fresh dressings on his wound . . . both Zanker and I had a couple of black-outs during it. We had now used two of our last three dressings so felt none too happy. About 10 o'clock a bush native came to us with a bunch of vegetable bananas and we managed to rake up 1/7d. for him. In the evening we duly boiled them and enjoyed a tasty few mouthfuls. The lads had run out of smokes too, and I collected a few likely-looking leaves but I'm afraid they weren't quite the right type. Diarrhoea broke out . . . during the day and we were lifting the poor lads for the next 24 hours with no respite.

After spending most of the night on the go, Friday dawned with a blazing hot sun and millions of flies. Again I spent the night with Corporal Williams and at 0800 hours he had a drink and at 0810 hours we found him dead. We immediately dug a grave approx. 3 ft. deep by the means of a tin hat and machete. It was a hard hour's work. At 0930 we buried him with just a little prayer. The event cast a gloom over the whole of the party . . .

The 25th arrived and only after what seemed to be the longest and hardest night of my life. Zanker and I managed about two hours' sleep during the night, but the poor lads on the stretchers couldn't get off. Private Burke of the 16th Battalion [2/16th] had taken a definite step towards the end at this stage and he lapsed into semi-consciousness. He was in a bad way. There was nothing we could do for him except a dose of morphia to put him out of agony every now and then. It took Zanker and I all our time to hold him on his stretcher when he started throwing himself around . . .

After a night when no one slept again, Saturday arrived. Zanker and I were run off our feet during the night; the boys had re-developed diarrhoea and we would no sooner lift one lad back than the next man would call for us . . .

Burke also was gradually getting worse; he was going through a living hell; this was his second day of unconsciousness. A native from a nearby tribe visited us during the afternoon and I asked him if he knew his way to Itiki and he said 'yes' so I told him to come back the following morning and I would send the strongest of the walking cases. They had to take the chance which-ever course they undertook—stay . . . or break for safety—and it means less movement around the stretchers, so I sent them off . . .

On the 27th the native guide arrived at approx. 0800 hours and I saw the lads off on their way to what we prayed would be safety. Corporal A.G. Riches, Private C. Tee, Private Ashby and Private Corfield comprised the party. We gave the native 10/– for his trouble.

Private Burke kept Private Zanker and me busy all night and Private Martlew was also weakening. We boiled a little water and gave Burke a spongeover, put my spare shirt on him and put him in a new stretcher. We then gave him a needle and he slept in peace—a real blessing for everyone . . .

The 28th, and we were a sad party once more; our pal Private Burke passed away at midnight and at dawn Zanker and I dug a grave with our only implements—the tin hat and machete. We buried him beside Corporal Williams. We then washed and shaved the lads and made them as comfortable as possible. The flies were at us in a big way again. The native boy who took our boys off on their return arrived back during the morning and brought seven sticks of trade tobacco; it was like a Xmas dinner for the boys; the only smoke I had seen in days appeared.

Tuesday the 29th finds the planes bombing and strafing just opposite us down the river; they were trying to get something as they returned again about 11 o'clock. We kept ourselves well out of sight. About 1400 hours a native policeman arrived and I asked him would he try and obtain some food and dressings from the nearest outpost and he said he would, and off he went. The boys' spirits were falling flat at this stage and Zanker and I found it more difficult to instil any confidence into them. We read the New Testament as much as possible and had general discussions on different subjects to try and keep their minds occupied. The strain was beginning to tell on us, too; we were becoming very weary.

The 30th September finds the boys' morale and spirits very low. We shaved and sponged the lads again but the smell was getting too strong to stay beside them for long. If only we could have had some dressings for them. There was no sign of our policeman friend but one of his tribe visited us and said he had gone to find out for us . . . Private Martlew took a turn for the worse and we had to watch him very closely . . . The yam stock was beginning to run low and we were praying for help more than ever.

Thursday morning the police boy turned up with three tins of Army rations. He told us the Japs had taken all the food from the camp. He also told us that two policemen and 25 bearers would arrive at ten the following morning to take us away. I thought he had

> rounded up a party for us. After the policeman's departure I occupied their time by giving a talk on the finer points of baking [Burns was a baker by trade] and then we had a discussion on the merits of the different books of the New Testament. It helped to pass away the long hours. At 1600 hours Zanker and I cut up enough yams for we stronger lads and flavoured it with a little M. & V. ration. For the weaker boys I made some M. & V. broth . . .
>
> It usually took us an hour for all the lads to have a meal; five of them had to be fed by us as they couldn't move, but this meal took me almost two hours.
>
> Friday, 2nd October . . . Our first job at dawn was to go down and fill the bottles and then give all those who could eat them a roasted yam for breakfast. At 0950 Zanker and I were making a new stretcher for Private Martlew when in ran our police friend and he was most excited. At first I thought he meant the Japs were coming and I ordered those men who could walk to hide in the thick undergrowth nearby while Zanker and I stood by the stretchers. Soon afterwards I saw a line of troops moving across the garden, but couldn't identify them until I recognised Sergeant Ray Koehne and Captain Joe Cuming and I knew all was well [both 2/27th Battalion] . . .
>
> The doctor, Captain R.S. Wilkinson of the 2/4th Field Ambulance, immediately set to and gave attention to the lads whilst Sergeant Koehne boiled a billy of beef tea; the tin of bully we had been longing for was still denied us—the Doc. wouldn't play.
>
> At 1230 hours [Friday 2 October] the first stretcher moved off and we were on our long trek to safety. It wasn't until 1730 hours that the first halt was called. We had covered a lot of ground . . .

It would be no small march and carry for this party. On 4 October, the third day of the return journey, Doctor Wilkinson decided to stop and rest and wait for Corporal McGregor's condition to stabilise before completing his journey to hospital. The last part of Burns' report:

> After a good meal on the 7th day we were away at 0600 hours. It was raining, but everyone forgot all about the rain; the hospital was all they were thinking of . . .
>
> At 1700 hours I handed over the wounded to Captain Ryan of the 2/4th Field Ambulance and they were given a hot bath and a pair of pyjamas, then put on the ambulance to the hospital.
>
> When the party with Corporal McGregor, who unfortunately died 3 days later, arrived in on the evening of the 9th it brought to a close a chapter of hardships . . . No tribute can be paid which is too high for those native bearers, for without them it would have been impossible to have reached safety in time to save the lives of two of our men. As for their master, W.O. II Ron Preece, M.M. of NGF., his name will be a byword with the boys of the stretchers for a long time.[7]

For their sterling efforts in the care of the wounded, Corporal John Burns was awarded a Military Medal and Private Alf Zanker was mentioned in dispatches.

Potts to his wife:

> . . . I've just heard that Cooper and most of his crowd are 'in' and I'll see them tomorrow . . . Porter [Brigadier Porter, who had relieved Potts] is finished looking after odds and ends and comes down tomorrow and that lets me get back to start reorganising my toughs. They are feeling so damned sure of themselves that once they put on a bit of meat again they'll take quite a bit of restraining . . .
>
> Charlie Booker [Potts' batman] is in hospital with dysentery and I was jolly lucky to get off with twelve days, though as I say it was probably more a case of change of diet and a spot of worry chucked in. The last has gone thanks to a first class team.

> It looks as if Key is gone. Oh hell. And he did such a good job and made his Battalion into a fighting Battalion for all time. Makes me want to howl like a kid . . .
>
> I hope too that Albert [Caro, CO 2/16th] and his lads get back to a rest tomorrow and then I know where to lay my hands on the lot . . .
>
> Just slipping off to contact Cooper and then I hope to rejoin my family.[8]

Brigadier Arnold Potts and his 'family' were about to experience the shock of their lives.

I'LL FRY HIS SOUL . . .

12

When Potts handed over his command to Brigadier Porter on 10 September 1942 near Nauro, the Australians were almost at that critical point of time and place where they could halt the Japanese and then turn them back.

Report Into Operations, 21 Brigade—Owen Stanley Campaign:

> At this stage it was decided to combine 2/14th and 2/16th Bn into one bn. under Lt-Col. Caro. The strengths were approx 100 and 200 respectively. The disposns. at nightfall were, 2/14th Bn. elements holding F.D.L.'s [Forward Defended Localities], Bde HQ and two coys. 3rd [Militia] Bn approx. 3/4 hr along the track towards Ioribaiwa. The plan was to hold this position for as long as possible to allow 25th Bde which was moving up to commence offensive ops. from a suitable jumping off place. In view of the incidents 8/9 Sept. Bde Comd decided it would be impossible to counter-attack along the track in the event of the Jap. getting behind 2/14th, 2/16th Bn posn. He therefore decided to withdraw to the high ground at Ioribaiwa which offered far more tactical possibilities.[1]

The first thing Porter did when he assumed command of Maroubra Force, therefore, was to withdraw. His orders were to firstly stabilise the situation and then gain what ground he could. It is easy to give orders, but often much harder to carry them out. Porter withdrew because he quite simply had to.

The ground he occupied was nothing more than a short-term delaying position. No commander worth his training and rank and responsibility would attempt to hold an untenable locality. Porter knew that the high ground at Ioribaiwa offered him a decent defensive position so he withdrew to it. Further, his force consisted of the debilitated and grossly under strength composite 2/14–2/16th 'Battalion', and the 3rd Militia Battalion. In short, until a suitable defensive position could be occupied at Ioribaiwa, and the three fresh battalions of the 7th Division's 25th Brigade could concentrate there, Horii still retained the initiative. All this is but standard military strategy—and the very same strategy that Potts had applied with tremendous acumen from Isurava to Menari.

Therefore to order Porter to stabilise the situation was one thing, to order him to gain as much ground as possible was quite simply a ludicrous notion.

By the early morning of 11 September, the 2/14th elements held the rearguard post while the 2/16th had passed through the 3rd Battalion and had set up ambush positions in considerable depth on a ridge approximately 45 minutes march north of Ioribaiwa. What then transpired is ample testimony to the 21st Brigade's still considerable fighting qualities:

> The withdrawal was carried out successfully, 2/16th moved back leaving C Coy and A Coy in extricating posns. about 20 mins and an hour respectively along the track. Remainder of Bn. passed through 3rd Bn which was in posn. further back and took up another extricating posn. to cover the withdrawal of the 3rd Bn. 2/14th Bn elements moved back direct to the slope fwd. of Ioribaiwa . . . Immediately on their heels a strong Jap patrol coming from the Eastern Flank behind the posn which had been occupied ran up against C Coy 2/16th posn. and were shot up severely, and they lost 22 casualties. Without further incident the rest were leapfrogged back to the Ioribaiwa posn. leaving an ambush party of 2/16th Bn right on the crossing. This party late in the afternoon sighted a large party of the enemy on the other side of the creek moving down to the water's edge. The ambush party withheld their fire

> until the Japs were grouped at the Xing, then opened fire and killed approximately 25, wounded others, then withdrawing into the Bde. posn. At 1845 a further Jap patrol of 5 working up the track were also killed by a small ambush party fwd. of our F.D.L.'s. Further Jap activity for the night was limited to a noisy patrol which worked up on the right flank of the spur calling on our men in good English to withdraw. The attempt met with no response, and the Japs themselves withdrew.[2]

On 12 September, the Composite 2/14th and 2/16th Battalion and the 3rd Battalion positions were sited on the spur just north of Ioribaiwa, pending the arrival of the 25th Brigade. During 12–13 September the Japanese concentrated repeated mortar, mountain gun and machine-gun fire on the Composite Battalion positions, while also probing their defences with patrols. While booby traps were used with telling effect against those patrols, the Japanese in turn inflicted tragic and ever-mounting losses on the 21st Brigade, particularly with their quick-firing mountain gun.

But still the enemy could make little ground and he was made to pay a heavy penalty for every yard. His attempt to cross the creek in front of the Composite Battalion position was met with a savage wall of fire and short, sharp counter-attacks blunted his attempts to pierce the Australian lines. The exhausted defenders lost eleven men killed and 29 wounded in their last actions near Ioribaiwa. The 2/14th Battalion history:

> This evening in the twilight I buried two Headquarter Company chaps. A very sad business, as they had been terribly knocked. A shell had caught them in their slit trench. One of the chaps lending a hand fainted for a moment or two at the graveside. No one said a word—we just helped him to his feet. I noticed tears in the eyes of quite a few of the troops.[3]

If ever New Guinea Force Headquarters or for that matter General HQ South West Pacific Area had required some strong evidence as to the superb efforts of Potts and

Maroubra Force, then that evidence was immediately forthcoming with the initial deployment of Brigadier Eather's 25th Brigade at Ioribaiwa. It should be emphasised that Eather was in a position to commit all three of his battalions—his complete brigade—to the battle at the one time and, further, he had the additional force of the 3rd Battalion at his disposal, and the Composite Battalion. And his line of communication and supply was very short in relation to that of his adversaries, whereas Potts had begun his campaign at far-distant Isurava, and had been forced to commit his troops company upon company upon their immediate arrival while suffering under an appalling supply debacle in the process. And, critically, Eather could not have encountered Japanese in anything like the physical condition that they must have been in at and after Isurava, for that bloodied and costly advance had been contested to the point where the Japanese timetable had been shattered.

Eather's plan envisaged a right flank movement by his 2/33rd Battalion through the 3rd Battalion; a thrust through the Composite Battalion positions northward along the main track by his 2/25th Battalion, and a left flank thrust by his 2/31st Battalion. Two events brought him unstuck. The first was the fact that his 2/31st Battalion became disoriented and briefly lost in that extremely tough terrain while attempting to outflank and then encircle the enemy positions. The second problem occurred when the inexperienced 3rd Battalion was routed from one of its positions on the eastern high ground, when a strong Japanese patrol engaged it while it was digging defensive positions, and it was out of reach of its weapons and with less than fully alert sentries.

Eather's offensive suddenly became a worrying instability of control of the Ioribaiwa feature. Despite counterattacks he could not evict the Japanese, who had dug in on the high ground between the 3rd Battalion and the 2/31st. It is basically from this point on that the controversy of the Kokoda campaign begins. The first issue concerns the withdrawal of Eather's force back to Imita Ridge.

Eather to Allen, 16 September 1942: 'Enemy feeling whole front and flanks. Do not consider can hold him here. Request permission to withdraw to Imita Ridge if necessary.

Porter concurs.'[4] Although the request was granted, Rowell sent Allen a firm order: 'Stress the fact that however many troops the enemy has, they must all have walked from Buna. We are now so far back that any further withdrawal is out of [the] question and Eather must fight it out at all costs. I am playing for time until 16 Infantry Brigade arrives.'[5] Eather moved his force back to Imita Ridge and had completed the deployment of his force by 11.00 a.m. on 17 September. This action was a sound military decision, and Eather was merely placing himself into a position where he could create a reserve and then push out strong fighting patrols and begin the task of wresting the initiative from Horii.

By 12 September, the 14th Field Regiment had manhandled two 25-pounder artillery pieces through the mud to the high ground between Illolo and Uberi. The belated entry of Australian artillery into the Kokoda campaign was in fact an anti-climax.

In order to wrest a degree of the initiative from the Japanese, the American Navy had embarked upon an ambitious invasion of the Solomon Islands on 7 August 1942. Using their crack marine troops under the command of Lieutenant-General Vandergrift, the Americans effected a crucial landing at Guadalcanal Island. This battle involved a see-sawing, grim and protracted fight which consumed a critical number of Japanese troops and placed a telling drain upon their supply capability. With Guadalcanal in the balance and the failure of their invading force at our soon to be visited battle at Milne Bay and, conscious of MacArthur's potential to stage a seaward landing somewhere along that northern beachhead, the Japanese ordered Horii to stage a fighting withdrawal back over the Kokoda Trail to his Gona–Sananada–Buna beachhead.

But the Japanese had not abandoned their desire to capture Port Moresby. By landing a limited number of fresh troops at the beachhead and by concentrating Horii's force at that venue, it was anticipated that, in the event of a victory against the Americans at Guadalcanal, a fresh assault on Port Moresby might be achieved.

Strategic considerations aside, the Japanese force that swarmed over the Ioribaiwa feature had run its race. Captured diaries demonstrate the point: 'We gave some dry bread to the

Engineer Tai at the foot of the hill. They had not eaten anything for two days, and said it was delicious.'[6] The breakdown in the Japanese line of communication had become so serious that orders were issued to commanders to crack down on troops in the rear rifling the limited supplies coming forward to the combat troops.[7] The official Japanese ration around 20 September 1942 was two *go* of rice per day for troops 'engaged in great physical exertion',[8] and 1.5 *go* a day for 'others generally'.[9] One and a half *go* of rice is about 500 grams in its boiled or cooked state. In other words, by the time the Japanese had arrived at Imita Ridge the private soldier was consuming about four tablespoons of cooked rice twice daily—if his comrades hadn't pilfered a portion of his forward travelling ration on the way. In terms of calories, he was consuming about 550 calories a day—if he was lucky. Further, continuing bouts of dysentery were working against the benefit of his 'meal'.

The fact that the Japanese were soon to engage in cannibalism is further proof that Maroubra Force's fighting withdrawal had accomplished precisely what Potts had planned.

The Japanese war correspondent Seizo Okada reported the impact of the order to withdraw upon the forward commanders and their troops:

> On a thin straw mat in the tent the elderly commander [Horii] was sitting solemnly upright on his heels, his face emaciated, his grey hair reflecting the dim light of a candle that stood on the inner lid of a ration can. Lieut-Colonel Tanaka, his staff officer, sat face to face with him also on a mat. Two lonely shadows were cast on the dirty wet canvas . . . The staff officer was silent, watching the burning wick of the candle as though to avoid the commander's eyes, when a rustling sound was heard in the thicket outside and the signal squad commander came in with another wireless message. It was an order from the Area Army Commander at Rabaul instructing the Horii detachment to withdraw completely from the Owen Stanleys and concentrate on the coast at Buna. This message was immediately

> followed by a similar order that came from the Imperial Headquarters in Tokyo. It was now beyond doubt that the order had been authorised by the Emperor himself. His Majesty's order had to be obeyed. It is true there was a strong body of opinion among the hot-blooded battalion commanders advocating a desperate single-handed thrust into Port Moresby. But Staff-Officer Tanaka remained cool, and reasoned with them saying that it was a suicidal action even if everything went well except the supply of food, which was in a hopeless condition.
>
> The night was far advanced. It had begun to drizzle, softly. The headquarters was in confusion sending out messages to the front positions instructing them to make preparations for immediate withdrawal . . . The order to retreat had crushed the spirit of the troops which had been kept up through sheer pride. For a time the soldiers remained stupefied among the rocks on the mountain side. Then they began to move, and once in retreat they fled for dear life. None of them had ever thought that a Japanese soldier would turn his back on the enemy. But they were actually beating a retreat! There was no denying that. As soon as they realised the truth, they were seized with an instinctive desire to live. Neither history nor education had any meaning to them now. Discipline was completely forgotten. Each tried for his life to flee faster than his comrades.[10]

After having been in reserve since 16 September near Uberi, where they had resumed their separate identities, the 2/14th and 2/16th Battalions were relieved by the 14th Brigade's 36th Battalion on the 26th and then moved to Koitaki. Their ordeal was finally over. David Horner:

> Brigadier John Rogers, Blamey's Director of Military Intelligence, was in Moresby at this time and saw some of the troops coming back from the fighting. Rogers and the Americans, who had heard tales of the Anzacs and their fine record in Syria, were dismayed at what they saw. 'Never in my life', said Rogers, 'in the worst

> part of Gallipoli, or anywhere, had I seen soldiers who looked so shocked and so tired and utterly weary as those men'.[11]

Blamey had planned to visit Port Moresby before the politicians panicked. But as a result of the Advisory War Council's concerns during a meeting on 9 September, his visit was put forward. Before leaving by air for Port Moresby on 12 September, Blamey had sent the Minister for the Army, Frank Forde, a letter reassuring him of the situation on the Kokoda Trail.

Blamey arrived at Port Moresby from Brisbane on 12 September. It will be recalled that at this time Maroubra Force had withdrawn to Ioribaiwa but that Eather's 25th Brigade was set to begin operations near that village the following day. Blamey and Rowell visited Allen at his HQ on the 13th and, according to Allen, 'all seemed pleased with the situation'.[12] By this time, Rowell had conferred with Potts after the latter's return to report to him; he knew that he now had four fresh battalions disposed on a short line of communication, and that the enemy was now critically extended from his far-distant base over the Owen Stanley Range. With this knowledge, he and Allen were able to thoroughly brief Blamey. It is little wonder then that 'all seemed pleased with the situation'.

At a press conference later that day, Blamey told reporters that Port Moresby was 'in no danger and I think we shall find that the Japs will be beaten by their own advance with its attendant problems of supply . . . It will be a Japanese advance to disaster, an Australian retreat to victory.'[13] Allen was not the only member of the gathering to record that the visit by Blamey had gone well, as during the course of a letter to his old friend Cyril Clowes, Rowell wrote that he had 'had a pleasant day with the little man'.[14]

Blamey arrived back in Brisbane on 14 September. The following day he delivered a national radio broadcast which again praised Rowell and his troops and 'was widely covered in the newspapers the next morning'.[15] But the real problems began when Blamey faced the Advisory War Council in Canberra on 17 September. Part of his report stated that:

> On the 17th of August the Japanese made a heavy air raid on Port Moresby and destroyed Allied land transport aircraft. This disorganised our forward supply arrangements, with the result that supplies could only be made available for 1500 men in the forward area.
>
> The 53rd Militia Battalion was infiltrated by the Japanese, and the 39th Militia Battalion was attacked. The Commander, 21st Brigade, A.I.F., was unable to deploy his Brigade to make a fight, as he had to extricate the Militia Battalions . . .
>
> The 25 A.I.F. Brigade, which recently arrived at Port Moresby, and the A.I.F. Pioneer Battalion were sent forward on the 15th September and deployed for an attack on the Japanese. The attack began yesterday, but no great progress has been made . . .
>
> Lieut-General Rowell, Major-General Allen and the troops are confident that the Japanese will not be able to take Port Moresby from the land. General Blamey shared their confidence. The Air Force has improved 100% and there are adequate landing grounds and sufficient aircraft, while Military Forces were there in sufficient strength to render the capture of Port Moresby a very difficult operation.[16]

It must have been a rather testy meeting. Former Prime Minister Billy Hughes, who was one of the United Australia Party representatives on the council, and John Beasley, one of the Labor Government members, were particularly aggressive—and ill-informed. Hughes asked Blamey why the Japanese were not having the same supply problems as the Australians. Blamey's reply was a touch shallow: that the enemy could carry seventeen days' supplies on one soldier. We have just identified the condition of the Japanese at Ioribaiwa and, therefore, the state of their supply line. Beasley questioned whether the Australians possessed any real plan for movement through the country where the fighting was taking place. Blamey strongly denied this.

Blamey should be given high praise for his conduct leading up to, and during, this meeting of the Advisory War Council. First, he had gone to Port Moresby, met his commanders, and satisfied himself as to the conduct of operations. Secondly, under the most intense political scrutiny of events in New Guinea, he had supported both his commanders and troops. His conduct and subsequent support of his Australian commanders was therefore commendable. The matter should have been closed. Fair and reasonable time should have now been given for the fresh troops on the Kokoda Trail to make an impact on the operation there. Such a show of confidence was not unwarranted, as the battle for Milne Bay had been won well before this time. The recent news had not, therefore, been all bad.

But these events, and Blamey's hard work, were worth little when MacArthur contacted Curtin the night of 17 September by 'secraphone' to inform him that despite the deployment of fresh Australian troops, there had been another withdrawal: Eather's withdrawal to Imita Ridge. MacArthur told Curtin that Blamey should go to New Guinea to 'energise the situation' and to 'meet his responsibility to the Australian public'.[17]

And whose responsibility and interests was MacArthur representing? His own. By suggesting to Curtin that Blamey return to Port Moresby, MacArthur could then assert, if Port Moresby were to fall, that he had told the Australian Prime Minister to order his Commander Allied Land Forces to take personal command. Any resulting scrutiny and possible blame would thus be Blamey's. During the conversation with Curtin, MacArthur was having a bet each way, by saying that 'the Australian command [Blamey] might be right'[18] but that he still had the gravest concern about the state of affairs.

Curtin had two choices—he could support his Australian commander or MacArthur. He chose MacArthur. It should also be noted that around this time, Curtin had been making disparaging remarks about Blamey in terms of his private conduct as well as the situation on the Kokoda Trail. In fairness, it must be stated that Blamey's personal behaviour was something well known throughout Australia from his far-distant time as Police Commissioner in Victoria and, for that matter, during his time in the Middle East. Such knowledge had not prevented Curtin promoting Blamey to Commander-in-Chief of the Australian Army upon his return from the Middle East.

For his part, Blamey now knew that his position was in jeopardy—if the tone of the Advisory War Council meeting of the 17th had not been proof enough, then the fact that the Prime Minister was ordering him *back* to Port Moresby only a few days after his return would have provided ample evidence.

But like MacArthur and Curtin, Blamey also had a clear choice: back Rowell or cover his own position. He chose the latter. However, there is evidence to suggest that Blamey was attempting to buy time for events in New Guinea to strengthen his stand, and thereby prove his appreciation correct. He received Curtin's order to fly to Port Moresby on either the 17th or 18th. He arrived in Brisbane on the 19th and did not arrive in Port Moresby until late on the 23rd. But the point is that if Blamey had supported Rowell, he would have gained two tremendous outcomes: a vindication of his judgment as a commander and, critically, high praise and respect and standing within his army for his loyalty. Like MacArthur and his Prime Minister, Blamey had much to gain but did not possess the moral strength nor complete loyalty to his subordinates to seize the moment. Blamey wrote to Rowell on 20 September:

> The powers that be have determined that I shall myself go to New Guinea for a while and operate from there. I do not, however, propose to transfer many of the Advanced HQ Staff . . . At present I propose to bring with me only my P.A. [personal assistant] Major Carlyon, two extra cipher officers and Lieut Lawson. I hope you will be able to house us in your camp and messes.
>
> I hope you will not be upset at this decision, and will not think that it implies any lack of confidence in yourself. I think it arises out of the fact that we have very inexperienced politicians who are inclined to panic on every possible occasion, and I think the relationship between us personally is such that we can make the arrangement work without any difficulty.[19]

The tone of Blamey's letter is conciliatory to say the least. But Rowell did not see either Blamey's letter or his visit in the same light. His attitude is best portrayed by a letter he sent to Clowes on the 22nd:

> The plain fact is that he [Blamey] hasn't enough moral courage to fight the Cabinet on an issue of confidence in me. Either I am fit to command this show or I am not. If the latter, then I should be pulled out. He comes here when the tide is on the turn and all is likely to be well. He can not influence the local situation in any way, but he will get the kudos and it will be said, rather pityingly, that he came here to hold my hand and bolster me up. Shades of Greece in April 41!![20]

Rowell saw Blamey's visit as a poor return for the service and loyalty he had given him and the indicated personal and professional flaws of his superior. In the Middle East the proud, austere, highly principled Rowell had noted the opposite behaviour in Blamey with regards to the latter's conduct; he had noted, with professional disdain, Blamey's inability to cope with the pressures of battle during the crisis in the Pinios Gorge during the Greek campaign; and he had further noted Blamey's reluctance to use Lavarack and an Australian Corps HQ in the early stages of the Syrian campaign because of what he perceived as nothing more than professional rivalry. Above all, he saw Blamey's behaviour during all this as merely self-serving and to the detriment of the Australian Army and its war effort. He believed he had carried Blamey before and would now be made to do so again. From Rowell's perspective therefore, Blamey's visit to Port Moresby is no isolated, annoying sojourn, but the despicable act of a man whom he loathed and felt was being totally disloyal to him.

The night of Blamey's arrival saw a frank and bitter discussion between the two men. Over the next few days the relationship soured further.

On 25 September Blamey flew to Milne Bay and ordered Major-General Clowes to deploy a battalion at Wanigela. Rowell saw this action as the final usurping of his authority.

Rowell: 'I fairly rose. I then got off my chest what I'd been storing up since April 1941. Told him he's already dumped me twice and was in the process of doing it a third time, as I hoped he would.'[21] The argument then centred around how the command structure would work. On 28 September Blamey's patience ran out. He informed Rowell that he had relieved him of his command and had written an adverse report to the Prime Minister. Rowell to Clowes later that day: '. . . I am sacked. So the fight is on and one of us will go down. I pray that I am successful and that this bad man and his rotten influences will be out of public life for ever. Like all crafty gangsters he got his blow in first, but I'm much happier that he felt he had to take action than that I had to ask to be relieved.'[22] Blamey wrote to Curtin on 1 October:

> I would like to say that the personal animus displayed towards me was most unexpected . . .
>
> In regard to his [Rowell's] . . . claim that I had failed to safeguard his interests in accepting the direction of yourself and the C-in-C S.W.P.A., I informed him perfectly frankly of the exact incidence of events which led me to come to New Guinea, and there appears to be no ground for any resentment or objections on his part. It seemed to me when I received your directions and those of the C-in-C S.W.P.A., that it behoved me to carry out those instructions, and there can be no doubt that when the consequent instructions were given to General Rowell, it was his duty to also carry them out without question, cheerfully and cooperatively. I endeavoured to induce him to see this point of view, but his resentment was too deep.
>
> I informed him that I did not propose to make any alteration in the method of command, and I would do nothing that would derogate from his authority. He asserted his intention of refusing to accept the situation and remain in New Guinea. I pointed out that such an attitude would be unacceptable to any Government and that it would certainly mean his retirement from the Forces . . . This was the substance of my interview with him on the day of my arrival on the 23rd September.[23]

Rowell's was the first head to roll during the Papuan campaign. Amongst all the animosity and controversy surrounding his dismissal, one point remains undeniable: on 28 September 1942, Australia—and Blamey—lost the services of a soldier whose record during the Second World War had been exemplary. Throughout the most extraordinary pressure in conducting the battles of the Kokoda Trail and Milne Bay (which we will examine shortly), he maintained a professional and competent conduct and was thoroughly loyal to his subordinates—Potts included, after Rowell had taken the trouble of listening to Wilmot and Potts himself. MacArthur, Curtin and Blamey could make no such claim.

When Blamey removed Rowell, he appointed Lieutenant-General Herring as his successor. David Horner in *Crisis of Command*: '. . . Blamey had chosen his man carefully and he knew that Herring would be completely loyal . . . this was to be his first operational command of a formation . . . he had never had to bear the responsibility of independent decisions, but for a while at least, Blamey would be at his shoulder to offer advice and encouragement.'[24]

Captain Ken Murdoch was Arnold Potts' new staff captain. On 9 October Murdoch was a solitary witness to one of the most extraordinary conversations of the Papuan campaign. Murdoch:

> Shortly after the 21st Brigade had reached Koitaki plantation area—even before the scattered parties of the 2/14th and 2/16th Battalions had made it to base, a parade was organised to allow an address to be given by Major-General 'Tubby' Allen, the then commander of 7th Australian Division. At this parade the G.O.C. gave the commander, the officers and men of the 21st Brigade, a personal message from the Prime Minister extending the nation's thanks to the brigade for 'saving Port Moresby and thus Australia'.

What a fillip this was for the troops—despite the difficulties and turmoil of the time the morale was high—it was tops, the veterans of the Middle-East had shown their worth under terrific odds and the Kokoda Trail must always be remembered with pride in the annals of their families.

Shortly after this episode and with little warning to the Brigade Headquarters, a visit by the Commander-In-Chief was announced. At the time I had just been appointed Staff Captain of the brigade . . .

The above is explained to create the atmosphere of the time. The Commander-In-Chief's arrival was heralded by the arrival some minutes before of his personal assistant and some aides including, if I recall correctly, some military police. Unbeknown to me at the time, the personal assistant issued instructions that the headquarters was to be vacated by all ranks except Brigadier Potts. At that time the Staff Captain's job was reasonably onerous with a reorganisation of the brigade and other problems, time was precious—I recall I kept working not having nominated my presence to any of the visitors—before I could move out the Commander-In-Chief was present in the adjacent room having been welcomed at the front door by Brigadier Potts. The C in C's first words were—'Is everybody out?' As the Brigade Commander was not aware of my presence, he answered in the affirmative. My position was delicate—I could not move and thus I became an unwilling eavesdropper. I was trapped. The conversation, with both officers standing, was completed in a matter of a few moments.

I am of the belief and remain to this day that Brigadier Potts thought the C in C was visiting to extend congratulations to him for the efforts of the brigade. His first remark of substance after greeting was to the effect that the men were wonderful—there was no doubt that their spirit and showing would bolster up the morale of the whole of Australia. The C in C replied that he was on other business—he pointed out that the Prime Minister and War Cabinet had instructed him to say that failures like the Kokoda Trail (it was the Owen Stanley's

Campaign then) could not be tolerated—the men had shown that something was lacking—the C in C blamed the leaders—he further stated that he was relieving Potts forthwith. Naturally Brig. Potts expostulated—he said that if any blame was attachable to anybody then it was to him and him alone. The battalion commanders were not at fault—the officers and men were exceptional as had been shown.

The C in C was adamant and said that Potts was to leave the brigade forthwith and move to Darwin—a plane would be made available. Potts asked could he stay to meet his successor—this request was denied—the C in C said Potts was to hold himself available for immediate movement. Brigadier Potts did not have time for further remarks, the C in C departed abruptly—in fact, the Brigadier did not accompany him past the front door.

On the return of the Brigadier to the main room I made my presence known. The Brigadier expressed his personal feelings, but, ever the soldier, he said he accepted the position. As his movement was pending he said he would see the Battalion Commanders and the Brigade Major but other than that he would leave quietly, without any farewell parade or review. He asked that an order of the day be prepared for his signature—to thank the troops and to ensure that they continued their loyalty and support to his successor.

From memory, the time of the visit was approaching noon. The word spread rapidly throughout the brigade—many questions were asked—then came the resignations—most of the brigade staff paraded to 'Pottsy' and requested that they go with him—officers of the units tended their resignations in writing—almost certainly overlooking the fact that in war the gesture was meaningless. Within hours, as staff captain, I received resignations from a large number of the unit officers—I advised the brigadier and also made a request to go with him. He was very overcome by the loyalty of his officers but insisted that no resignation be handed to him—I was to tell all officers that the papers were not acceptable—as many had said at the time of

> handing in their resignations—'they had volunteered in—they were now volunteering out'.
>
> The morale of the brigade hit a very low level and remained that way for some time. From memory again (much water having passed under the bridge) Brownie, Pottsy's batman accompanied him on the move. He, like Brigadier Potts and the C in C have now gone to their higher reward.
>
> I need swear no affidavits to the above, none can deny what I have said, none can confirm my recollections of the day. I state simply that they are correct . . .[25]

As late as 1957 Herring would make a pathetic attempt to justify the fact that it was he who had pressed for Potts' dismissal with Blamey: 'Neither of us [Herring and Blamey] was looking for anyone's head on a charger. But we wanted to make 21 Bde as efficient as possible, we had a war and a very tough war to win, and it was our job to call in the best man we could. It would have been wrong for us to allow ourselves to be influenced by Potts' feelings.'[26] This outrageous statement deserves the closest scrutiny. The 21st Brigade's performance in Syria was first class. We have recorded the fact that Blamey erected a monument to its performance and that of its 7th Division at Dog River; its brigadier during the Syrian campaign, Brigadier Jack Stephens, had been promoted to major-general for his leadership of that brigade in Syria; Potts had been awarded a DSO for his performance and promoted *twice* to the final position of brigadier of that formation; and, finally, we have recorded the extraordinary performance of Potts and his 21st Brigade during the Owen Stanley campaign. And where was Herring during this campaign?—in Darwin and later Queensland! As for calling on 'the best man we could', Brigadier Ivan Dougherty had been in Darwin, which hardly bore any resemblance to the conditions found on the Kokoda Trail. Herring's action at the time, and his jaundiced view in hindsight, amounts to little more than a denial of natural justice and an assessment that he was in no position to fairly make.

It is staggering to contemplate that an Australian brigade commander could be thrust into a campaign with such a damning inadequacy of military intelligence, support and equipment and yet fight a near flawless fighting withdrawal where the military and political stakes were so terribly important and that he could then be relived from his command as a reward. Brigadier Arnold Potts is quite simply an Australian hero. His performance will be recorded as one of the most critical triumphs in Australian military history and one that an apathetic nation has still to honour.

Denied the right to address his soldiers personally, Potts left them an emotional farewell, the content of which is reminiscent of the soldier, the man, and the magnificent troops he was privileged to command:

> Special Message To Officers, N.C.O.'s and men.
>
> HQ 21st Aust. Inf. Bde.
>
> 23rd Oct. 42.
>
> On relinquishing my command of the 21st Bde, it is impossible to express my feelings adequately to all its members.
>
> Though in comd of you for only six months, my association has been for the full period of service of the Bde. It has so grown to be part of my life, that even when not facing you or speaking directly to you, the task of saying goodbye is the hardest job in my life and one I funk badly.
>
> This much I can say—that I regard this Bde. as the best fighting formation in the A.I.F. and second to none in this war or the last. Your new comd. will be proud of it. Its discipline and tone is obviously high and that is not meant as praise—it is as it should be.
>
> Be loyal to all the ideals we have built up around this Bde. of three hard-hitting, hard-marching and hard-living Bns, and nothing in your lives will give you so much pleasure as belonging to it or so much pain as leaving it.
>
> Thanking you for your loyalty and cooperation; you are a great team and I'm proud that I was one of you. Thanking you and goodbye.
>
> A.W. Potts[27]

Perhaps one of the real tests of a fighting commander is the attitude of his soldiers, especially if they are veterans who are hard-nosed enough and experienced enough to know their man and what is required of him. A sample of his officers—Lieutenant-Colonel Geoff Cooper, CO 2/27th Battalion:

> Arnold had an inferior force which he handled splendidly. He kept a fighting force going which was deteriorating with sickness, injuries, was split up, grossly overworked physically and with everybody in it half-blind with intense fatigue. I don't know of anybody who could have done any better.[28]

Captain Stan Bisset, 2/14th Battalion:

> A leader, a man to be admired and respected, always mindful of the welfare of the troops under his command; courageous and could not be faulted in any way for his leadership in the Owen Stanleys.[29]

Lieutenant-Colonel Ralph Honner, CO 39th Battalion:

> Admiration for Potts went beyond his own brigade. I served under some distinguished brigade commanders; Morshead, Robertson, Savige, Vasey, Porter, Eather, Dougherty—under six of those in action. But to follow and to fight beside in a hazardous campaign, I could not have preferred any of them to Arnold Potts. He had a magical, yet natural, charisma of leadership that inspired confidence and loyalty and devotion. To me, he was the Bayard of them all—'sans peur et sans reproche [without fear and without reproach].'[30]

A sample of his soldiers—Sergeant John Burns, 2/27th Battalion:

> Brigadier Potts was held in the highest esteem by every man in the brigade. He was every inch an infantry soldier. Of great personal courage, his only thoughts

> were for the care of his men whose personal problems and outlook he personally understood. The battalion held him in great affection and said goodbye to him with a heavy heart.[31]

Sergeant, later Captain, Bob Thompson, 2/14th Battalion:

> Excellent—loved by all the men. Even when men were on the point of exhaustion, the call 'Pottsy ahead!' made men straighten up.[32]

It was a perfect night last night. You'd flown from Popondetta across the Owen Stanley Range, and landed relieved but contented with your completed trek over the Kokoda Trail. A magnificent meal at the Port Moresby Yacht Club followed in what seemed almost colonial surroundings.

As you lie on your bed next morning, the stick in the corner is a lasting memory of the exertion, the pilgrimage and the history. But Frank Taylor has one more moving experience before tomorrow and your flight to Cairns. You're up early and once again in the back of the ute.

When you stand on the open ground here, it is not hard after all the interviews and letters and questionnaires to reconstruct the scene and the history of this place. The old 1942 narrow bridge is there. The open ground is now used to graze a few cattle and is interspersed with a few fruit trees. A thin windbreak of rubber trees is a lonely reminder of the grandeur of this place in its heyday.

David Lewis in his *The Plantation Dream* has given us an insight into Koitaki before the war, and its manager, Tom Sefton:

> Ausa Songoro . . . worked for Tom Sefton of Koitaki as a boss-boy before 1942 . . . he remembered Sefton as a 'strong' or hard man . . . 'Mister' Sefton valued good workers and rewarded them. He was harsh with those who were lazy or rough with the rubber trees. He ensured that Koitaki labourers were well fed and when they were sick he visited them each afternoon. He kept

> two 'shooting boys' constantly out in the bush after game to provide variety and interest in the plantation diet . . .
>
> Indeed Sefton came to epitomise the more successful Papuan planter. In 1935 he had a cricket ground with a concrete pitch made at Koitaki where 'all hands, European and Papuan, practice together . . . on Saturday and Sunday and play matches against neighbouring plantations'.[33]

And not unlike the Kokoda Trail, there was a Seventh-Day Adventist presence in this area. The prewar church plantation was just up the road.[34]

When Potts and his 21st Brigade camped in this Itiki–Koitaki area and prepared themselves for their momentous march into Australian history, you can easily picture the sense of urgency, the equipment being measured and haversack contents packed. The stone grinding wheel is busily employed, as one man gently tips water over the stone and others take their turn winding the handle or applying their bayonet to the stone for an edge that will have to substitute for a machete on the trail.[35]

That last church parade was intensely moving. We can see the 2/14th church service—there is drizzling rain and darkness punctuated by a thin veil of light from the odd hurricane lamp as groups gather into their denominations.[36] They are all so typical of soldiers before battle: quiet, reflective and, thankfully, unaware of the trauma that lies ahead. And they are bronzed and hardened and supremely confident after their service in Syria and their training in Queensland. They cut imposing physical images.

Your mind now turns to the aftermath of battle. Some of these same men return to Koitaki, utterly exhausted and their ranks tragically reduced. The ordeal is at last over. Gone are the cold, wet sleepless nights; the soul-destroying, mud-ridden climbs and the steep, slippery descents; the monotonous and meagre diet; the filthy stinking clothes; and, above all, gone is the seemingly endless slaughter of their comrades. And, at last, gone is the sight of their wounded mates, literally dragging themselves and sometimes each other for days on end along the trail rather than deprive someone worse off of a stretcher. These blokes defy the term 'walking wounded'.

This place is not Tel Aviv: no bars, cafes and tourist spots and various other pursuits, but there are long-denied, more simple pleasures. You can see these soldiers having a thorough, unhurried wash, changing clothes, and savouring the jam, biscuits, butter, a bit of chocolate and a letter from home and the joy of sending one back. But it's the chance to sleep that is the initial joy, hours of uninterrupted sleep. All this is heaven—unless you cop another dose of dysentery.

You will end up at 'lightning ridge' if you're a hard case. The stench is bloody terrible. They will want a sample every morning here, and then they'll work out your 'diet'. If you're a hard case it's arrowroot and beef tea and then, with luck, arrowroot, beef tea and your familiar dog biscuits. And when you really start to pick up it's the usual 'bully' or perhaps a bit of meat and veg and tea.[37]

Mister Sefton's Koitaki Plantation sportsfield is the logical place for a parade. Many of the sick and wounded are back here now and the order comes to fall in—the Commander-in-Chief is coming. The expanse of adjacent tents is a hive of activity. The veterans of Kokoda are no mere collection of raw recruits, but a proud formation who have distinguished themselves. They are convinced that Blamey is here to commend them for their deeds.

He arrives. The men are smartly turned out and stand to attention. Their officers stand just in front of them. They are now told to stand at ease. Blamey is standing on a wooden platform.

What now occurs is the greatest dressing down of all time.[38] Blamey tells them that their country has been defeated, that he has been defeated and that they have been defeated. The 'stand at ease' order of a minute or two ago now becomes a contradiction in terms. There is a growing restiveness in the ranks. Muffled insults begin to be heard from the rear. The body language of the troops is also becoming restless and aggressive. Whispers are issued from junior officers to the troops to hold their anger, to maintain control. The 2/16th are particularly incensed. So Pottsy *was* sacked, *was* humiliated, and *was* sent away. And now it's their turn.

Blamey cannot quite fathom the men's open hostility towards him. He tells them that they are each worth three Japanese. More restiveness, more muffled comments. They know they have been worth more like five Japanese each. Blamey now tells them that there must be no more withdrawals, no more retirements, no more failures. And then the comment comes that will blow like a whirlwind through the scattered ranks of the entire 7th Division—the entire army in Papua. 'Remember,' he says, 'it's not the man with the gun that gets shot, it's the rabbit that is running away.' This is quite simply dynamite. It is taken as a charge of cowardice, and it infuriates everyone present.

This isn't the British Army. Australians are egalitarian by nature and have, throughout their brief history, tended to express themselves and their views openly. As the soldiers of the 21st Brigade march past Blamey many refuse to give 'eyes right'.[39] There will be a hospital visit by Blamey not long after and the nurses will smuggle in lettuce leaves and soldiers will nibble on them and twitch their noses.[40] As he walks out of the hospital there'll be faint but still audible whispers, 'Run rabbit, run.'

But Blamey hasn't finished. After the other ranks have left the scene he addresses the officers. He tells them that they have let their men down; he questions whether they are worthy of their men; he says he is giving them another chance and that their performance must improve.[41] If the officers, like their troops, are infuriated by Blamey's comments to the brigade, then they are molten with rage concerning his comments about the standard of its leadership. Potts to his wife on hearing of Blamey's Koitaki diatribe:

> Hugh [Challen, Potts' Brigade Major on the Trail] sent me a precis of his ('T's') [Blamey's] speech to the old team and to the officers. Hells Bells, it was a cowardly bit of work and untrue in every detail. I'll fry his soul in the next world for that bit of 'passing the buck'. Surely a man in his position is big enough to carry his own mistakes.[42]

It is all too easy to become so impassioned by the slur of Koitaki that its real historical significance is lost. Blamey's

Koitaki address was not the first time that a commander had disparaged his soldiers—and, sadly, it will not be the last.

The real and relevant shame of Koitaki lies not only upon the slur, but its dramatic impact upon the soon-to-be-fought battle for Gona. Here, during November–December 1942, the 21st Brigade's—and the 39th Battalion's—climactic Papuan destiny will be tragically, and yet triumphantly, played out.

If you can keep your head when all about you
Are losing theirs and blaming it on you,
If you can trust yourself when all men doubt you
But make allowance for their doubting too . . .

Rudyard Kipling, 'If'

PART TWO

MILNE BAY

If you can keep your head …

OUTPOST OF THE EMPIRE

13

It will be remembered that on 29 June 1942, General Blamey had ordered Major-General Morris to deploy an occupying force at Kokoda to secure its airfield, and subsequently protect a proposed airstrip to be built at Dobodura near Buna. Captain Sam Templeton's B Company, 39th Battalion was the force chosen. To further secure Port Moresby, the 14th Militia Brigade was sent to reinforce the 30th Brigade (comprising the 49th, 39th and 53rd Battalions) at that location.

On 14 May, MacArthur had requested that Blamey supply a force to defend a proposed air base at Milne Bay on the eastern tip of the island. Blamey chose the 7th Militia Brigade, which had then only just arrived in Townsville. By securing air bases at Milne Bay, Dobodura and reinforcing Port Moresby, MacArthur believed that he could carry the air offensive many hundreds of miles into enemy territory and help facilitate his intended, if highly ambitious, invasion of Rabaul.

Both the Japanese and the Allies appreciated the strategic significance of Milne Bay. From an Allied perspective, an air base there could dominate the vital eastern sea lane between mainland Australia and Port Moresby, and also facilitate an offensive arc of air power to the north and north-east. From a Japanese viewpoint, the acquisition of airfields at Port Moresby and Milne Bay would enable them to bomb northern Australia, harass its shipping lanes from the United States, and help protect their right flank.

Milne Bay dominates the south-eastern extremity of mainland Papua. Its entrance, between East Cape and China

Strait, is about seven miles wide. The bay extends westward to a distance of approximately twenty miles to its deep-water head and varies in width from roughly five to ten miles.

The densely timbered and rugged Stirling Range, rising to summits of about 5000 feet, encloses the head of the bay from three sides, leaving a narrow coastal corridor which consisted in 1942 of numerous villages, a few coconut and rubber plantations amidst thick jungle and scrub, and mangrove and sago swamps.

In 1942, Samarai, a small island in China Strait, was the Eastern District capital and the most populous centre outside Port Moresby. Here, as in other Papuan districts, the resident magistrate, his assistant magistrate and a patrol officer were to be found, as well as the necessary number of Papuan police boys. There was a hotel, various warehouses, a wharf and a memorial hall.

When ANGAU was formed in March 1942, its operating role in this Eastern Division of Papua was of no less importance than elsewhere. It was strongly represented at and around Samarai—it would be destined to select sites for, and then assist in, the deployment of part of the legendary coastwatcher system, it organised both the indentured and local native population, and it carried out regular patrolling. As was the case in other Papuan regions, ANGAU was manned by a mixture of administrators, plantation owners and white supervisors along with a number of devoted missionaries who had refused outright to leave their congregations for the safety of Australia.

Gili Gili lies on the broadest portion of the coastal plain near the head of Milne Bay. By the outbreak of the war, Lever Brothers were operating one of the largest coconut plantations in the world at this location. From Gili Gili, along the narrow coastal ledge on the north shore, ran a ten-foot-wide government track which rarely meandered more than one hundred yards from the shoreline. This track traversed a multitude of streams and ran roughly ten miles through the native villages of Kilarbo, Rabi, KB Mission, Goroni, Waga Waga and then to Ahioma before finally extending to the tip of East Cape. Although these villages were not unlike those found along the Kokoda Trail in terms of size and population,

Milne Bay, July 1942

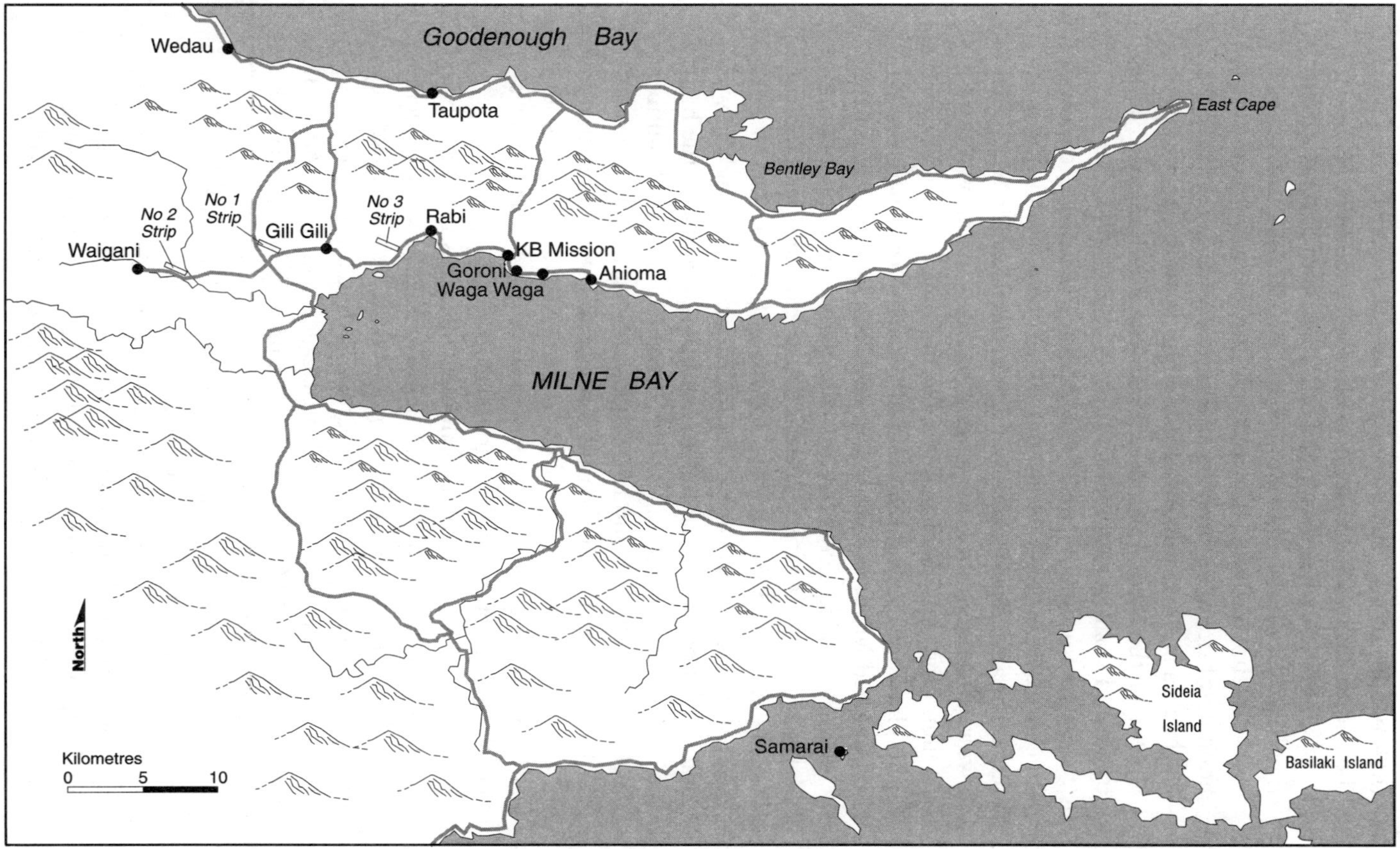

their occupants had the added advantage of trade by sea and the additional food supplies provided by it.

Unlike Port Moresby, which lies in a rain shadow, Milne Bay has a very high rainfall of around two hundred inches per year which, in those days, caused the frequent and rapid flooding of the many streams along the coastal corridor. Low-level cloud and swirling mist often prejudiced the operation of aircraft in the area and most movement was limited to foot traffic and small coastal craft.

In response to General MacArthur's May 1942 decision to construct an air base in the Milne Bay region, the first reconnaissance of the area was undertaken on 27 May. That investigation identified the village of Abau in the vicinity of Mullins Harbour as being a suitable site.

However, Major Elliott-Smith of ANGAU had already approached Major-General George Vasey, Deputy Chief of the General Staff, concerning an alternative location. Elliott-Smith's choice was situated at the Lever Brothers plantation at Gili Gili. He had two reasons for his option: the first was its firm soil in comparison to other local sites—although it was still susceptible to regular boggy conditions because of the high rainfall—and the second was the existence of a small number of buildings, sheds, a modest 'road' system, a few small jetties, and a ready supply of coral to assist in the road construction that would immediately follow a build-up of a base at the airfield site. Another reconnaissance of likely areas merely confirmed Elliott-Smith's astute selection.

The construction of the landing strip was assigned to a part of the American 46th (General Service) Engineers Regiment. Security of this construction force was to be undertaken by A and C Companies and a section of E Company (Vickers machine-gunners) from the 14th Brigade's 55th Battalion, then deployed in Port Moresby, and the gunners of the 9th Battery, 2/3rd Light Anti-Aircraft Regiment.

Construction on what was to become known as Number 1 Strip began on 28 June 1942. The American engineers performed magnificently. They set to their task with a limited supply of mechanised assistance: two motor graders, a number of dump trucks, one power shovel and some D4 Cats. Warrant-Officer Geoff Baskett of ANGAU watched them at work:

> We were amazed to see the way they removed coconut palms. One engineer would move along a line of ten coconut palms using a power drill to make a deep hole at the base of each palm. He was followed by other engineers who dropped several plugs of gelignite into the holes and connected the plugs with a long electrical lead. When all the palms had been 'mined' in this way . . . one of the engineers pushed down hard on an electric charger to detonate the gelignite . . . every coconut palm shot vertically into the air, hung there . . . then with its fronds waving helplessly, crashed to the ground.[1]

Pick and shovel work also saw drainage ditches and trenches dug and the eventual draining of a nearby swamp.

It is all too easy to underestimate the logistical nightmare that was the Papuan campaign. It is one thing to operate in Greece where the roads are too narrow; where there is but one train line north; where the port system is overloaded; or in places in the Middle East where the road network and ports and rail systems are antiquated. But it is a far more daunting challenge to supply a major force where there is no real infrastructure at all. The identified desire for tracks—not roads—and ports, airfields and even basic buildings at first necessitates a hurried reconnaissance and then an equally hurried construction. And all of this has to be accomplished against an unforgiving climate and tough terrain that will also impact upon the health of the soldiers and Papuans who work in it.

Lieutenant Jim Ross was one of the ANGAU soldiers who helped organise this amazing transformation:

> . . . the response was gratifying. This in no small way was a result of the confidence they [the natives] had in the . . . administration (ANGAU) personnel who they had come to know . . . The lack of sufficient and proper tools did not hamper the work; native baskets were used for carrying stone filling; canoes were used to transport coral from nearby islands and used after the style of tip drays; hoop iron knives were used to cut the heavy grass and undergrowth. The concerted efforts of the 800 natives brought in from all villages in Milne Bay, supervised by

> the District Officer personally, and his staff, resulted in the completion of the task (of building a wharf) in 4 days. The native carpenters under . . . supervision . . . completing the large pontoon wharf only 12 hours before the arrival of the first convoy . . .
>
> This labour line was allocated to the increasing military requirements . . . it was clearly understood by units receiving labour that ANGAU officers were in charge.[2]

Nor was the recruitment of native labour a straightforward concern. Warrant-Officer David Marsh, ANGAU:

> If you have a village of 100 people, under normal circumstances 20 out of 100 will be able bodied men.
>
> So that is one man looking after four dependants—old men and women, wife and kids and you take 20 men out and there's no one to look after the others.
>
> There's no one to pull a canoe into the water to go fishing, there's no one to cut down trees to make gardens, no one to repair a house, no one to hunt, no one to dance, no one to dance for and everything falls apart so fast . . .
>
> You have to be careful how many people you recruit.[3]

The soldiers of the 7th Militia Brigade began arriving at Milne Bay on 11 July. First impressions can often be misleading. Private Allan Dolly, 9th Battalion:

> To enter the bay . . . you had to go through . . . China Strait . . . at 1500 hrs looking at palm fringed . . . beaches and the bluest water you ever saw. Here was peace, tranquillity, nothing could happen here. Like bloody hell! When you disembark at Gili Gili at 2000 hrs, black as all hell and raining—make that pouring—and you finally put foot on ground, almost up to your waist in mud . . . what a let-down!
>
> . . . And so to the base area, the last place God made and didn't finish . . . excessive rain also took its toll. It was

> impossible to keep dry and one was wet for a lot of the time . . . the whole atmosphere tended to wear one down if you let it.[4]

Private Eric Mortensen, 7th Brigade Signals:

> . . . you'd have inches of rain overnight . . . we'd still have to get around on bloomin' motorbikes. And you'd pull into an office, and you got off the bike, you didn't have to pull it up on the stand, it just stood up in the mud on its own![5]

The 7th Militia Brigade was commanded by Brigadier John Field. The tasks that confronted him upon his arrival at Milne Bay were both complex and diverse. The appointment, whether made by an astute judgment on General Blamey's part or merely by chance, was to prove a good one. Field had been a mechanical engineer and university lecturer in Tasmania before the war—his skills were thus ideally suited to the further preparation of a base at Gili Gili.

The new commander's military qualifications were also impressive. His prewar service consisted of sixteen years in the militia and he had seen active service in the Middle East as CO of the 18th Brigade's 2/12th Battalion, AIF. Field's appointment to command the 7th Brigade had occurred only weeks before its arrival in Papua. Major James Mahoney, brigade major, 7th Brigade:

> On arrival Field established his HQ in the plantation manager's house at Gili Gili, a high-set, white painted, wooden house on a hill rising out of the palm-trees, and, for obvious reasons marked as 'Target House' on the first map. The Brigade Commander quickly had constructed by native labour well-hidden palm-frond huts for his HQ.[6]

Field found the construction of Number 1 Strip at an advanced stage. Steel mesh, known then as Marsden Matting, was nearly ready to be laid upon the prepared earth runway. However, to compound his already daunting challenges, he was ordered to reconnoitre a site for a second airstrip within days of his arrival. An area near Waigani, about four miles west from Number 1 Strip, was chosen.

But the 'road network' was Field's most pressing problem. He decided, with the limited time at his disposal, to employ two processes to upgrade it. The first was the employment of coral or coconut logs as a base for construction. Captain Alan Harlen, 7th Brigade Signals: 'They used coral for making the roads . . . later on when the roads got torn up, the jeeps would be one wheel right down in a rut, and you'd be scraping your bottom along, and leaving white coral in the middle of the road.'[7] The second was the building of a limited number of loops and passing arcs to attempt to increase the speed and efficiency of movement. The great majority of vehicles sent to Milne Bay were two-wheel driven and were therefore subject to almost constant bogging. And the infantry at Milne Bay were two-leg driven. Theirs would be the energy-sapping and time-consuming task of literally dragging their bodies and equipment through sometimes knee-deep mud over what appeared to be relatively short distances. The gruelling reality of fighting was destined to severely contradict the calculated theory at an impatient headquarters in Australia.

Bridges in and around the base area presented an additional problem: approximately eighteen in the Gili Gili area were too light for military employment and the new strip at Waigani would require the construction of two new bridges.

Although a coral shelf running to within about ten yards of the shore provided a deep-water dock for shipping of up to 5000 tons—the vessels were often moored by being tied to coconut palms—the resulting pontoon system caused an enormous drain upon the manpower and time of the garrison, as all cargo had to be manhandled from the pontoons to waiting vehicles. Gili Gili required a wharf building program urgently.

There were no maps of the base area and its hinterland. This lamentable state of affairs at both Milne Bay and on the Kokoda Trail and, to a lesser degree, at the later beachhead battles at Gona–Buna–Sanananda, was to inhibit operations and reflects the almost total lack of Allied preparedness for a military campaign in Papua. Amongst the multitude of other pressing problems, the soldiers of Milne Force were thus required to set to the task of producing maps quickly, and with only elementary equipment and training—largely by God and by compass.

The health of the rapidly increasing garrison was also a matter of crucial concern. The 11th Field Ambulance, commanded by Lieutenant-Colonel J.M. Blair, had arrived at Milne Bay on 11 July. Owing to the strict security and the speed of the build-up of the garrison, Blair observed that anti-malarial equipment and medicines were scarce—quinine was in use as a suppressive, but it had not been supplied until a week after the troops' arrival and sufficient stocks were not in place until 25 July. By then the damage was done. Nor had the soldiers of Milne Force a high level of personal malarial discipline or general hygiene. Allan S. Walker, in *The Island Campaigns*:

> This laid stress on the personal use of suppressive quinine in daily dosage of 10 grains, and the wearing of protective clothing, and on the methods of adult and larval mosquito control. However, there were no nets available for use when the force arrived, and very little protective clothing: the men wore shorts and had their sleeves rolled up.[8]

And when some mosquito nets did arrive, some were for double beds—a sick joke.[9]

The soldiers of the 7th Brigade, not unlike their militia comrades in Port Moresby, became wharf labourers, road makers, bridge builders and airfield construction workers on their arrival at Milne Bay. And if literally carving a military base out of a high-rainfall tropical coconut palm and jungle area was not a difficult enough task, then Field's deployment and training of his 7th Brigade and the rapid arrival of additional units presented an enormous challenge.

The 7th Brigade consisted of the Queensland 9th, 25th and 61st Militia Battalions. The 9th had been raised from the Brisbane and Nambour areas; the 25th from the Darling Downs; and the 61st had been originally raised as the Queensland Cameron Highlanders.

As has been mentioned, during early April 1942 Major-General Vasey had requested a rating, from A to F, regarding the level of training of all formations in the Australian Army. The 30th Brigade in Port Moresby had been graded at 'F': 'Unit training is not yet complete'. We have seen the consequences of this assessment on the Kokoda Trail with regards to the performance of the 53rd Battalion, and the triumph over such a level of training by the 39th Battalion.

When those April 1942 assessments were given, the 7th Militia Brigade was graded at 'D': 'Individual brigades are efficient in a static role. Additional brigade and higher training is required'. The 'D' grading given the 7th Brigade seems open to some question. Major J.C. Mahoney, brigade major, 7th Brigade:

> We were given to understand that on the basis of its manning, equipment, training and readiness for battle, 7 Bde was selected for the task from the formations available in Queensland at that time. The units of the Brigade had had a long period of training in the Brisbane area; two full-scale Bde Group exercises had been held with supporting arms and services. In North Queensland, at Rollingstone, the Bde had dug and wired a defensive position to cover Townsville from a landing north of the city.[10]

The private soldier often has a different perspective. Sergeant Colin Hoy, 61st Battalion:

> ... I'd only fired seven shots out of my rifle prior to Milne Bay! I could salute well, I could march well . . . you see it's very hard for people to understand that in those days every round of ammunition had to be accounted for . . . we just didn't have much of it.
>
> When I joined up we went up to Fraser's Paddock and we were out there complete with kilts . . . we were trained by 1914–18 old Sergeant-Majors and they were tough bastards . . . the point was, that they taught us discipline; that is the big thing. Whether they were any good on the battlefield . . . well, we'll never know because they never ever went away.[11]

Sergeant Jack Capper, 9th Battalion:

> I believe we were very fit and well trained with our weapons to platoon and company level, but not beyond that . . . we had never advanced over covering fire of any kind . . . mortar, Vickers [machine-guns], artillery, carrier, tank or aircraft. And with our World War One weapons, unsuitable clothing . . . shit! What more disadvantages do you want? Shorts—Bombay Bloomers—short sleeved shirts . . .[12]

The 7th Brigade was, in mid-1942, an astute choice amongst the available militia brigades for deployment to Milne Bay. However, like all militia formations at the time, it suffered from two distinct handicaps. First, it had a drastic deficiency of seasoned, well-trained and youthful officers. Brigadier Field was the only officer in his brigade who had seen action in the present war, and there were only four other officers who had seen action in the Great War. This was no small handicap, as the Papuan campaign was almost totally unforgiving of a lack of physical and mental robustness among officers. The second problem was the second-rate priority given to the militia with regards to its equipment, as the AIF, being first committed to action in the Middle East, had received the best of Australia's limited supply of resources.

Brigadier Field's arrival at Milne Bay coincided with increasing Japanese interest in the base area. An enemy air reconnaissance took place on the same day.

On 21 July, the Japanese landed at Gona on the north coast of Papua. Their arrival constituted the advance party of General Horii's South Seas Force, sent to ascertain the feasibility of an overland assault upon Port Moresby. Three days later, Lieutenant Alan Timberley, the ANGAU officer in charge of the Trobriand Islands (about 150 miles north of Milne Bay), reported that the Japanese had conducted repeated and painstaking air reconnaissance over the area during the period 13–22 July.

On 25 July 1942, the American engineers and Australian soldiers of Milne Force were rewarded for their intense labour in completing Number 1 Strip and the base area by the morale-boosting arrival of 76 and 75 Kittyhawk (P-40) Squadrons, RAAF. On 6 August, the 46th Engineers were able to report:

> This aerodrome now has a completed steel-mat [Marsden Matting] runway of approximately [5100 feet × 100 feet] in excellent condition. The lengthening of the runway by the removal of the rise at the West end is now under way and will be completed to make a total length of 5400 [feet] and rates third priority after the widening to 100 [feet] and the construction of bomber bays as per instructions by General Casey . . .
>
> Two fighter dispersal strips are completed, to handle two fighter squadrons, and the clearing and grading of the new bomber dispersal strip is well under way.
>
> Nine steel-mat bomber bays have been constructed adjacent to the steel runway to allow bombers or fighters to be parked just off the actual landing strip.[13]

Although the construction of Number 1 Strip had been a remarkable effort, the strip was, by normal standards, a tough proposition from which to operate. The Official Historian:

> No. 1 Strip . . . was virtually under water. Interlocking steel . . . alone made landing possible. The pilots, few if any of whom had landed on such a runway, touched down with their aircraft spraying water like so many hydroplanes. On landing the aircraft skidded, often so violently that they swung off the runway and became bogged in the morass at the side of the matting. The ground staff and all others who could help laboured in deep mud, dragging out bogged aircraft to what firm ground there was and laying further sections of steel matting for taxiways to the dispersal areas among the coconut plantations.[14]

The operational experience of the two squadrons differed markedly. The Battle for Milne Bay was to be 76 Squadron's first fight, although some of its pilots had served either in the Middle East or in Britain. Notable among them was Squadron

Leader 'Bluey' Truscott, a prominent prewar footballer with the Melbourne Football Club and a pilot who had excelled in the skies over Britain and France. The CO of 76 Squadron was Squadron Leader Peter Turnbull. Pilot-Officer Bruce 'Buster' Brown remembered his CO as '. . a marvellous man! A guy who could keep everybody together. An excellent leader; he had an understanding of men; he could spot a weakness, and he'd endeavour to overcome that weakness . . .'[15]

75 Squadron had taken the brunt of the Japanese air assault upon Port Moresby. It was commanded by Squadron Leader Les Jackson. Pilot-Officer David Pank: '. . . he was tough . . . when his brother was killed in Port Moresby, and I knew his brother very well, after that, Les went off his rocker . . . I mean the risks he took were incredible, even stupid at times. He was determined that he was going to win the war by himself . . . to avenge his brother.'[16]

Milne Bay made no more favourable impression upon the pilots of the RAAF than it had upon the infantry. Pilot-Officer David Pank:

> Absolutely bloody terrible! . . . the rain just didn't stop . . . we simply had tents with a stretcher in it and a mosquito net . . . they sent us up there without a long-sleeve shirt between us or a pair of trousers—the only long trousers we had were our flying suits . . . we wore shorts and flying boots so we could get through the mud. And so to get to bed at night your trick was, and there was nothing on the floor, it was just mud, you'd get into the bloody bed, take everything off, and the last thing you took off was your boots . . . the water just flowed straight through the tent.[17]

Pilot-Officer 'Buster' Brown:

> My best description of Milne Bay would be that if you were going to give the world an enema, that you'd push it in at Milne Bay. It was bloody terrible . . . malaria . . . and dysentery was rife—some of us were flying with guts that would swell out, and you'd dirty the cockpit or your trousers . . . you take off and you feel all right and

> suddenly your belly starts to rumble and the gases in your stomach . . . you see the food was bloody awful![18]

Perhaps one of the advantages that the pilots of 75 and 76 Squadrons had was confidence in their aircraft. The Kittyhawk fighter plane was an American single-seater fighter which had a maximum altitude of about 29 000 feet, and at about 15 000 feet it was able to reach its maximum speed of 340 m.p.h. It was about 20 m.p.h. faster than a Japanese Zero fighter, and at either low altitudes or in a dive could therefore outpace the enemy plane. The Kittyhawk carried armour plating behind the pilot, three potent .5 calibre Browning machine-guns on each wing, self-sealing fuel tanks and armoured glass windscreens. The plane was powered by a usually reliable V8 Allison engine. But its robust engine, armour plating and its resultant weight prejudiced its ability to manoeuvre against the lighter and easier-to-handle Zero. The trick of combat, therefore, was to engage the Japanese from superior height and avoid dogfights. For all this, after the recent history in the Middle East, Greece, Crete and the early battles over Port Moresby, the infantry saw one priceless quality in the Kittyhawk pilots and their planes: 'they were ours'.

The early days of August saw increasing Japanese air activity over Milne Bay. David Pank's logbook:

> Aug 4th—zeros strafed. 76 shot down 2 confirmed. Peter Ash one & Paddy Dempster one. Frank Grosvenor shot up but landed OK.
>
> Aug 12th Zeros strafed. P/O Angus McCloud, F/O Mark Sheldon, Sgt Inkster & Sgt Shelley shot down . . .
>
> Descended through cloud—lost—crash landed & spent 3 days at Suav [sic].[19]

A pilot's logbook is often an excellent record of one man's war: the number of sorties flown from day to day and, in basic terms, which pilots might have scored 'kills' and the names of those who did not return. But some idea of the strain on the two squadrons can be gauged from the 75 Squadron doctor's account of the death of one of those pilots mentioned briefly in Pank's logbook. W. Deane-Butcher, in *Fighter Squadron Doctor*:

> A message came through that an aircraft on the way back was streaming smoke. My medical orderly, Jack McIntosh, was on stand by in the ambulance. I jumped in and we drove half the way along to the side of the strip and watched. We saw the aircraft coming in at low altitude with smoke billowing behind. Our radio picked up the voice of the approaching pilot talking rapidly on the intercom. He was agitated as fire was taking hold.
>
> There were a few hundred yards to go and then he would have the long run before he could escape. The smoke was black and more intense now. Suddenly, the aircraft changed posture and with nose up climbed steeply to gain height. It stalled and turned above us as he baled out. The aircraft crashed behind us. The pilot dropped fast as his chute streamed out behind him. Before it had time to open, only twenty yards from us, he struck the ground. We ran forward toward the motionless crumpled heap. Sgt. George Inkster was dead.[20]

When two companies of the II Battalion of the American 43rd Engineer (General Service) Regiment arrived at Milne Bay on 7 August, one was employed at the site of a proposed third airstrip, to be aptly named 'Number 3 Strip', roughly three miles south-west of the village of Kilarbo and extending nearly to the coast, while the second company was deployed at Gili Gili for the purpose of additional work upon Number 1 Strip and the ongoing improvement of Gili Gili's docking facilities.

With the build-up of his base well under way, and two of the three airstrips planned and the first completed, Brigadier Field had given considerable thought to both an early warning system of approaching enemy infantry and to the protection of his outer defence. To this end, he deployed the 61st Battalion's B Company (Captain Bicks) at KB Mission, Captain Davidson's D Company at Ahioma, and a platoon of the 61st across the Stirling Range to the north-east on the coast at Taupota. To further cover the far northern approach, he sited a company and a machine-gun platoon of the 25th Battalion at Wadau.

All of this was standard and prudent military planning. But one of the recurring problems facing commanders in Papua was communication. The harsh terrain and debilitating climate and the consequent slow and cumbersome transport network, all conspired to give added significance to Milne Force's communication system. The challenges confronting the 7th Brigade Signals were enormous; it was equipped as a brigade unit, but was, at Milne Bay, required to provide communication from Field's HQ to all formations in the base area. Captain Allan Harlen, 7th Brigade Signals:

> Our switchboard capacity was two 10 L [line] boards . . . because of the restrictions on the capacity of the switchboards it was obvious that we would have to party to as many lines as possible.
>
> Goodness only knows what the higher ups did in peace time, but the provisioning of equipment was unbelievably bad. We were sent to this theatre with 6 smooth tyred W/T [wireless transmitter] vans, 6 motor cycles and a four wheel 30 cwt truck for cable laying and a water cart. Ideal for the desert conditions but completely unsuited to the terrain.[21]

But the major communication problem was that orthodox signal equipment which was tried and tested in desert conditions was found wanting in Papua. Allan Harlen:

> . . . little reliance could be placed on the wireless sets. The 101 set was of low power, the antennae equipment was cumbersome—a jointed arrangement with radial spokes—and the sets were vulnerable to moisture damage. Furthermore they required two 6 volt accumulators with two being charged and the noise of the chargers could direct enemy action to the W/T site. The 108 set was nigh on useless, requiring heavy dry batteries with an antennae which rose above the head of the operator. They were cumbersome and a dead giveaway when trekking through jungle.[22]

Consequently, when there was insufficient cable or time to lay it, communications were maintained by runners.

When the Battle for Milne Bay began, the engineers had cleared the ground for Number 3 Strip and had bulldozed the graded earth into an almost continuous mound along the strip's western side. They could not have known that, in so doing, they had in fact prepared a landing ground that would not be employed by the RAAF but by the infantry. That conscientious grading of an airfield was in fact the timely construction of a future killing ground.

As Field's limited time passed, the now complete arrival of further American engineers had brought the total Allied personnel at Milne Bay to 265 officers and 5947 other ranks.[23] On 8 August 1942, Field was further informed that his infantry force was to increase again.

When General MacArthur had finally consented to deploy the 7th Division in Papua, Arnold Potts' 21st Brigade had already left Brisbane and sailed to Port Moresby. At the same time, the 18th Brigade had also set sail northwards, but had sailed to Milne Bay. Its complete disembarkation was anticipated by 21 August. The 18th Brigade was commanded by Brigadier George Wootten. The Official Historian:

> Wootten was a heavily-built man who had served as a regular officer with the first A.I.F. and in 1923 left the Army for the Law. He had sailed with the 6th Division in 1940 in command of the 2/2nd battalion. Subsequently he took command of the 18th Brigade and led it in the Middle East desert fighting. He had a reputation as an able and resolute leader, for an energy which belied his bulk, and a quick and discerning eye.[24]

Colonel Fred Chilton remembered Wootten:

> . . . as a huge man—he was known to the troops as 'Two-Ton-Tony' or 'Mud-Guts'. But he was popular with them, and greatly respected. And he was a formidable man indeed—I have never met a man of stronger will and personality. He had a 'very short fuse' but his anger soon subsided.
>
> He had a first rate brain and a very sound judgement in military matters. I once heard that MacArthur had

> said he was the best of the Australian Generals—I am unable to discover the source. He was a mighty man in all respects.[25]

It is at this point that one of our central commanders from the former fighting in the Middle East re-enters our story. With the build-up of two of the three 7th Division brigades to Papua, Lieutenant-General Rowell had been ordered to Port Moresby to assume command of New Guinea Force. With him went Major-General 'Tubby' Allen, the commander of the 7th Division. Major-General Cyril Clowes was appointed to command Milne Force.

Clowes' calm and astute operational control when put to the test at the Pinios Gorge in Greece has been mentioned, as have his most impressive prior achievements in both the Great War and the early campaigns in the Middle East. In short, Major-General 'Silent' Cyril Clowes, a permanent soldier, had had an impeccable record.

The new Milne Force commander's journey and eventual arrival at Gili Gili's Number 1 Strip on 13 August was less than relaxed. His American pilot became disoriented in the rain and cloud-covered skies over Milne Bay and landed with a near empty fuel tank. In his usual understated manner, Clowes wrote to Rowell:

> Dear Old Syd,
> Thankyou for yours of 14 Aug. Nice hearing from you in one of the real outposts of Empire!
>
> Yes we did get here safely in the end largely by guess and by God though. Pouring rain the landing strip covered with water a ceiling of a hundred feet and a complete lack of knowledge of the country and no maps in possession of the pilot, all helped to add interest to the trip . . .
>
> One lesson sticks out though. I suggest that our allies be impressed with the fact that senior officers are perceived to be valuable and that reasonable precautions should be taken when they are moved by air. Majors-General may be two a penny but . . . before taking to the air with these people in future I recommend prior

> enquiry to ensure a reasonable degree of safety.
>
> This place in particular is generally clouded low down and with high ranges in close proximity is not an easy proposition for strangers.[26]

In planning his defence of Milne Bay, Major-General Cyril Clowes had one overriding strategic responsibility: the airfields. The whole purpose of Milne Force was to construct, then employ and obviously hold, the air potential of that location. His vital ground was therefore Number 1 Strip, his one now fully operational RAAF site. The other two strips, 2 and 3, although still under construction, were his two further priorities.

In framing his defence, Clowes was confronted with two radically different and changing scenarios which would occur *every day*. During daylight hours, the Allies held almost total air superiority, which would cause the Japanese to conduct daylight naval operations in the bay at their peril. But by night Clowes' aircraft were almost superfluous. Under cover of darkness, therefore, the Japanese were at liberty to sail into the harbour, land or evacuate troops at any spot, or shell Allied dispositions almost at will. Provided the Japanese naval forces were out of the bay before sunrise, they could engage in whatever activities they desired. This see-sawing ascendancy would add the crucial ingredient of a certain degree of guess-work as to the size and the ongoing tactical intention of the enemy force. Throughout most of the Battle for Milne Bay the so-called 'fog of war' made planning extremely difficult.

Clowes' tactical defence of Milne Bay's vital ground displayed this astute soldier's understanding of the capabilities of his units. Graded at 'D'—'Individual brigades are efficient in a static role. Additional brigade and higher training is required'—the 7th Militia Brigade was deployed by Clowes in precisely that capacity.

He sited his 9th Militia Battalion on the western shore of the Bay, stretching from roughly Ladava Mission around Gaba Gabuna Bay; the 25th Militia Battalion occupied an area about three miles due west of Number 3 Strip and about a mile north of Number 1 Strip; and the 61st Militia Battalion had two of its companies deployed around Number 3 Strip, with its B Company at KB Mission. Clowes was not content with the earlier siting of D Company of the 61st Battalion at far distant Ahioma, and therefore ordered Field to return it to Number 3 Strip. Essentially, therefore, the 7th Brigade was sited for a static defensive role.

The 18th Brigade's 2/9th, 2/10th and 2/12th Battalions were quite clearly Clowes' trump card. In terms of training—graded 'A': 'Efficient and experienced for mobile operations'—leadership and combat experience, this AIF brigade was at least the equal of any formation in the Australian Army at this time. He planned its employment accordingly.

Clowes deployed Wootten's 2/12th Battalion at Waigani; the 2/9th Battalion less one company at his Force HQ at Hagita House (one company was deployed at Number 1 Strip); and the 2/10th Battalion was stationed in the Gili Gili base area between the 25th and 61st Battalions.

The beach defence area stretched approximately one mile on either side of the Gili Gili wharf where the 7th Brigade machine-guns, the American maintenance units and one troop of 25-pounder artillery guns were sited.

The 18th Brigade was therefore deployed to not only directly defend his vital ground, but for 'counterattack in any direction'[27] and for 'special operations as may be required'.[28] Clowes thus maintained the elite component of his force for decisive defensive and/or offensive action once the enemy had shown his hand. However, this sound plan required a further ingredient: a cool, cautious and calculated appreciation of the battle as it unfolded. If the 18th Brigade was committed too early to an offensive operation and away from Milne Bay's vital ground, and the Japanese first thrust or a subsequent push was a feint, then disaster might well follow.

The critical element of Clowes' defensive plans was the realisation that the Japanese were at liberty to attack him from any direction, and with naval superiority. From the outset, he was also very mindful of the propensity of the Japanese to employ outflanking movements. The Japanese could attempt such a tactic through the nearby Stirling Range, and it was therefore at the forefront of his thinking. After five days at Milne Bay, Clowes wrote to Rowell:

> Dear Old Syd,
> Operationally, I have sorted things out into a reasonable shape. A lot still remains to be done to turn the place into a decent fighting proposition, though Field, to my mind, has done a good job of work here, particularly on the organisational side. In general, I have based my plans on possible Jap action from Milne Bay (in particular), from the north across the Stirling Ra., and via Wedau (Dogura Mission). Fwd areas lightly held with bulk of troops in reserve. Patrolling from Wedau along the foreshores to East Cape, hence along North coastline from Milne Bay with standing posts on latter about 12 miles from Gili Gili. Constant patrolling of tracks leading over Stirling Ra. (2 day's trekking time). Also patrolling south shore of Milne Bay to pt about 15 miles from Gili Gili.
>
> Lack of decent water tpt is a great difficulty here. A few fair-sized launches would be worth their weight in gold.[29]

But there was one perceived weakness in Major-General Cyril Clowes' make-up. Colonel Fred Chilton, Clowes' chief staff officer:

> . . . a fine commander and a steady man. He was a cautious man . . . this was reflected in his dispositions. The only thing I think he can be criticised for, is his lack of public relations—for not sending back phoney reports about what a wonderful job he was doing and how many Japs they'd killed and all this sort of thing. But his reports were confined to the purely military operations and didn't give the boys back in Melbourne what they wanted. At that stage most of them didn't have a clue about fighting battles anyway . . .[30]

Chilton might well have provided a rider to his comment. The 'boys in Melbourne' most certainly did not have a clue about the conditions in Papua, let alone battles in general terms.

Another most pressing problem facing Clowes and Chilton was the immediate task of establishing a separate Milne Force HQ at Hagita Plantation, when both they and

Milne Force Dispositions, 25 August 1942

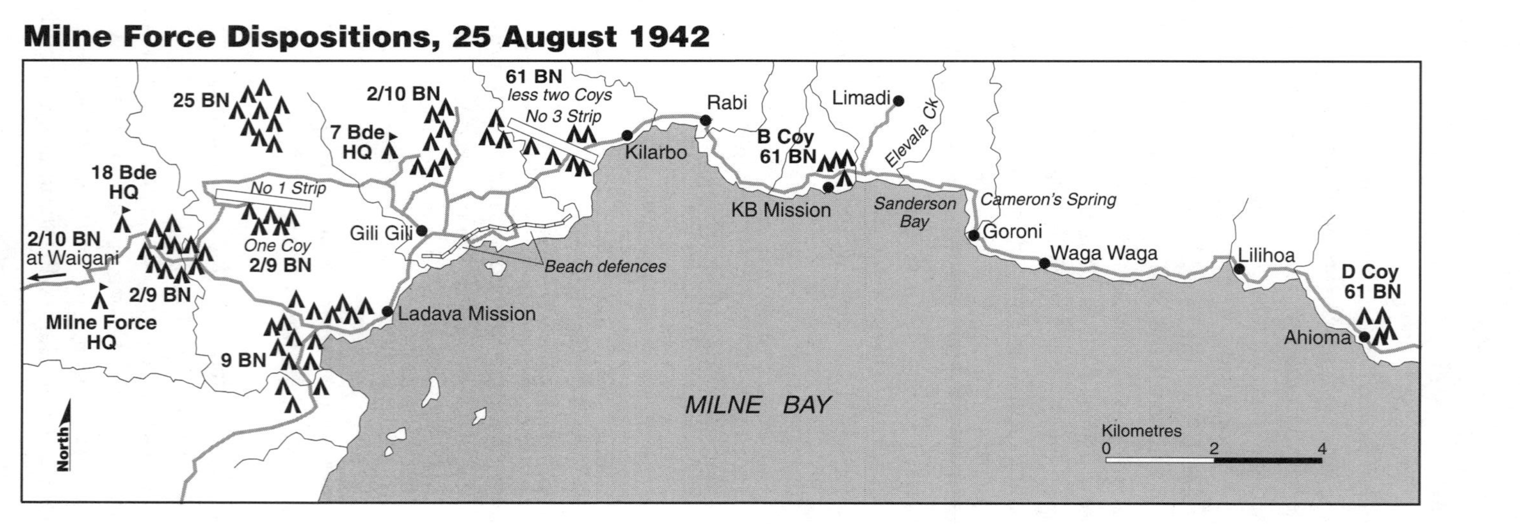

their staff had arrived only a few days before an anticipated battle. Until that vital HQ could be established, Clowes and his staff were forced to share the limited facilities of Target House with Field and his staff.

Such a predicament, and the limited time available, might have been difficult enough for a highly trained and experienced staff, but Clowes' HQ staff were not only inexperienced, they had also been formed from far and wide. Milne Force Signals (as distinct from the already described 7th Brigade Signals) was a case in point. Its commander, Lieutenant-Colonel Clementson, had assumed command of the unit on 6 August, and it had not arrived at Milne Bay until the 21st of that month. This unit had been formed using mostly young Western Australian militiamen. Brigadier Field made his own observations in his diary:

> Force Signals have occupied a large area around No. 1 House in white tents pitched cheek and jowl and with no attempt at track discipline or camouflage.
>
> Further down the road, the Force HQ people have dumped all types of stores, adding to the 'Target Area' . . . a very amateurish show and even allowing for the weather difficulties it looks a fortnight might elapse before this HQ becomes established.[31]

Cable laying from Force HQ to the 7th and 18th Brigades began on 23 August and lines were established by 6.00 p.m. on the 25th, less than 36 hours before the commencement of the battle.[32]

The weather conditions continued to hamper all forms of military endeavour. One pilot placed an empty can outside of his tent and noted thirteen inches of rain in a little over 24 hours.[33] Baker and Knight in *Milne Bay 1942* quote driver Colin Henry:

> . . . many a hole in boggy mud had to be filled with whatever was to hand, food cases, boxes of shells, undoubtedly buried under the road as they were constructed . . . tracks between the trees soon chopped up, impossible for ambulances to negotiate. The gun tractors

> with their big wheels were called in . . . then a matter of put it into gear, make sure you kept hands clear of the steering wheel (easy to break an arm) as you just followed the deep mud tracks through the trees.[34]

Such were the transport problems within the confined base area. Outside of that perimeter, the ordinary infantry digger would rely only on his legs to traverse the bog-ridden terrain.

The arrival and deployment of the 9th Battery, 2/5th Field Regiment was also a major administrative calamity. The battery arrived at Gili Gili on 21 August. John O'Brien, in *Guns and Gunners*:

> The battery had thought mostly in terms of open warfare . . . It was intended that the guns should be sited to give artillery support to whatever forward infantry positions might be established from the northern to the southern shores of the Bay. Headquarters said, 'Go there.' It was not as easy as that.[35]

The now familiar Milne Bay scenario of bogged vehicle traffic and poor prospective sites inhibited the battery's early and efficient deployment. The original allotted position was unsuitable because of a swamp between it and the main 'road'; no liaison with the infantry was immediately possible; no reconnaissance of the area could be made; and the route from the staging area near the dock where the battery's guns and stores were stationed entailed a six-hour journey some five miles inland to the proposed site.

By 10.00 p.m. on the 25th, Captain Tinkler and his A Troop deployed one gun at the coast end of Number 1 Strip, one positioned approximately a mile east of the Gili Gili jetty and the remaining two guns south of the jetty. Captain Stevenson had his B Troop in position by midnight—protecting Number 1 Strip. Despite the frequent bogging of vehicles and traffic congestion, ammunition was moved forward by sunrise.

The Japanese had a two-pronged assault plan for the capture of Port Moresby.

On 12 June 1942, just six days after the Battle of Midway, the commander of the Japanese 17th Army, General Hyakutake, was ordered to ascertain the feasibility of an overland crossing of the Owen Stanley Range, and then, if a positive assessment was forthcoming, commit General Horii's South Seas Force to the operation.

The Milne Bay troop component of the plan for the capture of Port Moresby consisted of Major-General Kiyotake Kawaguchi's 124th Infantry Group (Kawaguchi Force), which had fought in Borneo and the Philippines. The two-pronged plan envisaged Horii and Kawaguchi converging on Port Moresby after the former had nearly reached that objective via the Kokoda Trail and the latter had captured Milne Bay and moved westward. However, the landing of the US marines on Guadalcanal caused the Japanese to change tack.

Despite the fact that General Vandergrift's force quickly captured both islands that comprised Guadalcanal, the American carrier fleet was forced to withdraw late on 8 August. The disastrous Battle of Savo Island, fought on that very night, caused the loss of four Allied cruisers including the Australian cruiser *Canberra*. Vandergrift's marines were destined to be subjected to a protracted and bloody defence of their conquests against an enemy who still possessed a potent naval capacity and a resultant ability to reinforce its troops. As a consequence of the American capture of Guadalcanal, the Japanese decided to commit Kawaguchi Force against the Americans on Guadalcanal and compose a new Milne Bay force.

The Japanese now decided to mount a two-part assault upon Milne Bay. The first part of the infantry force was to consist of the 5th Kure Special Naval Landing Force (Commander Hyashi), which numbered about 600 marines; around 200 members of the 5th Sasebo Special Naval Landing Force (Lieutenant Fujikawa); approximately 350 marines of the 10th Naval Landing Force; and, finally, about 100 personnel of the 2nd Air Advance Party. The selected landing point for the invasion was to be in the Rabi area, near to where the Japanese believed the Allied air base to be located. The date set for the invasion was 25 August 1942. It was anticipated that this initial 1250-strong force could effectively storm the nearby air base and rapidly overwhelm its defenders.

Meanwhile, Major-General Horii's timetable for his assault across the Kokoda Trail was to begin with the attack upon Potts' Maroubra Force on 27 August at Isurava; he then allowed ten days for his troops to complete the crossing. The Japanese assault upon Milne Bay was timed for 25 August. It is highly likely that the enemy therefore considered ten or twelve days ample time for the capture of, and planned movement from, Milne Bay to link up with Horii's force at Port Moresby.

The Japanese operation order for the capture of Milne Bay was rather imaginative:

> At the dead of night quickly complete the landing in the enemy area and strike the white soldiers without remorse. Unitedly smash to pieces the enemy lines and take the aerodrome by storm. In the event of an enemy counter attack before the landing do not get flustered, but under cover of a smoke screen (according to the circumstances use rifle smoke cartridges) go forward to the appointed spot and force an advance.[36]

The landing procedure had been well rehearsed during exercises in Rabaul. It was decided that two companies of the 5th Sasebo Special Naval Landing Force would spearhead the landing, and that tanks, the medical unit, pay corps personnel (to be used as labourers), engineers, explosives and fuel would be landed in that order. The plan called for great speed by the initial landing force and a rapid build-up through a green landing navigation light on the beach. Elements of the 5th Sasebo Naval Landing Force had spearheaded the first Kokoda Trail assault against the 39th Battalion near the village of Kokoda. This unit's record of war atrocities was abysmal during the whole Papuan campaign. Its behaviour at Milne Bay was to be no exception.

The second component of the enemy landing force consisted of a further 350 marines of the 5th Sasebo Force (Commander Tsukioka), which was ordered to move by barge from Buna along the north-eastern coast of Papua via Fona and Goodenough Island, and then to Taupota. From Taupota, this force was to cross the Stirling Range and assault the Allied base from its rearward flank.

But not all Japanese commanders or other ranks had been happy with the preparations for the landing at Milne Bay. Lieutenant Chikanori Moji was the paymaster—and therefore destined to be involved in the logistical side of the operation—with the 5th Kure Special Naval Landing Force. Moji witnessed some of the officers' concerns before leaving Rabaul:

> As the CO poured beer for us, he said that nothing was known yet about the enemy situation in the relevant area. When I glanced at him, I saw in his eyes, as he said this, that he seemed near tears. He had been unable to recce the area by air, nor could any special aerial photographs be taken. Of course there were no accurate maps and enemy strength was not known either. We were setting out in such conditions to make an assault. The CO's feelings of dissatisfaction and impatience were conveyed to us too.[37]

Although the Australians had been very careful to disguise their total air force presence at Milne Bay, and had also similarly taken pains to conceal the size of the infantry force there, the Japanese inability to assess the correct location of the operating airstrip and the size of Milne Force is ample evidence of a poor reconnaissance effort and further demonstrates their preoccupation with Guadalcanal and their Kokoda Trail operation. They were to pay very dearly for that oversight.

The main Japanese invasion force sailed from Rabaul at 7.00 a.m. on 24 August 1942. The fleet consisted of the two light cruisers *Tenryu* and *Tatsuta*, the transports *Nankai Maru* and *Kinai Maru*, the destroyers *Urakaze*, *Tanikaze* and *Hamakaze*, and two submarine chasers. The convoy was commanded by Rear-Admiral Matsuyama.

His fleet was first sighted and its presence reported back to Gili Gili by the pilot of a patrolling Australian Hudson Bomber at 8.30 a.m. near Kitava Island (in the Trobriand Islands). Barely 90 minutes later, three coastwatchers confirmed the earlier intelligence. The second seven-barge

Japanese force, which had sailed from Buna, was observed by three additional spotters on Goodenough Island as it landed there to prepare food and rest before its planned assault on Taupota that same night.

The RAAF Kittyhawks were immediately alerted but could not take off because of poor weather. However, despite low-level cloud cover still over the base area at midday, ten Kittyhawks of 75 Squadron did take off and headed for Goodenough Island. They were in luck. Finding clear skies over the island, they attacked in two flights led by Flight-Officers Piper and Atherton. It was an unequal contest. Pilot-Officer John Pettet would later record in his logbook: 'Strafing barges at Goodenough Island 2 hours 10 minutes. 10 P40's versus 7 landing barges, massacre!'[38]

With the supporting force from Buna now destroyed, the main Japanese invasion fleet was obviously the critical target. It eventually transpired that a number of Flying Fortresses took off from northern Queensland but were unable to locate the fleet. But after one available Hudson Bomber and a dozen Kittyhawks managed to take off from Number 1 Strip at around 3.00 p.m., the main enemy fleet was attacked. Although a small number of Japanese marines were hit by the resultant strafing, no bomb hits were actually registered. Baker and Knight in *Milne Bay 1942* recorded Flight-Lieutenant Jeff Wilkinson's experience:

> We were all bombed up with 250 lb bombs but unfortunately none of us had ever dropped a bomb from a Kittyhawk before. We were told that the only way to do it was to line up the target—go into a steep dive—start pulling out and count three and pull the lever and let the bomb go . . .
>
> There seemed to be numerous small ships around and at least two transports. We went in one after the other and I went down firing all my guns at a transport that was heavily laden with Japanese, dropped my bomb and pulled around.[39]

Aboard one of the transports, Lieutenant Moji, after hearing the piercing sound of bugles, was on the receiving end:

> To control our feelings, my friend and I said to each other 'Well it's come'. We could still not hear the sound of engines . . . we began to hear the sound of AA guns. It was a period when our nerves were exhausted with the stifling feeling that something we could not see was pressing down on us from above . . . the hammering of the machine guns got on my nerves.[40]

As the afternoon of 25 August passed, HMAS *Arunta* and the transport *Tasman* were forced to exit the bay and sail for Port Moresby. The military tables were about to be turned: the Japanese were on their way for a landing under the cover of darkness, and the RAAF, after having accomplished the destruction of the Japanese Goodenough Island second invasion force, was now forced to return to base.

At 5.35 p.m., HQ 7th Brigade issued the following message:

> Every indication attack by enemy imminent tonight or early hrs tomorrow. Tps will stand-to in battle posns until further notice. Attack may be supported by fire from warships and bombers. All localities will push to completion for all round def through-out night. Amn, rations and water supplies will be placed in fighting positions with utmost vigour and determination. Half hourly reports from 1800.[41]

The Japanese invasion of Milne Bay was now only a few hours away.

14 SPIRITS GOOD HERE

After Major-General Clowes had arrived at Gili Gili, he had adjusted the original infantry dispositions and had ordered Brigadier Field to recover his 7th Brigade's D Company, 61st Battalion, which had been stationed at far-distant Ahioma since that battalion's arrival at Gili Gili in early July. Clowes considered that it was far too isolated from potential support and had therefore ordered its return to Number 3 Strip, thus leaving B Company at KB Mission as his most distant eastern force.

D Company's main purpose had been to provide east flank protection for the main base and to patrol the East Cape region and approaches over the Stirling Range. It had been an energy-sapping and morale-testing time for its soldiers, who had experienced infrequent supplies and monotonous food. D Company's only contact with its rearward comrades had been by runner or bicycle courier from KB Mission, where the signal cable communication ceased.

On 25 August 1942, D Company's 17 Platoon was making its weary way back from an extensive eastward patrol. Sergeant Jack Newcomb was amongst them:

> We had been sent down there . . . up onto the range to look for lights on the sea. And we were coming back, still hungry, two quinine tablets, some still with fever, and many of us felt crook. And it rains and it rains and it rains! There were planes going over, water running into the beach and your boots full of gravel, and after a while you give up—you didn't change them, so you're getting real

> cranky! We hadn't seen a Jap and we hadn't heard about a Jap. No tucker and no communications—and what was wrong with a boat to bring us back![1]

There were boats coming, but not for everyone. At dawn on the 25th, Corporal Bert Bradford, Private Kevin Hazel and the OC (officer commanding) D Company, Captain Davidson, met Newcomb's exhausted patrol. They had set out to commandeer a small motor launch called the *Dadosee*. But there was only room for five malaria-ridden men and Lieutenant Tom O'Keefe. O'Keefe simply had to go, as he had repeatedly become delirious during bouts of malaria, resulting in Newcomb taking his pistol from him on a number of occasions. Newcomb and the remainder of his platoon were now forced to march back to Ahioma from the East Cape peninsula.

By late that afternoon, more water transport was finally found. Major Wiles, the second-in-command of the 61st, sailed to Ahioma with the luggers *Bronzewing* and *Elevala*. Major Wiles:

> Going down our Hudsons were flying low with their cargo of bombs & the flashes as they exploded out to sea being visible by the party in the boats. Darkness fell before Ahioma was reached & the hour was late. Only a portion of D Coy was in the Coy area, the rest including the OC & 2/ic being away on patrol. One pl had only just returned . . . Lt Richie was the only officer & Jock McMillan and Jack Newcomb the senior NCO's.[2]

Major Wiles immediately encountered Sergeant Jim MacKenzie and his just arrived 18 Platoon. Jim MacKenzie:

> I was told to have the *Bronzewing* loaded immediately with all supplies . . . and that all arms were to be below decks out of sight so that if it was looked at and examined by anybody, you wouldn't have thought they were soldiers and that we were to keep out of sight . . . and of course we were wasting time loading the galley iron from the cookhouse and all this sort of stuff aboard.[3]

Wiles must have suspected that the enemy invasion was near, as he had very recently witnessed the 'flashes as they exploded out to sea'. He made two errors of judgment at Ahioma. The first was that soldiers should have their weapons at hand in a situation such as that faced by his men, and the second was that the loading of anything not absolutely necessary was costing him time that he could ill-afford. While this process was in train, Sergeant Jock McMillan was attempting to stir the exhausted remnants of 17 Platoon into another long march. It was no easy task as these soldiers had literally collapsed from exhaustion upon their arrival back at Ahioma.

But when further flashes out to sea interrupted a conversation between Newcomb and Wiles, the protracted loading of the *Bronzewing*, the slow stirring of the remaining soldiers of 17 Platoon and the final loading of soldiers aboard the *Elevala* developed a greater sense of urgency.

Sergeants MacKenzie and McMillan and twenty other ranks of D Company immediately assembled on board the *Bronzewing* and cast off; Major Wiles and approximately eight sick soldiers then followed, not far behind, on the *Elevala*; and bringing up the rear came the *Dadosee*, which had very briefly called into Ahioma for fuel. The last group to leave that village were the seemingly luckless members of 17 Platoon, who faced a tremendous ordeal on foot back to KB Mission. Sergeant Jack Newcomb, who had been ordered aboard the *Bronzewing*, 'jumped ship' at the last moment to join his fatigued platoon members on their forthcoming march.

Events now moved very quickly for all members of D Company. Sergeant Jim MacKenzie, aboard the *Bronzewing*:

> . . . and we were told to keep as close to the shore as we could. So I was up with the skipper because I liked yachting . . . we'd come around one little point, and we were making for the next little point, and all of a sudden this native captain said, 'One! Two! Three! Four! Five! How many boats?' And I said, 'Eleven! Eleven!' And by that time we looked to shore, and there were just spots of light coming from shore—galore! . . . and all of a sudden of course Crash! Crash! Crash! The bullets were hitting the boat![4]

When you stand on this fateful little black-pebbled beach near the village of Waga Waga, the terror of that night is not hard to fathom. The distance between the two points of the small bay is not far, and each is rimmed on its extremities by thick mangroves and shallow, swampy ground. Once inside the bay, and caught between the enemy fire on the beach and the barges revisiting the shore with further fresh invaders, the *Bronzewing* simply had to come to grief. Imagine MacKenzie and his few on board almost transfixed by the small flashes and then watching and hearing the bullets ripping into the *Bronzewing*.

MacKenzie then quickly goes below and finds a Bren gun. His short burst is met by such a voluminous counter fire that he refrains from further action. Another comrade, Private George Thurlow, also tries to return fire. A rapid burst of enemy fire quickly kills him.

It is McMillan who now takes control and hurriedly orders everyone overboard, and thus it is now every man for himself. Jim MacKenzie:

> . . . and I'm not a really good swimmer, but I tell you what, could I swim that night! Every time I put my head up there were bullets. So I swam under water until I hit the shore, and then clambered through, looked around, and I said, 'Is that you Jock?' 'Come on hurry up!' . . . 'No,' he said. 'I'm going to wait here a minute.'[5]

For all the high drama of these moments, the Australians do have a few advantages: the masking darkness and the fact that thick vegetation comes almost right down to this pebble beach. It doesn't take long for a desperate soldier to scramble over the beach, through the first line of vegetation, dash across the narrow government track and into the relative safety and security of the bush. It is, perhaps, a fifty-to-sixty yard sprint for salvation through partly covered ground.

MacKenzie makes it. He catches his breath and ponders his position. A mixture of curiosity and the desire to assist others in their flight causes him to return to the government road. But he 'trots'[6] down and in his haste almost falls over a

Japanese soldier who is doing precisely what he himself was doing only moments ago: taking a breather and assessing the situation. Some actions in war are pure instinct. MacKenzie lashes out with his bare feet, bowls the enemy soldier off guard and off balance, and sprints back to where he had come from earlier.[7]

Sergeant Jim MacKenzie is one of the few lucky ones. Some of the luckless members of D Company die on board the *Bronzewing*; others are shot while trying to swim for shore; and others still will face the lottery of freedom or capture as they come out of the water and onto that small beach and approach the government track.

Major Wiles and his ill and helpless few aboard the trailing Elevala have witnessed the carnage ahead of them. Yet again it is an ANGUA soldier who renders priceless help in this Papuan campaign. Private Albert Ramsden and his native crew successfully beach the Elevala and disappear into the darkness with all the men except for Wiles and two other soldiers. Ramsden will return to safety some days later with this party.

Wiles and his companions will return to KB Mission the next day after a passage through a sago swamp and some high ground to the west.

During the firefight that had caused the abandoning of the *Bronzewing* and the beaching of the *Elevala*, Captain Davidson and his small crew aboard the *Dadosee* had experienced far better fortune. Corporal Bradford was amongst them:

> After we had called at Ahioma I started to look for diesel fuel and couldn't find any. I didn't have enough sense to go and get my rifle . . . I was more concerned with keeping the blasted boat going with fuel. And then we pushed off. We hadn't been going very long and the next thing I was conscious of was . . . a Japanese transport. And I hadn't had much sleep for a couple of nights or food for a hell of a time . . . we had this tent up as a sail, and I think they discounted that we were anything more than a native lugger. And then we beached and 17 Platoon elements and other members of Don Company were standing near the jungle.[8]

During those last dramatic minutes of the night of 25 August 1942 and the early hours of the 26th, the soldiers of the 5th Sasebo Special Naval Landing Force and their comrades of the 5th Kure Special Naval Landing Force committed savage atrocities upon both the innocent Papuans who were unfortunate enough to be caught in the immediate area of the enemy landing site near Waga Waga and upon some of the luckless soldiers of D Company, 61st Battalion.

A Papuan who had been forced to accompany the invasion force as a guide was executed for supposedly directing the fleet to the wrong place; numerous others were tied to trees and used for bayonet practice; a young boy was executed by the use of a flamethrower, his only crime being that he happened to live in the path of the invaders; Papuan women were sexually assaulted and then mutilated; and the captured soldiers from the *Bronzewing* and other isolated prisoners from the confused fighting during those early hours of the 26th were interrogated while tied with signal wire to coconut trees and subsequently executed with a bayonet. The Webb Royal Commission would later document 59 atrocities against the indigenous population and 36 against the soldiers of Milne Force in the twelve-day period 26 August to 6 September 1942. Jock McMillan, who had waited on the shore, was amongst them.

From the time of their landings in the Buna–Gona area to their advance along the Kokoda Trail and their invasion of Milne Bay, the Japanese indulged in an orgy of torture and summary executions against combatants and Papuans alike. When the Australians witnessed the Japanese atrocities they reacted ruthlessly. The Papuan campaign was to be characterised by one simple and precise maxim: kill or be killed, with no quarter asked for and none given. Chikanori Moji noted a different attitude in the Australians:

> A young Australian soldier was tied to a palm tree. I was told that when the first phase landed, an enemy boat was encountered and those aboard captured. One had been taken by the first line as guide and the other left here.
>
> I looked at an 'enemy' for the first time. He was a young man of about twenty with blonde hair and a pale

> face. I tried asking him in broken English where our position was and where the Rabi airfield was, but he did not reply.
>
> But when a nearby soldier tried to take a fountain pen from his breast pocket, he shook his head saying, 'No! No!' This gave me a peculiar feeling. He showed none of the solemn realisation that having been captured, he could not remain alive. I thought this attitude to be very different from ours.[9]

Excluding some small number of isolated groups each comprising two or three soldiers, two main parties of the hapless survivors of D Company—the soldiers of the three vessels and Sergeant Newcomb's men—later met up and were subsequently faced with a tortuous trek back along the Stirling Range until they were able to regain their battalion lines on 27 August. And the much-needed qualities of leadership and fitness and inspiration for that desperate group came from their NCOs. Jim MacKenzie was amongst them and indeed one of the NCOs in question:

> . . . in the morning, I got onto a bit of a kunai ridge and I saw another fellow . . . this turned out to be a stretcher-bearer . . . we had a saying in our platoon, 'Who's up who?' Nobody ever knew what was going on . . . we laid low for a while and then off we went . . . I was barefoot and the kunai grass shoots are like chisel points, so that the soles of my feet were getting cut to ribbons . . . then we eventually, next morning, joined up with Jack Newcomb and the party that hadn't come by boat.
>
> At this stage, poor old Captain Davidson got into a panic. The Japs had stolen his grenades and he was wanting to go off and search for them with a pistol . . . Jack and I had a bit of trouble placating this old bloke because I think by this stage he'd gone a bit troppo . . . so we had to take Davo's revolver off of him and we had less sleep than the others that night.
>
> Jack [Newcomb] actually was the leader of the whole thing.[10]

When warning was received that the enemy invasion fleet was near, and that D Company was in the process of being brought back behind his lines, the OC of B Company, Captain Bicks, immediately adjusted his dispositions. He sent a standing patrol of just over section strength (fourteen men), under Lieutenant Bert Robinson, to a position near Cameron Springs late that night (Cameron Springs was about two miles east of KB Mission).

Sergeant Ridley's section remained not far behind in the platoon area. Bicks also sent a patrol along Homo Creek just to his rear to secure his rear and flank, and he cancelled a proposed patrol over the Stirling Range. The rest of B Company now formed a perimeter at KB Mission.

Robinson chose the best defensive position available for his standing patrol: an area where a spur of the Stirling Range ran down to the track. On that spur and near to the track, he deployed Private Latorre with his Bren gun. The rest of the patrol was positioned on either side of the track and spaced along roughly forty-five yards of ground between the track and the beach. He also placed Private Whitton about twenty yards forward of the spur as a sentry.

When you stand by this spur at Cameron Springs it is not a dominating feature nor a high or rugged climb near the track, but it does command a reasonable view over the area and it would have deterred an enemy force from an out-flanking movement too far inland, as the spur climbs more abruptly the further it travels inland away from the track.

At about 1.00 a.m. on the 26th, Private Whitton was alerted by noises directly in front of him. Corporal Bill Wilson was one of the forward members of the standing patrol:

> Robby, through inexperience, sent Wally Whitton forward as a kind of sentry. Now, as we knew later on, you didn't post sentries out in the bloody jungle . . . preferably, you got into a platoon area . . . Now, we had before, and whilst we were waiting, heard quite a deal of war-like noises emanating from eastward of where we were. I remember particularly hearing what I thought to be barge engine or engines but it subsequently turned

> out to be a light tank . . . after a while . . . noises of troops were coming from the east towards us.
>
> Now Bert Robinson had no idea who would come up that track, D Company or the Japs, and he had to avoid firing on our own troops at all cost. Wally unfortunately, instead of coming back to us, challenged the approaching troops in the darkness and was promptly shot and apparently killed on the spot.[11]

Whitton was killed by forward patrolling Japanese scouts. The Australians behind the slain Whitton immediately returned the enemy fire, which resulted in the deaths of at least a few Japanese. During the eerie silence that ensued, Robinson again committed the sin of challenging the oncoming men. When the enemy advanced, Robinson's soldiers opened fire again. Although the enemy force, probably at about company strength, took further casualties, it now rapidly put in heavy counter fire and began to outflank the Australians.

While the distance from the road to the beach is only about ninety yards, that ground could not be held by a force of Robinson's size. The encounter should have been very short, sharp and lethal and followed by a rapid retirement.

Private Latorre, the Bren gunner stationed on the spur near the road, was attacked and not seen again; movement in the dense undergrowth could be heard between the track and the beach; and the enemy now began to wade through the sea towards Robinson's rear. During that confused action, two further soldiers of Robinson's 11 Platoon went missing.

Robinson's surviving soldiers began to fall back. Private Bill Wilson and two of his comrades, realising that there were enemy in their rear, moved into the Stirling Range and would rejoin their B Company at KB Mission next morning.

Sergeant Ridley and Private Fraser, deployed not far back from this action, were soon infiltrated, then surrounded, by the fast-moving Japanese forward elements. In desperation they feigned death. Both men were prodded with bayonets, but when Ridley was actually stabbed in the thigh and still managed to remain motionless, the enemy lost interest in these 'corpses' and moved on. It is a commonly told story in the ranks of the 61st Battalion veterans that Ridley's hair changed to a grey colour quite soon after this terrifying experience.

It is at this point that the Japanese now brought forward their two light tanks against the Australians. The tanks were Type 95 light tanks, which weighed about nine tons; contained armour of about a half-inch thickness; were able to travel at around 18 miles an hour on a favourable surface; and carried a 1.5-inch turret gun and two 0.25-inch machine-guns. The tanks were each manned by a crew of three. But the characteristic of these light Japanese tanks that was to repeatedly frustrate the Australians was their reflector light system. Despite repeated attempts to shoot the lights out of action the Australians were unable to do so, as the position of the lights meant that they could not be directly targeted.

KB Mission was perhaps the scene of some of the most repeated, and also controversial, actions of the Battle for Milne Bay. Its basic fighting perimeter stretched from its back on Motieau Creek about a thousand yards forward to its front on Eakoekonai Creek. The government track run through the Mission at a distance of only about forty yards from the beach near Motieau Creek, and moved gradually more inland as it neared the front creek. A small jetty was sited not far from the rear Motieau Creek ford—only about twenty feet in length. Towards the beach, the Mission ground finally gives way to a short, steep bank of about five feet in height, before it joins a very short pebble beach. The track in 1942 wound its way through a coconut and small rubber plantation and a number of huts. Until then KB Mission had been the base of successive London Missionary Society and Catholic Missions. The coconut and inner rubber plantation was at that time well manicured by native labour, resulting in very short foliage between the neat, orderly rows of palms.

The Japanese employed the basic tactic of moving their tanks alternately along the government track with their infantry hard at their rear. When the first tank reached KB Mission's front eastern creek, it was forced to negotiate a small, narrow log bridge. In order to safely travel across this bridge, the Japanese commander recklessly exposed his upper body above the turret. Lieutenant Bert Robinson, 'a gentleman, with not much to say but a man of action',[12] had provided inspired if inexperienced leadership for his young 11 Platoon charges that night. But there was one military skill that Robinson possessed to a high degree: he was a crack rifle shot. As the tank began its crossing of that narrow bridge, Robinson, possibly assisted by the lights of the tank, took careful aim and incredibly, from a distance of around 130 yards, shot the tank commander. The tank almost immediately ran off the log bridge and into the shallow water of the creek.

By dawn on 26 August the position was that after the Japanese had landed near Waga Waga, D Company, 61st Battalion had been broken up and scattered into the Stirling Range, and B Company's 11 Platoon, deployed near Cameron Springs east of the company perimeter at KB Mission, had been assaulted by the leading elements of the enemy force moving westward. After a series of engagements, the remainder of Lieutenant Bert Robinson's small group had regained their company lines at KB Mission. At this point in time, neither Captain Bicks nor Robinson had any real idea of the strength of the enemy force.

The performance of the advanced elements of the 61st Militia Battalion's fighting on the night of 25–26 August 1942 deserves high praise indeed. The battalion was trained for and initially deployed with a forward, defensive stand in mind, not a series of fluid movements for which it was not trained or prepared.

The Japanese base personnel had worked feverishly during those action-packed hours immediately after their landing. A small sandbag jetty was hurriedly constructed before dawn on the 26th, and on this and the nearby beach the rations, ammunition, medical supplies, bombs and fuel—and the tanks—had been quickly deposited. But time worked against them. Knowing that they were falling behind in their ambitious timetable, they allowed drums of fuel to be tossed overboard from their barges close to shore, to be gathered as they floated inwards. Not long before dawn, the invasion fleet moved at top speed for the entrance to the bay and the safety of the open seas in anticipation of RAAF sorties to contest its exit.

At first light, the menacing roar of the Kittyhawk fighters sounded across the Gili Gili area. Pilot-Officer 'Buster' Brown, 75 Squadron:

> I was in the first lot on the morning after the night they landed. I happened to be the duty officer that night. It was sometime between midnight and two o'clock on the morning of the 26th . . . this shell started to fly over the top of the strip from the cruiser or destroyer in the bay . . . I got on to Les Jackson . . . and he said, 'Do you think I'm bloody deaf!' . . . so as soon as first light took place we took off . . . as soon as we could safely get off![13]

Pilot-Officer John Pettet, 75 Squadron:

> What strafing at Milne Bay involved . . . it was like taking off from the Sydney Cricket Ground and strafing at Darlinghurst . . . just a few kilometres at the most before you were firing.
>
> The Jap barges were all drawn up on the beach and some on shore a little bit and it wasn't a very long beach as I remember . . . and so we were strafing the barges and the beach itself; their hardware; their equipment up on the beach . . . on that first day I strafed only the landing point.[14]

Flight-Sergeant Bob Crawford, 75 Squadron:

> I didn't start my two hours fifteen minutes of strafing the landing point until around ten o'clock in the morning . . . and from then on you never left your aircraft.[15]

The pilots of 75 and 76 Squadrons were now beginning a pivotal contribution to the defence of Milne Bay. But the pressure upon the ground staff, although different to that of the pilots, was no less exhausting. Warrant-Officer Ted Bambridge, 76 Squadron:

> . . . how the armourers slaved—I had every available person belting up ammo—cooks and all and I was flat-out with a ute just delivering ammo from the belting-up area to the aircraft. The only way I could see which was the latest returning aircraft was to observe which one had

> the most smoke belching from the gun barrels. They no sooner took off, before they had wheels up and nose down firing—35 000 rounds in one day is a lot of bullets![16]

The maintenance of the Kittyhawks' machine-guns was only one of many ground staff concerns—keeping the planes in the air was the major one. Baker and Knight in *Milne Bay 1942* quote from the diary of Flight-Lieutenant Ron Kerville, 76 Squadron:

> Water on the runway was inches deep in places and caused damage to flaps when landing aircraft were covered in mud. This hardened on the wing tips when airborne, slowing down the forward speed considerably. Windscreens and perspex were always filthy—brakes 'bound' due to mud intruding and frequently tyres would skid for distances of 100 yards—the metal mesh [Marsden Matting] tearing great pieces out of them.[17]

Corporal Jim Millar:

> All the time while the battle was on, we were flat out repairing the flaps to keep the aircraft airborne. With all the rain, the force of water and mud that hit the flaps when the aircraft were landing and taking off—the flaps were bent all ways. We were repairing mud damage as often as the damage done by bullets.[18]

As a consequence of the fact that the entire Battle for Milne Bay was confined to an elongated, narrow coastal corridor between the sea and the close-by Stirling Range, the Kittyhawk pilots were able to concentrate their fire. During the daylight hours of 26 August 1942, the pilots of the two squadrons wrought utter destruction upon the Japanese landing area. And their attention was initially attracted by a lack of discipline by a Japanese anti-aircraft machine-gunner at the base area, who fired at the Kittyhawks, thus exposing the Japanese position. Lieutenant Moji was on the receiving end of the RAAF strafing:

> The enemy's attention was drawn straight away to our stores dump . . . it was less than five minutes later that the en ac [enemy aircraft], sudden as a hailstorm, attacked . . . when the first one or two ac [aircraft] began strafing with a comparatively mild noise . . . I was not very disturbed . . . However, when the MGs of the third, fourth, and fifth ac came to bear successively, the hitherto relaxed mood around the landing-point suddenly lapsed into a state of tension, panic and confusion.
>
> I felt a severe cramp in the stomach, everything disintegrating and all order lost. The . . . feeling that if we went on we would certainly succeed had completely disappeared . . . we sat on fallen trees and remained silent.[19]

There were a number of dire consequences for the Japanese as a result of the havoc rained upon them by the RAAF that day. The first was the obvious loss of valuable stores that would inhibit future operations. The second was the destruction of their Daihatsu landing barges, which was to prevent any contemplation on their part of 'coast hopping', and thereby bypassing Australian coastal forces, as they had so successfully done on the Malayan peninsula. They were to be confined to movement by foot over bog-ridden terrain which made a mockery of the seemingly small distances involved. The Kittyhawks had, therefore, made life much more difficult for the invading force.

The sterling work of those Kittyhawk pilots also had an immediate impact upon the morale of the infantry at Milne Bay. For the militiamen, particularly those far forward, the results were obvious. But for the veterans of Tobruk, the 18th Brigade, AIF, the close proximity and resounding success of the strafing and the future ground support capability of 75 and 76 Squadrons were heartening indeed—there had been an air force presence at Tobruk, but it had been German.

The scene was set. Any ground gained by the Japanese at Milne Bay was now to be chiefly won by night when the RAAF was basically impotent, while any ground stabilised or gained by the Australians was to occur during daylight, when the RAAF could offer potent strafing support and force the enemy to take cover in the jungle and off the track.

With the Japanese stunned and far from their objective, Captain Bicks was intent on assessing where, and in what strength, his enemy was deployed. Just after 6.00 a.m. on the 26th, a 10 Platoon reconnaissance patrol under Lieutenant Sanderson left KB Mission. With Sanderson journeyed Corporal Cyril McCulloch and six other ranks. McCulloch:

> We made our way along the track, half on the left side and the other on the right . . . the jungle was very dense . . . our forward scout was approximately 20 yards ahead of the patrol.
>
> Lt Sanderson had ordered us to fix bayonets after contact with the enemy and all to finish on the side of the road where the Japs were situated. After about 500 yards our forward scout was fired on . . . we never saw him again . . . it was at this stage that we fanned out and entered the jungle in a straight line to engage the enemy. I was about 20 yards in on the left flank. The jungle was very thick and it was impossible to see any further than about 10 feet . . . I could hear Lt Sanderson firing his Tommy-gun (he was the only one with an automatic weapon) . . . all this time the Japs were jabbering endlessly and telling us in very good English 'To give up the fight.'[20]

During this brief and confused action, Lieutenant Sanderson and one other soldier were killed, and for all the effort put in the Australians were none the wiser as to the enemy strength before them. And in the process of withdrawing, McCulloch and a private accompanying him were raked by concentrated tank machine-gun fire and forced to take to the jungle.

This action clearly demonstrates the difficulty of reconnaissance work in jungle terrain, particularly for troops who are not trained for such operations. Japanese patrols or forward defensive set positions were often able to disguise the main force's positions and strength.

These first twelve hours of fighting must have been a decided strain upon Major-General Cyril Clowes and Colonel Fred Chilton. There were many questions, but few answers. What was the Japanese strength? Was the first landing merely the vanguard of a later and imminent decisive build-up? Was this landing a feint, designed to draw them into a strong commitment away from their vital ground, thereby exposing the critically important Number 1 Strip? Or would the enemy soon descend from the Stirling Range in an outflanking movement upon their vital ground? The action taken late on 26 August 1942 by the Australians reflects this great unknown. Brigadier Field to Colonel Chilton, 11.40 a.m., 26 August:

> I am treading warily. Do not want to leave drome [Number 3 Strip] in case of wide encircling movement. I now have . . . 25 Bn supporting 61 Bn. Arty has F.O.O. [Forward Observation Officer] with B Coy 61 Bn. My Bde Major went fwd to clarify. 61 Bn has asked for bombing at rear of enemy. I am not certain of numbers landed. Jap may be quiet awaiting reinforcements.[21]

Field then signalled Lieutenant-Colonel Meldrum, the CO of the 61st Battalion:

> Take your C and A Coys and push them in. Watch your control road and get cooperation of F.O.O. who is with Capt Bicks and may be able to help you. B Coy 2/10 Bn now forward around drome. No worries about coastal strip. We must get job done today in case reinforcements arrive tonight.[22]

This was an ambitious order. 'We must get job done today' presumably means destroy or at least defeat the enemy in battle.

At around midday Bicks did get some insight into the enemy strength. The battalion second-in-command, Major Wiles, returned to KB Mission after his gruelling escape from the enemy landing site. He informed Bicks that he thought the enemy might have a strength of about a thousand men.

Field's order to Meldrum was issued at 11.54 a.m.[23] The proposed concentration of force was impressive on paper: two fresh companies of the 61st Battalion had arrived in the area and one 25th Battalion company was also assigned to Bicks. The plan was that Bicks' B Company would mount an attack along the inland side of the track and that the 25th Battalion company would move along the coastal side of the track. The support for the assault was to be provided by artillery fire and Kittyhawk strafing. But there were some critical flaws in this plan. The first was the size of the attacking force. Two companies moving against a set-piece defence of ground occupied by a force at least in battalion strength was ambitious. The second was the military quality of the attacking force. As already stated, the soldiers of the 61st and 25th Battalions were not in any way trained for offensive operations, and certainly none of this kind.

But the implementation of the plan was also severely flawed. The vital support offered was in one case late, and in the other far too limited. It was to be a critical four and a half hours after the order to attack had been given before it was effected. The reasons for this crucial delay are unclear. Captain Bicks did have a signal line back from KB Mission to his Battalion HQ. The signal would therefore have arrived in ample time for an early attack. But the RAAF Kittyhawks may well have been preoccupied with their ongoing strafing of the Japanese landing site near Waga Waga. It would be 4.30 p.m. before the attack got under way. And the allotted artillery support proved to be threadbare indeed. The Australian force therefore had only a short period of daylight left in which to move on to their enemy, attack him, and recover the security of their base before dark—a very tall order. Private Dick Connelly, B Company, 61st Battalion:

> Bicks had his company attempt an advance from the mission area of the coconut plantation, in KB Mission, into the jungle . . . that advance began at twenty past four in the afternoon, and we knew having been there for several weeks that it would be quite dark by six o'clock . . . here was an attempt to advance a company in line abreast . . .[24]

Private Jim Byrnes, B Company, 61st Battalion:

> . . . we did have some 25-pounder support but because of the heavily wooded timber and the limited number of

> rounds that could be fired, it was more morale-boosting than anything. The Kittyhawk support came just as we advanced to the far edge of the coconut plantation . . . the airmen . . . were flying in gathering dusk, through the rain clouds and skimming along the top of the tall coconut trees and perhaps in danger more from the elements than from the enemy. They seemed to have a complete disregard for their own lives.[25]

Private Roy Hildred, 11 Platoon, B Company, 61st Battalion:

> We were just going side by side and then crossed the front creek and had to climb a bank to get up the eastern side. We were dead lucky because there were sticks and leaves and bark falling like confetti . . . their firepower was unbelievable! . . . eventually everything stopped. I was given a Bren gun . . . and they left me there . . . I didn't see which way they went. I was near a bit of a track near some kunai grass . . . and time goes on and time goes on, and it was almost dark, and I see two heads coming down . . . from there we withdrew.[26]

At this point the situation deteriorated further. As Lieutenant Bert Robinson and his remaining few from 11 Platoon fought a series of rearguard actions, Bicks and the remainder of his force now withdrew to the western bank of Motieau Creek.

Lieutenant McCoy's 12 Platoon, B Company, 61st Battalion had also taken part in that inland left-flank attack. Corporal Ellenden was amongst them:

> During the retreat to the original start position east of Eakoekonai Ck [the front creek at KB Mission], our platoon became separated from Coy HQ and Lt Robinson's platoon. As we trampled through the undergrowth Sgt Clarkson and some of the wounded & others became separated . . . and were not found until many days later.
>
> By the time we reached our start position East of the KB Mission yard it was dark & we immediately went into

> a defensive posn from the road to the beach still east of the mission house . . . we were not to know that enemy patrols were following our withdrawal. We also were not aware that the Coy HQ & the RAP [Regimental Aid Post] had been moved. Pte Miles asked me to let him retire to have medical attention to a flesh wound . . . he had been hit by a sniper's bullet.
>
> Shortly afterwards McCoy ordered us to retire behind C Coy's position at the western end of the KB Mission yard. As we moved out . . . we noticed a number of shadows who went to ground . . . McCoy went over to investigate.[27]

The shadows were of the Japanese variety. An alert but startled McCoy fired into them and the tempo of his platoon's withdrawal increased rapidly.

Bicks' retreat to Motieau Creek was a smart decision, because the area chosen provided the best ground to contest the advance of tanks at KB Mission. The distance from the creek and track junction to the sea was not a great one and the ground inland became marshy and the bank of the creek increased in height the further inland it travelled. And across the front of the new perimeter lay a sizeable killing ground where the approach of the enemy could be readily seen.

Captain Ken Campbell's C Company, 61st Battalion had established a defensive position on Motieau Creek astride the track. Campbell:

> This creek was a wide swampy area and we were lying in water, and I was concerned about the Japs getting around my flanks, so I had a section by the water and a platoon slightly behind, not far, and another section on my left flank [inland]. The terrain was so boggy and wet that nobody could move quickly.[28]

Captain Gowland's A Company was the third 61st Battalion company allotted to the defence of KB Mission. One of its three platoons had been deployed at Taupota on the far north coast as a standing patrol before the Battle for Milne Bay had commenced. It would have had to face a company of the 5th Sasebo Naval Landing Force if that formation had not been stranded on Goodenough Island by the Kittyhawks on the eve of the landing. Gowland's remaining two platoons were placed astride the track and along the Mission fence.

It is at this point that the almost inevitable confusion of conducting a battle in this area at such short notice and with darkness approaching—and with such poor methods of communication—came into play. Brigadier Field had already sent a company of the 25th Battalion forward to assist in Bicks' attack ahead of KB Mission late that afternoon. The 25th Battalion's C Company had been selected for that role. When the 61st had moved forward along the inland side of the track, the 25th Battalion's C Company had been ordered to move forward between the track and the sea. C Company had experienced an equally testing time during its baptism of fire. Lance-Corporal Errol Jorgensen was amongst them:

> I didn't know B Company 61st Battalion were there. Never had a bloody clue! That's why we were so confused . . . we advanced in extended line; we were from the beach to the road . . .
>
> When we hit this bit of a creek, the corporal that was in charge of the section I was in . . . he was out in the open, and he came under heavy fire, which we all did . . . they ambushed us . . . I was left in charge of about eight blokes . . . we just kept firing and it started to get dark . . . in the jungle and rain, the darkness set in quickly, and we were still in extended line . . . the Japs used mostly sniper fire and a few grenades . . .
>
> And then everything went quiet . . . we could hear all their bloody jabbering all round us and at about six o'clock I went back to find that the Japanese were behind us . . .
>
> So I went back to the fellas . . . I told them there was only one thing we could do . . . we went out to sea and got back like that . . . The company had been told to withdraw about five hundred yards and that order had never got to me.[29]

Bicks' attack forward of KB Mission on 26 August had therefore materialised without the soldiers of the 25th Battalion's C Company having any real idea of the presence of the force across the other side of the track; the attack had gone in very late given its task; and the soldiers undertaking this difficult mission had not in any way been trained for their role.

In the very late afternoon of that fateful day, Bicks decided to re-enter KB Mission for the purpose of recovering the company records and a ute that had been stranded there. His choice of soldiers to accomplish this mission that should have been done when the company first withdrew to Motieau Creek was extraordinary. He not only went himself, but took Captain Campbell, Lieutenant Robinson and Private Jackson.

Corporal Bill Wilson was on other business. Two captains and a lieutenant should not be exposed to an unnecessary risk such as this. And they very nearly came unstuck. Corporal Bill Wilson:

> I remember striking one of our men in the RAP tent which was at the junction of the main track and the track leading north. [This was Private 'Boxer' Miles, who had requested attention for a flesh wound after the attack and whom McCoy had sent to this tent.]
>
> I left him to go north up the track to get the platoon back . . . I told him what I was doing. I went up and saw Ken Jackson and saw Charlie Bicks, Bert Robinson and Ken Campbell. As I got there, there was westward movement by the Japs on the main track and Bert Robinson lined one up and shot him from about 100 metres. The point is that the Jap had cut off access to the man at the RAP tent, Boxer Miles, who the Japs slaughtered on the spot. The vehicle wasn't bogged, it just had to be abandoned. We made our way back to Motieau.[30]

The Japanese had followed the retreating Australians into their perimeter at KB Mission because they knew that the entire possession of the initiative was about to change hands—it was getting dark. After lying low in their jungle cover and surviving the limited Australian artillery barrage, and having also weathered the Kittyhawk strafing, they had not found it difficult to deal with the disjointed Australian infantry attack. Back near the main Japanese base, Lieutenant Moji was also feeling decidedly more confident with the onset of darkness:

> Finally evening came, and when the locality grew dim, the sound of en ac [enemy aircraft] vanished from the sky. My over-stretched nerves were suddenly loosened, and I felt relaxed and realised the stomach cramp had gone . . . and I returned to normal.
>
> . . . we again crossed the stream and went to the original dump area . . .
>
> Some of the palms had collapsed . . . the accumulated stores had either been blown out of sight or incinerated . . . the wooden cases were still burning, giving off crackling flames.
>
> The situation at the front was unknown. The group who had carried amn and rats [ammunition and rations] up had not returned.[31]

After the return of Bicks' small party into the defensive positions at and just forward of Motieau Creek, a prolonged and eerie silence descended over KB Mission. The Japanese were probably using this time to concentrate their force ready for an attack. At around 9.30 p.m. their navy revisited the bay, which resulted in a shelling of the general KB Mission area—without any real success—and a further shelling of the Gili Gili area, which also failed to unduly worry its defenders.

The Japanese ashore managed to signal the destroyer *Tenryu* requesting further food supplies to replace those destroyed by the Kittyhawks. They must have been relatively disappointed with the supply of dried bread that came ashore in exchange for their wounded.[32] In a move which perhaps illustrates their acknowledgement that the mission to capture the airstrip might take longer than originally expected, the Japanese also returned their airfield ground staff to the fleet for the immediate future, as they were an unnecessary drain on food supplies until the infantry mission had been accomplished.[33]

At about 10.00 p.m. on the 26th the Japanese launched a concentrated and determined attack upon Bicks' force. Its main effort fell upon Gowland's A Company force astride the track and near the Mission fence. As the intensity of their firepower and their steady approach to the Australians increased, Lieutenant King's and Lieutenant Tomlinson's C Company platoons moved slightly forward to bolster the A Company front. Lance-Corporal Jim Whybird of A Company:

> We were lying down behind what I call a cattle fence, just a three strand wire fence at KB . . . they began hitting us with machine-guns and tracer. There was also a flame-thrower, and I remember throwing a grenade over there and it was silenced. Their fire was very heavy—we held ours until they got close. One Jap got one side of the cattle fence . . . I shot him through the fence. They seemed to concentrate on coming down the track most of the time.[34]

Private Eddie George was on the right flank, near the track:

> . . . we had moved into position just before dark . . . we didn't have time to do any digging in . . . Eric Peters and I were the Bren gunners of 14 Platoon and we sort of set up a bit of a barricade of old coconuts. They began by sniping and then came in with a flamethrower. He was about 30 yards away and set some fronds on fire. Now, we got him pretty quickly. Everyone fired, Brens and rifles and grenades. One sniper got in behind us because I heard him firing behind me.[35]

As the battle raged in ever increasing intensity, Lieutenant Klinger's mortar platoon, deployed near the bridge at Motieau Creek, and artillery fire from the base area began to bombard KB Mission. Not long after C Company's move forward to strengthen A Company's front, Lieutenant Eddie King was badly wounded. Private George Lorimer was the stretcher-bearer who came to his aid:

> . . . he was standing up behind a coconut palm and firing an automatic weapon. He slightly moved . . . and was shot

> across the throat. I found Lt King being supported by someone. Either his batman or I applied a large field dressing around his throat . . . it was a main artery bleeding so I immediately applied firm pressure on it by pushing a closed fist down on the dressing . . . Lt King, his batman and I, started back to the Regimental Aid Post at Battalion Headquarters, a long way back . . . I heard that Lt King had died . . . there was a shortage of blood for field transfusions.[36]

The Japanese at KB Mission were engaged in their standard drill: strong frontal fire in conjunction with an outflanking movement. As the battle raged, small numbers of the enemy were able to wade out from the shore and gain the rear ground, while a quite troublesome further few were able to move to the inland rear and begin sniping at the young Australians. But when a few of the enemy 'ordered', in very good English, the Australians to withdraw, some began to do so. And to make matters worse, once one or two soldiers obeyed the 'order', others passed it on to still more of their comrades. Such can be the confusion of close-quarter combat in jungle vegetation in almost pitch-black darkness. Private Jim Watt was one of them:

> There was some confusion and there were fellows coming back from Motieau Creek telling us that we were to withdraw. I, with a couple of others, started back to Bicks' headquarters and there is Bicksie with a rifle and he said, 'Where do you think you're going?' We said, 'Sir, we were told to withdraw.' 'Like hell you are! This is where you stay!' So we went into a defensive position at his headquarters.[37]

At a conference at about 4.00 a.m. on the morning of 27 August, Bicks took the only course of action open to him. Knowing that his front was beginning to be outflanked, he ordered a withdrawal to the Gama River, where he hoped the wide, faster flowing and deeper water of that obstacle might slow the enemy force down further.

Unbeknown to Captain Bicks, his steadfast stand at KB

Mission had delayed the enemy long enough for a critical reprieve for the Australians—with the rapidly approaching daylight, the initiative would now swing back to the Australians. The Japanese did not follow him up, but consolidated just to the rear of KB Mission in the thick cover of the rearward jungle. They were only too well aware that the break of dawn would bring Kittyhawk fighters their way.

If there was a certain amount of understandable confusion at Milne Force HQ during 26 August and the very early hours of the 27th, there was, at least, professional calm. Clowes had put in train the best dispositions possible given the training and size of his force. His base area was defended in depth by his elite troops; the enemy had, thus far, landed well to his east and away from his vital ground; he had air superiority; and he knew that if he panicked and deployed his 18th Brigade too far east and far too early, he was unnecessarily exposing his airstrips and particularly his operational Number 1 Strip. And he was astute enough to know that the whole purpose of Milne Force was to keep control of the airfields—at all costs. Major-General Cyril Clowes was in these early hours of the Battle for Milne Bay doing what he did best—behaving in a measured, professional and, above all, completely calm manner. The atmosphere was quite the opposite at Supreme Allied Headquarters in Brisbane.

At around midday on the 26th MacArthur's chief of staff, Sutherland, issued Major-General Vasey with an order to 'take energetic action'[38] against the Japanese Milne Bay invaders. David Horner, in *Crisis of Command*: '. . . Landops signalled Rowell that the "enemy landing at Milne Bay may be a prelude to landing in numbers. The landed force must be attacked with greatest vigour and destroyed as soon as possible." '[39] Rowell would have none of it. He did what MacArthur and his hyperactive colleagues in Brisbane should have been doing—he backed and supported his subordinate at this early part of the battle when the 'fog of war' was arguably at its thickest. He sent Clowes a short, supportive and encouraging signal at 10.00 p.m. on the 26th: 'Confident you have situation well in hand and will administer stern punishment.'[40]

Clowes then signalled his immediate superior, Rowell, in Port Moresby. The signal is a revealing insight into the thinking of the commander on the spot:

> With information at my disposal, find it difficult to understand the Wog actions—especially as to why he didn't effect (or try to) other landings.
>
> Spirits good here—all in good heart. Do wish, though, that the bombing were more effective. How about torpedo carrying craft—torpedoes held here.
>
> Had assumed command of whole show early yesterday afternoon when attack seemed definitely indicated. Had no intention of letting fighters leave here, except as a last resort, though they were very reluctant to stay. They have done and are doing a grand job—a great lot of chaps. Am writing this in their Ops room.
>
> Weather foul here—inches of rain daily and country and roads are foul.[41]

During the early hours of 27 August 1942, an operation was being proposed to Brigadier John Field at his 7th Brigade HQ. The advocate was Lieutenant-Colonel Jim Dobbs, and his plan, with later brigade and Milne Force adjustments, was about to bring the 18th Brigade's 2/10th Battalion into the Battle for Milne Bay. And the site for one of the most action-packed and controversial battles of the Papuan campaign was yet again KB Mission.

LEFT HIGH AND DRY

15

The 2/10th Battalion had been the first AIF infantry battalion raised in South Australia in late 1939. It had seen distinguished service during the famed Siege of Tobruk and had, as part of the 7th Division's 18th Brigade, been stationed in Queensland prior to its departure in August for Milne Bay.

The 2/10th was commanded by Lieutenant-Colonel Jim Dobbs. An original company commander with the 2/27th Battalion, Dobbs had been promoted and given command of the 2/10th in early 1942. Known as 'The Sheriff of Sandy Creek', after personally rounding up a group of AWL soldiers at Sandy Creek during the battalion's stay north of Adelaide (before its move to Queensland), Dobbs was renowned as a strict disciplinarian and an excellent trainer of troops. Captain Geoff Miethke, 2/10th Battalion:

> . . . he was an exceedingly brave man and also very witty, particularly when hearing charges against his soldiers . . . he was very popular with the battalion. He was also very good—and strict—in bringing the battalion to physical fitness which helped us in the really dreadful conditions in New Guinea.[1]

Lieutenant Murray Brown, C Company:

> I knew him very well, I'd served with him pre-war . . . I think his two great qualities were firstly administration, and secondly, his ability to inspire troops. I don't think his tactical ability was equal to those two qualities.[2]

After having arrived at Gili Gili aboard the SS Both on 12 August 1942, the 2/10th Battalion had been deployed in thick jungle at the end of Route 8, about four miles to the north-west of the main base at Gili Gili. The occupation of that perimeter was designed to secure the northern approach via the Stirling Range to the vital base area and to provide flank protection for the 61st Battalion's Number 3 Strip perimeter. The main tasks of the 2/10th in the period leading up to the enemy landing near Waga Waga on 25 August had been reconnaissance patrolling through the Stirling Range and wharf labouring duties.

At 2.15 a.m. on the 26th, the 2/10th was informed that the enemy had landed east of Gili Gili. The battalion was immediately ordered to a position about a half-mile south of its camp area. By 6.00 a.m. a perimeter defence had been established. Later that day, as Captain Campbell's C Company, 61st Battalion moved forward in support of Captain Bicks at KB Mission, Brigadier Field assumed command of Captain Miethke's B Company, 2/10th Battalion and deployed it initially at his HQ and later at Number 3 Strip.

At 6.30 p.m. on the 26th, the 2/10th was yet again ordered to move, on this occasion to an area near Number 1 Strip. That order would have been the result of the 25th Battalion having been ordered east to bolster Bicks' force at KB Mission. The battalion's occupation of its new perimeter was completed by 11.00 p.m. Lieutenant-Colonel Dobbs was not amused:

> It is seriously advanced that such an occupation by night, without the opportunity for prior recce [reconnaissance], would not have given the Bn a fighting chance to do a sound job had it been called upon to deal with an enemy attack at dawn on that ground.[3]

As events were unfolding at KB Mission on the night of 26 August, Dobbs decided to volunteer his battalion for an offensive operation against the Japanese. He visited Brigadier Field at his headquarters at 4.13 a.m. on the morning of the 27th. The circumstances of that meeting are interesting. Sergeant John Andrews was at that time in charge of the 2/10th Signals:

> Things were pretty quiet around the place and I was about to turn in . . . I'd been out helping two of my men get cable to one of the companies . . . to my knowledge everyone had turned in . . . and Dobbs turned up and said, 'I want you to come with me Andrews, down to Brigade Headquarters.'
>
> . . . we went in there and I don't think we were expected . . . as far as I can remember they were in a house . . . we were stopped by a sentry just outside the house and Dobbs identified himself and the sentry called the duty officer . . .
>
> And Dobbs said to Field almost immediately, 'Listen Sir, I want you to let me take the battalion out and have a crack at the Jap!' . . . or words to that effect. And Field declined saying that he'd only brought the 10th down to fill up the hole created by him sending the 25th down to KB. He said that he had no authority to do so.[4]

However, at 10.57 a.m. on 27 August, Dobbs was summoned back to Field's HQ for another conference. It was at this meeting that an offensive operation was planned. What had changed between 4.13 a.m. and 10.57 a.m.? The answer is simple: the arrival back into the base area of Major Wiles, second-in-charge of the 61st Battalion, who had escaped capture at the Japanese landing site on the night of the invasion. Major-General Cyril Clowes:

> During the early hours of 27 Aug several men who had previously been cut off, rejoined our forward troops, and reported that east of KB Mission they had observed large parties of Japs moving eastward. This, and the fact that there were no visible signs on the morning of 27 Aug of additional stores etc, having been landed, seemed to indicate the possibility of an enemy withdrawal during the night 26/27 Aug.[5]

Wiles estimated (quite accurately) that the enemy force was around a thousand soldiers. The reference to 'large parties of

Japs moving eastward' might well have come from Wiles and other Australians observing the enemy making a limited withdrawal at night to escape detection and obtain cover from the Kittyhawks next morning.

It is at this point that we see an operation planned which attempts to cover every contingency and in the end covers none well.

The operation was to be undertaken by the 2/10th, as it was the most easterly AIF formation and therefore closest to the advancing Japanese. Further, its B Company, under Captain Miethke, was at that time deployed at Kilarbo just east of Number 3 Strip. The remaining three rifle companies of the 2/10th could therefore gather it in as they moved east.

The plan had two central aims. The first was to find out, once and for all, the enemy's strength. This would finally allow the Australians a better chance to then plan offensive operations or, critically, further plan their defence of the base. There was still, therefore, a distinct need for accurate intelligence. But the second option was also appealing. If the size of the enemy force was indeed a modest one, the 2/10th might have an opportunity to mount an attack in battalion strength upon the enemy—Milne Force would thus be going from defence to attack in strength.

At the brigade planning level, Field now ordered Dobbs to trek down to the village of Rabi with his three companies now in the base area, and then strike north into the Stirling Range, move along it to draw level with KB Mission, and then attack the enemy there. And in so doing, if the Japanese were making a western movement through that range to attempt to outflank the forward troops, Dobbs could attack them. Miethke's forward B Company based at Kilarbo was to move straight along the coast and occupy KB Mission. On paper it was a sound if ambitious plan that appeared to cover almost any eventuality.

At the battalion planning level Dobbs made a number of critical decisions. The first was to streamline his battalion to a strength of about 420;[6] each soldier was to carry one emergency ration; no signal cable was taken; additional Thompson sub-machine guns were carried as well as mortars. Lieutenant-Colonel Dobbs:

> If time and space meant anything, we must move lightly weighted . . . after having wandered up hill and down dale through jungle looking for Japs.
>
> I was of the opinion that in close jungle a Thompson gun [Tommy sub-machine gun] would be quite as useful as a Bren, and the carrying of a good supply of ammo. made easier for the use of the weapon. An addition to the establishment of Thompson guns, made later during the war, tells that somebody up at the top thought on similar lines.[7]

Given the paucity of the rations to be carried, the conscious attempt to lighten haversacks and the decision not to take signal cable (since they were to travel up onto and along the Stirling Range), the object of the operation was therefore to attack the enemy in force and then to regain their base area. Importantly, the nearest Australians to the 2/10th Battalion's KB Mission perimeter on the night of the 27th would be one platoon of the 25th Battalion deployed at Rabi, and another of the 61st Battalion at Kilarbo.

Moreover, there was another important decision taken that fateful morning by Dobbs. To organise a lightly equipped and mobile fighting patrol, he decided to discard his Boyes anti-tank rifles in favour of twenty sticky bombs. The Boyes anti-tank rifle was a long, very heavy, lethal but often unreliable anti-tank weapon. Its bullet was about six or seven inches long and, when fired, could often pierce the armour of a tank such as that used by the Japanese at Milne Bay. The British 74 sticky bomb contained a core of nitroglycerine and when placed on an enemy tank was supposed to stick to it before the five-second fuse detonated the charge. In Dobbs' planning, the sticky bombs were preferable to the Boyes rifle because they were easier to carry.

The whole question of the Japanese tanks was clouded in some mystery. The intelligence up to about midday on 27 August as to their presence near KB Mission was at best confused and at worst contradictory. There had certainly been one at the front creek at KB Mission on the first night of the battle which had been put out of action. However, no enemy tank had taken part in the fighting against Bicks on the night of the 26th. But Dobbs did not discount their presence but simply chose a lighter, more mobile anti-tank weapon as a precaution should tanks be deployed against him.

The 2/10th left the Gili Gili base area at noon on 27 August 1942. The battalion's second-in-command, Major Martin, led the main formation while Dobbs, the adjutant, Captain Theo Schmedje, and the intelligence officer, Lieutenant Teedsdale-Smith, travelled ahead in a Bren gun carrier to reach Miethke and his B Company at Kilarbo. But events took a turn for the worst almost immediately. Captain Theo Schmedje:

> There was a sentry posted somewhere on our way down. And he reckoned that there was an anti-tank mine there on the road. I said, 'Are you the only one guarding it?' 'Where is it?' he said, 'I don't know, it's somewhere around here, and I've got to warn people.'
>
> So I said, 'You make sure you're here all the time . . . and I suggest your officer takes it out!'[8]

Sometime later a carrier with the doctor from the 2/10th and eight of his staff on board hit that very same mine and all were either directly killed as a result of the vehicle's petrol tank exploding, or subsequently died of burns within days of this tragedy. The 2/10th was now destined to be without critical medical care at KB Mission that night.

After having concentrated at Kilarbo, at the end of the vehicle-accessible section of the track, the now complete 2/10th Battalion (having added Miethke's B Company to its force) headed eastward. But just west of Rabi, the point at which Dobbs and his A, C and D Companies were to have turned and climbed onto the Stirling Range, Dobbs was called back to a telephone. Brigadier Field was the caller, and he had information that was to change the whole concept of the 2/10th Battalion operation.

While the 2/10th had been making its way eastward, Captain Davidson of D Company, 61st Battalion had arrived back at the base area and told Field that his estimation of the enemy landing force was around five thousand! He was in no physical or mental state to make such an assessment. The reader will recall that Sergeants MacKenzie and Newcomb had been forced to relieve Davidson of his revolver on the first night of their flight onto the Stirling Range after the Japanese landing, because he had 'gone troppo'. Unfortunately, given his condition, Davidson's intelligence assessment had also 'gone troppo'.

Thus the whole concept of the 2/10th operation was now changed from a mobile fighting patrol in strength to a set-piece defence of KB Mission.

As 27 August dawned, the RAAF immediately began to fly sorties over the Japanese landing area to ascertain whether the enemy had made a further landing. Its Kittyhawks also scanned the jungle around the KB Mission area for any signs of massed infantry. Shortly after 8.00 a.m., eight Japanese dive-bombers and twelve escorting Zeros attacked the Gili Gili base area, concentrating their fire on Number 1 Strip. They were unable to inflict much damage and one of the dive-bombers was shot down. The RAAF Official Historian:

> The strain was beginning to tell on both aircraft and men. On the ground the squadron's armourers, riggers, fitters, engineers, even transport drivers and messmen joined in the almost ceaseless work of belting ammunition and manhandling bombs and fuel drums. They worked with their clothes and bodies caked in mud and sodden with sweat and rain.[9]

The reports of an enemy tank presence near KB Mission prompted Squadron Leader Peter Turnbull to undertake a two-plane flight in the company of Lieutenant Kerville to try to locate and attack the tanks. Turnbull and Kerville took off at 5.00 p.m. Kerville:

> It was about dusk when we took off together to attack a Japanese tank located on the roadway right on the shore at Milne Bay. Peter was in good spirits and we talked over the method of attack. As we flew out to locate the target

> he told me exactly what to do if my engine failed—'Hop out old boy and swim for it.' He was really happy to be flying again after a day on the ground. He told me to keep top cover, watch his attack and then follow him in. I saw his aircraft dive from about 600 feet up and from about 500 yards out to sea. His guns opened fire in a long burst—tracer could be seen flying in all directions from the tank and I could not tell whether it was return fire or Peter's own fire. He carried the dive very low and his aircraft, during the recovery, turned over, hit the trees and disappeared into the dense undergrowth. I called up on the radio in the hope that perhaps he was not badly hurt—but unfortunately he was killed.[10]

Turnbull's loss was very keenly felt by the pilots of both Kittyhawk squadrons.

The 2/10th soldiers would have either seen Turnbull's plane dive to its doom, or have at least heard the distant crash. Upon arrival at KB Mission at around 5.15 p.m. on the 27th, Lieutenant-Colonel Dobbs immediately dispatched two patrols. The first was under C Company's Lieutenant Murray Brown, which was ordered to reconnoitre the ground over the front creek ahead of the Mission and to look for Turnbull's crashed Kittyhawk. This patrol found neither the enemy nor Turnbull. The second patrol under Lieutenant Parkinson was sent along a track to the north to investigate the ground on the battalion's inland flank. It too reported no contact. The inhibiting factor for both patrols was the limited amount of daylight available when each had departed.

But perhaps contact had been made. Private Summers of the 61st Battalion's Intelligence Section was a 2/10th guide to KB Mission: '. . . we did encounter a native who was smoking a Jap cigarette—with our limited "Pidgin" we could not find out how far away the Japs were or how many he had seen. I've often wondered that perhaps he reported back to the Japs about our strength & dispositions.'[11] It is highly likely that the Japanese had the Australians under observation as they moved into the Mission. The Australian detection of the enemy force would have been very difficult indeed given their limited time and the fact that they would have stuck to the tracks for more rapid movement. However, the Japanese would have only needed a small number of standing patrols in the jungle to have observed the Australians.

Dobbs' decision to deploy his battalion in the actual confines of KB Mission did not impress his adjutant. Captain Theo Schmedje:

> . . . the first thing I thought when I saw the mission was that it was a killing-ground, but whose killing-ground?
>
> I was busy when he [Dobbs] was disposing the battalion. I was hoping . . . that we'd be only bivouacking there . . . but like everyone else, I was taught to look for the unexpected. So I went around to the rear . . .[12]

Schmedje, as Bicks had done during his time at KB Mission, reconnoitred fall-back positions along the rearward Motieau Creek, where the more swampy ground and the creek itself might offer a better chance of operations against the possibility of enemy tanks.

The 2/10th perimeter at KB Mission formed an ellipse occupying most of the coconut plantation. B Company occupied the forward positions; 10 Platoon covered the area just inland from the coast to a point near the track; 11 Platoon was astride the track stretching a small way inland; and 12 Platoon was deployed inland and stretching around to the rear. Looking further around inland, and stretching back towards Motieau Creek, A Company's 7 Platoon formed a 'track block', with its soldiers facing inland, near to where its earlier patrol had travelled. D Company completed the inland perimeter with its 17 and 18 Platoons; and A Company's 8 and 9 Platoons were deployed in the rear along the Mission fence running from the coast around to 17 Platoon. C Company's 14 Platoon, commanded by Lieutenant Murray Brown, was disposed along the small beach bank and facing the sea to prevent an enemy infiltration along that narrow pebbled beach. This allowed the remaining 13 and 15 Platoons of C Company to congregate in the coconut plantation as the battalion reserve. And the one unaccounted for platoon, D Company's 16, was deployed back along the western or base side of the main track into KB Mission as a track block to the rear.[13]

Dobbs placed his HQ in the rubber plantation, which was enclosed in the larger coconut plantation and to the rear of the forward B Company. The carrier platoon was given the role of HQ security. The battalion mortars were sited in the HQ perimeter and in some cases on the edge of that area and near the coast.[14]

Not long after dark, the forward observation officers, Lieutenants Baird and Gilhooley, and six of their comrades of the 2/5th Field Regiment (the artillery) arrived at the Mission. They took possession of a hut in the main Mission area and also brought with them the welcome addition of a signal line which ran back to the 61st Battalion foremost dispositions. However, given the enveloping darkness and the nature of the vegetation in the area, the artillery was unable to select targets and find the appropriate range.

When you stand in the confines of KB Mission during darkness, it seems such a small battleground for a force of this size. And it is difficult to appreciate that while for some 2/10th soldiers on that fateful night of 27 August 1942 the ensuing hours were to comprise some of the most action-packed and dramatic moments of their lives, for others quite nearby the whole night would pass without their having to fire a shot. Despite the relative proximity of the forces involved, communication between HQ and the companies, or within companies, was always going to be difficult, mainly because there was not enough cable brought by the artillery personnel to be used by the 2/10th. Sergeant John 'Andy' Andrews was in charge of the battalion's signals that night:

> When the companies went forward to their positions, I sent two runners with each company, and one was to remain with the company and one was to come back, so that they both knew the way. But then of course, what happened very early in the night . . . they got tied down and in two cases, they got killed.[15]

The 2/10th BN at KB Mission, 27–28 August 1942

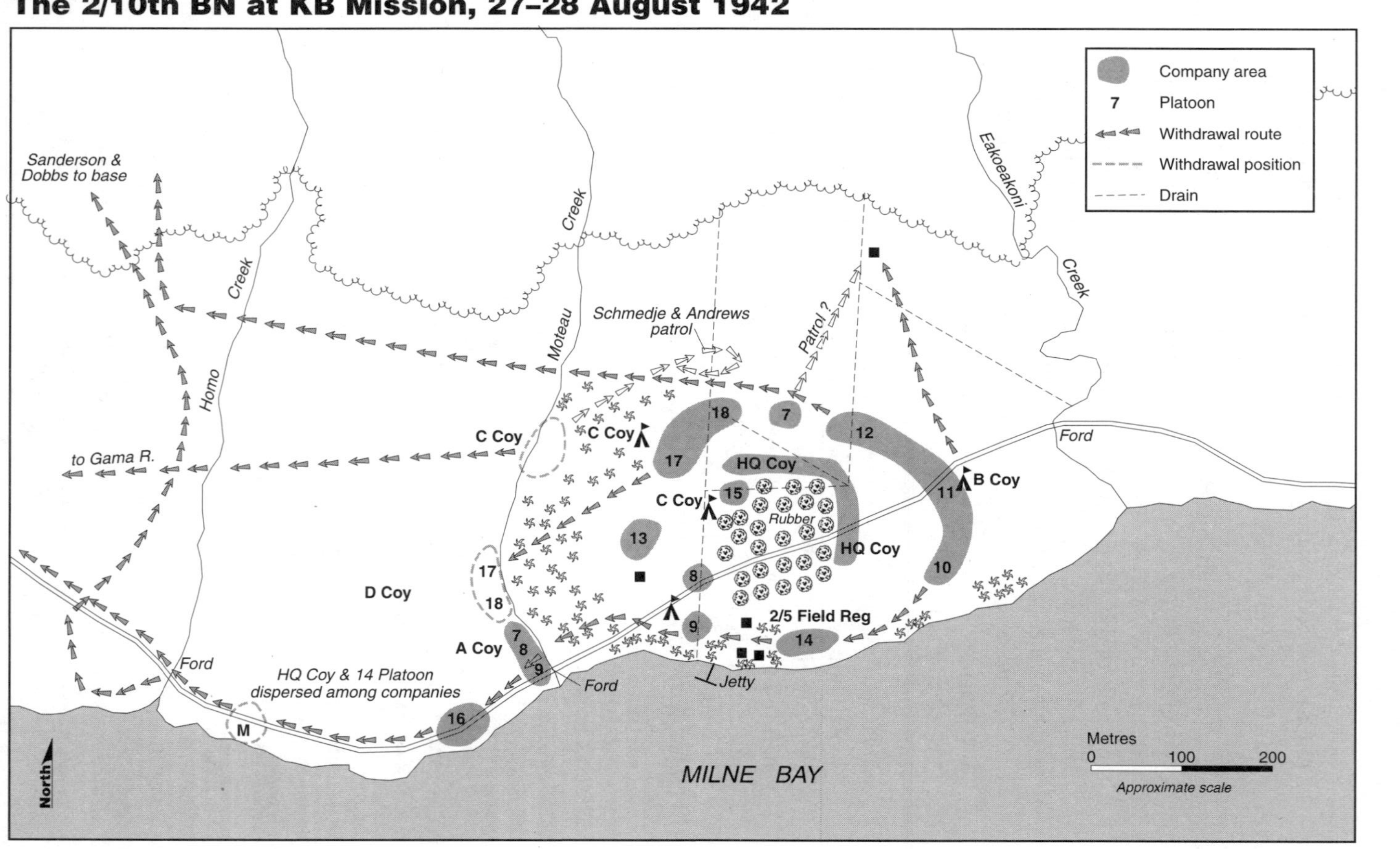

When the soldiers of the 2/10th were deployed in KB Mission that night, they were sited in threes around the coconut palms. The matted soil around those palms made the task of digging in almost impossible. The palms themselves became their best cover. Most of these soldiers had had little or no sleep for 48 hours, so that orders were issued for two soldiers of every three to sleep, while one remained alert. There was to be absolutely no movement—anything that moved was to be shot—no smoking, no noise, and all positions were under voice control from commanders.

That pitch-black night, which was occasionally interspersed by dim moonlight, was at around 7.45 p.m. interrupted by the distant sound of a revving engine. Not long after, the distant lights of a vehicle were seen. Lieutenant-Colonel Dobbs was not impressed: 'Put out that bloody light!' The Japanese refused to obey his order. The humour of the moment aside, Dobbs' order was a response to the fact that he had been told that there might be a 61st Battalion Bren gun carrier in the area.[16]

The beginning of the 2/10th Battalion's battle for KB Mission was unlike anything those soldiers had experienced. Sergeant 'Andy' Andrews:

> . . . and there was all this luminescence on bits of bark . . . quite bright . . . and insects making all sorts of noises . . . but strangely enough, just before the tank came on the scene or before we heard the tank, those noises stopped. And I think possibly, there were Japs infiltrating by this time.
>
> And then we had the 'Barber Shop Quartet', where the Japs went through their chanting procedure . . . it was a most unreal thing . . . it was a bit off-putting in a way because it was something we'd never heard before . . . it was a sort of ritual I think, or perhaps a passing down of orders, because there was a big voice back in the distance and some other high-pitched voices in various other positions . . .[17]

At 8.00 p.m. the Japanese launched their attack. Sergeant Len Tabe, who was commanding 10 Platoon, was not far from the front line:

> Burridge and I weren't on the track, we were about five yards or so off into some bushes. We could see the outline of the tank and then behind the tank were all the Japs. They'd come in between the two sections that I'd put further out and they hadn't fired. I thought, 'Well, I'm not going to fire now, let them get in, and then we've got 'em!' The two tanks had passed and then the Jap must have seen the glint of a rifle or something, and he yelled and came straight over to me! All I could do was up and shoot him. Burridge started firing and then there was sort of a lull. Then the other platoons opened up . . . and she was on![18]

Private Joe Coombe, 10 Platoon, was positioned between the track and the beach:

> . . . you could see the flashes going and almost immediately, Freddie May, my number two [Coombe was a Bren gunner and May his assistant] got shot. It was difficult . . . was he killed instantly or what? I mean it's as dark as a dog's guts! . . . the Japs fired a burst of machine-gun fire into the top of the coconut tree . . . we were getting bombarded with coconuts . . . so we backed off a bit. By this time the tank had backed off a bit. And then it comes in again and it turned its headlights on, and it's spotlight shooting! I did a lot of spotlight shooting in my youth—it's not much fun when you're on the other end.
>
> And I pumped a couple of magazines straight into it and it wasn't thirty yards away, straight into the lights . . . you couldn't shoot them out. We backed away into some tall grass . . . perhaps three foot high in front of us . . . they couldn't get a low enough trajectory to get us, but mowed the grass down above us . . . then they stopped again right alongside us . . . then the Jap took off.[19]

The Japanese tactics at KB Mission that night relied upon the close coordination between their two tanks and the infantry. The tanks performed two decisive tasks. The first was the identification of the Australian positions. With their lights on, and usually operating one at a time, the tanks first fired tracer at the suspected enemy position. Once identified, the Australians were then subjected to prolonged tank machine-gun fire. The tank then turned its lights off, and during that short pause its infantry were able to deploy a machine-gun crew near to the desired Australian position. As each tank ran out of ammunition, it withdrew and allowed the second tank to continue the manoeuvre. On some occasions the tanks worked together, and on others they operated without infantry support.

Not long after the battle commenced, Dobbs sent his intelligence officer back to the rear to bring up an anti-tank gun and to arrange for rations and ammunition to be brought up by motor launch to the KB Mission jetty.

It took an action-packed but short 30 minutes for the vulnerable members of B Company's 10 Platoon to be overrun. Hemmed in by the coast on their right and the Japanese on the track on their left, all manner of escape routes were employed. Private 'Blue' Clarke, 10 Platoon:

> And I thought . . . 'well gee, this is nice! I'm here on my own' . . . after about an hour, I saw four figures coming. I thought they were Japs, and got a grenade out . . . and someone sang out, 'Where are you B Company?' . . . And they came up to me, and it was Bob Fee and Snow Evans. I can't remember the others . . . They said, 'Well, you'd better come with us.' I said, 'You've got no bloody hope of getting rid of me!'[20]

That small group consisted of six men, half from 10 Platoon and the remainder from its rearward 14 Platoon. Corporal Bob Fee calmly led the group forward towards the enemy-occupied front creek and then along it and into the Stirling Range to effect their escape back to the main base area. The very dark night, thick vegetation along the creek, and the enemy preoccupation with their forward movement into the Mission saved these soldiers.

By around 9.00 p.m., barely an hour into the battle, 10 Platoon and the most easterly section of 14 Platoon had been broken up and scattered. The brunt of the fighting now fell upon 15 Platoon, which was holding the forward drainage ditch at the Mission, and the remaining two sections of 14 Platoon along the coast.

There were two drainage ditches that ran from the higher ground inland to the beach. At that time, when the coconut and small rubber plantations had been in recent operation, these ditches allowed the ground to remain firm enough for the native labourers to work. The two ditches were joined by a further ditch inland which ran across them. The ditches are there today, but are far more shallow after years of neglect. When you stand in this forward ditch, you realise that even at its 1942 depth of about three feet it could not have offered much cover. But it did provide some, and it also was an easily identified perimeter line and a later rallying point for the wounded and the retreating soldiers forward of it.

Lieutenant Murray Brown was stationed along the beach bank with his two intact sections of 14 Platoon:

> Our main task was to face seawards to prevent any landing or any approach along the beach . . . two sections facing seaward . . .
>
> The tanks got through B Company . . . I had to reverse my platoon . . . there was a certain amount of hand-to-hand fighting going on in the darkness and I was shot up by one of the tanks; a top of an ear shot off and one through the right ankle and one across the forehead, rather like being touched with a red hot poker.
>
> There was intermittent rain . . . at times the clouds would part and there'd be starlight and pale moonlight—it varied . . . there was a tank there with its headlights off. Exasperating! I did the most futile old thing in the world. I emptied my pistol into it. I might as well have pissed on it! I was just furious because there was nothing you could do![21]

As each Japanese tank sortie crept ever closer to the besieged defenders of 11 and 15 Platoons, determined attempts were made to destroy the tanks by the use of the sticky bombs brought as lightweight substitutes for the Boyes anti-tank rifles. But they proved futile because the moist, humid, tropical conditions had ruined the internal mechanism of the bombs. The other problem was the fact that the bombs relied upon the ability of a soldier to stick then onto the tanks, which was a task beset by the difficulties of the nearby, following Japanese infantry and by the firepower of both them and their tanks. Lieutenant Scott of B Company made two attempts, and on C Company's front Sergeant 'Boof' Spencer and Lieutenant Mackie also made a further two. Private Todd, C Company:

> And then 'Boof' Spencer came up to me and he said, 'When the tanks return, well, here you are, go and stick this on a tank Toddy!' . . . but the damn thing wouldn't stick . . . there was a hell of a lot of noise and fire but you didn't take much notice. They were running everywhere, they got in behind us and were throwing crackers and making all sorts of noises.[22]

While the Japanese had been able to quickly overrun the 10 Platoon positions just by the track and between it and the sea, they found a swift penetration of 11 Platoon's perimeter—near the track and a short distance inland—much more difficult. Their intent was clear: they wanted the track, the limited ground between it and the coast, and some ground on their right inland flank astride the track for security. Any 2/10th troops further inland were of a trifling concern, since a speedy acquisition of the track and security each side of it negated the threat of troops inland. The stubborn 11 Platoon resistance was therefore denying them part of their vital ground.

On this 11 Platoon front Lieutenant Scott led four desperate counterattacks against the advancing enemy. And Private Jim Kotz, who had taken over his section's Bren gun after three of its previous users had been wounded, single-handedly pushed forward to destroy a troublesome Japanese machine-gun post. Kotz later grenaded a second three-man post which had been firing on his company HQ.

As the fighting on 11 Platoon's front hung in the balance, the Japanese were slowly making further ground down along the coast. Lieutenant Murray Brown now turned his men around facing the inland rather than the sea. Brown:

> My chaps were actually kneeling in the sand shooting over this embankment, into the hut area . . . there weren't many people firing and you didn't fire unless you could see something. You couldn't see any more than about ten paces really.
>
> The right hand section started to fall back a bit, and I said, 'Where's Sergeant Gardner? Where's Jack?' . . . the sea was calm and he was in about an inch of water. So I went up to him, crawled along behind this bank and said, 'How are you Jack?' He said, 'I'm stuffed Boss'. And as he said that, a Jap stepped out from behind a palm tree and fired two shots. One hit Jack between the shoulders; he was in my arms and died like that. The second shot hit me. The bullet must have hit a rock or something, because it broke up, fragmenting in my chest. I shot the Jap. By this time I'd lost quite a bit of blood. I went back and saw Dobbo . . . he said, 'You're no bloody good to me tonight boy, back you go!'[23]

At approximately 11.30 p.m. disaster struck at the Mission hut occupied by the forward observation officers of the 2/5th Field Regiment. A Japanese party managed to bring that small group under heavy fire, and in the ensuing firefight Lieutenants Gilhooley and Baird were killed. Signaller Clem Constable was also involved:

> . . . all hell broke out. Someone let out a yell, 'Bloody Japs—take cover!' I saw Lt Baird firing his pistol and running forward. Lt Gilhooley I could not see.
>
> The Japanese were everywhere and seemed to be running and I said to myself, 'This is it!' and emptied my rifle at them, and jumped towards the jetty. Then there's a bang and I only remember getting a hell of a whack on the boot heel. I did not move for a while then as things were very quiet, I sneaked towards the jetty and there I found Vic Horsnell.[24]

Constable rallied his remaining four artillery comrades and three 2/10th soldiers and took to the sea, wading for some distance before the party was able to take to the track further down and later reach the comparative safety of the Homo River.

The confusion on that fateful night was intense. As the tanks made their sorties into various parts of the Mission, selected their targets and then fired and facilitated their infantry deployment, the resulting action might only last for a short time before the tank and most of the following infantry retired. Gains were made in some forward areas, while short sharp Australian counterattacks sometimes restored the position. The battle was characterised by localised confrontations and fighting at close quarters. It ebbed and flowed from one section to another as the enemy tanks in turn swung away, to return later. Two soldiers to the extreme left (inland) side of B Company's forward positions did not see an enemy soldier all night and did not fire a single shot, although the battle raged for over four hours only seventy or so yards away against their 11 Platoon comrades. Not more than 400 yards to the rear, the soldiers of the rearward sited A and D Companies simply lay flat on the ground and listened and watched the flashes of tracer or explosives ahead of them—and, on occasions, the ever-changing paths of the tank lights.

The withdrawal of the 2/10th Battalion from the confines of KB Mission began at about 11.30 p.m. on 27 August. The aspect of that withdrawal which made the whole operation a confused nightmare was the lack of communication. All communication between sections and platoons was by voice. At the company level the problem magnified enormously. The only identified fall-back position was the rear creek. Dobbs sent his second-in-charge, Major Martin, back to that creek to deploy the rearward companies and receive the forward companies as they withdrew.

As the remnants of the 2/10th left their perimeter, the Japanese set fire to the Mission hut near the jetty. The whole area bound by the coast, the Mission fence stretching northward to the track and eastward along the track to the extremity of the coconut plantation now became a macabre illuminated stage where the players enacted a desperate and confused withdrawal under fire. Groups large and small moved to gain the perceived security of the jungle and scrub and, beyond that, the further security of the rear creek. And about two hundred yards to the east of that blazing hut, the two Japanese tanks had now been positioned on the track with their infantry massing behind them—the track and the coast were their objectives and any interest in the ground inland was seen as almost irrelevant to the prime objective of a push to the base area and its prized airstrip.

When you stand at the Motieau Creek and main track junction and then walk inland along the creek, its boundary is at first very easy to see, but when you travel further inland the creek becomes far more shallow and wider and eventually gives way to boggy, marshy ground surrounded by thick vegetation—at that point the creek now becomes very hard to identify.

Although HQ Company and the four rifle companies all had the task of withdrawing to Motieau Creek, that withdrawal was not staged by four complete or identifiable companies. It was more a story of small groups often composed of a hotchpotch of soldiers each doing his best to find his sub-unit, his officer or, in some cases, any company officer.

A Company had the easiest task, as their withdrawal was essentially straight back and not far away. Its soldiers congregated in Motieau Creek and were then moved about 250 yards north of the track junction. The plan was that the tanks would be allowed through. It was the Japanese infantry that the reassembled 2/10th planned to fight.

D Company, further inland, also deployed themselves in the creek bed, but much further inland. But it was the heavily engaged C and B Companies at the front that were the chief concern. Captain Geoff Miethke had tried to contact his 10 Platoon to issue the order to withdraw, but the journey was in vain since its members had either been broken up early in the fight, had taken to the bush, or had in some cases joined their C Company comrades in the drainage ditch to their rear. Miethke, now under extreme pressure on his 11 Platoon front, withdrew. Private Jack Thomas, 11 Platoon:

> . . . they cut us off from the other company [C Company] . . . they were trying to fire from our rear . . . they definitely cut us off, but they weren't able to do it fully . . . Miethke had to get out . . . I just got up to get behind

> a tree . . . and as I stood up, I got hit in the jaw, the stomach and my arm. I think he [Miethke] went straight back . . . I crawled back into the drainage ditch . . . and Langy Slade and a young lad called Hilet, came back to get me with a ground sheet . . . and I said to Langy Slade, 'I'm done for, best you get out' . . . you looked into the darkness and you could see the shadows coming . . . and two Japs picked me up and tossed me into one of the huts . . . I was expecting the bayonet any second . . . from them bending down looking at you . . . and they kicked hell out of me . . . I heard someone call out to them and they were off . . . I crawled to a tree and stayed there till morning.[25]

Incredibly, after a few days of discomfort, Thomas was later rescued and did survive.

Miethke's main B Company group, numbering only about thirty soldiers, travelled well inland, and in the dark overshot Motieau Creek and eventually stopped at the more distant Homo Creek, believing this stream to be the fall-back position.

After most of C Company had withdrawn, its commander, Captain John Brocksopp, and John Andrews, the signals sergeant, each journeyed along the drainage ditch to recover any stragglers. Andrews was rewarded with the task of carrying a wounded comrade to safety on his shoulders.

By approximately 1.30 a.m. on the morning of 28 August near KB Mission, a mainly A Company remnant, including Dobbs, was deployed in Motieau Creek about 250 yards north of the road; a small B Company group under Captain Miethke were to their west at Homo Creek; a mainly C Company group under Captain Brocksopp was making its way through dense jungle and then along the main track towards the base area with the intention of further contesting the enemy advance; and a mainly D Company group under Captain Seddon had settled not very far north of Dobbs' group in Motieau Creek.

Having travelled past Homo Creek and then having arrived at the farther westward Gama River, Brocksopp's group met a D Company contingent under Captain Matheson (this group had originally manned the track block at the

Motieau Creek ford). And there was one further addition to this growing group. When Dobbs had ordered his intelligence officer to journey back to the main base area and obtain a Boyes anti-tank rifle at the beginning of the battle, that officer had sent Corporal John O'Brien on the mission. O'Brien:

> I knew where a Boyes Anti-Tank Rifle was. It was back in a Bren-gun carrier at Number 3 Strip. I knew it was there because I'd seen it . . . I was glad to do something.
>
> It was a good stretch of water the Gama. I thought, 'Now here's a beaut place, the strip side of the river.' I'd had a little bit of instruction, but I'd never fired a Boyes in my life. I did a foolish thing . . . one of the things you're trained to do is that if you lie in wait for a bloke, you've always got to make sure you can get away . . . but I got down, I got stuck behind this bloody great bush, and the tanks came along and the Japs came along . . . and there was a tank sitting across the other side of the river, about ten or fifteen yards, and there was a bit of jabbering going on there . . . I could see the tank . . .
>
> And it's a funny thing, when I thought I was going to die I wasn't frightened, it was only when I realised that I might live, I got scared . . . I fired at this tank . . . it stopped all the talking anyway! . . . I fired two shots at the second tank . . . And there was an almighty bang . . . they'd thrown this grenade at me and wounded me in the arm . . . and I started to feel a bit faint, I was bleeding . . .[26]

But O'Brien's bravery did not really change the train of events at the Gama River that night. Although Corporal Mick Winen and around twenty-five of his comrades managed to evade the infiltrating enemy by heading straight for the beach and then trekking back to the base area, the adjutant of the 2/10th, Captain Schmedje, Brocksopp, Andrews and those near them took to the Stirling Range, and carrying the wounded O'Brien managed to meet up with Miethke's group and the later arriving Dobbs, Sanderson and the main battalion body. After a tortuous climb, the 2/10th regained its base area on 30 August.

It is interesting to note that when an operation does not go according to plan, the perceived blame rapidly journeys down through the line of command to those fighting the battle—no mistakes could possibly have been made by those in higher places.

On the night of 27 August 1942, the 2/10th Battalion was left high and dry at KB Mission. The causes of this state of affairs are to be found at the divisional level, the brigade level and, lastly, at the battalion level.

From Clowes' perspective, the operation which employed a trained, competent and experienced AIF battalion was designed to furnish him with two crucial outcomes: a reconnaissance in force, and the possibility of attacking the Japanese in considerable strength. At this time, he had no reliable way of knowing whether the Japanese invasion was complete in terms of strength and location or whether they were withdrawing, or indeed whether or not the enemy operation thus far was a feint. His 2/10th operation, therefore, might begin to force the issue.

At the brigade level, Brigadier Field made three decisive errors. First, he placed an unreal expectation upon Dobbs of the accomplishment of his mission within the time span allotted. As it was, the 2/10th was only able to reach KB Mission by dark that day—it could never have climbed onto the range, moved along it, and struck down on the enemy in a half-day, and with only an emergency ration and with no means of communication. This was faulty planning.

Second, when the whole concept of the operation was changed by Field late on the afternoon of the 27th and he ordered Dobbs directly to KB Mission, a long-range fighting patrol suddenly became a set-piece defence of a locality. And with that change in orders the gap between the 61st Battalion, which had previously asked to stay forward, and the 2/10th in the Mission should have been greatly reduced.

The third error related to the enemy tanks. It would be just after 10.00 p.m. on the night of the 27th before 7th Brigade HQ made its move to send the requested Boyes rifles to KB Mission. A launch was dispatched, but did not arrive at KB Mission. Lieutenant Tom Abernethy:

> . . . at no time did I set foot in KB Mission, not before, during or after the action. What we thought to be KB Mission . . . was in fact Rabi Village . . . It should be remembered that maps and info were scarce. I can't recall having seen a map and relied on the boatman to take us to the right place. I had not been forward of No. 3 strip before.[27]

Those Boyes rifles should have been dispatched far earlier and, in fairness to Lieutenant Abernethy, under the direction of an ANGAU, or native, or 61st Battalion guide who had actually been to KB Mission and therefore knew that location.

At the battalion level Lieutenant-Colonel Dobbs made three additional mistakes. The first was his refusal to allow the 2/5th Field Regiment's forward observation officers to call in range-finding artillery fire upon the area. This could have been done in darkness by firing into the adjacent sea as was done later in the campaign. The second error of judgment was the failure to take a Boyes rifle into the Mission. The original plan envisaged Miethke's B Company moving directly to KB Mission. Therefore the seemingly sound reason for Dobbs not taking that cumbersome weapon into the range with him did not apply to his B Company. The last error was the failure of the 2/10th to adequately reconnoitre and identify the withdrawal perimeter behind its Mission dispositions. The battalion's subsequent withdrawal at midnight was prejudiced by this oversight.

The action at KB Mission on the night of 27–28 August 1942 cost the 2/10th 43 killed and 26 wounded.

It was one thing for a militia battalion to have been steadily pushed back towards the base area during the early part of this Battle for Milne Bay, but it was quite another for an experienced and highly trained AIF unit to be ejected from KB Mission. The panic of the powerful in Brisbane would now, in conjunction with the onset of a titanic struggle at Isurava on the Kokoda Trail, cause great consternation back in Australia.

Milne Bay, 1942. AWM 026600

The base area, Gili Gili, with Number One Strip inland. AWM 026598

The main 'road', Gili Gili. AWM 026679

A Kittyhawk riding on the Marsden Matting to a dispersal bay at Number One Strip. AWM 013329

A wrecked Japanese barge and wrecked stores at the landing point. AWM 026620

One of the Japanese tanks used at KB Mission. AWM 026631

Number Three Strip. Stephen's Ridge is in the foreground. AWM 014700

Major-General Cyril Clowes, the victor of Milne Bay. 'If you can keep your head . . .' Photo courtesy of Ms Lis Blake (nee Clowes).

PIG'S ARSE YOU ARE!

16

When the Japanese formed up behind their two tanks near the blazing KB Mission hut, late on the night of 27 August 1942, they thought that they had just won the decisive Battle for Milne Bay. Their pre-battle intelligence had estimated that between two and three companies of Australian infantry would contest their capture of the airfield.

The 2/10th Battalion fought at KB Mission with a reduced, streamlined force of roughly that number of soldiers—and they had been pushed back by the enemy. It is little wonder then that the Japanese now formed lines four-abreast behind their tanks and dog-trotted with great anticipation towards Number 3 Strip, and what they thought was the one and only operational strip at Milne Bay.

While the 2/10th had been marching to KB Mission during the afternoon of the 27th, a change in dispositions at, and near, the critical Number 3 Strip had been made. The now exhausted 61st Battalion had more than earned a rest. The 25th Militia Battalion was sent forward from Gili Gili to replace the 61st. Two of its companies were deployed east of the airfield. A Company (Captain Ryan) deployed a platoon forward of Rabi village, a second platoon and his HQ at that village, and his third platoon on the track to the rear of Rabi. C Company (Captain Steel) was the next company in line, with its platoons stationed successively at Duira Creek, Kilarbo, and finally Poin Creek, just east of Number 3 Strip. The final stretch of the track between Kilarbo and Number 3 Strip had also been extensively mined.

Captain Ryan had an ambitious plan to contest the Japanese advance. Rather than perform a standard set-piece defence of a perimeter, he decided to spread his company along the inland side of the track, let the Japanese pass and then ambush them. But the deployment of a force in the dark, the level of training required by officers and other ranks using such a tactic and the swift enemy movement all worked against him. Private Jim Hilton, A Company, 25th Battalion:

> The officer's theory was quite good. When the first Jap met our last fellow down there he'd open fire and then we'd push them into the sea. They were still getting instructions on what to do from these officers . . . we were all in a bloody huddle—we hadn't spread out at all. And by the time that happened, half the Japs had passed us! I could have touched them, they were from me to you . . . they seemed to be going past us for bloody hours . . . they were making that much of a bloody racket they felt they owned the place![1]

The ambush failed. Quickly bypassed and cut off from their rearward troops, Ryan could do nothing more than gather his men and move north-west and further off onto the high ground to rejoin his battalion via a trek through the Stirling Range. After the Japanese had speedily moved through Ryan's positions, they also managed to repeat their performance against the main A Company positions near Rabi.

To further strengthen his Number 3 Strip defence, Brigadier Field had also sent a further anti-tank gun from the 101st Anti-tank Regiment to cover the minefield at Kilarbo, along with a truckload of sticky bombs, Molotov cocktails and further supplies of ammunition. The bog-ridden main track caused this truck to become immobilised, and after it had been disabled it was abandoned and used as a track block by Lieutenant Schlyder's platoon. However, only a platoon strength track block merely invited the inevitable Japanese outflanking movement, which caused the Australians a further withdrawal to C Company's positions at Kilarbo.

The detachment from the 101st Anti-tank Regiment sent by Field to Number 3 Strip was commanded by Lieutenant

Keith Acreman. The establishment of an anti-tank regiment consisted of four batteries, each of four troops with four 2-pounder guns. Keith Acreman commanded D troop's four 2-pounders—guns D1, D2, D3 and D4. Lieutenant Keith Acreman:

> When you deploy them, under normal circumstances, you put them on the ground and fold their legs out, and they sit on their legs so you get three-hundred-and-sixty degrees traverse, and you camouflage them, so that you're actually firing very low . . . but you transport them by either pulling them behind on wheels, which you can take out, or you can put them on top of a Portee [a flat topped truck] . . .[2]

At around midnight on the 27th—just after the 2/10th had withdrawn from the confines of KB Mission—the battery commander arrived and Acreman was ordered to site two guns forward of Number 3 Strip. He deployed guns C4 and D4 covering the bridge across Anabila Creek and its adjacent beach. As the latest intelligence indicated that the Japanese tanks were fast approaching his positions, he decided to leave the two 2-pounders on their Portees and deploy them off the track with the intention of firing the guns over the back of the trucks. A section of infantry from the 25th Battalion accompanied Acreman as protection for the guns—sparse protection indeed. Keith Acreman:

> . . . the Japs hit us . . . we heard them but didn't see them except their gunfire . . . suddenly we realised there was no 303's firing against them. What happened I don't know. So we had to open fire . . . and then we ran out of ammunition. Then I tried to get the guns out. The layer on the other gun, was dead. He'd been shot. Then I tried to get the other gun out and it bogged. There's a fire mechanism on the gun which you can take off very quickly and that immobilises the gun . . . so we took that and we decided, well the only thing we can do is walk back to the strip . . .[3]

Milne Force Dispositions, 28 August 1942

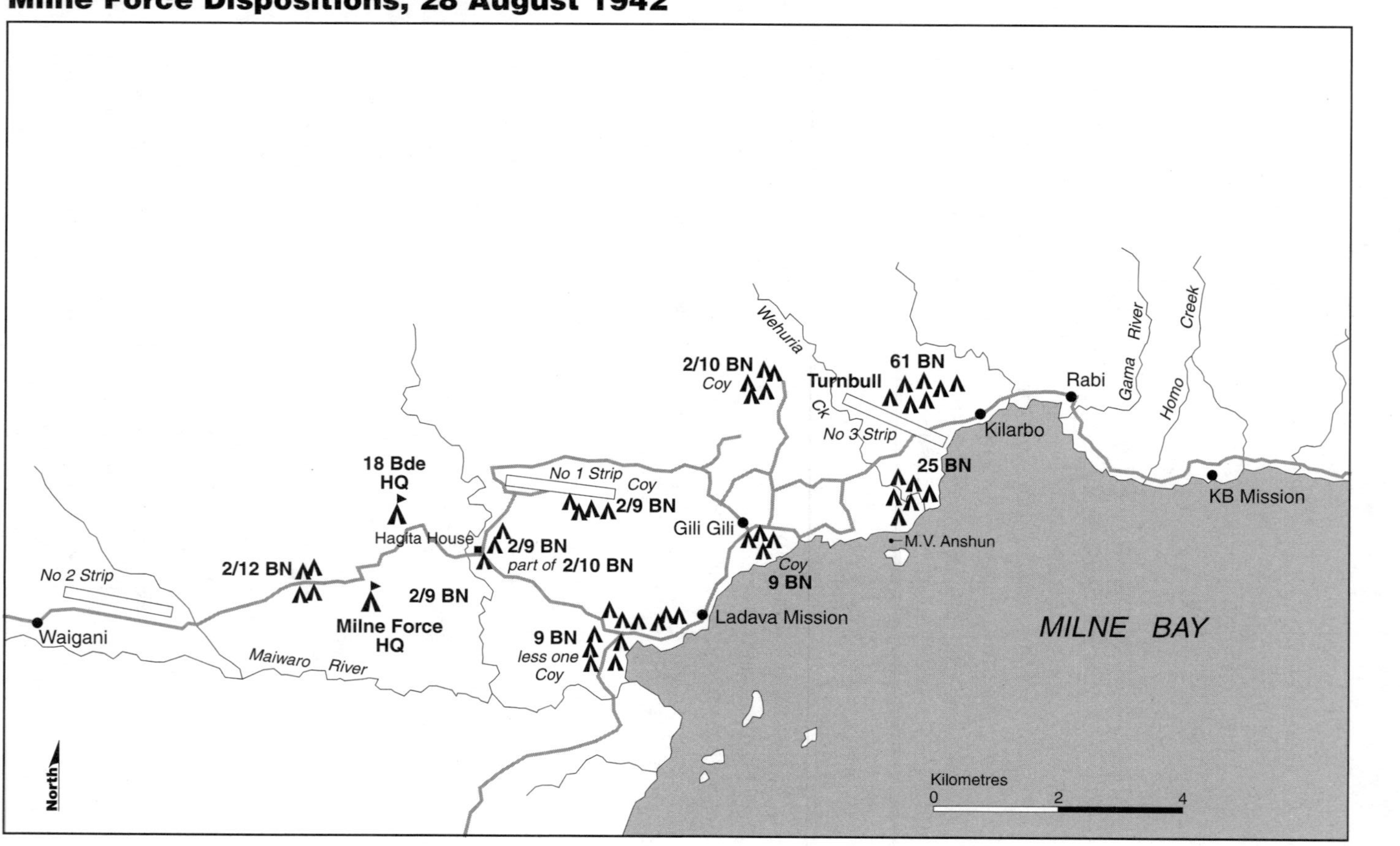

Acreman's small force withdrew successfully under enemy fire. In all this, Acreman might have been forgiven for thinking that his mission had failed dismally, and that his action in the Battle for Milne Bay was over. But a quick decision taken by him not only saved his little group from being fired on as they moved back to Number 3 Strip, but would greatly influence the eventual outcome of the battle. On the way back he seconded a 25th Battalion signaller who was able to tap into the line and warn the defenders at the strip that his group were coming through. Unbeknown to the Australians, by around 5.30 a.m. on 28 August the Japanese tanks had also become bogged near Rabi.

By the time the enemy forward elements had reached Kilarbo, the narrow coastal corridor between Number 3 Strip and that village had become a jumbled conglomeration of soldiers from both sides. Lance-Corporal Errol Jorgensen, C Company, 25th Battalion: '. . . it was that bloody well confused that there was Japanese coming back, the 2/10th fellas behind them, and Japanese behind them. And we didn't know who we were shooting at. Didn't have a clue—we could have killed some of our own fellas . . .'[4] To this hotchpotch of soldiers from both sides should be added a certain number of 25th Battalion soldiers who were also by now scattered and making their way back. The confusion and nerve-racking nature of that night actually caused an Australian manning a machine-gun to be bayoneted by his comrades as they came back and on to his position.[5]

Once again, as had occurred during the 61st Battalion's early actions, it was the steadying influence of an 'old hand' that rallied and inspired the young soldiers of the 25th Battalion. As the soldiers of C Company arrived near a just-cleared proposed dispersal bay for future aircraft on Number 3 Strip, an imposing figure materialised from the darkness. Lance-Corporal Errol Jorgensen:

> We were forward of that [the dispersal bay] . . . at about three or four o'clock in the morning, after this confusion, we thought it was time to go! . . . there was about fifteen or sixteen of us, there might have been a few more. And all of a sudden out of the bushes comes the RSM [the

> Regimental Sergeant Major]—Barnett . . . 'Where are you so-and-so fellas going! I'll shoot the first fella that bloody well takes another step!' And he says, 'Right follow me!' And this is where he put us in this dispersal bay there, just off the road. He laid us out in about six fellas. And he said, 'When one fella gets killed the next moves up.' That's how it was. And the Japanese came along and swung right into us.[6]

Sergeants Ludlow and Steel and their men of this small force were able to inflict telling casualties upon the Japanese from this position. When a number of enemy soldiers climbed trees to snipe at the Australians, Ludlow hurled four-second fuse grenades into some of the trees.

This engagement not only cost the Japanese casualties but critical time. With the arrival of sunrise, the Kittyhawks once more took to the skies over them and began their seemingly ceaseless patrolling and strafing. The Japanese dispersed into the surrounding jungle. The young soldiers of the 25th Battalion withdrew across Number 3 Strip at around 8.00 a.m. on 28 August.

Chikanori Moji, 5th Kure Special Naval Landing Force:

> Next morning our light sleep was disturbed by the sound of en [enemy] engines. The airfd had still not been taken and the prospects of taking it had seemed doubtful since yesterday. Nevertheless we were downcast again when we heard the engines.
>
> . . . those in the front line must be exhausted. I was also concerned about the rats [rations]. There would by now, be very little dry bread left in their haversacks. I was very much on edge. In regard to rats, the rear was in the same plight.[7]

At Milne Bay, 28 August 1942 was a day of consolidation for both sides. The Japanese were tired and still far short of their objective. They concentrated on moving their limited rations forward to their front line, while the Australians now strengthened their Number 3 Strip perimeter. Given the need to maintain a strong Gili Gili base area protection, the 61st

Battalion, although fatigued from its eastward campaigning, was moved back to the Number 3 Strip perimeter. Arthur Ballard of the 2/2nd Heavy Anti-Aircraft Regiment witnessed their return:

> We were horrified by their condition. They were asleep on their feet, mud caked and they seemed in a state of shock. Worst of all was their age. They seemed only kids and these were the thin red line between us and the Japanese army. Anyway they moved into our tents, blankets, ground sheets and collapsed from fatigue after a feed.[8]

> To NG FORCE from MILNE FORCE 27 August. Private for GEN ROWELL from CLOWES. Still no repeat no definite indication whether further landing effected last night. Tpts [tranports] not repeat not seen but could have been present and landed trps well east of our left flank. Jap inactivity and certain other indications may possibly mean re-embarkation portion of troops landed night 25/26. Several tanks active at present against 2/10th Bn vicinity KB Mission . . .[9]

Rowell to Vasey, 27 August:

> I took a lousy view of your signal telling us to be offensive as the convoy might be a prelude to further landings.
>
> . . . you must move slowly in 2 feet of mud however much you desire to run. Again if the bombers can't sink ships, what about some navy (is there any left?) or torpedo bombers. There are torpedoes at Milne Bay but all the Beauforts are apparently being kept for exhibition in Sydney.
>
> To cut a long story short, I refused to send a copy of the signal to Cyril, in its place assured him of my complete confidence in his ability to administer stern punishment.

> We're still guessing at the size of the force & I can only hope that the Wog has been completely surprised as a result of his inability to make air recce & didn't know what was there. Perhaps in a few moments I'll be able to send Cyril another 'good luck' signal. It's a great life.[10]

General Sutherland, MacArthur's chief-of-staff, to Blamey, 28 August:

> The commander-in-chief requests that you instruct Major-General Clowes at once to clear the north shore of Milne Bay without delay and that you direct him to submit a report to reach General Headquarters by 0800K/29 [8.00 a.m. 29 August] of the action taken together with his estimate of the enemy's strength in the area. Please further request General Clowes's opinion as to the possibility that a second movement of enemy shipping into Milne Bay was for the purpose of withdrawing forces previously landed.[11]

Vasey to Rowell, 28 August:

> Dear Syd,
> The lack of information from you on the operations at Milne Bay has created a very difficult situation here. GHQ get through air sources various scraps of information. The source of these is usually not given and they generally indicate a lack of activity on the part of our troops in the area. Our view is that these are not worth anything, but in default of authentic information from you we are not in a position to combat GHQ, whose outlook is based on these sundry reports.
>
> Only two minutes ago I have been phoned by Sutherland asking me what reports I had, and what offensive action had been taken by Cyril. I was compelled to answer that I was unaware. Sutherland stated that MacArthur was very concerned about the apparent lack of activity on Cyril's part. I replied that it was not necessarily a lack of activity, but a lack of information.
>
> . . . You possibly do not realise that for GHQ this

> is their first battle, and they are, therefore, like many others, nervous and dwelling on the receipt of frequent messages . . .
>
> By the tone of this morning's conversation with Sutherland, I feel that a wrong impression of our troops has already been created in the minds of the great, and it is important for the future that that impression be corrected at the earliest possible moment.[12]

Clowes to Rowell, 28 August:

> My Dear Syd,
> The situation seems to grow curiouser and curiouser down here. Find it very difficult with limited inform at hand to determine what Moto is up to.
>
> He has made three visits here and yet to date has not made any real attempt to deal with the situation, though he succeeded in cleaning up the 2/10th with tanks . . .[13]

And later on the same day:

> Dear Old Syd,
> Things are not so hot really in these parts. You will have had the story in sitreps [situation reports] & have given the ALO the sitn. as of 1600 hrs. True to style, the Jap is doing his dirty work by night, and seems to be getting much the better of it against our chaps.[14]

Advanced LHQ (Land Headquarters) G Branch, 28 August (author unknown):

> MACARTHER [*sic*] becoming very perturbed. ROWELL has acknowledged receipt our instn for offensive action. Have wired ROWELL for immediate report.[15]

A small Papuan community now lives at this beautiful village. It sits right where the end of the 1942 Number 3 Strip ran to the sea. When you walk from the narrow beach onto the small rise, past a canoe and through the huts, you immediately notice the extensive gap in the otherwise thick jungle vegetation on either side. This was Number 3 Strip, which is now a swathe of waving kunai grass stretching inland. And when you drive through and flatten some of that grass, some concept of its 1942 significance dawns on you.

By the beginning of the Battle for Milne Bay, the American engineers had bulldozed a strip roughly two thousand yards long and about eighty yards wide, running inland right from the beach. At the north-eastern end of Number 3 Strip is Stephen's Ridge, which runs about a third of the way down the strip's eastern side. On that ridge, in 1942, was Stephen's House. The site of this once elegant home is now overgrown with jungle, but the evidence of its grandeur remains. Its steps are now embedded in the earth; old flower tubs, bottles and rock garden perimeters are still visible; and watching over the land is Stephen's grave, still set apart by a circle of small rocks from the enveloping jungle. As you walk down a little way from Stephen's House you arrive at a small creek, which is either the start of Poin Creek or perhaps a small tributary of it.

The 61st Battalion deployed a platoon upon and around this ridge, dug in and sited two Bren guns. The remainder of the 61st dispositions ran down from Stephen's Ridge along the base side of the strip.

The defensive line running from the beach inland to join the 61st Battalion's dispositions was also impressive. The 25th Battalion was deployed in depth from the sea along the strip to the road and back to Wehria Creek, and an awesome array of 25th and 61st Battalion Vickers machine-guns, American half-track vehicles, mortars and infantry stretched along the entire length of that feature.

This was no hastily prepared defence of a position where the enemy could outflank the Australians because of superior concentration of force, or where he could infiltrate through thick vegetation. Both flanks were covered: one was the sea flank covered by the open strip killing ground running right down to it, and the other was the high ground on Stephen's Ridge where the Australians were well dug in. And here, finally, was an impressive perimeter defence. When the enemy came to cross that consummate killing ground, the Australians would have the firepower to combat him.

Lieutenant John Paterson, officer commanding 21 Platoon, E Company (the machine-gun company), 61st Battalion:

> Generally, Vickers guns are quite unsuited for jungle warfare. They lack mobility in that they have to be carried in two sections. The tripod approximately 50 lbs, the gun weighing approximately 30 lbs, plus a condenser can holding about 2 gallons of water, plus several metal ammunition boxes each holding a belt of some 200 rounds. However at Number Three Strip, they were ideally suited to the task . . . the cleared strip presented a perfect killing ground. From memory the strip was about 80 yards wide . . . my field of fire was the track and either side of it. The other two platoons of the coy were positioned, one on my right [southern] side of the track, and one on my left [northern] side. Their fields of fire were to right and left respectively. All guns were sited so that their zones of fire over-lapped creating a solid blanket of fire.[16]

In addition to this impressive array of firepower, the 25th Battalion mortars were stationed on the inland side of the track and just to the rear of the strip, and the American half-track vehicles, with their armour plating and 50 and 30 calibre machine-guns, were ahead of the mortars on the edge of the strip. In addition to these defences, Major-General Clowes, while leaving his 2/9th Battalion, AIF in its original positions, now brought forward his 2/12th Battalion to a point just west of Milne Force HQ to enable him to begin offensive operations if the opportunity presented itself.

It is at this point that a certain degree of panic and rumour—one usually follows the other—broke out at Milne Bay. The first was the decision to fly out the air force on 29 August 1942. There has been some conjecture as to the source of the decision. Colonel Fred Chilton:

> I could never understand why the order was given to recall the aircraft. I don't think it came from the airmen on the

> spot. As far as we were concerned, the battle was contained and we were winning—we had the thing under control, unless the Jap reinforcements came in. Somebody, for some reason, without knowing the situation sent back a panic signal; it may have come from the air force or more likely, it may have come from the American engineering unit. I don't think Clowes was consulted but if he was I don't recall any discussion on the subject.[17]

Group-Captain Bill Garing was the RAAF commander at Milne Bay:

> Clowes told me that the situation was critical and that he couldn't guarantee that the Japanese wouldn't get onto the airfields that night. I can remember that very distinctly. I thought, well if that's the case, I shouldn't leave aeroplanes on an airfield that can be captured. That had happened in previous battles.[18]

The reaction from the pilots was mixed. Pilot-Officer David Pank, 76 Squadron:

> . . . we were ordered to fly all serviceable aircraft to Port Moresby that night. Now, Truscott refused to go. But the point was, you can look at it either way you like, the army were a bit cheesed off because they'd say, 'The bloody air force is deserting us!' But I firmly believe it was the right thing to do; we knew we were going to come back the next morning, assuming that we could get back the next morning. In other words, that they hadn't taken the bloody airstrip in the meantime . . . but the last thing we wanted to do was catch all the bloody aircraft on the ground that night and lose the lot. That was the danger! Truscott objected to it and he stayed with the troops. Now that was great from his point of view. It was a gesture. But I still believe that he was wrong really, because we had to save those aeroplanes.[19]

The decision to send the Kittyhawk fighters from Gili Gili to Port Moresby in no way affected the outcome of the battle. Given that the battle for Number 3 Strip would almost certainly occur during darkness, the planes would have found it almost impossible to have taken off during the night, as it was difficult enough to either take off or land during daylight. Second, although Chilton seems to have had no recollection of the order coming from Clowes, Garing distinctly remembers it being made by that commander. In the event the decision was a sound one, because it influenced the battle not a bit but covered all contingencies.

The arrival and subsequent proceedings in the RAAF mess at Port Moresby demonstrates the stress and strain that the pilots had endured at Milne Bay. Their doctor noted the proceedings:

> This [the mess in Port Moresby] had become quite 'Proper' since our last visit several months earlier. The squalor and heat of battle were only a couple of hours behind. Several of the pilots wore wide felt hats known as 'Gili Gili hats' and they were unshaven with a variety of beards and moustaches. All wore .38 revolvers, mud covered flying boots and filthy shorts and shirts . . . Then the bawdy songs started . . . General Kenny was in command of the US Army Air Force . . . it was unfortunate that he chose this moment to visit Moresby and walk into the Mess with his staff. He showed great interest in this unusual motley collection of Australian pilots, enquired carefully about their activities . . . However, after watching their uninhibited antics and conscious of an element of Aussie disrespect he and his entourage walked out. The party continued well into the night. Bruce Brown reported, 'They wanted to shut the bar but we just showed them our .38s' [revolvers].[20]

The second event which indicates the panic in some quarters was the rumour that Major-General Cyril Clowes had made a contingency plan to evacuate Milne Bay himself. The rumour was widespread, as many veterans recall, but it was totally without foundation. No commander would abandon a perimeter which had not, in any way up until now been breached, where he had total air superiority and where he had not as yet been forced to commit his best trained and experienced troops to his battle. And the prime point is that such an action would have run against the character and grain of this most calm, assured and capable officer. We have noted his perfectly composed demeanour at Pinios Gorge in Greece, his decorations for coolness and competence under fire throughout his career, and the nature of the man himself. It would have taken a lot more than the events at Milne Bay up to this juncture—however confused they were—to cause panic in this distinguished Australian commander. In fact, a similar dose of coolness and confidence might have been a desirable state of mind for those in Brisbane to have possessed. Further, Lieutenant-General Rowell, during the whole course of the Battle for Milne Bay, displayed absolute confidence in his old friend and colleague, for no other reason than that Clowes had repeatedly earned that respect and trust.

We have witnessed the signal exchanges between Brisbane and Port Moresby on 28 August. That day, apart from the exit of the planes from Number 1 Strip, was a quiet one at the front. The reasons are clear. The Japanese were busily engaged in resting in the jungle and seeking its cover by day from the Kittyhawks. Lieutenant Moji had begun to notice the effects of the environment on himself and his comrades:

> It was about this time that everybody's feet started to become swollen and inflamed. This area was in the middle of the rainy season and the weather was unpleasant. There was no heavy rain but it was always overcast and showers fell frequently so that it was muddy underfoot.
>
> Since we were crossing streams and constantly walking through mud wearing shoes or 'heavy' (outdoor) socks, the ankles would swell and something like ulcers formed on them. Those who suffered most severely could not get their boots on and they wound gaiters around their ankles instead of shoes. I did not suffer much with my feet, but as I was often sitting in damp spots, much the same happened to my buttocks.[21]

On 29 August forward patrols of the 7th Brigade found the two bogged Japanese tanks near Rabi and destroyed their tracks and engines. But when an RAAF reconnaissance plane identified an enemy convoy consisting of a cruiser and nine destroyers heading for Milne Bay, Clowes suspended plans for his 18th AIF Brigade to commence preliminary offensive operations from Number 3 Strip to KB Mission, which he had hoped might begin the next day.

The third instance of panic erupted on the morning of the 29th when someone in the base area decided to blow up the main base canteen. This was the result of an inexperienced staff and a lack of discipline after a rumour had spread through the base that an enemy patrol had pierced the Number 3 Strip perimeter. The explosion destroyed the canteen building but not the RAAF beer stores. Pilot-Officer David Pank, 76 Squadron:

> . . . the AIF blokes got into this very smartly, and they were going away with bloody cases on their shoulders; all the air force beer! And I remember looking up the 2/10th blokes [South Australians like Pank], Austin Ifould and all of those blokes and saying, 'Please can we come and visit you and have some of our beer?' . . . and out of the goodness of their hearts they'd give us a drink of our own bloody beer![22]

At around midnight, the Japanese convoy sighted by the RAAF that day shelled the base area but caused no casualties and little damage. However, an RAAF crash boat sent out onto the bay to report on any enemy approach was sunk prior to the midnight shelling.

The arrival of the Japanese convoy saw a significant and much-needed infantry reinforcement for their Milne Bay force. At about 2.00 a.m. on the morning of 30 August, around 550 troops of the 3rd Kure Special Naval Landing Force and about 200 soldiers of the 5th Yokosuka Force landed near KB Mission. While fresh troops were entirely welcome, the selection of their disembarkation point did not impress Chikanori Moji:

> It seems to have been about noon 29 Aug that a wireless message arrived 'reinforcements being sent, secure

> coastline'. We were first told by Lt Fujikawa in the native huts at Hilna [KB Mission] that 3 K SLF would land that night as reinforcements . . . but were our reinforcements to land in this area, it would still be a long way to the airfield, and they would be advancing from a direction for which the enemy were prepared. The failure would be repeated unless the reinforcements landed the other side of Rabi or immediately in the vicinity of Rabi [the Japanese referred to the main base area as 'Rabi'] . . . Lt Fujikawa . . . immediately gave orders to a sig to be ready to pass this view by visual sigs to Tenryu as it came in.
>
> We were surprised however when the first flight of barges with the reinforcements came in towards the sig light, arriving at the coast with fully-armed pers [personnel] of 3K. Our thought was 'It's no good landing here'. . .[23]

When CO Hayashi of the now sorely tried 5th Kure Special Naval Landing Force (SNLF) met his opposite number of the newly arrived 3rd Kure SNLF, Moji witnessed the conversation:

> CO 3K, in white crossed webbing and a moustache suggesting great and fearless vigour, was saying to Hayashi, 'Let's go into the atk [attack] straight away.' Hayashi was subdued in front of this imposing CO 3K, and quietly said, 'They're all exhausted. It would be unreasonable for them to atk the airfd straight away with the rnfts' [reinforcements].
>
> This was an attitude I had not previously seen in a fully-fledged comd. My sympathies were with him and I felt a certain animosity towards the CO of 3K. I even had the mischievous thought of 'You'll soon get it too.'[24]

As Moji hurried off to organise his soldiers to collect the newly arriving supplies of 'tinned food and dried bread',[25] the two commanders decided to move their force forward and hide them in the jungle for an attack late on the night of 30 August. By undertaking this advanced deployment, it was hoped that the Kittyhawk fighters would firstly not find them in the jungle, but also not strafe them so close to the Australian Number 3 Strip perimeter.

On 30 August the Australians engaged in further patrolling. A 61st Battalion patrol under Captain Charlie Bicks travelled as far as KB Mission. Captain Bicks:

> With [Bert] Robinson and 2 OR's I went on, finding a Jap hospital at Gama River. Here I saw evidence that they'd killed their wounded. Several men, neatly laid in a row and naked with bandaged legs and in one case a head wound, had bullet wounds in the vicinity of the heart. We pushed on across the Gama River to Motieau Point without seeing any live enemy. Here we saw the first dead native who'd obviously been taken prisoner by the Japs as his hands were tied behind his back with sig wire. Shot and bayoneted! We were at K.B. about midday and gained first-hand information of Thursday night's fight there when the 2/10th were over-run. Many of our dead and enemy dead! We found bodies of two FOO's [Forward Observation Officers] of the 2/5th Field Regiment. Also found several of *my* battalion men (who were in shorts) their features no longer recognisable. They may have been from 'D' or 'B' Company. Their hands were tied behind their backs, arms had been broken by gunshot wounds and they'd been bayoneted. Pushing on . . . we approached 11 Platoon's old bivouac position. Here we encountered three enemy moving towards a hut there. Robinson and I killed two at 40 yards but the third got away.[26]

These men were probably base soldiers engaged in either taking rations forward or moving back for more. The patrols were ignored by the jungle-hidden Japanese, who went to great pains to avoid both detection and Kittyhawk attack.

Blamey to Rowell, 29 August 1942:

> In my view . . . 26 Aug cannot understand apparent piecemeal action by bns at Milne Bay vide your sitreps

> 113 and 114 and G3568. greatest vigour must be used immediately to exterminate enemy before further reinforcements arrive.[27]

Rowell to Vasey, 30 August:

> Dear George,
>
> . . . Let me say at once that I appreciate your position as regards pressure from above for information. But I have been giving you all I have got from Cyril. This problem is an old one. We had just the same trouble in Greece and it will happen again. As I told the C in C [Blamey] in a signal tonight, it is taking up to 7 hours to get a message through . . .
>
> It is perilously easy to criticise a commander for his actions at a distance of 250 miles . . .
>
> I'm sorry that GHQ [the Americans] takes a poor view of Australians. In some cases this is all too true, but I wish Chamberlain & Co could visit the jungle to see what conditions are, instead of sitting back and criticising. It is obvious also, that the Japs are the very highest class of troops, as the 2/10th were well above the ordinary . . .
>
> PS. I'm personally very bitter over the criticism from a distance and I think it damn unfair to pillory any commander without any knowledge of the conditions. It has rained for ten days at Milne Bay and it keeps on raining.
>
> I suppose there will be heresy hunts and bowler hats soon. I hate to think what would have happened with our allies in charge up here.[28]

By about 3.00 a.m. on the morning of 31 August 1942, the Japanese had concentrated their assault force opposite Number 3 Strip. Private Jim Hilton, of A Company, 25th Battalion was almost opposite the enemy forming-up position:

> . . . a mate of mine and I were under a ground sheet having a smoke and another mate of mine, Alec

> MacKenzie, he was watching, standing-to . . . The next thing he gives us a nudge with his foot and we put the cigarette out quiet, and we were listening. No, couldn't hear anything. And I said, 'Don't let it get to you boy, you'll be right in the morning.' Do you know I still don't remember whether I saw or heard something . . . I passed word up the line . . . Company Headquarters sent a very light up . . . and she lit up all these bastards over there.
>
> There was no chant to start with, but they did yell, and one Jap sang out in pretty good English, 'It's no use . . . we're coming across!' And the RSM said, 'Pig's arse you are! Hit 'em with everything you've got!' And then everything opened up.[29]

The Japanese had formed up where the track and the eastern end of the strip met. Given the tremendous Australian—and American half-track—fire that now ranged at them, telling casualties had to follow. But it was the decisive action of Lieutenant Keith Acreman that hurried their fate. During the preceding hours of daylight, Lieutenant Ernie Bain, the 25th Battalion's signal officer, had run a line to Acreman just forward of the western or base side boundary of the strip. Keith Acreman:

> And I'm there with the signaller that I purloined—he's still with me. And I said to him, 'Get on to the mortars and tell them I want them to give me a ranging shot on the road and the strip.' The next minute over came this mortar.
>
> Bang! It hit . . . on our side of the ruddy strip! Lucky it didn't go off. We all cowered there waiting for it . . . I gave the order, 'Up two hundred!' That actually was effective, the first one, and I just said, 'Gunfire!' It was devastating . . .[30]

Lieutenant Aubrey Schindler, Mortar Platoon, 25th Battalion:

> . . . We had a lot of bombs which we had brought up and put in the back of the pits. We were sitting on them as a matter of fact . . . we had very close to a hundred bombs . . . between the two pits . . . Rapid fire! And away she

> goes! And then another correction . . . and that went on for about an hour. And then there was a gap of about half an hour and the second wave of Japs came in . . . we received a new supply of ammunition from Battalion Headquarters.[31]

If the KB Mission battleground had been brilliantly lit by the Japanese setting fire to one of its huts four nights earlier, then it was now the Australians who took centre stage on another illuminated battlefield. Tracer fire from the American half-track vehicles was answered by similar fire from the Japanese trying to eliminate them. Flares, tracer fire and mortar explosions lit the whole scene to the point where one Australian has claimed that he was able to read a map by the light provided.[32] And the Japanese assisted the Australians in their endeavours by forming up and attempting the impossible not once, not twice, but three futile times. And they paid an horrendous price.

After these three misadventures, the Japanese now tried a last desperate tactic: an outflanking movement via Stephen's Ridge. Bill Wilson and his 61st Battalion comrades were waiting for them:

> I was well forward of Stephen's House on the ridge . . . we had at least two Brens with their crews and other Brens behind us . . . it was a crown of a ridge, so you didn't have a lot of land . . . the firing on the strip ceased and after a short period of time, it might have been half an hour, we heard movement coming up the track . . . and when the movement got close, probably a matter of twenty or thirty yards, I ordered the Brens to start firing. The Bren on the right jammed. Now, I went forward to try and clear it . . . after a couple of minutes, a flare went up . . . the Japs saw his movement . . . he and his number two were killed . . . those two posts were about fifteen feet apart . . . they [the Japanese] must have been sickened by what had happened to them on the strip . . . they did not persist.[33]

Not long before dawn, a forlorn bugle call signalled the end of the Japanese attack upon Number 3 Strip. Amongst the enemy dead lay Commander Hayashi. The scenes that awaited the Australians across the strip next morning, after the 2/12th had commenced its offensive, appalled the most hardened amongst them. Private Jim Hilton, 25th Battalion:

> There were bloody bodies around like logs. There was one Japanese machine-gun lined up there and I'd say at least twenty blokes killed in a row behind that. One bloke must have strapped on and then he'd get killed, and then another bloke would take over and he'd get killed. There were even blokes . . . with legs crossed over each other . . .[34]

Lance-Corporal Errol Jorgensen, 25th Battalion:

> . . . next morning I went over with about twenty Yanks and the bloody slaughter over there turned you up. It turned about fifteen of the Yanks up, they just got sick and went back. There were legs up in trees, arms, heads everything. It was repulsive really.[35]

TIME FOR A CAPSTAN

17

Vasey to Rowell, 1 September 1942:

> My Dear Syd,
> Thanks for your letters sent by Wilson. I am afraid the last week was a trying time for many of us. I appreciate your forbearance. GHQ [MacArthur's HQ] is like a b_____y barometer in a cyclone—up and down every two minutes.
>
> When C-in-C [Blamey] returned from there yesterday he said one would have thought they had just won the battle of Waterloo. They're like the militia, they need to be blooded. They also need to realise that they are not commanding a besieged force where front line reports come in every few minutes.
>
> I am glad you stopped AAF [American Air Force] sending their news flashes. They were part of the trouble. Also, I am more convinced than ever that our reports need to be written in Americanese. They don't understand our restrained English . . .
>
> I am convinced there will be no heresy hunt or bowler hatting. The only possible sphere where that might take place is in Signals . . .[1]

Ever calm and measured, Major-General Cyril Clowes was now thinking ahead. He signalled Rowell at about 1.00 a.m. on 1 September:

> Dear Old Syd,
> The thing that concerns me at present is that there is a limit to the distance I can go along the shore without uncovering this place and if you get a signal from me asking which is to be my task:—
>
> A. clean up the Japs on the north side (there is no limit within reason to the distance they can go back) . . .
>
> Or B. What I have always regarded as my primary role—to keep MB itself intact. I can't do both old son and I can't go very much further along the coast as I can't clean him up without doing so. LHQ have said 'clear the Japs off' which is all very easy for them. I think it is a matter for them to say whether I am to chase the Japs as far east as they like to go or get them back a reasonable distance and make reasonably sure of this Milne Bay area itself. Will you think about it? Suggest they should be asked if you agree to this so that my position will be clarified.[2]

At this point in time, Clowes could look to two of his three AIF battalions for use in an offensive capacity. On 29–30 August, the 2/10th was regaining the main base area after their torturous trek through the Stirling Range. For the time being, therefore, they were not considered for such a role.

When the Japanese had shown little inclination to proceed with their offensive on 28 August, Clowes had moved his 2/12th Battalion, AIF from Waigani to an area immediately west of Milne Force HQ, in readiness for his offensive along the north shore. On the 29th, he ordered Wootten to attack the enemy up to and including KB Mission. But when the Japanese Navy reappeared in the bay late that night, Clowes was forced to suspend this plan.

The 2/12th had been raised in 1939 predominantly at Brighton, Tasmania, but because of the lack of available personnel in that state it also enlisted volunteers at Redbank in Queensland. While Brigadier Field had commanded it during its service in the Middle East, the battalion at Milne Bay was led by Lieutenant-Colonel A.S.W. 'Wolf' Arnold.

Private Bert 'Ack Ack' Treschman, 2/12th Battalion: 'Wolf . . . was a South Australian, one of the best officers we had. He was a man's man; he mixed with you . . . you could talk to him.'[3] Captain Angus Suthers remembered Arnold as 'A good tactician, top line, respected by the blokes'.[4]

The battalion's available intelligence forecast little if any resistance between Number 3 Strip and KB Mission. Bicks' patrol had sighted only three Japanese at that location. Ideally, the 2/12th would have been barged down to KB Mission, which would have allowed it to secure that position and then begin offensive operations almost immediately. But the decided lack of water transport at Milne Bay—which Clowes had earlier complained about—precluded this tactic. The 2/12th Battalion would therefore be required to march forward and secure the Mission by 4.00 p.m. on the 31st.[5]

The unit left its reception camp at 6.30 a.m. on 31 August. Its passage to Number 3 Strip was a nightmare journey. By this time, Milne Force's vehicles, the constant movement by the 7th Brigade's soldiers, the American engineers and other odds and sods had turned a humble government 'road' into a bog. A relatively short distance on a map at Supreme HQ in Brisbane, therefore, bore little practical relationship to the burdensome foot-slogging of infantry who were in the mud and not on the map. Corporal Roy 'Buck' Rodgers, D Company, 2/12th Battalion:

> I was concerned about the weight of the Boyes Anti-tank Rifle (plus the ammo) and I took action to ensure that it was constantly swapped around amongst members of my section. We had the usual section Bren gun plus reserves of ammunition and the remainder of my section were equipped with rifles and bayonets . . .
>
> Reserves of ammunition plus magazines for the Bren were spread throughout the section and we all carried hand grenades, at least two per man . . . carrying reserves of ammunition within the rifle section is a problem in so far as weight is concerned, and takes on great significance when attempting to move quickly through thick foliage and/or muddy conditions underfoot.[6]

Lieutenant-Colonel Arnold's order of advance saw D Company and a platoon of B Company cross the strip first, followed by Battle HQ with the Commando Platoon, the remainder of B Company, C Company, HQ Company and finally A Company. The creation of a commando platoon was an 18th Brigade idea that was to prove very shrewd. Lieutenant Mike Steddy commanded the 2/12th Commando Platoon. Captain Angus Suthers:

> The idea of the Commando Platoon was A: protection of Battalion Headquarters, and B: it was a force that the CO had at his disposal that you kept separate from anything to do with the companies . . . so if there was . . . something causing a lot of trouble he'd say, 'Take it out Mike!' They did terrifically well . . . about thirty men . . .[7]

At 9.09 a.m. D Company moved through the 61st Battalion positions and began crossing the strip in extended line. Why the Japanese chose not to contest their advance is clouded in some mystery—the very same killing ground that had been so ruthlessly exploited by the Australians only hours before could have equally been used by the Japanese. Perhaps the thorough mauling they had received the previous night had caused them to withdraw in strength and merely seek to delay the Australians, rather than engage in a set-piece battle.

But the Japanese did employ three very clever, disciplined and determined methods of delaying the approaching 2/12th, which reflect their almost unique attitude to warfare and how little value they placed upon the ordinary soldier's life.

Trained and well-deployed snipers are a familiar facet of warfare. However, under normal circumstances, the sniper reconnoitres his position most carefully: he looks for a place of concealment from which he can observe the enemy and, usually, a path for his undetected escape. The Japanese were very good snipers, but they were more than prepared to forgo the luxury of an undetected escape. During the Battle for Milne Bay, but particularly along our soon to be travelled Gona–Buna–Sananda beachhead, the Japanese found their ideal deployment in any number of the numerous coconut palms along or near preferred Australian tracks or other infantry routes. They strapped themselves high among the fronds of these trees or palms, and because of the light nature of their equipment and their frugal food supplies they were able to stay deployed until the Australians not only approached them, but passed them. This gave them ample time to choose a quality target: usually a machine-gunner or, if possible, an officer. The Australians learnt very quickly during the Papuan campaign to mask the presence of their officers by having them dispense with their insignia of rank. Moreover, they often carried the common rifle rather than the obvious officer's revolver. The Japanese snipers were, therefore, a formidable opponent in this form of warfare.

The second ploy used by the enemy was to have troops lying 'doggo'. Not unlike the sniper, this Japanese soldier, once discovered, could only have one fate. And on Number 3 Strip during the immediate hours after the carnage of the previous night, there were no shortage of corpses for the 'corpses' to lie among. As the troops from the various 2/12th companies crossed, the grisly game began. Captain Swan of D Company was the first casualty. As the Japanese began to pull the pins from their grenades, the 2/12th started shooting. But Swan and a small group with him were hit when an enemy managed to throw his grenade as Swan fired at him. It was only the prompt action of Private Joe Eager—aptly named—who managed to locate a pressure point near Swan's wound that saved this officer's life. There was only one course of action open now. The Australians mercilessly put to the bayonet absolutely any Japanese soldier who looked remotely alive.

The second-in-command of D Company, Captain Ivey, assumed immediate command and pushed on. The Japanese ploy of feigning death continued for some time and claimed the life of Lieutenant Tietzel, which resulted in Lieutenant Neil Russell assuming command of both 16 and 17 Platoons. Although Captain Suthers' A Company was the last to cross Number 3 Strip, the necessary elimination of the 'hidden' enemy had not finished. Suthers:

> On the way up I met an I Section man who said the track to K.B. was clear. As he said this our leading platoon did over an L.M.G. [light machine-gun] and five men! They

> spotted them first. A man saw an apparently dead Jap move and shot him. Others came to life and they shot them and found an L.M.G. mounted. They were lying on their faces and backs as though dead. There were 12 to 20 dead Japs lying about . . .[8]

The third Japanese tactic consisted of cutting a small number of firing lanes at right angles to the track, or using the occasional track junction for ambush purposes and occupying them in groups numbering from three to full section strength (about twelve). Corporal Roy 'Buck' Rodgers:

> During one of these actions a very good friend of mine Cpl Charlie Koppie was killed when he ran into the enemy who were completely concealed.
>
> Between Gama River and KB Mission . . . the enemy fired . . . (including LMG fire) from the left side of the track. Also there was clearly movement at fairly close range and voices farther in the distance. (Talking indiscriminately was a definite weakness of the Japanese at Milne Bay.) We appreciated that the enemy was withdrawing on our flanks as they had been doing for most of the day.
>
> We came across a number of dead bodies of Papuan natives some of which were badly mutilated. One younger female had her breasts badly cut about either by the use of a sword, knife or bayonet.[9]

Along its path to KB Mission, the 2/12th was subjected to a brief strafing from the Kittyhawk fighters. One explanation for this error was that one of the infantry's red Very light signals—one to be fired for every hundred yards estimated distance to the enemy—failed to ignite, while another was that the battalion had moved beyond its anticipated position of advance and was mistaken for the enemy.

The advance elements of the 2/12th, D and A Companies and Battle HQ, approached KB Mission at around 4.30 p.m. D Company's 16 and 17 Platoons were leading that movement, and after crossing Motieau Creek 17 Platoon deployed to the inland side of the track and 16 Platoon to the seaward side. Lieutenant Neil Russell: 'Several Japs showed themselves as we approached the Mission clearing and we lost two or three men including Artie Carnell, a popular figure in 16 Platoon. I then had the idea of a bayonet charge to frighten the Nips.'[10] What then transpired is a fairly good illustration of the influence upon his men of a competent, calm and brave platoon leader. Corporal 'Buck' Rodgers:

> Just after we got into position our own air force [Kittyhawks] came over low and strafed the area, generally just forward of our positions and in depth into the coconut plantation.
>
> Also at this time, several enemy advanced on foot towards us, moving quickly through the coconut trees and taking cover as they moved forward. I can recall making a guess that one of the leading Japs was an officer, as he was carrying a pistol.
>
> There was some other Japanese fire at the time but this was mostly going just overhead, as you could hear the 'crack' of the rounds. We returned the enemy fire and I know that a number of Japanese were killed in this fire fight . . .
>
> Lt Russell was fairly close to me—say about twenty yards or so—and I can still see him as he clearly . . . took charge of the situation. Just before he led us in, he calmly said, 'What time is it?' 'Time for a Capstan!' [A 'Capstan' was a popular brand of cigarette at the time.] He then coolly led the charge. He was an inspiration.[11]

The bayonet charge undertaken by Russell and the soldiers of 16 and 17 Platoons on 31 August at KB Mission cleared the enemy from that location. By 5.00 p.m. that afternoon, the 2/12th advance guard consisting of D and A Companies and Battle HQ were employed—with darkness approaching—in siting and occupying a perimeter defence of the Mission.

While these events had been unfolding at KB Mission, the remainder of the 2/12th—B and C Companies—were in the process of forming a night defensive position at the Gama River.

Gama River, 31 August 1942

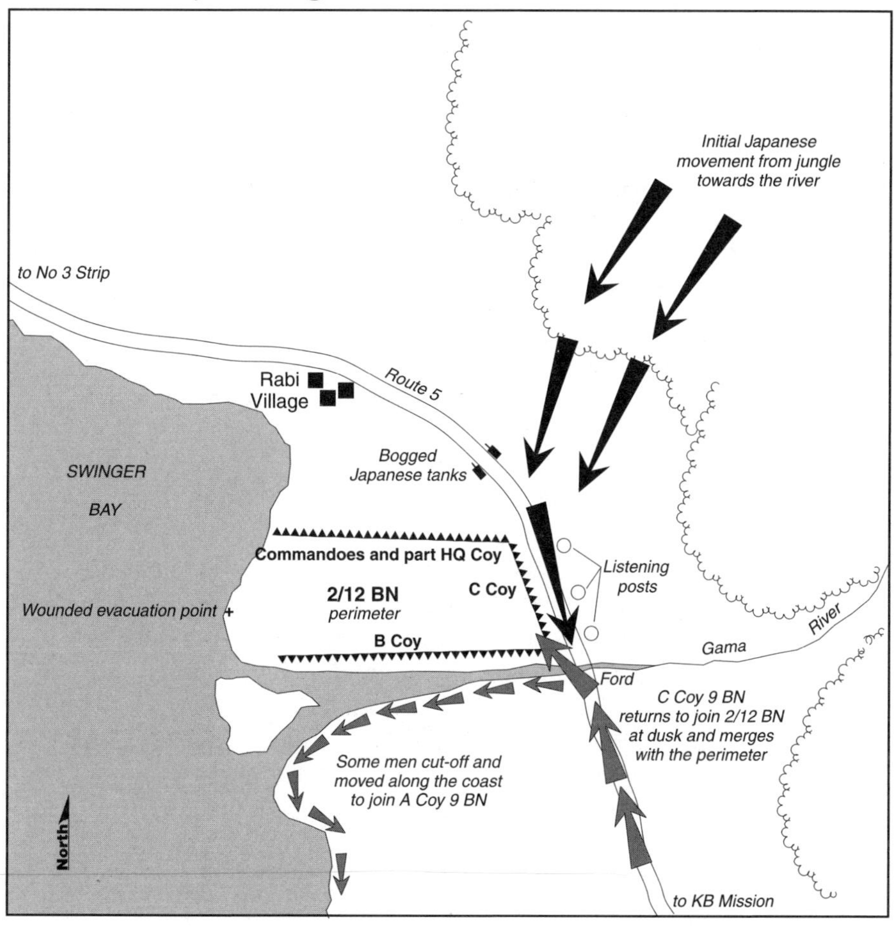

The 2/12th Battalion's perimeter employed the natural feature of the river as its eastern flank. If the enemy chose to breach this flank, he faced a scramble down its two-yard bank; a roughly twenty-yard passage through the sandy-bottomed, fast-flowing and roughly knee-deep water; and finally a climb up a short bank before he could face the 2/12th Battalion's B Company, spread along the ground from its mouth back to the track. The Japanese would do well to avoid it.

The western or base side of the perimeter ran from the track back down to the coast, a distance of around seventy yards. Along it, the battalion deployed its commandos and HQ Company. Private Paul Hope was on this western flank:

> The whole area between the road and water was light jungle with odd big trees. The company cleared a field of fire from the perimeter to a small creek or drain running roughly parallel with the perimeter but cutting in towards the perimeter as it ran closer to the sea. Its entrance there was only a few yards from the perimeter itself but 25 to 30 yards near the road . . .
>
> I don't recall a beach just a shoreline of shingle.
>
> We were spread out mostly in pairs but close enough to each other to prevent infiltration by the Japs. I believe this was standard for the whole perimeter. Coy HQ and the OC Capt Maurice Boucher were about 20 yards in from the perimeter . . .[12]

The track perimeter was the obvious front that any infiltrating or attacking force would use to confront the 2/12th. Although the track—about four yards wide—provided a modest killing ground, the thick jungle on the other side provided ample cover for the enemy right up to the track. To effect some form of early warning defence, the 2/12th deployed four listening posts spread evenly (about 25 yards apart) along this northern part of the perimeter. C Company's 13 Platoon was deployed from the western or base side of the perimeter to the middle, and 15 Platoon stretched from the middle to the Gama.

It is at this point that another Milne Bay battalion enters our story. At around midday on the 31st, the 7th Brigade's 9th Militia Battalion was ordered to send its A and C Companies forward to occupy and secure a number of points between Number 3 Strip and the remaining 2/12th force at KB Mission. This occupation of ground would allow the 2/12th to continue its eastern assault the next day. The 9th Battalion's C Company's 15 Platoon was the first to stop—it settled at Kilarbo, providing a link between the defences at Number 3 Strip and part of the 2/12th at the Gama River. The battalion's A Company, out ahead, settled near Homo Creek, not all that far from KB Mission.

It had been a successful day for the Australians. After the carnage at Number 3 Strip during the previous night, they had occupied a series of positions from the strip moving eastwards: Kilarbo, Rabi, the Gama River, Homo Creek and, lastly, their objective for the day, KB Mission. But few nights during the Battle for Milne Bay had been uneventful, and the night of 31 August–1 September was to be no exception.

When the Japanese had been reinforced just prior to their fruitless assault upon Number 3 Strip, its fresh reinforcements from the 3rd Kure SNLF (Commander Yano) had attempted an outflanking movement on Stephen's Ridge against the 61st Battalion. When that Japanese attempt to both cross and outflank the Number 3 Strip had failed, a bugle call had signalled the enemy withdrawal. The enemy soldiers who had contested the 2/12th Battalion's progress once they had crossed over the strip had been the original force remnants. But the fresh force which had assaulted the 61st at Stephen's Ridge had been forced to take to jungle cover during daylight on 1 September. During the course of that day, it had gradually made its weary way through the jungle, had skirted any sign of its detection near the strip, and had moved further east under cover past Kilarbo and on to Rabi. Commander Yano reasoned that he might gain a far more speedy access back to the KB Mission area by taking to the main track past Rabi—he was both unaware of any Australian offensive and would have thought that, had there been one, it would not have reached as far east as the Gama River.

Just on dusk, Private Merv McGillvery was perched high in a coconut palm on the north-west corner of the Gama River perimeter—on the base side and near the track—busily engaged in removing some fronds for his night's shelter, when he spotted the Japanese force approaching. He passed the word to those below him. What followed was extraordinary.

The 2/12th Battalion was very fast and very quiet indeed in readying itself for an ambush. But the first voices they heard were Australian. 15 Platoon from C Company, 9th Battalion had overshot their area for the night, back near Rabi. As they were making their way back towards the Gama River from the west, the Japanese were coming the other way in front of the 2/12th track portion of their Gama River perimeter.

Sergeant Lucas, 2/12th Battalion, in *Of Storms and Rainbows*:

> . . . we could still hear the voices of some of our chaps moving along the roadway [15 Platoon, 9th Battalion]. There seemed to be a quiet, or more of a dead silence for a minute or so, and then other voices could be heard, coming . . . from the direction of . . . our left flank [from the west, or base side of the perimeter] . . .
>
> These voices sounded somewhat different, higher pitched perhaps . . . Apparently all our men had realised what had happened, and all kept quiet.
>
> After a brief period . . . when the head of the Jap column had neared the ford, right at our right flank, someone started firing . . .[13]

'Someone' fired at precisely the right time. It requires tremendous discipline to remain quiet, to know where and when to fire and, above all, fight the natural impulse to open up when you see a formidable group of the enemy in your sights. The Japanese were caught at very close range and in close formation. It was a slaughter. And in all this, they deserved what they got. Had they had a forward scout or a forward reconnaissance patrol they might have seen McGillvery high among the coconuts, or they may have at least heard some giveaway noise, some movement, within the Australian perimeter.

Lieutenant David Radford was near the ford with 15 Platoon, 9th Battalion when the 2/12th ambush was sprung:

> And when the firing broke out we just instinctively and immediately jumped into their [the 2/12th] pits! . . . after the firing had eased off, I asked a 2/12th bloke to take me to their company headquarters . . . my reason being that as a 2/ic or as an officer, I had a responsibility to let their CO or Company Commander know whatever knowledge I had.
>
> This bloke took me in, I found out later it was Captain Kirk, reported to him, told him what I knew . . . didn't know where my Company Commander was

> because he was forward . . . I asked him for instructions. He said, 'Fix your bayonets, stay here, and if any Japs break through, take 'em with the bayonet because if you shoot you're liable to hit some of our own fellas.'
>
> I deduced that all those who were in the immediate vicinity of the 2/12th perimeter would have done exactly the same thing. Now, next morning, that deduction in my opinion was confirmed because they were all there except for Frank [Sergeant McCosker] and a few others . . . we had one killed and one wounded. Had any great number of our fellows been unable to get into the 2/12th perimeter, and been in the immediate vicinity of it, they would have been annihilated.[14]

While Radford's small group and various other stragglers of the 9th Battalion's C Company had dashed into the 2/12th perimeter, Sergeant Frank McCosker, further advanced down the track towards KB Mission, noticed the flashes of fire to his rear. Frank McCosker: '. . . I went back down the creek bank, crossed the river and held up there, until the Japs started coming round. We then copped it from both the 12th and the Japs, so we moved farther up, and eventually finished with A Company [at Homo Creek] next morning.'[15]

When the surviving Japanese recovered from the initial shock of the 2/12th ambush, most rushed across the inland side of the track and into the far more secure jungle. To accomplish this, they had to scramble up and over a small rise. In so doing, some of their number almost immediately encountered the listening posts stationed in that area, which had been deployed as an early warning defence against a Japanese inland infiltration. And in one case, the Japanese landed virtually in a listening post pit. George Lucas, in *Of Storms and Rainbows*: 'In one post I had put out there were a couple of tough Tasmanians, Pug Gleason and young Franklin: the Japs apparently landed on top of these two. Next morning Pug was found dead with a large number of dead Japs around him. He was a hard man and apparently went the hard way.'[16] Private Franklin, although badly wounded, did crawl out of his listening post and managed to cross the track. Lucas reached him, but was unable to save his life. The remaining soldiers in the three other listening posts miraculously managed to gain the main perimeter during a lull in the action.

The Japanese now began to probe the 2/12th positions looking for a vulnerable point. Private Paul Hope noted their efforts on his western side of the perimeter:

> When the Japs came around . . . we refrained from firing so as not to disclose our positions. But many hand grenades were thrown. They were obviously unaware of our exact position and proceeded to set up a machine gun not ten yards from the water's edge. The machine gun . . . was sited to shoot up the full length of the perimeter from the water to the road. Luckily it did not get into action and was removed without firing a shot . . .
>
> I was aware of Japs wading through the water while trying to infiltrate our bivouac. They too were stopped with grenades.[17]

The Japanese tried to breach the 2/12th perimeter on a number of occasions but failed. They broke contact at around 1.00 a.m. on the morning of 1 September and took to the inland side of the track with KB Mission as their objective. These enemy soldiers almost certainly used a narrow track that ran parallel with the main government track. It had been used by elements of the 2/10th Battalion to withdraw from KB Mission during the early morning of 28 August.

When the members of the 2/12th Battalion Gama River perimeter examined the results of their ambush at first light on the 1st, they found Japanese corpses literally piled on the track in front of their dispositions—about a hundred in all. In that confined, narrow place, the enemy had suffered critical losses that he could ill-afford, given the size of his original, and later reinforced, Milne Bay force.

The Japanese must have taken their wounded with them, or eliminated some of them, as the Australians found none at the scene. From a Japanese perspective, the losses were tragic enough, but the fact that they consisted of the 'fresh' arrivals only landed a few nights before must have been particularly galling.

While the Japanese Stephen's Ridge contingent had been thus ambushed at the Gama River, the KB Mission component of the 2/12th had formed its night perimeter at the Mission. However, their late arrival at that place, after Lieutenant Russell's spirited bayonet charge, had given them only limited time to organise their dispositions. Corporal Roy 'Buck' Rodgers:

> . . . the best that can be said for the defensive positions of 17 Platoon on the first night [at KB Mission] was that it was a fairly 'quick fix'. We hurriedly scraped out a bit of earth and tried to provide a little protection using fallen coconut husks and coconut tree fronds. All the platoon were in pairs and the pairs were at about 10/12 yard intervals. We checked lines of fire etc and followed as closely as possible normal defensive procedure. But the position was definitely a 'preliminary' one and needed development the next day.[18]

Captain Angus Suthers and his A Company were a little more fortunate as they were able to occupy some shallow pits which had been dug by either the 61st or the 2/10th soldiers during the previous fighting at the Mission.

The Australians' perimeter at KB Mission was partially held by Captain Ivey's D Company, which stretched from the sea around the outskirts of the coconut plantation to about halfway along its northern boundary. Captain Suthers' A Company bordered the western perimeter from the sea around the plantation to link up with Ivey's soldiers.

At around 8.00 p.m., the Japanese started to infiltrate the KB Mission perimeter. They were primarily engaged in allowing their far distant rear force to recover their lines—this was the force ambushed by the 2/12th at the Gama River. The 2/12th Battalion CO would later report: 'Japanese harassing tactics at KB took the form of letting off delayed action crackers, while the attention of our troops were thus engaged, infiltrators, armed only with a bayonet, would attempt to come in from a flank, and attempt to stab our men.'[19] The strain upon those 2/12th soldiers was severe. Any movement that night attracted fire. A small number of men were shot by other defenders who, because of the limited amount of time before darkness, did not always have a clear idea of the positions of some of their comrades. And the Australians in KB Mission were also aware that the enemy was moving inland past their perimeter. Corporal Roy Rodgers:

> We could hear them quite plainly. They seemed to be chattering all night and at times called to us in such terms as 'Hello Aussie' or the like.
>
> . . . they came close to our perimeter and also, I believe, many moved along the line of the coconut trees and jungle which was a couple of hundred yards down from our front.
>
> There was a certain amount of enemy fire during the night—coming from that direction . . .[20]

The harassing tactics employed by the Japanese through most of that night were designed purely to facilitate the recovery of their Gama River force and any other stragglers. The 2/12th actions at both the Gama River and KB Mission—on top of the mauling of the enemy force at Number 3 Strip during the previous night—crippled the Japanese Milne Bay force and then scattered and fragmented it.

During the early morning of 1 September, Major-General Cyril Clowes ordered the 7th Brigade to assume responsibility for the ground from Number 3 Strip to the Gama River, which would subsequently facilitate further offensive operations by his 18th Brigade past KB Mission. The 2/12th Battalion was able to concentrate at KB Mission for the purpose of patrolling east of that position.

While the 2/12th Battalion began this process almost immediately, Clowes was frustrated in his plans to deploy fresh troops for this offensive. On 1 September he received yet another message from MacArthur: 'Expect attack Jap ground forces on Milne aerodromes from the west and north-west supported by destroyer fire from bay. Take immediate stations.'[21]

This signal proved to be flawed. There was to be no north-west attacking force (through the Stirling Range), no fresh force of any kind, and no additional landing. But Clowes, forced to take MacArthur's 'intelligence' seriously, delayed by 24 hours his movement of the 2/9th Battalion forward to KB Mission. But when that battalion did arrive on 2 September 1942, the Battle for Milne Bay was destined to enter its final phase.

THE GLASSY STARE OF DEATH

18

The 2/9th Battalion was raised in November 1939 at Redbank Camp near Brisbane, as part of the 18th Brigade, AIF. It had first seen action at Giarabub against the Italians holding that Libyan fortress. During the subsequent siege of Tobruk, the 2/9th had seen tough fighting in the Salient and had returned from that famous siege with an outstanding reputation. Perhaps one of the main reasons for its success was the high standard of both its officers and NCOs.

The battalion's original CO was Lieutenant-Colonel Eric Martin, who was affectionately known as 'February' Martin after his frequent use of 28-day field punishments. Martin instilled tremendous discipline and training into the unit. Its second CO was Lieutenant-Colonel Clem Cummings, who retained Martin's strong discipline but also impressed his soldiers with his own personality and style. Warrant-Officer 2 Vince Donnelly remembered Cummings:

> . . . [he was] no flamboyant or gung-ho commander, but his quiet insistence and determination, his calmness and coolness in threatening situations, his quick and clear thinking and rapid counter action when required, radiated confidence which carried on down to the section commanders and individual soldiers. Wherever the action was hottest, Clem would arrive and his effect on morale was immediate. If Clem said it was on—it was on—and they made it happen.[1]

Colonel Fred Chilton:

> In my book he was one of the best infantry commanders that I met in six years of war—a mighty soldier. The troops swore by him. He was a very brave and competent soldier, outstanding for his personal qualities and leadership—he gave me a lot of confidence at Milne Bay.[2]

The 2/9th had been stationed for much of the Battle for Milne Bay near the vital Number 1 Strip. And with good reason. Lieutenant-Colonel Clem Cummings:

> If the Japs . . . instead of bashing, bashing, had gone round the top [through the Stirling Range] and came down on the airfield there . . . it would have been a bloody difficult defence. There were all these bloody gullies . . . that they could sneak down; plus the jungle . . . they could have at least got in there and blown up the planes . . .[3]

The stranded Japanese force on Goodenough Island had been assigned precisely that task. It will be remembered that it was MacArthur's inaccurate message, warning Milne Force of an enemy attack through the range, which had caused Clowes to abandon the early deployment of the 2/9th at KB Mission on 1 September. General MacArthur was entitled to send Clowes intelligence information—the purport of which Clowes was bound to take most seriously. However, the inaccuracy of such signals completely undermines the credibility of MacArthur's criticism of Clowes' lack of offensive action. The 2/9th Unit Diary, 2 September 1942, tells another story:

> A Coy still at Drome and remainder of Bn at staging camp. Bn under orders to move and C Coy embarked for KB Mission at 1430 hrs. B Coy with C.O. Adjt and I.O. embarked at 1630 hrs.
>
> A Coy recalled to staging camp and arrived at 1930 hrs. Bn less two coys spent night at staging camp.[4]

While the 2/9th Battalion was finally being barged down to KB Mission during the afternoon of 2 September, the

2/12th had resumed its fighting eastward. By nightfall, Captain Kirk's B Company, Captain Gategood's C Company and Lieutenant Mike Steddy's commandos were deployed at the fourth ford east of KB Mission. The remainder of the 2/12th were at KB Mission. It was here, late that afternoon, that Cummings, his adjutant, intelligence officer and his C and B Companies arrived by barge.

The 2/9th moved forward from KB Mission early on the morning of the 3rd, with the task of pushing through the advanced elements of the 2/12th and taking the fight to the enemy. The remaining A, D, HQ and rear Battalion HQ were barged to the Mission at 11.00 a.m.

It was roughly at this juncture that the fighting at Milne Bay changed. Other than for the purposes of a static defence of a night-time perimeter the Australians were now the aggressors, and were therefore required to move forward, seek out the enemy and destroy him. News of the Japanese tactic of feigning death and then firing on the unsuspecting Australians had reached Cummings. His orders were quite simple: 'I don't want any bloody prisoners—and I don't think you will get any!'[5]

The soldiers of the 2/9th were fast learners. They quickly noticed that a number of their casualties had gunshot wounds where the point of entry was higher on the body than the point of exit. This obviously indicated sniper fire from the treetops. The solution was measured, meticulous and highly organised. The Australians learnt to watch for the telltale signs of chopped palm fronds or tree foliage on the jungle floor. When they spotted it, the chances were that an enemy sniper was nearby. Accordingly, as the men advanced, usually in line of sight and in line abreast, some would be ordered to scan the trees for snipers while others looked for likely support positions or ambush sites.

This was a workable system given that the enemy were not in great numbers and were not engaged in prolonged set-piece defence of their ground. The Japanese could at best hope to delay and frustrate the Australian advance—and create time for an evacuation. They therefore rarely operated more than 150-odd yards inland from the track, and as the distance between the track and the sea was never much more than 100 yards, their fighting withdrawal moved through a coastal corridor of only about 250 to 300 yards of thick jungle and scrub.

However, the terrain on the north shore of Milne Bay did offer the Japanese one critical advantage. Small streams and creeks abounded in this area of high rainfall. They were so copious (and the maps of the region so rare) that the Australians took to expressions such as 'the third ford from KB Mission', or 'the sixth ford'. These obstacles were numerous enough and just wide enough to cause a slowing of the Australian pace and, most serious of all, exposure; often they became killing grounds.

Captain Marshall's C Company and Captain Anderson's B Company, 2/9th Battalion found the advanced elements of the 2/12th about five hundred yards ahead of the fourth ford, near a small stream just west of Elevada Creek. The 2/12th had killed about twenty of the enemy but had lost a section of men from fire across the creek. This area was only sparsely covered with timber and secondary growth and small clumps of grass.[6] The Japanese positions across this creek ranged from the coast to about a distance of 130 yards inland from the track, and the stream was dominated by a machine-gun and a 20-millimetre field piece.

For his attack on this position, Marshall sent Lieutenant Fogg's 13 Platoon in on the coastal side of the track and Lieutenant Heron's 14 Platoon on the inland side. He held his 15 Platoon in reserve. The attack was timed for 10.10 a.m., and was to follow an artillery barrage.

The sixty Queenslanders comprising these two attacking platoons set the scene for the 2/9th Battalion's Milne Bay fighting. As they slowed down to cross the stream, they were met with concentrated machine-gun and small arms fire. Private Bill 'Soda' Fountain, 13 Platoon:

> The creek might have been waist-deep; running very fast and the Nips was on a scrubby mound.
>
> They were in that, between the track and the coast. It happened so bloody fast. First thing I knew, was that we went over this bloody creek and I see a joker jump up into the air and flop into the creek . . . all hell blew, they shot us up.[7]

Lieutenant Fogg, Fountain's platoon commander, was one of the first hit. Shot in the head, Fogg was dragged back out of the water by his batman, Private Reid, who was also almost immediately shot in the arm. Lieutenant Heron's 14 Platoon fared no better—within minutes Heron, his sergeant and a number of other ranks were casualties.

In a trained, disciplined and experienced infantry battalion, a situation such as this requires the immediate initiative of a junior leader to immediately assume command, otherwise the impetus of the attack wanes and the momentum is lost. Corporal Gordon provided that dash and determination as he led his section hard against the Japanese positions over the eastern side of the creek. The Official Historian:

> Notable among the many brave men in that company were the giant Lance-Corporal John Ball and Lance-Corporal Allen. Ball's body was found later 25 yards across the stream, right among the Japanese machine-gun positions—so far across, indeed, that he had outstripped all others and none had seen him die. There was no mark on him and it was thought that he had thrown an anti-tank bomb and that the blast had killed him. Allen lay dead almost at the muzzles of the guns.[8]

Needing reinforcement, the two platoons withdrew across the ford while elements of Captain Anderson's B Company and Captain Hooper's D Company made an outflanking movement inland. During this move, one Japanese soldier was killed. The Japanese had, however, withdrawn to their next holding position, leaving about twenty of their dead as testimony to the persistence of the original Australian assault upon their positions. The action advanced the 2/9th around five hundred yards to Sanderson's Bay, where they formed a perimeter defence for the night. But sleep never came easily to Australians in a night position at Milne Bay.

When you stand along this coast during darkness, barely able to see a hand in front of your face, you can readily imagine the sheer mental anguish experienced by soldiers who had to maintain such a perimeter throughout the night. Your company or platoon commander will give your section its ground. Some of your comrades occupy the immediate ground running to the beach. This is usually a very narrow pebble beach, and is one of the more highly fancied spots. With some observation over it, the Japanese are unlikely to get past you here. Your backside is covered and any enemy attempt to breach your ground will more than likely come from further ahead. But as the company perimeter moves inland, you occupy the ground using pairs of men dug in to the best of their ability behind some vegetation. These blokes are conscious of the fact that they must not fire their weapons, because to do so will almost certainly cause 'friendly fire' deaths or maiming—a sick term this, because a bullet's a bullet no matter what its source. Forward of your perimeter, your mates have cleared a small but crucial killing ground. If threatened, the machine-gunners and riflemen will provide your company's firepower. But if the perimeter is breached your role, if you are back, will be to fight with the bayonet. As you lie there, busting for a smoke, every sound of nature—the noises of insects and especially the wind rustling through the vegetation—conspires to convince you that a Jap is coming for you. And through the night you take turns as one or two sleep and one or two remain totally vigilant. This goes on all over the perimeter. Now off to sleep—if you can.

On the night of 3 September 1942, the enveloping darkness brought only a disturbance from the sea. The Japanese Navy paid its now customary visit to the bay not long before midnight and shelled the north shore. There were no casualties. But the soldiers in that forward 2/9th perimeter did hear the faint, distant sounds of motor launches but could only guess at their purpose: were the Japanese bringing troops in, or taking them out?[9]

At 7.00 a.m. on the 4th, Lieutenant-Colonel Cummings moved Major Peek's A Company and Battle HQ through B Company to join Captain Hooper's D Company as the forward force. His plan involved Peek thrusting forward astride the track with Hooper moving on his flank to a point where that coastal corridor widened, and then moving inland to secure Peek's flank. At 8.20 a.m. Hooper's men reached Goroni.[10] Forty minutes later they struck heavy opposition past the village and were forced to withdraw. In so doing,

Lieutenant Scott's 18 Platoon lost contact with Hooper's other two platoons.

It was at this point in the Battle for Milne Bay that a vital change in tactics was employed. At no time during the 7th Brigade's fighting had an outflanking movement been employed in strength against the Japanese. There are a number of reasons for this. For much of the time, the battalions involved were fighting defensive rather than offensive actions. The 61st and 25th Battalions' thrust forward of KB Mission late on 26 August presented just such an opportunity but was not taken by Captain Bicks, probably because of the difficulties in communication and the unknown strength of the enemy. The 2/10th Battalion's ambitious operation of the 27th was indeed originally seen as a battalion-sized outflanking movement, but was changed in conception during its march to KB Mission. Moreover, the 2/12th had been in no position to attempt such a tactic as it had been attacked at both the Gama River and KB Mission.

Thus, the first real attempt to outflank the Japanese along the coastal corridor at Milne Bay was now to be undertaken by the 2/9th. The potential for success was enormous. Apart from the obvious opportunity of inflicting telling casualties, this movement offered the chance to cut off a large proportion of an already sick, exhausted and rapidly dwindling force. With luck, they could even totally annihilate the enemy.

Cummings' plan envisaged Hooper moving about four hundred yards inland from the track and then a similar distance eastward (parallel to the direction of the enemy withdrawal). He then would move back onto the track to cut them off. But there were limiting factors. First, Hooper would have no communication with his rear. Signal cable could not be dragged through this jungle terrain, and radio equipment was both ineffective and too cumbersome to carry. The second problem was mobility. When you see this terrain, the tremendous difficulty of moving quickly and silently becomes immediately apparent. The third problem was navigation. Once again, to be immersed in the vegetation of Milne Bay is like wearing sunglasses in a railway tunnel. A high degree of jungle training navigation is required—which had been denied to the Australian Army at this time.

Cummings reasoned that Hooper's two-platoon movement and subsequent attack might materialise somewhere between 11.00 and 11.30 a.m. The supporting frontal assault from the 2/9th Battalion's current positions would be undertaken by Peek's A Company.

Corporal Ron Fitzpatrick was a member of the 2/9th Battalion's Intelligence Section and accompanied Hooper: 'The ground was very slippery—very wet—tiring to walk over. Visibility was not good because of the foliage of trees shut out the views once you left the track. There were so many changes of direction . . . navigation was by having a forward scout and moving forward in short distances.'[11]

By midday Cummings had had no word from Hooper—understandable given that communication relied upon runners who would have found navigation, distance and time all working against them. Cummings now called up Captain Anderson's B Company to the front with the intention of putting in a frontal assault with two companies instead of the originally planned one. At this time, Lieutenant Scott's 'lost' 18 Platoon returned from the attack earlier that morning.

Not long before the attack was set to start, Hooper and his 16 and 17 Platoons returned to the battalion's HQ. Hooper told Cummings that he had penetrated to a distance of about 1250 yards, had found enemy supply dumps, had been engaged by the enemy, and had subsequently withdrawn. Cummings was not amused. He relieved Hooper of his command and ordered Captain Barnes to assume command of D Company.

It is not hard to feel some sympathy for Hooper's plight. In addition to the difficulties described, he had been retarded in his speedy movement back with the encumbrance of a wounded soldier. However, from Cummings' perspective, Hooper had failed to execute his orders. Fitzpatrick was present when Cummings relieved Hooper and illuminates these events further: 'My memory of the meeting is that Cummings told Hooper that he (Hooper) had lost contact with Bn HQ, thereby holding up the proposed attack. (There was a plan to call in an air strike before the attack, I believe.) And so Hooper was relieved.'[12]

The attack began at 3.00 p.m. with an artillery and mortar barrage with Peek's A Company astride the track and

Anderson's B Company on their left, inland flank. Captain Anderson was wounded during this engagement. The bullet's point of entry and its lower point of exit indicated that the enemy were employing sniper fire as well as machine-gun and small arms fire. Captain Benson now took over B Company. But the enemy firepower proved too strong, and the 2/9th withdrew into high kunai grass. A second assault was soon mounted which was described by the intelligence officer, Lieutenant Tony Worthington, as 'a Chicago gang-fight'.[13] Private Frank Rolleston was a member of Scott's 18 Platoon, sent in to bolster the numbers for this second attack: 'As our men reached the other bank and clambered up, the din was terrific, with long bursts of fire from the Bren guns, the rattle of sub-machine guns, combined with the noise of exploding hand grenades, while amongst the noise could be heard the lighter, whiplike crack of the Japanese rifles.'[14]

Again the intense enemy fire drove the Queenslanders back—two attacks, two withdrawals. The Japanese, convinced that they had won the day, now made the costly error of leaving the concealed positions which had brought them such striking success and attempted to rout the 2/9th. The Australians met them with a steady and determined resolve. Battles are often won or lost during one decisive individual or collective action. During this climactic fight, as its very outcome hung in the balance, one Australian seized the moment.

Amidst that inferno of heavy fire Corporal John French reacted to the peril of the moment. Seeing that his section was pinned down by three Japanese machine-gun posts, he rose and attacked the first with grenades. Private Arthur Hinz was watching him: 'Johnny French ordered us down, and he went in and got the first two posts. And for the next one, he came back and got a grenade off us and finished the other one off. And that was the finish, when we advanced, he was dead.'[15]

Lieutenant Tony Worthington: 'He wiped out the three [machine] guns and crews of nine altogether. To me, this incredible action of sacrifice by a usually quiet, smiling, young soldier, stands out as a highlight of the campaign . . . Late in the day, the Jap resistance seemed to weaken. One could feel them begin to give way.'[16]

Corporal John French was subsequently awarded the Victoria Cross for this pivotal moment in the fighting. It was the second Victoria Cross—after Private Bruce Kingsbury's at Isurava only six action-packed days before—to be won during the Papuan campaign.

There is a monument to the deeds of French and his 2/9th Battalion just near that fateful creek and its nearby battleground. The heavy jungle still envelops the narrow track; the creek and its surrounds, still untouched, give the visitor some idea of the incredible intensity of a battle fought in such confined circumstances. About sixty Japanese died there, knowing that they had to make a prolonged stand to have any chance of evacuation later. The Australians paid dearly too. In company with the brave French, the 2/9th lost seventeen other ranks killed, Lieutenant Salisbury died of wounds, and Captain Anderson and Lieutenant Paterson and thirty-two other ranks were wounded.

Cummings ordered a slight withdrawal late on the afternoon of the 4th to secure a defensive position for the night. The next morning reconnaissance patrols revealed that the Japanese had withdrawn again. One patrol managed to reach Waga Waga without encountering any enemy presence.

At 9.15 a.m. Cummings resumed his advance with his D Company on the coastal side of the track and his A Company on the inland side. Later that morning Brigadier Wootten ordered him to secure the Japanese main base area and inform him of that occupation immediately.[17] But the Japanese had one last, desperate fight left in them.

When Captain Barnes' D Company crossed the creek east of Waga Waga, it had its 17 Platoon (Lieutenant McDonald) leading the advance, its 16 Platoon (Sergeant Roberts) on the inland flank and 18 Platoon (Lieutenant Scott) on the seaward side. Lance-Corporal Steve McCready was amongst those of 17 Platoon leading the way:

> . . . McDonald led us forward across the creek. We were at that stage quite a distance ahead of Company HQ and Lieutenant McDonald was concerned at the ominous quietness, almost a hush, and lack of contact with the Japs. He returned across the creek to confer with Company

> HQ leaving Sergeant Irving in charge of the Platoon.
>
> No sooner had he left than 'all hell broke loose' with the Japanese amid blood curdling yells and very heavy fire attacked 17 Platoon from across the creek behind us on the left. This was eventually repelled presumably by A Coy on our left and our own platoon. But casualties were heavy and those who could returned across the creek to Coy HQ. I was the only NCO left and McDonald called across the creek instructing me to move the remainder of 17 Platoon about 8 or 9 men from memory, back to Company HQ . . . this was done with a little sporadic Jap fire from ahead along the track.[18]

Scott's 18 Platoon lost seven men—Scott included—before it too withdrew, which now brought D Company's casualty count for the engagement to twenty-six. However, the Japanese had been forced to pay a heavier price. The 2/9th later found about forty enemy corpses in the area. D Company withdrew to Waga Waga, where Cummings decided to mount a second and much stronger attack during the afternoon which, given the earlier stiff enemy resistance, would be supported by Kittyhawk strafing and subsequent artillery and mortar fire. When the 2/9th advanced the destruction caused by that support was immediately apparent. Private Frank Rolleston:

> . . . we again moved forward with great caution, this time with the support of C and A Companies. We fully expected to meet opposition but when we reached the spot of our recent action, we found that the enemy had withdrawn. Just as I crossed the creek I came on about half a dozen Japs lying around a light machine gun, grim evidence of the effectiveness of our counter fire. Their eyes shone in the jungle gloom with the glassy stare of death, but they were not all dead for I recall that one lifted his head at the sound of our approach.[19]

Back at Waga Waga, the Australians now had a chance to observe the Japanese base area. Private Frank Rolleston was amongst them:

> . . . bicycles, small arms ammunition, big fibre bales of rice, cooking utensils and also Japanese invasion money, as well as post cards . . . several barges were beached nearby and everything, even the mess gear, appeared to bear the insignia of an anchor. Nearby was a Japanese first aid centre, in which several kinds of surgical instruments could be seen . . .[20]

Sergeant Bill Spencer, Intelligence Section, also examined the hospital area:

> One shelf held a large number of small bottles branded 'quinine, property of HM Forces Singapore'. Another item of interest was a bundle of maps, which included detailed maps of Queensland overprinted with arrows sweeping from Port Moresby to various centres along the Queensland coast.[21]

But the curiosity of others was less academic. Corporal Ernie Randell, A Company:

> Positions unoccupied, having trouble with sore feet. Dumps showed that the Japs had brought along their saki and we had a swig. Worried then about it being poisoned. Fair risk![22]

Lieutenant-Colonel Clem Cummings and his 2/9th Battalion settled into their defensive perimeter on 5 September with every reason to assume that the Japanese had been comprehensively defeated by their determined advance over the preceding three days.

Some idea of the sufferings of some of the Japanese might be gauged by Lieutenant Chikanori Moji over this period, as his hopes were raised and then dashed with successive barge arrivals and departures until his turn finally came. Moji, 4 September:

> Lts Nagata and Fujikawa were class-mates at the academy, but Nagata had the senior appointment. He stubbornly opposed our suggestion, saying that as senior officer he

> could not leave everyone in the area and go back himself. The chief MO and the rest of us stressed that at this stage, when positive operational action was no longer possible, it did not matter which of them remained behind . . . Nagata's voice grew tearful, saying that this was not the right way, but, yielding finally, to everyone's argument . . .
>
> As the cutter finally withdrew, we felt left alone at last, and sure that those remaining would die within the next few days . . . We could not imagine being able to hold out until the army came . . .
>
> The chief MO noisily drew his pistol and, as he wiped it with a rag, said in a tone between serious and joking, 'I hope it will fire once at least.' I too, thinking that my pistol might be rusty, took it out and had a look, but was not feeling very happy and just wiped it briefly before putting it back in its holster.
>
> It was not as if death was actually staring us in the face, but rather that we still had a few hours or days of leeway which made us think even more intensely about death.[23]

Moji, the night of 5–6 September:

> Soon the black shape of a barge appeared before my eyes. On board it there was a pl [platoon] to cover the wdl [withdrawal], led by Lt Suzuki . . . They spread out from the wdl-pt [withdrawal point] on landing, deployed for surveillance. These fresh tps, fit but few, made us feel secure. A launch drawing two or three cutters also arrived at the shore. The wounded . . . were withdrawn in the first stage . . .
>
> To us this peninsula at the East end of NG was a nightmare of a place. After waiting patiently we boarded the cutters. The pace was slow as the launch towed the cutters. We moved out over the dark sea. The members of the P-M [paymaster] unit were aboard the various vessels. Including the wounded, a total of about 600 were evac . . .
>
> The cutters reached *Tenryu*. I grasped a hand extended from the side of the ship and was dragged up

> onto the deck where there were those previously evacuated, some lying, some seated . . .
>
> They had the air of a defeated force.[24]

Although Cummings and his 2/9th Battalion—and Milne Force HQ—did not know it, 5 September 1942 had seen the last effort by the Japanese at Milne Bay. There would be no more major actions, no more set-piece defences, and no more major evacuation of their survivors. The Japanese who did remain behind were now essentially foodless fugitives, doomed to a hidden existence and to either a long trek along the north coast or extinction where they stood.

On 6 September, the 2/9th fought isolated skirmishes. However, that night the Japanese entered the bay yet again, with the result that the *Anshun*, which had been unloading supplies at Gili Gili, and the hospital ship *Manunda* were illuminated by searchlights. The Japanese spared the *Manunda* but sank the *Anshun* at its mooring. The enemy ships then proceeded to illuminate the shoreline for targets and to shell them, which resulted in two 2/12th deaths and twelve other casualties.

If the battle was all but over at Milne Bay it was still very much on in Brisbane.

> To NG Force Milne Force from Land Ops
> 5 Sept
>
> Personal for comd MILNE BAY FORCE. Indication from MOST SECRET sources 200 repeat 200 reinforcements will be landed MILNE BAY in 3 patrol boats from light cruiser on 5 Sept. Same procedure probably repeated 6 Sept with one light cruiser & destroyer. On 7th & 8th Sept one light cruiser & destroyer will anchor MILNE BAY view evacuation wounded & possibly pioneer force.
>
> Additionally or alternatively patrol boats may be sent.
>
> White repeat white light will indicate RY with destroyer. Army reinforcements will arrive 12th Sept. Until then reinforced landing force will retire to a safe camp in mountains . . .[25]

Clowes replied the following day to Rowell at New Guinea Force HQ in Port Moresby:

> Apparent our Naval and Air Forces at present unable prevent almost complete freedom enemy movement by sea and must anticipate possible further landings early anywhere this area shortly.
>
> In view of this and disposition considerable portion this force so far from vital area consider can NOT repeat NOT safely continue advance indefinitely further along NORTH shore. Regard security vital area incl No 1 strip as my primary role.[26]

Clowes reacted to the signals from MacArthur and Blamey on 7 September by beginning the process of recovering his distant 18th Brigade 2/12th and 2/9th Battalions. The 2/9th arrived back at Gili Gili on the 8th and the rearguard of the 2/12th, after destroying or salvaging all discovered Japanese supplies and equipment, completed its movement soon after. The Official Historian:

> Clowes now busied himself with preparations for the new attacks he had been told to expect, but which never materialised. Thus far the defence of Milne Bay had cost the Australians 373 battle casualties. Of these 24 were officers; 12 officers and 149 men were either killed or missing. Of the Americans one soldier of the 43rd Engineers was killed and two more were wounded in the ground actions; several more were killed or wounded in air raids.
>
> Of the Japanese casualties Clowes reported: 'It is conservatively and reliably estimated . . . that enemy killed amount to at least 700.'[27]

The reader could be forgiven for thinking that this Milne Bay victory was the stuff of celebration—and commemoration. Here was the first land defeat of the Japanese in the Pacific War. And its significance and inspiration was not lost on those elsewhere during that war. Field Marshal Slim would later write:

> We were helped, too, by a very cheering piece of news that now reached us, and of which, as a morale raiser, I made great use. In August and September 1942, Australian troops had, at Milne Bay in New Guinea, inflicted on the Japanese their first undoubted defeat on land. If the Australians, in conditions very like ours, had done it, so could we. Some of us may forget that of all the Allies it was Australian soldiers who broke the spell of the invincibility of the Japanese Army; those of us who were in Burma have cause to remember.[28]

Blamey to Rowell, 1 September 1942:

> My Dear General,
> I would like to congratulate you on the complete success of the operations at Milne Bay. It, of course, is extremely difficult to get the picture of the whole of the happenings, but it appeared to us here as though by not acting with great speed Clowes was liable to have missed the opportunity of dealing completely with the enemy and thus laying himself open to destruction if after securing a footing, the enemy was able to reinforce their first landing party very strongly.[29]

This signal does nothing other than bring great discredit on Blamey and MacArthur. Clowes should speak on his own behalf. In 1956 he wrote to Gavin Long, the Official Historian:

> I would refer generally to several features of the campaign which are most significant. These are:—
>
> (a) The complete control, for all practical purposes by the Japs of the sea. Consequently, the initiative in reinforcing or breaking off the operation rested with them throughout. We had no similar opportunity, and any serious miscalculation and reverse could have produced catastrophic consequences.

> (b) The 'fog of war' is never entirely missing in warfare, but it was never thicker and more opaque than in this case, due to the nature of the terrain, lack of communications, impossible weather and no maps. Information took a long time to get back, and even then, owing to the conditions, it was difficult to build up a true picture of the situation. It was, further, a very slow process to have Force HQ decisions implemented, since, owing to the all-pervading mud, movement was necessarily at snail's pace. To make matters worse . . . there were, during the operation, no 4 wheeled drive vehicles available . . .
>
> (c) The force was very hastily improvised—not a cohesive well-trained formation. This was a very severe handicap. The battle followed immediately after the arrival of Force HQ and 18 Inf Bde.
>
> (d) The operations were conducted on our part from initial dispositions to final victory on the basis of the original plan and operation instruction issued by me two days prior to the landing. A clear and definite policy was followed throughout.
>
> . . . the criticism from GHQ at the time—and after—appears to have stemmed from a complete ignorance or lack of appreciation by them.
>
> . . . the 'flap' messages . . . were decodes of 'most secret' Jap signals, but whether they were correctly interpreted or other wise the fact remains that they were of little use to us and served merely to hinder and hamper the development of our counter-attack which, otherwise, I feel, would have reached its conclusion days earlier than it actually did.[30]

When the contents of Clowes' letter are examined, the baseless speculation of Blamey's signal is realised. The overriding point concerning the Battle for Milne Bay is the fact that the Japanese had the initiative. If Clowes had reacted quickly to the first assault and committed his 18th Brigade to the offensive, and the Japanese had staged a further landing or landings, he could so easily have lost his vital ground. He could not move far or fast or in great strength, because he was denied naval craft with which to do it.

It should also be appreciated that had the enemy landed with any force up to division strength, Clowes' dispositions and appreciation of the Japanese options would still have proved successful. His original plan and dispositions were first class, and he stuck to them—he was, at all times, in total command of the situation.

However much the 'fog of war' operated at Milne Bay, the enemy would still have had to breach his Number 3 Strip perimeter and/or have infiltrated via the Stirling Range where he had an early warning system to detect any approach. And he kept his elite 18th Brigade deployed right on this vital ground.

Three last points should be made. The first is the strategic situation in August 1942. The Japanese had moved through South-East Asia with startling and frightening rapidity. In that context, Clowes' battle was absolutely critical to the war at that time. What was needed was a calm, clear-thinking, competent general who retained a decisive grip upon his battle at all times, because so much was at stake. Major-General Cyril Clowes did precisely that.

The performance of the RAAF at Milne Bay is the second point. The tireless and skilful service of the pilots of 75 and 76 Squadrons was of paramount importance to the defeat of the Japanese. The Kittyhawk pilots had destroyed the enemy barges at Goodenough Island on the day preceding the battle and had, therefore, also prevented the Japanese attempt at an outflanking movement through the Stirling Range. Further, those same pilots had destroyed the enemy invasion barges at their Waga Waga landing point, and had therefore rendered them useless for the purposes of moving the enemy troops along the bay by night. In addition, the Japanese were strafed and harassed during daylight hours and forced to conduct their infantry operations by night, a severe handicap during the entire battle. We have witnessed Lieutenant Moji's chagrin at the presence of the aircraft, a presence focused upon a narrow coastal corridor of operations where the intensity of fire was most severe. And during all this, the ground crew and pilots worked under the most appalling conditions, where the mere act of landing a plane was a hazard in itself. Some of the RAAF pilots during this unique campaign gave their lives merely trying to land on, or indeed find, their airfield.

The last point concerns the performance of the infantry at Milne Bay. High praise should be given to the 7th Militia Infantry Brigade. Clowes both deployed and employed it shrewdly. It was not a force trained for offensive operations, and the 61st Battalion's limited offensive operations aside, it was essentially used in a defensive role in which it excelled. If the Australian nation is to commemorate the deeds of the 39th Militia Battalion on the Kokoda Trail, it should not forget the excellence of the campaigning of the 7th Brigade—particularly the 61st Battalion—at Milne Bay.

The 18th Brigade was quite clearly Clowes' trump card. When he finally and astutely committed it to battle, its results were startling. In country ideally suited to short, sharp and costly ambushes, the 2/12th and 2/9th Battalions routed the enemy with a determination and professionalism of the highest order.

Perhaps Major-General Cyril Clowes might have anticipated some commendation, some decoration for his victory. None was forthcoming. Not only was Clowes not given another field command, but not long after his evacuation from Milne Bay with malaria there was an enquiry into the high rate of that disease amongst the personnel under his command. The fact is that the troops sent to Milne Bay from August 1942 onwards arrived without satisfactory anti-malarial medicines and instructions.[31] To therefore hold Clowes in any way responsible for the high incidence of this disease at Milne Bay—highly prevalent throughout the Papuan campaign—is quite simply ludicrous.

Major-General Cyril Clowes was posted to the position of Commander, Victorian Line of Communication Area in 1943, and remained there for the duration of the war. His removal should be attributed to two main issues. The first was the fact that he had incurred the displeasure of General MacArthur for his failure to 'clear the north shore immediately'. We have noted the ignorance and the panic and the self-serving reasons for MacArthur's attitude during the Papuan campaign thus far. In all this, Blamey saw his own position first, and not the welfare of his own Australian subordinates. Second, by the time Clowes was removed, Blamey had sacked Potts and, more importantly, Rowell.

Blamey was only too well aware that Clowes and Rowell were firm friends and colleagues of over 30 years' standing. In removing Clowes, he was also getting rid of a Rowell supporter.

We have seen two heads roll in this Papuan campaign—Potts and Rowell—and Clowes will sit at Milne Bay awaiting his just described fate. Thus far then, three heads.

By mid-September 1942 the tide has turned. The Japanese will retreat to their Gona–Buna–Sanananda beachhead. Our 7th Division AIF, and various militia units including the 39th Battalion, will journey to this beachhead. If the Papuan campaign to this point has been a desperate and controversial affair, the battle for the beaches will see its final bloodied and contentious conclusion. And General MacArthur will have his first opportunity to commit his American troops to the Papuan campaign after his contemptible criticism of the Australians.

With never a sound of trumpet,
With never a flag displayed,
The last of the old campaigners
Lined up for the last parade.

The Last Parade

A.B. 'Banjo' Paterson, 1900

PART THREE

GONA–BUNA–SANANANDA

The last of the old campaigners . . .

. . . COME UP HERE AND BLOODY TRY!

19

The great one arrived in Port Moresby on 2 October 1942. MacArthur should, in fact, have journeyed to Port Moresby far sooner, given his uneducated but forthright comments and intervention during Potts' campaign, but he 'had an almost unreasonable fear of flying'[1] and had had to be coaxed into the flight by his air chief. The next day MacArthur, Blamey and Frank Forde, the Minister for the Army, visited Ower's Corner, the last stage of the motorised section leading to the Kokoda Trail.

Forde, dressed like some latter-day African explorer, complete with pith helmet and side-strapped pistol, informed Brigadier Lloyd's 16th Brigade that they were now facing their baptism of fire. Many of these soldiers were original members of the 6th Division AIF, who had fought through Bardia, Derna, Tobruk, in Greece and Crete and Syria.[2] MacArthur was a much more impressive and dramatic speaker than Forde. As Brigadier Lloyd passed him he said: 'Lloyd, by some act of God, your brigade has been chosen for this job. The eyes of the western world are upon you. I have every confidence in you and your men. Good luck and don't stop.'[3] The great one flew back to Brisbane on 4 October.

On 25 September, Blamey had outlined his plan for the Allied thrust to the Gona–Buna–Sanananda beachhead. It envisaged a three-axis approach. The first was the obvious one, an Australian assault back over the very ground that the Japanese had used: along the Kokoda Trail to Kokoda and then on through Oivi, Gorari, Wairopi, Awala and on to Gona. Brigadier Eather's 25th and Brigadier Lloyd's 16th Brigades were to accomplish this task. The second axis entailed a much more ambitious trek by the Americans to the east of the Kokoda Trail via Jaure–Wairopi or Jaure–Buna. The third advocated a combined sea and land route via Milne Bay–Wanigela–Pongani–Buna, involving the Americans or the Australians and Americans. To initiate action along the final axis, the 2/10th Battalion was sent from Milne Bay to Wanigela to establish a base there.

While the Australians were guardedly optimistic about the time frame and the suitability of all three axes of approach to the beachhead, the Americans—despite early problems with their 2nd Battalion, 126th Regiment on the route to Jaure, who were finding the terrain and their poor levels of fitness and training a severe handicap—were supremely optimistic of an early result at Buna.

As these plans were being formulated, events at Guadalcanal in the South Pacific theatre of operations during that month lent an increased sense of urgency to MacArthur's desire to take the Gona–Buna–Sananada beachhead.

Japanese naval guns and bombers shelled Henderson Field on Guadalcanal and rendered it unserviceable on 13 and 14 October. The Japanese then began to land troops in anticipation of yet another ground offensive. The precarious manner in which the American Navy marines were maintaining their hold upon the prized Henderson Field, and the scale of the fighting, indicated that both sides were utterly determined to produce a favourable result at Guadalcanal. The ramifications for MacArthur were that, should the Japanese prove victorious there, they would then be poised to deploy vast numbers of troops to recontest the hard-won gains in Papua. Speed was of the essence.

Thus in October 1942, it was against this strategic background that MacArthur sought to push the Australian advance far harder over the Kokoda Trail and also develop his other two thrusts towards Buna.

When Brigadier Eather mounted an attack on Ioribaiwa on 28 September 1942, he found the Japanese had retreated. After congregating his entire 25th Brigade and the 3rd Militia Battalion on that feature the following day, patrols were reporting that the enemy had also withdrawn past Nauro.

The Japanese had had no alternative but to retreat. The first factor was the breakdown of their own line of communication. By this time, the Allied air forces were inflicting telling damage upon their supply lines, particularly with the continued bombing of the Wairopi bridge at the Kumusi River. The second was the Japanese failure to use the Kokoda airstrip, much less the advanced Myola dry lake bed or any other locality for the air dropping of supplies, which meant that they relied exclusively upon the ability of their Rabaul labourers and those Papuans whom they had press-ganged into carrier service. But the third and most critical reason for their withdrawal had been Potts and his Maroubra Force fighting withdrawal. And the evidence of the pitiful plight of the Japanese was almost immediately obvious to the advancing Australians.

From this time on, the Australian advance from Ioribaiwa to Templeton's Crossing became the familiar Owen Stanley story of difficulty of supply. Bert Kienzle of ANGAU was still on the job:

> 5th October. I inspected all stations between '66' and Nauro and arrived there at 1915 hrs. and was told to see Brigadier Eather and Brigadier Lloyd 16 Bde.
>
> Owing to the shortage of carriers forward Brigades had been held up, so made immediate arrangements for more carriers to come forward and assemble at Nauro, leaving enough to maintain essential supplies on L of C. I also appealed to H.Q. for more carriers . . .
>
> (On the way through Ioribaiwa I inspected the ridge, Jap defences, and abandoned material. There were many Jap graves. Before arriving at Nauro I observed the first Jap prisoner lying on a stretcher . . . in a very weakened condition.)
>
> At Nauro I interrogated rescued Rabaul natives who were in a terrible state. They had all been half-starved. One showed me wounds in the back where he had been prodded by Japs forcing him to carry when utterly exhausted. They gave some harrowing accounts of Jap

> brutalities. No medical attention when sick and death by the bayonet. Their faces showed what they had been through. They were glad to be with us again. I immediately used this evidence as propaganda for our carriers who were quick to take in the fact, that their treatment was totally different . . .
>
> The only Orokaiva native (Kokoda Village) who was impressed by the Japs fell by the wayside exhausted and was rescued by us. He is able to give exact information of tracks taken by the enemy and confirmed Jap brutalities.[4]

The next few days saw Kienzle busily engaged in trying to gather sufficient natives. He had employed the new technique of allotting certain numbers of them to specific battalions and headquarters, as well as overseeing sufficient numbers to work at various dropping grounds. An ANGAU soldier was stationed at each dropping ground, or accompanied each carrier group for a battalion formation. In that way there was someone able to converse with the carriers and to understand their needs and capabilities. The practical situation, of course, was not in any way understood by the new commander of New Guinea Force (Lieutenant-General Herring), let alone the other and more powerful recent visitors to Ower's Corner. Allen to Herring 7 October:

> Implementation of air-dropping programme causing gravest concern. Under present system it would appear that air force cannot supply planes necessary to assure dropping of 50,000 pounds daily weather permitting. (2) 50,000 pounds daily covers maintenance only and does not repeat not provide for building up a reserve. It does however allow for 30 per cent wastage due to destruction by dropping. Actual daily requirements for delivery to units etc for maintenance is 35,000 pounds [15 000 pounds wastage through inaccurate dropping or destruction upon impact!] (3) Understood it is intention to build up 21 days' reserve supplies ammunition etc forward under existing system. This is quite impossible as supplies etc dropped during first two days of programme less than 50% of requirements for daily maintenance only.

The Kokoda Trail

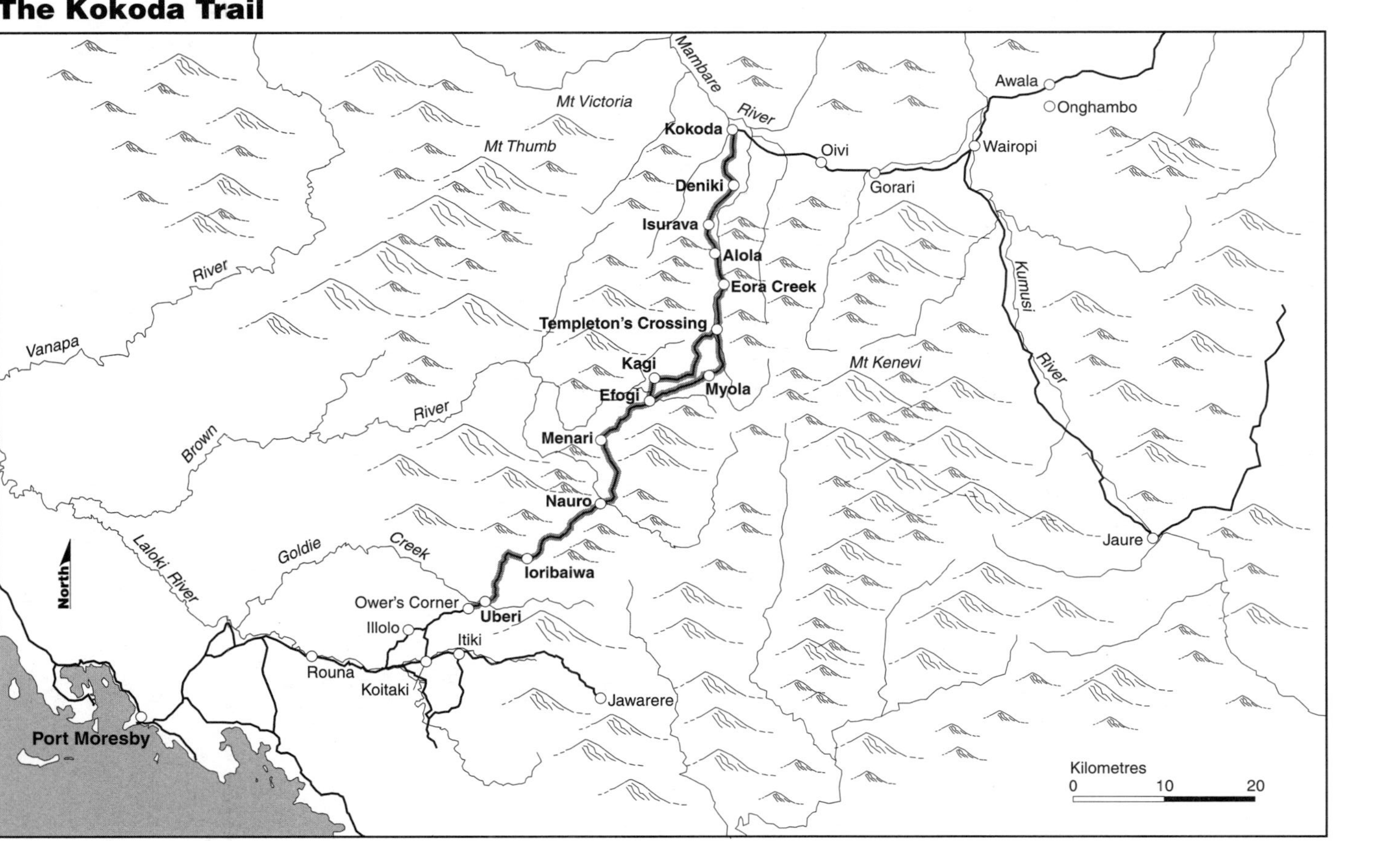

> (4) Unless supply etc dropping of 50,000 pounds daily plus additional to build up reserve is assured complete revision of plans will have to be made and large proportion of troops withdrawn to Imita Ridge position. Any attempt then to hold a determined enemy advance Kagi–Templeton's Crossing–Myola area and to occupy Kokoda will be jeopardised beyond all reason.[5]

On 11 October 1942, MacArthur had signalled Blamey demanding to know why Allen's advance had not been far faster. In turn, Blamey signalled Allen:

> Your order definitely to push on with sufficient force and capture Kokoda. You have been furnished with supplies as you requested and ample appears to be available. In view of lack of serious opposition your advance appears much too slow. You will press enemy with vigour. If you are feeling strain personally relief will be arranged. Please be frank about this. Dropping arranged only at Myola . . . As soon as you can arrange more advanced location will arrange to drop there.[6]

Allen replied the next day:

> My outline plan . . . is designed to capture Kokoda as soon as possible. Apparently it has been misunderstood. Nothing is being left undone in order to carry out your wishes and my brigade commanders have already been instructed accordingly. The most serious opposition to rapid progress is the terrain. The second is maintenance of supplies through lack of native carriers. Reserve supplies have not repeat not been adequate up to 11 Oct. Until information of recoveries today am unable to say whether they are yet adequate. Rate of advance does not entirely depend on air droppings. Equal in importance is our ability to carry forward and maintain our advanced troops. Notwithstanding that men carry with them up to five days' rations maintenance forward of dropping place is still necessary. This country is much tougher than any previous theatre and cannot be appreciated until seen.

> From all reports the worst is north of Myola. The vigour with which we press the enemy is dependent on the physical endurance of the men and the availability of supplies. Our men have pressed so far with vigour consistent with keeping them fit to fight. With regard to my personal physical fitness I am not repeat not feeling the strain. I never felt fitter nor able to think straighter. I however feel somewhat disappointed on behalf of all ranks that you are dissatisfied with the very fine effort they have made.[7]

On 12 October Brigadier Eather had his 2/33rd Battalion moving along the main track from Myola towards Templeton's Crossing and his 2/25th moving along the track from Kagi. His third battalion, the 2/31st, was moving on Kagi while the 3rd Militia Battalion was at Myola. Constant patrolling had been carried out in an attempt to keep in touch with the rapidly withdrawing enemy. And because of the critical supply situation, the 16th Brigade was also held at Myola. The point Blamey could not grasp was that, given the acute supply situation, only one brigade could be maintained at the front at a time—and this by a tenuous carrier line through appalling mud, rain and horrendous terrain. Allen planned that the 16th Brigade would soon take over the front and push on to Kokoda.

Not long after midday on the 12th, the 2/33rd came across a point on the track between Myola and Templeton's Crossing which negotiated the top of a narrow, densely covered ridge. Here was an ideal ambush position in terrain where the thick undergrowth negated movement other than by the main track and a small number of localised paths. It was here in the Templeton's Crossing area that the Japanese, dug in often in single-soldier pits and well camouflaged by vegetation, had decided to contest the Australian advance. They had the familiar Owen Stanley defensive advantages: the high ground, ample vision, concealment and cleverly dug pits.

When you stand in many of the Japanese pits on the trail, they are far more narrow than their Australian counterparts, which made the destruction of their occupants difficult by grenade burst. Frequently, pits were joined by very narrow and shallow crawl trenches—just large enough for the relatively quick and covered movement of occupants and automatic weapons from one point to another.

By nightfall on 12 October, the 2/33rd had lost four men killed and twelve wounded after attempting to clear the enemy from this troublesome ridge. Attempts to outflank the positions were frustrated by the difficulty of having to negotiate the steep approaches.

Progress was equally difficult on the track from Kagi, where the 2/25th had encountered telling sniper fire which masked well dug-in holding positions on the high ground. Although little ground was gained, a disturbing discovery was made. During the course of a patrol, a 2/25th Battalion section leader discovered a 'parcel of meat'. This was taken back to the battalion doctor, who made the following declaration: 'I have examined two portions of flesh recovered by one of our patrols. One was the muscle of a large animal, the other similar muscle tissue with a large piece of skin and underlying tissues attached. I consider the last as human.'[8]

On 15 October Lieutenant Crombie, 2/25th Battalion, filed the following report:

> I was the officer in charge of the burial party of two 3 Battalion militia personnel killed on 11 Oct 42 and, on examination of the bodies, found that one of them had both arms cut off at the shoulders and the arms missing and a large piece cut out of one thigh as well as one of the calves of one of the legs slashed by a knife. The other body also had a large piece cut out of one of the thighs. These mutilations were obviously made by a sharp knife, and were not caused by bullets or bayonets. The men's deaths were caused in one case by a burst of MG fire in the chest and the other in the head.[9]

This would prove to be no isolated incident.

The fighting near Templeton's Crossing during the period 12–17 October by the 25th Brigade and 3rd Militia Battalion continued to reflect the basic problems of maintaining a force of that size forward of its supply base: the tremendous drain on the health of a force operating in that unique terrain for a prolonged period; and, at the tactical level, the difficulty of shifting a smaller, well dug-in and determined force from the high ground when that ground and vegetation impaired rapid outflanking movement.

From a supply perspective, Blamey and MacArthur's signals also demonstrate little if any understanding of the multitude of day-to-day practical obstacles that men like Bert Kienzle were facing and fixing. The fact is that Kienzle and his ANGAU personnel, the carriers and soldiers were not only responsible for the gathering and moving of supplies, but for the very infrastructure that facilitated it. It was they who had to organise the clearing of sites, the building of camps, the allocation and deployment of the carrier line, the movement of casualties, and the very backbone of the transport system: the carriers. To Blamey and MacArthur's distant and ignorant eyes, the whole issue was merely concerned with dropping supplies, adding them up, and then concluding that they had furnished the forward force with the ample implements of war. Kienzle:

> 11th October. I went forward with Maj-General Allen, Col. Spry and Brig. Lloyd to Menari where Brig. Eather awaited the G.O.C's arrival, for a conference. I moved the 2/1 Bn and Bde H.Q. with 375 native carriers; Police-Sgt. Bagita was in charge. At 2000 hrs. I was called to G.O.C. and told by Col. Spry, G1, to . . . make a reconnaissance of that area [Myola] to make a possible landing ground . . .
>
> 12th October. I left Menari at 0815 hrs for Efogi Nth. On the track I noted many dead, skeletons, and graves . . .
>
> I also noted Jap camps at Efogi, large ones; the evacuation of which were completed. The stench was terrible. I arrived at Efogi Nth at 1600 hrs where I met Brig. Eather and camped the night with W.O. Davies.
>
> 13' October. At 0815 hrs. I left for Myola accompanied by Brig. Eather and party and arrived at Myola 1 at 1100hrs . . . Found the organisation not very satisfactory and the need for a completely new camp after the Jap occupation. W.O. Davies and Angau personnel

> were detailed with carriers to get this in hand and to organise the collecting of stores dropped and scattered over the wide area of swamp at Myola. I left Myola 1 for larger area Myola 2 where we arrived at 1600 hrs. With Lieut. Dawe, R.A. Engineers I measured up 800 yds of the best ground available.
>
> 15 October. I reconnoitred Myola 2 and visited Myola at 1430 hrs to inspect the native labour camp where I found good progress had been made. Shelters were built for 2/3 Bn at Myola 2.
>
> 16th October. I ordered 100 natives to clear site for landing ground and good progress was made. Natives can clear 3 times as quickly as troops. Returned to Myola and saw G.O.C, G1, Brig. Eather and Lloyd and had conference regarding native carrier position.
>
> 17 October. I went forward and selected a site for a new dump at first crossing of Eora Creek on way to Templeton's Crossing to be known as 'Station 1' and returned to Myola. On the trail I noted several Jap camp sites, graves, Japanese and Rabaul boys dead. I also reconnoitred a short cut along the ridge separating the 2 Myola areas and ordered natives to clear and widen the same day . . .
>
> 18th October . . . Planes were now dropping supplies at Myola. 274 carriers to station 1 were sent. 75 carriers with 16 bde H.Q. 50 carriers with 2/2 Bn.
>
> . . . We were now having a nightly conference where the days activities were discussed and plans for the next day formed. The carrier position played a big part at these conferences.
>
> 19th October. I was ordered to accompany Col. Spry and other staff officers to select a dropping area and camp site on Myola 2, as this area was found to be more suitable and closer to our present scene of operations. Planes were dropping at Myola 1 and a trial drop at Myola 2. Capt. Vernon returned from Efogi Nth and went down with malaria.[10]

While Kienzle, his ANGAU personnel and the carriers were busily occupied in their vital activities, the 25th Brigade and the

3rd Battalion were gradually closing on Templeton's Crossing.

The 25th Brigade, but not the 3rd Militia Battalion, was relieved by the 16th Brigade on 20 October. Eather's soldiers had performed magnificently given their supply situation, the debilitating conditions and the closeness of the fighting. After a number of further stiff engagements, the Japanese withdrew to the Eora Creek crossing. More determined resistance was to follow.

After another aggressive Blamey message on 17 October—and a reply from Allen which listed his casualties and the startling sickness wastage as 24 Officers and 706 other ranks for the 25th Brigade and 1 and 38 for the 16th Brigade—Blamey signalled Allen again on the 21st:

> During the last five days you have made practically no advance against a weaker enemy. Bulk of your forces have been defensively located in rear although enemy has shown no capacity to advance. Your attacks for most part appear to have been conducted by single battalion or even companies on narrow front. Enemy lack of enterprise makes it clear he has not repeat not sufficient strength to attack in force. You should consider acting with greater boldness and employ wide encircling movement to destroy enemy in view of fact that complete infantry brigade in reserve is available to act against hostile counter-offensive.
>
> You must realise time is now of great importance. 128 US already has elements at Pongani [on north-eastern Papuan coast on the way to Buna] Capture Kokoda aerodrome and onward move to cooperate with 128 before Buna is vital portion of plan.[11]

And later that day Blamey, feeling further intense pressure from MacArthur, sent yet another signal:

> The following message has been received from General MacArthur. Quote. Operations reports show that progress on the trail is NOT repeat NOT satisfactory. The tactical handling of our troops in my opinion is faulty. With forces superior to the enemy we are bringing to bear in actual

Kokoda Trail—Efogi to Templeton's Crossing

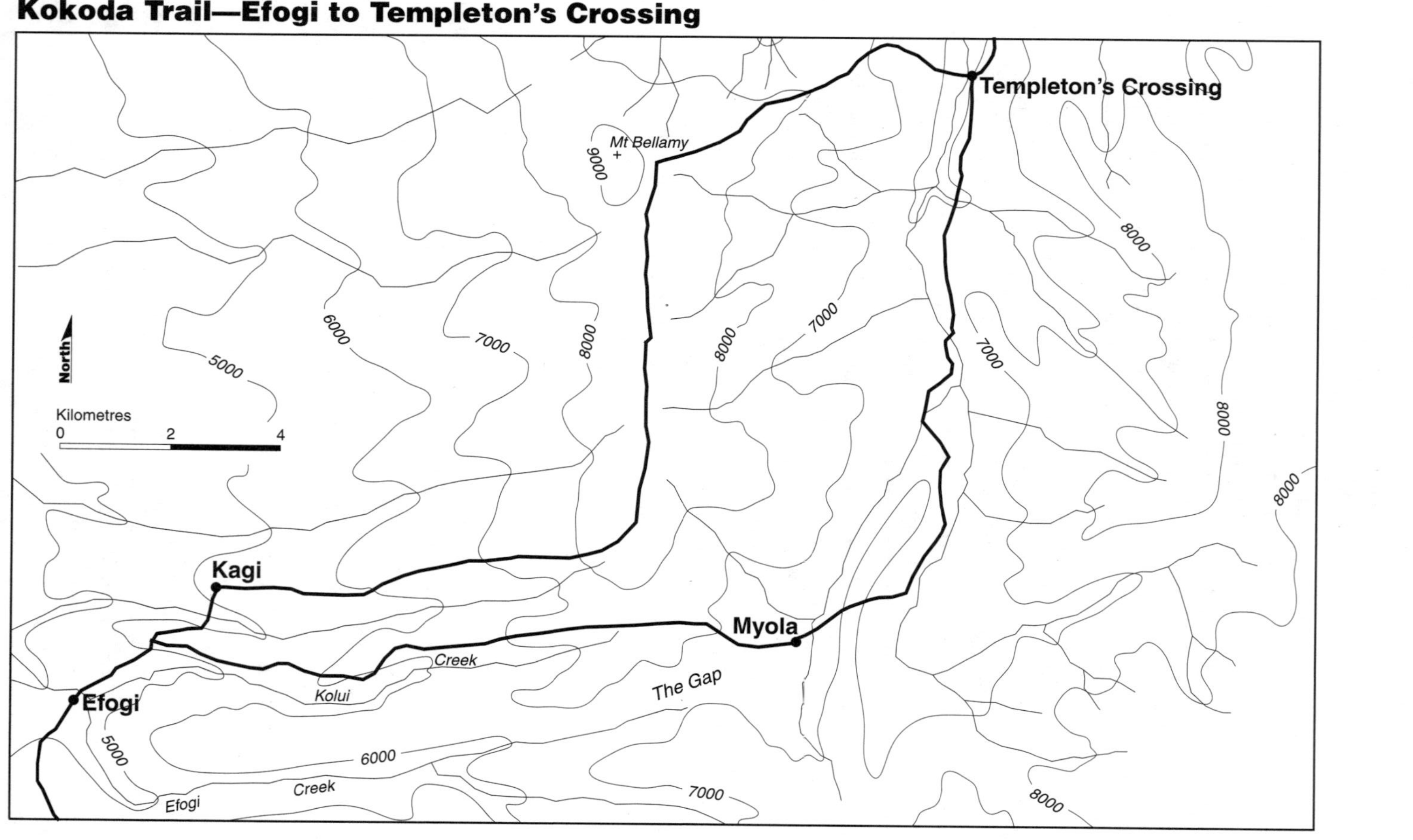

Kokoda Trail—Kokoda to Eora Creek

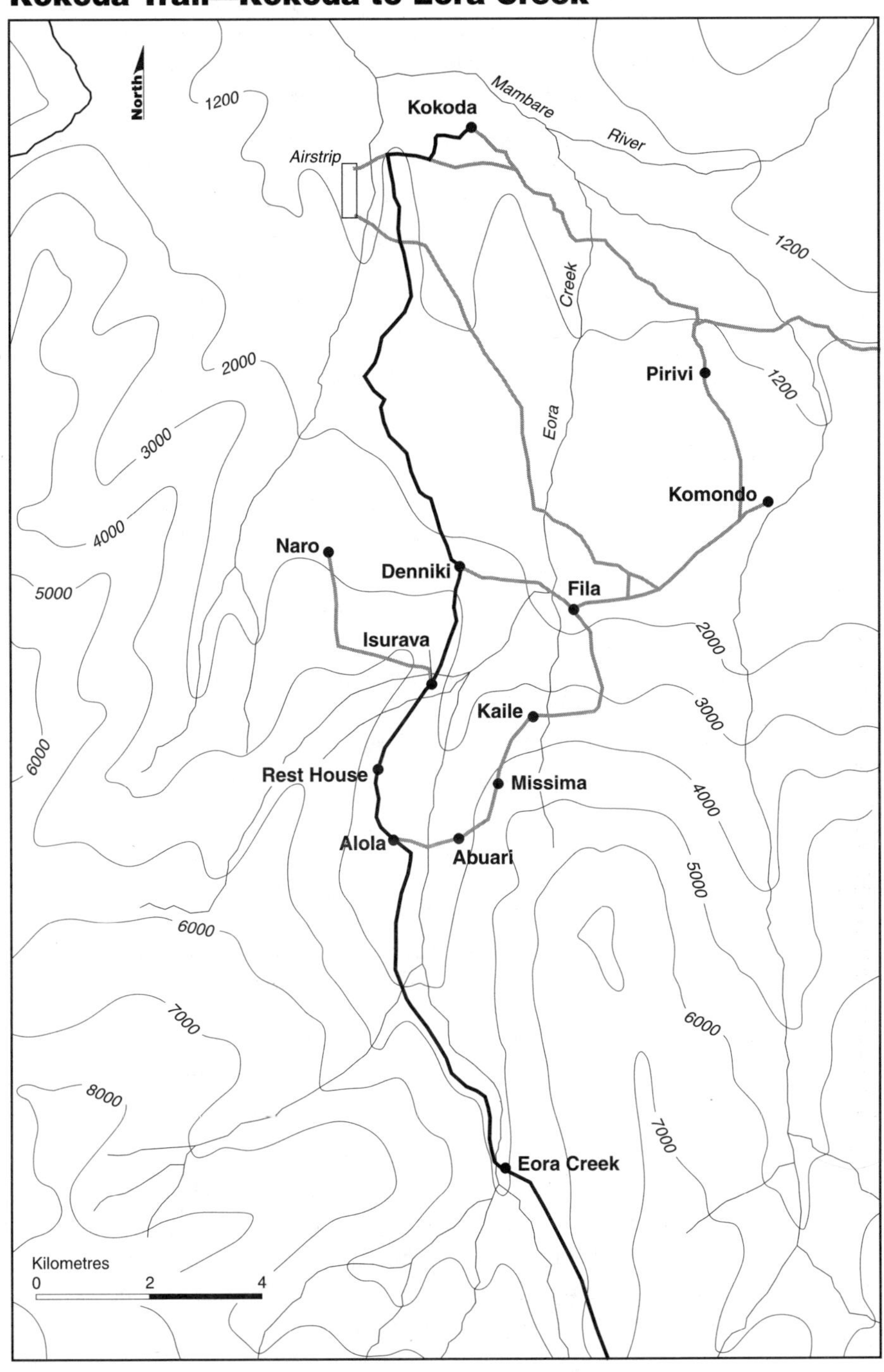

> combat only a small fraction of available strength enabling the enemy at the point of actual combat to oppose us with apparently comparable forces. Every extra day of delay complicates the problem and will probably result ultimately in greater casualties than a decisive stroke made in full force. Our supply situation and the condition of the troops certainly compares favourably with those of the enemy and weather conditions are neutral. It is essential to the entire New Guinea operation that the Kokoda airfield be secured promptly. Unquote.[12]

Allen attempted to once again educate both Blamey and MacArthur concerning his legitimate problems and concerns, but the signal fell on deaf ears. And the signal might have been radically different if Allen's Chief Staff Officer, Spry, had not convinced Allen to change his first draft: 'If you think you can do any bloody better come up here and bloody try.'[13] Blamey was also losing patience with his subordinate. He would soon tell a member of the press: 'If it wasn't for the fact that it takes six days to send in a relief I'd sack the old bastard.'[14]

In the end he did anyway. After a further signal exchange between the two of them, Blamey, just as Allen's troubles were about to wash away in the final tide of victory, sent him another signal on 27 October:

> Consider that you have had sufficiently prolonged tour of duty in forward area. General Vasey will arrive Myola by air morning 28 October. On arrival you will hand over command to him and return to Port Moresby for tour of duty in this area. Will arrange air transport from Myola forenoon 29 October if this convenient to you.[15]

Allen could only reply that:

> It is regretted that it has been found necessary to relieve me at this juncture especially since the situation is improving daily and I feel that the worst is now behind us. I must add that I feel as fit as I did when I left the Base Area and I would have preferred to have remained here until my troops had also been relieved.[16]

Rowell, Potts, Clowes and now Allen—four Papua senior commanders' heads had now rolled.

It will be remembered that as Deputy Chief of the General Staff in Brisbane, Major-General George Vasey had exchanged a number of intriguing signals with Lieutenant-General Rowell regarding the Battle for Milne Bay during late August and early September 1942. When the 16th Brigade had been sent to Port Moresby in September, Vasey was chosen as the new 6th Division commander and was promptly sent to Port Moresby. And when Blamey decided to relieve Major-General 'Tubby' Allen as commander of the 7th Division he simply swapped the two commanders: Allen to the 6th Division, and Vasey to the 7th.

When Vasey assumed command of the 7th Division at 8.00 a.m. on 29 October, he received a message from MacArthur via Blamey: 'Feel sure General Vasey will take his force through without delay. Please give him my felicitations and tell him of my confidence.'[17] The irony is that Vasey immediately put Allen's plan into practice. After the 16th Brigade's bloody battle to capture Eora Creek had concluded, Allen had recognised that with two brigade, he could send one around the loop in the trail via Alola–Missima–Abuari–Oivi, and thus bypass Kokoda, while sending the second brigade along the Kokoda Trail and into that village. This was nothing new—it will be remembered that General Horii had done precisely the same thing coming the other way in an attempt to outflank Potts during the Battle of Isurava. Vasey sent the 16th Brigade along the route to Oivi and the 25th Brigade towards Kokoda.

Eather's 25th Brigade entered Kokoda—it did not capture it—on 2 November 1942. The Japanese had abandoned that village in anticipation of the outflanking movement to the east. In short, had Blamey held off for six days, Allen would have entered Kokoda—and received the resulting praise. In the event Vasey did.

You are standing on the Kokoda Plateau. The village today consists of a memorial site, a number of rough buildings on the plateau itself, a museum and, as you gaze to the west, you can see the airfield in the distance, ringed by oil palms. Off to the east is the track to the Gona–Buna–Sananda beachhead. There is an abundance of fibro houses stretching in front of the plateau and around to its east.

But it is this Kokoda Plateau and the airstrip that sets you thinking. Lieutenant-Colonel Owen stood just near where the museum is now. 'Sir, I think you're taking an unnecessary risk walking around amongst the troops like that,' said the 39th Battalion's Lieutenant 'Judy' Garland. You can picture Owen then being shot and taken to the police house that Doctor Vernon has occupied as an RAP. And then there is the stealthy withdrawal of the young soldiers of the 39th under Jim Cowey—and the still inspirational Doctor Vernon—creeping out from this eerie, mist-covered plateau.

The Australian Army paid such a heavy price defending and then retaking this place. The 39th gamely tried to recapture it and awaited reinforcement by air that never came; Potts was ordered to retake it, but was forced into a fighting withdrawal that should live forever in Australian folklore. Finally, the 16th and 25th Brigades and a militia unit, the 3rd Battalion, paid so very dearly in both battle and sickness casualties to return here.

There are nearly always official ceremonies which mark great moments in history. Kokoda was no exception. On 6 November some troops gathered around, the flag went up the pole and General Vasey made a speech—all entirely appropriate. The Papuan carriers were most deservedly praised, and everyone probably felt that appropriate acknowledgements had been made to all concerned. But two people who had given so much returned to Kokoda after its occupation by the Australians and to this day have received scant recognition for their unique service.

Doctor Geoffrey Vernon remains a prime example of the paradox of war. Throughout this campaign he had rendered selfless help to the Papuans. At Eora Creek, Vernon had silently slipped down to see a native who had pneumonia and had placed his blanket over him, so that this carrier's last hours might be a touch more comfortable. He had tended them, nursed them and treated them with the most basic of medicines, and to the very best of his ability he had safeguarded their interests.

When Vernon returned to Kokoda in early November 1942, the Papuans, decked in flowers, ran to honour him with shrubs and further flowers and, in a gesture befitting a king, hoisted him onto a derelict Japanese bicycle, bare rims and all, and wheeled him triumphantly into Kokoda. The old man must have been moved. Today, a native hospital at Maipani in a remote part of Papua serves as his only memorial.

Bert Kienzle was the other:

> 2nd November.
> . . . The climate was much warmer and the carriers cheerful and eager to get to Kokoda. The news arrived of occupation of Kokoda without resistance.
>
> 3rd November. With Col. Spry and Lt-Col Cannat I left Deniki early and arrived at Kokoda in 1 hr. 35 mins at about 0830 hrs. It was a relief to see it again even though all the buildings were demolished. The native carriers came in later bedecked with flowers and shrubs and all smiles. They knew they had done well. Even here we could not rest for it was most urgent that supplies be landed on the landing ground as quickly as possible. All available carriers which I could muster were put on during the afternoon weeding the landing ground which was overgrown. The Japs had not used it. I also selected a labour camp site near the aerodrome. The local village people, whom I had known for years, came in to welcome our return. They told me pitiful tales of hardship and the losses of villagers who were killed by the Japanese. Some immediately joined up as carriers to come to the coast with us. Our carrier lines started to swell from then on. Morale was high. The white man had proved a superior fighter.
>
> 5th November. With permission . . . I went to Yodda to visit my home and plantations. I found 2 houses burnt to the ground and my house riddled with machinegun and cannon fire and all contents removed and destroyed.

> The rubber trees were still standing, a few mutilated, and secondary growth was taking charge. Planes landed at Kokoda bringing much needed supplies.[18]

However, even the energetic and resourceful Kienzle failed to execute one of his July 1942 orders. By August of that year he had still failed to build a road from Ilolo, outside Port Moresby, over the Owen Stanley Range to Kokoda.

Major-General George Vasey was no fool. He had witnessed MacArthur's harassment of Clowes during the Battle for Milne Bay while he (Vasey) had been Deputy Chief of the General Staff; he had been in Port Moresby when Rowell had been sacked; and he had been flown into the Kokoda campaign to take over 'Tubby' Allen's command of the 7th Division. Recent history had therefore shown him that anything other than fast, decisive movement—whether it was possible or not—might end in dismissal.

During early November 1942, the fortunes of war now favoured Vasey, as he was not locked into a precarious mountain advance such as Allen had faced but was out into more open ground east of Kokoda. He sought a decisive outflanking movement that might cripple the Japanese. The opportunity came at Oivi–Gorari, and to Vasey's great credit he took it.

Using Brigadier Lloyd's 16th Brigade, which had moved along the right side of the loop in the track bypassing Kokoda and had travelled to Oivi, Vasey now moved Eather's force forward. While the 16th Brigade maintained pressure on the Oivi front, Eather's 25th Brigade and one 16th Brigade battalion (the 2/1st) marched south to move around the Japanese defences. It was a bold move, as by doing so Vasey had committed his whole force to the battle and was left with no reserves.

By dark on 9 November, Eather had two of his four battalions holding a dug-in Japanese force deployed about a mile south of Gorari, while his remaining two battalions were sited just near that village. Away to the rear, the 16th Brigade's 2/2nd and 2/3rd Battalions faced the Japanese at Oivi. The enemy had now been caught in a well-sprung pincer movement—and they reacted with desperate efforts to break out and back towards the Kumusi River. The Oivi–Gorari battle became a grim killing ground as the Australians, many of them sick and running very low on rations, not only held their line but proceeded to constrict the enemy perimeter.

By dark on 11 November, it was apparent that the Japanese force at Oivi–Gorari had been shattered—the Australians later estimated about six hundred Japanese had been killed. Why Horii chose to contest Vasey's advance in this area is hard to fathom. He should have crossed the Kumusi and used that natural barrier to contest Vasey's eastward progress with fighting patrols, which would have gained him more time with far fewer casualties. The chaotic crossing of the fast-flowing Kumusi River swelled the Japanese losses, as many were overwhelmed in its turbulent waters which swept their rafts away. The most notable drowning casualty was Major-General Tomitaro Horii himself.

As early November 1942 passed, Generals MacArthur and Blamey were filled with great optimism. The Japanese attempts to capture Port Moresby by an overland crossing of the Kokoda Trail and an amphibious landing at Milne Bay had both been utterly defeated. And General Vasey had inflicted a telling defeat upon the enemy at Oivi–Gorari.

The Japanese had retreated into the confines of their Gona–Sananda–Buna beachhead. Intelligence estimates of the Japanese strength at this beachhead varied considerably amongst the Allies. The 7th Australian Division's assessment was between 1500 and 2000; the 32nd American Division's calculation was approximately a battalion (about 1000) across the whole front; while General Headquarters Intelligence determined that 4000 of the enemy occupied the area.[19] There were in fact 9000.

The Australians, commanded by Vasey, were ordered to approach the beachhead from the south-west. The 25th Brigade (with the 3rd Militia Battalion attached) was assigned the task of capturing Gona, while the 16th Brigade was ordered to capture Sananda. The Americans were to attack and capture Buna. The Americans were certainly confident. Major-General E.F. Harding, the commander of the American 32nd Division, had written to MacArthur's chief of staff in mid-October:

> My idea is that we should push towards Buna with all speed, while the Japs are heavily occupied with the Guadalcanal business. Also, we have complete supremacy in the air here, and the air people could do a lot to help in the taking of Buna, even should it be fairly strongly defended, which I doubt. I think it quite possible that we might find it easy pickings, with only a shell of sacrifice troops left to defend it. This may be a bum guess, but even if it proves to be incorrect I don't think it would be too much trouble to take Buna with the forces we can put against it.[20]

Our Papuan journey thus far has chronicled the fate of the 7th Australian Division. We have noted Potts' 21st Brigade's magnificent fighting withdrawal along the Kokoda Trail during August–September 1942; we have followed the fight of the 18th Brigade at Milne Bay; and we have noted the struggle back across the Owen Stanley Range of this 7th Division's 25th Brigade. There has also been the sterling service of the 16th Brigade, their militia comrades, the 7th Brigade at Milne Bay, and the 30th Brigade (chiefly the 39th and 3rd Militia Battalions) along the Kokoda Trail. The losses to the 16th, 21st, 25th, and 30th Brigades from 22 July until 16 November 1942 were 34 officers and 607 other ranks killed, and 59 officers and 956 other ranks wounded, giving the Australians combined casualty counts of 93 killed and 1563 wounded.[21]

During November–January 1942–43, the 7th Division and their attached militia troops were faced with their final Papuan confrontation. At the Gona–Buna–Sanananda beachhead this splendid 7th Division, the victors of Kokoda and Milne Bay, would be bled white during a war of final victory and by further bitter controversy.

Few Australians have heard of Gona, Buna and Sananada—or for that matter Milne Bay. In commemorating the Papuan campaign we have, as a nation, got lost on the Kokoda Trail.

I KNOW THEY'LL FIGHT

20

The Allied operations to force the final defeat of the Japanese in Papua during the period November 1942– January 1943 at the Gona–Sananaanda–Buna beachhead were confined to an area about fifteen miles long, stretching from Cape Endaiadere on the north-east coast to the Amboga River.

Prior to the outbreak of the war, Buna consisted of a native village and a government administration station about half a mile to its east. It was from this station that the district magistrate and his staff operated. About two and a half miles to the west of Buna lay Sananda Point, where a corduroy track was used to transport goods from as far as Soputa to waiting small coastal craft. Five miles further west again was the Anglican Mission at Gona.

Scattered along this Gona–Sananda–Buna beachhead were groves of coconut palms, often up to a depth of about a hundred yards. Dispersed through many of the coconut belts were tall banyan trees, which had extensive foliage and large, protruding roots. Inland the terrain consisted of a mixture of swamp, scrub and jungle and patches of kunai grass.

The swamps varied in size but displayed some common features. All were fetid and mainly tidal. Most were quite shallow but, in some places, they were impossible to wade across. A number of these swamps were both bordered and interspersed by sago palms or mangroves, giving them a dark, dank and claustrophobic character. That also enhanced their obstructive potential. Areas of jungle and scrub ran inland from the coconut groves and were of sufficient height and density to conceal movement, concentration and occupation. Thick, stifling areas of sharp-edged kunai grass were also scattered throughout the beachhead area, usually to a height of about seven to eight feet.

This beachhead region is chiefly the home of the Orokaiva Papuans. A substantial number of the Orokaivas had been indentured labourers who had, at the outbreak of hostilities, been working away from the beachhead area with ANGAU on the Kokoda Trail. Some had remained in their villages under Japanese occupation, while others had remained with their administration employers and had undertaken patrol work. A small number had cooperated with the Japanese and had betrayed a number of missionaries, spotters and shot-down airmen.

Although the three battles for the beachhead were fought at the same time, in the interests of clarity we will join the Australians at the three battles in turn.

During the half-hour flight from Port Moresby across the Owen Stanley Range to Popondetta, vivid recollections of the gruelling but rewarding trek over the Kokoda Trail just three short months earlier come flooding back.

Frank Taylor of Kokoda Treks and Tours is on the trail and cannot take this beachhead tour. But he has taken care of everything. When you arrive at the Popondetta terminal, Adrian is there to greet you. This strong, smiling and affable Orokaiva with the Bob Marley haircut and matching Marley T-shirt has *wantok* contacts across the beachhead. Adrian is from Buna and will live with you at the motel, accompany you each day in the cabin of your four-wheel-drive, and has two Buna relatives staying with *wantoks* in Popondetta each night as extra help. You will, for every moment of your time here, feel totally safe and secure.

This is not the Kokoda Trail and, therefore, you only need your maps, water, camera, first aid kit and lunch. There'll be two days each at Gona, Sananada and finally Buna. And each night there is the comfort of the motel at Popondetta after your drive back. This beachhead visit will enthral you no less than Kokoda and is far more accessible.

The Beachhead

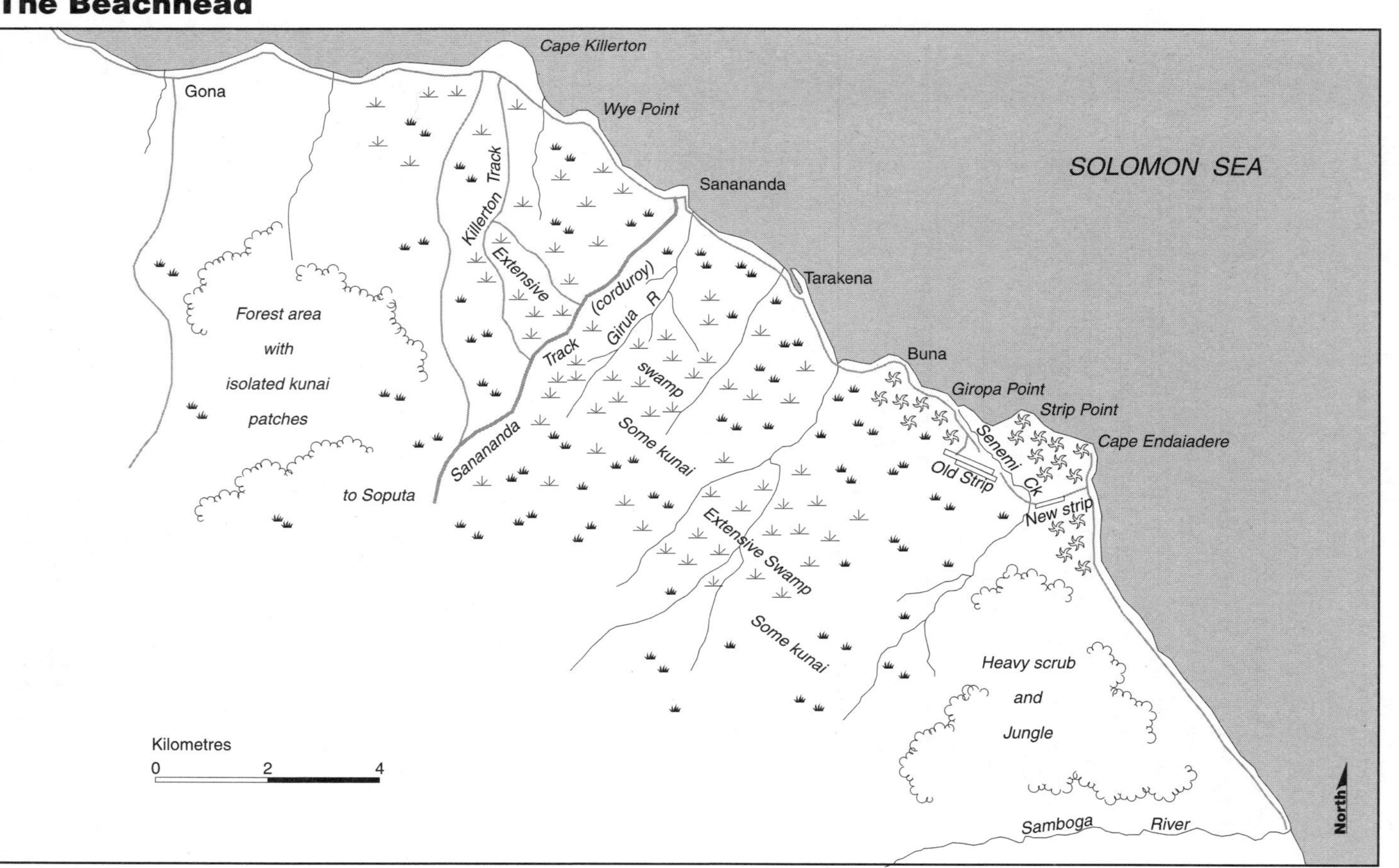

SOLOMON SEA
Cape Killerton
Gona
Wye Point
Sananananda
Tarakena
Buna
Giropa Point
Strip Point
Cape Endaiadere
Killerton Track
Extensive
Sananananda Track (corduroy)
Girua R
swamp
Some kunai
Extensive Swamp
Some kunai
Old Strip
Senemi Ck
New strip
Forest area
with
isolated kunai
patches
to Soputa
Heavy scrub
and
Jungle
Samboga River
Kilometres
0
2
4
North

Prior to the war, Anglicans Father James Benson, Miss Mavis Parkinson and Miss May Hayman lived and worked among the Papuans at Gona. Benson had a large, beautifully woven sago-leaf church and a Mission house with a red tin roof nearby. The two women ran a small Mission school made of 'reedy walls of sago-stalk'[1] and, in addition to their teaching obligations, administered a little hospital serving the natives in the region. There was also a carpenter's shop and a small number of native houses. They were built around a pretty path bordered by crotons and red hibiscus and a number of scattered high trees and palms which had given Gona the reputation of being one of the most picturesque places on the north-eastern coast of Papua.[2]

About the time of the Battle of the Coral Sea in May 1942, Captain Tom Grahamslaw of ANGAU had tried to persuade the female missionaries to return to Australia. Grahamslaw:

> The most telling point I made was that if the enemy landed, lives of ANGAU personnel could be endangered while endeavouring to rescue the womenfolk. Benson said that he had already taken up the matter . . . but the Bishop considered it was their duty to remain. Miss Hayman and Miss Parkinson being dedicated women, elected to remain.[3]

When the Japanese landed near Gona on 21 July 1942 Benson and the women fled, but they were later captured by the enemy. Grahamslaw was able to discover their eventual fate:

> Perhaps the most harrowing evidence was that given by a native from Kakendatta (near Popondetta), concerning . . . Miss Hayman and Miss Parkinson.
>
> This man was lying in the undergrowth near the coffee buildings at Popondetta observing the movements of Japanese troops stationed there. (. . . Orokaiva natives made a practice of doing this without being seen or heard by the Japs), when he saw the two European women

> being led out from one of the coffee buildings. As I recall it, the witness said that the women had been incarcerated in the building for a full day and night. He was unable to describe what happened within the building, but saw a number of Japanese enter and depart.
>
> When the women came out a Japanese stepped forward and seized Miss Parkinson and started to hug her. She pushed him away. He thereupon drew a bayonet or dagger from his scabbard, and stabbed her in the throat. She gave a slight scream and dropped dead.
>
> Another Japanese, who was standing near Miss Hayman, drew a handkerchief from his pocket and handed it to her, indicating at the same time that she was to blindfold herself. She did so and then stood with head upright facing the Jap, and without speaking. The Jap then bayoneted her in the breast and she fell dead. The bodies were buried in a shallow grave at Popondetta. This, to the best of my knowledge, was the only factual eye-witness account of the deaths of those dedicated and courageous young Australian women.
>
> Incidentally, the Kakendatta witness had previously reported the matter to ANGAU and he led Dr. Vernon to the place where the bodies were buried.[4]

The fate of these two Australian missionary nursing sisters is recorded in a memorial register in the Nurses' Memorial at Westminster Abbey in London.

For reasons known only to themselves, the Japanese spared Father Benson's life (although Grahamslaw has stated that Benson's advanced years might have been the reason).[5] He survived the war, worked for some further years postwar at Gona, and having returned to England in 1955 he passed away the following year.

The Japanese Gona defenders consisted mainly of the 41st and 144th Regiments. Some had endured the Kokoda Trail fighting, others were fresh reinforcements, and the remainder were base personnel who had been in the area since the original landings. This Japanese Gona force numbered around 1000–1200 defenders and was commanded by Lieutenant-Colonel Yoshinobu Tomita.

The location of the Japanese defences and their resulting fire-plan were the result of a masterly use of both the ground and its vegetation, as well as the available personnel at Tomita's disposal.

About seventy yards west of Gona Mission lay Gona Creek, which was wide enough both at its mouth and for a distance just past the Mission to prohibit an Australian attack across it. The Japanese therefore had a reasonably secure right flank. A coconut grove that was about a hundred yards in depth ran roughly 750 yards along the coast to a small creek, which the Australians duly named Small Creek. Gona beach is only about seven or eight yards wide before the coconut belt begins.

The Mission was about seventy yards inland from the coast and from it, roughly parallel to Gona Creek, the main track from the village ran south to Jumbora. The ground around Gona Mission was dominated by areas of jungle and swamp. The Battle for Gona Mission would therefore be fought in three basic areas: along the coconut belt from Small Creek to the Mission and its Gona Creek mouth; the area between Gona Creek and the track; and the central or inland area between the track and the coconut belt. Using the natural features between Gona Creek and Small Creek, the Japanese toiled long and hard on a fire-plan that concentrated their defence in three key locations.

Their first positions consisted of numerous machine-gun posts stretching approximately a hundred yards along the eastern bank of Gona Creek to its mouth and then along the coastal coconut belt to Small Creek. Throughout this area, shallow slit trenches had been dug to allow the Japanese to move from one position to another, most critically to also allow the infantry to support the machine-gun posts. A double shallow trench system stretched from due west of the Mission along Gona Creek and the coast to a position slightly north-east of the Mission.

The second position formed a semi-circle around the south-eastern and eastern sides of the Mission. A network of slit trenches and a shallow trench system, often filled with water, linked the numerous machine-gun posts in the area.

The third and final position, at the southern edge of the smaller scrub area between the creek and the main track south, consisted of a line of slit trenches fortified by machine-gun posts and larger strong posts.

Posts in adjacent areas and within all areas were able to assist each other with enfilading fire—arcs of fire which crossed each other. Any Australian soldier approaching such posts was therefore subjected to telling fire ranging across his front. To add to this considerable curtain of firepower, the Japanese deployed snipers high up in coconut fronds who were able to fire both at targets in the coconut belt and at those approaching through the more open ground between that belt and the central jungle and scrub approach. Understandably, those Japanese snipers took a considerable interest in approaching Australian Bren gunners, whose death or wounding could cause a temporary lull in offensive firepower while a new soldier armed himself with the weapon and carried on the fight.

The Japanese also used the natural camouflage of banyan trees as cover—they dug around the protruding roots of those trees to form further posts and small trenches.

Imagine attacking these Japanese positions. Some had multiple machine-guns, infantry rifle support and connecting crawl trenches. Anywhere between twelve and twenty Japanese might have occupied such a position. Each post was camouflaged, well dug and had walls and a roof made of coconut palm logs. The firing slit was quite narrow, perhaps made by the removal of one log from the wall, and the post was impervious to grenade bursts or machine-gun fire. Perhaps a direct hit from air bombing or an artillery shell might have destroyed them outright. But the artillery shells were mostly high-explosive shells which exploded on impact—usually in the thick foliage above and not where they were needed, on the bunker itself. Whatever form these defences took, all of them were difficult to see until it was too late. Many a wounded Australian at Gona failed to see either a bunker or a Japanese soldier.

But excellent defensive fire-plans are one thing, the psychology of the defender himself is another. Under most circumstances, when a position becomes untenable and only futile death or maiming can result, the enemy will surrender. Not the Japanese. Those soldiers' posts variously became latrines, rice larders and morgues. The enemy at Gona was a totally uncompromising soldier who saw his death as the logical result of his obligation to stay and fight to the end if ordered.

If the Japanese were a formidable enemy then the ravages of tropical disease were no less so. For every battle casualty during the Papuan campaign there were 4.8 tropical disease casualties, and the ratio of battle casualties to those of malaria was 1 to 3.6—in fact, the Medical Official Historian has claimed that these figures are conservative.[6] And the beachhead fighting would produce even more staggering statistics as malaria, scrub typhus, tropical ulcers, dysentery and dengue fever took their toll on the Australian forces.

Immediately prior to crossing the Kumusi, Vasey's force had lost 53 officers and 900 other ranks as battle casualties in addition to crippling sickness casualties. As the 25th Brigade and the 3rd Battalion approached Gona, the soldiers of Chaforce were added to their ranks. That unit had been formed in October 1942 from members of the 21st Brigade—each battalion supplied one composite company. The original aim of Chaforce was to harass the Japanese line of communication over the Kokoda Trail. However, the rapid Japanese withdrawal prevented its deployment. One company of Chaforce was now allotted to each of Eather's battalions to bolster their strength. Even with the addition of Chaforce soldiers to its ranks, the 25th Brigade was at only comparable strength to the Japanese Gona defenders.

During the afternoon of 18 November, the 2/33rd Battalion, 25th Brigade had reached Jumbora. A reconnaissance patrol composed of Captain Clowes (the brother of Major-General Cyril Clowes) and 60 men pushed on towards Gona to establish the position and strength of the Japanese Gona defences.

The initial plan was that the 2/31st Battalion would then pass by the rest of the 2/33rd and press on to Clowes at Gona. Brigadier Eather and his HQ were about two miles to the rear with the 2/25th in reserve.

When the 2/31st arrived on the southern track approach to Gona, Clowes was under heavy fire in a kunai patch. Lieutenant-Colonel Miller pushed Captain Thorn's company

Gona Mission, 1942

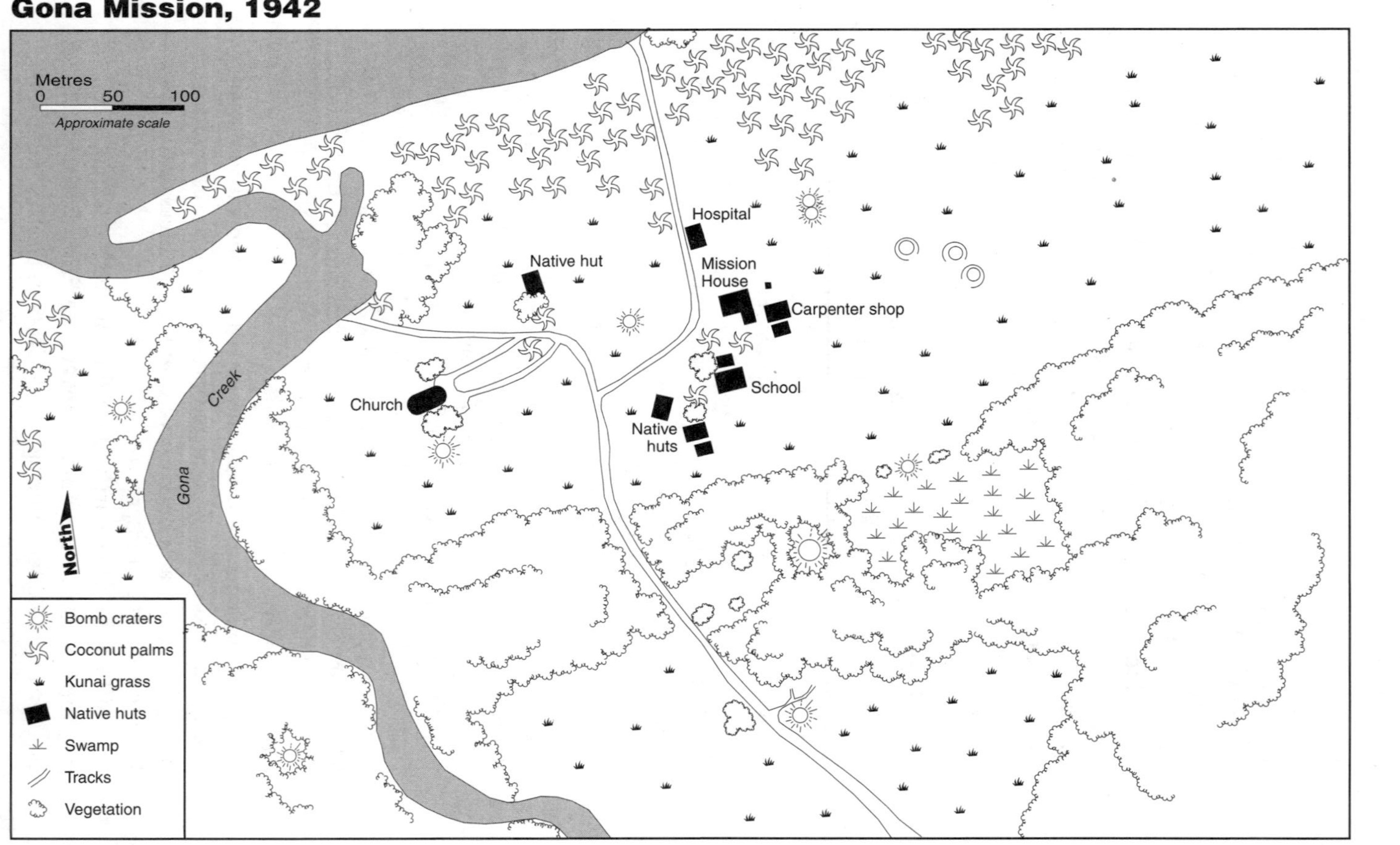

Metres
0
50
100
Approximate scale
Hospital
Native hut
Mission House
Carpenter shop
Church
School
Native huts
Gona Creek
North
Bomb craters
Coconut palms
Kunai grass
Native huts
Swamp
Tracks
Vegetation

Gona—the Japanese defences

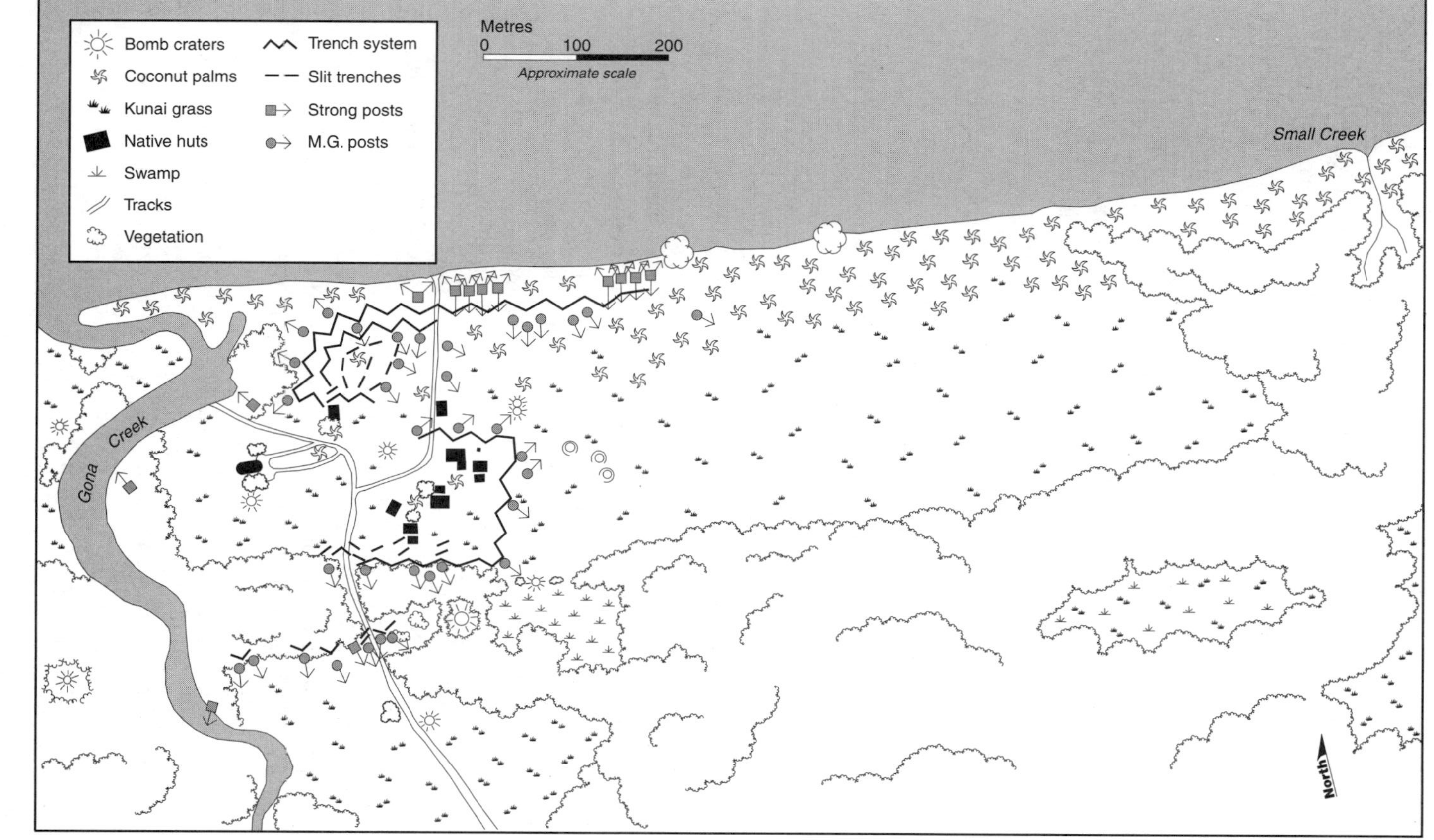

through and, when it ran into a daunting fusillade, his other companies fanned out on either side of the track. Captain Cameron's Chaforce company then led the advance on the right until it emerged from the scrub on the southern outskirts of the Mission. Warrant-Officer 1 Jack Glavins was with them:

> We attacked along the right of the track . . . our forward section, from Lt Pearce's platoon, broke through to within a few yards of the Mission Hut, but was stopped by very heavy fire . . . the Chaforce Coy, then taken over by Capt Thurgood, held their positions and dug in where they were, a matter of yards from the enemy positions . . .[7]

Cameron was wounded, Thorn was dead and two of Miller's other company commanders were down with raging fever; 32 more of his men had been killed or wounded and most of the rest were wasting from malaria; food was low and his ammunition insufficient for another fight.

Before midnight Eather ordered Lieutenant-Colonel Miller and his 2/31st to break contact and fall back behind the 2/25th some two miles to the rear. The recurring problem of supply had inhibited further offensive action. This train of events further supports Major-General Allen's handling of his command on the Kokoda Trail only weeks before. Had Allen pressed his troops any harder without adequate supplies it can be imagined what condition these soldiers might have been in, since they were wasted and diseased as it was.

The 2/33rd set to work to prepare a dropping ground for the biscuit bombers. Heavy rain prevented a supply drop until late on 20 November when food was received. The next day saw the arrival of significant supplies of ammunition, rations, medicine and tobacco. But the cost of this familiar supply problem was valuable time. A company of the 2/33rd was left to guard the supply dump while the remainder of the 25th Brigade pushed on.

On 22 November Brigadier Eather attacked from the south with the 2/33rd Battalion while directing his main thrust from the east, again using his 2/31st Battalion and the Chaforce company now commanded by Captain Thurgood. Jack Glavins participated in this attack:

> 2/14th Chaforce was to move about 50 yards in rear of the left forward Coy led by Capt Clowes. This Coy was stopped in its tracks by heavy machine-gun fire of all calibres coming from heavily reinforced firing positions. The Chaforce Coy however pushed through into the enemy trenches and some were seen pushing grenades down the firing slits into the Jap trenches. However the enemy had done his ground work and all the kunai grass had been cut giving 180^0 field of fire and with his back to the sea, he was impregnable. Through heavy casualties 2/31 had to be withdrawn as it was now too weak to capture the position.[8]

They were enveloped and enfiladed by such intense fire that they were forced to withdraw to the cover of the narrow scrub corridor to the south, backed by the confining swamp. The 2/31st had lost another fourteen killed and 43 wounded. Thurgood's Chaforce company, on top of the four dead or dying and seven others wounded from its first action, had lost another nine killed and fourteen wounded. In the absence of adequate reconnaissance or support, the confused slaughter at Gona was well under way.

For his attack on 23 November, Eather decided to move his 2/25th Battalion north past the 2/31st to attack to the west with the 2/31st providing supporting fire. The plan failed because of the same disadvantages that the brave 2/31st had had to contend with the previous day. As a result the 2/25th lost twelve killed and two officers and 50 other ranks wounded.

By nightfall on 23 November 1942 at Gona, Brigadier Eather was faced with a number of critical problems. The first was the rapidly diminishing size of his force. In the period 19–23 November, his already greatly debilitated troops had suffered losses of seventeen officers and 187 ranks in battle. This was distressing enough, but his losses due to sickness further exacerbated the problem. The 25th Brigade had arrived at Gona in a very poor physical condition, as the Kokoda Trail campaign had severely impacted upon them. In addition to the poor condition of his force upon arrival, his soldiers now began to suffer from a rampant outbreak of malaria and other tropical ailments. By the morning of the 24th Eather was informed that his total brigade strength was now 35 officers and 701 other ranks. These casualties and sickness losses now meant that his force was a little under battalion strength.

This unhappy state of affairs might have been more palatable had satisfactory progress been made. It had not. Vasey to Herring, 23 November 1942: 'The Jap is being more stubborn and tiresome than I thought and I fear a war of attrition is taking place on this front. The Jap won't go till he is killed and in the process he is inflicting many casualties on us. I am beginning to wonder who will reach zero first.'[9]

Late on 23 November Brigadier Eather made fresh plans. He decided upon mortar support and limited fighting patrols in cooperation with an air bombing and strafing of the Japanese dispositions for a six-hour period starting at 8.00 a.m. on the following day. Sixteen sorties were flown by the fighters, followed by the heavy bombers. On paper in some far removed headquarters, divorced from the battle raging in that unique environment, such 'support' might have seemed substantial but it was not. Against a well dug-in enemy, precise knowledge of his positions is critical and accuracy in bombing execution is also crucial. Neither was the case at Gona, and the support provided that day was not followed up by an infantry attack.

During the mid-afternoon of the 25th Eather unleashed what could have been his fourth major Gona attack. The 3rd Militia Battalion had arrived in the Gona area two days earlier. During this attack the 3rd Battalion was given the key role of attacking the enemy from the south-west supported by machine-gun and mortar fire from the 2/33rd and 2/25th Battalions and by 25-pounder artillery fire recently deployed at Soputa. The 3rd Battalion attacked at 4.00 p.m., came against strong defences and withdrew at 5.40 p.m.

By 26 November 1942, it was painfully clear that the Allied operations at the beachhead had become bogged down, and they were taking heavy casualties. At Sananada, the brave but exhausted 16th Brigade had come up against strong Japanese positions on the Sananada Track. At Buna, the Americans, who had previously disparaged the Australians' efforts at Milne Bay and along the Kokoda Trail, were subjected to a bewildering reality check with respect to jungle warfare and the ability of their Japanese enemy to deny them ground. At Gona, Brigadier Eather's debilitated soldiers were simply being asked to capture their objective with too few soldiers and support. Including his diminished 3rd Battalion, Eather could now muster little more than a thousand soldiers.

On 23 November Vasey had requested that General Herring send him his 21st Brigade forthwith. It was the 21st Brigade that had fought under Brigadier Arnold Potts on the Kokoda Trail.

If the mood at the beachhead was grim, it was even more so in Port Moresby.

On 20 November MacArthur had ordered forces to attack at the beachhead and that 'all columns will be driven through regardless of losses'.[10] On the following day, the 21st, General Harding at Buna was told: 'Take Buna today at all costs. MacArthur.'[11]

After visiting the American front on 25 November, General Herring had returned disturbed by their lack of offensive spirit and morale. But a letter from Vasey to Blamey added real fuel to the Australian fire: 'The situation on the front of 126 U.S. Regt remains inactive and unsatisfactory. I saw Tomlinson this afternoon and he said he was "embarrassed" by the present situation. I said I was too.'[12] The letter also stated that the American infantry had 'maintained a masterly inactivity'[13] at Buna. The tables had been turned and the Australians made the most of it. General Berryman told General Eichelberger that: 'The jokes of the American officers in Australia, making fun of the Australian Army were told all over Australia . . . Therefore . . . when we've got the least thing on the American troops fighting in the Buna sector, our high command has gone to General MacArthur and rubbed salt into his wounds.'[14]

A chance came at this conference. When MacArthur offered Blamey the 41st American Division as a beachhead reinforcement Blamey declined, saying that he preferred the understrength 21st Brigade 'as he knew they would fight'.[15] It should be pointed out that while Blamey was busily engaged in having a cheap shot at MacArthur, he was actually contradicting himself. He had sacked Potts in late October and had in fact called the 21st Brigade 'running rabbits' at the

Koitaki parade on 9 November. In sixteen short days assessments of troops can radically change, especially when self-serving generals are making them.

The 21st Brigade was now about to be plunged into the military mincing machine that was Gona.

A VULGAR PUBLIC BRAWL

21

After Brigadier Arnold Potts had been removed from his command of the 21st Brigade, Brigadier Ivan Dougherty was flown in from Darwin to replace him. Dougherty brought with him a most distinguished record from the Middle East. He had journeyed to war with the 6th Division and had seen testing action in Cyrenaica, Greece and Crete. He had commanded the 2/4th Battalion and, on his return to Australia in early 1942, had been given command of the 23rd Brigade in the Northern Territory. Lieutenant-Colonel Ken Murdoch, then staff captain, 21st Brigade:

> His tremendous personnel attitude; aptitude towards the officers and men of the brigade and his perspicacity, his patience and his fairness in overcoming the difficulties and the feelings of the officers and men, welded the brigade once again into a fighting machine.[1]

Captain Frank Sublet, 2/16th Battalion:

> He commanded 21st Bde from Gona to war's end. When I commanded the 2/16th Bn, I found him very supportive while also being very decisive. His responses were calm and measured and he was always ready to explain his decisions. Though quiet and unobtrusive, he seemed to have the capacity to absorb 'atmosphere' and spot strengths and weaknesses.[2]

When Dougherty assumed command of the 21st Brigade he was immediately conscious of the situation confronting him:

> . . . I realised that I'd supplanted someone who was a hero amongst the troops, and rightly so, in Arnold Potts. I knew how they liked him. My job was to overcome anything that was there. They were intensely loyal to Potts. I knew I wasn't going to be welcome. There was some later point, I don't know when, I think it might have been on the Sananda Road, that the Brigade seemed to swing in behind me, and for the next three years I could never have wished to have better support from that Brigade.[3]

If Dougherty was therefore placed in an unenviable position—which he handled with great diplomacy and tact—Potts' removal and the Blamey diatribe at Koitaki caused a far greater obstacle at Gona that was not overcome.

> When Potts was taken off from command of the Brigade and Allen the division; leave Rowell out of this, it's a separate issue, there were other factors in it; now the only story I heard was a story Herring told me. There was criticism within New Guinea Force and Supreme Allied Headquarters, concerning the leadership of 21st Brigade. Much of this criticism arose from that particular withdrawal from Efogi. [Dougherty was referring to the battle at Brigade Hill, near Efogi.] And I know at the time I was summing things up.[4]

This story has chronicled the performance of Potts and his battalion commanders and the soldiers of the 21st Brigade on the Kokoda Trail. We have further witnessed Rowell and Allen's support—if belated—for Potts and his brigade after their relief, and the fact that neither saw any reason for the removal of the former, and certainly not any basis for criticism of the latter. The source of this poisoning of Dougherty's perception of his commanders was therefore Blamey in the first instance, and Herring in the second. Blamey had been in Brisbane while the critical battle for Port Moresby had been in progress, and Herring and Dougherty had been in Darwin. While it should be recognised that Dougherty would have been negligent in his command if he had not been 'summing things up', it is clear that the Blamey slur at Koitaki on 9 November 1942 had impacted upon the relationship between the new brigadier and his three battalion commanders before Gona was ever reached by the 21st Brigade.

And the whole sad, sorry and tragic episode did not end with Dougherty and his battalion commanders. Captain Harry Katekar, Adjutant 2/27th Battalion:

> And they [the junior officers] were absolutely ropable! Incensed! In fact I claim to this day that some of the officers whom we lost at Gona did so because of the effect of Blamey's unfair criticism. He was sheltering, trying to in effect pass the buck to our officers instead of accepting it himself.[5]

Captain Frank Sublet, 2/16th Battalion, recalled a slightly different Koitaki influence:

> Well I'd tackle it this way. Many of the young officers who were killed at Gona weren't on the Owen Stanley track anyway. But those officers who were at Koitaki and heard Blamey's speech were very, very incensed and they were really carrying on about it. Almost mutinous in their feelings! What I did see at Gona was that a number of the young officers and sergeants who had not taken part on the Kokoda Trail were determined to show their mettle at Gona, because they knew what the battalion had gone through on the Kokoda Trail and they'd been left out of battle; they were determined to redeem the battalion; put the battalion back on its mantle.[6]

And Sublet's observations were not limited to his own battalion:

> I can quote one! Stan Bisset [2/14th Battalion] used to jump up and down with rage every time he talked about it. Stan was absolutely ropable because his own brother had been killed up there. And a great bloke, Stan! A strong man, strong in will; strong in resolve; strong in every way.

> Actually the whole brigade was in the mood to show the Commander-in-Chief. And of course the opportunity arose at Gona.[7]

The 21st Brigade had paid a heavy price on the Kokoda Trail. When the 2/14th Battalion, now under the command of Lieutenant-Colonel Hugh Challen (Potts' former brigade major), emplaned for Gona, it numbered nineteen officers and 322 other ranks; the 2/27th, still commanded by Lieutenant-Colonel Geoff Cooper, numbered 22 and 301; and the 2/16th (Lieutenant-Colonel Albert Caro) numbered 22 and 256. Therefore, the losses on the trail and the supply of officers and other ranks for the establishment of Chaforce meant that the 21st Brigade numbered little more than one full battalion upon arrival at Popondetta.

While the three battalions were emplaning, Brigadier Ivan Dougherty had flown over early to confer with Major-General Vasey:

> On the morning of 25th Nov. I moved to Popondetta by plane, and thence by jeep to Div. HQ at Soputa where I met General Vasey there late in the morning . . .
>
> He told me what the situation was at the time. 25th Aust. Inf. Bde, depleted and suffering from malaria and fatigue was in contact with Jap. Forces holding Gona Mission area . . .
>
> 16th Aust. Inf. Bde, with some Americans of 126th Regt. U.S. 32nd Div, were astride the Sananda Road about 3.5 miles north of Soputa. 16th Aust. Inf. Bde, also depleted in strength and suffering from malaria and fatigue, was unable to make further progress. Two companies of the Americans were then attempting to do an encircling move, but their whereabouts in the jungle were not known, beyond the fact that someone had an idea they were out on the left flank and getting in behind the Japs . . .
>
> On the Buna side 32 U.S. Div less attachments on Sananda Road were unable to make progress. General Vasey told me that he was considering using

> 21st Aust. Inf. Bde to capture Sananand by means of a wide encircling move—moving first via Jumbora to rear of 25th Aust. Inf. Bde, thence diagonally towards the coast about Basabua or Garara, and thence to Sananada . . .
>
> As an alternative means of using us, the General was considering our capturing Gona Mission Area, supported by 25th Aust. Inf. Bde.
>
> As it would be some time before my Brigade had finished its move, he suggested that I remain at his HQ until the following morning, and then that I move to Gona to meet Brigadier Eather. He wished me to discuss the two alternatives with Brigadier Eather, and then advise him of what I thought best, when he would give me his decision.[8]

After arriving at Eather's HQ on the afternoon of 26 November, Dougherty further contemplated the tactical situation:

> . . . Gona was held up and 25th Brigade was exhausted. Vasey at one stage thought of going across to get Sananada. I felt 'Well if we do that, we're likely to start a fourth situation if we run into enemy positions which are too strong for us to knock over.' . . . So I did say to him that I thought it was a better thing to finalise one of them straight away.[9]

All this was sound, considered command by a competent divisional commander and his brigadiers, who were very well aware of the problems they were facing: the lack of concentration of force and the poor physical condition of their troops. The same cannot be said of either the high command or certain officers from the brigade level down.

The 21st Brigade's first fight at Gona had been tentatively planned by Vasey for 29 November. Dougherty, however, rightly concluded that as his battalions would not arrive until late on the 28th they would be tired from their march from Popondetta. Therefore, the attack should be delayed until the 30th. Dougherty:

> I told General Vasey that I thought the attack should be postponed till 30th, and he agreed with me. He left me intending to discuss the matter with higher authority and make strong representations for the postponement. He was to ring me when a decision had been made. At 0700 hrs on the 28th of November he rang me to tell me that in view of certain information that higher command possessed, the attack on Gona must take place on the 29th. I had an idea that this information had something to do with the Japanese attempts to reinforce their Gona–Buna troops.[10]

This order to attack came from MacArthur to Blamey, then to Herring and on to Vasey. And it was nothing more than an elaborate smokescreen. There are a number of points worthy of mention. The first is the strategic situation at this time.

The battle for Guadalcanal was, in late November 1942, still delicately poised. The Japanese were still pouring resources into the battle, while the American marines, still holding Henderson Field, were able to fight on. The Japanese could not hope to substantially reinforce their Papuan beachhead until Guadalcanal had been won.

Second, the Allied air forces held air superiority in this beachhead area. Although the enemy had managed to reinforce his Gona–Buna front earlier, he was now under constant harassment in his later efforts to do so. On 27 November four Japanese destroyers left Rabaul and were turned back on the same day with two of their number damaged. A convoy which left the following day was also engaged on or around the 30th, and only managed to land about five hundred troops. A third attempt was to be undertaken on 7 December.

But the critical point is surely that reinforcement of an enemy force is always a possibility in war—all the more reason to conduct the operation along established and prudent lines. And prominent Gona veterans knew it. Lieutenant-Colonel Ralph Honner would soon arrive at Gona:

> I didn't need to be told about this [Japanese reinforcement], there is always such a possibility . . . that there

> might be some pressure to get a quick solution before the enemy reinforcements could arrive. But none of this could justify unmilitary procedure of attacking without proper preparation.[11]

Captain Harry Katekar, adjutant, 2/27th Battalion, witnessed the 'preparation':

> All those involved at command and staff level in a normal properly conducted operation, first of all have an appreciation of the situation; from the enemy's point of view and our own troops' point of view. That wasn't done at Gona. We were thrown in with scant information about the enemy; no aerial photographs, nothing to go on. I don't recall ever seeing a proper plan of the area showing where 25th Brigade was at that time when we were supposed to go in, or in fact, what the 2/14th were doing . . . The whole of the thing was rushed and therefore one can expect there to be what actually transpired—a slaughter of good men! The correct way to get the information was to send in recce patrols. That's always the way you do it, because you get the enemy to disclose where he is. You don't go in with a full company rushing in against something you know nothing about.[12]

And Ralph Honner adds yet another damning indictment on those at the rear:

> And after the campaign was over of course, we were shown the aerial photographs which had been taken months before, and presumably put up on someone's wall as decorations when they would have been of invaluable assistance to us.[13]

Honner and Katekar's views are not brilliant or original examples of military genius, but simply reflect standard military procedure. The truth is that an attack on the 30th would still have been a foolhardy rush. There is an old saying amongst soldiers: time spent on reconnaissance is never wasted. At Gona the maxim would be tragically illustrated.

When Dougherty learnt that he must attack on the 29th, the only 21st Brigade Battalion to have arrived was the 2/14th. He now ordered Challen, who had left his Chaforce to command the 2/14th, to deploy the battalion at a 'lying up point' four hundred yards south-east of Small Creek, and then secure a start line just west of Small Creek for the attack next day. Dougherty was attempting to secure the area at that creek and the ground to the west. In addition, he wanted a start line established from which the 2/27th could move west to Gona Mission the next day.

However, instead of using the scrub cover along his approach to Small Creek, Challen journeyed through the kunai grass. When an earlier 25th Brigade patrol reported that the area around Small Creek was free of the enemy, Dougherty told Challen to go straight to the creek and secure the ground. But some small number of Japanese had almost certainly been lying 'doggo' when the 25th Brigade patrol had moved near the area, and therefore would have spotted Challen's approach in force. In the interim, they would have had ample time to deploy troops in their pre-prepared positions.

Challen's final movement was a trying one. His troops had to make their way through jungle for about three hundred yards and then wade in single file across a waist-deep sago swamp which was almost two hundred yards wide. By the time the advanced elements of B Company, under the command of Captain McGavin, had crossed that obstacle it was approaching dusk. When McGavin's forward scouts spotted a small group of the enemy on the beach the Australians attacked. Captain Stan Bisset:

> I was acting as adjutant to Challen, and it was on the late afternoon and night that the disastrous attack was made by our troops on orders from Brigade. No proper recce of the Jap positions had been made and at Dusk moving at times through waist deep swamp, the attack was made through light scrub and tree cover into the well sited enemy positions, no-one knowing their exact whereabouts. Our troops were caught in enfilade fire from several bunkers and in the dark it was impossible to locate them. We lost six of our best officers and forty

> other ranks in this abortive and ill-conceived attack. It became necessary to withdraw and try to extricate our wounded.[14]

Valiant attempts by the 2/14th to identify and then outflank the Japanese positions were both costly and fruitless. The ground in front of the enemy positions was littered with the dead and the wounded and any attempt to recover the casualties was met with concentrated fire. A striking feature of this action was the high casualty count amongst the junior officers and NCOs. Bisset, supported by Lieutenant Clarke and Private Boys, a signaller, guided the wounded to a signal cable which provided a lifeline back through the swamp and scrub. Corporal Ted Sheldon, 2/14th Battalion:

> . . . walking wounded started to trickle back; we were sent to help carry in others, four of us carried big Bill O'Brien, all 15+ stone of him, on a ground sheet, his upper leg was mangled, the track was narrow and it was very dark . . . The Bn withdrew. We retained our position on the track for the night—a night made eerie by occasional shots, and weird calls from the Jap stronghold. The efficiency and coolness of officers and other ranks, whether wounded or not, was an encouragement . . .[15]

Against a resolute, well-concealed foe who has a magnificent fire-plan, any attacking force that confronts it with no prior intelligence, with no opportunity for reconnaissance and with no support must fail. The 2/14th lost a tenth of its already diminished force at Small Creek, including the tragic slaughter of 32 per cent of its officers.

Dougherty issued fresh plans for 29 November. He ordered the 2/14th to attack the same ground again east of Small Creek to secure that area. The incoming 2/27th was ordered to attack west of Small Creek and capture Gona Mission. All available mortar fire was assigned to the 2/14th while the South Australians were to be supported by an air strike. After the 2/27th had advanced, an artillery forward observation officer, Major Hanson, was to meet Lieutenant-Colonel Cooper and then direct that fire support. A guide was assigned to take Hanson to Lieutenant-Colonel Cooper.The 2/27th was to be in position on its start line at 11.00 a.m. Lieutenant-Colonel Cooper:

> The unit commanders were given no say; they weren't even consulted . . . very unusual; you can't have a battle without having a command group of commanders of units . . . to discuss what they can and cannot do and how long they'll need to make a reconnaissance. Oh yes, that was pretty unusual, but everybody seemed to be panicking to rush this operation.[16]

The air support was impressive on paper:

> 0930–0950—12 fighters each dropping a 300lb bomb.
> 0930–1015—3 A20s drop parachute bombs and give machine-gun fire.
> 1000–1100—6 B17s each eight 500lb bombs.
> 1055–1110—33 A20s bomb and machine-gun fire.[17]

The Official Historian would later claim that the 'perfectly executed air strike' was not followed in by the 2/27th Battalion on time and that the artillery officer, Major Hanson, missed Cooper because of his guide's inability to find him.

The truth is that the attack should have occurred one to two days later when Cooper's reconnaissance patrols might have identified the enemy positions. Second, Major Hanson should have been brought forward hours before the attack, and not upon its commencement. Third, we have noted the splendid ground support provided by 75 and 76 Squadrons RAAF at Milne Bay when smoke flares were fired forward of advancing Australian troops, thereby pinpointing that support. There was no communication between the ground and its air support at Gona—further evidence of the haste in both the planning and execution of the attacks. Captain Harry Katekar, Adjutant, 2/27th Battalion: 'You see the whole thing was, at that stage, no one had exactly pin-pointed the area. If it had been defined as the coconut area, they might have done some good . . . in the event, I think you can say that that kind of support was ineffective.'[18]

Cooper had reorganised his understrength battalion into three rifle companies, A and D consisting of five officers and 77 other ranks each, and C Company with four officers and 77 other ranks. For the attack on 29 November, Captain Charlie Sims and his A Company were to attack through the coconut belt, while Captain Joe Cuming and his C Company were to attack along the beach on Sims' right flank.

At 11.00 a.m. on 29 November the forward elements of the 2/27th arrived at the beach. However, the battalion could not reach its start line, well to the west, before the end of the bombing due to the boggy ground and the fact that the unit was being guided in.

Not long after midday both Sims' A Company, still moving through the coconut belt, and Cuming's C Company, which had swung around from the totally exposed beach on the right to press its attack through the only partial cover of the kunai fringe on the left, were pinned down by withering machine-gun fire from both the beach and from the Mission area. There was also sniper fire from the coconut belt. Lieutenant Bob Johns, 9 Platoon, A Company, was in the van:

> My platoon was to lead the company attack; Peter Sherwin's Platoon was to be on my left flank to the rear; Joe Flight's platoon was to be on my right slightly to the rear. So we went in arrow head formation of platoons . . . I was not far from the beach . . . I was moving as the point platoon . . . with a section ahead, platoon HQ at their rear and the other two sections on my left and right so, in effect, we were in arrow head formation, and . . . the sections as they went were also in arrow head formation.
>
> . . . we were hit with a withering fusillade of fire right across our front from positions, basically, we couldn't see . . . and this first fusillade of fire, of course, took a lot of casualties . . . at that point in time the other two platoons went to ground also . . . we got a message from Charlie Sims at Company HQ . . . to report back . . . We got back to Charlie and he changed the plan. I was furthest forward; I was to give support fire while we then mounted a leap-frog attack, and the other two platoons came past me on my left and right as my forward sections

> gave support fire. Joe Flight and I ran together and when we were almost back to Joe's platoon on the right he went down thomp! And I rolled him over and he'd taken one through the heart
>
> . . . I got the news to his sergeant and told him what was expected of him, and went on to my platoon . . .
>
> My point section Bren-gunners and most of the section had been wounded . . . I sent blokes from the left section to take over the gun and continued with the support fire . . . I think I saw Peter (Lt Sherwin, left flank platoon) and one or two blokes on the left go down . . . the second lot of machine-gunners were wounded and came crawling back and I thought I'd better keep that Bren in action, so I started crawling forward to that Bren, and I got hit myself. The same burst hit my batman . . .[19]

Lieutenant Peter Sherwin, 8 Platoon:

> We had not a single idea where they were located; what sort of defences they had there . . . the coconuts were to the right of us. We suddenly came under fire and hit the ground. My main objective was to try and locate some source of all this lead flying around.[20]

Shortly after, Sherwin was shot in the knee by sniper fire, which would eventually cost him a leg. At this stage, heavy small arms fire to the rear indicated that the 2/14th was also in action.

With the assistance of additional artillery support, C Company was slowly able to gain about fifty yards of critical ground near to where a number of the Japanese posts were sited. Its commander, Captain Joe Cuming, then sought permission to attack to the north, across A Company's coconut belt front, in an effort to clear a corridor for the battalion to establish a firm base into enemy territory. Corporal Ray Baldwin, 13 Platoon, C Company:

> The ground was fairly flat; it was covered on our left flank with kunai grass . . . it was a typical native village scene, flat beach-head, palm trees and so on . . . we came in

The 2/27th at Gona, 29 November 1942

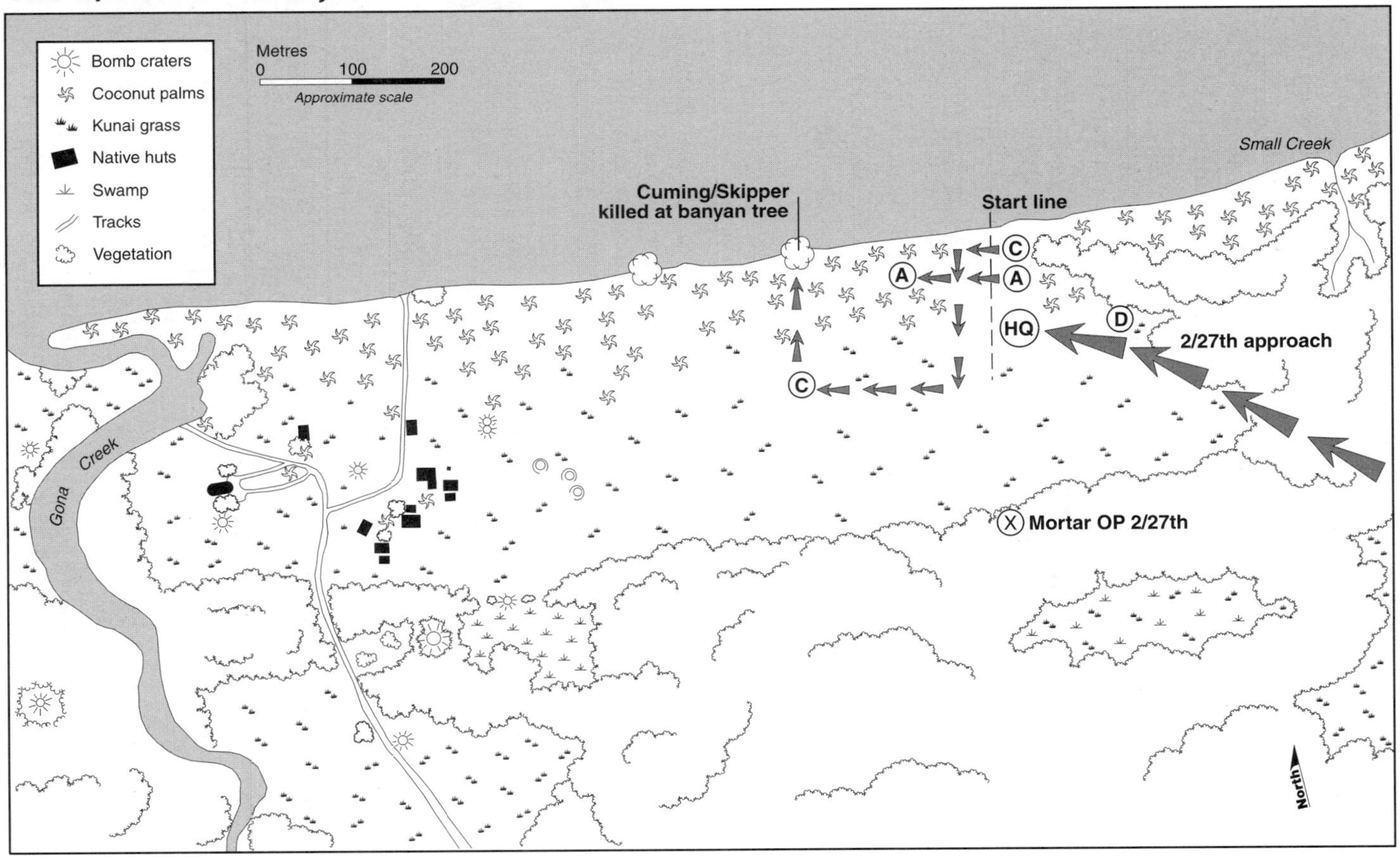

> under cross fire from positions in front of A Company and from our western flank . . .
>
> The fire was very intense; it was very, very concentrated, and all those innocent looking palm trees that were fallen down were in fact not fallen down—they were deliberate fire traps. In short, the Japanese had enfiladed all those fallen palm trees, so that if you took cover behind what you thought was cover, in fact it was a fire trap, and that is where so many of C Company died.
>
> I saw Justin Skipper, he was on the left flank of this position we were attacking, and he was calling out 'Come on 13 Platoon, come on C Company!' . . . Joe Cuming, when I went in with my rifle, he was actually poised over a position, this fortified position, bayoneting Japanese. I saw that, and I remember it very clearly. After that, I don't know, I was knocked off with a blast from two hand grenades, and everyone about me seemed to be hurt or dead . . .[21]

The 2/27th Battalion's A Company attack in the coconut belt at Gona on 29 November 1942 was brave and persistent; its C Company's attempt to break the resulting impasse was audacious in the extreme; but, in the event, both were doomed to costly failure because of the unprofessional and impetuous desire of high command for a quick victory at any cost. As a consequence, the lives of well-trained and well-led infantry were, in the end, squandered for no gain.

C Company lost Cuming and Skipper. Their bodies were found days later, lying tragically in front of posts they very nearly captured but were destined never to seize, let alone hold. The two Australians were found ringed by dead Japanese. Lieutenants Bennie and Caddy were wounded, Bennie mortally, and in A Company all three platoon commanders were hit—Sherwin and Johns wounded and Flight killed. The final cost was seven officers killed or wounded and fifteen other ranks killed and a further 33 wounded.

If the carnage at the front was severe, then the rescuing of the wounded was fraught with little less danger. Private Paul Robertson, a former league ruckman with the Sturt Football Club in Adelaide, who had repeatedly carried the wounded on his back up steep gradients which stretchers could not negotiate on the Kokoda Trail, surrendered his life at Gona while attempting to rescue Corporal Henderson, who later died of his wounds. The Japanese were always alert to the potential of sniping at stretcher-bearers—or selfless soldiers such as Robertson.

While the 2/27th had been thus occupied, the 2/14th Battalion had been assaulting the Japanese to the east of Small Creek. Supported by brigade mortar fire, the 2/14th moved round wide to the east and cut through to the beach. A standing patrol was deployed there to secure the Australians' extreme right flank. The remainder of the 2/14th pushed on towards Small Creek. But once again, just as that objective was in sight, the battalion came under stiff resistance from concealed posts. Corporal Ted Sheldon was at the forefront of the movement:

> . . . my platoon was on the left flank of the attack, close to a kunai patch. We got to within 15 yards of the nearest Jap position and held a line there till withdrawn later in the day. Jack and I, crouched behind coconut trees, were the only ones not killed or wounded in our area . . .
>
> The one big handicap on our flank was that the Jap positions were so strongly fortified and camouflaged that it was difficult to locate them.[22]

Lieutenant-Colonel Challen now brought his brigade mortar fire to bear on the Japanese positions and pushed Captain Treacy's A Company through B Company. But that mortar fire was not specifically aimed at identified targets, and the outcome was almost predictable—more fine soldiers put to the slaughter. Treacy was killed within 25 yards of an enemy bunker; Privates Valli and Thompson managed to destroy two posts before being killed by snipers; and Lieutenant Kolb was slain leading a bayonet charge. That brave but blind attack also claimed the lives of a further two NCOs and seven privates, with a further one officer and sixteen other ranks being wounded.

The day of 29 November 1942 was a dark one. A number of the heroes of Isurava, Brigade Hill and Mission Ridge had been senselessly sacrificed at Gona.

The news was no better elsewhere. On that same fateful day the 2/33rd Battalion and the 3rd Battalion had attacked Gona from both sides of the main track leading into the village, only to be stopped by strong posts which brought a withering fire upon them.

On the 29th Lieutenant-Colonel Albert Caro's 2/16th Battalion completed the 21st Brigade deployment at Gona. Dougherty gave it three roles: one company was placed under Cooper's command for further operations in the coconut belt; another was to provide Brigade HQ protection; and the third was stationed to reinforce the 2/27th Battalion's rear on the western side of Small Creek.

For his dawn attack on 30 November, Lieutenant-Colonel Cooper decided to employ his ten minutes of available artillery support on the Japanese beach posts and his three-inch mortar barrage upon the Mission defences. His infantry plan centred on the use of his fresh D Company for an attack on the beach posts with his now diminished A and C Companies ready to exploit any gains.

At 6.15 a.m. Lieutenant Inglis' 16 Platoon mounted its attack on the left through the scrub and then across a low kunai patch. Lieutenant MacDonald's 17 Platoon moved to Inglis' right through the coconut belt. Sergeant Roy Thredgold, D Company:

> We got within about a half a mile of Gona. And the crack, crack, cracks are coming out of the coconut palms. So we'd spread. We could see the beach away at about a hundred yards. If you didn't keep your head down a sniper would just pick you off. Now after we'd got to the edge of the kunai grass, we've got no alternative but to cross this stubble paddock . . . and the snipers are banging like hell, and the pillboxes are banging shit out of us; bullets going round our heads. We made about fifty yards, and jokers were going down like bloody rabbits, getting killed! So we ended up going back to where we bloody well started.[23]

The Japanese snipers had two priority Australian targets: Bren gunners and officers. Perched high in the coconut palms, snipers could readily identify the Bren-gunners, and any telltale command or gesture also brought their fire. And the soldiers approaching them through the scrub and particularly the nearer low and then burnt-off kunai grass were sitting ducks. Private Bert Ward was an 18 Platoon Bren gunner:

> It was simply a matter of going over this cleared kunai . . . partially cut down, three to four feet. But then when you got over that you got the burnt kunai where it was cleared; where there was absolutely no cover.
>
> Well, we got going and there was a terrific amount of fire, it was just like being attacked by a hive of bees—you weren't conscious of intervals; it was a constant stream of bullets going through. And it must have been Roy [Thredgold] who yelled out, 'Go to ground!' At that stage you're out of the fire of the machine-guns . . . but then the snipers took over. We'd got to the very edge of the kunai and the burnt kunai.[24]

In all this, the Bren gunners could not easily identify targets, but the Japanese snipers could. Ward was shot in the head and evacuated. It later transpired that all but one of the battalion's Bren gunners were killed or wounded at Gona. The officer casualty tally continued unabated. The OC of D Company, Captain Gill, and his 17 Platoon commander, Lieutenant MacDonald, were both wounded, and Captain Best of A Company was killed. And when the assistant-adjutant, Lieutenant Pickering, was also killed by a sniper, the casualty count for the 2/27th rose to four officers and 42 other ranks.

But amongst the courage and carnage of 30 November, there was heartening news from the 2/14th's front. Brigadier Dougherty:

> Later in the day I made the artillery available to 2/14th Aust Inf Bn . . . I discussed with Colonel Challen the possibility of him doing a sharp attack on the enemy pocket, assisted by 40 rounds of 25 pr. Ammunition (this was all I could spare, plus what was required for ranging). I felt this would successfully overcome the enemy provided the artillery was followed in smartly by the bayonet.[25]

While the 2/27th was busily engaged in its attack on 30 November, the 2/14th was doing what should have been done from the outset at Gona: conducting reconnaissance and fighting patrols. The enemy positions in front of it were identified and harassed, and when the final attack came, supported by concentrated if limited artillery and mortar support, the soldiers of the 2/14th now triumphed in their area. Lieutenant Bob Thompson, signals officer, 2/14th Battalion:

> This was a tremendous victory, achieved with only two minor casualties. Had other commanders been allowed time for reconnaissance and planning I am sure the victory could have come much earlier and without such heavy losses . . . worst of all was the prior loss of first class officers and men who were virtually irreplaceable.[26]

By dark on 30 November, the rear Small Creek position was secured.

Dougherty now issued fresh orders for 1 December. In basic terms it was the same old plan, using the same uncovered approach which came on in the same old way. And on this night enemy barge movement was heard off Gona. To once again bolster the rapidly dwindling supply of soldiers within Cooper's ranks, Caro's last company under the command of Major Robinson was placed under Cooper's command. Dougherty:

> For this attack 150 rounds of 25 pounder were allotted.
>
> I requested Brigadier Eather (25 Aust Inf Bde) that 3 Aust Inf Bn should contact 2/27 Aust Inf Bn's left flank and move as far as the track running north-south through the village. I was desirous of 25 Aust Inf Bde cooperating to this extent so that 21 . . . Bde's left flank would be protected, by destroying and neutralising enemy positions south and southwest of the village, when the village area was entered . . .
>
> Following artillery preparation the attack was made at 0600 hours.[27]

Sergeant Jack Scott, 2/16th Battalion, has given a unique insight into the soldiers' minds the night before the attack:

> It was like World War One. It was open ground against fixed positions. We knew the Japs had been preparing for months. That was the part we couldn't understand, it was beyond comprehension. And even if we got through we had no idea what we'd find when we got there. We were apprehensive to say the least, but like trained soldiers we had a job to do for our country and we believed those in high command had good reasons for ordering us to go. And, I suppose, while there's life there's hope.
>
> I didn't think I'd sleep a wink that night. But there was an officer who walked up and down behind us during the night. 'Relax, boys, get some sleep, it'll be alright,' he'd be saying in a soothing tone. I've never met Colonel Geoff Cooper and I wouldn't know him if I ran into him, but I'd probably recognise his voice even now. Surprisingly I did get to sleep . . .
>
> Brigadier Dougherty must have been under enormous pressure. You could hear him on the phone . . . just behind us. His voice was raised with the strain. It must have been terrible for him, a real quandary.[28]

Cooper's third Gona attack was to be undertaken by two movements. The first was a repetition of the first two—another assault through the coconut belt. The second was to have Captain O'Neil's 2/16th Company and the left flank portion of Lieutenant Egerton-Warburton's 2/27th D Company sweeping along the edge of the scrub area to the south-east of Gona and, in the process, linking up with the 3rd Battalion in the scrub. Major Robinson's 2/16th company was to act as a reserve.

Despite the assistance of a smoke barrage, the 2/27th's A Company in the coconut belt, and D Company near the shaven kunai grass about 50 yards from the Mission, both became pinned down. Private George Atkinson, D Company, 2/27th Battalion:

> I was . . . by a big log; and there was a palm tree . . . there was three or four of us there . . . there was also a bomb crater, and one chap tried to make a run back to get behind this scrub. He got back about fifty yards and he

> got hit by a sniper. The shot came from high up so I automatically looked up, and I saw the puff of smoke . . . I gave him four bursts; one in each corner of the puff of smoke . . . he was definitely gone, I saw him drop, fifty yards away . . .[29]

Sergeant Roy Thredgold, D Company, 2/27th Battalion:

> We came out of the kunai and were tearing through this bare patch of ground. And the next thing whack! One in the leg; ten past six in the morning. I just lay there from ten past six in the morning till lunch. And Derek Parsons said 'Try and make it over to me Threddy!' The blood had congealed around the wound and so I tried to crawl over to him. The bastards must have been having a little sleep because Derek got right out of his shell hole he was in and pulled me back into it with him. This shell hole was full of muddy water and he kept pouring water out of his dixie over my head all day. Then at half past eight that night he said 'We'll come back for you Threddy!' Late that night I thought I'd had it. And the next thing I hear was 'Threddy!' 'Where are you Threddy?' It was black as pitch, and stinking hot. Derek saved my life. They took me back on a stretcher. And through three attacks at Gona I didn't even see a bloody Jap![30]

But amidst the futility and resulting slaughter of this day came a stirring breakthrough that so typified the aggression of the 21st Brigade. Captain John O'Neill's 2/16th Company and a portion of Lieutenant Warburton's 2/27th Company made a spirited and audacious dash into Gona Mission against all the odds.

As the artillery barrage lifted at dawn, there was no sign of the 3rd Battalion on the left flank. But this did not deter O'Neill. Cheering, the soldiers of the 2/16th ran forward into a withering curtain of fire. Lieutenant Peter Gorrie and Lieutenant Lea Allnutt's platoons were all but obliterated, except for those lucky enough to be wounded but covered from further fire by shell holes into which they fell. But O'Neill, Lieutenant Leo Mayberry and four others from his eighteen-man platoon incredibly survived not only the charge through that concentrated Japanese fire, but also the fire fight to overcome some of the village defences. On the right flank the 2/27th's Lieutenant Harold Inglis was killed, leaving only three of his soldiers to burst through the enemy defences to reach O'Neill.

Private Jack Breakey, 2/27th Battalion, was amongst them:

> We started to walk, and then the Western Australians started to run and they were doing this yelling out, so I began doing it with them! When we got through the kunai grass there was the area of burnt off grass and two rows of native huts. And there were two Jap machine-guns that we had to go through. You could feel the bullets around you; you could actually feel them! And after we came through this enfilading fire there seemed to be considerably less of us around somehow or another.[31]

If these soldiers had not endured enough, their fleeting moment of seeming triumph was shattered by their own artillery, which now rained down upon the already captured ground for ten minutes. They ran for cover. Sergeant Jack Scott, 2/16th Battalion, was amongst them:

> When the artillery barrage opened up (our own) I took cover in a bomb crater—the theory being 'they never land in the same place twice.' I was joined By Lt Leo Mayberry, Sgt Ted 'Skeeta' Herold, L.G. Morey and A.G. Sage (all 2/16th). Sage then was wounded. The barrage was very heavy and seemed to go on for some time. When it lifted we came out and took up a position on a small mound overlooking Jap bunkers.
>
> As soon as it lifted the Japs started coming out in single file along communication trenches. L.G. Morey opened up with his .303 and of course drew the enemy fire. Sage was wounded again and Morey was hit twice and I think that was when he was killed. Mayberry, Herold and myself moved in a westerly direction taking Sage along with us.

> When we reached the river if it had not been that Ted Herold who was slightly behind us, recognised Charlie Bloomfield and yelled out at them Chaforce [across Gona Creek] would have opened up on us. There were four of us including Sage who was pretty far gone by then. We supported him in the water while we swam the river. He must have died soon after if he was not already dead.
>
> . . . Johnnie O'Neill was nowhere near us; he was further down the river on the Gona side [the Japanese or Mission side], because the Chaforce boys could hear him calling out and Tom McMahon and another bloke went out after dark and got him out. I saw him at the CCS [casualty clearing station] just before he died; he was my first cousin . . .[32]

While the bravery of the still-alive few amongst the 2/16th had carried them in and rapidly out of Gona Mission, the even smaller surviving 2/27th contingent of the attack also found themselves on the objective but with few familiar faces. Private John Hobbs was one of the few:

> We passed through this blanket of fire into the Mission . . . we were well trained troops with good leadership and we had our objective in mind and we knew we couldn't bloody stay where we were, so it was just head down and arse up sort of thing. We lost contact spreading out.
>
> I saw this white post with Japanese writing on it. I thought, I'll have a bit of a spell here', and the next thing somebody else came along. And then Jack Breakey came along.[33]

Breakey led this party to Gona Creek, where it was hoped that a safe passage across that obstacle could be found. Along their path a wounded Western Australian was added to their number. Hobbs:

> Where we crossed the creek there was some scrub country, and we came under some fire. What I think happened there was they must have either seen some

Preliminary plan for attack on 1 December 1942

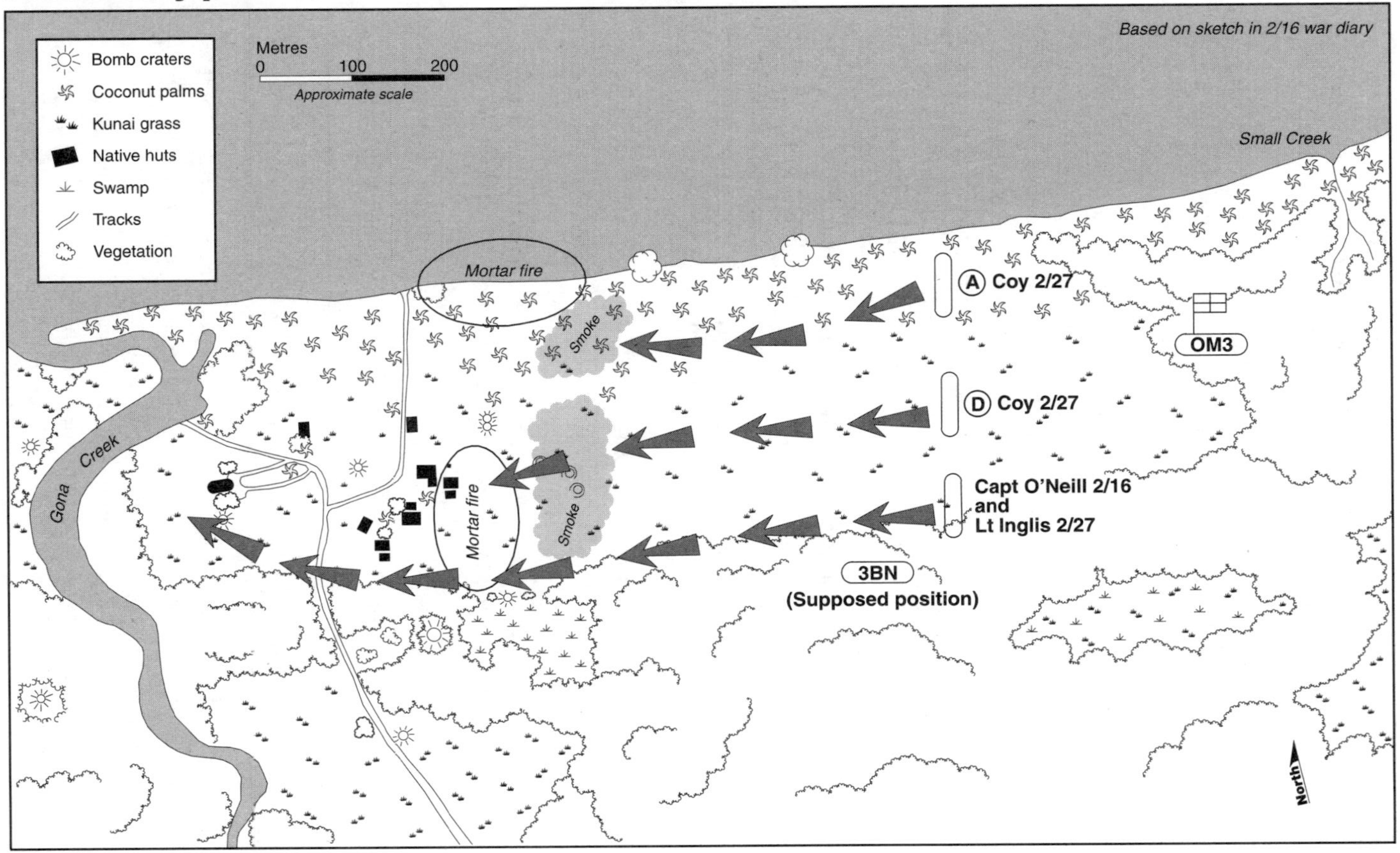

> movement or thought that there was some movement there and given the trees some whacko on the off chance, because we didn't get any direct fire . . . that spurred us on a bit! . . .
>
> We all got through and I was with Breakey at this time . . . we realised that the 16th joker was missing, so then Jack went back; swam across and got him.[34]

Lieutenant-Colonel Cameron's 3rd Battalion was located, out of contact with the enemy, in the scrub on the east of the track leading north into Gona. It was to have moved north, skirting the east flank of the Japanese positions between it and the Mission area, to join in the combined 2/27th and 2/16th attack. But it was not as close to the battle area as the 21st Brigade had been led to believe. Brigadier Dougherty:

> And he [Cameron] was to liaise with them on the left flank . . . the crux of the thing is he didn't do that, and when O'Neill's company got into Gona, instead of him going forward, he hadn't gone forward . . . and I don't think he was ever forward where he said he was.[35]

The 2/27th Battalion War Diary:

> 0645 hrs C.O. 3 Bn. Rang to say that his Bn had NOT advanced as arranged because our left flank had also not moved. However position at this stage was 2/16th Coy & D Coy 2/27th had not only moved but had reached Gona and fought their way through the village, with NO support from 3 Bn. 0700 hrs fighting still heard in village. Severe casualties due to NO support.[36]

And the slaughter at Gona on this day was not yet complete. Ordered yet again to repeat the folly of the previous two days, Major Robinson attacked through the coconut belt with his reserve 2/16th Company and sustained further casualties—they captured a post, but were forced to withdraw when the Japanese counterattacked in considerable strength. Robinson was wounded on the way in and again on the way out.

The remainder of this brave but pointless day was spent in gathering in the wounded, which was burdened by the now usual enemy machine-gun fire and made costly by its accompanying accurate sniper fire. One of the wounded was Lieutenant-Colonel Cooper. A bullet hit the butt of his revolver, fragmented, and 20 pieces were later found in his hip. After persevering with his duties for two hours, he was evacuated. Major Ben Hearman, 2/16th Battalion, now assumed command of the 2/27th–2/16th force.

During that night the Australians heard the explosions of bombing out to sea as Allied aircraft forced a Japanese convoy away to the north-west. But despite that forced delay, the Japanese managed to land about 500 reinforcements at the mouth of the Kumusi River on 2 December. Brigadier Dougherty:

> I rang General Vasey at 1700 hrs on 1 December and discussed the situation with him. He told me that he felt too many casualties were being suffered at Gona Mission, and that he was considering leaving a force to contain Gona Mission while another force moved east from that area to towards Sananda.[37]

During the morning of 2 December Lieutenant Hicks of the 2/16th Battalion, with a platoon of twenty men, made a successful attack on a major Japanese beach post at a cost of nine wounded—Hicks mortally. A platoon of D Company of the 2/27th bolstered the newly won position.

When you walk this Gona battleground the futility of the Australians' attacks between 18 November and 3 December becomes immediately apparent. Two or three huts are sited near to the 2/14th's area of operations near Small Creek. The locals gladly take you to the nearby swamp—it is still a stagnant, foul-smelling obstacle that should have been far more carefully reconnoitred before such a risky and costly operation was mounted.

The distance between Small Creek and Gona Creek is only about 750 yards. It might just as well have been 750 miles when the tactics used to capture this ground are examined. The Japanese had the sea as a secure left flank and, using the cover of the coconut belt and its scattered banyan trees, sited mutually supporting strongposts to provide a sweeping arc of fire that meant death or maiming for any attacker who persisted in massed frontal movement. And the really clever aspect of these posts was their superb camouflage. You have to see a target before you can offer a decent standard of counter-fire. The Australians often could not see their foe and his positions until it was too late. When you walk along this coconut belt and then inland and out into the kunai grass, the real madness of this approach becomes obvious. Any walk through this grass—then cut or burnt down—was vulnerable to concentrated fire from both the coconut belt posts and the ever-present snipers, who were firing from close range. The enemy wanted, indeed hoped, that the Australians would use this almost perfectly prepared killing ground. And the Australians accommodated them, not once, not twice, but over and over again. As the casualties mounted, tomorrow was always another day of ignorant hope and desperate anticipation for those who planned these misplaced and ignorant assaults, and acts of great courage but inevitable carnage for those who had to carry them out.

There is absolutely no evidence whatsoever that either Eather or Dougherty ever saw the ground upon which they committed their soldiers. There can be no excuse for their lack of professional support for their men—Eather's HQ was little more than a mile from the Mission and therefore less than a mile from his front; and, later, Dougherty's was little further. And their trek, had they made it, would have been over flat ground that could hardly have overtaxed them.

We have noted that no intelligence was passed on from 25th Brigade to the incoming 21st Brigade upon its arrival. No opportunity was given the battalion commanders to reconnoitre their battleground. No Officer Group conferences were held to determine where the enemy was vulnerable, where he could be defeated, and at the least cost, because the basic function of reconnaissance patrolling was not undertaken. And the lesson is simple: the harder and more urgent the military nut is to crack, the more astute, the more cunning and the more professional its master plan must be. Failure to conduct any military operation with astute planning can produce a wanton waste of fine, experienced infantry who deserve better.

When you walk along the western ground between Gona Creek and the track into Gona, the same limiting factors apply—the creek forms your left flank, and the ground between the track and the creek is not all that wide. And here, too, the Japanese had cut and burnt the kunai grass, created their killing ground, and manned their posts hoping the Australians would walk into their enfilading fire. The Australians again accommodated them.

But when you walk through the covered jungle and swamp approach running south-east through this battleground, you realise that here there is cover, no enemy killing grounds, and the chance to come in on the adversary and take the war to him. The aerial photographs would have shown this obvious approach—or some sensible, measured and professional reconnaissance would have found it.

By 3 December the 25th Brigade, which had fought almost from sea to sea across the Kokoda Trail to Gona, had suffered around 200 casualties from an already grossly debilitated force, and the newly committed 21st Brigade—only at about 1000 soldiers in total—had been forced to add to this register of slaughter by a further 340 men. Warrant-Officer 1 Jack Burnett, 2/27th Battalion, best sums up the battle for Gona to this point:

> . . . of all the training we had, and we had plenty of training . . . the reconnaissance; time spent on reconnaissance is never wasted; and we had the better weapons . . . it was a vulgar public brawl. And the lesson to be learnt is this—ensure that men do not walk straight into zones of fire . . . everything in the military sense was wrong . . . we paid for it.[38]

Cooper, Caro and Hearman also paid for it. After being wounded at Gona on 1 December, and after having been involved in an acrimonious discussion with Brigadier Dougherty while lying on a stretcher near HQ at Gona concerning the tactics employed during his battalion's fighting, Lieutenant-Colonel Cooper did not regain another battalion command—a great injustice to a soldier who had led his battalion with such zeal and competence both at Mission Ridge and Gona. Cooper's replacement was Major Ben Hearman from the 2/16th Battalion. Major Ben Hearman:

> Even at this stage [shortly after Koitaki] there were suggestions that there could be a witch-hunt for officers who were known to show an unconcealed respect for Brigadier Potts. I recall a conversation initiated by the 2/16th Bn Adjt., Capt. John O'Neill who was killed at Gona, along these lines . . .
>
> Both Lt-Col Caro and I were relieved of command of the 2/16th Bn. Without, so far as I am aware any very convincing reason being given to either of us . . .
>
> I can say that when I did eventually rejoin the 2/16th Bn in the beginning of April 1945, I was shown great consideration and kindness by Brig. Dougherty. I am sure that any differences we may have had at Gona stemmed from honest differences of opinion *and army politics*.[39]

Lieutenant-Colonel Albert Caro would pay for his protests by serving out the war in a details depot in Perth. By the time the battle for Gona had concluded, the Blamey slur at Koitaki had manifested itself in the interference in the command structure, and the resultant slaughter of soldiers. The 21st Brigade veterans of Gona all maintain one critical belief—such a command structure and uneducated series of assaults would never have occurred under Brigadier Arnold Potts. Arnold Potts could be a difficult and forthright subordinate. Perhaps one was needed at Gona.

By an ironic twist of fate the battle for Gona would now hinge on a militia battalion which had been decisively reinforced at Isurava by the very brigade that it was now sent to assist. Lieutenant-Colonel Ralph Honner and his 39th Militia Battalion were on their way to Gona.

THIS IS NOT A MOB!

22

At around midday on 2 December, General Vasey held a conference at Brigadier Eather's HQ. In attendance were Vasey and Brigadiers Eather, Dougherty and Porter. As the casualties at Gona had dramatically increased, it had been decided to emplane the 30th Militia Brigade from Port Moresby to relieve the 25th Brigade. The reader will recall that the 30th Brigade consisted of the 39th, 49th and now the 55th–53rd Battalion, after the disbanding of the ill-starred 53rd.

The outcome of this conference, however, was that Vasey now decided to contain Gona with the 25th Brigade and the composite 2/27th–2/16th Battalion, and march the fresh 39th Battalion and the 2/14th to Sanananda in an attempt to concentrate a force strong enough to cause Sanananda's capture.

Vasey's plans were to last but a day after it was discovered that an infantry route to Sanananda via the coast was not practical. The plan was now revised to relieve the 25th Brigade with the 39th Battalion and deploy the 49th and 55th–53rd Battalions at Sanananda. Their fate will be examined later.

After having his battalion strafed by a Beaufighter along its fruitless path towards Sanananda—miraculously at the cost of only four wounded—Lieutenant-Colonel Ralph Honner had an opportunity to observe the ground along which the 21st Brigade had been forced to attack Gona. Honner would later write that 'we didn't like the look of it at all'.[1]

Upon his arrival at Gona, fate dealt the commander of the 39th a fortunate hand. Ralph Honner:

> On the opposite side [from 21st Brigade's positions on the coast] the enemy were protected by a creek [Gona Creek]; our western company occupied its left bank but could not attack across it. The rest of the battalion was on the southern front which was divided into two sectors by a track running north to the mission and parallel to the creek. In the sector between the road and the creek was a broad belt of low kunai grass; and a long stretch of this grass in front of the timber line that marked the enemy's position had been cut off at ground level. To the right of the road there were covered approaches right into the enemy lines; this was obviously the best area from which to launch an attack.[2]

Thus Honner was allotted two assault approaches at Gona. The first, between the track and Gona Creek, was militarily useless because it suffered the same handicap as the 21st Brigade's ground—it was an open ground approach into well-sited enemy machine-gun posts. But his second option, the jungle and scrub approach east of the track, was militarily priceless. Honner:

> Strangely enough its possibilities seem to have been overlooked while bloody losses were sustained elsewhere. Brigadier Eather had told me that in this area the 3rd Battalion posts were so close to those of the Japanese that the favourite pastime of both forces was the throwing of grenades at one another. I relayed this information to Captain Joe Gilmore [ex-53rd Battalion] but when his A Company took over from the 3rd Battalion he immediately obtained my permission to move his company forward to make contact with the enemy and dig in there, not yet within grenade range but in what had been no-man's land.[3]

Clearly, Lieutenant-Colonel Cameron's failure to support the brave but ill-fated 21st Brigade attack on 1 December, his false reports as to his position in this area—for whatever reason(s)—and his reported 'grenade throwing' contests with the enemy, all conspired to mask the military potential of this sector.

However, if the aerial photos taken prior to the battle had been available, the potential of this sector would have been recognised.

But Honner was also initially ordered to attack at the wrong Gona location, and his failure to protest that order more strongly with Brigadier Dougherty remained a deep-seated regret.

On 5 December 1942, Honner received orders from Dougherty to attack the Japanese through the area between Gona Creek and the track. The attack was to be supported by yet another pointless assault in the coconut belt by the now rapidly diminished 21st Brigade's 2/27th–2/16th force.

When the attack was explained at a meeting of the 39th Battalion's officers, Captain Max Bidstrup, whose D Company was to mount the attack, protested strongly. Bidstrup's assault was to be undertaken through kunai grass and then over about sixty critical yards of bare killing ground facing the Japanese positions, which comprised a number of mutually supported bunkers with machine-guns operating on fixed lines. To support his attack, Bidstrup was allocated a 3-inch mortar barrage which was to be laid down just before daylight, and a smoke barrage at dawn to conceal the approach of his 16 and 17 Platoons as they advanced.

The attack was a costly disaster. Lieutenant-Colonel Ralph Honner:

> Our orders were to attack directly from the front. I do not know why, because I protested against the idea, but these were the orders and I take it that they must have fitted into some plan that was beyond my conception . . . the only support from another sub-unit was a section from B Company which was to provide flanking protection along the track should Don Company's attack succeed. That flanking protection which went in where the attack should have gone in, around the flank of the Japanese position, was able to get right through the jungle behind the bunkers, go on, find out what was there and get a sight of the village, but as the attack had failed, they had to come back.[4]

The haunting white Gona Mission Cross sits just above the jungle and scrub at Gona. AWM 013930

The bullet-ridden car used as a machine gun post by the Japanese during the final attack on Gona. AWM 013931

Evidence of the final Japanese attempt to break out of Gona. AWM 014012

'Gona's gone!' A part of the final carnage near Gona Creek. AWM 014028

Lieutenant McIntosh, D Company, 2/9th Battalion and Private Syd Bourne, Intelligence Section in Duropa Plantation, 18 December 1942. AWM 151329

A Japanese bunker, Duropa Plantation, Buna. AWM 013850

The point at Sememi Creek where the 2/10th Battalion crossed the swamp onto the Old Strip at Buna. The 2/10th signal cable can be seen. AWM 013881

Private Whittington and Raphael Oimbari at Buna (*Not Kokoda*). George Silk's most famous photo.
AWM 013878

Papua, Giropa Point. Australian-manned General Stuart Tanks attacking Japanese pillboxes in the final assault on Buna. Men of D Company, 2/12th Battalion, using Bren machine guns and rifles, fire on 25 Japanese (not seen), who are fleeing from a wrecked pillbox 150 yards away. AWM 014001

Corporal Roy Rodgers, 2/12th Battalion, warns the tank crew about another Japanese pillbox at right as the tank blasts away at a pillbox ahead. AWM 014002

Buna, Papua. Fighting during the final assault on Buna. Australian machine gunners in action around 5.30 pm New Year's Day. AWM 014037

George Silk. AWM 013757

Damien Parer on his last leave. Photo by Max Dupain. (Print Jill White) Courtesy Elizabeth Parer.

Lieutenant Doug McClean led 17 Platoon in this ill-fated attack:

> The Japs were in deep dug-outs protected with thick logs at ground level separated by other logs just to allow the weapons to protrude . . . providing a field of fire for the one hundred and eighty degrees facing the scrub. Now our troops as they attacked were hit in the lower leg and body . . . and I later found some of my boys lying against enemy positions with unexploded grenades in their hands. They were riddled with wounds but struggled as they died to get to the enemy . . . if ever blokes had earnt a decoration . . . one lad was shot twice in the same action . . . flesh wounds . . . and the tears in his eyes when he asked for a safer spot . . . 'Sir', he said crying, 'Every time I move some bastard shoots me!' . . . he was only eighteen.[5]

This attack was nothing more than a costly, vain and ignorant attempt to emulate—under almost the same conditions—the attacks which had preceded it in the coconut belt by the 21st Brigade. It cost twelve killed and 46 wounded for no ground gained. And yet again the 2/27th–2/16th attack in the coconut belt yielded nothing more than casualties: four killed and six wounded.

Dougherty ordered another attack for the following day. There was both good and bad news for Honner:

> . . . the scope of the attack was extended. We were this time allowed to attack on the right of the track, where we could attack through some cover . . . but we still had to attack on the left of the track where Don Company's attack had failed the previous day . . . I didn't know how to get out of this, I didn't want to disobey orders, I didn't want to have another company killed off, and I didn't know how to get out of it.[6]

Lieutenant-Colonel Ralph Honner's deliverance came from a quarter that was in startling contrast to his previous war experience. In the high passes of the mountains in Greece and

The 39th attack on Gona Mission, 6 December 1942

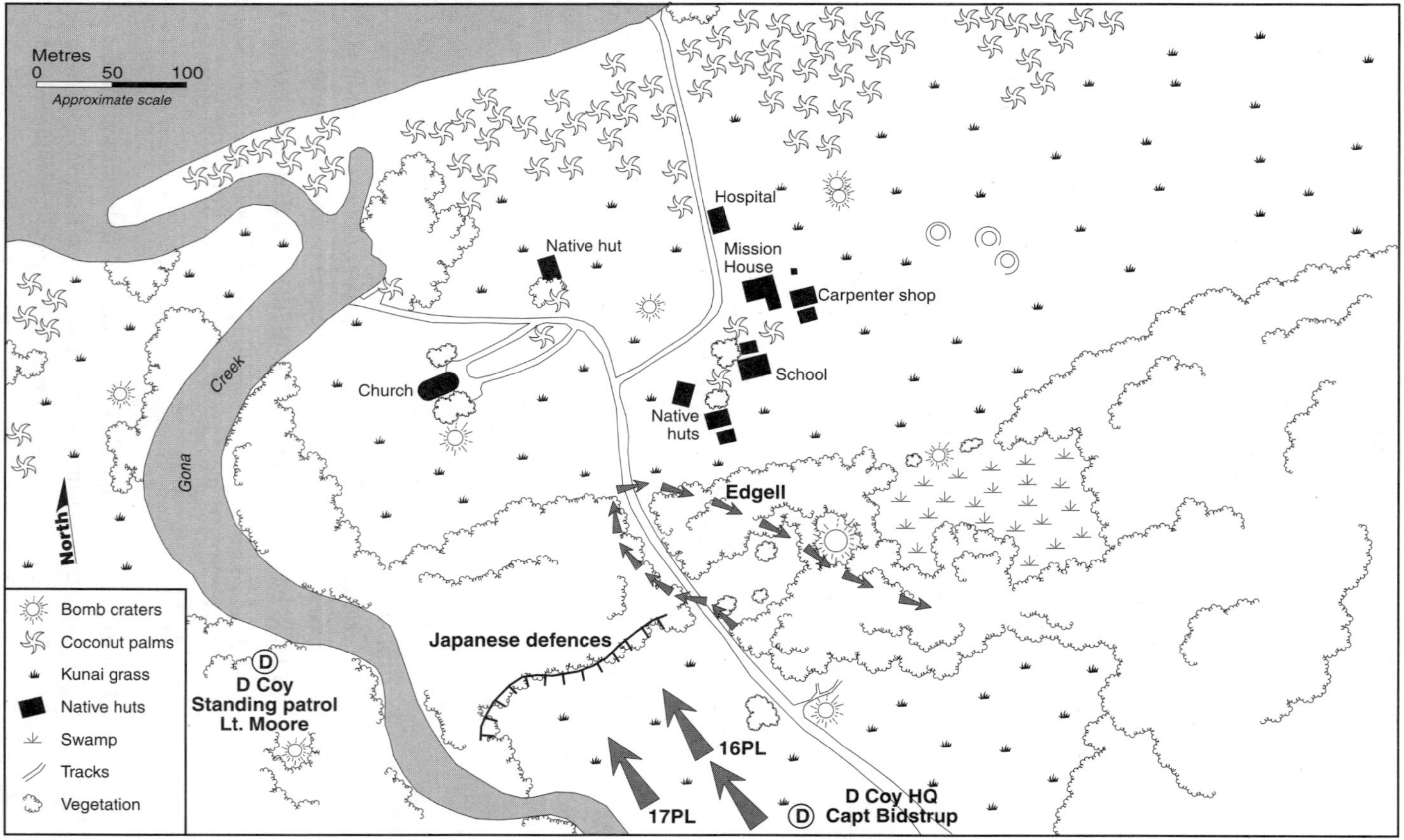

the vulnerable olive groves of Crete, Honner had been subjected to the terror of German Stuka dive-bomber attacks. At Gona on 7 December he was fortunate enough to be bombed by his own air support, which consisted of a paltry few bombs which landed harmlessly behind his own lines. Captain Bidstrup remembered his commanding officer's quiet but cutting statement: 'Give me a squadron of Stukas!'[7]

This 'air support' provided Honner with an excuse to cancel the attack. When Honner rang Dougherty to inform him of his decision, he attempted to decrease the potential wrath of his superior:

> . . . I had cancelled the attack because the mis-directed bombing attack had jeopardised its chances of success. This was a spurious pretext but the brigade commander accepted it and I tried to fortify it, or bolster it, by giving an optimistic assessment that if I were allowed to attack the next day through the jungle approaches on the right of the track and abandon the attack approach on the left which had already proved disastrous, I should have a good chance of getting into Gona Mission.[8]

Honner's decision had a positive effect upon the troops. Lieutenant Hugh Dalby:

> I think you could say that Colonel Honner's decision to scrap the attack which we were to have put in on the Japanese after an aerial bombardment, built up the troops' confidence. I think this permeated right through to the troops; that we were still going to attack, but it was to be with decent supporting fire . . .[9]

What had changed? Why were commanders less than a mile away not allowed to fight their battles with similar trust and confidence and independence? There are two simple answers. The first is the fact that Ralph Honner was well known to Dougherty because of their mutual experiences in Greece and Crete—as officers in the same 19th Brigade of the 6th Division. The second was quite simply that Honner was not Koitaki branded, as the 39th had not been involved in the

Brigade Hill battle and had not been disparaged by Blamey or Herring. Trust and confidence—or a lack of it—carry much influence. Dougherty supported Honner.

By 8 December the pressure to capture Gona was intense. Vasey yet again contemplated a containment of the Japanese at Gona and a concentration of force at Sananada. And further news that a fresh Japanese force had landed near the Kumusi River and was making its way towards Gona Mission only heightened that anxiety.

Dougherty still maintained his belief that Gona should and could fall first, and to this end he now ordered Lieutenant-Colonel Challen to deploy his 2/14th to the west of Gona. This movement was a response to the plight of Lieutenant Alan Haddy's Chaforce standing patrol on that western flank.

On 30 November Haddy had relieved a standing patrol at a small village near the Amboga River and about two miles west of his own Chaforce base. He had forestalled an enemy attempt at movement eastwards, sustaining two killed in action, and subsequently estimated that about 150 to 200 Japanese troops were west of the Amboga River. Lieutenant 'Kanga' Moore, 39th Battalion, was sent with his 18 Platoon to relieve Haddy on 4 December:

> Haddy's Village was a clearing on a beach about one hundred and fifty yards long; probably fifty yards in depth before you got near the swamp; right in the centre of it there were about half a dozen native huts that were on high stilts . . . and further along towards the Amboga River there were another couple of huts . . . Haddy to me was the tiredest-looking man I had ever seen, he looked exhausted . . . malaria; he hadn't eaten properly; hadn't slept, because there was no sleep in this position . . .[10]

Haddy's relief lasted but one night before he returned to again assume the defence of Haddy's Village on the 6th. In the middle of the rain-soaked night of 6 December, the Japanese converged on Haddy's position. Private Charlie Bloomfield was with Haddy:

> The attack came at the height of a storm. The Japs came in throwing grenades and in the attack one man was killed, presumably Stephens . . . four were wounded, among them being Haddy. As our lines of communication were cut one man was sent back to alert the company . . .
>
> Another attack came in shortly after but was unsuccessful, and during the lightning flashes we could see lines of Japs making their way along the beach. Haddy, who was badly wounded . . . decided to vacate the position; he ordered me to take the wounded and withdraw; two of the wounded—one with a groin injury and the other caught a bomb blast to the stomach—both seemed in a dazed condition and the other man had a leg wound and had to be carried.
>
> We hadn't left the position for many minutes when sounds of gun fire came again from where we had just left.[11]

Although there were only fifteen malaria-ridden 2/16th Chaforce soldiers on the western side of Gona Creek, Sergeant Jones lost no time in leading them to Haddy's rescue. In the resulting action, Jones accounted for four of the enemy while being bayoneted in the process. The Australians pressed on with such resolution that the Japanese were temporarily halted. But further help was on its way.

The 2/14th force sent by Brigadier Dougherty to reinforce Haddy was led by Lieutenant Bob Dougherty (no relation to the Brigadier). Dougherty's and his 50-strong contingent were able to surprise the enemy about a half mile south-east of Haddy's Village. Along the way, Lieutenant 'Kanga' Moore and approximately ten of his men were added to Dougherty's group. In spite of the fact that the Japanese outnumbered him by about four to one, Dougherty attacked. 'Kanga' Moore:

> I was beside him when a bullet cut a gouge about six inches long in his rifle butt. Dougherty was the coolest man I've ever seen in my life. He just sort of looked at it and said, 'Ah, look at that!' He put in a most remarkable

> attack . . . and I just couldn't believe that men were going in as Dougherty and his men were . . . They were actually walking through bullets flying around everywhere and not seeming to notice . . . a little fella of mine by the name of Reid was killed there . . .[12]

This impudent attack checked the enemy advance for the time being—long enough for Lieutenant-Colonel Challen to arrive on the evening of 7 December to strengthen the blocking position.

When Haddy's Village was eventually retaken the body of Stephens was found still at his post in the command hut, and beneath that hut's raised platform they found Alan Haddy ringed by dead Japanese. Haddy had fought to the last so that his comrades could withdraw.

Thus on the night of 7 December 1942 at Gona the position was that Brigadier Dougherty's planned attack on the 7th had been cancelled by Honner, the situation in the coastal coconut belt was essentially unchanged and, finally, Honner and his 39th Battalion were to attack on the 8th.

This was Dougherty's last throw, and he was still utterly determined that his attack for 8 December would be conducted across all three Gona fronts: the coconut belt, the area between the track and Gona Creek, and Honner's thrust through the jungle and scrub approach from the south.

Lieutenant-Colonel Ralph Honner had been fortunate indeed to have been allotted the prime offensive ground for his attack on Gona for 8 December. But he was given two further priceless privileges denied his colleagues in the 21st Brigade: the right and the time to conduct his own reconnaissance, and the freedom of action to plan and execute his own plan. It was standard military procedure, but it was long overdue. Honner spent the day reconnoitring his ground, particularly the scrub and jungle approach. He was accompanied by his intelligence officer, Lieutenant McNamara, but shared his thoughts with no one.[13]

Ralph Honner's plan for the capture of Gona Mission was a succinct employment of the principles of warfare and the invaluable use of his own comprehensive experience as a soldier in the Middle East. Honner's allotted jungle and scrub approach had a number of critical advantages. The first was the nature of the ground. Ralph Honner: 'It doesn't matter what cover you have getting close to the enemy if in the last stretch he's got an unbroken field of fire where he can mow you down. But if you've got a covered approach right into the heart of his defences he's gone!'[14]

The second advantage of this approach was that a breakthrough in this area would drive a wedge between the Japanese defenders between the creek and the track and those to their east.

Honner's next consideration was concentration of force. Captain Joe Gilmore's A Company was deployed in the southernmost area of this critical jungle and scrub sector. Therefore, it was logical to deploy that force to spearhead the attack. Late on 7 December, Honner moved the remnants of his decimated D Company—after its fruitless attack between the creek and the track the previous day—behind A Company. He proposed that as A Company gained initial ground at the onset of the attack, D Company was to follow hard on its heels to maintain the momentum of the break-in. And in order to maintain the violence of that break-in, Ralph Honner disobeyed his orders for an attack on the left between the track and the creek. Honner: '. . . I had made up my mind to modify the attack . . . I instructed C Company's commander [Captain Seward] who was to attack on the left, to attack with fire only; just enough fire, waste no ammunition, to keep his company intact, fully armed and ready to fight, but lose no lives.'[15]

When A Company followed by D Company had achieved their initial breakthrough, the fresh C Company was therefore to be rapidly moved over the track to that crucial jungle and scrub sector to maintain the impetus of the attack. But for all this, one recurring Gona obstacle had to be surmounted if the attack were to succeed, and with tolerable casualties. During previous Australian artillery attacks, the Japanese had simply gone to ground in their bunkers and trenches or moved to others nearby, waited for the conclusion of the shelling, and then regained their positions. They had then proceeded to blanket the ground between them and their attackers with telling fire. While a covered approach was far more desirable than advancing over cleared ground, it was the time taken between the conclusion of the barrage and the onset of the Australians across that intervening ground that was absolutely critical. If there was any delay it was usually very costly. Ralph Honner:

> . . . the plan was added to by a couple of significant factors. I knew from previous experience that infantry could fight under their own artillery bombardment, and using their own bombardment they could use surprise to catch the enemy unawares. I had arranged with the artillery FOO, the Forward Observation Officer, to have the artillery barrage on the Japanese defences use shells fused to burst eighteen inches or two feet deep in the soft soil. If they managed to break through the roofs of the bunkers they would damage the bunkers, if they dropped into the soft ground alongside the bunkers, they would stun the defenders. Now, in either case they'd distract the defenders while our troops reached the defenders. And to capitalise on that I arranged my timetable for our troops who would be lining up about a hundred yards away from the Japanese defences, to move two minutes before the barrage lifted, so that they had one minute to get into the Japanese defences and one minute to fight among them with the artillery shells still dropping.[16]

Honner had witnessed troops going in under their own barrages in Libya—usually because of mistakes in planning. But he hadn't ordered them. This decision was not only one of shrewd planning, it was also one made with great guts. The possibilities were daunting. He stood the chance of inflicting significant casualties upon his own soldiers. The men were not told of his decision. However, had Honner known what two of his platoon commanders were planning, he may have been considerably more concerned.

Lieutenants Dalby and Kelly of A Company had been considering the same problem—how to gain ground and minimise the time given for the enemy to implement their fire-plan. The two enterprising officers therefore decided that while the barrage was in progress they and their soldiers would creep towards the enemy. Honner had no idea of their plan and they were equally unaware of his. One critical and life-saving—and life-threatening—minute at Gona Mission under their own artillery barrage was about to become two.

The artillery ranged at about 11.30 a.m., and the barrage began at 12.30. Twelve minutes later, and not fifteen as planned, Kelly and Dalby attacked. Hugh Kelly:

> . . . they were spot on with the barrage, and actually, it didn't worry us all that much; the ground was a bit soggy and there was just a bit of a soggy thump as it hit and then the explosion. I suppose if it'd been on hard ground there would have been a hell of a lot more noise and it might have been a bit more dangerous too.
>
> We went in two sections forward and one section in reserve. When we actually stood up to move across the ground, this car body (across the swamp near the school) came to life by machine-gun fire and my right hand section got into strife . . . that's when I yelled out to a Bren gunner in the reserve Platoon, that was 'Darky' Wilkinson, he was within earshot of me, to tell him about this. In typical fashion he made a remark, 'What's wrong with your rifle!' . . . that's when he moved forward to a little peak of scrub there . . . there was an old fence that petered out and he stood up and put the Bren on a post. He quietened that and when we got to the edge of the Jap weapon pits we just met up with Dalby. He struck the heavy opposition; he had the heavy machine-gunners in front of him . . . I saw him once on my left; where his platoon was there was a weapon pit, an obvious weapon pit; it was round and raised up . . . I saw Dalby stand up in front of it and on the off chance he chucked a grenade into it. And a body came hurtling out of it and he just fired from the waist with his rifle. There's no doubt about him, he was right into it.[17]

Lieutenant Hugh Dalby has left a succinct insight into the platoon commander's role in such fighting:

> We had our bloody objective, and I think once you got committed, and you got in among being shot at, and shooting at . . . you just hoe in . . . it was pretty close warfare; there wasn't the room to manoeuvre beautifully like you could in the desert . . . unless the platoon commander and the platoon section leaders were not of a mind to charge in, well then how do you expect the troops to? . . . and so really there was no set formation as far as I was concerned . . . we got in a reasonably straight line, the two forward platoons, and charged straight in at the bloody Japs. We had to get in among them while the artillery was firing.
>
> . . . the Japs still had their heads down and in the pillboxes. They didn't come out until we started shooting . . . the first gun that I ran into, I was on top of them as the last shell exploded. And I started shooting and the bloke on the left and the bloke on the right and everyone else got in for the bun fight![18]

The point is that the hitherto predictable and futile Australian mode of attack had been abandoned and the priceless military ingredient of surprise had replaced it. It is not known if any Japanese were killed by the artillery, but the point is that the enemy were driven to ground with many of them in a heads between the knees, or crouched, position. Dalby remembered shooting Japanese who were almost in a state of shock and looking at the ground. The Australians were not expected until after the barrage. Many of the Japanese were therefore shot at ranges varying from two to fifteen yards. Others died in groups by grenade bursts in the close confines of their logged bunkers. And once the momentum of this audacious assault gained real speed and concentrated fire-power, the Japanese, with their extended killing grounds lost, were systematically slaughtered. Lieutenant-Colonel Ralph Honner:

> A Company's initial attack had an extraordinary success. Post after post fell to them. But there was a severe time gap between their attack and the arrival of C Company from across the other side of the track to support them.

> Into that time gap the reinforced D Company, including the platoon which was not engaged in the attack on the 6th of December, were thrown in straight after A Company to maintain and expand the impetus of the attack, and behind Don Company came C Company, pouring across from the other side of the track fully armed and rearing to go. The impetus of the attack carried them through the Japanese network of posts until they reached the sago swamp which was an integral part of the Japanese line of defence. There the A Company attack had to branch into two. Hugh Dalby's platoon went around the left of the swamp to clean up the network of enemy posts between the swamp and the main track into the Mission. On the right Hugh Kelly's platoon went around the right of the sago swamp up through the cover there, and turned west across the north of the sago swamp through the timbered corridor leading to the Mission school.
>
> And so the attack continued in two prongs around the sago swamp. That attack went on through the day and at the end of the day, the 39th Battalion had captured the centre of the Japanese defensive positions right up to the Mission school; had captured all the jungle around the sago swamp on the right of the track; had isolated the unattacked Japanese bunker line on the left of the track which had been our disaster on the 6th of December and by-passed it; and as night fell, we had already taken about half of the Japanese perimeter and had hit right into the heart of the defences.[19]

Predictably, the attack on the coast, despite the unfailing aggression and bravery of the composite 2/27th–2/16th Battalion, came to a grinding and costly halt because of the recurring factors of open ground and poor support. On the left of this coconut belt assault Captain Atkinson's 2/16th Company pushed north-west into a storm of machine-gun fire. The Official Historian:

> Once again Lieutenant Mayberry shone out even in that brave company. With a scratch crew of six men he

The 39th attack on Gona Mission, 8 December 1942

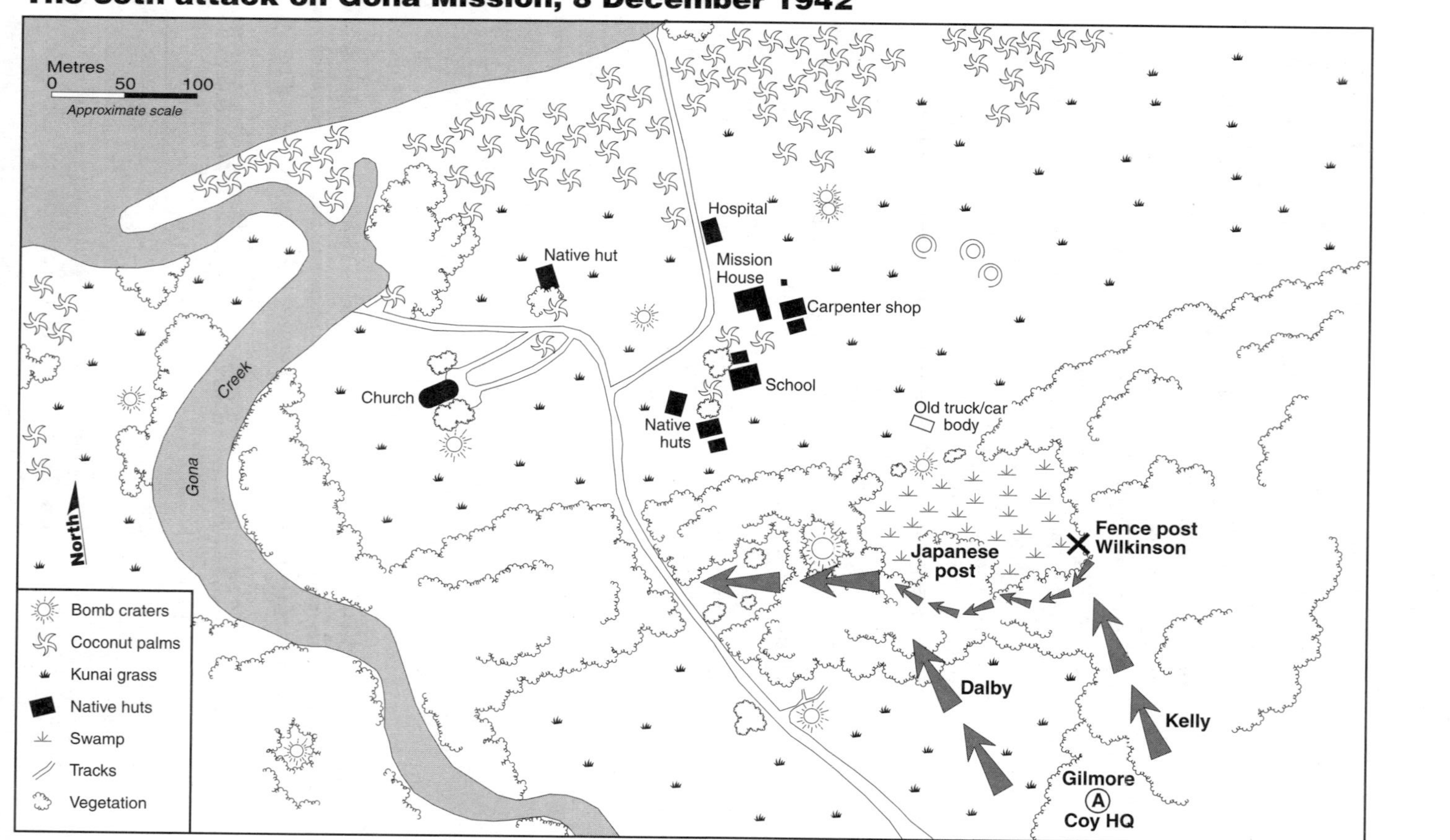

> stormed headlong against a key position. Badly wounded in the head and right arm he still fought on and urged his men forward. His shattered right arm refusing its function, he dragged the pin out of a grenade and essayed a throw with his left hand. But the arm was too weak. He forced the pin back with his teeth and then lay for some hours in his exposed position before he was rescued . . . The other two platoon commanders also went down, Lieutenant Inkpen mortally wounded.[20]

The composite 2/27th–2/16th Battalion had been struggling for numbers well before this juncture. To bolster its ranks, the 2/27th had taken a small number of soldiers from the mortar platoon. When George 'Babe' Luscombe had joined the battalion in Adelaide in May 1940, it will be recalled that he had shown a willingness to perform any role: 'mortar, bricklaying, anything you like boss'. At Gona, he was needed as a rifleman. On 8 December 1942 at Gona, Luscombe was shot through the heart while trying to gain ground in the coconut belt. His mate from the mortar platoon, Roy Borchers, assisted in his burial.

The former seemingly impregnable Japanese Gona defences were now decisively ruptured through their middle. To the west lay the untouched but trapped defenders between the track and Gona Creek—their bare killing ground would claim no more Australian lives, but would now act as an Australian killing ground which they dare not cross. And to the north-east, stretching some small distance along the coconut belt, the remaining enemy soldiers were faced with the debilitated but steadfast 21st Brigade and the 39th closing in on the Mission.

Calm, measured reconnaissance, a sound plan employing concentration of force at Gona's most vulnerable point, and a brave storming of bunkers under an artillery barrage using delayed action fuses had won a stirring victory.

But there was one nerve-racking experience to come.

The Japanese survivors of this action-packed day, knowing that they had inflicted as many deaths upon the Australians as had been possible, now determined that they would break out in the hope of joining their comrades at Sananada.

Two passages were chosen for their escape. The first was through the kunai grass corridor between the Australians occupying the scrub and the coastal fringe, and the second was by wading out to sea in an effort to bypass the 21st Brigade remnants in the coconut belt. The breakout began at midnight on 8 December. Brigadier Dougherty:

> And at the end of the day I had to report that the attack was unsuccessful whereas in fact it had been successful . . . Frank Sublet [now commanding the Composite Battalion] rang me and told me that they were being infiltrated. And I said, 'Frank, just order your men to stay in their holes and just shoot anything that moves on top of the ground, it doesn't matter what it is, shoot it!' These men were the Japanese remnants of Gona, they were finished![21]

Captain Harry Katekar, the 2/27th Battalion Adjutant, was well forward and remembers the beginning of the breakout:

> . . . I remember the deathly silence being broken by one of our chaps yelling out, 'He's stabbing me!' And I said 'For Christ's sake shut up you stupid bastard'. Someone else said, 'He's having a nightmare'. We soon learned that he wasn't having a nightmare; it was a Jap with a sword having a go at him![22]

Private O'Connor, A Company, 2/27th Battalion, was in the coconut belt:

> We were close to the beach . . . there was a group out on patrol . . . the next minute three or four blokes went past our post, and we thought, 'Ah back early!' . . . of course they went out into the sea further on . . . the 2/16th got most of them . . .[23]

Corporal Jim Hardie, 39th Battalion, was further inland:

> . . . Company HQ was involved . . . on my left there was a section . . . one Jap got in with these blokes on the left;

> they suddenly found they had a stranger in their midst . . . somebody fired a Very light which lit up everything and there in front about twenty yards from the company HQ were these little groups of Japs looking for a way through. Of course they were all killed . . . not too many people got any sleep . . .[24]

Lance-Corporal Bill Pannell, 2/27th Battalion, had taken detailed precautions and was ready for night-time action:

> . . . I had a ground sheet laid on top of the slit trench with a Bren on it and a spare barrel and I got four magazines and I had my rifle alongside it with bayonet on it . . . I was set!
>
> We could hear all this firing out on the beach . . . Doug was in there with me, shoulder to shoulder . . . and all of a sudden he said, 'Look out Bill, right in front of you!' And with that a sheet of flame went between our bloody heads . . . I just went with the Bren and probably got rid of half a magazine . . . everything went quiet for a couple of minutes . . . it was still going on the beach . . . come daylight there was three dead there . . . one bloke had a revolver in his hand; one of the other blokes had a sword in his hand and a grenade with the pin still in . . .[25]

The 2/16th had a Bren gun sited on the edge of the beach and coconut belt. As the noise of the breakout and the consequent movement of the Japanese came closer, they noticed a number of 'coconuts' moving slowly out in the sea. The 'coconuts' were nearly all shot at and eliminated.

On the morning of 9 December, the Australians were able to see the result of that night's climactic action. About a hundred enemy corpses were discovered in the coconut belt, across the kunai patch and along the beach. While most of the Japanese engaged in that breakout were killed, some small number may have escaped the almost-closed net and made their way to Sananada.

On 9 December 1942, as the 39th moved from its scrub positions towards the beach, it was able to see groups of comrades from the 2/27th–2/16th Battalion also closing in on the

Mission beach. But even now, when continued fighting meant nothing more than continued and pointless slaughter, those Japanese who had been too sick and enfeebled to attempt their breakout, fought on rather than surrender to the oncoming Australians. Lieutenant Bob Sword led his platoon to the beach, where he was killed taking the last defiant post.

Ralph Honner sent a two-word message back to Brigade HQ that so typified his feel for the moment: 'Gona's Gone!'

Gona Mission was a grotesque and nauseating field of slaughter—from both an Australian and Japanese perspective. Lieutenant Alan 'Kanga' Moore, 39th Battalion:

> My enduring memory is of the beach itself, which was the greatest shambles you've ever seen in your life . . . it had been bombed and strafed on a number of occasions; just back from the beach amongst the coconut trees they had a lot of stores . . . they had a bit of food there, there were some bags of rice . . . there was quite a few bodies lying around; the stink was horrible, I don't think they'd ever had latrines or anything; Gona beach was a dirty, filthy mess.[26]

Lieutenant Doug McClean, 39th Battalion:

> They seemed to want to die and we were delighted to oblige them. They didn't give in, they didn't surrender and therefore there is no point in saying we showed them mercy. I found troops [Australians] with grenades unexploded in their hands who'd been trying to push them through these narrow apertures in the logs that the Japs had dug in so well. If ever anyone had earnt a VC those blokes had![27]

Lieutenant-Colonel Ralph Honner:

> We reverently buried our gallant dead and moved out as burial parties went in to dispose of the Japanese—they had buried 638 of them by the end of the next day, but many days later we still stumbled over the ones they didn't find, or momentarily stopped brushing our teeth in the lagoons as decayed bodies nudged past us. We did not

> envy the burial parties their task. We had seen the Japanese put on their respirators when our bombardments churned up the stench of their comrades' rotting corpses. And many of our battle-hardened veterans, fighting their way forward over that polluted ground, were unable to face their food. It was sickening to breathe let alone eat.[28]

Sergeant John 'Moey' Manol, 39th Battalion:

> I'll never forget the feeling of revulsion I had when Gona fell. Gona was a terrible sight to behold; most of the coconut palms, etc. were blown apart by bombs and artillery and mortar fire. Rotting corpses were everywhere, scores of bodies. The huts and water tanks were riddled with bullet holes and the stench was terrible. Gona had been taken at a terrible cost of lives. Walking past Jap positions I saw so many corpses; their mouths, eyes and nostrils full of maggots in that heat; every dead body was putrified in such a short time.
>
> Walking along the beach the next day I was amazed to find a white painted cross, outside a chapel, the only thing at Gona that had not one single scar or bullet hole in it. And at the time it gave me an eerie feeling.[29]

On 10 December 1942, the 39th and 2/14th Battalions journeyed to Haddy's Village where, during a further eight days of fierce fighting against the Amboga River Japanese force, that village finally fell.

On 16 August 1942, Brigadier Arnold Potts had led two of his proud, battle-tested and victorious 21st Brigade Battalions onto the legendary Kokoda Trail. The 2/14th Battalion had totalled 24 officers and 577 other ranks, while his 2/16th had totalled 600 soldiers all told. And by the time the battle for Brigade Hill had occurred in early September, his 2/27th Battalion had been committed to the campaign with 28 officers and 560 other ranks—in total approximately 1800 fit, young Australians of an elite brigade. The 2/14th Battalion left

Gona with 21 soldiers, and when it gathered in its walking wounded and various holding camp personnel its numbers grew to 57. The 2/27th left Gona with three officers and 67 other ranks, and Potts' original command, the 2/16th Battalion, left Gona with eight and 48.

The horrific casualties suffered during the Kokoda campaign and at Gona, in unison with their high sickness casualties, had reduced those proud battalions of August 1942 to three exhausted, ragged groups of malaria-stricken skeletons. But in all this, the spirit of the 21st Brigade was to live on. After leave in Australia, the 7th Division would take in reinforcements from the motorised division: the 'forty thousand horsemen'. The slaughter at the beachhead would be put behind them as they added fresh laurels to their record of achievement in the Ramu–Markham Valley campaign and at Balikpapan. And through it all, Brigadiers Eather and Dougherty would remain with them, serving with great distinction until war's end in Dougherty's case, and until July 1945 in Eather's.

The haunting white Mission cross stands fixed to a timber pole not far from the beach at Gona. And barely 30 yards away from the memorial plaque is a medical aid post and a midwife centre for the people of Gona. It has been funded by some of the soldiers who fought there and by Rotary.

At midday every day, a large metal chime is hit. The sound reverberates across Gona. It is rung for an Anglican angel—perhaps it rings also for Mavis Parkinson and May Hayman, the Anglican missionaries who gave their lives in the service of these people. But it is hard not to think that that chime might not also ring in commemoration of the lives of the desperate Australian soldiers who fought not only their Japanese enemies here, but also the ravages of malaria and scrub typhus—and who died in their droves so that an American general could claim his first beachhead victory before Guadalcanal fell to the American Navy marines.

When the 2/14th Battalion survivors were still some distance from Popondetta airstrip, an American jeep stopped alongside Lieutenant Bob Thompson. The officer in that jeep enquired as to whether the unit would like transport sent out to drive it to Popondetta. Thompson was asked the name of his unit. He replied, 'The 2/14th Battalion.' The American could not have contemplated the casualties the 2/14th had suffered, could not have guessed at the sacrifice. Some time later about twenty trucks arrived to take the 2/14th to Popondetta—all 57 of them.

When you travel to either Sananada or Buna, after a relatively comfortable drive along a picturesque bitumen road, a turn-off takes you along a rough, pot-holed clay track towards those destinations. And then you arrive at a rough bitumen road running across your path. Your guide tells you to turn right. But when he then tells you that you are now driving along the 1942 Dobodura airstrip you must stop. You look to either side of the 'road' and the dimensions of this airstrip become obvious. Kunai grass has pushed up through the old bitumen tarmac on either side.

It doesn't take much of an imagination to see those haunting ghosts. The 39th Battalion had finished its brief campaigning at Sananada after moving from Gona. Let Lieutenant-Colonel Ralph Honner describe one of the great moments in Australian history:

> Down to this point, the war was almost becoming a farce for us; we were only a remnant, and we were malaria-ridden. But as we marched back towards Soputa, we were told that we were to march to Dobodura the next day to the airfield to be evacuated.
>
> Our RMO reported to brigade that some of our troops were not capable of marching to Dobodura and would have to have transport, because they were tottering with malaria—they could hardly stand let alone walk. The edict from Brigade was that transport would be provided to pick up all stragglers, but the battalion would march to Dobodura. I said, 'The 39th Battalion won't have any stragglers, you won't need to pick any of them up.'

> We marched all the way to Dobodura. It was a hot day, a long march. We marched all the way, but mostly we marched in columns of three, two blokes supporting one bloke in the middle. And truckloads of cheering troops went past us. These were the stragglers, who hadn't seen, many of them, much campaigning and less fighting.
>
> When we got to Dobodura, we made an effort, we went back into parade ground formation—one single file . . . We marched across Dobodura airfield and the spectators came out to see this unusual sight . . . and one of them said, 'What mob's this?' And we ignored them, looking straight ahead and marching at attention. But my 2/IC marching at the end of the line barked, 'This is not a mob, this is the 39th!'[30]

There would be no fresh laurels, no further fields for the 39th Militia Battalion. In July 1943 it was disbanded by an army that could have made so much more use of its distinguished commander and his magnificent battalion. At Dobodura on that fateful day the 39th Australian Infantry Battalion not only crossed an airstrip, but crossed also into a priceless place in Australian history.

The first beachhead battle was over. If MacArthur had brief cause to celebrate one victory, then the fall of Buna and Sananda still seemed a remote dream rather than an immediate possibility.

At Buna the Americans were confused, inactive and demoralised. Blamey would now turn to the 7th Australian Division's 3rd Brigade to break the stalemate. The 18th Brigade veterans of Milne Bay would write another stirring if costly chapter in the Australian story.

BOTH IMMEDIATE AND ENDURING

23

It is not a long drive from the Dobodura airstrip to Buna. But it is slow, and as you arrive within a mile or so of the village the track narrows to a pot-holed path that is bordered by thick jungle. The scrub, in fact, comes right up to the sides of the four-wheel-drive. The Papuans fill the holes here and there with stones and pieces of timber.

Both during the wet season and for a period shortly after it you can't get a vehicle into Buna, so you have to wade through waist-deep water to get to the village. But we are visiting during October, and apart from a shallow pot-hole full of water here and there the track is firm.

Like so many other war-ravaged villages, Buna has been relocated. As you swing into the approach to it, you cross a wheel-deep ford and subsequently come upon a substantial collection of raised huts.

You do not stop at the village because this Buna pilgrimage demands that you begin at the beginning. As you follow the course of this 1942 battle, you will retrace your steps. After passing through Giropa Point and Buna, another very narrow track bordered by tall, thick kunai grass takes you alongside the Old Strip and down to the remnant of the bridge crossing the Sememi Creek. The crossing takes you to a track heading north through kunai grass. It is a hot, humid walk, but the anticipation of your arrival at the coast pushes you along quickly.

You enter the coconut plantation. It was planted by Leslie 'Jumbo' Joubert and 'Ernie' Oates in 1917 as a commercial venture which produced 70 tons of copra in 1940.[1] The men planted and managed their Duropa Plantation at Cape Endaiadere for the British New Guinea Development Company, and they also recruited native indentured labour for other enterprises.

Duropa Plantation is essentially neglected now. The orderly rows of palms stand very straight and tall, and provide a shady walk along a narrow footpath through thick, tangled vines and grass. After a short walk you come out onto a beautiful beach. It has black sand, and is narrow but leads to a glorious, dark-green stretch of some of the clearest sea water imaginable.

And then you notice a solitary lean-to and a small, swirling fire about a hundred yards away just in from the beach. As you approach you notice a young mother and her two toddlers curled up together sleeping the heat of the early afternoon away. You look out to sea and the woman's husband is in his canoe, fishing about 350 yards out.

You gaze up and down this beach. Idyllic. Silent. The only thing that violates the serenity of this place is the occasional falling coconut. And then you look up. High in the palms are the bullet scars and holes. If you have stood at Brigade Hill or Isurava—or a score of other places—on the Kokoda Trail—and have been deeply moved, you will be no less moved here, because along this beach from 18 December 1942 the 18th Brigade's 2/9th Battalion transformed this tranquil scene into a shattered, splintered killing ground. This is Cape Endaiadere. Australians should know about it; should revere those who fought and died here; and should also commemorate the larger Battle for Buna.

In their attacks upon Buna during November and early December 1942, the American 32nd Division employed two formations. The first, codenamed Urbana Force, was deployed against the Buna village/government station area. The second, codenamed Warren Force, was directed at the Duropa Plantation–Cape Endaiadere–Strip Point region.

The American Official Historian, summing up the first days of the contest, would later write:

> The men on both the Urbana and Warren fronts were tired and listless. They had not been sufficiently hardened for jungle conditions and, with few exceptions, had not been fresh when they reached the combat zone. Thrown into battle in an exhausted state, most of them had been living on short rations for weeks and their food intake since the fighting began had averaged about a third of a C ration per day—just enough to sustain life. They were shaggy and bearded and their clothes were ragged. Their feet were swollen and in bad shape. Their shoes, which had shrunk in the wet, often had to be cut away so that the troops could even get their feet into them . . . morale was low. Instead of being met, as they had been led to expect, by a few hundred sick and starving Japanese, they found themselves facing apparently large numbers of fresh, well-fed, well-armed troops in seemingly impregnable positions, against whom in almost two weeks of fighting they had failed even to score one noteworthy success.[2]

The Americans hadn't really stood a fair chance. These troops were National Guardsmen from Wisconsin and Michigan, whose lack of basic training and poor standards of physical fitness had made them greener than the jungles and kunai grass in which they were deployed.

They had not fought their first battles in the Middle East, as had the Australians. Therefore, they had not been tried and tested; and most importantly, their officers had predominantly been elevated from the promotion list and not from the crucible of battle. And to add to their degree of difficulty, these unseasoned troops were facing their baptism of fire in a campaign that was proving a terribly exacting test for the tough, experienced Australians of the 7th Division.

MacArthur's patience and preparedness to lose further face had evaporated. Late on the afternoon of 30 November, he summoned General Robert Eichelberger to Government House in Port Moresby and delivered another famous order:

> 'Bob', said General MacArthur in a grim voice. 'I'm putting you in command at Buna. Relieve Harding. I am

> sending you in Bob, and I want you to remove all officers who won't fight. Relieve regimental and battalion commanders if necessary, put sergeants in charge of battalions and corporals in charge of companies—anyone who will fight. Time is of the essence; the Japs may land reinforcements any night . . .
>
> 'I want you to take Buna, or not come back alive'.[3]

The next day MacArthur informed Eichelberger that if he captured Buna he (MacArthur) would decorate him and release his name to the press. This was an enormous concession on MacArthur's part—from the onset of the Papuan campaign only he had been writing the press releases. All wireless and newspaper reports had to 'bear out the tone of the official communiques'.[4] Reports from correspondents from Papua were constantly held up 'for a week or more in Townsville or Brisbane—mainly Brisbane, because they do not agree with the communiques'.[5]

Here is the sad and sorry result of a supreme commander who, in command of a multinational force, has failed to select a multinational staff, has failed to engender an atmosphere of teamwork and cohesion, and has disparaged a coalition power's performance for his own politico-military gain. Now, when the tables have been turned, and his soldiers have failed and have been justifiably criticised, he orders Eichelberger to unravel a military mess that he, MacArthur, has created. A promise of a decoration and the release of Eichelberger's name to the press is nothing more than the act of an egotistical general who assumes that his subordinates' are similarly motivated by purely egotistical incentives.

Eichelberger arrived at Dobodura on 1 December. He acted decisively and with great speed. He relieved General Harding the following day and replaced two of his senior Warren Force commanders with members of his own staff.

When success at Buna still did not eventuate, General Blamey conceived of two ill-considered and desperate measures to break the stalemate. The first was a proposal that the 2/9th Battalion be used to stage an amphibious landing at Buna. Had that plan gone ahead, that magnificent unit would have been butchered as it attempted to take the entrenched and impregnable Japanese positions. Even with the planned support of the Americans, the Australian attack would have failed.

The second plan did eventuate and it, too, failed dismally. On 5 December 1942 on Warren Force's Cape Endaiadere front, five Bren gun carriers were used to support the American infantry's attempt to prise open the Japanese defences. Bren gun carriers were designed for speedy reconnaissance work and the transportation of infantry across contested ground. They were open-topped, had low sides, and their armour was not thick enough to withstand anything more lethal than small arms fire. The predictable slaughter transpired. The Australian Official Historian:

> . . . within half an hour, the five vehicles lay abandoned, proof of the dictum that carriers were not tanks. And, just in rear of them . . . [the] leading company was shot to pieces from Duropa Plantation or from behind the log barricade . . . [the] whole attack was halted before it was well begun; the blazing sun now sickened the discouraged survivors.[6]

These brave Australian carrier crews had no real chance: they were highly vulnerable to sniper fire from the coconut fronds and to grenade lobbing by the enemy. And once the crews left their vehicles, which were often immobilised by fallen logs or tangled vines, they were exposed to bunker and further sniper fire. At Buna today, the visitor will notice remnants of carrier tracks used as garden borders and as supports for outdoor cooking equipment.

Blamey, to his great credit, realised that the Warren Force Buna sector was the key to the final capture of Buna. Such a conquest would obviously assist the Americans, but would also render the nearby Allied airstrips far more secure. With these points uppermost in his thinking, he now determined that a fresh force would be committed to the Warren Force area, and that this time tank support would mean just that: tanks.

Blamey chose Brigadier Wootten's 18th Brigade as his infantry force and the 2/6th Armoured Regiment as the tank unit. And he demanded that Wootten was to have command of Warren Force.

On 11 December, Wootten made a reconnaissance of the Buna area and decided that the Cape Endaiadere area was the most suited to the critical employment of the tanks. His proposal was adopted.

> The camera is part of you, it's your skin! Emotions are powerful, they hit hard, they wash over you. They can't overwhelm you, you're doing a job . . . Sometimes it was an emotion that took the picture.[7]

George Silk was three years younger than Damien Parer and had worked with him in the Middle East. Born in New Zealand, he had learned photography while working in a camera store where the proprietor encouraged him to try out the more complex cameras such as the Rolleiflex, the Contax and the German Leica. Silk was just beginning to acquire a reputation as a still photographer when the war broke out. He felt it was his duty to join up but there was one problem: he was scared of firearms!

George Silk: 'The only way I could go to war was to photograph it. And indeed it was important someone should photograph it. Instinctively I had developed this documentary sense. I had been following documentary movies and had made some documentary films.'[8]

He first tried the New Zealand recruiting office but distrusted the promise 'sign here and you'll be a photographer tomorrow'. So Silk decided to go to Australia, and if all else failed join the AIF, as he did not have the fare to go back to New Zealand. After wandering around Sydney for three weeks he finally took a train to Canberra to see the prime minister. Silk got as far as Menzies' private secretary who, incredibly, agreed to show the prime minister the album of photographs he had brought with him. After showing the shots to the Cabinet, Menzies instructed his secretary to send Silk to Melbourne.

Upon their arrival in the Middle East, Silk and Parer found that covering the desert war was frustrating. The action took place over huge distances, and the war always seemed just outside their grasp. On his return from the desert campaign, Silk missed the Kokoda campaign because he had taken leave back in New Zealand. Silk: 'By the time I got up there the Australians had pushed across the top of the ranges and were about to take over Kokoda Strip. The Army told me to wait and within a couple of days I'd be able to fly into Kokoda. And so I flew into Kokoda and joined General Vasey . . .'[9]

At Gona George Silk took some impressive stills, but he seemed to just keep missing out on the action. It was always a case of finding out a battle was on after it had started. After the fall of Gona, Silk found out that the Australians were to be sent to Buna, where the Americans were bogged down. If Gona is seen as some of Silk's best work—near the action but not in it—his Buna shots were to prove some of the most outstanding of the Pacific War. This time, Silk was not going to film the aftermath of war, he was going to stand up in the middle of it and do some shooting of his own.

Blamey's original orders for the capture of the Warren Force sector at Buna had envisaged an initial infantry force consisting of the 18th Brigade's 2/9th Battalion and one battalion of the 7th Brigade—both formations being from Milne Bay.

But Wootten immediately requested the use of the assigned three corvettes, *Broome*, *Ballarat* and *Colac*, to also pick up his 2/10th Battalion from its Wanigela and Portlock Harbour positions and bring it forward to Buna immediately after the 2/9th had landed there. Wootten's request was granted.

At Milne Bay, the 2/9th Battalion boarded 26 officers and 638 other ranks on the three corvettes from 6.00 p.m. on 12 December. The three vessels left Milne Bay at 3.00 a.m. the following morning. Although conditions were extremely crowded, the troops had an uneventful passage until nearing Cape Sudest. There an unidentified aircraft dropped a flare, and a report was received that an enemy convoy was steaming towards them. The three corvettes withdrew, with the intention of landing the 2/9th at Portlock Harbour.

Before the ships departed, Lieutenant-Colonel Cummings, his adjutant, intelligence officer and a small party, including the 2/10th Battalion's CO, Lieutenant-Colonel Dobbs, and his intelligence officer were landed at Cape Sudest. That party spent a cheerless night in a shallow swamp not far from the Americans.

On 15 December 1942, the 2/9th, after having spent the previous day confined aboard the three corvettes in extremely hot and humid conditions, marched in full battle order to Hariko. This entailed a chest-deep crossing of the Samboga River and the traversing of stifling scrubland. It arrived at Buna during the late evening of 16 December.

While the 2/9th Battalion had been thus engaged, the 2/6th Armoured Regiment had had a much more challenging time arriving at Buna. The 2/6th had been formed in NSW in 1941 in anticipation of service in the Middle East. Its training had been for desert warfare. Trooper John Wilson, 2/6th Armoured Regiment:

> In 1942 we received Stuart (U.S.) light tanks and trained with them at Singleton and Narrabri (NSW) in open country with the emphasis on training for the Middle East and defence of Australia. There was no training with infantry. Solid training took place with the tanks for about a six month's [*sic*] period mostly at troop, regiment and brigade level. The equipment was fair, some of it was old. There were a few different marks of tanks, some tanks had flat rivet six sided turrets; they were the older ones. The rest had round turrets. The U.S. wireless sets were replaced by British No. 19 Sets . . . The Stuart Tank was about 14 tonnes, with 1½" of rather soft steel armour plate. These tanks were designed for fast running in open country, mainly for reconnaissance. They were powered by a seven cylinder radial airplane engine, high revving, and running on high octane fuel . . . The guns were 37mm cannon and two Browning Machine Guns of .30 calibre. One MG mounted in the turret alongside the 37mm gun and the other a free operating hull gun. There was a five man crew as follows: Crew Commander, who could either be an officer, a sergeant or a corporal; a turret

> gunner, a turret gun loader and wireless operator, driver and hull gunner. The driver and hull gunner were seated, the other three crew members had to stand. All crew members were trained to be interchangeable . . .[10]

While the tanks were certainly an improvement upon Bren gun carriers, they were not suited to the assigned Buna task. They were designed purely for fast reconnaissance over open ground, where speed—and not thick armour plating protection—was the priority. Further, the 2/6th had not undertaken infantry support training.

By 15 December, four tanks of the unit's C Squadron, under the command of Captain Whitehead, had arrived at Oro Bay from Port Moresby aboard the Dutch freighter *Karsik*. They were deployed at a lying-up position behind Brigade HQ. Four more tanks from B Squadron, under the command of Lieutenant McCrohon, were at that time making their way from Milne Bay. The primitive nature of the docking and landing facilities in the Buna region made the selection of the General Stuart tanks the only viable option for this Buna operation. There was no available method of landing the heavier conventional infantry support tanks.

By nightfall on 16 December, Wootten had the 2/9th Battalion, a squadron of the 2/6th Armoured Regiment, detachments of the 2/4th Field Regiment (artillery), five Bren gun carriers and the 2/5th Field Ambulance deployed at Buna. He proposed to use the American force of just over two battalions and the 2/10th Battalion as his reserve, when it arrived.

Wootten's orders were to capture the area between Cape Endaiadere, the New Strip, the Old Strip and the Buna government station. He planned that the operation would have three phases. The first was the capture of the tongue of land which stretched from the eastern end of the New Strip to the coast, then along to the mouth of the Sememi Creek and back again to his start point. The second phase involved the capture of the area bordered by the western end of the New Strip running along the southern perimeter of the Old Strip to its north-western end, and back along the inland side of Sememi Creek. The third and final phase was the capture of the area from the end of the Old Strip through Giropa Point, and then over the ground leading to the Buna government station.

From the Duropa Plantation inland the ground becomes gradually less firm, with belts of kunai grass and scrub. As the area of Sememi Creek is gained the ground becomes swampy, so much so that infantry access to the Old Strip from the inland side appears impossible.

In much the same vein as their masterly Gona fire-plan, the Japanese used the natural features of the Buna area to their utmost advantage. Also, the bunkers at Buna were fortified by 44-gallon aviation fuel drums, which had been filled with earth, tied together, and employed as formidable defences. Corrugated iron was used in conjunction with palm logs in some of these bunkers to assist in roof making. Some small number of the Buna bunkers were of concrete construction. Entry to these posts were by side and/or small rear doors. Firing slits, narrow in height but long in width, facilitated a wide arc of fire, and the bunkers could be manned or left vacant according to their changing tactical need. These structures were mutually supported and often connected by crawl trenches, which were just deep enough to avoid Australian fire. And as at Gona, the bunkers were magnificently camouflaged by earth and coconut fronds and other selected vegetation. Any approaching soldier had to be virtually next to them before he could sight them—usually too late to avoid strong, enfiladed fire.

The sniping at Buna would have two forms. The first was the obvious: snipers strapped high in the Duropa Plantation coconut palms. The second was more devious. Scattered throughout Duropa Plantation and later along the thick jungle positions on the western side of the Old Strip were small one-man pits from which enemy snipers could shoot at the Australians after they had passed. They could then cover the top of their position and so repeat the exercise until they were sooner or later discovered and eliminated.

The enemy could also mortar an approaching force and further bombard it by the use of two anti-aircraft guns, one deployed at the top of the Old Strip and the other along its western side, although these guns were more suited to an

Warren Force—Brigadier Wootten's plan

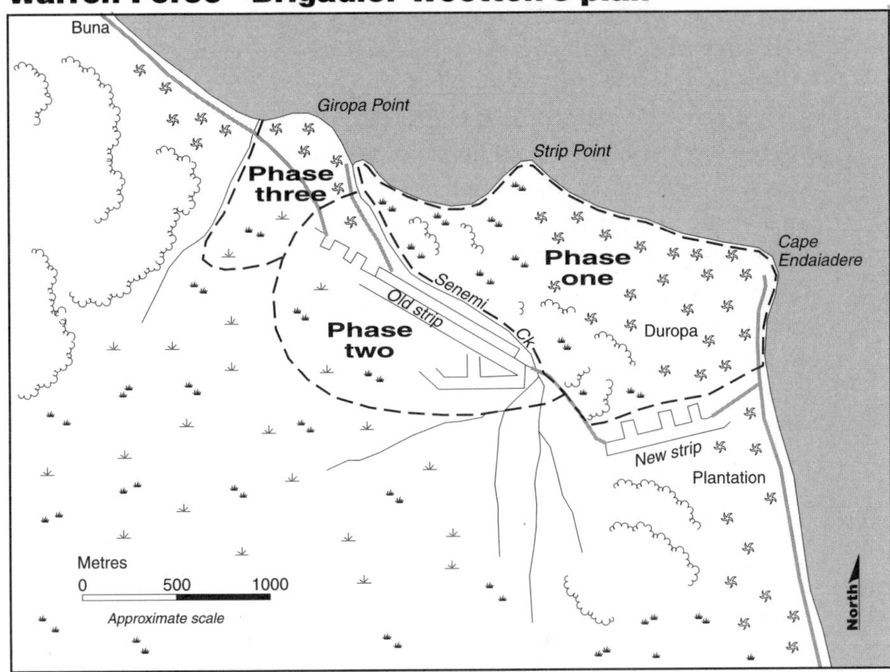

Warren Force—the ground

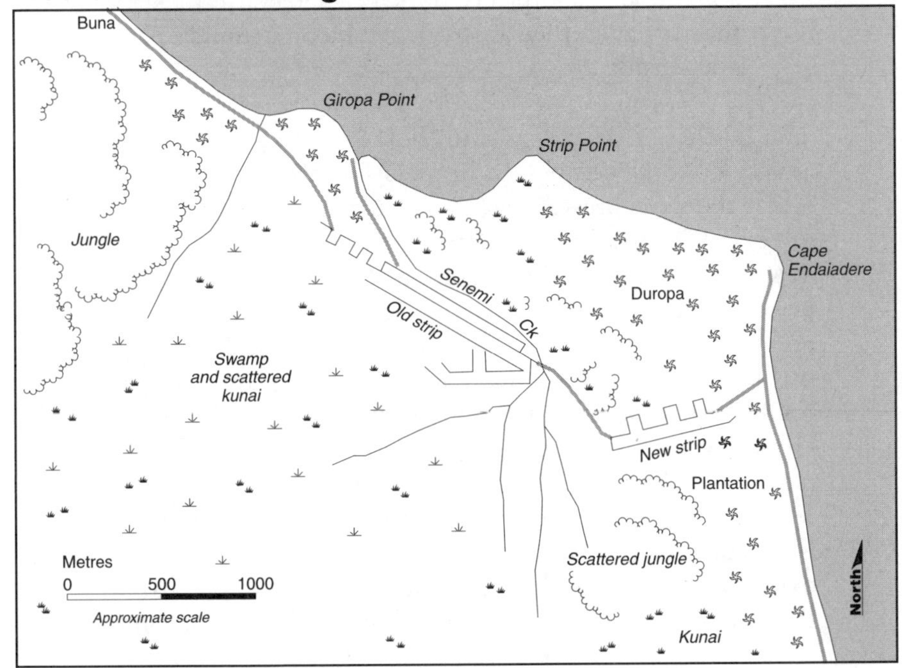

enemy force moving on the Old Strip itself. They could also concentrate their infantry in any desired area in already dug and prepared fortifications according to the nature of the Allied thrust.

Given the nature of the ground, the lack of American success over it and the excellence of the Japanese fire-plan and the numbers of Japanese defenders, detailed reconnaissance and astute planning were, as was the case at Gona, critical prerequisites to any sensible attack. MacArthur had already issued Eichelberger with orders that hardly encouraged a measured American approach to Buna's capture. And the Australians' approach was no less rushed and ill-considered—and unprofessional.

Upon the arrival of the 2/9th at Buna, Wootten ordered its commanding officer to attack the following day. Strains of Gona. Lieutenant-Colonel Cummings:

> And my battalion had to march all the bloody way twenty miles across tidal creeks . . . and Wootten ordered them to go in the next morning . . . and this was one of my other arguments with Wootten! I said, 'They've got to have a good sleep and plenty of tucker, and warm tucker . . . the day after they'll go in. It's bloody stupid! They're buggered![11]

The truth is that it was also 'bloody stupid' to stage the attack on 18 December. In his decision, Wootten was surely under the same pressures as Dougherty and Eather had been under at Gona. An experienced commander such as Wootten would not have committed his brigade without prior intelligence and planning. There can only be two reasons for his haste. The first was that he felt that the task was in fact an easy one; that experienced elite troops such as his 18th Brigade would automatically and speedily succeed. Given events across the beachhead up to this time, and during the Americans' fighting at Buna, this theory would seem unlikely. But the second reason is more plausible. It is simply that Wootten was reacting to the repeated demands by MacArthur and Blamey to quickly capture Buna. Wootten had conferred with Blamey on 10 December in Port Moresby when he had received his orders. It is hard to believe that similar pressure was not placed upon him as had been placed on others at Gona and upon the Americans at Buna.

The fact that Wootten was also prepared to stage his first-phase attack using the 2/9th Battalion before his two remaining 18th Brigade battalions had arrived at Buna also demonstrates the point. Captain Tom Parbury, OC C Company, 2/9th Battalion:

> As far as I know, no recce of the Japanese positions was made. If there was, I was left in ignorance about it. There was no indication of the Jap bunkers; where they were, nothing of this was given to me.[12]

Private 'Chalky' Morris, Intelligence Section, 2/9th Battalion:

> Intelligence. Nil! I think they were driven that hard by the higher ups . . . none of us had any idea of what we were going into. We knew it wasn't going to be easy, but I don't think that we expected the casualties that we had there that morning.[13]

Private Bill Spencer recalled the beginning of the battle in his memoir, *In the Footsteps of Ghosts*:

> On the afternoon of 17 December Lieutenant-Colonel Cummings, Major Maloney, Sergeant Elliot and I moved out towards the Japanese lines to mark a start line. I carried a sandbag full of start line lights (a small single-celled torch with a red glass). We stopped and climbed up onto the stumps of coconut palms to have a better view of the terrain. We remained there for some ten minutes and neither saw nor were fired on by the enemy. After we climbed down and were talking, Lieutenant-Colonel Cummings remarked, 'It's going to be tough over that patch tomorrow!' A decision was made that the start lamps would not be used . . .
>
> The start line ran in a dog-leg from the end of New Strip to the coast.[14]

A commanding officer and various intelligence personnel mounting a number of coconut palm stumps and gazing in the general direction of the enemy does not constitute adequate reconnaissance before a vital military assault. Further, such behaviour fails dismally to show sufficient respect to an enemy as competent and resolute as the Japanese at Buna in December 1942.

To comply with Wootten's first-phase plan, Cummings ordered a three-company assault. His D Company, commanded by Captain Griffen, had the task of pushing through the roughly two hundred yard front along the coast to Cape Endaiadere. In short, Griffen was to capture most of Duropa Plantation. In the centre, A Company, commanded by Captain Taylor, was to capture the inland fringe of the plantation and an adjacent 150 yards of grass and scrub ground running alongside Griffen's area. On the left flank Captain Parbury's C Company was ordered to gain 150 yards of ground to the north of the coastal end of the New Strip. Parbury's soldiers were to comprise a pivot upon which a 2/9th arc would swing north-west to the mouth of Sememi Creek. Captain Benson's B Company was to act as the battalion reserve.

In the dimming light of 17 December, the 2/9th moved near the coast to its assembly point, about three hundred yards from its start line. Wootten's remark that 'There'll be no turning back tomorrow!',[15] which was overheard by his officers, was a sad indictment of the pressure that had been placed on him.

Think of it. Battalions of Americans who had made no ground. No reconnaissance, no measured planning, questionable support consisting of reconnaissance tanks, not infantry tanks. And above all else, a movement into an enemy position brilliantly fortified with numerous bunkers and snipers and an enemy who will not withdraw when the pressure mounts, but will carry on his war with a terrible resolve. The Queenslanders of the 2/9th Battalion had the odds of war stacked inexorably against them. These soldiers were arguably an elite battalion of an elite AIF brigade—they had served at Tobruk, Milne Bay and later would fight at Sanananda, Shaggy Ridge and Balikpapan. But none of the survivors of 18 December 1942 at Buna would ever forget this day; it was and still is burnt forever in their minds.

Bill Spencer, from the Intelligence Section, stood near the start line as his battalion crossed:

> At 7.00 am I was the spellbound onlooker to actions the likes of which I had never witnessed before—or have witnessed since—as the tanks moved forward into a barbarous inferno ahead of the walking paced infantry. The roar of their engines added to the mounting crescendo of noise from both Vickers and enemy machine guns and a wall of small arms lead—it was like nothing the 2/9th Battalion had experienced. The sky seemed to rain debris as small pieces of undergrowth and bark floated down like confetti, and the repeated crack of bullets and chatter of automatic weapons and explosions close by, the acrid smell and eye-irritating smoke from discharging weapons and grenades, added to the extreme discomfort experienced by the men. Soldiers were dropping like sacks. There appeared to be utter confusion, but among all the chaos the courageous men moved resolutely forward . . .
>
> There were no sounds from the wounded, as the pain of a gunshot wound comes later; sudden death was always silent. Our casualties were immediate and heavy as the thin, green, determined line moved forward. The bodies of those who had fallen became sprinkled with leaf and bark litter ripped from the undergrowth by bullets and shrapnel, which somehow softened the starkness of death.[16]

Private George Walpole, who was with the Machine Gun Platoon, also witnessed his battalion's extraordinary advance:

> You'd swear they were going in for a cup of tea! We laid down a barrage of Vickers and of course we were sitting watching . . . the way I explained that to my mother, when I saw it, and, I was crying at the time, they went in just cool and calm as you like.[17]

Telling casualties will often either stop an advance in its tracks, or at least severely hinder its momentum—but there was not a bit of it on this stirring but tragic day.

When the 2/9th crossed its start line, George Silk had decided that this was one battle that he would not miss. Incredibly, he was just *forward* of the troops when they crossed the start line. Perhaps he liked the look of his chances of both surviving and taking gripping photographs that day in the Duropa Plantation. His startling shots—which capture nearly everything bar the flying bullets—were taken at enormous personal risk.

In his attack along the coast, Captain Griffen ordered Lieutenant MacIntosh's 18 Platoon to the right or beach side of the plantation with Corporal Barnet's tank in support; Lieutenant Sivyer's 17 Platoon to the left flank with Lieutenant McCrohon's tank in support; and Warrant-Officer 2 Vince Donnelly's 16 Platoon to move behind the forward two platoons. The third allotted tank, Sergeant Lattimore's, was between the other two tanks. Thus, the forward platoons attacked the Duropa Plantation with two platoons forward and three tanks offering support.

While senior commanders were either too hard pressed to order or conduct even fundamental reconnaissance, there were various junior commanders whose initiative was most impressive. On the night of the 17th, an early success on the following day was engineered. Corporal Barnet:

> Lieutenant MacIntosh, who was the platoon commander . . . he and I crawled forward on the evening of the 17th in the dark. We found that in front there were some very heavily armed Japanese pillboxes. We veered off to the right and crawled up and found no Japanese and so we actually walked up and found that right up to nearly Cape Endaiadere we found . . . no Japanese . . . but there were these rows of pillboxes almost right up to the beach. They were at right angles to the beach so that when we drove up the beach next day, we were firing down their lines . . . we created quite a bit of havoc by doing that.[18]

Warren Force—Phase 1— 2/9th Battalion

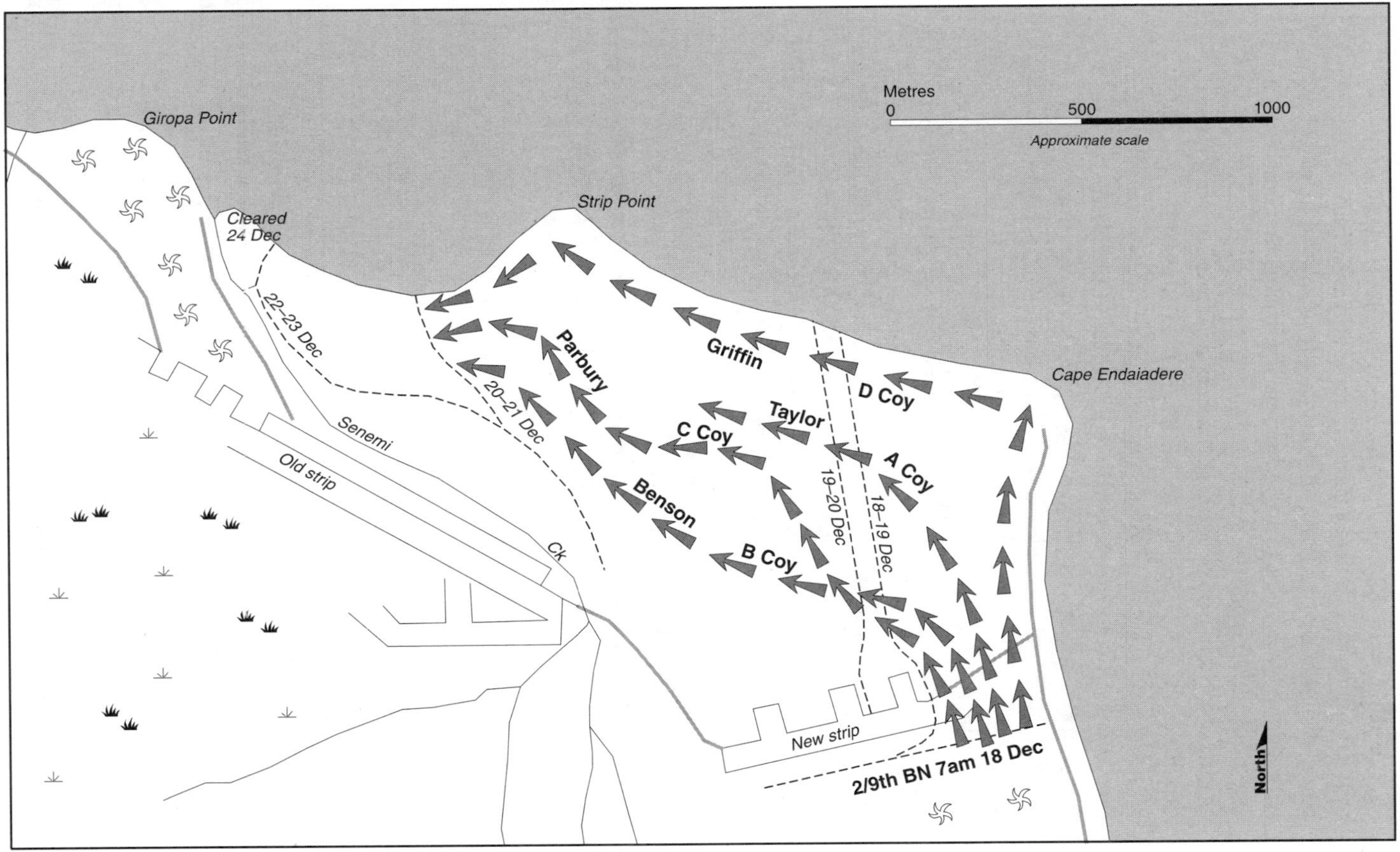

With the benefit of the previous night's reconnaissance uppermost in their minds, Barnet's tank and MacIntosh's men made straight for the first pillbox noted the night before. The tank began firing at the log joins, or the firing slits, and thus under fire the Japanese were unable to prevent the infantry closing on their bunker and grenading it. The tank crews and the infantry soon learnt to simply cover the sides of the bunkers—when any survivors ran out of the side or rear doors, they were mowed down with a cold-hearted purpose.

Barely seventy minutes after the start of the assault, MacIntosh sent a signal back to Cummings: 'Kilcoy taken.' The 2/9th had a foothold on Cape Endaiadere.

While MacIntosh had made rather rapid ground adjacent to the coast, Sivyer's platoon had faced a more torrid time. Without the advantage of a secure seaward flank, they had been moving through coconut and secondary growth and striking concentrated enfiladed bunker and sniper fire.

Moving in the vicinity of one of the burnt-out carriers from the ill-fated attack on 5 December, Sivyer was killed and his platoon sergeant wounded. Before long, 17 Platoon had lost its officer and about twenty of its approximately thirty members were killed or wounded. Sergeant 'Shorty' Walters assumed command of the survivors but was killed soon after.

Given that it was estimated that there were 36 bunkers in the area, the tanks could not account for them all. But both the soldiers of the 2/9th and their tank comrades soon worked out a suitable method of eliminating those they found. Trooper Wilson was in McCrohon's tank:

> . . . the crew commander worked out with the infantry leaders a plan as follows—the infantry leader would indicate the bunker which was holding him up by firing a Very pistol at it, or throwing a grenade, or just pointing. We would advance within 10 or 15 feet so that we could line up the 37mm cannon at the correct angle . . . using AP and HE shot to enlarge the opening. This usually took ten rounds. An infantry volunteer would then crawl forward . . . The Japs inside who survived would usually attempt to leave by the side entrance, which we would cover with our MGs. Very few escaped. This was the basic

> routine for a couple of hours, and then we would have to pull back about 50 yards or so to our base, refuel, and replenish ammo. The infantry often ran short of ammunition so we hung cloth bandoliers with 303 ammunition on the back of the tanks hanging down about 2 feet off the ground so they could reach up and grab same.[19]

Donnelly, following his two lead platoons forward, accounted for one bunker that had been missed. When he and his platoon reached Cape Endaiadere, they found MacIntosh's men holding the objective. But when they looked for the other platoon, 17 Platoon, they could not find them. Nine survivors out of a total platoon strength of about thirty-five are not always easy to find. D Company's assault was a startling but costly endeavour.

But the further inland the fighting, the greater the degree of difficulty the 2/9th faced and the greater its casualties became.

After having no sooner finished his fighting on MacIntosh's front, Barnet received a distress call:

> We got a call from Jack Lattimore's tank which was straddled on a coconut log and he called us for help . . . we started shooting at the Japanese and hunting them away, and I said to my gunner Rod James, who was an excellent gunner, 'Take the paint off Jack's tank, and hunt those Nips back!' . . . we ran out of ammunition, and we heard Lattimore calling out for help, 'Don't leave us Splinter!' He couldn't hear us, so as soon as we replenished we came back and gave covering fire while Lattimore's crew got out of their tank.[20]

When MacIntosh had signalled 'Kilcoy taken' at 8.10 a.m., progress in the centre of the 2/9th Battalion's first-phase attack—A Company's front just inland from Duropa Plantation—had been less spectacular. Corporal Ernie Randell of 7 Platoon was one member of a rapidly diminishing force which was fighting desperately about two hundred yards behind D Company:

> The ground was strewn with old trunks of coconut palms making it difficult for the tanks to manoeuvre. I had lost a couple of my section killed before we got near the Jap defences. Suddenly, my mate waved me urgently to his side.
>
> Here in an open slit trench in full battle order were ten or a dozen Japs. They were watching a tank go by and hadn't noticed us. We took care of them. Now that we had reached the pillboxes we hurled grenades down through the slits but they were promptly thrown back at us. Ever try holding a grenade for a few seconds?
>
> As the battle grew we formed small groups. There were only two of my section left. Myself and Les Judd . . .
>
> There was so much small arms fire around it was not possible to tell if snipers were operating. However, during a lull in which our troops who were totally exhausted, rested for a while, a sniper started to operate. A shot rang out. Lyle Hicks was kneeling beside a coconut palm. I yelled, 'Did you see where that came from?' 'No' he replied, 'But it was damn close to me.' As he spoke another shot rang out and Lyle slumped forward shot through the temple. We up and dived for the cover of the tank. This sniper killed more men that same afternoon despite our efforts to locate him. I had a tank knock out several palms that could have been hiding him. When we went forward next morning, we found his hiding spot.[21]

There were two main reasons for A Company being further behind their D Company comrades. The first was the ground. A Company was not lucky enough to have a closed right sea flank, and the ground itself over which they fought had more scrub and kunai grass than the more covered coconut palm and secondary growth of the Duropa Plantation. The second limiting factor was the fact that A Company's three tanks ran into considerable trouble.

Within about thirty minutes of the advance from their start line, Lieutenant Curtiss' tank bellied on a stump. Although infantry covering fire allowed the crew's flight from that now stationary tank, the Japanese managed to burn it out. Later during that fateful morning, Corporal Cambridge's tank was also lost. That left Sergeant Church's tank as the surviving A Company support tank. Late that morning, after MacIntosh had signalled 'Kilcoy held', two of his tanks were transferred to Taylor's A Company sector. The battle raged on.

But it was along C Company's perimeter that the real trouble, and tragic slaughter, reached its appalling climax.

Captain Tom Parbury's C Company began taking casualties from the moment it crossed the start line. As its dogged soldiers continued to push on through the first hundred yards of kunai grass, the Japanese laid a continuous blanket of fire across its unsupported front, which resulted in 46 of the 87 in the company lying dead, dying or wounded in that relatively small area.

Worst hit was Lieutenant De Vantier's right flank platoon, which lost its commander and all of its NCOs except one—who was wounded. Parbury called his men to ground. Time to assess the situation. Harry 'The Wog' Dixon, so named because of his fascination with all things Middle Eastern, was a member of the Mortar Platoon and went in with Parbury's men:

> It was bloody time to do it wasn't it? There was nothing left! . . . I never expected to live . . . but things turned out differently. Tom Parbury called out to Corporal Les Boylan, 'Call the roll!' And he rolled over on his side in this grass, he got it out of his haversack and called the bloody roll. You wouldn't believe it! And some wouldn't call out of course, and some would sing out, 'I'm wounded!' And then another bloke would say, 'He's dead!' And the Japs weren't any more than fifty yards in front of us! They had us pinned down and we couldn't move. We knew the bastards were there, but you couldn't actually see them . . .[22]

Captain Tom Parbury:

> I advised Cummings by phone that we had suffered frightful losses and were unable to proceed further until tank support was furnished. He told me to try infiltration,

> which would not be possible, because the bunkers were close together and self-supporting, and the tree snipers had every inch of ground covered, and we had no cover to advance. I reluctantly sent Sgt Morey in to do this . . . I still feel remorse about this.[23]

Sergeant Morey and a section from Warrant-Officer Jesse's reserve platoon attempted to carry out the order. They were all dead by the time the last of them had covered twenty yards of worthless kunai grass.

B Company had supposedly been deployed as the battalion reserve for that fateful day. The fact is that this company took casualties almost immediately the battle started, and was committed to action shortly after zero hour. 'Snow' Hynard of B Company made diary entries each day at Buna:

> 7 am we moved into front line and the Japs threw everything they had at us, they were zinging over my head like hornets. We had a few tanks and moved up behind them. In the first ten minutes my officer was killed and my corporal was cut in the head with a grenade. The first 'deadun' I saw was a Jap, who had been that way for weeks. I surprised myself by my lack of emotion. We were pinned down by a sniper who was only a few yards away in front in a sangar.
>
> I saw Scotty our stretcher bearer walking back with a wounded arm, he had just passed me when this sniper got him in the stomach. It was terrible to hear his groans, but we had orders not to help anyone, but keep going. We disposed of the sniper with hand grenades and moved from one coconut tree to the other. The Japs had innumerable machine gun nests in concrete sangars and they had coconuts and creepers growing over them so we could not see them until we were right on them.[24]

Rapidly following up the forward D and A Companies, B Company employed a well-learnt Milne Bay lesson. All ground taken was carefully examined, as the enemy often left snipers or isolated small pits whose occupants shot selected rearward troops coming through. B Company's fighting, hard on the heels of the two forward companies, was fraught with little less danger and tension. And to look was not necessarily to find. Vernon Hansen, 2/9th Mortar Platoon:

> I remember one sniper there. He would only fire now and again. But when he shot, the man he shot, he killed him. He was always shot through the heart. He might go and lay there for an hour. They found him under a couple of palm leaves.[25]

Private 'Chalky' Morris was with B Company as their Intelligence Section member:

> Actually their fire power, their machine gunners were some of the best that I ever came up against. And their snipers were good . . . they had little foxholes. In some cases they had crawl trenches . . . I shot one trying to get out of his foxhole into a pillbox. Then we went through that . . . and I got wounded, through the elbow, no bones broken, but I lost the feeling in my hand . . .
>
> As I was walking out, I passed Eichelberger with Wootten talking to him. And Wootten said to Eichelberger, 'Now! Say my men won't fight!' I heard him say that! I was seven or eight feet from them. I also heard one Yanky say, 'Ah, that's what they did on the Somme!' Because they were supposed to follow us in and do the mopping up, the little foxholes we missed, but they sat down where they were . . . and this is why the four companies went straight up. B Company wasn't in reserve. I went in with the last tank on the left.[26]

'Say my men won't fight!' said Wootten. 'Chalky' Morris' eavesdropping is terribly significant. Wootten's comment to Eichelberger demonstrates the sheer intensity of the feeling against the Americans and their unfair, misguided and counterproductive criticism of the Australians along the Kokoda Trail and at Milne Bay. And when the Americans had had their opportunity to show the Australians how it was to be done, they had shown themselves to be rank amateurs.

But the hurried, unmilitary beachhead methodology

reflects no less poorly on the Australian command than it does upon the Americans. The savage professionalism and sheer guts of the 2/9th Battalion and their tank comrades at Cape Endaiadere on 18 December 1942 should have been capitalised upon. They should have been reinforced by the 2/10th to maintain their hard-won momentum. And it took two enterprising young soldiers, one from each unit, to show yet again the priceless value of reconnaissance along the beach the night before the attack. Reconnaissance, astute planning and concentration of force should always come before the guts and determination. Wootten's comment to Eichelberger, therefore, smacks of an understandable reaction to the Americans; but, sadly, it also indicates a willingness to sacrifice priceless infantry for senseless and essentially unproductive speed. Strains of Gona.

When, at 1.00 p.m. on that fateful day, three tanks were shifted across to Parbury's C Company remnant, a dramatic change occurred. Parbury:

> I then outlined a plan to Curtiss for Jesse's Platoon to advance in line with the tanks with a section between each tank and the remnants of De Vantier's Platoon on the right and Lt Pinwell's behind the tanks.
>
> An hour after the tanks arrived the recommenced attack, with Jesse firing Very lights into the Jap bunkers, began. Tank shells poured into the bunkers setting several alight. Everyone seemed to be firing, creating a crescendo of noise, eventually breaking the Japanese resistance. They fled from their posts.
>
> It was a very successful action and the remnants of C Coy were grateful. If only we had had the tanks for the first attack, what a difference it would have made.[27]

The point is that Parbury's C Company could have merely held its front and kept the enemy pinned down by fire, while the breakthrough—which did transpire—had occurred through Duropa Plantation. The exercise undertaken at 1.00 p.m. could then have occurred anyway without the tragic casualties of that morning.

At Buna on 18 December 1942, the 2/9th Battalion lost five officers and 49 other ranks killed in action and six and

111 wounded, giving it a total casualty count of 171. Statistics. Bill Spencer, Intelligence Section, 2/9th:

> Moving around between the companies was a macabre and at times hair-raising task. It was sickening to see the number of mutilated, dead bodies lying everywhere, together with the torn undergrowth, blood-stained clothing and discarded utensils of war. Some of the dead lay or were slumped in natural positions, appearing to be in a deep, peaceful sleep. I thought one of our lads, Jack Hardwick, was asleep, and I had to gently push him to make sure. Poor old Jack did not wake up. Any thoughts of peace were driven from your mind when you heard the sharp crack of a sniper's bullet. Although you knew that it was not the one you could hear that claimed you, you still instinctively ducked . . .
>
> On 19 December the 2/9th took stock of its gained ground, reorganised, and continued to clean out all the enemy defences encountered the previous day. Burial parties were kept busy with their sad, noisome task.[28]

Wootten's orders to Cummings on 20 December anticipated the completion of his first-phase plan: the capture of the remaining ground along the coast to the mouth of Sememi Creek and back along that creek to the airstrips. To support the advance, an artillery and mortar barrage and Vickers machine-gun fire were to be used just before zero hour at 7.00 a.m. The 2/6th was ordered to supply four tanks with Lieutenants Gunn and McCrohon in command.

At first the ground gained was impressive. After some time spent in fighting out of the Duropa Plantation, the forward companies broke out into marshy scrub and kunai grass which spread all the way to Sememi Creek. At this point, Captain Taylor was wounded and Parbury took over the inland thrust.

While Griffen rounded Strip Point and pushed on, Parbury's Company, closely followed by Benson's B Company, began a movement through very marshy country, which resulted in their two supporting tanks becoming bogged. The remaining two tanks now pushed along the firm coastal ground. As Parbury's unsupported C Company moved into a further belt of kunai grass they met strong opposition. Tom Parbury:

> We came under machine gun fire from the enemy whose line ran from Sememi Creek north to the coast. Pinwell's Platoon came up against the Jap positions, with one post being knocked by a grenade thrown by Sgt MacCarthy. The platoon came under flanking fire and was pushed back. Pinwell was killed along with 3 others and MacCarthy was wounded in the face.[29]

As Private Jock Milne of the Intelligence Section moved forward to re-establish contact with Pinwell's platoon, he was shot by a sniper. When he crawled further forward to gain that line, he missed it, and was bayoneted by the enemy. Milne lay doggo in the kunai grass within earshot of the Japanese. Somewhere to his left in the haven of that grass, Milne knew that Private Jack Allen also lay wounded. But each could only guess at the other's fate.

Later, a conference was called between Cummings, Parbury and Griffen. Almost immediately the Japanese mortared the area with the result that Parbury and a number of other ranks were wounded. At 1.50 p.m., with Parbury unable to continue and the number of C Company ranks very rapidly dwindling, Captain Griffen assumed command of the now amalgamated C and D Companies.

Under covering Vickers and mortar fire, Benson's B Company attempted an attack on the enemy line. But without tanks, and with the Japanese skilfully using their enfilading machine-gun fire from the south-west and from in front of the Sememi Creek mouth, the Australians were beaten back with further casualties.

By nightfall on 20 December, the 2/9th had secured about eight hundred yards of priceless coastal ground which left it with a staggered line running back south-east to Sememi Creek. In front of it lay a narrow tongue of land still in Japanese hands, extending about four hundred yards from the Sememi Creek mouth.

By the 21st, the 2/9th once again needed a day to consolidate and rest and take stock. Unsurprisingly, the gruelling nature of their campaigning was beginning to take its toll. Private Bill Spencer:

> Your physical condition's one factor and your mental condition is another. You feel mentally flogged! You don't want to give up, but you wish to Christ you were somewhere else! In the night you're on stand-to and with a mate in a pit you wonder what is going to happen next.[30]

Early that morning there was news of Jock Milne and Jack Allen. Bill Spencer:

> Unfortunately, instead of moving through the scrub line, he walked straight through the kunai . . . he walked into the Nips. They shot and bayoneted him but he didn't die . . . he had his own bayonet out, I know, because I wasn't with Jock when he was killed, but I was out there in the morning looking for him . . . he must have turned around and they bayoneted him in the back again . . . he must have been alive at dawn, and he must have been hungry, and with his own bayonet he was trying to open some raspberry jam.[31]

When Milne's mates examined his belongings, they found a humble diary made of pages of lined paper bound together with string. The diary contained a two-page account of his last hours. As his strength deserted him, Milne's writing became weak and almost childlike: 'Should I be dead when you find [me] search the surrounding bush carefully for wounded men. Jack Allen is somewhere on my left.' And on the next page: 'Bombs are dropping all around me but somehow I feel quite happy about it.'[32]

A search of the nearby grass found the mortally wounded Allen.

On 22 December the 2/9th resumed its push to the mouth of Sememi Creek. The tanks were still counted on to provide critical support. Trooper John Wilson:

> We advanced with the infantry, some small arms fire was received. We could not see anything because of the grass, likewise the Japs were in the same position. A couple of MG posts were overcome. It was very hard to observe in which direction the fire was coming from. We continued on as before at times coming under heavy MG fire and kept getting bogged, until we could make no further progress because of the soft ground. During this time some of our tank crews not engaged in tank work volunteered to act as stretcher bearers and form small parties, and did anti-sniper patrols.[33]

If the boggy ground and resultant lack of tank support proved difficult enough, then the sudden entry of a Japanese anti-aircraft gun into proceedings at around 10.00 a.m. that morning both hampered and shocked the 2/9th. The gun was able to bombard the battalion's start line, with the result that twenty Vickers and mortar personnel were killed or wounded. When the Japanese had observed and heard the tanks withdrawing to their refuelling point at around noon, they set fire to the kunai grass, which caused an Australian withdrawal to the scrub line.

The steady demise of the officers of the 2/9th had been tragically under way since the first stirring attack on the 18th. When Captain Griffen was killed trying to direct tank fire onto a bunker and his second-in-command, Captain Roberts, had an eye blown out by a shell fragment, Sergeant Steve McCready took over. Warrant-Officer Jesse, who had fought so tenaciously on C Company's front on the first day, now took over command of the Composite Company. Such are the actions, the esprit de corps, and the training and discipline of an elite unit such as the 2/9th—every soldier knew his role in the war, and each man merely faced adversity and the challenge of higher command and responsibility, as the situation demanded.

By 5.00 p.m. on 22 December, the day was won. The Japanese resistance on Wootten's first-phase ground had finally crumbled. Lieutenant Thomas recalled that: 'Sememi Creek was muddy, very smelly and cluttered with broken and twisted timber. It was alive with rats and vermin and totally unfit for consumption.'[34]

On Christmas Eve 1942, Lieutenant-Colonel Clem Cummings was wounded by fire from across the Sememi.

By the time Buna finally fell on 2 January 1943, the 2/9th had paid a heavy price for its distinguished campaigning: 23 officers and 351 other ranks as battle casualties. And then there is the aftermath, both immediate and enduring. Bill Spencer on the immediate aftermath:

> Usually there are bodies to be removed from your position—sometimes anonymous enemy bodies and sometimes those of a more personal nature. In death, friend and foe alike exude a sickening, sweet stench from their decaying flesh, which pervades the air. You are unable to wash that presence away—in either its physical or emotional form. Once again you prepare yourself for what in truth is going to happen again in the future. You wait, recounting in your mind the faces of those who fell, those you will never see again. No matter who you are, that future excites in you a certain trepidation. This feeling remains in you until you move on.[35]

But there is the haunting, long-lingering memory of both the pride of achievement and also the tragic cost of Buna for these veterans. Spencer on the enduring aftermath:

> 'The 18th of December is a day we will remember,
> When the ninth moved up on Cape Endaiadere,
> With Jap bunkers by the hundred,
> Where the Yankee boys had blundered,
> The ninth moved in where no one else had
>   dared.'. . .
>
> Over 50 years after the end of the fight for Buna, the content of my unfinished verse still haunts me.[36]

I'VE NEVER GOT OVER IT

24

While the 2/9th had been engaged in its first-phase fighting, the 2/10th had arrived at Buna on 21 December 1942. It concentrated in the already captured Duropa Plantation, between Cape Endaiadere and the eastern end of the New Strip.

The dynamic employment of the General Stuart tanks, in unison with the magnificent performance of the 2/9th Battalion, had brought a stirring victory during the first-phase operation. Lieutenant-Colonel Jim Dobbs and his 2/10th now faced their Buna challenge: the capture of the Old Strip.

The Old Strip at Buna was about 850 yards long and about 125 yards wide, with an access strip about 170 yards long leading to dispersal bays at its north-western end, and a similar access track with dispersal bays on either side leading to a small log bridge at its south-eastern end. This log bridge linked the Old Strip with a track which led to the western end of the New Strip.

At the top end of the Old Strip lay a coconut plantation established on relatively firm ground. Near its northern side lay Sememi Creek, which passed through a fetid swamp bordered by mangroves. The swamp varied from about three to nine feet in depth. A narrow corridor of ground ran from the swamp to a bank and then onto the strip. At the bottom end of the Old Strip the boggy ground was dominated by Sememi Creek, which traversed it but was approached only by the narrow log bridge. The southern side of the strip was bordered by a further significant area of swamp and thick jungle. And the ground sloped from the plantation at the top end back down to the log bridge.

The strength of the Japanese defensive positions at the Old Strip at Buna reflected the fact that they had had plenty of time to prepare before the Americans' arrival in November. Moreover, there were many advantages for the defender. Sememi Creek made an attack from the north-eastern flank unlikely. Thick scrub and jungle and a difficulty in an approach to it seemed to rule out a southern assault, and the narrow log bridge at the bottom end meant any attacking force would have to congregate along that narrow approach and risk heavy fire in the process. The Americans had tried and tried to force a passage at the bridge but had taken casualties for no gain.

With the advantages of the ground in mind, the Japanese were able to focus their firepower upon the strip itself. And they now had a critical advantage denied them when the 2/9th attacked in the Duropa Plantation: they knew the Australians had tanks. Further, the open strip gave them a magnificent view of a tank approach and accordingly, they had two anti-aircraft guns sited at the top of the strip against that eventuality.

A network of bunkers and trenches ran along the Old Strip, all well concealed in the kunai grass. Further well-disguised posts were sited towards the top end of the jungle-covered left flank, each expertly camouflaged and placed to provide mutually supportive fire. There were also the now mandatory snipers, deployed in the coconut palms around the top end of the strip. However, the most telling array of bunkers, and therefore firepower, awaited the Australians at the top end of the strip, expertly deployed to cover the obvious passage along that feature.

By 21 December, Wootten knew that it was only a matter of time before his first-phase operation would be completed. With the Americans still stalled at the log bridge, he now ordered Dobbs to find a passage through the swamp and onto the strip. Dobbs ordered his A Company's Captain Sanderson to find it. Private Peter Bowden, A Company, 2/10th Battalion:

> And Tim Hughes, an Aboriginal, Captain Sanderson asked him to go and have a recce . . . and we knew if anyone could find a way across it was Tim. And he came back within a few hours I think . . . and we went across

> one by one. I had to hold the Bren gun over my head, up to my neck in water . . . I've never been so hot in my life, it was like walking into a bloody great oven, going through that mud and shit and then the sun beating down on that bloody great high kunai and I can remember digging into that sandy ground and making a little place for my Bren gun.[1]

Virtually under the noses of the Japanese, Bowden's section had crossed by 11.00 a.m.; within a quarter of an hour his platoon was across complete with a Vickers gun crew, and, by 1.40 p.m. the remaining two platoons of A Company were staggered across the swamp or on their undetected way along it. By 11.00 p.m. that night two companies were across.[2]

Corporal Gerry Robinson was a Vickers gunner: 'I remember men coming across well into the night and 3 times during the night as more arrived we moved our line further out into the kunai and dug in, all this time at night I don't remember a shot being fired. Even though the ground was only hard packed sand we were very tired by morning.'[3] This was stirring stuff. When Captain Ifould completed his B Company movement across the swamp and wheeled away to the bottom of the strip on the 23rd, the Japanese trapped between the log bridge and the approaching Australians fled into the jungle and scrub to the south. Around 250 yards of priceless Buna ground had been captured without a casualty. Immediate repairs were made to the log bridge and the Allies now had both a tank and infantry access point to the Old Strip.

More priceless Old Strip ground was gained when an artillery barrage hit Japanese bunkers about a hundred yards forward of an old tin hut on the Sememi side of the strip. By 4.00 p.m. on 23 December, the 2/10th was deployed 350 yards along the Sememi Creek side of the strip, and about 150 yards along its centre.

So much had been gained for so little cost. But the continual beachhead concern with speed now came into play. No patrolling to ascertain the enemy's positions. No patrolling to find his anti-aircraft guns. At 7.30 p.m. on the night of 23 December, Wootten ordered Dobbs to attack along the Old Strip next morning.

Dobbs had lost his C Company, which had been assigned the task of covering the bridge area, and therefore he determined that Major Trevivian's D Company would attack along the Sememi Creek side of the strip, Captain Ifould's B Company would strike along its centre, and finally that the Americans would assume responsibility for the scrub and jungle left flank. Captain Sanderson's A Company was to act as the battalion reserve.

Although eleven tanks were then leaving Milne Bay, the potential use of his remaining four tanks at Buna was a matter for Brigadier Wootten's keen consideration. Although he did not know where the enemy anti-aircraft guns were, he knew of their existence. They had fired on the 2/9th towards the end of that unit's assault upon the Sememi Creek mouth. However, the guns had been silent for a couple of days, which might mean that they had been eliminated by bombing, or perhaps by artillery fire, or that possibly they had run out of ammunition—or perhaps their silence was a ruse.

Wootten told none of this to Lieutenant McCrohon, who was to lead the tank support. In fact, both Wootten and his brigade intelligence officer told McCrohon that he could 'disregard any threat from these guns which were known to be sited on the left of the advance'.[4] Lieutenant McCrohon argued that he would require all four tanks to adequately assist the whole 2/10th front, and after some discussion it was decided that all four would indeed be committed.

At around 9.30 a.m. on Christmas Eve 1942, after a twenty-minute artillery barrage, the attack began. Church's tank moved forward on the right or Sememi Creek side of the Old Strip, and Lattimore, Barnet and McCrohon were each spaced about fifty yards apart and in line abreast.

The Japanese immediately brought tremendous fire to bear, particularly upon the most vulnerable portion of the advance, which was Captain Justin Ifould's movement through the kunai grass along the centre of the strip. Private Joe Coombe, 10 Platoon, B Company, was not far from Ifould:

> Ifould stood up and said, 'It's time to go!' I don't think he got out of his hole actually. You couldn't see the bloody snipers . . . I'll tell you what, all that first day going up the

> strip, I didn't see a bloody Jap! The shit hit the fan, but you couldn't see them![5]

Captain Murray Brown, who had rendered distinguished service at KB Mission at Milne Bay, now assumed command of B Company:

> . . . I heard the orders for the attack along the airstrip, and it seemed to me the craziest orders I'd ever heard, for troops to advance against dug-in machine guns on either side. I ran over and there was Justin Ifould with a bullet through the forehead . . . it was not possible to evacuate the wounded because we were on open bullet swept ground, it was kunai grass about waist-high. As soon as you stood up you were under cross-fire.[6]

Whether or not the Japanese anti-aircraft gunners decided to allow a modest advance along the strip before firing so as to ensure their maximum effect upon the Australian advance is not known, but there was a pause before their fire began. But when it did, all hell broke loose amongst the advancing but helpless tanks. Trooper John Wilson was the gunner in McCrohon's tank on the extreme left:

> . . . we moved down the strip at about 5 miles per hour, with the infantry following. Heavy machine gun and mortar fire was received and we had only proceeded a short distance when McCrohon . . . ordered the driver to swing left in the direction of where we knew the Ack-Ack gun was situated. The turret gunner opened fire with the 37 and only got away a couple of shots when he had a misfire, in that the round failed to go off . . . Next thing we knew there was a loud explosion, the tank shook and we knew we had been hit. This happened as the tank was making a full circle to the left and the shell struck the centre side of the tank near the track about level with my head and the radio equipment. Radio and other stores were blown out of the compartment, the radio struck me on the head and I was knocked out for a few seconds. The next thing I knew the crew commander had me by the

Warren Force—Brigadier Wootten's plan

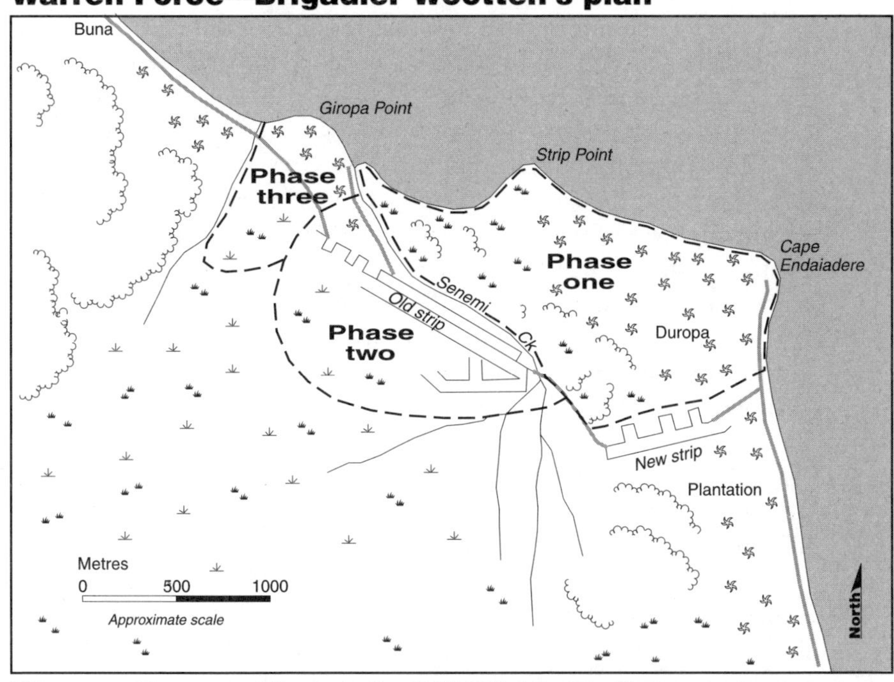

Warren Force—Phase 2—2/10th Battalion

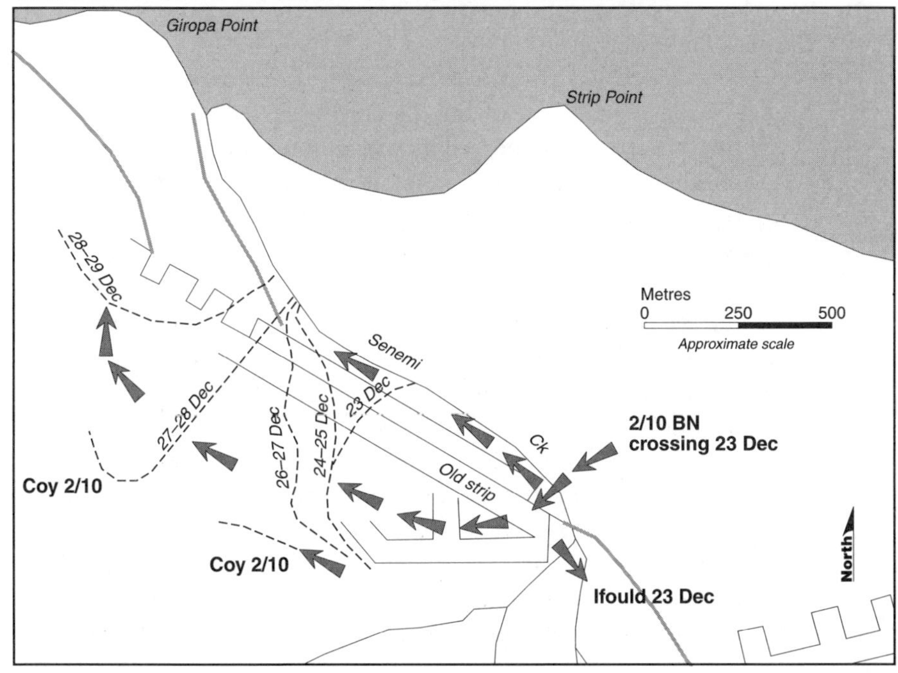

> hair shaking my head to see if I was all right . . . as my eyes came into focus I saw that the side of the tank hull had opened up and I could see up along the strip we were supposed to be advancing.[7]

To compound their problems, McCrohon's crew also discovered that their tank had suffered steering problems. The driver shortly informed his commander that he had lost control of the vehicle. When their tank veered over the lip of a bomb crater which was half filled with water, it tilted to the left, which resulted in water entering through the driver's visor. After deactivating the guns, the crew escaped through Wilson's visor exit, which was the only escape not visible to the enemy.

McCrohon's crew had to now contend with the possibility of being shot by the advancing Australians as well as Japanese machine-gun and sniper fire. They yelled to the 2/10th soldiers to warn them of their presence, and Wilson remembered a laconic South Australian infantryman offering him a bet of ten shillings that he and his crew would never regain their start line! He should have taken the bet. They made it.

The Japanese gunners now turned their attention to Barnet's tank. Barnet:

> . . . the missile sort of hit the turret, circled around the turret like a tin opener, killing my gunner, Jones, who was standing immediately in front of me and thus protecting me . . . instructions had been given to my driver that if we were hit at any time . . . to turn and go for hell out of it, which he did do, but at the same time when the tank was hit, the top, the lid of the tank was thrown open, and I was thrown halfway out of the tank . . . when the tank turned I was thrown out onto the ground . . . I had difficulty deciding which direction was the enemy and which direction was our own troops . . . I took pot luck and turned around and headed in a direction. Because of the kunai grass . . . they couldn't see me . . . my arm was shattered and I carried my arm . . . Kevin Kennedy, my hull gunner, and my whole crew had come looking for me. My arm was amputated on Christmas Day.[8]

And then there were two. The next tank in order of line across the strip was Sergeant Lattimore's. A shell hit his hull gunner's flap, killing Trooper Forster and mortally wounding Trooper Leggart. Lattimore had a leg blown off. The final unequal tank contest on the Old Strip at Buna on Christmas Eve 1942 was resolved when Sergeant Church's tank was knocked out. And then there were none—all within thirty minutes.

The 2/10th were left to advance along a 125-yard wide front of waist-high kunai grass into enfiladed machine-gun and sniper fire. Such grass and the odd bomb crater were poor protection from such withering fire.

If the 2/9th had won a unique place in the annals of its nation's history in the Duropa Plantation just one short week earlier, then the undaunted soldiers of the 2/10th were no less resolute. While the Vickers gunners maintained concentrated covering fire at both identified and suspected enemy posts, the infantry continued their snail-like advance, grenading and firing at posts as they approached them.

To compound an already daunting state of affairs, the Australians' allies on their left flank were less than persistent. You have to keep up before you can 'mop up'. The failure of the Americans to push their advance with suitable vigour caused Brown's B Company to sustain casualties from both flanking and sniper fire.

It was a costly day. B Company lost its commanding officer killed, two of its three platoon commanders wounded, and suffered heavy casualties amongst its other ranks.

On the right flank, running adjacent to the Sememi Creek, Major Trevivian's D Company enjoyed a little more success, as had the 2/9th Battalion advance adjacent to the sea at Cape Endaiadere.

In his advance along this right flank, Trevivian deployed his 16 Platoon on the right, bordering the swamp, his 17 Platoon was spread from the embankment to the right flank of B Company, and his 18 Platoon was just behind in reserve. Some measure of the carnage on B Company's fire-swept central strip front can be gauged from the account of Lance-Corporal Bill Maroney of that D Company reserve platoon, after it had been sent to plug a hole in the B Company line:

> I was going up to find the gap in the line, crawling through the grass and I struck Frank Duffy, who was a bloke I knew extra well, he was the Mortar Sergeant. And he's trying to get a pit settled up so he could put a mortar in it . . . He said, 'You got a match on you?' So I gave him my lighter, and he lit his smoke and put the lighter in his pocket. He said, 'You're going up there aren't you?' I said, 'Yeah.' He said, 'You won't bloody well need this then!' . . .
>
> I struck Wally Cramey of B Company . . . there weren't many of his platoon left in the pits. The rest had been left behind dead or wounded.[9]

The attack gradually lost any real momentum. By 9.00 p.m. that night A Company had thickened the B Company line, which now stretched in an arc back from D Company's front back along the strip. The day had cost the 2/10th one officer and twenty other ranks killed in action and four officers and 87 other ranks wounded, giving it a total casualty count of 21 dead and 91 wounded. And to this tragic tally must be added the brave but futile loss of three killed and at least three wounded from the ranks of the 2/6th Armoured Regiment. The thoughts of Captain Theo Schmedje, the 2/10th Battalion's adjutant:

> You've got no idea what it's like to lose blokes like Ifould and Bunny Wilson because of these terrible tactical blunders, and this is what I can never forgive Brigade for. Nobody's got any idea of tactics . . . alright, we'll hold the line there but we'll go around their flanks! But get behind them! Then you've got them! It's our operation! I never knew him [Wootten] to interfere like this . . . From then onwards, you'll appreciate that our companies were reduced to platoons. And this broke my heart, I've hated Buna. To think of it ever since . . . all those blokes that died. It's tragic, I've never got over it.[10]

High casualties may not necessarily be the measure of high success or even of high endeavour; they can be merely statistical evidence of poor planning, and of the squandering of unvalued lives. They can also be the result of a commander turning a Nelsonian blind eye to standard, prudent and responsible command procedures, because he is under perilous pressure from a chain of high command demanding speed, demanding success, and accomplishing little more than unnecessary slaughter.

During Christmas Day 1942, the 2/10th made modest ground in employing what the Official Historian called 'soft-spot tactics'.[11] A more blunt and accurate interpretation might be that they were 'buggered and licking their wounds'. A small number of 18th Brigade veterans remembered receiving a small number of boiled lollies for Christmas.[12] Even the lollies were hard work at Buna.

George Silk: 'After I did Cape Endaiadere, and the mass of casualties, and I came out of there pretty shot up emotionally and everything else, I took a couple of days at Battalion Headquarters or regimental headquarters . . .'[13]

Providence had probably saved Silk's life. Had he continued his 2/9th assignment, his limited luck would almost certainly have run out. And when the 2/10th and its supporting tanks had advanced along the Old Strip, Silk's chances of survival would most certainly have been even less. However, on Christmas Day 1942 at Buna, George Silk took not only one of the most compelling stills of the Pacific War, but one that was destined to be almost universally mis-attributed. George Silk:

> As I remember that incident it was Christmas Day and I had been walking back to Battalion Headquarters and I think I was sleeping mostly at Battalion Headquarters [probably the 2/9th Battalion HQ] . . . and I was making my way up to the front, at that moment, the front being only a few hundred yards away, across this field of kunai, tall kunai grass [probably not far from the Old Strip] . . . I was the only person on the path and suddenly I saw these two people walking towards me . . .

> I remember feeling there was something distinctive about these two people . . . here is this tender scene . . . this native is helping this man so tenderly . . . I saw all this just in a flash and I felt it in me! And for a second I thought, 'God! You know, I've got to take a picture!' But I sort of didn't want to. I didn't want to interfere!
>
> . . . I squatted down beside the track and set the camera at ten feet, the Rolleiflex at ten feet, and as they went by I didn't even look through the finder . . . and as I remember I took one shot . . .[14]

Incredibly, this photo first appeared not in Australia but in the United States. The Australian Department of Information suppressed the still for more than two months. Finally, a friend of Silk's submitted the still, which would become known as Silk's 'Blinded Digger Shot' to the American censor, and it appeared shortly after in *LIFE* magazine as Picture of the Month.[15]

The photo has *absolutely nothing* to do with the Kokoda Trail campaign, despite having been linked to it on numerous occasions. And there is an interesting story behind the Australian soldier in Silk's still. Bill Spencer, *In the Footsteps of Ghosts*:

> The MV *Tarooma* arrived at Gili Gili during the final stages of the action at Milne Bay with an unusual cargo: apart from ammunition, fuel and general supplies, there were six soldiers who had deserted from their duties guarding various military establishments in Townsville. Tom Franks, Jackie Cassidy, Sergeant Keith Quirk, 'Duke' Neilson, 'Snow' Oliver and Dick Whittington had grown sick of parades and camp life while their comrades were fighting in New Guinea, and so the momentous decision to desert and join a fighting unit was made. They were eventually paraded before [Lieutenant-Colonel] Clem Cummings, who was at a loss to understand why men would desert to face the rigours and dangers of service in New Guinea. These men were subsequently taken on strength by the 2/9th Battalion—except Dick Whittington, who was posted to the 2/10th Battalion.[16]

Whittington was wounded on the Old Strip at Buna on Christmas Eve 1942. He could not have guessed that he would, as a Queenslander, be posted to the South Australian 2/10th and, further, that he would later feature in a George Silk still that would become one of the most famous photos of the Pacific War—or that he was to die, not from his head wound, but from a bout of the dreaded scrub typhus. Sergeant Quirk would later lose his life serving with the 2/9th and Oliver, Neilson and Franks survived the war.[17]

On Christmas Day, after the repeated and costly casualties at Buna over the preceding seven days, the potential to gain ground by a movement through the cover along the left flank of Old Strip began to dawn on the 18th Brigade Headquarters.

It was now decided to employ C Company of the 2/10th Battalion in this role, as that force had been occupied in guarding the log bridge area at the foot of Old Strip. At 5.00 p.m. on Christmas Day, Captain Matheson's men began moving around the south-western side of the strip to eventually pass through the Americans to a lying-up point about 125 yards inland from the strip. Here was a sensible, considered attempt to eliminate the troublesome Japanese naval gun and penetrate the Japanese defences using a covered, outflanking approach. But as had been done at Gona, the 2/10th was still ordered to also attack along the strip in the same old way, causing the same old cost.

At 6.00 a.m., one hour before the scheduled battalion assault, Lieutenant Rudall's 14 Platoon, C Company undertook a fighting patrol to attempt the elimination of the enemy gun. It failed.

Sanderson's A Company attacked along the middle, the most open part of the strip, and suffered high casualties. On the right Sememi Creek flank, D Company managed to occupy one of the Japanese dispersal bays near the top end of the strip. But Wootten was still impatient for a final breakthrough. He ordered Dobbs to press on and eliminate the naval gun and a supporting bunker near it.

At 3.00 p.m. a smoke barrage was laid down and Sanderson's A Company went in again along the centre of the strip. Lieutenant Gray's 7 Platoon, fighting on its left flank, ran into not only intense machine-gun fire, but also the fire of the naval gun. Private Frank 'Pud' Gray participated in this costly attack:

> We got to about 30 feet, a little closer maybe, from that post and that's when we got all the casualties. But that's where we reckon they were firing a gun without any shells in it, it was killing blokes outright, but there were no wounds anywhere on 'em. The blast was killing them.[18]

While A Company was thus occupied, C Company again attacked the naval gun. Private 'Snow' Evans watched his 13 and 15 Platoon comrades go in:

> . . . we flanked the box. Then we cut in until we found a track that had been used from the pillbox back . . . they attacked the pillbox, and they raced out to the pillbox all right and they started feeding grenades in. But the Japs were pretty smart—they chucked them back again. And that cost us a lot . . .
>
> So our people were holding the grenades for a couple of seconds before feeding them in. It went on for quite a while, but eventually they were successful, but they lost a platoon doing this, killed or wounded.[19]

Quite a number of the C Company casualties were taken during heavy and close fighting near the pillbox and naval gun. The Japanese were up to their recent Cape Endaiadere tricks: the occupants of one-man-covered sniper pits were bobbing up to fire and then seemingly disappearing after a kill. It was only a matter of time before such individuals were sighted and eliminated, but in the process there were further Australian casualties.

After the troublesome naval gun was eventually seized, a priceless 220 yards of ground along the edge of the Old Strip was taken.

If events in the centre and along the left flank had been costly, then D Company's second attack on 26 December was no less so. When 18 Platoon moved forward, an enemy post bordering the coconut plantation and its accompanying sniper in its right-hand corner took such a heavy toll amongst the oncoming Australians that the platoon was nearly wiped out. Gained ground is of little use if the attacker has been reduced to such numbers that he has difficulty securing his conquests. Both A and D Companies were forced, late on that day, to withdraw to their original positions.

After a day of 'soft-spot tactics' on the 27th, C Company was able, during the following day, to traverse an amazing six hundred yards of uncontested territory along the jungle fringe on the southern side of the Old Strip. A southward track was found that Matheson felt sure ran from a major Japanese position further in toward the coast. Although the Americans were immediately ordered to block this potentially dangerous track, Matheson was only too well aware of the enemy's potential to soon use it.

With events now turning swiftly against the Japanese, they decided to mount a counterattack against D Company on the edge of Sememi Creek. At 9.00 p.m. that night, they overran the right forward D Company perimeter. Sergeant McAuliffe, stationed on the left flank, heard the din of the action and telephoned for help. However, well before Battalion HQ could react to the threat, Captain Murray Brown took the initiative.

Captain Murray Brown had already displayed an almost bloodthirsty willingness to participate in all manner of confrontations at KB Mission on the night of 27 August 1942. When the situation hung in the balance near the top of the Old Strip at Buna on the night of 27 December, he and a band of willing comrades provided the necessary initiative and courage. Murray Brown:

> And a man come running back and flung himself down and said, 'The Japs have counter-attacked and taken the forward positions!' So there was no time for dithering. One couldn't see far. I came across a couple of Japs with a light machine gun. I attacked them with a machete and shot a couple of others with a pistol and then someone

> shot me through the left lung. And then some of our stretcher-bearers came who were wonderful.[20]

Sergeant Len Tabe was with Brown:

> The Japs had these positions that Don Company had had. They were in trenches, there were no pillboxes there. All the vegetation had been more or less wiped by gunfire. There was just stalks of young saplings standing up all over the place. He would have been in the same strength as us, about twenty.[21]

Private Joe Coombe was also a member of Brown's group:

> The shit hit the fan as usual. I was a Bren gunner. And when we got to this place, I remember Browny getting hit and he said, 'Get these bastards out of here and I'm with you, and if you don't, I'm stuffed!'[22]

After a short, swift encounter where much of the fighting was hand-to-hand, the surviving Japanese fled. Brown refused to be evacuated until the position had been stabilised. By the end of this action, the 2/10th Battalion numbers were down to about 170 all ranks.

Such heavy battle and sickness casualties placed an enormous strain on the battalion's doctor and medical staff. Lieutenant John 'Andy' Andrews, signals officer, 2/10th Battalion:

> Geoff Verco [the battalion doctor] was doing a fantastic job. He had a trench there dug out with a bench down below ground level where they could put a stretcher and that was his operating table. And the RAP was under fire more or less. And he couldn't have had a touch of rest from one day to the other . . . the most terrible wounds I think I've ever seen, hit in the stomach, and they were two men from D Company and their names were Watkins and Goodgame, and they were only lads . . . they were inseparable cobbers, mates. They came to put Watkins and Goodgame on the stretchers and they rolled

> one of them onto the stretcher and his intestines stayed on the ground, and they were still conscious both of them. And each was saying, 'Never mind about me, look after my mate.' I didn't realise it at the time, I should have known, Geoff Verco told me afterwards that he looked at these blokes and they were hopeless . . . so he kept shooting them with morphine . . .[23]

On 28 December, the 2/10th attacked again. The end of the enemy resistance on the Old Strip was in sight, and there was the prospect of seizing the north-western dispersal bays. During the morning D Company became separated from its left fighting A Company force and, later that same morning, a similar gap developed between Sanderson's left and Matheson's right. The Americans were given the task of closing these gaps. However, the Americans lacked both the training and the inclination to push forward with sufficient energy. Dobbs went forward to examine his ground and dispositions that afternoon—it would be 3.45 p.m. before he returned.[24]

At 6.15 p.m. Captain Matheson attempted to drive a wedge north-east into the coconut grove, while the formation on the right pivoted around in support. Matheson was actually able to travel all the way to Giropa Creek—and cross it—before coming to the realisation that he was dangerously far from his main force. When he retired over the creek and found the track which led to his front and into Giropa Point, he was ordered to hold his position astride the track. He assigned this task to Lieutenant Rudall and the remnants of his 14 Platoon.

Late that night the Japanese again counterattacked. They assaulted D Company again on the Sememi Creek side of the strip, but were driven back by that company remnant and a number of A Company reinforcements. But when the enemy attacked an American command post situated near to where Matheson had handed over control the day before, it was quickly overrun. Rudall and three other 2/10th wounded comrades were put to the bayonet as they lay on their stretchers. On 28 December the 2/10th lost a further nineteen killed and 23 wounded. The Official Historian:

> . . . Wootten sought Dobbs out on the morning of the 29th. He was 'bouncing the ball' impatiently, critical of Dobbs and his battalion. Dobbs was sick, worn with strain, heart-broken over the loss of so many of his men, only his courage sustaining him. There was heat in some of their exchanges until Dobbs finally received his orders for the afternoon.[25]

The adjutant of the 2/10th had a different perception of the meeting:

> Poor old Dobbsy! I kept saying to him, 'Brigade's running our operation.' I admired him with his illness the old bugger, and he was standing up to the Brigadier and standing up to the BM [Brigade Major] . . . he was aggressive towards them. He'd lost too many lives . . . he knew it. He was happy with the way we'd started but bloody miserable with the way we'd finished.[26]

Dobbs had every fair reason to defend his unit's fighting on the Old Strip. The 2/10th Battalion's crossing of the swamp onto that feature had been brilliantly executed and accomplished with no casualties; the critical tank support had lasted but a half-hour, and above all the decision to subsequently push the 2/10th along the strip instead of engaging in some measured reconnaissance and outflanking of the Japanese was Wootten's idea and not Dobbs'. Wootten's criticism of both Dobbs and his battalion, therefore, smacks of an unforgivable measure of injustice and ignorance. That Wootten was under intense pressure from Blamey is undeniable, but he could have taken little pleasure or pride out of his Buna command.

But the really damning attribute of Wootten's orders to Dobbs on the 29th was that he was ordering his subordinate to execute his third-phase operation—with the 2/10th now numbering a paltry 46 men per company in each of his A, C and the now amalgamated B and D Companies. In short, Wootten's interference and senseless desire for speed had, between the 24th and 28th, decimated the 2/10th. To then allot it the third phase of the capture of Buna was quite simply ludicrous. The assignment given to Dobbs on 29 December—with about 138 weary soldiers—was the same task allotted by Wootten to the 2/12th Battalion three days later with 34 officers and 592 other ranks.[27] And that assignment was still to prove a tough one.

However, there was one sorely missed and critical element added to the operation for 29 December: tanks. The remainder of B Squadron, 2/6th Armoured Regiment had arrived from Milne Bay in time for this final push to the sea. Wootten ordered B Squadron's Major Tye to allot four of his tanks to the operation, with the remaining seven under Captain May being sent as a reserve to the New Strip area.

The infantry plan envisaged Captain Matheson and his 46-strong C Company advancing through fairly open kunai grass into the coconut plantation and then pushing through to the coast. On his right, Captain Sanderson's A Company was to perform exactly the same function. Another paper plan. Matheson was under no illusions as to the difficulty of the operation, as he had performed a rehearsal of it the previous day. Lieutenant 'Andy' Andrews, signals officer, vividly remembered Matheson's reaction to his orders:

> . . . Dobbs was told he had to do it. When Matheson got his orders, I was there at the O Group conference when Matheson actually got his orders, and Matheson actually had tears in his eyes, knowing what was going to happen. And Dobbs said something to the effect, 'Well, it's got to be done, you've got to do it.' And Matheson said, 'We can't Sir, we can't do it!' And Dobbs repeated, 'We've got to do it!'[28]

The attack was a disaster. And there were some very good reasons for it. Dobbs held a conference at his HQ at 8.30 a.m. on the morning of the 29th. Three tank officers were present. Plans were issued to both the 2/10th officers and their tank colleagues for the attack, which was timed for 11.00 a.m. But as the conference was concluding, the tank officers informed Dobbs that their crews actually conducting the operation were not present at that conference. Dobbs immediately ordered that those missing officers be brought forward and shown the start line, the ground, and meet their infantry counterparts. After the 'missing' officers arrived, and the timing of the attack had been changed to 4.00 p.m., they informed Dobbs that they could not reach the start line by that time. Dobbs immediately informed the brigade major of these circumstances, and ordered his company commanders to await the tanks' arrival at the start line.[29]

In their delayed passage along the Old Strip, Sergeant John Gollan's tank became bogged. Trooper Cec Ganderton was its driver:

> . . . neither myself or John had spotted this bog-spot and we were trapped in seconds. A spare tank was soon brought up and we transferred to it and off we went. I might add until that day we had had next to no training with the hatches fully closed and the driver-commander using the periscope. We proceeded up the strip through very heavy kunai grass, I driving on my commander's instructions as I could only see a few feet in the grass.[30]

The three tanks eventually arrived on the American flank of the front at about 4.45 p.m. and began firing into the coconut plantation at identified bunkers. Nearby, C and A Companies of the 2/10th Battalion then began their attack. Within a short period of time two of the three tanks left the area to replenish their ammunition supply. The third tank moved in on C Company's front.

Sanderson's 46 soldiers from A Company immediately ran into very strong machine-gun fire and found it extremely difficult to make ground. That enemy fire was coming from dug-in positions only about five yards into the plantation. But both striking and unexpected success came on Matheson's front.

Sergeant Mitchell's 13 Platoon actually pushed right through to the coast, with Sergeant Bob Fee's platoon remnant at his right rear, and Sergeant 'Boof' Spencer's at his left rear. But just as Mitchell's objective was realised—a precarious victory since he reached it with only himself and twelve soldiers—tragedy struck. Private 'Snow' Evans was coming in with Fee's left rear support group:

> And we moved into the coconut grove, which I was very happy about because we got the protection of the trees, and we sort of came to a halt. The attack stopped. The tanks were still shooting and a chap alongside me yelled out, 'Snow!' he said, 'They're shooting our own blokes!' So I raced out, without thinking of course, and I belted with my Tommy gun on the side of the tank and yelled out to them. It went on . . . and then I realised that the pinging I could hear was the Jap bullets flying off the tank, they were trying to nail me, so I got the hell out of there fast![31]

By 6.30 p.m. it was obvious that this brave but baffled attack had failed. Literally shot off their hard-won objective—with Sergeant Mitchell and nine of his men killed or wounded—the three survivors of that small force had no alternative other than to surrender the ground they had so bravely gained. When Private 'Pud' Gray shot a green Very light into the darkening sky, the remnants of the 2/10th Battalion's force withdrew. There were 22 survivors of Matheson's original 46-man force.

There are a number of damning pieces of evidence which explain Brigadier Wootten's imprudent impatience at Buna. David Horner, in *Crisis of Command*:

> Already he [Wootten] had begun to feel the pressure for quick results which affected his predecessors. He knew that MacArthur was urging Eichelberger forward and was anxious lest Blamey thought that with tanks and five battalions under his command he was going too slowly. His main worry, however, was that he did not believe that he could rely on the three American battalions for offensive action.[32]

MacArthur to Eichelberger, Christmas Day 1942:

> You have probably eight or nine times the strength of the enemy . . . I feel convinced that our time is strictly limited and that if results are not achieved shortly, the whole picture may radically change.[33]

David Horner has shown that MacArthur's pressure persisted on the 26th:

> Before returning to Dobodura on 26 December Herring called on MacArthur whom he found greatly disturbed. He told Herring: 'This situation is becoming very serious. If we can't clear this thing up quickly I'll be finished and so will your General Blamey.'[34]

And so each day is characterised by a rushed, desperate and ill-conceived attempt to 'clear this thing up quickly' at the cost of seasoned, expert troops who offer experience, skill and guts and, in the end, far, far too many of their undervalued lives.

During its campaigning on the Old Strip at Buna between 22 December 1942 and 2 January 1943, the 2/10th Battalion lost eight officers and 83 other ranks killed in action, one officer and twenty other ranks died of wounds, and twelve officers and 207 other ranks wounded: 331 casualties.

Lieutenant-Colonel Jim Dobbs cut a lonely, tragic figure as he trudged back along that Old Strip at Buna on 5 January 1943. Depressed, malaria-stricken and utterly exhausted, his battalion doctor had insisted upon his evacuation. The slaughter of his 2/10th Battalion on that Old Strip, on orders from above, would linger with him for years. And like a number of his colleagues at Gona, his sensible protests aimed at reducing the terrible losses were not forgotten: as a consequence he would never regain a battalion command.

. . . NINE, TEN . . . OUT!

25

After the Battle for Milne Bay, the 2/12th Battalion had been sent to Goodenough Island to deal with the Japanese force that had been trapped there. On the morning of 28 December 1942, their mission completed, the 2/12th embarked on the corvettes *Broome*, *Colac* and *Whyalla* at Beli Beli, Goodenough Island and landed at Oro Bay late the same day. After a strenuous eighteen-hour march from Eoro Mission, the battalion took up defensive positions in Duropa Plantation at Buna at about 1.00 a.m. on 30 December. Wootten now ordered Lieutenant-Colonel Arnold to accomplish the third phase of the capture of Buna.

This last remaining Japanese position in the Warren Force sector at Buna stretched from the mouth of Giropa Creek around Giropa Point eastwards along the coast to the mouth of Sememi Creek. It then curved along the inland side of the Sememi to a point near the end of the Old Strip proper, and then about 160 yards inland. Finally, it extended back for about six hundred yards parallel to the coast to Giropa Creek.

This third-phase ground was dominated by a coconut plantation which was about 140 yards deep and had a track running roughly halfway through it and parallel to the coast. The main track into the area ran about halfway between the two creeks and south-east out of the plantation.

Within a short distance of the mouth of Sememi Creek, the plantation gave way to tangled vines and mangroves. A seventy-yard belt of kunai grass separated the Japanese defences in the plantation from any would-be attackers.

Captain Angus Suthers, HQ Company, 2/12th Battalion:

> Where we went in it was mostly in the coconut plantation . . . and the Jap was up in the trees . . . now the coconut plantation itself was neglected, and there was scrub there, up as high as your crutch . . . he had you under observation.
>
> The way he'd built the pillboxes . . . they wouldn't have been any more than four or five feet above the ground, he'd planted coconuts, so when you looked at the bloody things, depending on the age of the sprouts, often a couple of feet high . . . you were right on top of the bloody pillbox before you saw it.[1]

The bunkers in the plantation varied in width from two to five yards and housed anything up to seventy Japanese, according to the size and position of the bunker. In the larger posts the weaponry often consisted of six light machine-guns and two medium machine-guns, with the remainder of the occupying enemy acting as riflemen.[2]

While the Japanese command post area was sited in the Giropa Creek portion of the perimeter, the bunkers were most numerous in the Sememi Creek part of that area. A maze of crawl trenches gave the enemy the potential to move his soldiers from bunker to bunker and also support those structures with covering fire. A number of shallow but serviceable drainage ditches in the plantation also provided cover.

In planning the last phase of his conquest of Buna, Brigadier Wootten envisaged a concentrated push through the middle of the plantation, the purpose of which was to punch a 250-yard corridor to the sea. In a perimeter that was by far the smallest of the three assaulted at Buna, such a corridor would then create two distinct enemy pockets. The first would be the western area, between Giropa Creek and that corridor, and the other would be between Sememi Creek and the corridor. The Japanese would be bottled up between each creek, the sea, the kunai boundary (the Australians' start line) and the central corridor. It was then a matter of attacking up the two pockets and exterminating their occupants.

And the lessons of the first and second phases were applied with some sensible, considered planning. With the tank failure of 29 December uppermost in his mind, Wootten now ensured that close liaison and briefing (with the relevant personnel this time) between the infantry and tank crews was established, and that the forming-up point was far closer to the start line. There were also going to be more tanks for this operation; nine tanks were to be deployed with six operating at any one time and three being kept in reserve. However, the greatest single Australian advantage during this third-phase fight was the simple realisation that the enemy did not possess anti-tank weapons, the likes of which had devastated that support on the Old Strip.

To further assist the infantry, the tank crews were to hang bandoliers of ammunition from the rear of their tanks and carry significant grenade supplies inside them. Given the much smaller dimensions of the third-phase battleground, the increased number of tanks, the more astute planning for their liaison with the infantry and the stockpiling of extra ammunition and grenades for the infantry, the Australians' firepower and concentration of force was impressive.

A further critical addition to the available arsenal of weapons for the assault upon the Japanese bunkers was the timely invention of a lethal, new bomb. Captain Angus Suthers:

> . . . like gelignite. Basically it was a tin, like a tin of baked beans but a bit fatter, and it's got a lid on it and you have a hand grenade and there's a base plate that goes on to the hand grenade . . . you make a little hole in the lid of this tin; you put the threaded plate through the inside of the tin and you screw the grenade on top. The tin itself has got two pounds of ammonal and you put an instantaneous fuse round the grenade and into the ammonal . . . so that when the grenade goes off the instantaneous fuse sets the ammonal off.[3]

The ammonal charges were to have two decisive effects upon the Japanese in the bunkers. The first was the obvious one: an increased charge exploding in a confined space. But such charges also had the additional advantage of stunning those Japanese not killed or wounded. The only problem was getting close enough to the bunkers to drop the charges in through the firing slits.

At 7.00 a.m. on the morning of 31 December, the 2/12th took over the positions of the 2/10th and sustained five casualties in the process. During that night, the 2/5th Field Regiment bombarded the Japanese defensive perimeter.

At first light on New Year's Day 1943, further artillery fire was brought down on both sighted and suspected enemy bunker positions in the plantation. At 7.40 a.m., the 2/12th employed their Vickers machine-guns to spray the tops of the coconut palms in an attempt to destroy as many enemy snipers as possible. Ten minutes later the artillery laid down another ten-minute barrage into the plantation.

When zero hour arrived at 8.00 a.m., in a dramatic replay of the stirring advance undertaken by the 2/9th at Cape Endaiadere on 18 December, the tanks began their slow, measured advance across the kunai grass belt, followed by the infantry. Captain Murray's A Company had the task of pushing through the central corridor to the coast and then swinging left to Giropa Creek, while Captain Kirk's B Company was to swing right along the coast to the Sememi Creek mouth. Applying the lesson learnt at Milne Bay—and by the 2/10th on the Old Strip—the 2/12th Battalion's D Company was to move behind its leading A Company to the left, and C Company to the right, to eliminate still-surviving Japanese bunkers and snipers missed by their comrades.

The critical crossing of the kunai grass belt leading to the coconut plantation cost the 2/12th dearly. Despite the Vickers gun supporting fire of six guns on either side of the advance, 88 casualties were taken before the leading two companies could gain the confines of the plantation. Lieutenant Duncan Clarke, A Company:

> Captain Murray didn't last long. He was killed soon after we started. The enemy fire was sustained and quite heavy, but what I did notice was that it was damn accurate, as though they were experienced troops, and they weren't wasting ammunition. It soon became

> apparent that there were a lot of snipers around in the trees . . . they had a magnificent field of fire.[4]

One well-hidden and disciplined Japanese sniper shot and killed Lieutenant Mike Steddy, Captain Murray, an A Company runner and a Vickers machine-gunner all within a small area and in a brief period of time. Captain Angus Suthers recalled the recurring Japanese sniper tactic of letting the infantry pass:

> Their snipers were bloody good! . . . there was one bastard who laid doggo the whole of New Year's Day, and on the second, he shot one of our blokes . . . he let the whole of the bloody fight go on for a day! We knew bloody well that it was only a matter of time before we got it too! They went in an extended line and just took it![5]

A Company's thrust to the coast was quick but costly. The distance to travel was not great, but the density of the Japanese defences and the intensity of their fire in that confined area caused heavy casualties. The snipers were operating in near perfect conditions: a confined area with magnificent cover. Their preparedness to die only added a further dimension to their effectiveness. Lieutenant Clarke, A Company:

> . . . we got to the beach and there I lost the last officer that I had, Tim Logan . . . I had the phone and I was talking to the old man, when Tim suddenly stood up. And I yelled out, 'For Christ's sake get down!' And as I did so, to this day I'm quite convinced that I could actually see the discolouration on the side of his neck as the bullet either hit him or was coming out the other side.[6]

Clarke assumed immediate command of his A Company, and despite a glancing bullet wound through his helmet rallied his men and led them through the assault upon the remaining twenty or so enemy bunkers.

Warren Force—Phase 3—2/12th Battalion

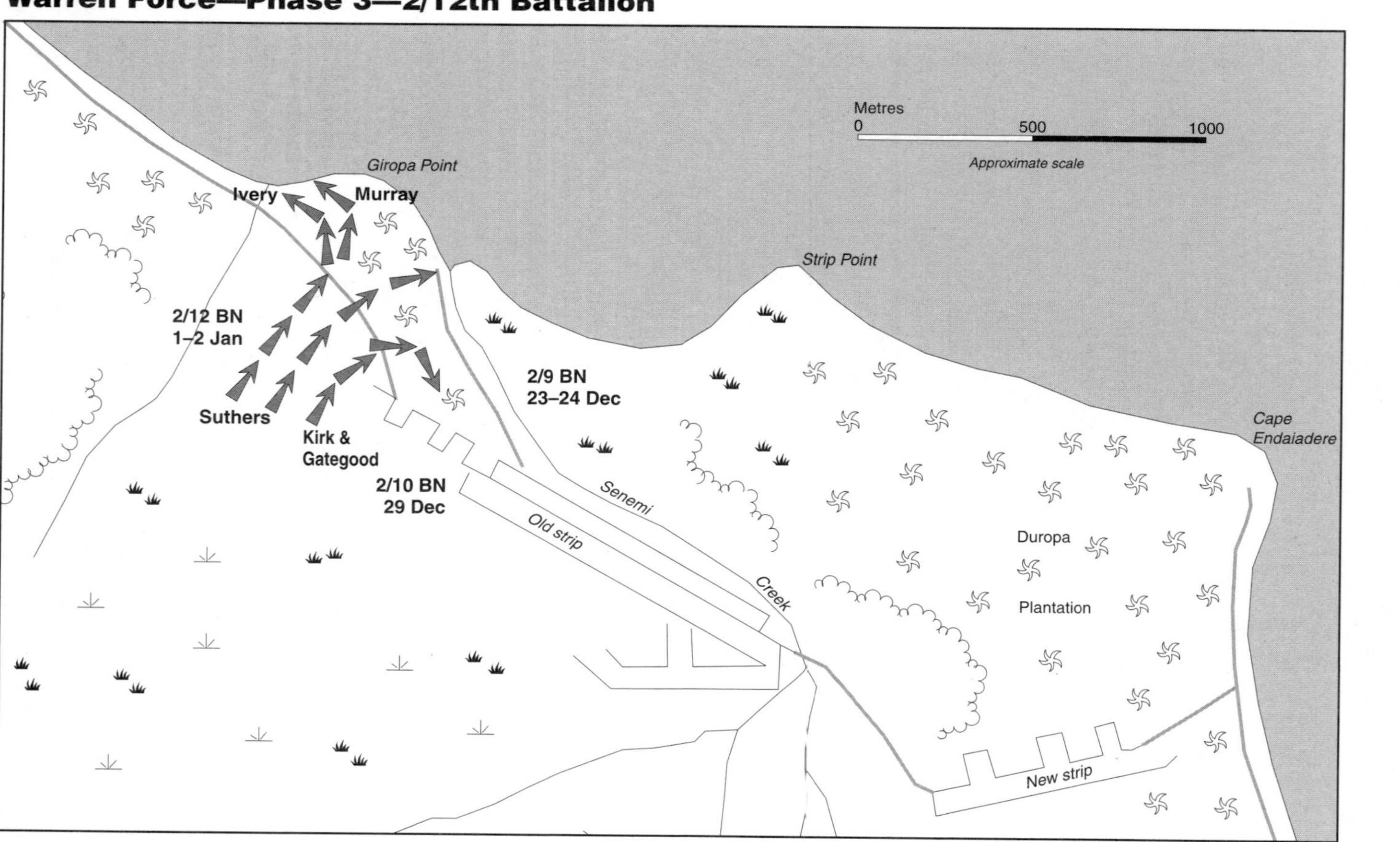

While the A Company front had reached the coast and had begun to move west to Giropa Creek, their supporting D Company followed them in. Corporal Roy Rodgers, 17 Platoon, D Company:

> After we had advanced about 150 yards through the kunai grass we turned partly left and advanced approximately in a NW direction towards Giropa Point. (We did NOT follow A Coy through towards the beach.) We moved towards the lines of Japanese Pill Boxes which defended Giropa Point in great depth. We were caught continually under enemy fire from this point on for some hours, however it was pretty difficult to ascertain what fire was being directed at us, due to the constant noise of the battle, which was concentrated into a relatively small area. The noise of course was coming from our own tanks, and our 2 inch and 3 inch mortar fire and grenade explosions, plus machine gun, sub machine gun and rifle fire, not forgetting the enemy fire.[7]

As D Company forged ahead, it encountered lines of enemy bunkers about twenty yards apart and connected by crawl trenches. Each post was engaged according to the availability of the tank support, the size and firepower of the post, and the available machine-gun support for the attackers. But no matter what the circumstances, there was one critical common denominator in the fight against all of them: the sheer courage and initiative of the 2/12th soldiers. Roy Rodgers has left an absorbing account of the destruction of a number of those enemy bunkers:

> . . . I received information from Capt Ivey at D Company Headquarters that accurate enemy fire from pillboxes slightly to the left of my section's axis of advance was seriously holding up some elements of the company . . .
>
> Captain Ivey directed me to attempt to make contact with the tank commander with a view to having this tank engage the enemy elements with both gun and machine gun fire. I approached the tank from the rear and attempted to draw the attention of the crew by hitting

> the rear and side of the tank with the butt of my sub machine gun. This was unsuccessful.
>
> With some caution and difficulty I was able to climb the rear of the tank and was able to make contact with the commander (or gunner) through a small opening (or shutter) in the turret. Because of the noise of battle plus the engine noise of the tank we found voice communication very difficult and at times impossible. I therefore decided to use a combination of hand signals, voice and finally and most importantly, some rough sketches which I hurriedly made on pieces of note pad paper from my note pad which as a section commander I always carried . . . I do recall one of the more unpleasant aspects of the operation was that the metal of the tank was pretty bloody hot on hands & body . . . I was pretty happy to get the 'thumbs up' from the tank commander and apparently my messages had been received and understood. The tank redirected its fire—both accurate gun and machine gun fire—with most unfavourable results for the enemy. Those elements of the Company that had been held up now continued to move forward.[8]

Although George Silk had missed the 2/10th action on the Old Strip, he had taken, however unwittingly, one of the great stills of the Pacific War when he captured the wounded Whittington and Raphael Oimbari making their way out of Buna. But his still shots of the 2/12th Battalion's fighting at Giropa Point on New Year's Day 1943 provide an intimate record of infantry tactics conducted during some of the toughest fighting of the war in the South-West Pacific.

Silk decided to attach himself to Corporal Roy 'Buck' Rodgers' D Company section. It was a calculated but still enormous risk—he was not going in with the lead A Company, but he was, whether he could have guessed it or not, still going into the inferno of close and immediate Buna fighting. Silk:

> It's a busy little scene! Someone's just been hit here; someone's been hit there; and here's another guy behind a tank shooting . . . I mean I was very much aware that this was an amazing position to be in, where you could stand up and take pictures and not get immediately shot! I expected to be shot, because look what's going on![9]

Bravery takes on many forms in battle. As Rodgers is lying on that hot, uncomfortable tank, passing messages to one of its crew, Silk is crouching near the tank looking into a narrow viewfinder. Bunker occupants and snipers and riflemen are killing soldiers around him while he freezes and captures that intense moment in history. And when he arrives at a Vickers machine-gun position, a soldier has already been taken by a sniper and a Vickers crew are desperately trying to locate and kill the sniper. And Silk stands up to get the shot! Silk:

> The machine gunner said, 'What the hell do you think you're doing?' as out of the corner of his eye he spotted my camera. 'Get down you bloody fool. They've just shot my cobber.' He swung his gun viciously across the tree tops to revenge himself on the hidden Jap snipers.[10]

Some photos are a result of pure instinct or perhaps a subconscious desire to capture much more than one split second of action. Silk:

> . . . because of reading about Gallipoli and World War One; the Somme and things, you often came across references to machine gunners getting killed and another one moving into his place and then he gets killed and another one moves into his place, and here it was happening in front of me—I was watching it! I mean, I was photographing a cliché which is what you should avoid photographing. But I'd never seen pictures of a machine gun surrounded by dead gunners, so I just stood quickly up with the open Rolleiflex, with the open finder shot only one picture and down again . . .

> That's the one that caused all the fuss. The arm is a dead soldier and they didn't want the picture to be used at all so . . . I just got a pair of scissors and cut it off . . .
>
> I understood that you couldn't use dead bodies, and so I tried to get part of the dead body in, but not the whole thing. I could argue with them that it was only half a dead body; something like that . . .
>
> Instead of that they [the Australian Department of Information] carefully sat there and censored the pictures! . . . [they] said, 'They're not fit and proper pictures! . . . This guy has a mother. You can't publish his picture, what will his mother say? What will she think?' Well, you know, that's what the war was about.[11]

Late on New Year's Day 1943, Silk's energy ran out: '. . . I turned around and wanted to go back. I'd had enough. I only went a short distance and I passed out.'[12] After his evacuation to Australia, Silk learned that the Department of Information had suppressed his pictures: 'My fight with the department was entirely around the fact that they wouldn't release the pictures that I took. Here I was risking my life to do the job . . . that they accepted me for . . . and they wouldn't release the pictures!'[13]

There was no surrender at and near Giropa Point on New Year's Day 1943. The Japanese died in their bunkers or trenches or sniper positions. Had they attempted to retreat by leaving their covered positions, they would still have been doomed to death. Some actually charged forward to a defiant, faster finish.[14]

By late afternoon, the 2/12th Battalion's A Company had consolidated its positions about sixty yards east of Giropa Point, and D Company held their gains about 125 yards from the mouth of Sememi Creek—the 2/9th was across the other side.

While A and D Companies had been thus engaged, the right flank assault by B and C Companies towards Sememi Creek had been the cause of grave concern. The crossing of the exposed kunai grass in their right-flank approach to the plantation was as costly an exercise as had occurred on the left. Not long after gaining the confines of the plantation, B Company's commander, Captain Kirk, was dead and all of his officers wounded. Within minutes of that crossing, C Company's commander, Major Gategood, was also a casualty.

Although the two companies pressed on, their attack quickly became bogged down against a wall of magnificently concealed bunkers and a daunting screen of accurate sniper fire. When communication between the right flank companies and Battalion HQ became tenuous, Lieutenant-Colonel Arnold was forced to adopt a desperate measure.

Just as Brigadier Potts had done at Brigade Hill on the Kokoda Trail when reinforcements seemed non-existent, Arnold decided to send into battle 'the old and bold', or 'the toothless and the ruthless'. Captain Angus Suthers, HQ Company, 2/12th Battalion:

> . . . the assault wire broke and we were out of contact. And Arnold said to me, 'look, all the odds and sods, get them in there and straighten it out!' So I got in there . . . with perhaps 50 men, cooks, transport drivers, batmen . . . anyone who could carry a rifle . . .
>
> . . . we swung right and there was this large bloody pillbox holding us up. So I just said, 'Come on fellas, I want a couple of volunteers to come with me, and we'll take this bloody thing out!' I don't know who the blokes were to this day. They got up and I had one of these blast grenades, and I told the blokes to give us covering fire, and they beat up the front of it, and as we got near they stopped firing. And we went in and down the smoke hole! They had the door shut and it blew the door out! You imagine the equivalent of four sticks of gelignite going off in a confined space! I took one right through the side about twenty minutes before that . . . just a flesh wound . . . you couldn't pull out because we were losing too many NCOs and too many good officers. You had to stop there. But the blokes were good, by Christ they were good!'[15]

Later that day, to add yet further impetus to the right flank thrust, Suthers' HQ Company contingent and the remnants of B and C Companies were reinforced by two platoons from the 2/9th under Lieutenants Thomas and Tippetts. Vic Thomas, 2/9th Battalion:

> . . . Captain Angus Suthers required thickening on the right flank of the action. His eastern drive was a sticky one contested by bunkers and pillboxes supported by strong earthworks and myriads of fanatical Japs eager to do and be done. The fighting was very severe but ground was slowly being won and casualties inevitable.[16]

At dusk Suthers pulled his force back one line, or row, of coconut palms from the Japanese positions and formed a night perimeter. That position was manned by a mere 35 survivors of his original 2/12th force and the survivors of the 2/9th who had reinforced them. The Australians were only a hundred yards from the mouth of the Sememi and the Japanese perimeter now occupied about eighty yards of ground to that feature. Suthers' men had three problems that night: the proximity of the enemy, the weather and their American allies.

Not long after dark, thunder and lightning and very heavy rain set in, which provided a dramatic backdrop for isolated small bands and individuals among the enemy to attempt to break out along the beach towards Sananda. Such a situation requires tremendous fire discipline. The old hands among the Australians employed it, the Australian reinforcements soon learnt it, but the Americans were inclined to shoot at sounds rather than shapes.

One small band of Japanese entered the confines of Captain Sampson's 2/12th Regimental Aid Post. But the battalion's medical personnel were armed and gave an impressive account of themselves as they shot down the intruders—mainly during the numerous lightning flashes. Padre Roy Wotton's night was interrupted by an enemy soldier who fell into his water-filled weapon pit. The intruder was gone in an instant and Wotton is said to have gone back to sleep. The 2/12th Unit Diary, 2 January 1943:

> Orders were issued at first light for a continuation of the attack. Zero to be at 0800 hours. Tank support to be two tanks on each flank, and two in reserve. Strong enemy opposition was encountered from remaining pillboxes on Giropa Point. At 0945 hours, this flank was reinforced with one platoon of 2/9th under command of Lieut. Giezendanner (2/12th), and all pillboxes were captured by 0955 hours, but mopping up in this sector was not completed until 1400 hours. On the right flank [Suthers], the advance continued steadily during the morning, and at 1200 hours, this flank was reinforced by a Coy of 2/9th Aust Inf Bn, and at 1415 hours contact was made with the 2/10 Aust Inf Bn, but mopping up areas continued to 1700 hours, when the Bn assembled and consolidated Giropa Creek area. Estimated Jap casualties on 1 and 2 Jan, 600 killed, 23 POW.[17]

The final curtain was drawn upon the 18th Brigade's Buna fighting in an action that so typically portrayed the Japanese martial code of conduct. Captain Angus Suthers:

> . . . and we got through to Sememi Creek. And across the other side [on a small island, the 2/9th were on the far side], there's a bloody officer, all done out in his finery . . . obviously a Staff Officer from Headquarters . . . and he came out with a big sword and he made a sign that he wanted to have a fight.
>
> He went whoosh with the sword, and he carved all the bits off the side of the palm fronds. Now, at this time the old man arrived up—Wolf Arnold. And I said, 'Bugger 'im we'll give him ten to surrender!' There was one other Jap behind him, and I had a Vickers gun brought forward. And I said to him, 'Righto, one, two, three, four . . . nine, ten!' And this Jap said, 'Out!' And we just opened up and that was it![18]

When the Australians crossed the intervening ground they discovered the other Japanese officer had hung himself from a tree.

On 2 January 1943, the final Warren Force sector at Buna had been captured. And when the Americans of Urbana Force captured the Buna government station and later linked up with the Australians late on the same day, Buna had fallen.

The 2/12th Battalion took a further eight casualties securing the area during the following three days. During its distinguished Buna campaigning the battalion lost five officers and 61 other ranks killed in action or died of wounds, and seven and 126 wounded in action, giving it a total casualty count of twelve officers and 187 other ranks—a heavy price indeed given its short time in action.

During fifteen days of bitter fighting, the three battalions of the Australian 7th Division's 18th Brigade had accomplished a magnificent feat of arms. But the casualties were heavy and tragic: 56 officers and 840 other ranks.

Of course the accolades flowed thick and fast after the fall of Buna. Stimson, the US Secretary of State, wrote to MacArthur, saying that: '. . . it is a tremendous satisfaction to feel that the American fortunes in SWPA are in such skilful hands'.[19] John Curtin also congratulated the supreme commander.

But many of MacArthur's orders weren't all that skilful: '. . . put sergeants in charge of battalions and corporals in charge of companies'; 'I want you to take Buna, or not come back alive'; 'drive through to objectives regardless of losses'; 'take Buna today at all costs—MacArthur.' And all this from a supreme commander who *not once* visited his subordinates or saw the front.

Blamey was no less culpable. After finally visiting the front—on 5 January, after the fall of Buna—he gave a press conference in Port Moresby two days later. David Horner in *Blamey: Commander-in-Chief*: '. . . that evening [he] told war correspondents that he had "never seen so many strong earthworks packed into such a small area. In the face of these defences the time taken by the Australians and Americans to clear out the Japanese had been good".'[20] If Blamey and MacArthur had trusted in their local commanders who were confronted by those 'strong earthworks', if they had allowed them time for reconnaissance and studied planning, and if they had supported and encouraged them, the desired results would have come far quicker and with far fewer casualties.

The 2/9th Battalion was hurried into its Buna fighting, and when, through the magnificence of that effort, it forced a decisive breakthrough at Cape Endaiadere on 18 December, it lacked a force to exploit its startling success.

When the 2/10th outflanked the Japanese by its audacious crossing of the swamp adjacent to the Old Strip, it was subsequently ordered to advance along that fire-swept feature when it could have advanced along the left flank where Captain Matheson's C Company was later able to make such striking ground. And when the last of Wootten's elite 18th Brigade battalions arrived at Buna, that fresh unit was given the task of capturing an area that the brave survivors of the 2/10th had been ill-equipped to secure.

The failure of the Allied senior commanders to concentrate their force, coupled with their preparedness to order frontal attacks over relatively open ground, cost the Australians dearly.

The rushed and costly attacks at Buna—a carbon copy of similar attacks at Gona—were nothing more than the tragic expression of MacArthur's burning desire to conclude his Papuan campaigning before the American marines on Guadalcanal could complete theirs. And with that race seemingly won, MacArthur believed that he could expect a corresponding reward in terms of the amount of material that would thus be directed to his theatre of operations. The costly victories at Gona and Buna were little more than the appalling expression of his limitless and egotistical ambition.

At the bloodied interface of battle, the 18th Brigade's startling success was due to the studied expertise of the platoon commander and, especially, his sergeant, corporals and their sections. In that final, critical confrontation, the capture of Buna came down to sections fighting in small pockets of coconut plantation, kunai grass, jungle or swamp. Perhaps Corporal Roy Rodgers, D Company, 2/12th Battalion, best encapsulates the experience of many of his comrades:

> At Buna the operation was a set piece attack and that attack was carried out against well prepared enemy positions and within a particular concentrated area. This concentration of the attack . . . within a limited space of time, has meant that I think of the 2/12th Infantry Battalion on that day with a feeling of relative closeness—perhaps it's a feeling of togetherness. Perhaps it has given me another dimension to the aspect of mateship. And then our casualties were heavy, both killed and wounded. This happened relatively quickly. It may be that there was a greater feeling of loss in the knowledge that so many of one's comrades died or were wounded so close by. The feeling of loss, and the pain of that loss is still high . . .
>
> The noise of the battle . . . was deafening, and it seemed never ending and at times the noise still rings in my ears. I have this memory of grenades bursting, the machine guns chattering, the crack of enemy fire and the mortars, guns and tanks blasting away . . .
>
> The Japanese soldiers whose bodies littered the coconut plantation and the Giropa Point area . . . bloody, battered bodies of Japanese soldiers seemed to be everywhere.
>
> Buna was a bloody and noisy battle and so it remains in my memory.[21]

The present-day village of Buna sits neatly between the 2/10th Battalion's objective—the top of the Old Strip—and Rodgers' final Giropa Point fight. A new school has been built within yards of the rusted Japanese anti-aircraft gun, and a small number of shells litter the immediate area. The children play here, acceptant of the danger. The same applies to distant 2/9th pits and mortar shells near Cape Endaiadere. And across from the garden bordered by carrier tracks in the village, the small island can be seen at the Sememi Creek mouth—'. . . nine, ten . . . out!'

INTENSIVELY TRAINED

26

As the crow flies, Sananda Point lies a little over five miles east of Gona and about three miles north-west of Buna. During peacetime, there were three practicable landward approaches to Sanananda. The eastern approach from Buna wound its way along the coast via Tarakena–Giruwa, while the western coastal route from Gona passed through Basabua–Cape Killerton–Wye Point. The third or inland approach was undertaken using a twelve-foot-wide 'road' which ran from the village of Soputa about six miles to the coast. Before the war this rough road was used to carry goods from the hinterland to the small trading post that was Sanananda. These commodities were then taken by native canoe to light vessels lying off the coast.

A little over halfway between Soputa and Sanananda Point, the narrow Killerton Track ran from the road to Cape Killerton. From near the Sanananda Road–Killerton Track junction, the remaining portion of the Sanananda Road to the coast was of corduroy construction.

The terrain of the region was characterised by kunai grass, very thick scrub and swamps. This was a not uncommon beachhead combination. But there were a number of other factors which made the ground on which the Japanese sited their Sanananda defences the most formidable of the three beachhead battlefields.

Unlike Gona and Buna, access to the near coastal confines was very difficult. Nearly all of the territory within the triangle bounded by Cape Killerton, Tarakena and the

Killerton Track–Sananda Road junction was swampland, and because this track junction was about three miles from the coast the junction was pivotal to any inland approach. The swamps were shallow when the tide was out and deeper when it was in. The incoming tide stopped the flow of waters from inland, but after heavy rain the swamps deepened rapidly. The flow of swamp water was from west to east in the Sananda area. To compound the problem, at the time of the battle for the beachhead the wet season was at its peak. Thus, when torrential tropical downpours occurred, and that was quite frequently, the numerous patches of kunai grass were subject to rapid flooding.

The coarse, white sands of the beach along the Sananda coast extended only about five yards up to a low bank which was higher than the immediate swamp-dominated hinterland. The ground for a short distance inland was covered by reasonably tall tropical growth and the occasional coconut palm and banyan tree, though it soon degenerated into scrub and swamp.

When Generals MacArthur and Blamey determined that General Vasey, after having re-entered Kokoda on 2 November, would assume responsibility for the capture of Gona and Sananda, and that the fresh Americans would capture Buna, it was estimated that the Japanese had deployed about 1500 debilitated and diseased troops across their beachhead. In early November there were actually 5500 desperate defenders at Sananda alone, and by early December 1942 that formidable force totalled about six thousand. Although some significant number of the Sananda defenders were hospital cases, subsequent events were to demonstrate that, where possible, they were also combatants.

After General Horii had perished in the turbulent waters of the Kumusi River, command of the Japanese forces west of the Giruwa River—west of Buna—fell to Colonel Yokoyama. After deploying about a thousand of his defenders at Gona, he set about the task of defending Sananda—the site of his main headquarters and base hospital.

Yokoyama concentrated his forces in four main positions. The first was the main base area, stretching in a semi-circle from Wye Point around to about halfway between Giruwa and

Tarakena. The second was on the fourth small track junction back from the coast along the main road. The third was stationed about a thousand yards back from that junction while the fourth, and most formidable, was the Killerton Track–Sananada Road junction itself. In this critical junction area alone there were 1700 Japanese defenders.

The really telling factor, however, that made the Japanese task of defending Sananada far easier than Gona or Buna was the fact that they were able to occupy key areas where the ground was slightly elevated, such as the junction perimeter, and were therefore able to deploy only small outposts and snipers on isolated small 'islands' otherwise protected by the extensive swamplands. The Japanese knew that any Sananada attacker was bound to secure the critical junction area before he could move along the Killerton Track and the main Sananada Road.

Within that roughly half-mile ellipse, the Japanese concentrated their mutually supporting pillboxes, their extensive linking trench network, their close and concealed snipers, and their rearward supporting mortar fire—and, as usual, brilliantly camouflaged all positions and personnel.

It is little wonder that from the beginning of the battle, Sananada provided General Vasey with more casualties and frustration than progress. By early December 1942, after about two weeks of tough fighting in the area, it was clear that the 16th Brigade's long campaigning from the Kokoda Trail up to the beachhead had taken its toll. The Official Historian, Dudley McCarthy:

> It was clear that this spent formation, willing though it was, could do no more to affect the course of events along the Sananada Track.
>
> Between 3rd October and 6th December . . . it lost about 29 officers and 576 men in action. Fifty-six officers and 922 men had been evacuated through sickness.
>
> The total of these figures represented approximately 85 per cent of the strength with which it had set out on the campaign.[1]

The next phase of the fighting at Sananada saw the introduction of two battalions of the 126th American Regiment.

After nine days of indecisive probing rather than concerted fighting, the only American gain was their tenuous hold of a small roadblock on the Sananda Road about half a mile north of the critical Sananda Road–Killerton Track junction. The Americans exploited a weak spot in the Japanese defences to gain and hold this position, which they called Huggins' roadblock. Although the roadblock was a worrying incursion into the Japanese perimeter, the defenders were always able to hold the Americans in check by constant counterattacks. As a result, the Americans found it difficult to even supply this outpost.

During a frustrating duplication of their efforts at Buna, the Americans were severely handicapped by their soft physical condition, their lack of high quality infantry training and, most of all, by their uninspired and bewildered leadership. Geoffrey Perret, MacArthur's most recent biographer:

> As the Louisiana maneuvers [*sic*] in the fall of 1941 had shown, Guard Divisions [the 32nd US Division at the beachhead was a guards division] tended to have a large number of political appointees filling senior posts. The hometown character of many companies and battalions was also a source of weakness. Officers tended to go easy on discipline because Guards companies reflected political, social and business relationships back home. It was too much to expect a man to antagonize his friends, customers and voters over Army regulations.[2]

On 4 December 1942, Blamey wrote an extraordinary letter to Prime Minister John Curtin:

> . . . I had hoped that our strategic plans would have been crowned with complete and rapid success in the tactical field. It was completely successful strategically in as much as we brought an American Division on to Buna and an Australian Division on to Gona simultaneously. But in the tactical field after the magnificent advance through the most difficult area, the Owen Stanley Range, it is a very sorry story.

> It has revealed that the American troops cannot be classified as attack troops. They are definitely not equal to the Australian militia, and from the moment they met opposition sat down and have hardly gone forward a yard. The action, too, had revealed a very alarming state of weakness in their staff system and in their war psychology. General MacArthur has relieved the Divisional Commander, and has called up General Eichelberger the Corps Commander, and sent him over to take charge. He informs me that he proposes to relieve both the regimental commanders, the equivalent of our brigade commanders, and five out of six of the battalion commanders; and this in the face of the enemy. I am afraid now that the bulk of the fighting will fall on our own troops in spite of the greatly larger numbers of the 32nd U.S. Division.
>
> The brigades that went over the mountain track are now so depleted that they are being withdrawn and I am utilising the only remaining AIF Brigade in Port Moresby and a brigade of Militia, that has been intensively trained here, and I think we will pull it off all right . . .[3]

Blamey's comments concerning the Americans were fair. At the time of his writing, all three beachhead battles were undecided and little progress was being made. But Blamey's comments concerning his own forces were an appalling twist of the truth. And there can only be two explanations for them: he was either culpably ignorant of the state of his own forces, or he was misleading his prime minister. On either or both counts he deserves the strongest condemnation.

It is a gross distortion of the facts to suggest, as Blamey did, that he had brought 'an Australian Division on to Gona'. In fairness to Blamey, his statement *may* have referred to the Gona–Sananada front and not just Gona. However, even allowing for this concession, his statement is still a fabrication of the truth. His 'Division' was, in fact, two brigades: the 25th Brigade and the 3rd Militia Battalion and Chaforce at Gona, and the 16th Brigade at Sananada.

Even the term 'brigades' is misleading. The official historian lists the strength of the 16th Brigade at the onset of its Sananada fighting as 67 officers and 974 other ranks.[4]

At Gona, Brigadier Eather's original force was approximately 1350 all ranks.[5] Therefore, the 'Division' referred to by Blamey was actually equivalent to one full-strength brigade—a third of a division. And that force was split (and therefore diluted) between Gona and Sananada. It was all very well for Blamey to claim that the movement onto the beachhead had been 'completely successful strategically' and then denigrate the tactical application of this force, when in fact it had been his and MacArthur's distant and ignorant interference in the tactical handling of the battles which had been largely responsible for those failures.

Moreover, Blamey's last paragraph contains two blatant distortions of fact. The first refers to 'the only remaining AIF Brigade in Port Moresby' and the second to the 'intensively trained' militia brigade.

The only AIF brigade left in Port Moresby at the time of his decision was the 21st Brigade. This brigade comprised Potts' 'running rabbits' and battalions commanded, in some cases, according to Blamey, by officers who 'were not worthy of their men'. Our story has chronicled the fact that the 21st Brigade arrived at Gona with barely a thousand soldiers—it was therefore a *battalion,* and not at brigade, strength. The manner in which this splendid formation was subsequently put to the sword in rushed, ill-considered and irresponsible attacks along the coast towards that Anglican Mission at Gona has also been recorded.

The 'intensively trained' militia brigade from Port Moresby was the 30th Brigade. That formation consisted of the 39th, 49th and 55/53rd Battalions. In December 1942, the 39th Battalion was sent to Gona while the 49th and 55/53rd Battalions were sent to Sananada. And as the casualty count tragically grew at Sananada, the 36th Battalion and 2/7th Cavalry Regiment would be added to the battle from Port Moresby. By December 1942, Blamey was scraping the bottom of the infantry barrel in an effort to supply a force strong enough to bring about his long sought after beachhead victories.

There can be no doubt that the 49th and 55/53rd Battalions were intensively trained—in wharf unloading and ditch digging.

The 49th Battalion had experienced a sad and sorry period of service in Papua. Many of its soldiers had endured twenty months' service in and around Port Moresby as part of the first unit to garrison that town. Fred Cranston, in *Always Faithful*:

> The unit had . . . dug defences in all areas of Port Moresby and surrounding districts. In relation to this, Bill Noyes recalls that his company dug defences from Bootless Inlet to Port Moresby and was then given the task of erecting a rest camp at Koitaki (after winning the brigade competition for the best prepared defensive area). From there they were soon ordered to join the rest of the battalion to commence jungle training.
>
> Though jungle training would have been a great morale booster for the troops after months spent in digging, they had no sooner arrived in the training area and dug the battalion latrines, when they were ordered to move again. This was the end of jungle training for them even though almost all of Bill Noyes' company (and no doubt others) never fired an Owen or Bren gun on a range . . .[6]

The 55th and 36th Militia Battalions were part of the 14th Brigade, which had been committed to the Port Moresby garrison in May 1942. Both had been assigned new commanding officers. Lieutenant-Colonel John Lovell had only been commanding the 55th Battalion for a few weeks when he was given command of the newly established 55/53rd Battalion. Lovell had been an original member of the 2/1st Battalion and had seen extensive service in the Middle East. Lieutenant-Colonel Cedric Isaachsen had been an original company commander with the 2/27th Battalion and had seen action during the Syrian campaign. He was posted as CO of the 36th Battalion at the end of August. Lieutenant-Colonel John Lovell:

> I had no opportunity to really carry out any intensive training for two reasons; firstly they were being employed as wharf-labourers unloading ships, and secondly, in

> October and November, we were employed on the construction of the defence of Tuaguba Hill.[7]

Lieutenant-Colonel Cedric Isaachsen:

> When we flew over to Sananada, when Brigadier Porter found that quite a few of the fellows had never fired a Bren gun or Tommy gun—never thrown a grenade—he ordered that these fellows come back not far from Brigade Headquarters and be given actual experience in firing a Bren, a Tommy gun and throwing a few grenades. This was within a few days of us arriving at Soputa.[8]

It is also salutary to note that when Lovell and Isaachsen had requested ammunition for the purpose of zeroing their rifles (adjusting the sights for accuracy after firing) in Port Moresby weeks earlier, that request had been denied by Brigadier Smith.[9]

When the slaughter at the beachhead had impacted upon the Allies during late November and early December 1942, the militia battalions in Port Moresby became the last resource—one that had been tragically neglected and denied the basic training essential for active service in a war zone.

Round one at Sanananda had seen the brave but worn, diseased and under-strength 16th Brigade grind to a halt in front of the brilliantly sited and camouflaged enemy defences. Round two had seen the introduction of the fresh but frail Americans—poorly trained, poorly led and, in the end, inactive. Round three at Sanananda was to be undertaken by Blamey's 'intensively trained' militia.

By 7 December 1942, the Australian positions at Sanananda had formed a rough horseshoe shape around the Killerton Track–Sanananda Road junction, with the base of the 'horseshoe' stretching across the Sanananda Road and about four hundred yards from the junction.

Brigadier Porter's plan for the 49th and 55/53rd Battalions' assault on 7 December envisaged a movement by the 49th to the right-hand side of the road and a corresponding left thrust by the 55/53rd. Because Porter had no third battalion for his attack, he ordered that the militia battalions attack one at a time while the other attempted to 'divert Japanese attention'.[10]

The 49th Battalion was given the task of commencing the attack on the right or eastern flank. Its A and C Companies were to commence the attack, with D and B Companies ordered to follow them in after a brief pause.

In a carbon copy of prior beachhead operations, the preparations for these militia attacks were rushed and ill-considered. The CO of the 49th, Lieutenant-Colonel Kessels, was not in a position to brief his company commanders until 6.00 p.m. on 6 December. The resultant meeting was undertaken in 'a badly lit shelter',[11] and by the time the company commanders arrived back at their lines—only occupied that day—there was no opportunity during darkness to either brief their men or reconnoitre the ground.[12] And when, after a rain-soaked night, the attack commenced, it was found that insufficient signal cable had arrived to enable adequate communication.[13] The 49th Battalion was therefore to put in an attack without accurate intelligence, without the opportunity for reconnaissance and, to further compound the degree of difficulty, without adequate signal equipment.

Despite these handicaps, there was no shortage of brave 49th Battalion soldiers that day. Fred Cranston, in *Always Faithful*:

> Jim Bryce [Captain, OC A Company] had not gone far when he was badly wounded by an explosive bullet, but fortunately the bullet hit his hands and the stock of the Owen gun he was carrying. This absorbed the shock and probably saved his life even though his face was peppered with fragments. Jack Dunne had the ground sheet which was rolled and attached to the back of his equipment shot to pieces, and was later wounded badly in the left arm, although not before firing his Owen gun in action for the first time in battle. Russ Forster, leading C Company, had advanced some 400 yards, and had knocked out a Japanese bunker with grenades. When his men reached a kunai patch near a small creek, he raised his head to investigate and received a bullet in the jaw. He continued to lead his men, holding a field dressing to the wound . . .[14]

But positions such as the Japanese junction defences required more than bravery if they were to be overcome.

As the attack pressed on, the two following companies lagged five hundred yards behind the lead two, instead of the proposed two hundred yards. And the main enemy positions were found to be on the left flank, and not on the right, as had been indicated by the Americans. With identification of the Japanese positions increasingly difficult as thick jungle and scrub was entered, and with communication now conducted by runners and hand signals, the attack ran into a wall of concentrated and enfilading fire.

The action was a comprehensive failure—however brave and determined its soldiers were on that fateful day. On 7 December 1942, in its first action after about twenty months of service in Papua, the 49th Militia Battalion lost fourteen officers and 215 soldiers killed or wounded in a period of five hours. This tragic tally constituted 48 per cent of the battalion's strength and between 55 and 60 per cent of its attacking force.[15]

Despite the failure of the 49th Battalion's role in the attack, Brigadier Porter decided to push ahead with the 55/53rd component of it; he reasoned that the potential for success of this second attack was not contingent on the success of the first.

Brigadier Porter's orders to Lieutenant-Colonel Lovell for his afternoon attack on 7 December near the junction reflect the lack of prior intelligence and 'detailed' planning: '55/53rd Battalion will attack enemy positions astride the road.'

Two companies of the 55/53rd Battalion moved forward at 3.15 p.m. on 7 December. Their objective was three 'suspected' enemy machine-gun posts near a feature called 'the big white tree', which was on the right of the track.[16] Lovell's orders were to then press on past this feature along the Sanananda Road towards Huggins' roadblock.

Some idea of the complete lack of training in this 55/53rd Battalion might be gauged from the experience on 7 December 1942 at Sananada of Private Kevin Barry:

> When we arrived in Port Moresby I was in the signals and I was only there a couple of weeks and I got malaria and I was crook for weeks. I ended up at Koitaki

> convalescent camp. Then I was seconded away to join a group to put up a telegraph line ten miles out of Moresby into Moresby . . . Then when that was over we were walking up and down Mount Tuaguba digging defensive positions outside of Moresby. Wake up in the morning, dig and walk back down again that night.
>
> Bearing in mind at this time I'd never held a rifle in my hand, never ever fired one—didn't know anything about it . . . Then when the Japs started coming over the Range [Kokoda Trail], out we go to a rifle range somewhere . . . Next minute we're over there [Sananandal] and we're lining up at 3.15 p.m. on the 7th of December, fixed bayonets, and I'm a forward scout with Johnny Achbold; we both got wounded the same day—so out we go and they say charge—into the jungle we go . . . and all of a sudden the shit hits the fan. Machine-guns; and I'm going along and I can hear this and I'm hanging on to the rifle and I'm shit scared—then in the next minute I'm up in the air—lost the rifle, lost my tin hat—hit in the shoulder . . . that was the sum total of my war time experience . . .[17]

Sergeant Clarrie Meredith had been an original member of the 53rd Battalion and had been posted to the 55/53rd after his former unit's disbandment. As the 55/53rd did not attack until the afternoon of 7 December, some minor reconnaissance did take place:

> Sanananda was really Kokoda all over again. No specific training, new weapons on the eve of departure . . .
>
> December 6th—my role as Cpl . . . we were immediately allocated an area on the left side of the track and dug in and consolidated our position, and were to await further instructions. My section plus one other under Lt Travis had to do a reconnaissance patrol forward as far as possible that afternoon. We went about 200 yds when we came under heavy fire but could not locate the actual position from which the firing came from. We attempted to probe further but we had to return to our position.

Sananda, 19 December 1942

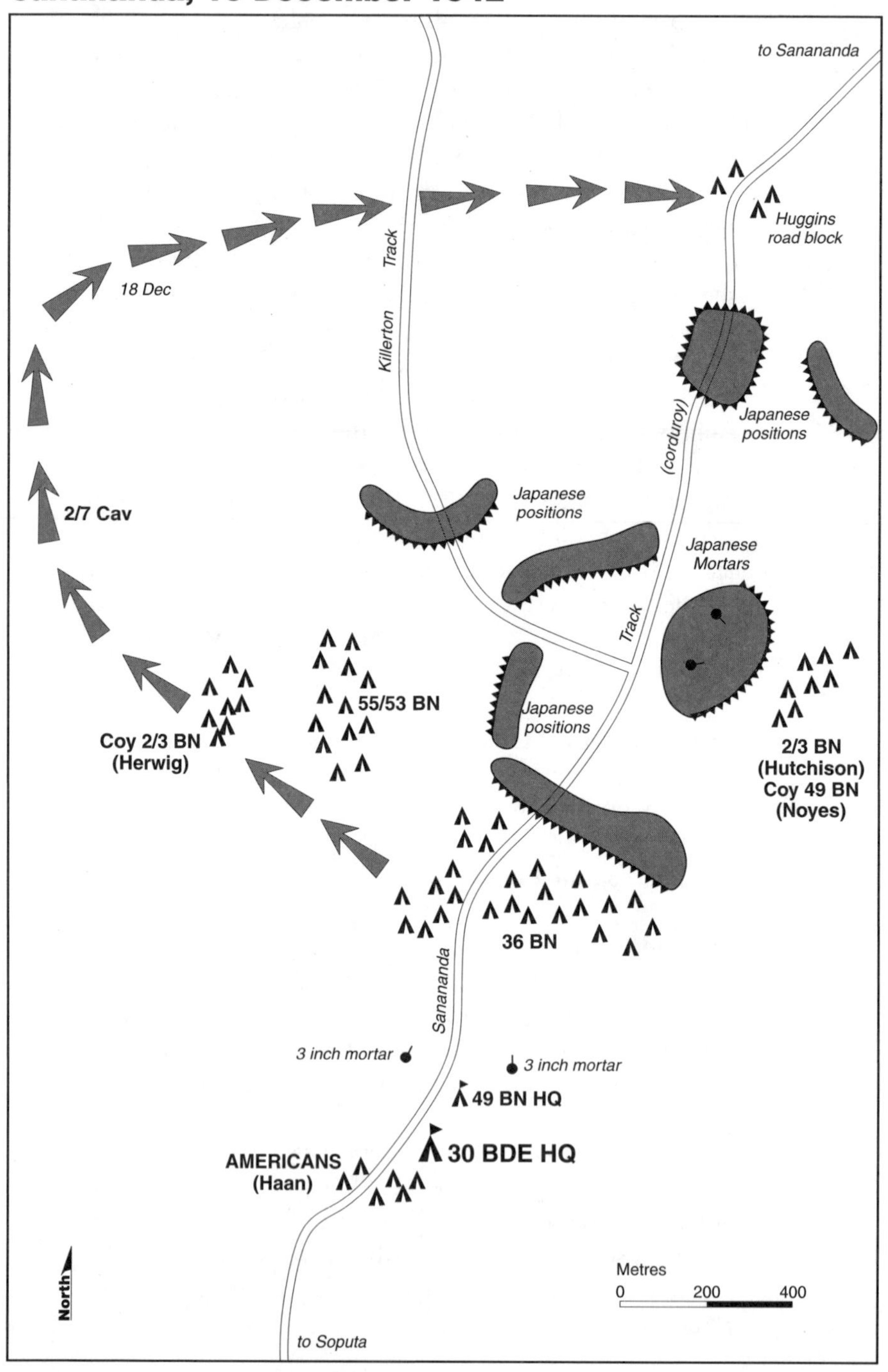

> The area around the Sananada Track was reasonably flat and although not as thick jungle as the Trail there was still a very limited vision. The rain kept the soil in such a state that any movement turned the soil to mud. The water table level was only about 18 inches to 2 feet below the surface and when you tried to dig a 'fox' hole you nearly always sat in water. The Track was kept passable by the use of timber forming a corduroy surface. It seemed the growth was such that you could almost believe you saw it grow.
>
> December 7th— . . . A and C Company were to advance to endeavour to take the area 200 yards ahead if possible to the 'big white tree'. We had only moved 80 yds when we had all hell belted out of us. I lost my Owen Gunner, Joe Paull, before we had gone 50 yards—badly wounded in his right thigh. I took his Owen gun and we only moved forward about another 30 yds or so when we were forced to try and dig in as you could not see any more than 10 ft in front of you. We had only about 36 men on their feet at dark—out of approx 120 . . .
>
> Our first real contact with the enemy as 55/53 and our worst. Next morning we returned to our original positions . . .[18]

The Official Historian talks of these soldiers' 'inexperience' which caused them to 'bunch together' and that only a handful of one of the two attacking companies crossed the track, which brought the second company under further sustained fire.[19] The experiences of Kevin Barry and Clarrie Meredith are illuminating. 'Inexperience' is an understatement. And a further point should be made. When the 53rd Battalion was disbanded in October 1942, some of its failed Kokoda Trail officers ought to have been replaced. The reality of war is that some officers are not equal to their tasks. They should be removed for their own sake and for the welfare of their soldiers. At Sanananda on 7 December 1942, a very small number of such officers were *still* in command of troops in action. Sergeant Clarrie Meredith:

> _______was not a leader in combat. I have memories of him in action on the Sananada Track, sitting behind a large fallen tree in a small creek, purely dead scared, which we all would have been to some degree, just telling us 'Keep moving forward boys, you mustn't stop.' He did not lead us in at all . . . enough said.[20]

The officer in question was a senior commander. Some small number of the 55/53rd Battalion did indeed lose their purpose, did lose their will to push on. In view of their lack of training, their often unfamiliar weapons, the lack of reconnaissance, the questionable leadership of at least one of their officers, and last but by no means least the fact that previous attacks by tried and tested AIF troops had failed prior to their arrival at Sanananda, the results of 7 December 1942 at Sanananda are hardly surprising. On 7 December 1942 at Sanananda, the 55/53rd Battalion lost eight officers and 122 other ranks either killed, wounded or missing. Of those listed casualties, 28 were NCOs—the junior leaders whose example and inspiration are critical to a unit's success in action.

This dark day at Sanananda caused Major-General Vasey and Lieutenant-General Herring to call a halt to the carnage. They now determined that for the immediate future, all Allied actions at Sanananda would constitute patrolling only. Porter would later write:

> Since our first assault, [his 30th Brigade] we have used a 'stalk and consolidate' type of tactics, combined with fire concentrations on enemy positions, as discovered. We have patrolled deeply and over wide areas. Several raids have had the effect of killing some enemy, but his well constructed MG positions defy our fire power and present a barrier of fire through which our troops must pass. We have attempted to seize these in failing light, but they are too numerous to deal with by other than an attack in great strength. One of these attempts silenced one MG but others supported from flank positions. On the latter occasion own troops [*sic*] avoided fixed lines by crawling back to cover in the bad light.[21]

This is an extraordinary statement. And it is typical of the almost bewildering command approach taken by the Australian senior officers at the beachhead. The very approach outlined by Porter *after* the 30th Brigade had taken such heavy casualties was, in fact, the procedure that should have precluded the attacks of 7 December.

By mid-December 1942, Lieutenant-General Herring realised that he had almost expended the available pool of infantry troops in Port Moresby and Milne Bay who might be committed to Sananda. Knowing that a portion of those available troops must be kept to secure those places, he decided to commit the 36th Militia Battalion and the 2/7th Cavalry Regiment to Sananda. The Official Historian:

> The 36th, a militia unit from New South Wales, had arrived in Port Moresby late in May as part of the 14th Brigade. The 2/7th Cavalry was part of the 7th Division and had been formed in May 1940. Though the regiment had left Australia in that year, battle had so far eluded it. It trained in Palestine and Eygpt, went to Cyprus in May 1941 to augment the slender garrison when that island was threatened with airborne invasion, and then rejoined its division in Syria. After their return to Australia with other units of the 6th and 7th Divisions early in 1942 the cavalrymen spent a period in south Queensland training in infantry tactics before they set out for New Guinea in September. Their work and training at Port Moresby continued into December and, when orders to move forward arrived, their spirits rose high. Some 350 of them were flown across the range.[22]

On 17 December, Major-General Vasey issued orders for another Sananda attack on the 19th. Vasey:

> Our immediate enemy has been in position without reinforcement of personnel, material and supplies since 21–22 November. During the intervening period the enemy has been continually harassed by air, artillery or mortar bombardments and subject to infantry attacks and offensive patrols. From information obtained from

> prisoners of war and captured natives it would appear that he is now short of supplies.
>
> The enemy, therefore, should now be considerably weaker although his strength in automatic weapons has NOT been greatly reduced in the areas which he is still holding. However, in spite of great tenacity, past experience has shown he has a breaking point and it is felt that this is now close. Adverse local conditions and the ever present possibility of him receiving reinforcements makes it imperative that the complete and utter destruction of the enemy in the Sananada area should be carried out at the earliest possible moment.[23]

Vasey's plan envisaged the 2/7th Cavalry undertaking a wide encircling movement around the left, or western junction flank, occupying Huggins' roadblock and then pushing through to the coast along the Sananda Road. At the same time, Brigadier Porter's 30th Brigade was to attack the junction area, eliminate the enemy occupying it, and then destroy the Japanese between Giruwa and Garara. Porter's attack was to be undertaken again by the 55/53rd and the 49th Battalions, with the newly arrived 36th Battalion assigned to either assist where needed or exploit gains.

On 18 December, the 36th Battalion moved forward and occupied the positions held by the 49th and 55/53rd Battalions astride the road. The 30th Brigade plan was that the 49th was to attack from the right or eastern flank and occupy the Sananda Road about five hundred yards north of the junction. The 55/53rd was sent around the left or western flank with orders to attack eastwards and clear the Sananda Road up to the junction.

The attack by the 30th Brigade in the junction area on 19 December was a virtual replica of those which had preceded it. The 49th made some small ground early, as its control of its sub-units was maintained. However, after eliminating a number of Japanese posts, the momentum of the attack waned as the volume of concealed enemy fire increased and communication became more difficult. Although a patrol of the 49th did make contact with the Americans at the Huggins' roadblock, little ground was gained. Porter sent

Major Douglas and his A Company, 36th Battalion to take over the slightly advanced position of the 49th.

On the left flank, the 55/53rd Battalion attack also faltered after only one of the Japanese posts had been taken. The company lost its momentum after its commander was mortally wounded and his second-in-command also hit. And when a number of the NCOs were soon killed or wounded, the company assault became a confused number of small groups who lost contact and therefore their cohesion and ability to communicate.

When Lieutenant-Colonel Lovell ordered a second company forward, its movement to the front was slow. The Official Historian:

> In the early afternoon Captain Henderson came forward to hurry them along. But some of the men were reluctant to advance and Porter wrote bitterly later: 'Captain Henderson lost his life as he bombed an enemy LMG post. The remainder of his party left him to the task without aiding him.'[24]

The attack was called off. It cost the 55/53rd a further six officers and 69 other ranks either killed or wounded. The 55/53rd fell back about a hundred yards and Captain Stan Powers, 36th Battalion, moved his B Company around the front of the 49th. Late that day, and in fading light, Powers' men occupied a small perimeter astride the road.

When Powers and his B Company attacked towards the southward junction at first light on 20 December, the Japanese were ready for them. The company gained some ground but found itself fired on from both sides as well as the front. And when Major Douglas and his A Company also attempted to move on B Company's flank, they too came on to heavily concealed and defended positions.

Orders then came back for the two companies of the 36th Battalion to break contact—B Company was needed to join its C and D Companies in an attack the following day in front of A Company's perimeter.

For its attack on 21 December, the 36th Battalion was required to move from about two hundred yards east of the

Sananananda Road, south through the jungle, and eventually arrive at the junction. Lieutenant-Colonel Isaachsen allotted his C Company (Captain Andy Powers) the left flank and his D Company (Captain Ted Elphick) the right. Captain Andy Powers was an identical twin to Captain Stan Powers of B Company. B Company was to act as the battalion reserve. A creeping artillery barrage and mortar fire were arranged to support the attack.

The attack went in at 3.00 p.m. Although D Company made about three hundred yards, it took heavy casualties. But it was along C Company's front that the carnage and confusion reached its peak. Private Ken Hamilton, 14 Platoon, C Company, 36th Battalion:

> In our first frontal attack C Coy lost our full Coy HQ including Captain A.M. [Andy] Powers. A hell of a lot of noise, smoke, mortars and grenades—my rifle platoon worked its way down the edge of the fire trail, to get at the guns, but very thick jungle, no visible contact . . . the Coy HQ must have staggered into the face of the guns. In this, and other attacks, we made ground, only to be pulled back so not to have our flanks exposed . . . not many of the dead or wounded ever saw a Japanese . . . in that first attack it was so confused, and the jungle so thick, that my best friend Pte Glenn Wall, made his way around the left side of a large tree—and I went right, and did not see him again![25]

Private Jack Jackson, 13 Platoon, C Company, 36th Battalion:

> Our advance got nowhere. I was pinned down with bullets flying everywhere. You could hear them zipping into leaves and trees. We couldn't see the Jap positions and their snipers were active till they were taken care of. The attack was a disaster as we had to withdraw and lost a lot of good mates.[26]

The 36th Battalion's baptism of fire took little or no ground for the cost of 55 killed, wounded or missing. And most of those casualties occurred within the first ten minutes of the attack.[27]

The Official Historian:

> By this time Brigadier Porter had become bitterly critical of both the 36th and 55/53rd Battalions. He said that any success which was theirs was 'due to a percentage of personnel who are brave in the extreme'; and 'the result of unskilful aggression'. He was caustic in referring to their deficiencies of training and spirit.[28]

Lieutenant-Colonel Cedric Isaachsen, CO 36th Battalion:

> If he said those words at that time then it was a grossly unfair comment . . . we had been mucked about by him, with companies taken away from us and put under command of other units then switched around. There was a hell of a lot of messing around that went on. Unnecessary in my view.[29]

This 'messing around' should be examined. It had not started at Sanananda. It is interesting that Porter's comments were confined to the 36th and 55/53rd Battalions—both members of the 14th Brigade. His 30th Brigade's 49th Battalion had achieved little more. We have noted the 'training' given to Porter's 49th Battalion prior to their deployment at Sanananda. It should also be stated that a significant number of the 55/53rd Battalion were ex-members of the 53rd, who had also been under his command since May 1942. When that battalion had been withdrawn from the Kokoda campaign in September, we have noted its subsequent 'training': wharf unloading, labouring and guard duties. We have further noted the tragic transfer of a small number of officers from the 53rd who had failed dismally on the trail, and who subsequently found their way into the 55/53rd and action at Sanananda.

Brigadier Porter must take some measure of responsibility for the subsequent unpreparedness of both the 49th and 55/53rd Battalions for action at Sanananda. Further, Isaachsen's concern at the 'switching around' of companies under differing commands is entirely valid.

To have soldiers learning how to throw a grenade, learning how to operate Thompson machine-guns and Bren guns for the first time near Brigade HQ at Sananandajust prior to their first action is a damning and unforgivable indictment upon any army. Not long after Christmas 1942, some members of C Company, 36th Battalion refused to mount an attack. Some members of the 55/53rd had also shown a reluctance to advance after their costly attacks of 18 December. They were not cowards—that had been proven during their initial attacks.

It is hard to escape the conclusion that when Major-General Vasey had destroyed a substantial number of the enemy at Oivi–Gorari in early November, and when Allied intelligence had estimated the Japanese strength across the whole beachhead at about 1500, that New Guinea Force in Port Moresby did not contemplate that their militia units would be committed to the fighting. The wharf labouring was allowed to continue; rifles did not need to be zeroed; grenade throwing did not need to be learnt; and new weapons such as the Owen gun and the Bren gun did not need to be mastered. Incomplete platoon training was ample preparation for wharf labouring, but most definitely inadequate for action on battlefields such as Sananda during December 1942.

Of the total losses sustained by the Australians and Americans when Sananda eventually fell, nearly one-third of them were Australian militia.[30]

It was a nightmare of a journey just to get to Huggins' roadblock, let alone fight a war there.

When the 2/7th Cavalry Regiment made its wide, western flanking movement to cut the Killerton Track and arrived at Huggins' on 18 December—to put in its attack from Huggins to the coast—the approach to the roadblock had still not been secured. The move entailed the crossing of numerous areas of swamp, often up to arm-pit depth, along a track known as 'the Track of Dead Men's Bones'. The Americans at Huggins' were resupplied every three days—if the supplying force could get through. The 2/7th attempted to secure the final crossing point into Huggins'. They could not. Chaplain Hartley described the last required movement into Huggins':

> The signal was passed in whispers, from man to man, down the long line. 'When you get to the kunai patch, get down on your belly and crawl—go over the first log, don't touch the second and under *the third* . . .'
>
> At last the first log—over!—then the second, don't touch!—then the just around a bend in the Kunai patch our last symbol, came into view . . .
>
> Through the cover of the trees the track now wound through deeper swamps. The vivid meaning of the track now impressed itself upon us. On making the cover we first had to step on a Japanese body to clear a deep water hole.[31]

At every subsequent bend in the approach to Huggins' the 2/7th soldiers found green and rotting corpses. Upon their arrival at the roadblock, the unit prepared for its first attack.

If the 30th Brigade's attacks on the junction on 19 December 1942 ran into heavy resistance, then the wall of fire that awaited the 2/7th was no less testing. Chaplain Hartley:

> Dramatic messages began to drift back to Huggins. 'Advanced H.Q. Surrounded, send out "C" Squadron for protection—"D" Squadron cross to right of the road in an outflanking movement.' 'D' Squadron immediately crossed the road but 'C' Squadron were unable to carry out the C.O.'s orders. And so the gruelling day ended in a haze of uncertainty. We did not know what had happened to the boys further up.[32]

The 2/7th had gone into their attack with extraordinary courage. By the end of the day, despite the fact that the majority of the 2/7th were forced to fall back on Huggins', a further tenuous position on the Sanananda Road had been established. Known as James' post, about a hundred men from Captain James' B Squadron held a perimeter about four hundred yards further along the Sanananda Road from Huggins'.

By the end of Christmas Eve 1942, the 2/7th Cavalry Regiment had managed to concentrate nineteen officers and

205 other ranks at James' post. During six days of tough fighting the cavalry had therefore advanced some four hundred yards and had secured a post forward, but the intervening ground between Huggins' and James' was still separated by strong Japanese positions. Those savage actions had cost the 2/7th seven officers and 33 other ranks killed and about forty wounded.

The evacuation of the wounded from this forward post on Christmas Day gives some indication of the ground forward of the junction, and the nightmare that was Sananada. Chaplain Hartley:

> It was a slow, tedious and nerve-racking journey. The patients were heavy. Four men were required for each stretcher. These bearers had to carry their arms in their free hand. These arms caught in the creepers and caused no end of irritation. Then the track was for single file . . .
>
> Whenever there was a stop for rest, armed men would penetrate the jungle off the track and silently watch against a possible ambush . . .
>
> We now came into view of the Jap camp that had been shot up on the first of December in an American attack from Huggins Perimeter . . .
>
> There were mangled and rotting corpses scattered everywhere. Blank-eyed skeletons stared with sightless eyes from beneath the broken shelters. Bones of horses with their saddles and harness rotting around them shone white as the morning sun peering through the creepers caught them in her beams. We actually welcomed this gory sight . . . Huggins was but a hundred yards beyond.[33]

Round three of the battle for Sanananda had seen the 49th, 36th and 55/53rd Militia Battalions and the 2/7th Cavalry Regiment committed to the fighting. But by the time those formations' first fights had concluded, it was clear that other measures would have to be employed if Sanananda was to be taken. The Official Historian:

> New plans were again being made to end the ghastly nightmare which the Sananada affair had become. The primaeval swamps, the dank and silent bush, the heavy loss of life, the fixity of purpose of the Japanese for most of whom death could be the only ending, all combined to make this struggle so appalling that most of the hardened soldiers who were to emerge from it remember it unwillingly and as their most exacting experience of the whole war . . .
>
> . . . Herring visited Vasey on the 20th. The two Generals agreed that further major offensive action on this front was not possible with the troops available. Herring said that he would try to bring tanks and fresh infantry into the fight, but that it could not happen before the 29th at the earliest.[34]

The tanks referred to were those of the 2/6th Armoured Regiment. And the 'fresh' infantry—considerably less fresh by January—were none other than the 18th Infantry Brigade. While the 2/9th Battalion was busily engaged in fighting at Buna on 20 December 1942, the 18th Brigade was already earmarked for operations at Sananada. It is little wonder, therefore, that by 29 December Brigadier Wootten was pushing Lieutenant-Colonel Dobbs into speedy attacks along the Old Strip at Buna in the mad rush that was the battle for the beachhead; and, before Buna was captured, Sananada awaited the 18th Brigade.

We have seen the magnificent performance of the 18th Brigade at Buna. But in the fetid swamps and dense scrub at Sananada, this tried and tested formation was to experience battlefield conditions and privations that constitute a unique chapter in the history of Australia's wartime experience.

THE PASSING OF COMRADES

27

The 18th Brigade received its orders to march from Buna to Soputa to break the Sananananda deadlock on 4 January 1943. The 2/9th and 2/10th Battalions left on the 5th and 6th and the 2/12th followed on the 7th. Lieutenant John Andrews, 2/10th Battalion:

> The track was awful, it was knee deep in places and ankle deep anywhere, and the mud, it was an effort to take each step. And of course we were buggered from Buna . . . I think that was the toughest walk I did in my life. I was rotten with malaria, I think that was my first real bad attack, and how I got to Soputa I'll never know.[1]

Sergeant Bill Spencer, 2/9th Battalion:

> It was only a 15-mile march. During training both at home and in the desert, such a trek was no more than a half-day's wander for fit and well-trained troops. But Papua wasn't the desert—and we weren't fit. Like many other Buna survivors, I cannot remember one incident or feature about that march, as my high temperature, malaria, physical and mental exhaustion and sleep deprivation turned a 15-mile slog through stifling jungle, foetid swamps and mud into an eternal, sepia blur.[2]

Trooper John Wilson, 2/6th Armoured Regiment:

> The movement of tanks . . . from Buna to Soputa and then to Sananandа was an epic in itself. The first portion of the trip covered several miles of corduroy roads, swampy areas and then quite a distance through kunai grass . . . we had to cross several small rivers and creeks. When we reached these obstacles, the crews would dismount except for the driver, who would drive down the embankment which was usually very steep down to the border of the creek . . . we worked out a system where we placed a rope at the front of the tank with approximately 100 native bearers, who would take up the weight of the tank when it got to the stage where it started to slide backwards . . . the tank would be actually physically pulled with muscle power up the remaining slope slipping and sliding until it got onto level ground . . .
>
> The overall trip took several days, and we camped by the tanks at night . . .
>
> I remember one day coming on to a swampy corduroy road area and we found Brigadier Wootten, his driver, and 2 escorts in a jeep and trailer with all his maps and equipment bogged to the axles. We hooked the tank on and pulled them out.[3]

After the slaughter at Buna, the 18th Brigade had been substantially reinforced. The 2/9th received reinforcements at Buna and also three officers and 118 other ranks at Soputa during 6–8 January;[4] the 2/10th received six officers and 200 other ranks at Buna and five and 150 at Soputa;[5] and the 2/12th gained 25 on 7 January, 44 on the 8th and five on the 9th.[6]

The military quality of this 18th Brigade reinforcement varied. Some of the new arrivals to the 2/10th, for example, had only received basic training in South Australia and a further six weeks in Victoria.[7] Where possible, such soldiers were allotted to their own state's battalion: South Australians to the 2/10th and Queenslanders to the 2/9th. However, the contingent sent to the Tasmanians and Queenslanders of the 2/12th were Victorians. As far as was possible, the reinforcements were spread evenly amongst the companies and platoons so as to have a mixture of 'old hands' and new arrivals.

After Lieutenant-Colonel Cummings had been wounded at Buna, his second-in-command, Major Parry-Okeden, had assumed command, and Major Geard from the 2/12th had taken over the 2/10th from Lieutenant-Colonel Dobbs after his evacuation from Buna due to illness.

The initial objective of the 18th Brigade's operation was easy to identify: the infamous Sanananda Road–Killerton Track junction. After its seizure, Brigadier Wootten knew that he could move in two critical directions—down the Sanananda Road and along the Killerton Track. Once movement along those two routes was established, he could roll up the entire Japanese Sanananda defences from the east (via Cape Killerton) through the centre (the Sanananda Road) and, eventually, move westwards along the coast towards Tarakena.

Wootten's plan to break the stalemate at the junction hinged entirely on the ability of his tanks to force a passage down the Sanananda Road and blast the Japanese bunker network as they had done so brilliantly at Buna. He deployed the 2/9th Battalion facing slightly to the south-east of a strong network of enemy bunkers, with the 2/12th linking up on its left flank and stretching back and parallel to the Sanananda Road. Facing the 2/12th was a further network of bunkers which lay astride the road. The all-important Australian attack on the junction was planned for 12 January. The tanks were also to facilitate the advance of the 2/12th to the junction.

But there was one burning question: did the Japanese have a gun or guns such as those which had destroyed his tanks on the Old Strip at Buna? If they did, the same fate awaited those lightly armoured and vulnerable General Stuart tanks. The Sanananda Road was a mere narrow corduroy track—not the wide Old Strip at Buna—and it fell away to bog-ridden ground that would not allow for tight tank turning. Wootten simply did not know the answer to this critical question, so he made his plans on the basis that such a gun or guns did not in fact exist.

The crucial 18th Brigade attack on the junction at Sanananda began at 8.00 a.m. on 12 January 1943. Lieutenant Heap's tank was first in. Corporal Lloyd Thomas was Heap's driver:

The Junction attack—2/9th, 2/12th BNS, 12 January 1943

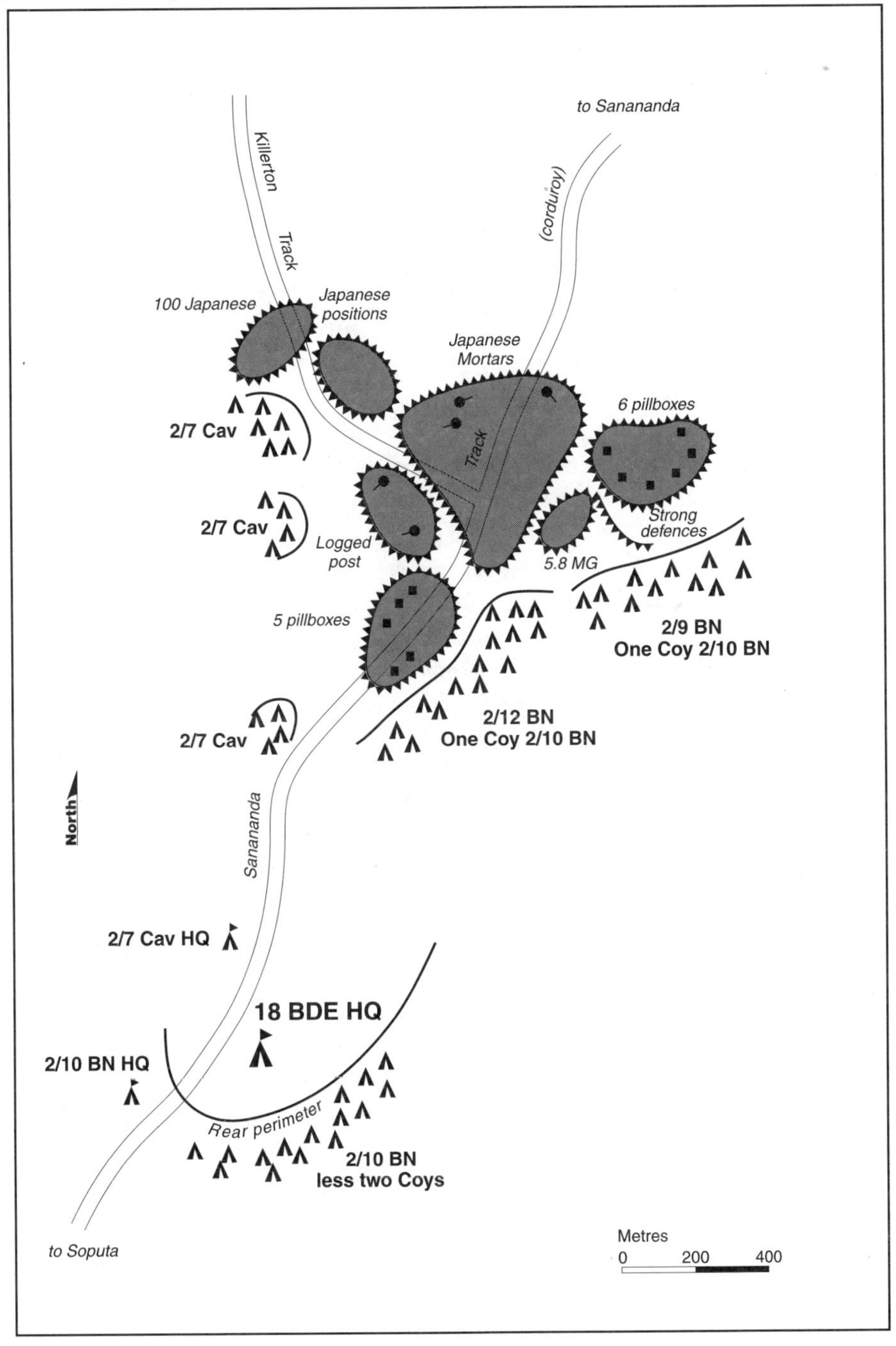

> As we crossed the start line we closed up and I drove using the driver's periscope which did not give much vision, and I had to totally rely on the crew commander for main directions . . .
>
> The track was very narrow and rough and we crept along slowly watching as much as we were able to. The first thing I can remember was there was a very loud explosion and my driver's flap flew open, but I was able to close it quickly before machine gun fire hit the tank. Seconds after that, the hull gunner's flap flew open from another direct hit and it took both of us to pull it down again. Another A/P shell went through the front of the tank . . . I was able to turn the tank with great difficulty to go back to our lines . . .[8]

Corporal Boughton's tank was moving about twenty yards behind Heap's. Trooper Jim Wood was Boughton's gunner:

> No report was received regarding the enemies [*sic*] positions or strength. We were definitely told there were no A.T. [anti-tank] guns against us . . .
>
> Cpl. J. Boughton apparently saw something suspicious, as he told me to traverse left to the base of a big tree. Before I picked up anything in my scope we were hit. I think on the turret just above my head. I certainly saw sparks. Then we got a direct hit just to the right of the driver's head (Ray Lynn's). I wasn't sure where the shells came from but assumed it must have been what Jeff Boughton had seen, so I proceeded to plaster that area with H.E. [high explosive] shells, as best I could, as I didn't have a loader. Geoff Hemphill was doing his best (damnest) to contact the other tanks.
>
> Ray Lynn's periscope was RS (rat shit), so I looked through the hole in the front to see what he was doing whilst he turned the tank. I kept traversing the turret so I could hopefully score a hit on the gun I couldn't see, or at least make them pull their heads in. I must have succeeded to some extent, as we didn't suffer any more damage.[9]

Lynn's driving under pressure was extraordinary. Ray Lynn:

> There were quite a few armour piercing points in my tank which I knocked out with a hammer, at a later date—they almost went through the armour plating. The gun was only 30 or 40 yards in front of us . . . we got one on the armour plating of my periscope. It left me with a small slit in the armour plating to see through—the shell came in the tank straight past my ear—singed my hair and back into Cpl Boughton's knee which left it dangling by a tendon.
>
> I immediately swung the tank off the track still leaving the track on the edge of the corduroy. It was at this stage a miracle happened for us. McGregor's tank bellowed out over the mike, to 'hold her there.' And I did till they came past and then I gave her all she had and got back on to the track and crept back with very little vision to an R.A.P. station where we pulled Geoff up through the turret. He was very weak with loss of blood and died later. Jimmy Wood got shrapnel in the legs and I got some on the side of my face, neck and arm.[10]

Shortly after MacGregor's tank entered the fight, it was seen to burst into flames. It remains a matter of conjecture as to the crew's fate, as neither their remains or personal effects were ever located—in or outside their tank.

When the tanks were destroyed, the 2/12th met the same fate as others which had attempted to make inroads directly into the junction area—and they took 70 casualties in the process.

But the 2/9th made ground through its now customary skill and aggression. Parry-Okeden's plan was that his C and D Companies were to hold their positions facing the enemy, while his A Company (Lieutenant Lloyd) and his B Company (Lieutenant Jackson) were to skirt around his right flank and attack the enemy bunkers. When that movement had begun, C and D Companies initially were to assist the right flank attack with supporting fire and then move to close the left flank. It is worth recording that lieutenants were now often in command of companies and sergeants of platoons at Sanananda—such had been the loss of officer ranks at Buna. Private Chalky Morris, Intelligence Section, 2/9th Battalion:

> In the centre of C Company's positions the jungle came right down to the creek. There was a very big tree right on the corner where the Japs had dug in a position for a machine gun. It had a bird's nest in the top of the tree and for artillery purposes we called it 'Birdsnest Tree'. On the right of this down to Jock Hart's platoon, the jungle was stunted and very thick . . . to the left was a high part of the ground, very firm footing . . .[11]

On the right flank of the 2/9th Battalion's attack Lieutenant Jackson's B Company made impressive progress. After eliminating a number of Japanese bunkers, the company reached its objective by midday. While journeying back to HQ Jackson was shot and killed by a sniper. But progress on A Company's front was less impressive—Japanese positions in the Bird's Nest Tree area pinned the Queenslanders down and Lieutenant Lloyd was killed. Warrant-Officer Jim Jesse from C Company was given command of A Company and, after a series of determined assaults, A Company was able to link up with B Company and thereby complete the capture of the 2/9th Battalion's objectives. The cost was two officers and 27 other ranks killed or wounded.

The failure by Wootten's elite 18th Brigade on 12 January 1943 to capture the junction at Sananananda was perhaps a low point of the campaign in terms of the high expectations of the senior commanders. If Wootten's men couldn't capture the junction—and with tanks—then the tactics, the concentration of force and the available support for both past and future operations had to be finally questioned. And such assessments were long overdue.

On 13 January, a spirited debate took place between the American commander (Eichelberger), Herring, Vasey, Berryman (who had been sent as Herring's new chief of staff to Vasey's HQ) and Colonel Pollard (Vasey's chief staff officer). Vasey wrote an appreciation:

> As a result of the attack by the 18 Aust Inf Bde on 12 Jan 43, it is now clear that the present position which has been held by the Jap since 20 Nov 42 consists of a series of perimeter localities in which there are numerous

> pillboxes of the same type as those found in the Buna area. To attack these with infantry using their own weapons is repeating the costly mistakes of 1915–17 and, in view of the limited resources which can be, at present, put into this area, such attacks seem unlikely to succeed.
>
> The nature of the ground prevents the use of tanks except along the main Sananada Track on which the enemy has already shown that he has A-Tk guns capable of knocking out the M3 light tank.
>
> Owing to the denseness of the undergrowth in the area of ops, these pill-boxes are only discovered at very short ranges (in all cases under 100 yards) and it is therefore not possible to subject them to arty bombardment without withdrawing our own troops. Experience has shown that when our troops are withdrawn to permit of such bombardment, the Jap occupies the vacated territory so that the bombardment, apart from doing him little damage, only produces new positions out of which the Jap must be driven.[12]

Major-General George Vasey's comment that 'To attack these with infantry using their own weapons is repeating the costly mistakes of 1915–17 . . .' was an extraordinary statement to be making at this time. Troops under his command had been doing precisely that at Gona from 21 November until 8 December: eighteen days. And troops under his command at Sananda had also been doing precisely that from 20 November until 12 January: 53 days.

The truth is simple. From the outset of the beachhead battles, the commanders had relied on faulty intelligence which asserted that the enemy were few in number and sick and therefore set for slaughter. However, when, on each costly day, the success they so keenly desired—and were unreasonably pressured by MacArthur and Blamey into achieving—did not eventuate, the feeling prevailed that each new day might bring that elusive victory. But each new day brought nothing more than the inexcusable 'costly mistakes of 1915–17'.

Vasey's solution to the problem was to offer two alternatives. The first was a movement around the junction along the Killerton Track to the coast, followed by a thrust along the beach to Sananananda. His second option advocated a landing from the sea in the Cape Killerton area. He readily conceded, however, that his first option was prejudiced by difficulties of supply, and the second by a lack of landing craft and shipping.

Berryman favoured a blockade of the junction area to starve the Japanese. Eichelberger tended to agree with Berryman but was more circumspect, and wanted more patrolling and assessment. Vasey and Pollard seemed against a blockade. The result of the meeting was that preliminary orders were given to commence a blockade.

In the end the Allies did not determine the outcome of the battle for the Sananananda Road–Killerton Track junction—the Japanese did.

On the very day of Vasey's meeting, 13 January 1943, the enemy realised that their operations on Guadalcanal were doomed. During early December, in the face of determined American naval and air strength, they were unable to reinforce and adequately supply their beleaguered troops on that island. Although the American marines were unable to make substantial ground, they were, by the end of December, in a position to plan a decisive January offensive against Japanese troops who were now starving and disease-ridden.

The Japanese ordered General Hyakutake to move his force towards Cape Esperance and be prepared to evacuate it by destroyer from Guadalcanal commencing 1–2 February 1943. The Japanese were eventually able to rescue 13 000 troops from the island.

With the Japanese decision to evacuate Guadalcanal came the almost simultaneous realisation that Papua was also lost. Their Sananananda commander was ordered to send his troops overland and by sea to Salamaua and Lae—no small trek. Small craft were also to be used for the wounded and some launches would attempt to remove as many troops as possible. The target date for this ambitious program was given as 25 January. Subsequent circumstances caused the Japanese to advance that date by five days.

After the depressed Allied command atmosphere of the previous day, Vasey was able to contact Eichelberger with exciting news on 14 January: 'the bugger's gone'. By nightfall on 14 January the junction was in Wootten's hands.

'The bugger' had suffered enormously at Sanananda. The Japanese had been forced into a static defensive position at the junction for weeks, and had been virtually surrounded by the Australians to the east and west and at the Huggins' and James' roadblocks to the north. Their supply and medical lines had failed, they were under artillery bombardment and had lived in swamp, mud and constant water for weeks. Towards the end, many a Japanese Sanananda soldier fought his fight naked from the waist down—rather than continually foul his pants. And once again, when forced to find food, he repeated his grisly Kokoda Trail behaviour. Chalky Morris, Intelligence Section, 2/9th Battalion:

> Then the Japs pulled out and we went through and they found Jack ______'s body with the fleshy parts off the back and buttocks and that cut off . . . I saw parts of Jack's body in the pot still on the fire.[13]

Sergeant Bill Spencer, Intelligence Section, 2/9th Battalion:

> . . . what he had been up to disgusted us and filled us with an utter determination to defeat him with no compassion or mercy . . .
>
> I found flesh in tin dixies wrapped in leaves in the possession of several Japanese. I also found a number of ten-shilling notes on the enemy bodies. There is always something to make you keep going, and perhaps this was the goad. I do know that this incident sealed the fate of any Japanese we came across in the future.[14]

Vasey assigned Brigadier Wootten the task of pushing down the Killerton Track to Cape Killerton, followed by an eastward movement through to Sanananda Point. The Americans were assigned two roles: the first was the destruction of the Japanese facing them at the Huggins' roadblock and a consequent movement down the Sanananda Road; and the second was a push from Buna along the Siwori–Tarakena–Giruwa path and along to Sananada. The 2/7th Cavalry Regiment was to mop up these track movements, while the 36th and 55/53rd Battalions of the 14th Brigade were to prevent any westward escape by the Japanese. The 30th Brigade was to protect the supply dumps in the Soputa–Jumbora area. Captain Geoff Verco, 2/10th Battalion doctor:

> . . . it was against all our bringings-up to sit in jungle and swamp and be rained on . . . it was just a completely foreign terrain, and nobody guessed that we would be going through the sort of jungles and swamps and mud and water, discomfort, heat and disease . . . it was unbelievable the whole thing! I've got the greatest admiration for the infantryman, he's the salt of the earth. And it was a terrible business to see them being knocked off like they were . . .[15]

Buna had been hard enough. But to the 'old hands' of the 18th Brigade the passage through the swamps, kunai grass and jungle, and the eventual passage to the coast at Sanananda, would be forever burnt into their memories. To the long-suffering infantryman this was the last throw, the last fight—and he was determined to see it through.

As the 2/10th had been the brigade reserve during the failed attack on the junction on 12 January, Wootten assigned it to lead the 18th Brigade advance along the Killerton Track. The 2/10th was to be followed by Brigade HQ, the 2/9th and lastly, the 2/12th. The South Australians began their advance along the Killerton Track at 7.00 a.m. on 15 January. Corporal Bill Neate, D Company, 2/10th Battalion:

> The Killerton Track was only a narrow, yard-wide track. Sometimes it widened a bit, muddy and slushy, and petered out into swamp up to your knees and deeper in places. It had jungle each side, streams, and about half a mile off the beach it was all swamp . . . And it was on the bloody nose! It also buggered up your feet—cracked heels.[16]

The 2/10th made steady progress until the track melted into a swamp. The scarcity of maps and a number of very poor aerial photographs did not assist their cause. The 2/10th Unit Diary gives a dramatic insight into the degree of difficulty faced by the battalion:

> 1115 D Coy reports track petered out in swamp
> 1130 D Coy instructed to send out two patrols to locate any tracks leading to coast. Bn held up until track can be established
> 1200 B Coy contacts Bn & is instructed to move east & locate Killerton Village.
> 1430 C.O. confers with Brigadier . . .
> 1700 B Coy movements, at 1445 hrs they reported having found a track about 300 yards South of Killerton Village. To help them find Killerton fired Village, Wirraway plane was instructed to fire very lights over the spot. Plane fired the lights over native garden approx 1000 yds. S.E. of K/V. B Coy after very rough going established itself here for the night . . .
> 1715 Lieut Scott-Mortar pln sent out with patrol to try & locate any tracks Nth of present posn.
> 1925 Lieut Scott's patrol returned after having found track to beach. D Coy patrols—nil findings.[17]

Over twelve hours through jungle and swamp for a gained distance of a little over a mile and a half. The already malaria-ridden and fatigued Buna veterans spent the first of a number of nights at Sananada clinging to protruding vegetation and sitting in a putrid swamp. Major Trevivian, OC D Company, 2/10th:

> Next morning we pushed on through the bloody mangrove swamps. It was the hardest job I ever had in the army. Sometimes the water was over our heads, most times up to our arm-pits. Our rate of progress was about 100 yards an hour and we had to cut down pieces of mangrove to get the stores across. At that stage we were carrying ammunition, mortars and the heavy stuff—and I would like to record the sterling job that the mortar chaps did in that show. If there was one bunch of fellows I had

> respect for it was the mortars, Eventually we struck a track which ran along the beach and ultimately into Killerton Village. We came on to that right by a Japanese position. The Japs were sunbaking at the time and it was a toss-up who got the biggest surprise . . . In the meantime, while the battalion was pushing along the coast, Cook's company was sent off to find Killerton Village.
>
> Until we found it we couldn't accurately determine where we were. Nothing seemed to make sense as far as our maps and photographs were concerned. Eventually an aircraft was sent out to help but by that time we were on the objective and the thing was plain sailing.[18]

Elements of the 2/10th reached the beach at Cape Killerton at 11.00 a.m. on 16 January and began moving east along the coast towards a track which led inland to Killerton Village. At about 7.30 p.m. B Company reached Wye Point, where they encountered Japanese outposts about 160 yards farther along the coast. The Australians had now secured the coastal left flank at Sanananda.

But if this audacious 18th Brigade move had brought such significant success, then the progress of the Americans at the Huggins' roadblock was an ongoing frustration. Vasey's situation report for 16 January concluded with a statement that masked his bitter disappointment with the American effort: '163 Regt, 41st Div, see Hebrews, Chap 13, Verse 8.' The lines are typical of Vasey's colourful language: 'Jesus Christ the same yesterday, and today, and forever!'[19] Two days later Vasey and Eichelberger inspected the American lines. General Eichelberger in *Jungle Road to Tokyo*:

> We went up the Sanananda Trail. American soldiers were lying across the road and firing: there was also American and Japanese firing behind us . . . Vasey and I . . . crawled down into a trench. This was Doe's command post . . .
>
> I said, 'Where are the Japs?' Doe answered, 'Right over there. See that bunker?' I saw it and Vasey saw it, and it was only fifty yards away. Doe was in the front line and

> so were we. He gave us some hot tea and then went on with the attack.
>
> Vasey was satisfied with Doe's determination and so was I.[20]

Vasey might well have been diplomatic with Eichelberger, but in private with his Australian subordinates he was under no illusion as to the performance of the Americans at, and near, Huggins' during January 1943. Vasey would have noted that the problem at the beachhead was not to gain positions within fifty yards from the Japanese—that was easy enough. The problem was the fifty yards of intervening ground. Staying put and offering concentrated small arms firepower is no hard task, but rising up to your enemy, being led by determined, capable junior officers and NCOs, and being backed by proficient fire and movement—these are the real ingredients for the acquisition of those critical yards. The Americans did not consistently possess those qualities.

This American failure seriously delayed success at Sanananda. In fairness to the inexperienced and poorly conditioned and led Americans, their orders for movement down the Sanananda Road were a tough task. The Japanese were withdrawing, but in so doing their rate of recovery of their troops—or the time needed to evacuate some of them on foot—was contingent upon the Allies being delayed as long as possible along that main track into Sanananda. The 18th Brigade's outflanking movements through the swamps was not expected, but the American thrust down the Sanananda Road was.

Vasey now reacted astutely to this impasse. In order to cut off the Japanese in the Huggins' roadblock area from their line of communication, and thereby facilitate operations on the northern portion of the Sanananda Road, on 16 January he ordered Wootten to deploy a force across from the Killerton Track to cut the road.

Captain Cook's A Company, 2/10th Battalion was assigned the lead role in this movement. Behind it that afternoon trudged the HQ and the C and D Companies of the 2/12th.

Easier planned and ordered than done. The task for the troops was a tedious and time-consuming one, since while the only available map certainly depicted the Killerton Track and the not-too-distant Sananda Road, it failed to make an allowance for the fact that the Killerton Track yet again petered out into swamp. And so the familiar Papuan navigation system—by God and by compass—again was put into use.

The track was not reached before dark, which resulted in another wretched night in that stinking swamp.

After further movement at dawn, Cook's men reached the Sanananda Road at 11.30 a.m. on 17 January. And not far behind them Lieutenant-Colonel Arnold's now complete 2/12th Battalion assisted in the occupation of a critical two hundred yards of that route.

Wootten now had his extreme left flank gained by three companies of the 2/10th at Cape Killerton, which was now moving east, and he had Cook's company of the 2/10th and the 2/12th astride the Sanananda Road north of Huggins'. With these significant gains, he now decided to push his 2/9th Battalion north-east through the swamp to capture Sanananda Point.

This was a bold and imaginative move. Wootten was relying on the fact that as the 2/12th had been able to cross the swamp to the road with little resistance, so his 2/9th Battalion might accomplish a similarly lavish gain. If successful, and with the anticipation of American gains along the coast from Buna, the enemy force would be fragmented and might consequently suffer a general disintegration of their defences—and annihilation.

Private 'Chalky' Morris, 2/9th Battalion:

> Sometimes you were walking through water ankle deep and suddenly you would be waist deep. The going was tedious as you would stumble over a log or a hidden bush . . . when it was nearing dark, we stopped for the night in the swamp. We sat down in the water, some of the fellas tried to climb into the bushes, but for most it was sit down and try and find something to lean against and rest.[21]

That night, known as the night of the big storm, is etched forever in the memory of all 18th Brigade Sananada survivors. Captain Angus Suthers, 2/12th Battalion:

> B Echelon, rear Bn HQ & the Regimental Aid Post with the RMO Capt MacDonald [the battalion doctor and his staff] were on a slight rise in the swamp at Stand to. By 2200 hrs we were up to our shins in water, and stretcher cases were being held above water level on ammunition boxes. Jack Hayward the cook, managed to keep one kerosene blower going & kept a dixie of tea hot for the fellows in the RAP. A most remarkable bloke.[22]

Bill Spencer, 2/9th Battalion:

> Suddenly there was a flash of lightning, as bright as day, and a roll of thunder like all the drums of hell let loose, then silence. As the night grew darker, the silence was broken now and again by the loud dripping of moisture from the shining leaves surrounding us, and the subdued chatter from troops sounding like birds looking for a place to roost. One wag likened us to a mob of bloody galahs. Then nature fell on us with a crushing of thunder and torrential rain, the likes of which I had never seen before. It poured buckets and it kept on pouring, and the thunder of that night almost drowned out an artillery barrage. Some of the men received electric shocks from lightning strikes on the water. The swamp began to rise and we all became worried that it would keep rising. We were perched on the roots of mangroves or shrub branches, hunched over, looking like deformed creatures from some weird fairytale.[23]

Private Stan Crowther, HQ Company, 2/12th Battalion:

> I had taken refuge in the roots of a tree, and I woke to find that I was now sitting in waist deep water. The lightning and thunder were virtually incessant, it was impossible to hear anything for the thunder, and the only time I could see anything was when the lightning flashed,

> and this had the effect of blinding me so I could not see anything until the next flash. I could feel something crawling on me and thought it was probably leeches. When daylight came . . . I discovered that it was maggots, about an inch long and as thick as my little finger. They had been washed off the bodies of the Japs which lay everywhere in that area.[24]

On 18 January, the 2/9th set about the task of gaining the village and the point. Private 'Chalky' Morris, Intelligence Section, 2/9th Battalion was leading the way:

> Daylight saw three of us sharing a tin of bully beef with biscuits and then we were on our way again. Nearing 9 am, I could see a change in the vegetation and the tops of a few coconut trees. I halted and Major Parry-Okeden and Captain Wills joined me, and word was sent out—no noise and no firing until we were out of the swamp . . . we carefully completed the last 30 yards or so and most of us crawled under the mass of small trees which formed . . . like a hedge growing along the bank of the swamp.[25]

The resulting 2/9th attack was achieved with almost total surprise. The enemy suffered 21 dead and 22 captured. There was an assortment of Japanese and Koreans, and 21 coolies.

Parry-Okeden immediately pushed his A Company about five hundred yards east along the coast to the mouth of the river at Giruwa, where relatively firm ground enabled those soldiers to dig in. He also immediately dispatched his C Company down the Sananada Road towards the advancing 2/12th Battalion. After clearing two pockets of Japanese along their path, C Company encountered far more formidable Japanese positions and were forced to a halt.

While the 2/9th Battalion was thus occupied on 18 January, the 2/12th advanced in a north-easterly direction at first light, with its B Company moving on the westward side of the Sananada Road, its C Company along the eastern side and its A Company and Battalion HQ advancing along the road itself. The battalion made about 150 yards before it ran into the inland end of the extensive Japanese positions that confronted the 2/9th that same day.

The 2/12th put in three spirited attacks on these positions, but the Japanese, still two days short of their evacuation timetable, resisted stubbornly to allow as many of their comrades as possible the chance of escape. During this tough day the battalion lost a further twelve men killed, one died of wounds and 21 were wounded. But the gap was quickly closing.

By 18 January the 2/10th was positioned away to the west, just east of Wye Point, facing strong Japanese positions. The enemy had the advantage along this narrow coast of the sea providing a secure right flank, and the jungle wall running only four or five yards in from the sea to the swampland protecting their left. Bunkers containing about four soldiers and sniper positions in that jungle wall allowed them to strongly contest any Australian advance along the narrow coastal corridor. Lieutenant Keith Davey, OC 18 Platoon, D Company:

> We did send patrols out through the swamp trying to get around. I was involved in one patrol, but it was absolutely hopeless. It's hard to find your way, you're up to your shoulders in water, and I decided that if we did run across anything we were in too bad a position to fight because we were in the swamp, so we returned back to the company. There were bunkers all along the beach.[26]

Despite every endeavour to make ground, the 2/10th remained hard against these enemy positions for the rest of the day.

By 19 January 1943, both the Australians and the Japanese were on the point of exhaustion. Sergeant Bill Spencer, 2/9th Battalion:

> The polluted water throughout the area had made dysentery endemic, and as the Japanese had no medication to control it they found it more convenient to wander around trouserless rather than continuously pulling their fouled garments up and down. We also

> suffered from dysentery at Sananada but were fortunate to have medication. There were times when we also would have found it more convenient to be trouserless, but our culture forbade it.[27]

On the 19th, only two large Japanese positions remained facing the 18th Brigade at Sananada. One was confronting Lieutenant-Colonel Arnold's 2/12th Battalion and Major Parry-Okeden's 2/9th two-company force on the Sananada Road, and a similar-strength force was facing the 2/10th away to the west near Wye Point.

Early on the morning of 19 January, when his patrols reported the enemy still in occupation of the main defence area, Arnold ordered Captain Cook's attached A Company, 2/10th Battalion to attack along the left flank. Arnold would later write that:

> The successful attack by 'A' Company 2/10th Battalion on the left flank was one of the outstanding features of this phase of the campaign. The position held by the Japs was almost entirely surrounded by water more than shoulder deep, except for a small tongue of dry land about 15 yards wide and which was covered by enemy LMG fire. Under cover of a mortar bombardment this company infiltrated by twos and threes along this tongue [of land] forming up within 25 yards of the enemy. On a given signal they rushed forward with the bayonet under their own hand grenade barrage. The enemy resistance collapsed and the company advanced . . . killing 150 Japs many of whom were hiding in huts and captured three large supply dumps of medical and other stores. As in many cases enemy wounded engaged our troops and had to be shot. This may give rise in the future to Jap propaganda but they are doing it so consistently that our troops cannot take any chances.[28]

Approximately 150 Japanese were killed in this area, in and around part of the hospital ground. The enemy in this position were a grotesque mixture of the dead, the dying and those weak but willing and able enough to fight to the last.

The truth is that *any* enemy soldier who looked to have even a remote opportunity to offer any form of resistance was killed on the spot. And the few captured were usually taken because they were physically incapable of resistance. It was a painstaking, dangerous, filthy and callous task, but it had to be done. And done it was.

After Cook's breakthrough had occurred, Arnold was able to push elements of the 2/12th further along the western side of the road to link up with B Company of the 2/9th. But stiff enemy resistance continued on the eastern side of the road despite a determined attack north by A and D Companies and a similar thrust south by the 2/9th.

At first light on 20 January, Arnold's patrols found that the Japanese were still in occupation of their reduced perimeter. Attacks by A and D Companies of the 2/12th made only slight gains, while a later attack put in by Cook's 2/10th Company also failed to break the deadlock. But later that day a company of the 2/9th linked with its 2/12th comrades on that right flank. The 18th Brigade's envelopment of the Japanese on the road was now virtually accomplished.

If the pocket of enemy resistance on the road remained stubborn and unyielding during the period 19–20 January, then such opposition was no less fanatical in front of the 2/10th Battalion near Wye Point.

However, the deadlock was finally broken on 20 January when D Company attacked along the coast after an impressive artillery and mortar barrage. Lieutenant Keith Davey, D Company, 2/10th Battalion:

> . . . we had an observation officer from the artillery with us, and I remember his name, it was Nix . . . their guns had to shoot over all this jungle and we're on the beach there and they hit the right places. Boy! Did that do a lot for the morale!
>
> As soon as the last shot went in, we went. Fix bayonets, charge! We just went absolutely mad. Grenades going in everywhere on every bunker we saw.[29]

Lieutenant Davey was amongst the 2/10th wounded.

As a result of this attack, the 2/10th advanced about three hundred yards east along the beach and, although A Company's advance was checked by the last remnant of the Japanese defences later that morning, the exhausted soldiers of the 2/10th were able to see their comrades of the 2/9th about a further two hundred yards further on.

The Japanese were now boxed in by the coast, the 2/10th, the 2/9th and the swamp, and were by this time occupying a paltry two hundred yards of ground. Wootten sent Captain Matheson's C Company, 2/10th Battalion through the swamp to the 2/9th.

After an inaccurate artillery barrage on the 21st a further effort was undertaken at 12.30 p.m. on the 22nd, and after about thirty minutes of tough fighting the last remnants of the Japanese force on the coast were crushed. Sixty-seven enemy corpses were found in the area. And in unison with those successful coastal attacks, Arnold's mixed 2/12th and 2/10th force finally staged their last attacks in the hospital area.

While these events along the coast and the Sananda Road had been unfolding, the 2/9th force which had been initially sent to meet the Americans moving west from Buna had been deployed at the river at Giruwa. During those four days, the 2/9th contingent had eliminated the odd enemy straggler attempting to cross the river, and had contested Japanese barge movement by night. Sergeant 'Lofty' Wells was amongst them:

> During the night barges were coming in to evacuate them and the barges were being guided in by the use of hand grenades thrown onto the beach. We now had a Vickers gun and crew in position with us, so on the second night we also threw grenades on to the beach when we heard the barges approach, resulting in one coming into the beach in front of our position. The Vickers crew with Cpl Alf Franklin in charge quickly moved into position along with Brens from 7 Platoon and when the ramp was lowered the barge crew were in for an unexpected welcome. The barge was quickly disabled.[30]

Sananda—the 18th Brigade, 15–23 January 1943

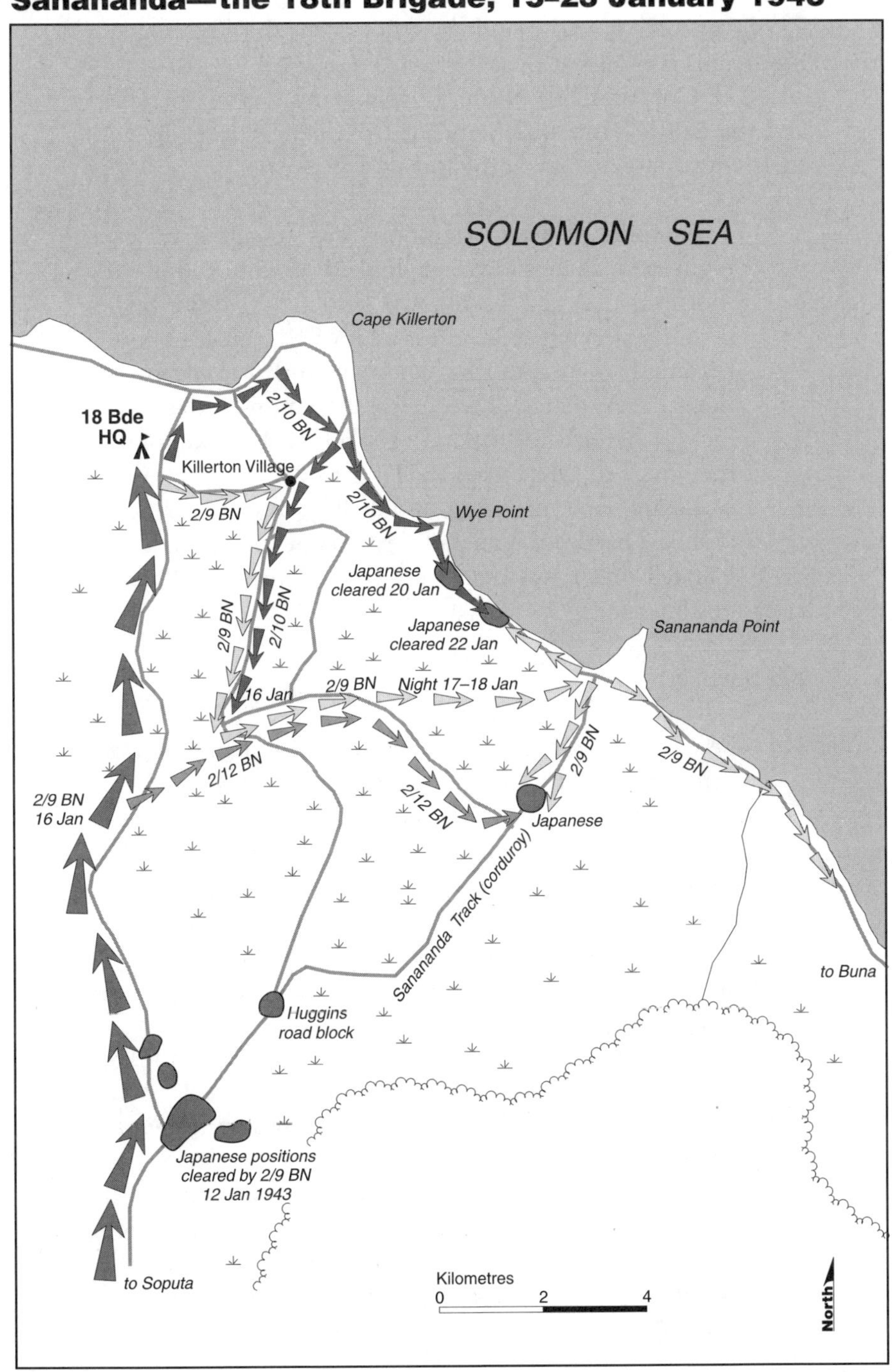

The approaching Americans were able to link up with the 2/9th on 21 January, and by the 23rd the fighting for Sananda was all but over.

Let Corporal Bill Neate, D Company, 2/10th Battalion and the 2/9th Battalion's Sergeant Bill Spencer leave us with their enduring Sanananda memories. Bill Neate:

> The moon. A beautiful moon used to come up each night and shine down. It looked lovely. And in the morning . . . ghastly, bloody battlefields, dead bodies floating everywhere. You lost a lot of your mates but you became hardened to that. You realised that it was part of the game. And lucky. I wrote home to mum, and said, 'I'm lucky, I haven't got malaria or scrub typhus like a lot of the boys. I'm OK. I'm lucky.' I'd hardly read my letter and woke up next morning and hell I was crook! Scrub typhus. Diarrhoea, you can't eat, dry retch, weak, all my hair fell out, I was practically bald, went deaf, deaf as a post![31]

Bill Spencer:

> Few of us are able to remember our movement back from Sanananda to the airstrip at Dobodura. I recall being rotten with dysentery and malaria, and feeling as if I was on fire. I remember waiting at the airstrip before boarding a DC3 aircraft for evacuation to Port Moresby, and someone saying 'You're as thin as a stick!' I was, too: a man of six feet three doesn't look too well when he weighs in at seven and a half stone [48 kg]. And I wasn't the only one . . .
>
> Eventually we travelled down the range to Port Moresby in trucks, and what little remained of the 18th Brigade embarked on the Dutch ship *Willis van de Vanter* . . .
>
> Those who remained [with their battalions] still played 'two-up'; still played poker; still complained about the tucker; still looked for their grog; and still told the same old yarns—and forever will mourn the passing of comrades.[32]

DANCING TO THE BEAT

28

The lies started before Sananada had fallen.

MacArthur flew back to Brisbane on 9 January 1943. With Buna now captured, it was important to return to Supreme HQ 'to demonstrate that the fighting was no longer a cause for concern',[1] and to 'ensure that the Joint Chiefs of Staff realised that he had obtained his victory while the troops on Guadalcanal were still preparing for their final offensive'.[2]

He told reporters that all that remained of the fighting in Papua was 'mopping up' at Sananada. After the war, Eichelberger would justifiably request that: 'If there is another war, I recommend that the military, and the correspondents, and everyone else concerned, drop the phrase "mopping up" from their vocabularies. It is not a good enough phrase to die for.'[3]

MacArthur released a communiqué in Brisbane on 28 January 1943—just five days after the fall of Sananada. Geoffrey Perret, in *Old Soldiers Never Die*:

> 'Our losses in the Buna campaign are low,' he [MacArthur] declared. 'As compared to the enemy they are less than half that of his ground force losses, including not only our battle casualties but our sick from natural causes . . . These figures reverse the usual results of a ground offensive campaign . . . losses to the attacker are usually several times that of a defender. Two factors contributed to this result: First, there was no necessity to hurry the attack because the time element in this case was of very little importance; and second, for this reason no

> attempt was made to rush the positions by mass and unprepared assault. The utmost care was taken for the conservation of our forces . . .'[4]

General MacArthur's influence upon the destiny of both the Australians and the Americans during the Papuan campaign was critical.

If the liberation of the South West Pacific Area and the Philippines is seen as his crowning achievement, then the campaigns on the Kokoda Trail, at Milne Bay, and at the Gona–Buna–Sanananda beachhead constituted his darkest hour.

Here was a theatre commander privy to first-class intelligence. The intent of the Japanese to mount an offensive over the Owen Stanley Range was presented to him. It was ignored until almost too late, because that intelligence did not lend support to his proposed foolhardy invasion of Rabaul. MacArthur's vain rejection of such accurate intelligence cost many lives on the Kokoda Trail.

However, MacArthur's most tragic and costly mistake during those campaigns was his failure to appreciate the ground and combat conditions encountered by the troops under his command. This ignorance did not, however, prevent him from critical interference in the conduct of those battles. William Manchester, in *American Caesar*:

> . . . MacArthur, in short, never saw the battlefield. Six days later the field commander [Eichelberger] wrote bluntly that the commander-in-chief hadn't visited the front once 'to see at first hand the difficulties our troops were up against', and later wrote bitterly that 'the great hero went home without seeing Buna before, during or after the fight while permitting press articles from his G.H.Q to say he was leading his troops in battle. MacArthur . . . just stayed over at Moresby 40 minutes away and walked the floor. I know this to be a fact.' After the war Douglas Southall Freeman . . . asked Eichelberger, 'Just when did General MacArthur move his headquarters to Buna?' Eichelberger dodged the question, and subsequently the General said to him, 'Bob, those were great days when you and I were fighting at

> Buna, weren't they?' and laughed. Eichelberger interpreted this as a 'warning not to disclose that he never went to Buna'.[5]

He didn't go to Gona either. Or Sanananda. Or Milne Bay. And a casual visit to Ower's Corner at the gateway to the Kokoda Trail is hardly an examination of that battleground. If a commander has no idea of the terrain on which his troops are committed—particularly ground so divorced from previous experience—he must surely falter in his appreciation of the required tactics. Manchester:

> Indeed, Eichelberger observed, 'the commander in chief's knowledge of details was so faulty that his directives to me, e.g. a letter of the 24th of December that spoke of attacking, "by regiments, not companies, by thousands not hundreds" indicated that he knew nothing of the jungle and how one fights there—that he had no detailed knowledge of how our forces were divided into many corridors by swamps.'[6]

The final and most revealing word concerning MacArthur's performance as commander in Papua should be left to his chief intelligence officer, Major-General Charles Willoughby:

> Buna was a head-on collision of the bloody, grinding type that MacArthur was henceforth to avoid, but it was necessary . . .
>
> It became a race between Eichelberger and the Marines under Admiral Halsey's command to see who would turn in the first important land victory in the Pacific War.[7]

This statement is both illuminating and a gross distortion of history. Some points, therefore, need to be made in response.

First, while there may well have been a race between Eichelberger and Halsey to get a victory on the board, the unavoidable conclusion is that it was the Australian troops who were being sacrificed to win such an event. Of this Willoughby seems totally oblivious.

Second, Willoughby's assertion that the manner in which the battles for the beachhead was fought was somehow 'necessary' only demonstrates that he could not conceive that a more professional approach to leadership on MacArthur's part would have seen superior tactics employed and the objectives attained at far less cost. There was no inevitability about it, as Willoughby contends.

The last point concerns 'the first important land victory in the Pacific War'. That victory was at Milne Bay in early September of the previous year. And then there was the victory at Kokoda on 2 November of 1942. And then Gona on 8 December 1942. Buna was the fourth important land victory of the Papuan campaign, but for the sake of American vanity the fourth victory has become the first. It should also be mentioned that the final victory at Sananda was, in fact, the end of the Papuan campaign. But that was only 'mopping up'.

The exasperating point that the Americans could not then, and still cannot, acknowledge is the fact that it was the Australians who won the critical battles at Milne Bay, along the Kokoda Trail, at Gona, and that they were primarily responsible for the victory at Buna and overwhelmingly in charge of the final victory at Sananda. And all this from a soldier who was MacArthur's chief of intelligence during the entire Papuan campaign—a contradiction in terms.

Not surprisingly, there have been other serious historical errors. After being sacked at Buna by Eichelberger and sent back to rest in Australia by MacArthur, Major-General Harding was posted to Panama. After the war, he was appointed the US Army's chief of military history. Harding 'made sure that the official account of the fight for Buna reflected the campaign as he saw it'.[8] So much for objectivity!

There is much to see at Sananda. Parts of one of the ruined tanks of the failed attack of 12 January are to be found near both Australian and Japanese pits. An old car brought by the Japanese to the beachhead lies rusted and bullet-ridden just off the 1942 Sananda Road.

Huggins' roadblock is a striking place to visit—'the land of plenty' has left plenty. The Americans did not have to account for the ordnance of war in the same manner as did their Australian comrades. Littered around the pits of their tight perimeter are dixies, spoons, belts, buckles, mortars, mortar bombs, tripods and all manner of associated implements of war.

When you approach the Sananada Road–Killerton Track junction at Sananada an American memorial stands before you. On it is this inscription:

> Capt. Meredith M. Huggins, USA
> 3rd Battalion, 126th Infantry Regiment.
> 32nd Division 'Huggins Road Block'.
>
> After his commanding officer was killed, Capt Huggins assumed command of companies of the 128th Infantry, 32nd Division. Tasked with securing a tactical choke point to thwart a rapid Japanese advance across the Kokoda Trail, Huggins' bravery under fire and his ability to hold a numerically superior Japanese force at bay, laid the groundwork for an American victory in New Guinea. The place where he fought and was wounded on 5 December 1942, now bears the name 'Huggins Road Block', in honour of his valor.
>
> With grateful appreciation
> The American Legion remembers
> Capt. Meredith M Huggins

After reading the inscription on the monument, one could be forgiven for succumbing to an overwhelming desire to get hold of the 'choke point' of the bloke who wrote this utter nonsense.

The truth is that throughout the battle for Sananada, the Americans retained an almost masterly inactivity at Huggins' roadblock. This was no tactical 'choke point' but simply a frustrating position where they had attempted to outflank the Japanese and had been unable to advance. And even after the Japanese had evacuated the junction, and the 18th Brigade had begun its wide outflanking movement through Sanananda's swamps, the Americans were still unable to advance until the last stages of the fight.

The notion that the Americans at Huggins' roadblock prevented a renewed Japanese thrust to Kokoda is quite simply laughable.

However, there was an American beachhead hero. Lieutenant-General Robert Eichelberger's degree of difficulty at Buna was extreme. He was placed in command of young National Guardsmen who had been neither adequately trained nor previously well led. Eichelberger was given the task of capturing a battleground where the enemy had a masterly defensive plan and a tremendous resolve, and his support was threadbare.

Forced to turn a near fiasco into a serious fighting concern, he quickly reconnoitred his battlefield and assessed the performance and abilities of his commanders and then, by his sheer leadership qualities, drive and personality, was able to reinvigorate his untrained and dispirited charges to far greater performance.

Eichelberger also had yet another priceless quality: the desire and ability to relate to, and cooperate with, his Australian peers, which was an attribute most decisively lacking in his supreme commander.

This Papuan journey of ours early identified six generals who were to play both key and controversial roles during the fighting in Papua. General Blamey was the first.

It should be acknowledged at the outset that General Blamey's command of the Australians during the Papuan campaign was a most difficult task. He suffered a lack of political loyalty from the Curtin Government. The fact that Curtin did not enforce the conditions of MacArthur's charter by failing to secure an Australian influence upon MacArthur's staff was a gross error in judgment. But of even greater significance is the fact that Blamey should always, as the Commander-in-Chief of the Australian Military Forces, have been Curtin's chief, and therefore first, adviser. He was not.

That critical influence fell to a foreign general: MacArthur. History has shown that Curtin's decision was tragically flawed.

Blamey, like MacArthur, failed to recognise and consequently react to the initial Japanese Papuan thrust, and therefore the defensive phase of the campaign—Kokoda and Milne Bay—was a costly condemnation of both men's surrendering of the military initiative.

Any fair assessment of Blamey's Papuan performance must surely focus upon his influence on the course of events and his exercise of command over his subordinates.

In the end, the command crisis which occurred in Papua could and should have been prevented by Blamey and not exacerbated by him. There can be no doubt that he knew the quality of the commanders he sacked. General Blamey had, after all, witnessed their performance as commanders in the Middle East and had promoted them accordingly.

Any force that is outnumbered by approximately five to one, which is incapable of being adequately supplied, which cannot effectively treat, let alone efficiently evacuate, its wounded, which cannot be given adequate artillery support and which cannot concentrate its force is incapable of offensive action.

The retreat from Mons in the First World War, the headlong retreat from Benghazi to Tobruk, and the fighting withdrawal in Greece during the Second World War—none caused disparagement of commanders or troops. Like the brilliantly executed fighting withdrawal along the Kokoda Trail by Brigadier Arnold Potts and his Maroubra Force, they were merely part of the ebb and flow of war. Of all these epic fighting withdrawals, which of them was the most critical to the Australian nation?

Blamey well knew the quality of the 21st Brigade and its commander. In Port Moresby in October 1942, he sacked Potts because he was quite simply more concerned with his own position than with the loyalty he owed to a subordinate, and indeed to the army he commanded. The ramifications of the Blamey slur at Koitaki impacted upon 21st Brigade's fighting at Gona, and Dougherty's poisoned perception of the brigade's senior officers was a direct result of it. During the defensive phase of the Kokoda campaign, Blamey, the

Commander-in-Chief of the Australian Military Forces, failed the Australian Army. History should condemn him.

Brigadier Arnold Potts is not commemorated in any significant way in Australia other than by Bill Edgar's biography, *Warrior of Kokoda*—a fitting title. At the time of writing, the Australian War Memorial has not commemorated Potts either by image or word in its relevant gallery. The Australian public who tour this gallery are none the wiser concerning Australia's esteemed 'Warrior of Kokoda'.

Brigadier Arnold Potts is an Australian hero. After serving in Darwin and Bougainville as commander of the 23rd Brigade, he returned after the war to his farm near Kojonup in Western Australia. Potts died as a result of a stroke on New Year's Day 1968.

Rowell's removal was more complex. Blamey's supporters would point to the influence of events in the Middle East and in Greece, and Rowell's distaste for Blamey's morality and lifestyle as contributing factors. They are valid points. The argument has been, therefore, that Rowell virtually sacked himself by his aggressive behaviour towards Blamey after the latter's arrival in Port Moresby on 23 September 1942.

But Blamey made two visits to Port Moresby during that fateful month. As a direct reaction to the events at Isurava and Myola and to the continuing withdrawal of Maroubra Force, the Advisory War Council thought it desirable that Blamey should travel to Port Moresby to examine the military situation there and then report back to the council. This was an Australian initiative and one the politicians were certainly entitled to undertake. General Blamey duly flew to Port Moresby, satisfied himself as to the conduct of operations and then returned to Australia. He then made a national radio broadcast on 16 September 1942 and also reported to the Council. Blamey had supported Rowell, Allen and his (Blamey's) troops. Loyal, commendable behaviour.

He returned to Port Moresby on 23 September—five days later. Brigadier Eather's withdrawal to Imita Ridge had precipitated panic among the powerful in Australia. Blamey's return heralded Rowell's sacking. His removal by Blamey, therefore, should be primarily seen as yet another example of a commander-in-chief who fails at the critical point of a crisis, who fails when the pressure is at its greatest. There had been strains of a similar failure in Greece.

In a letter to the prime minister after Rowell's removal, Blamey suddenly sighted command deficiencies in Rowell's performance[9]—only five days after he had solidly supported him in both the Advisory War Council and during a radio broadcast to the people of Australia. What had changed? The answer is simple: the security of Blamey's position. If Blamey's loyalty had lasted but a few more days, Rowell and his subordinates' campaign would have been entirely validated.

Rowell's subsequent posting was then fought over with unnecessary venom by Blamey. After considerable friction and debate between Blamey and the Curtin Government, Rowell's rank was reduced to major-general and he was posted to the Middle East. Rowell, in *Full Circle*: '. . . I was appointed general officer commanding AIF details in the Middle East and Australian liaison officer at GHQ Middle East—a complete sinecure since there were next to no Australian forces now in the area. In truth I was being sent into exile.'[10] Rowell spent the last two years of the war as Director of Tactical Investigations at the War Office in London. He would later return to Australia as Vice Chief of the General Staff in 1946 and subsequently served as Chief of the General Staff from 1950 to 1954.

Lieutenant-General Sir Sydney Rowell was the first Duntroon graduate to hold the army's highest post. He retired in 1954 and died on 12 April 1975.

Major-General Cyril Clowes was never given the recognition that he deserved. Nor were the victorious soldiers and airmen of his Milne Force.

His command future was affected by two key factors. The first was MacArthur's ignorant and therefore flawed assessment of his Milne Bay achievement. As a consequence, Blamey could not, in view of MacArthur's appraisal of Clowes, have considered him for Rowell's job. But a further compelling reason for Clowes' demise was the fact that he was perceived as a 'Rowell man'. Clowes and Rowell had been in the same Duntroon class together and were close friends for over thirty years.

After having commanded the 11th Division at Milne Bay until September 1943, Major-General Clowes was banished to Melbourne as GOC of the Victorian Lines of Communication. After a brief period as Adjutant-General in 1946, he was appointed as the Commander of Southern Command between 1946 and 1949. He retired from the army in 1949 and died on 19 May 1968. The victor of Milne Bay had faded quietly into Australian history, and remains relatively unknown to this day.

Major-General George Vasey's Papuan performance was varied. He did not, in any way, influence the Kokoda campaign. After replacing Allen, Vasey merely took possession of a deserted Kokoda.

The battle of Oivi–Gorari should be seen as his masterstroke. It was a bold move and a striking victory that cost the Japanese around six hundred casualties and hastened their withdrawal into the confines of their beachhead.

Four days after General Vasey replaced General Allen on the Kokoda Trail, he wrote: 'One of the grouses against Tubby [Allen] was that he let the situation control him instead of controlling it. I never believed in allowing that to occur and decided to take control quickly.'[11] On Christmas Eve 1942 Vasey wrote to Herring:

> My experience of the past two months convinces me that for success in jungle warfare, such is taking place in the Sananada–Soputa area, the first requisites for success in either attack or defence are high morale, a high standard of training, both individual and collective, and, for successful offensive action, superiority of numbers is also necessary. I regret to have to report that none of these conditions is present in my command.[12]

The fact is that the very criticism Vasey levelled at Allen applied to himself at the beachhead. General Vasey presided over the demise of his well-trained, well-led and highly motivated 7th Division. Initially, he had the necessary infantry resources to capture Gona. It is worth recording that the officers of the 21st Brigade and the 39th Battalion were adamant that Gona should have fallen far earlier and with far fewer casualties.[13]

Major-General George Vasey later led his 7th Division to stunning success in the Ramu–Markham Valley during late 1943 and early 1944. By the end of this campaign, Vasey's health had began to deteriorate. After being evacuated sick to Australia, he became stricken with polyneuritis in June 1944 and required the rest of the year to recover.

In early 1945 Vasey was posted to the command of the 6th Division. While flying north to assume that posting, he and all on board his aircraft were killed when it crashed off the coast of Cairns on 5 March 1945. This distinguished and colourful Australian soldier, who was probably the equal of any Australian divisional commander of the war, was sadly missed by the Australian Army. The fact does remain, however, that the beachhead was arguably the low point of an otherwise distinguished career.

Major-General Arthur 'Tubby' Allen spent the rest of the war in inactive commands in New Guinea and the Northern Territory. This demotion made him an embittered man until the war's end.

When the intense pressure of command reached its climax during the Kokoda Trail and Milne Bay battles from August to October 1942, Allen had performed capably. David Horner has raised a succinct point concerning Allen's dismissal:

> Few divisional commanders in history have been replaced by their army commander without having been visited by either the army or corps commander, or indeed by anyone above the rank of Lieutenant-Colonel.
>
> . . . Blamey felt that he *had* to relieve Allen to placate MacArthur. In other words Blamey displayed a remarkable lack of loyalty to his subordinate. Loyalty cannot be expected if you do not give it and it must start at the top.[14]

As had occurred with Rowell, if Blamey had waited but a couple of days Allen would have achieved the final Kokoda victory. In no small measure that final victory was indeed his.

In spite of the fact that Major-General 'Tubby' Allen was, at times, a difficult subordinate, he remains one of the best examples in Australian history of the citizen soldier, who had the tremendous distinction of commanding at every level from a platoon to a division during his distinguished, extensive and varied service in two world wars.

After suffering a heart attack in 1950, Allen suffered indifferent health until his death on 25 January 1959.

Lieutenant-General Sir Edmund Herring's performance as Commander New Guinea Force was nothing more than a masterly exercise in docility. David Horner in *Crisis of Command*:

> Blamey had chosen his man carefully and he knew that Herring would be completely loyal. It is true that this was to be his first operational command of a formation, for as CRA [Commander Royal Artillery, of a division] he had never had to bear the responsibility of independent decisions, but for a while at least, Blamey would be at his shoulder to offer advice and encouragement.[15]

Rather a different standard of support than that devoted by Blamey to Rowell, Allen, Clowes and Potts.

David Horner has provided telling evidence that in fact Blamey was the commander of New Guinea Force during the pursuit phase of the Kokoda campaign and the battles for the beachhead. The point is that after his part in the 'revolt' of the generals, Herring determined that never again would he be aligned with any effort to contest Blamey's almost absolute power.

Herring played a significant part in Potts' sacking. Allen's biographer, Stewart Braga, maintains that Herring had also developed a dislike for Allen in the Middle East and had later prejudiced his position as the commander of the 7th Division.[16] Herring's response to Blamey when the latter had suggested Vasey's possible but temporary relief due to the rigours of command in New Guinea—that he 'preferred Vasey tired to Allen fresh'[17]—would seem to support the point.

During his 'command' of New Guinea Force during operations at the beachhead, Herring also failed to provide adequate artillery support for his infantry. Both Berryman and the American Colonel Doe expressed surprise at this inability. And they levelled their criticism at Vasey. Vasey could only use the support provided him by his commander: Herring. Lieutenant-General Herring would later claim that a lack of available planes and the inhibiting weather conditions were the cause of that limited support. His assertion does not bear fair examination.

On 23 November 1942, three planes carried two officers, twelve other ranks, one 25 pounder, 1 jeep, 130 rounds of ammunition and a gun and signal stores under the command of Captain H.A. Manning (Bullforce) from Port Moresby to Dobodura. Two trips were made to double that force. Fifteen minutes later, Blackforce under the command of Major A.G. Hanson left Port Moresby with six allotted planes carrying three officers, 23 other ranks, two 25-pounders, two jeeps, 230 rounds of ammunition and stores. Thus, in one afternoon, four guns and 460 rounds and various stores and personnel were dispatched to the Gona–Sanananda front.[18]

Therefore, if the nine allotted planes had repeated the exercise on another given day—with the second contingent of six planes making two trips instead of one as the first contingent had done—General Herring would have deployed ten guns and 1300 rounds.

The standard level of artillery support in 1942 for a brigade in action was a regiment: 24 guns. In mid-1943, the army revised its prescribed level of artillery support for a division in jungle operations to 24 guns—therefore eight to a brigade. By any fair examination, therefore, the fact that Herring delivered only four for a divisional operation was inexcusable—by past or future standards.

Given that the beachhead fighting erupted from around late November and raged on until 22 January, the quantity of artillery support provided depended more on priority than feasibility.

The truth is that when a commander is willingly engaged in fulfilling such ill-considered, futile and rushed orders as those issued by MacArthur and Blamey for the immediate capture of the beachhead, considerations such as suitable artillery support get lost in that urgency.

The roles of senior Australian commanders through the Papuan campaign—Blamey, Rowell, Herring, Clowes, Allen and Vasey—were critical, and were also performed under enormous political as well as military pressure. Three of those who performed most credibly—Rowell, Clowes and Allen—were sacked, along with Potts, as a reward. Vasey, after a magnificent victory at Oivi–Gorari, became bogged down in the disjointed, rushed and expensive battles for the beachhead.

General Herring's command of New Guinea Force should be seen as nothing more than that of a loyal and faithful servant, sustaining MacArthur and Blamey in their quest for speed both along the Kokoda Trail and at the beachhead at the price of unnecessarily high casualties.

General Blamey presided over the Australian Army's offensives during 1943 and early 1944: Salamaua, Lae, Finschhafen and Sattelberg. His leadership and his army's great competence during this period reflect highly on both.

During the later stages of the Pacific War, Australian troops were essentially grounded by its receding tide, after MacArthur had determined that his Americans should have the glory of the capture of the Philippines and the final anticipated assault upon Japan. Australian forces served in Bougainville, Borneo and around Wewak—often tough, but almost irrelevant fighting. The Australians were out of the way, and where MacArthur wanted them to be.

Blamey was promoted to Field Marshal in June 1950. He died on 27 May 1951. As Chief of the General Staff, Lieutenant-General Sir Sydney Rowell was present at his funeral as the Australian Army's chief mourner.

Field Marshal Sir Thomas Blamey was a man and a commander of many parts. His First World War contribution was of the highest order; his largely competent raising of the Second AIF and his selection of its initial senior commanders were on the whole astute; his ability and determination to protect Australian interests through the enforcement of his charter also deserves high praise indeed; and a number of the campaigns conducted by the army under his command were most impressive.

However, if various aspects of the Greek campaign placed his command decisions and conduct under a cloud, then the

Papuan campaign should be seen as arguably his most critical and searching test. He failed it comprehensively.

During the tough and testing days of August to November 1942 in Papua, General Blamey could have restored a considerable amount of his lost prestige and poor standing among many in the army by a show of loyalty and steadfastness towards his senior subordinates and his soldiers. But as had been shown on a number of other occasions, he was not quite up to the task. Perhaps David Horner has left us with a final, succinct and fair assessment of Blamey in his first book, *Crisis of Command*: 'Blamey will, therefore, be remembered as the foremost Australian General of World War II but he will never be remembered as the greatest.'[19]

The fate of three additional Papuan campaign participants is of interest. Neil McDonald in *War Cameraman: The Story of Damien Parer*:

> One night in mid-September [1942] Alan Anderson heard a faint knocking on the door of his flat in Townsville. 'I opened the door to see a living wreck,' Anderson said. 'A black-bearded fellow looking more like a skeleton than a human being stood swaying there. "Sorry" he said, "Can't quite manage . . . to get me gear . . . up the stairs." Then I realised it was Damien back from the Kokoda Trail.' Alan and his wife Connie helped Parer inside and insisted the photographer rest with them for a few days before heading south.[20]

Parer, after returning to Sydney, set to the task of making a newsreel using his footage from the Kokoda Trail. In this Parer had three aims. The first was the obvious one: to portray the real nature of the Kokoda Trail fighting for an Australia hungry for news. The second and third are more interesting; and they had additional impact when the producer of the film, Ken Hall, decided to use Parer himself to give an opening and closing address to the newsreel. Neil McDonald:

> So, the line, 'when I got back to Moresby, I was full of beans with the knowledge General Rowell was on the job and now we had a really fine command' came to be included . . . He was also aware of the tensions between the AIF units and the militia so his narration emphasises how the Militia formations were acquitting themselves in the best traditions of the Australian army [Parer was obviously primarily praising the 39th Battalion].[21]

The impact of *Kokoda Front Line* was enormous. After opening to packed houses in Sydney on 22 September 1942, the film was most favourably reviewed by the *Sydney Morning Herald* and the *Daily Telegraph*.[22]

This was, from Blamey's point of view, poor timing by Parer. Blamey sacked Rowell in Port Moresby three days later.

When the army ordered 16 mm prints of *Kokoda Front Line* from Cinesound to use as a training film, and Blamey found out that the troops were cheering Parer's reference to Rowell at the beginning, the prints were removed and the Rowell reference was deleted.[23]

Parer later made further films concerning the commandos in Timor, the Battle of the Bismark Sea, and the fighting outside Salamaua. In 1943 *Kokoda Front Line* was awarded an Oscar for best documentary. Although *Kokoda Front Line* won an Oscar and Parer continued to produce first-class work, he had begun to fall foul of the Department of Information when he had defied orders to return to Australia prior to his work on the Kokoda Trail.

Three additional incidents caused Parer to leave the department. The first was the penny-pinching nature of its CEO, Bob Hawes, who refused to grant Parer additional funding. The second was the sacking from the department of his friend and colleague Alan Anderson, and the third was the department's censuring of George Silk's beachhead photography and its subsequent refusal to allow him to leave the department to work for *Life* magazine.

Damien Parer was killed while working for Paramount Pictures during the American marine landings at Peleliu on 16 September 1944. His extraordinary war photography is his enduring Australian legacy.

George Silk eventually found his way to the European theatre of war as a photographer for *Life* magazine, which saw him work in Italy and Western Europe. Coincidentally, Silk was able to undertake some of his assignments with Parer's former colleagues, Chester Wilmot and Osmar White.

Still working for *Life* magazine, Silk settled in America after the war and specialised in sports and recreation photography. At the time of writing he was living in Connecticut.

Chester Wilmot wrote a succinct report on the Kokoda campaign shortly after arriving back in Port Moresby. Rowell was impressed enough with its contents to include it with his final dispatches. The so-called 'Wilmot Report' is a masterly piece of research which was quite obviously undertaken by questioning both officers and other ranks during, and shortly after, the Maroubra Force fighting withdrawal on the Kokoda Trail. It would seem a fair observation that if a resourceful ABC correspondent might have found his way along the Kokoda Trail to report on operations, some responsible army liaison officers might have been dispatched to gather a similarly accurate impression of the campaign.

Wilmot had fallen foul of Blamey over his suspicions that Blamey had been involved in a picture print scandal—involving substantial sums of money—in the Middle East, concerning the exhibition of films for the Second AIF. Blamey accused Wilmot of undermining his position as Commander-in-Chief of the Australian Military Forces by both his investigations and discussions with various individuals. Neil McDonald, Chester Wilmot's biographer:

> Wilmot always insisted that Blamey's accusation, that the correspondent was dis-accredited because he continued to investigate the picture contract after being warned off by Blamey's solicitor, was a pretext. The real reason was Wilmot's support for General Rowell, and that the correspondent had gone to Curtin to urge the Prime Minister to reinstate Rowell after he had been sacked by Blamey. A further Blamey grievance was the perceptive Wilmot Report, which Rowell had included with his final despatches on the campaign in Papua.[24]

Chester Wilmot was rescued by the BBC, which employed him as a correspondent to cover operations in Europe. After landing with the 6th Airborne Division behind the German lines on D-day, Wilmot's work saw him report by radio and dispatch from Normandy to Berlin. His ground-breaking *Struggle for Europe* became an almost instant international bestseller.

Chosen by the Australian Official Historian to write the Tobruk volume of the Official History, Wilmot was tragically killed in a Comet jet crash on 10 January 1954. One can only ponder the resultant contribution to Australian military history had Wilmot arrived home and written about his experiences in the Middle East and Papua.

David Horner, in *Crisis of Command*:

> . . . the admiration in which he [Blamey] is held by a score of senior officers . . . after the war is an indication of the value of his work. Yet Blamey's detractors seem to believe that, as A.J. Sweeting [the Official Historian's chief research assistant] noted, 'by some mysterious power the senior officers still dance to the beat of the dead Field Marshal's baton'.[25]

General Herring's devotion to Blamey's cause extended well past the war—dancing to the beat . . .

Raymond Paull had been a junior officer serving with Potts in Darwin after Potts' removal from the 21st Brigade. Potts had often lectured the officers of his brigade concerning the Kokoda campaign.[26] Paull, a journalist by profession, must have recognised the potential for a book.

His bestseller, *Retreat from Kokoda*, was much more than an early account of the Kokoda campaign. He interviewed Potts for about two weeks at his farm at Kojonup in Western Australia, and was given access to Potts' diaries.[27] Rowell and Allen gave him 'their reminiscences and access to personal documents',[28] and Chester Wilmot made available copies of his notes and dispatches concerning the campaign.[29] Kienzle helped, as did Magarey, Norris and a steady stream of junior officers and other ranks.

Clearly, Paull's book was an effort to tell the story from the perspective of some of the senior officers who commanded the operation, the brigade commander, and a number of his junior officers and other ranks. This surely, while not being the only historical perspective, was an entirely legitimate one. It was a brave book, given that it challenged many of the decisions taken both prior to and during the Kokoda campaign, and that it was published in 1958—two years before the Official History and only sixteen years after the operation.

After its release, Herring entered the fray. In a letter to the editor a fortnight after the Melbourne *Age* had reviewed the book on Saturday, 26 July 1958, he and a number of Blamey's cronies took issue with it.

The point was that John Hetherington had written the review, which was high in its praise for Paull's treatment of the fighting soldier at the interface of battle but harsh on Paull's criticism of Blamey. Hetherington was hardly a balanced reviewer. He had written Blamey's biography in 1954 and would later write a revised edition which was published in 1972. The book lacks suitable documentation, undertakes a pathetic attempt to explain away the Koitaki parade, glosses over the events in Greece, and praises Blamey for his beachhead command performance. Wilmot referred to Hetherington as 'an artist in whitewash'.[30]

The thrust of the Herring letter was that Paull had seen fit to 'assail the honor [*sic*], capacity and reputation of the late Field Marshal Sir Thomas Blamey in a most bitter and partisan fashion'. The only point that Herring had of any real substance was the reason for Wilmot's disaccreditation. And the letter dwelt upon it.

The letter was written, so Herring and his associates claimed, so that 'some measure of justice may be done to the memory and motives of the Field Marshal'. In the course of their letter, they also stated: 'There are other unsatisfactory assertions in the text to which space does not allow us to draw attention.' What other assertions? If they did indeed have evidence, where was it? Why was it not included in a serious, lengthy article? As the then current Chief Justice of Victoria, a post he was to hold until 1972, and as a Rhodes Scholar, one would have thought that Herring's ability to write a long, thoughtful and well-prepared defence of Blamey might not have been beyond him.

It *was* beyond him because there was simply very little substance to his letter. Herring's fellow signatories actually formed a rather unique group of personalities who knew little of the Kokoda campaign. The first was Herring himself, in Darwin when Maroubra Force was conducting its Kokoda fighting. Brigadier Eugene Gorman was the second, whose post, according to the letter, was Chief Inspector of Army Administration. Another obvious Kokoda expert. The third was Brigadier John Rogers, Director of Military Intelligence, AMF. Arguably an intelligence expert, but not a Kokoda Trail campaign expert. The fourth signatory was perhaps the least qualified of a poor bunch. We have Colonel A.N. Kemsley, Business Advisor to the Commander-in-Chief, and later a member of the Military Board. Highly qualified to be debating the merits of Paull's book. The fifth was Major-General Sir Samuel Burston, Director-General of Medical Services, AMF. Any worthwhile contributions from Burston would have been trumped by Norris and Magarey, the medical officers who were actually involved in the campaign—and in Magarey's case oversaw the evacuation of the wounded on the trail. Both Norris and Magarey, it will be remembered, were contributors to Paull's book. The last signatory was Major-General C.H. Simpson, Signals Officer in Chief, Land Headquarters. Perhaps Simpson was fully conversant with the one and only signal line that ran over the trail to Maroubra Force during the campaign.[31]

Herring and his fellow 'experts' offered a trumped-up, *Boy's Own Annual* letter that had no thrust, had no argument, and was simply a pathetic attempt to white-ant Paull's book. That the above-named soldiers had otherwise distinguished army careers is not necessarily the point in question. But their 'dancing to the beat' over the Kokoda campaign most definitely is.

Brigadier, later Major-General, Sir Ivan Dougherty was a distinguished brigade commander during the Pacific War—and a great Australian. As Potts' successor, he led the 21st

Brigade for the remainder of the war. But for some reason, he felt duty bound to deny the content of Blamey's Koitaki diatribe in Hetherington's *Blamey: Controversial Soldier*.[32] Blamey's cronies, however, forgot to censor Norman Carlyon, Blamey's ADC, who was also at Koitaki. Carlyon's *I Remember Blamey*, an otherwise vigorous defence of Blamey's war service, actually gave an accurate account of the Koitaki harangue.[33] Dougherty died still supporting the Hetherington Koitaki account. Dancing to the beat . . .

The Official Historian for the fifth volume, *South-West Pacific Area—First Year*, Dudley McCarthy, had a terribly difficult task. His book is, on the whole, a magnificent piece of writing and a scholarly effort for the time, given the 'official' documentation available to him. The Koitaki parade is relegated to an obscure and inaccurate footnote.[34] McCarthy ends his narrative with the following tribute to Blamey:

> At the very peak of this leadership development was General Blamey himself. His greatness was demonstrated almost daily by a knowledge unparalleled in Australia of how an army should be formed and put to work; by his exercise of the vital field command at the same time as he kept within his grasp a vastly detailed control of the Australian Army as a whole; by his sagacity and strength in meeting the rapidly changing demands of a difficult political situation; by his ability speedily to encompass the requirements of the new war and plan far ahead of the events of the day as he controlled them; by his generally unappreciated humanity.[35]

Dancing to the beat . . .

The Papuan campaign from July 1942 until January 1943, fought along the Kokoda Trail, at Milne Bay and at the Gona–Buna–Sananada beachhead, constituted young European Australia's most critical test. War had come to Australia.

The first six months of the Pacific War had seen Japan sweep ruthlessly through South-East Asia, and with those fateful and fearful conquests the last vestiges of European colonialism in Asia were doomed to a protracted but inevitable death.

Australia quickly realised that the resources and manpower of a new and more powerful ally, the United States of America, were her only hope of salvation. But those resources only were brought to bear over time—the first critical onslaughts fell upon the Australia soldier. Papua New Guinea, after the crucial American naval victories at Coral Sea and Midway, became the stage for that ultimate and exacting trial.

The Australian soldier was plunged into the rugged and uncharted mountains, the jungles, the fetid swamps and coastal lowlands of Papua, ill prepared in terms of jungle training, equipment, support, intelligence and communication, and pitted against an enemy who had not known defeat on land.

That the Australian soldiers, both AIF and militia alike, were able to learn the lessons of jungle warfare on the spot, fight the Japanese in a totally foreign and hostile environment, hold them and then utterly defeat them at their own game speaks volumes for their initiative, cunning and sheer tenacity.

The crucial triumphs along the Kokoda Trail and at Milne Bay stemmed the Japanese tide of conquest, while the grinding and bloody beachhead victories signalled the enemy's final and irreversible loss of the military initiative. By the end of January 1943, the path of future conflict stretched away from Australia—not toward it.

The history of a nation is composed of the spiritual, intellectual and emotional energy of its citizens, both in the individual and collective sense, implanted into the building blocks of momentous events.

If Australia looks beyond the blunder to see Gallipoli as symbolic of the birth of a nation, the time has come to perceive the Papuan campaign not as a rival in importance, but as the vital historical building block of growing Australian adolescence. America did not save Australia in Papua in 1942–43. It certainly helped. But it should never be forgotten that during those critical six months of the Papuan campaign, Australians stood up and essentially saved themselves.

If it was a bastard of a place in 1942–43, it is now no less sacred ground than Gallipoli.

NOTES

1 SPREADING THE OIL

1 This narrative is derived from: Sergeant W.B. Spencer, 2/9th Battalion, letter to the author 2 June 1996; Corporal G.B. Robinson, 2/10th Battalion, questionnaire from Gorokan, New South Wales, 7 February 1996; and Sergeant A.A. Evans, 2/10th Battalion, taped reply to questionnaire, received from Melbourne, 31 July 1995.
2 This narrative is an actual account of the author's arrival in Port Moresby on 3 July 2002.
3 ibid. to Alotau.
4 Waiko, *A Short History of Papua New Guinea*, p. 4.
5 ibid. p. 8.
6 West, *Hubert Murray*, pp. 15–35, gives a detailed description of Murray's early life through to his arrival in New Guinea.
7 Waiko, *A Short History of Papua New Guinea*, pp. 57–60.
8 West, *Hubert Murray*, p. 125.
9 ibid.
10 ibid.
11 Waiko, *A Short History of Papua New Guinea*, pp. 69–70.
12 Lewis, D.C., *The Plantation Dream: Developing British New Guinea and Papua 1884–1942*.
13 West, *Hubert Murray*, p. 163.
14 ibid. pp. 225–7.
15 Quoted in Lewis, *The Plantation Dream*, p. 266.
16 ibid. note, p. 226.

2 THE DEEP THINKERS

1 Burns, *The Brown and Blue Diamond at War*, p. 8.

2 Hasluck, *The Government and the People 1939–41*, p. 4.
3 Greenwood, *Australia, A Social and Political History*, chapter 7.
4 ibid. p. 316.
5 ibid. p. 344.
6 Bartholomew, *The Times Handy Atlas, 1935*. Mortlock Library, Adelaide.
7 Ernest Rhys, *Everyman's Library*. The date is not shown on this atlas, but the Mandated Territory in New Guinea is shown as Dutch territory, suggesting that the atlas is pre-1920. Mortlock Library, Adelaide.
8 Central Schools were for those students who, in the main, were less likely to continue their schooling after the age of fourteen, either because they were destined for manual work or because of a desire to enter the workforce at the earliest possible time in order to contribute to the family income.
9 W. Oldham, *The Adelaide History Grade VII*, written for the Education Department of SA as both a text for students and a syllabus for teachers. It was published in 1930. Courses under the same format and title and written by the same author were published from 1920 to 1935. Mortlock Library, Adelaide.
10 Spencer, *In the Footsteps of Ghosts*, p. 7.
11 Knightley, *Australia, A Biography of a Nation*, p. 132.
12 ibid. p. 134.
13 Private Bert Ward, 2/27th Battalion, tel. con. 6 January 2003.
14 Spencer, *In the Footsteps of Ghosts*, p. 12.
15 Rowell, *Full Circle*, p. 43.
16 Russell, *The History of the Second Fourteenth Battalion*, p. 3. Burns, *The Brown and Blue Diamond*, p. 7.
17 Russell, *The History of the Second Fourteenth Battalion*, cites one section as having five soldiers in it ranging in age from fifteen to seventeen years. p. 4.
18 Long, *To Benghazi*, note, p. 58.

3 DOG RIVER

1 Long, *To Benghazi*, p. 57.
2 ibid. p. 46.
3 Monash, *The Australian Victories in France in 1918*, pp. 319–20.
4 Horner, *Blamey: Commander-in-Chief*, p. 56.
5 For a detailed account of Blamey's period as Police Commissioner see Horner, *Blamey: Commander-in-Chief*, chapter 4.
6 Hetherington, *Blamey: Controversial Soldier*, p. 55.
7 Horner, *Blamey: Commander-in-Chief*, p. 101.

8 ibid.
9 ibid. p. 102.
10 Hetherington, *Blamey: Controversial Soldier*, p. 56.
11 Horner, *Blamey: Commander-in-Chief*, p. 96.
12 ibid. pp. 96–7.
13 The charter is quoted in full in Long, *To Benghazi*, p. 101.
14 For an early example see Long, *To Benghazi*, pp. 103–4.
15 Long, *To Benghazi*, p. 50.
16 ibid. pp. 47–8.
17 It should be noted that Herring made some criticism of Allen's performance in Greece, and vice versa. However, the fact that Blamey chose to promote Allen during the fighting in Syria is surely proof enough of his overall performance.
18 Long, *To Benghazi*, p. 50.
19 Rowell, *Full Circle*, p. 79.
20 Horner, *Blamey: Commander-in-Chief*, pp. 159–60.
21 ibid. pp. 160–1. Also, Blamey's first biographer, Hetherington, acknowledges Blamey's behaviour: Hetherington, *Blamey: Controversial Soldier*, p. 117.
22 For example, Vasey in a letter to his wife March 1941, in Vasey Papers, National Library, MS 3782.
23 Long, *Greece, Crete and Syria*, pp. 6–7.
24 ibid. p. 7.
25 Horner, *Blamey: Commander-in-Chief*, pp. 186–7.
26 Long, *Greece, Crete and Syria*, p. 29.
27 Horner, *Blamey: Commander-in-Chief*, p. 196.
28 The Official Historian gives an account of both the problem and Clowes' handling of it: Long, *Greece, Crete and Syria*, pp. 95–6. Rowell relates the incident in Rowell, *Full Circle*, p. 74.
29 Long, *Greece, Crete and Syria*, p. 96.
30 ibid.
31 Horner, *Blamey: Commander-in-Chief*, p. 196.
32 ibid. p. 197.
33 Both of Blamey's biographers deal with this issue. Hetherington in *Blamey: Controversial Soldier* is full of generalisations and lacks documented sources and balance. See pp. 147–8. Horner, in *Blamey: Commander-in-Chief*, has detailed reactions of many of the chief characters involved. See pp. 196–9.
34 ibid.
35 Horner, *Crisis of Command*, p. 120.
36 Long, *Greece, Crete and Syria*, p. 151.
37 Spencer, *In the Footsteps of Ghosts*, pp. 22–3.
38 Maughan, *Tobruk and Alamein*, p. 332.

39 Rowell, *Full Circle*, p. 88.
40 Burns, *The Brown and Blue Diamond at War*, p. 39.
41 Long, *Greece, Crete and Syria*, p. 528.
42 ibid. p. 525
43 Edgar, *Warrior of Kokoda*, pp. 15–19.
44 ibid. chapter 3.
45 ibid. p. 66.
46 ibid. pp. 101–2.
47 Rowell, *Full Circle*, pp. 85–6. The Official Historian makes the same point and mentions Rowell's pre-battle criticisms. Long, *Greece, Crete and Syria*, p. 527.
48 Slessor, *Poems by Kenneth Slessor*, p. 108.

4 THEATRE OF WAR

1 Cranston, *Always Faithful*, p. 129.
2 Sturdee's assessment is well documented: see Long, *The Six Years' War*, p. 205; Cranston, *Always Faithful*, p. 137; and letters from 49th Battalion veterans to the author.
3 Horner, *Blamey: Commander-in-Chief*, p. 145.
4 ibid.
5 Sergeant K.J. Irwin, 53rd and 36th Battalions, letter to the author, 20 March 1989.
6 *Report of the Barry Commission on Cessation of Papuan Civil Administration in 1942*, paragraph 18.
7 Wigmore, *The Japanese Thrust*, p. 511. The *exact* figure may never be known. Also see the footnote on p. 511.
8 Horner, *Blamey: Commander-in-Chief*, p. 263.
9 Quoted in Churchill, *The Hinge of Fate*, pp. 138–9.
10 ibid. p. 141.
11 ibid. pp. 141–3.
12 ibid. p. 143.
13 Quoted in Churchill, *The Hinge of Fate*, p. 143.
14 ibid. p. 144.
15 ibid.
16 Perret, *Old Soldiers Never Die*, pp. 45–6.
17 Manchester, *American Caesar*, pp. 87–8.
18 Perret, *Old Soldiers Never Die*, pp. 116–17.
19 ibid. p. 134.
20 Two of MacArthur's most recent biographers give detailed accounts of this episode: Manchester, *American Caesar*, pp. 149–52; and Perret, *Old Soldiers Never Die*, pp. 154–61.
21 Perret, *Old Soldiers Never Die*, p. 173.

22 ibid.
23 Manchester, *American Caesar*, pp. 167–9.
24 ibid. p. 168.
25 Perret, *Old Soldiers Never Die*, pp. 249–50.
26 Edwin Ramsey in *MacArthur, Part 2, I Shall Return.*
27 Perret, *Old Soldiers Never Die*, pp. 271–2.
28 Faubion Bowers in *MacArthur, Part 1 Destiny.*
29 Edward H. Simmons in *MacArthur, Part 1 Destiny.*
30 Manchester, *American Caesar*, p. 276
31 McCarthy, *South-West Pacific Area—First Year*, p. 22.
32 Horner, *General Vasey's War*, pp. 168–9.
33 Rowell, *Full Circle*, p. 105.
34 Horner, *Blamey: Commander-in-Chief*, pp. 277–8.
35 Drea, *MacArthur's Ultra*, p. 230.
36 Hart, *Thoughts on War*, p. 219.
37 Rowell, *Full Circle*, p. 105.

5 BERT AND DOC

1 Dalby, interview with the author, 6 March 1986.
2 Ward, interview with the author, 8 December 1986.
3 ibid.
4 Horner, *Crisis of Command*, p. 304.
5 ibid. p. 302.
6 The author examined the unit diaries of the three battalions and recorded the names and checked each of them with battalion identities through interviews.
7 Dalby, interview with the author, 6 March 1986.
8 Austin, *To Kokoda and Beyond*, p. 79.
9 Sergeant K.J. Irwin, 53rd and 36th Battalions, letter to the author, 20 March 1989.
10 Garland, interview with the author, 7 June 1986.
11 McCarthy, *South-West Pacific Area—First Year*, p. 43.
12 This description of Kienzle was given to the author by Captain Noel Symington, 39th Battalion: interview with author, 15 July 1987.
13 Kienzle, letter to the author, December 1986. After having answered about 20 questions from the author's first questionnaire, Kienzle sent his complete files to the author in December 1986. It was a goldmine: 1942 original letters, orders, notes, diaries and the first twenty questions asked of him in the questionnaire. This voluminous collection will henceforth be referred to as 'the Kienzle File'.

14 The Kienzle File.
15 ibid.
16 ibid.
17 ibid.
18 The physical attributes of many of the Japanese in the 5th Sasebo Naval Landing Force was pointed out through interviews with Milne Bay veterans and Kokoda veterans e.g. Lieutenant Doug McClean 39th Battalion, interview with author, 7 June 1986, and Sergeant Bill Spencer, 2/9th Battalion, interview with author, 31 October 1994.
19 Paull, *Retreat from Kokoda*, p. 26.
20 The Kienzle File contains a copy of Wilkinson's diary. The passage used is from p. 3.
21 Bidstrup, interview with the author, 11 June 1986.
22 Garland, interview with the author, 7 June 1986.
23 Vernon's diary, the Kienzle File.
24 Wilkinson's diary, the Kienzle File.
25 ibid.
26 Austin, *To Kokoda and Beyond*, p. 113.
27 McCarthy, *South-West Pacific Area—First Year*, note, p. 136.
28 Austin, *To Kokoda and Beyond*, p. 114–15.
29 Brune, *Those Ragged Bloody Heroes*, pp. 68–9.
30 Wilkinson's diary, the Kienzle File.
31 Kienzle's diary, the Kienzle File.
32 *Medical Report on Native Carrier Lines of Communication Kokoda Front 2 July–12 October 1942, Captain G. H. Vernon*, the Kienzle File.

6 COURAGE FEEDS ON HOPE

1 Gwillim, letter to the author, July 1987.
2 Katekar, interview with the author, 12 July 1988.
3 Sublet, letter to the author, 10 July 1987.
4 Edgar, *Warrior of Kokoda*, p. 125.
5 ibid. pp. 120–1.
6 A copy of this report was most kindly lent to the author by Lieutenant-Colonel C. Isaachsen in January 2003.
7 Horner, *Crisis of Command*, p. 104.
8 ibid.
9 Clemens, letter to the author, 3 July 1987.
10 Thompson, letter to the author, July 1987.
11 Edgar, *Warrior of Kokoda*, p. 134.
12 *Report Into Operations 21st Brigade—Owen Stanley Campaign.*

A copy of the original was kindly lent to the author by Captain Ken Murdoch in 1987.

13 Murdoch, interview with the author, 25 February 1989.
14 McCarthy, *South-West Pacific Area—First Year*, p. 198.
15 Rowell, *Full Circle*, p. 115.
16 ibid.
17 ibid.
18 McCarthy, *South-West Pacific Area—First Year*, p. 197.
19 Lovett, interview with the author, 5 October 1998.
20 Honner, 'The 39th at Isurava'.
21 Ralph Honner, videotaped interview with the author for Headquarters Training Command, Australian Army, February 1993.
22 McCarthy, *South-West Pacific Area—First Year*, p. 44.
23 Lindsay, *The Spirit of Kokoda*, p. 18.
24 Confirmed with the battalion's adjutant, Captain Keith Lovett, tel. con. 16 February 2003. Confirmed also by Lieutenant Gough Garland, 39th Battalion, B Company platoon commander Kokoda Trail, tel. con. 16 February 2003. Lovett and Garland estimate the average age of the battalion at 'early twenties'.
25 Steward, *Recollections of a Regimental Medical Officer*, p. 108.
26 Sim, taped reply to questionnaire to the author, October 1997.
27 Brune, *Those Ragged Bloody Heroes*, p. viii.
28 Honner, interview with the author, 1 September 1986.
29 The 39th Battalion Unit Diary, the August Diary 1942.
30 Lovett, interview with the author, 5 October 1998.
31 Ralph Honner, 'The 39th at Isurava'.

7 GOD, KING AND COUNTRY

1 Signal, Potts to Allen, 26 August 1942. 7 Div Sigs Owen Stanley Campaign AWM.
2 Honner, 'The 39th at Isurava'.
3 Austin, *To Kokoda and Beyond*, p. 150.
4 Simonson, interview with the author, 3 July 1988.
5 Austin, *To Kokoda and Beyond*, p. 151.
6 Honner, 'The 39th at Isurava'.
7 Bidstrup, interview with the author, 13 March 1986.
8 McCarthy, *South-West Pacific Area—First Year*, p. 202.
9 ibid.
10 ibid.
11 ibid.
12 *Report Into Operations 21 Brigade—Owen Stanley Campaign*, p. 7.

13 Honner, 'This is the 39th'.
14 Sublet, letter to the author, 20 July 1987.
15 Dornan, *The Silent Men*, p. 115.
16 McCarthy, *South-West Pacific Area—First Year*, pp. 207–8.
17 Thompson, interview with the author, 19 February 2003.
18 Kingsbury's citation is sited in McCarthy, *South-West Pacific Area—First Year*, p. 206.
19 Thompson, interview with the author, 19 February 2003.
20 Honner, 'The 39th at Isurava'.
21 Barrett, *We Were There*, p. 13.
22 Honner, 'The 39th at Isurava'.
23 Sergeant R. N. Thompson, 2/14th Battalion, interview with the author, 19 February 2003.
24 ibid.
25 Sublet, letter to the author, 20 July 1987.
26 Gerke, letter to the author, 10 July 1987.
27 Sublet, letter to the author, 20 July 1987.
28 Fielding, letter to the author, 20 July 1987.
29 Gwillim, letter to the author, July 1987.
30 Sublet, letter to the author, 20 July 1987.

8 BOTH SIDES OF THE VALLEY

1 Sergeant Keith Irwin, 53rd Battalion, questionnaire reply to the author, 20 March 1989.
2 ibid. Also the battalion padre, Reverend Roy Wotton, confirms this element. Letter to author 22 February 2003, and tel. con. 28 February 2003. Also confirmed Irwin, tel. con. 1 March 2003.
3 Meredith, questionnaire reply to the author, March 1987.
4 Wotton, letter to the author, 22 February 2003.
5 Ahern is spoken very highly of in questionnaires and tel. cons by members of the battalion. Ahern later served with the 36th Battalion. He is spoken very highly of by its CO, Lieutenant-Colonel Cedric Isaachsen. Issachsen, tel. con. 2 March 2003.
6 Bisset, letter to the author, 28 June 1987.
7 Gwillim, letter to the author, July 1987.
8 WO 2 John Wilkinson, Diary, copy most kindly given to the author by Bert Kienzle, December 1987.
9 Sublet, letter to the author, 20 July 1987.
10 McCarthy, *South-West Pacific Area—First Year*, p. 202.
11 ibid.
12 Private R. A. Jones, 53rd Battalion, letter to the author, February 2003.

13 ibid.
14 Bidstrup, interview with the author, 14 July 1987.
15 The 53rd Battalion Unit Diary.
16 ibid.

9 . . . THE DEVOTION OF A MOTHER

1 Edgar, *Warrior of Kokoda*, p. 147.
2 Rosengren, interview with the author, 8 June 1986.
3 Dalby, interview with the author, 7 June 1986.
4 Austin, *To Kokoda and Beyond*, p. 171.
5 McCarthy, *South-West Pacific Area—First Year*, p. xi.
6 Paull, *Retreat from Kokoda*, p. 82.
7 Address by Neil McDonald with readings by Sally White, *Reporting the Papuan Campaign*, C.E.W. Bean Symposium, Canberra, 25 September 2002.
8 Horner, *Blamey: Commander-in-Chief*, pp. 133–4.
9 ibid. p. 134.
10 Rowell, *Full Circle*, p. 126
11 McDonald, *War Cameraman: The Story of Damien Parer*, p. 153.
12 ibid. p. 155.
13 ibid.
14 ibid. p. 156.
15 McDonald, *War Cameraman: The story of Damien Parer*, p. 156.
16 ABC Field Unit No. 1, *And Our Troops were Forced to Withdraw* by Chester Wilmot.
17 Quoted in Address by Neil McDonald, *Reporting the Papuan Campaign*, C.E.W. Bean Symposium, Canberra, 25 September 2002.
18 Lovett, interview with the author, 5 October 1998.
19 McDonald, *War Cameraman: The story of Damien Parer*, p. 160.
20 Brune, *Those Ragged Bloody Heroes*, p. 151.
21 Sim, taped questionnaire reply to the author, October 1997.
22 McDonald and Brune, *200 Shots*, p. 57.
23 McDonald, *War Cameraman: The story of Damien Parer*, p. 160.
24 Brune, *Those Ragged Bloody Heroes*, p. vii.
25 McDonald, *War Cameraman: The Story of Damien Parer*, pp. 157–8.
26 *Report Into Operations 21 Brigade—Owen Stanley Campaign*, p. 29.
27 Walker, *The Island Campaigns*, p. 34.
28 ibid.
29 *Report Into Operations 21 Brigade—Owen Stanley Campaign*, p. 39.

30 Magarey, interview with the author, 10 June 1987.
31 Edgar, *Warrior of Kokoda*, pp. 155–6.
32 *Report Into Operations 21 Brigade—Owen Stanley Campaign*, p. 42.
33 Walker, *The Island Campaigns*, p. 21.
34 Captain Darling's diary. Darling was Rowell's ADC. Kindly supplied by Neil McDonald.
35 Walker, *The Island Campaigns*, p. 21.
36 McDonald, *War Cameraman: The story of Damien Parer*, p. 157.
37 Steward, *Recollections of a Regimental Medical Officer*, p. 120.

10 . . . CALMLY BRAVE

1 Sublet, letter to the author, January 1988.
2 Quoted in Horner, *Crisis of Command*, p. 152. NB: Horner's author's bracket 'Colonel C.C.F. Spry' has been enlarged by Brune to read 'The 7th Division's Intelligence Officer, Colonel Spry'.
3 Horner, *Crisis of Command*, p. 152.
4 Sims, diary, copy most kindly lent to the author, October 1987.
5 Edgar, *Warrior of Kokoda*, p. 162.
6 Edgar, interview with Cooper, 4 January 1996.
7 Ward, interview with the author, 8 December 1986.
8 Edgar, *Warrior of Kokoda*, p. 162.
9 Little, interview with the author, 25 November 1986.
10 Sims, interview with the author, 24 August 1987.
11 War Diary, 21st Brigade.
12 *Report Into Operations 21 Brigade—Owen Stanley Campaign*, p. 12.
13 Quoted in Edgar, *Warrior of Kokoda*, p. 168.
14 ibid. p. 141.
15 McCarthy, *South-West Pacific Area—First Year*, p. 223.
16 Katekar, interview with the author, 12 July 1987.
17 Burns, *The Brown and Blue Diamond at War*, p. 120.
18 *Report Into Operations 21 Brigade—Owen Stanley Campaign*, p. 14.
19 Quoted in Horner, *Crisis of Command*, p. 147.
20 Quoted in Edgar, *Warrior of Kokoda*, p. 171.
21 ibid.
22 Horner, *Crisis of Command*, p. 151.
23 ibid.
24 ibid.
25 Darling, Rowell's ADC, diary entry. Copy kindly given to the author by Neil McDonald.
26 ibid.
27 Chapter 4 of this work.

28 McCarthy, *South-West Pacific Area—First Year*, p. 225.
29 ibid.
30 Quoted in Horner, *Crisis of Command*, p. 150.

11 MODERN DAY DISCIPLES

1 Russell, *The History of the Second Fourteenth Battalion*, p. 150.
2 ibid.
3 Keane, interview with the author, 24 November 1986.
4 ibid.
5 Williss, interview with the author, 25 November 1986.
6 Cooper, interview with the author, 19 September 1986.
7 Burns' report is quoted almost in full with kind permission from Burns and his 2/27th Battalion Association. The full text is to be found in Burns, *The Brown and Blue Diamond at War*, pp. 124–9.
8 Edgar, *Warrior of Kokoda*, pp. 181–2.

12 I'LL FRY HIS SOUL . . .

1 *Report Into Operations 21 Brigade—Owen Stanley Campaign*, p. 15.
2 ibid.
3 Russell, *The History of the Second Fourteenth Battalion*, p. 170.
4 McCarthy, *South-West Pacific Area—First Year*, p. 232.
5 Quoted in Horner, *Crisis of Command*, p. 166.
6 Quoted in Paull, *Retreat from Kokoda*, p. 228.
7 Paull, *Retreat from Kokoda*, p. 228.
8 ibid.
9 ibid.
10 Quoted in McCarthy, *South-West Pacific Area—First Year*, pp. 304–5.
11 Horner, *Crisis of Command*, p. 155.
12 Horner, *Blamey: Commander-in-Chief*, p. 323.
13 ibid. p. 324.
14 ibid.
15 Horner, *Blamey: Commander-in-Chief*, p. 325.
16 Minutes of Advisory War Council Meetings, Vol. V. Minute Nos 870–1073; 1st April–17th September 1942. pp. 510–645. Australian Archives, Canberra, CRSA. 2682/1 Minute No. 1067.
17 Quoted in Horner, *Blamey: Commander-in-Chief*, p. 327.
18 ibid. p. 326.
19 Quoted in McCarthy, *South-West Pacific Area—First Year*, p. 237.

20 Quoted in Horner, *Crisis of Command*, p. 171.
21 Quoted in Horner, *Blamey: Commander-in-Chief*, p. 330.
22 AWM, 3DRL 6673 The Rowell Papers, Rowell to Clowes, 28 September 1942.
23 McCarthy, *South-West Pacific Area—First Year*, p. 237.
24 Horner, *Crisis of Command*, p. 188.
25 After Potts' death in 1968, Murdoch saw fit to bring to light previously unrevealed evidence concerning Potts' sacking. The first publication of his account was in *Pigeon Post*, the official 2/16th Battalion newsletter. It was originally reproduced in the author's *Those Ragged Bloody Heroes*.
26 Quoted in Horner, *Blamey: Commander-in-Chief*, p. 348.
27 From a photostat copy of Potts' farewell address to 21st Brigade, kindly given to the author by Lieutenant-Colonel Ken Murdoch, August 1987.
28 Cooper, interview with Edgar, 4 January 1996.
29 Bisset, letter to the author, 28 June 1987.
30 Honner, letter to the author, June 1988.
31 Burns, *The Brown and Blue Diamond at War*, p. 137.
32 Thompson, letter to the author, June 1987.
33 Lewis, 'The Plantation Dream', p. 274.
34 ibid. p. 80.
35 Thompson, 2/14th Battalion, tel. con. 17 March 2003.
36 ibid. for the last 2/14th church parade.
37 Austin, *To Kokoda and Beyond*, p. 180.
38 The events of 9 November 1942 at Koitaki are taken from the author's *Those Ragged Bloody Heroes*, pp. 199–204. And also Carlyon, *I Remember Blamey*, p. 111.
39 Edgar, *Warrior of Kokoda*, p. 214. Also, Thompson, 2/14th confirms this, tel. con. 17 March 2003, and Burns, 2/27th confirms this, tel. con. 17 March 2003.
40 Paull, *Retreat from Kokoda*, note, p. 258.
41 Cooper, 2/27th CO, interview with the author, 19 September, 1986; Katekar, 2/27th Adjutant, interview with the author, 13 August 1988; Bisset, Adjutant (I Section Officer during the campaign), 2/14th, letter to the author, 28 June 1987; Thompson, 2/14th, tel. con. confirmed 17 March 2003.
42 Edgar, *Warrior of Kokoda*, p. 233.

13 OUTPOST OF THE EMPIRE

1 Quoted in Baker and Knight, *Milne Bay 1942*, pp. 27–8.
2 ibid. p. 30.

3 ibid. p. 31.
4 Dolly, letter to the author, 23 August 1993.
5 Mortensen, interview with the author, 2 October 1992.
6 Mahoney, letter to the author, 2 October 1992.
7 Harlen, interview with the author, 2 October 1992.
8 Walker, *The Island Campaigns*, p. 49.
9 Spencer, *In the Footsteps of Ghosts*, p. 95.
10 Mahoney, letter to the author, 6 September 1993.
11 Hoy, interview with the author, 3 October 1992.
12 Capper, interview with the author, 8 January 1994.
13 AWM 54 579/7/8 Messages Relating to Construction of Airfield Fall River, Milne Bay—June 1942.
14 Gillison, *Royal Australian Air Force 1939–42*, p. 605.
15 Brown, interview with the author, 1 April 1993.
16 Pank, interview with the author, 16 March 1992.
17 ibid.
18 Brown, interview with the author, 1 April 1993.
19 Pank, copy of logbook kindly given to the author, March 1992.
20 Deane-Butcher, *Fighter Squadron Doctor*, pp. 125–6.
21 From a copy of an ms sent to the author by Harlen, June 1994.
22 ibid.
23 McCarthy, *South-West Pacific Area—First Year*, p. 159.
24 ibid.
25 Chilton, letter to the author, 18 July 1994.
26 AWM 3DRL 6763 The Rowell Papers, Milne Force Letters and Signals.
27 AWM 52 1/5/25 HQ11Division GS Branch.
28 ibid.
29 AWM 3 DRL 6763 The Rowell Papers, Letters from Clowes.
30 Chilton, letter to the author, 18 July 1994.
31 AWM MSS 785 Brigadier Field's Diary, Letters and Articles.
32 AWM 52 7/26/1 Signals Milne Force.
33 Baker and Knight, *Milne Bay 1942*, p. 50.
34 ibid. p. 51.
35 O'Brien, *Guns and Gunners*, p. 150.
36 AWM 54 579/7/10 Notes from Milne Force Intelligence Log Diary. August–October 1942.
37 Captain Chikanori Moji, 'At The Ends of Sky and Sea', an unpublished account of his wartime experiences. Moji donated a copy of the Milne Bay section to Baker and Knight. Copy most kindly lent to the author, September 1994.
38 Pettet, interview 1 April 1993. This logbook entry was read during the interview.

39 Baker and Knight, *Milne Bay 1942*, p. 120.
40 Moji, *At the Ends of Sky and Sea.*
41 AWM 52 8/2/7 Headquarters 7th Australian Infantry Brigade War Diary, May–October 1942.

14 SPIRITS GOOD HERE

1 Newcomb, interview with the author, 3 October 1992.
2 Major H.J. Wiles, 61st Battalion. A personal account of his experiences at Milne Bay, copy kindly sent to the author by Sergeant Noel Worton, 61st Battalion, November 1992.
3 MacKenzie, interview with the author, 3 October 1992.
4 ibid.
5 ibid.
6 MacKenzie, interview with the author, 3 October 1992.
7 ibid.
8 Bradford, interview with the author, 1 October 1992.
9 Moji, *At the Ends of Sky and Sea.*
10 MacKenzie, interview with the author, 3 October 1992.
11 Wilson, interview with the author, 5 January 1994.
12 Quoted in Baker and Knight, *Milne Bay 1942*, p. 140.
13 Brown, interview with the author, 1 April 1993.
14 Pettet, interview with the author, 1 April 1993.
15 Crawford, interview with the author, 1 April 1993.
16 Baker and Knight, *Milne Bay 1942*, p. 148.
17 ibid. p. 47.
18 ibid.
19 Moji, *At the Ends of Sky and Sea.*
20 McCulloch, questionnaire reply to the author, 23 August 1993.
21 AWM 52 8/2/7 Headquarters 7th Australian Infantry Brigade.
22 ibid.
23 ibid.
24 Connelly, taped questionnaire reply to the author, 1993.
25 Byrnes, taped questionnaire reply to the author, 1993. (Connelly and Byrnes made a taped reply together.)
26 Hildred, interview with the author, 6 January 1994.
27 Ellenden, questionnaire reply to the author, August 1994.
28 Campbell, interview with the author, 4 October 1992.
29 Jorgensen, interview with the author, 6 January 1994.
30 Wilson, interview with the author, 5 January 1994.
31 Moji, *At the Ends of Sky and Sea.*
32 Baker and Knight, *Milne Bay 1942*, p. 150.
33 ibid.

34 Whybird, interview with the author, 3 October 1992.
35 George, interview with the author, 1 October 1992.
36 Lorimer, questionnaire reply to the author, August 1992.
37 Watt, quoted in Baker and Knight, *Milne Bay 1942*, p. 153.
38 Horner, *Crisis of Command*, p. 136.
39 ibid.
40 AWM 52 1/5/25 HQ 11 Division GS BRANCH August 1942 Messages in.
41 AWM 52 1/5/51 NGF War Diary, August 1942, Clowes to Rowell, 26 August.

15 LEFT HIGH AND DRY

1 Miethke, quoted in Baker and Knight, *Milne Bay 1942*, p. 167.
2 Brown, interview with the author, 4 October 1992.
3 AWM 52 8/2/18 HQ 18th Australian Infantry Brigade. The August Diary.
4 Andrews, interview with the author, 3 January 1994. The Official Historian claims that the first meeting was 'in the morning'. The 7th Brigade Unit Diary shows that conference to have been held at 10.57 a.m. But the same diary also confirms the earlier meeting at 4.13 a.m. Andrews told the author he thought the conference he attended with Dobbs was at '4.15 a.m.'.
5 AWM 3DRL 4143 The Clowes Papers *Official Report On Operations Milne Force*. (Will be referred to as 'The Clowes Report' and page number cited hereafter.)
6 Allchin, *Purple and Blue*, p. 248.
7 Dr Brian Clerehan turned over a considerable amount of correspondence between himself and Milne Bay participants to the author. These files will be identified citing the participant, Clerehan and a date. This first footnote then is 'Dobbs to Clerehan, 8 September 1976'.
8 Schmedje, interview with the author, 16 May 1992.
9 Gillison, *Royal Australian Air Force 1939–42*, p. 613.
10 Quoted in Baker and Knight, *Milne Bay 1942*, p. 168.
11 Summers wrote an account of his experiences at Milne Bay. A copy was most kindly given to the author in October 1992.
12 Schmedje, interview with the author, 16 May 1992.
13 The 2/10th Battalion dispositions at KB Mission for the night of 27 August 1942 have been reconstructed by veterans of each company from the post action reports (AWM 52 8/3/10) and the evidence assessed by Lieutenant John Andrews and the

author. The maps of dispositions and the withdrawal have been also assessed by members of the 2/10th Ex-Servicemen's Association.

14 Andrews, interview with the author, 3 January 1993.
15 ibid.
16 Dobbs to Clerehan, 8 September 1976.
17 Andrews, interview with the author, 4 January 1994.
18 Tabe, interview with the author, 11 June 1992.
19 Coombe, interview with the author, 19 June 1992.
20 Clarke, interview with the author, 17 June 1992.
21 Brown, interview with the author, 4 October 1992.
22 Todd, interview with the author, 5 March 1994.
23 Brown, interview with the author, 4 October 1992.
24 Quoted in Baker and Knight, *Milne Bay 1942*, pp. 175–6.
25 Thomas, interview with the author, 20 March 1994.
26 O'Brien, interview with the author, 8 August 1992.
27 Abernethy, letter to the author, 27 March 1995.

16 PIG'S ARSE YOU ARE!

1 Hilton, interview with the author, 6 January 1994.
2 Acreman, interview with the author, 3 October 1992.
3 ibid.
4 Jorgensen, interview with the author, 6 January 1994.
5 ibid.
6 ibid.
7 Moji, *At the Ends of Sky and Sea.*
8 Quoted in Baker and Knight, *Milne Bay 1942*, p. 185.
9 AWM 3DRL 4143 Papers of Major-General C.A. Clowes.
10 National Library of Australia, MS 3782. The Vasey Papers.
11 Quoted in McCarthy, *South-West Pacific Area—First Year*, p. 174.
12 The Vasey Papers.
13 AWM 3DRL 6763 The Rowell Papers.
14 ibid.
15 AWM 52 1/2/1 Advanced LHQ G Branch, August 1942, Appendix A.
16 Paterson, questionnaire reply to the author, 24 February 1995.
17 Chilton, interview by Baker and Knight, copy kindly given to the author.
18 ibid. Garing.
19 Pank, interview with the author, 16 March 1992.
20 Deane-Butcher, *Fighter Squadron Doctor*, pp. 143–4.

21 Moji, *At the Ends of Sky and Sea.*
22 Pank, interview with the author, 16 March 1992.
23 Moji, *At the Ends of Sky and Sea.*
24 ibid.
25 ibid.
26 Quoted in McCarthy, *South-West Pacific Area—First Year*, p. 176.
27 AWM 52 1/2/1 Advanced LHQ G Branch August 1942 Appendix 'A'.
28 The Rowell Papers.
29 Hilton, interview with the author, 6 January 1994.
30 Acreman, interview with the author, 13 October 1992.
31 Schindler, interview with the author, 7 January 1994.
32 McCosker, quoted in Baker and Knight, *Milne Bay 1942*, p. 227.
33 Wilson, interview with the author, 31 July 1993.
34 Hilton, interview with the author, 6 January 1994.
35 Jorgensen, interview with the author, 6 January 1994.

17 TIME FOR A CAPSTAN

1 The Vasey Papers.
2 The Rowell Papers.
3 Treschman, interview with the author, 3 October 1992.
4 Suthers, interview with the author, 8 October 1994.
5 Graeme-Evans, *Of Storms and Rainbows*, vol 2, p. 109.
6 Rodgers, questionnaire reply to the author, 21 August 1995.
7 Suthers, interview with the author, 8 October 1994.
8 ibid.
9 Rodgers, questionnaire reply to the author, 21 August 1995.
10 Russell, questionnaire reply to the author, 31 July 1995.
11 Rodgers, questionnaire reply to the author, 21 August 1995.
12 Hope, questionnaire reply to the author, 27 November 1995.
13 Graeme-Evans, *Of Storms and Rainbows*, p. 120.
14 Radford, interview with the author, 8 January 1994.
15 McCosker, interview with the author, 8 January 1994.
16 Graeme-Evans, *Of Storms and Rainbows*, p. 120.
17 Hope, questionnaire reply to the author, 27 November 1995.
18 Rodgers, questionnaire reply to the author, 21 August 1995.
19 AWM 52 8/3/12 The 2/12th Unit Diary, the August Diary, 1942.
20 Rodgers, questionnaire reply to the author, 21 August 1995.
21 McCarthy, *South-West Pacific Area—First Year*, p. 180.

18 THE GLASSY STARE OF DEATH

1 Donnelly, questionnaire reply to the author, 12 May 1995.
2 Baker and Knight, *Milne Bay 1942*, p. 255.
3 Cummings, interview Baker and Knight, copy most kindly given to the author.
4 AWM 52 8/3/9 The 2/9th Unit Diary, the September Diary 1942.
5 Baker and Knight, *Milne Bay 1942*, p. 257.
6 Captain Worthington, 2/9th Battalion, questionnaire reply to the author, 21 January 1996.
7 Fountain, interview with the author, 11 October 1994.
8 McCarthy, *South-West Pacific Area—First Year*, p. 181.
9 Worthington, interview with the author, 4 August 1993.
10 AWM 52 8/3/9 The 2/9th Unit Diary, the September Diary 1942.
11 Fitzpatrick, questionnaire reply to the author, 5 February 1996.
12 ibid.
13 Worthington, questionnaire reply to the author, 21 January 1996.
14 Rolleston, *Not a Conquering Hero*, p. 84.
15 Hinz, interview with the author, 12 October 1994.
16 Worthington, questionnaire reply to the author, 21 January 1996.
17 AWM 52 8/3/9 The 2/9th Unit Diary, the September Diary 1942.
18 McCready, questionnaire reply to the author, 20 February 1995.
19 Rolleston, *Not a Conquering Hero*, p. 88.
20 ibid.
21 Spencer, *In the Footsteps of Ghosts*, p. 107.
22 Randell, questionnaire reply to the author, 4 January 1995.
23 Moji, *At the Ends of Sky and Sea*.
24 ibid.
25 3DRL 4143 Papers of Maj-Gen C.A. Clowes, 11 Aust Div 2 AIF AWM 419/20/10 File 1 of 5.
26 ibid.
27 McCarthy, *South-West Pacific Area—First Year*, p. 185.
28 Slim, *Defeat into Victory*, pp. 187–8.
29 AWM 3DRL 6763 The Rowell Papers, Milne Force Letters and Signals.
30 AWM 67 3/74 Clowes to Gavin Long, 18 December 1956.
31 Walker, *The Island Campaigns*, pp. 47–8; Rowell, *Full Circle*, pp. 120–1.

19 . . . COME UP HERE AND BLOODY TRY!

1 Horner, *Crisis of Command*, p. 195.
2 ibid.
3 McCarthy, *South-West Pacific Area—First Year*, p. 280.
4 AWM 52 1/10/1 Kienzle's Report.
5 McCarthy, *South-West Pacific Area—First Year*, p. 268.
6 ibid. p. 269.
7 ibid.
8 McCarthy, *South-West Pacific Area—First Year*, p. 271.
9 ibid.
10 AWM 52 1/10/1 Kienzle's Report.
11 McCarthy, *South-West Pacific Area—First Year*, p. 290.
12 ibid.
13 Quoted in Horner, *Crisis of Command*, p. 210.
14 ibid. p. 211.
15 McCarthy, *South-West Pacific Area—First Year*, p. 307.
16 ibid.
17 Quoted in Horner, *General Vasey's War*, p. 207.
18 AWM 52 1/10/1 Kienzle's Report.
19 Milner, *Victory in Papua*, pp. 138–9; Long, *The Six Years' War*, p. 235.
20 AWM 581/3/5 Harding to Sutherland.
21 McCarthy, *South-West Pacific Area—First Year*, p. 334.

20 I KNOW THEY'LL FIGHT

1 Mayo, *Bloody Buna*, p. 14.
2 The description of Gona comes from Mayo, the Official Historian's aerial photo on page 130 and interviews with the participants.
3 Grahamslaw, 'Recollections of Angau', p. 17. A copy of this document was most kindly given to the author by Mr Michael Webster from Queensland.
4 ibid. p. 71.
5 ibid. p. 21.
6 Walker, *The Island Campaigns*, p. 122.
7 Glavin, letter to the author, March 1993.
8 ibid.
9 Horner, *General Vasey's War*, pp. 219–20.
10 Quoted in Horner, *Crisis of Command*, p. 226.
11 ibid.

12 ibid. p. 227.
13 ibid.
14 Quoted in Horner, *Crisis of Command*, p. 227.
15 ibid.

21 A VULGAR PUBLIC BRAWL

1 Murdoch, from his account of the removal of Brigadier Potts; copy sent to the author.
2 Sublet, letter to the author, 20 July 1987.
3 Dougherty, interview with the author, 12 November 1988.
4 ibid.
5 Katekar, interview with the author, 3 August 1988.
6 Sublet, interview with the author, 6 August 1988.
7 ibid.
8 'Report on Operations 25 November–14 January 1943' by Brigadier I.N. Dougherty, Commander 21 Aust. Inf. Bde (with appendices). See Appendix 2. A copy of this document was most kindly lent to the author by Major-General Sir I. Dougherty in Sydney, 12 November 1988. The report will be subsequently referred to as 'The Dougherty Report'.
9 Dougherty, interview with the author, 12 November 1988.
10 The Dougherty Report.
11 In February 1993 the author made a series of video-recorded interviews of Gona veterans for HQ Training Command, Australian Army, at Georges Heights, Sydney. Two of these interviews, with Ralph Honner and Ron Plater, 39th Battalion, were conducted at Georges Heights. The remainder were undertaken in Adelaide with 2/27th Battalion veterans at the Torrens Parade Ground Officers Mess. From hereon these interviews will be identified with the veteran's name and 'interview with the author, HQ Training Command'.
12 Katekar, interview with the author, 4 April 1989.
13 Honner, interview with the author, 1 September 1986.
14 Bisset, letter to the author, 28 June 1987.
15 Sheldon, letter to the author, July 1987.
16 Cooper, interview with the author, 10 March 1993.
17 The Dougherty Report, p. 5.
18 Katekar, interview with the author, 10 March 1993.
19 Johns, interview with the author, 15 March 1993.
20 Sherwin, interview with the author, 8 March 1993.
21 Baldwin, interview with the author, 16 March 1993.
22 Sheldon, letter to the author, July 1987.

23 Thredgold, interview with the author, 8 April 1989.
24 Ward, interview with the author, 8 March 1993.
25 The Dougherty Report, p. 6.
26 Thompson, letter to the author, April 1993.
27 The Dougherty Report, p. 6.
28 Quoted in Edgar, *Warrior of Kokoda*, pp. 226–7.
29 Atkinson, interview with the author, 17 March 1993.
30 Thredgold, interview with the author, 8 April 1989.
31 Breakey, interview with the author, 8 April 1989.
32 Scott, letter to the author, April 1993.
33 Hobbs, interview with the author, 9 March 1993.
34 ibid.
35 Dougherty, interview with the author, 12 November 1988.
36 AWM 52 8/3/27 The 2/27th War Diary, November–December 1942, the appendices.
37 The Dougherty Report, p. 8.
38 Burnett, interview with the author, 24 March 1993.
39 Hearman, letter to the author, 24 April 1989.

22 THIS IS NOT A MOB!

1 Honner, interview with the author, HQ Training Command.
2 Honner, 'The 39th At Gona'.
3 ibid.
4 Honner, interview with the author, HQ Training Command.
5 McClean, interview with the author, 29 March 1993.
6 Honner, interview with the author, HQ Training Command.
7 Bidstrup, interview with the author, 1 March 1989.
8 Honner, interview with the author, HQ Training Command.
9 Dalby, interview with the author, 23 March 1993.
10 Moore, interview with the author, 23 March 1993.
11 Bloomfield, letter to the author, March 1993.
12 Moore, interview with the author, 23 March 1993.
13 Lovett, the 39th Battalion adjutant, interview with the author, 5 October 1998.
14 Honner, interview with the author, 1 September 1986.
15 ibid.
16 Honner, interview with the author, HQ Training Command.
17 Kelly, interview with the author, 29 March 1993.
18 Dalby, interview with the author, 23 March 1993.
19 Honner, interview with the author, HQ Training Command.
20 McCarthy, *South-West Pacific Area—First Year*, p. 441.
21 Dougherty, interview with the author, 12 November 1988.

22 Katekar, interview with the author, 3 March 1988.
23 O'Connor, interview with the author, 24 March 1993.
24 Hardie, interview with the author, 27 March 1993.
25 Pannell, interview with the author, 24 March 1993.
26 Moore, interview with the author, 23 March 1993.
27 McClean, interview with the author, 6 June 1986.
28 Honner, *This is the 39th.*
29 Manol, letter to the author, March 1989.
30 Honner, interview with the author, HQ Training Command.

23 BOTH IMMEDIATE AND ENDURING

1 Lewis, 'The Plantation Dream', pp. 87 and 308. Duropa Plantation was originally spelt as 'Juropa' or 'Giropa', presumably after Giropa Point. In 1942 it was spelt as 'Duropa', which will be perpetuated in the narrative to this work.
2 Quoted in McCarthy, *South-West Pacific Area—First Year*, p. 369.
3 Quoted in Horner, *Crisis of Command*, p. 232.
4 ibid. p. 145.
5 ibid.
6 McCarthy, *South-West Pacific Area—First Year*, p. 378.
7 Quoted in McDonald and Brune, *200 Shots: Damien Parer, George Silk and the Australians at war in New Guinea*, p. 93. McDonald interviewed Silk in Connecticut, USA in July 1996.
8 ibid. p. 9.
9 ibid. p. 93.
10 Wilson, questionnaire reply to the author, 4 May 1995.
11 Interview, Baker and Knight with Cummings. Copy most kindly given to the author, October 1994.
12 Parbury, questionnaire reply to the author, 25 May 1995.
13 Morris, taped questionnaire reply to the author, May 1995.
14 Spencer, *In the Footsteps of Ghosts*, pp. 124–5.
15 Worthington, the adjutant of the 2/9th, questionnaire reply to the author, 21 January 1996.
16 Spencer, *In the Footsteps of Ghosts*, p. 126.
17 Walpole, interview with the author, 10 October 1994.
18 Barnet, taped questionnaire reply to the author, 16 May 1995.
19 Wilson, questionnaire reply to the author, 4 May 1995.
20 Barnet, taped questionnaire reply to the author, 16 May 1995.
21 Randell, questionnaire reply to the author, 4 January 1995.
22 Dixon, interview with the author, 6 November 1994.
23 Parbury, questionnaire reply to the author, 25 May 1995.

24 Hynard, quoted in Spencer, *In the Footsteps of Ghosts*, p. 131.
25 Hansen, interview with the author, 10 October 1994.
26 Morris, interview with the author, 17 January 1995.
27 Parbury, questionnaire reply to the author, 25 May 1995.
28 Spencer, *In the Footsteps of Ghosts*, pp. 132–3.
29 Parbury, questionnaire reply to the author, 25 May 1995.
30 Spencer, interview with the author, 31 October 1994.
31 ibid.
32 AWM 52 8/3/9 The 2/9th Unit Diary, the December Diary 1942. The appendices to this document contain Milne's original diary.
33 Wilson, questionnaire reply to the author, 4 May 1995.
34 Thomas, questionnaire reply to the author, 7 March 1996.
35 Spencer, *In the Footsteps of Ghosts*, p. 143.
36 ibid. p. 144.

24 I'VE NEVER GOT OVER IT

1 Bowden, interview with the author, 18 May 1995.
2 AWM 52 8/3/10 The 2/10th Unit Diary, the December Diary 1942.
3 Robinson, questionnaire reply to the author, 7 February 1996.
4 McCarthy, *South-West Pacific Area—First Year*, p. 469.
5 Coombe, interview with the author, 9 September 1995.
6 Brown, interview with the author, 8 January 1994.
7 Wilson, questionnaire reply to the author, 4 May 1994.
8 Barnet, taped questionnaire reply to the author, 16 May 1995.
9 Maroney, interview with the author, 10 September 1995.
10 Schmedge, interview with the author, 8 October 1992.
11 McCarthy, *South-West Pacific Area—First Year*, p. 471.
12 Allchin, *Purple and Blue*, p. 292.
13 Silk, interviewed by Neil McDonald, July 1996.
14 ibid.
15 McDonald and Brune, *200 Shots: Damien Parer, George Silk and the Australians at war in New Guinea*, p. 139.
16 Spencer, *In the Footsteps of Ghosts*, p. 108.
17 ibid.
18 Gray, interview with the author, 18 May 1995.
19 Evans, taped questionnaire reply to the author, 31 July 1995.
20 Brown, interview with the author, 8 January 1994.
21 Tabe, interview with the author, 8 September 1995.
22 Coombe, interview with the author, 9 September 1995.
23 Andrews, interview with the author, 4 January 1994.

24 AWM 52 8/3/10 The 2/10th Unit Diary, The December Diary 1942.
25 McCarthy, *South-West Pacific Area—First Year*, p. 477.
26 Schmedge, interview with the author, 8 October 1992.
27 Graeme-Evans, *Of Storms and Rainbows*, vol. 2, p. 251.
28 Andrews, interview with the author, 4 January 1994.
29 AWM 52 8/2/18 HQ 18 Australian Infantry Brigade. Appendices to the War Diary Part 4 of 5 Parts—HQ Barker Black (Codename for the 2/10th Battalion) Report on Tank Action 29 December 1942. The report was written and signed by Lt-Col Dobbs.
30 Ganderton, questionnaire reply to the author, 8 May 1995.
31 Evans, taped reply to questionnaire from the author, 31 July 1995.
32 Horner, *Crisis of Command*, p. 247.
33 ibid. p. 250.
34 ibid. p. 251.

25 . . . NINE, TEN . . . OUT!

1 Suthers, interview with the author, 8 October 1994.
2 ibid.
3 ibid.
4 Clarke, taped questionnaire reply to the author, 29 September 1995.
5 Suthers, interview with the author, 8 October 1994.
6 Clarke, taped questionnaire reply to the author, 29 September 1995.
7 Rodgers, questionnaire reply to the author, 9 December 1995.
8 ibid.
9 Quoted in McDonald and Brune, *200 Shots: Damien Parer, George Silk and the Australians at war in New Guinea*, p. 145.
10 ibid. caption p. 147.
11 ibid. p. 149.
12 Quoted in McDonald and Brune, *200 Shots: Damien Parer, George Silk and the Australians at war in New Guinea*, p. 154.
13 ibid.
14 Rodgers, questionnaire reply to the author, 9 December 1995.
15 Suthers, interview with the author, 8 October 1994.
16 Thomas, questionnaire reply to the author, March 1995.
17 AWM 52 8/3/12 The 2/12th Unit Diary, The January Diary 1943.
18 Suthers, interview with the author, 8 October 1994.

19 Horner, *Crisis of Command*, p. 253.
20 Horner, *Blamey: Commander-in-Chief*, p. 381.
21 Rodgers, questionnaire reply to the author, 9 December 1995.

26 INTENSIVELY TRAINED

1 McCarthy, *South-West Pacific Area—First Year*, pp. 407–8.
2 Perret, *Old Soldiers Never Die*, p. 310.
3 Australian Archives; A 5954, Box 532.
4 McCarthy, *South-West Pacific Area—First Year*, p. 394.
5 This total represents not only the 25th Brigade count, but the addition of about 180 members of the 3rd Battalion and the members of Chaforce. Given the sickness wastage of Chaforce, the figure might well be over the actual number. This total (1350) is also an approximate count. See McCarthy, *South-West Pacific Area—First Year*, p. 422.
6 Cranston, *Always Faithful*, p. 171.
7 Lovell, interview with the author, April 1988.
8 Isaachsen, interview with the author, June 1989.
9 Issachsen, tel. con. 8 June 2003.
10 McCarthy, *South-West Pacific Area—First Year*, p. 408.
11 Cranston, *Always Faithful*, p. 176.
12 ibid.
13 ibid. p. 177.
14 ibid. p. 179.
15 Cranston, *Always Faithful*, p. 181.
16 McCarthy, *South-West Pacific Area—First Year*, p. 410.
17 Barry, interview with the author, 13 November 1988.
18 Meredith, questionnaire reply to the author, March 1987, and tel. cons, January 2003.
19 McCarthy, *South-West Pacific Area—First Year*, pp. 410–11.
20 Meredith, questionnaire reply to the author March 1987. The officer in question's conduct was confirmed by a number of other company and battalion questionnaire replies and interviews and phone conversations.
21 Quoted in McCarthy, *South-West Pacific Area—First Year*, p. 412.
22 ibid. p. 497.
23 ibid. p. 498.
24 ibid. pp. 499–500.
25 Hamilton, questionnaire reply to the author, 22 March 2003.
26 Jackson, questionnaire reply to the author, 17 February 2003.
27 Isaachsen, tel. con. 14 June 2003.
28 McCarthy, *South-West Pacific Area—First Year*, p. 501.

29 Isaachsen, interview with the author, June 1989.
30 McCarthy, *South-West Pacific Area—First Year*, p. 501.
31 Hartley, *Sananada Interlude*, pp. 10–11.
32 ibid. p. 15.
33 ibid. pp. 34–6.
34 McCarthy, *South-West Pacific Area—First Year*, p. 508.

27 THE PASSING OF COMRADES

1 Andrews, interview with the author, 4 January 1994.
2 Spencer, *In the Footsteps of Ghosts*, p. 148.
3 Wilson, questionnaire reply to the author, 4 May 1995.
4 The author was unable to accurately ascertain the 2/9th Battalion's total reinforcements. The quoted figure for Soputa is taken from the 2/9th Unit Diary.
5 Allchin, *Purple and Blue*, pp. 307, 310.
6 Graeme-Evans, *Of Storms and Rainbows*, Vol. 2, p. 293.
7 This information was taken from interviews with Private L.A. Bennetts and Lieutenant K.J. Davey, 2/10th Battalion, and from Graeme-Evans, *Of Storms and Rainbows*, pp. 293–4.
8 Thomas, questionnaire reply to the author, 7 April 1995.
9 Wood, questionnaire reply to the author, 4 May 1995.
10 Lynn, questionnaire reply to the author, 4 May 1995.
11 Morris, taped questionnaire reply to the author, 4 May 1995.
12 Quoted in McCarthy, *South-West Pacific Area—First Year*, pp. 516–17.
13 Morris, taped questionnaire reply to the author, 4 May 1995.
14 Spencer, *In the Footsteps of Ghosts*, p. 154.
15 Verco, interview with the author, 13 May 1992.
16 Neate, interview with the author, 6 September 1995.
17 AWM 52 8/3/10 The 2/10th Battalion Unit Diary, the January Diary 1943.
18 Quoted in McCarthy, *South-West Pacific Area—First Year*, p. 519.
19 Quoted in Horner, *General Vasey's War*, p. 234.
20 Eichelberger, *Jungle Road to Tokyo*, pp. 60–1.
21 Morris, taped questionnaire reply to the author, 4 May 1995.
22 Suthers, letter to the author, 9 February 1996.
23 Spencer, *In The Footsteps of Ghosts*, pp. 155-6.
24 Crowther, letter to the author, 18 June 2003.
25 Morris, taped questionnaire reply to the author, 4 May 1995.
26 Davey, interview with the author, 4 September 1995.
27 Spencer, *In the Footsteps of Ghosts*, p. 158.

28 Quoted in McCarthy, *South-West Pacific Area—First Year*, p. 521.
29 Davey, interview with the author, 4 September 1995.
30 Wells, letter to the author, November 1994.
31 Neate, interview with the author, 6 September 1995.
32 Spencer, *In the Footsteps of Ghosts*, pp. 160–3.

28 DANCING TO THE BEAT

1 Horner, *Crisis of Command*, p. 257.
2 ibid.
3 Quoted in Manchester, *American Caesar*, p. 327.
4 Perret, *Old Soldiers Never Die*, p. 325.
5 Manchester, *American Caesar*, p. 330.
6 ibid. p. 326.
7 Willoughby and Chamberlain, *MacArthur 1941–1951*, p. 88.
8 Perret, *Old Soldiers Never Die*, p. 325.
9 McCarthy, *South-West Pacific Area—First Year*, p. 239.
10 Rowell, *Full Circle*, p. 133.
11 Australian Archives MS 3782, The Vasey Papers, Vasey to his wife, 6 November 1942.
12 Quoted in Horner, *Crisis of Command*, p. 247.
13 Interviews with the author. For example: Honner, 1 September 1986; Cooper, 4 April 1989; Murdoch, 25 February 1989; Katekar, 30 September 1988; and Hearman, letter to the author, 24 April 1989.
14 Horner, *Crisis of Command*, p. 213.
15 ibid. p. 188.
16 Braga, tel. con. with the author, 24 June 2003. At the time of writing, Braga's biography of Allen is in its final stage. Its publication is due for the first half of 2004.
17 Quoted in Horner, *Crisis of Command*, p. 242.
18 These figures are taken from the 2/1st Field Regiment's unit history: E.V. Hayward, *Six Years in Support*, pp. 144–5.
19 Horner, *Crisis of Command*, p. 187.
20 McDonald, *War Cameraman: The story of Damien Parer*, p. 163.
21 ibid. p. 164.
22 ibid. p. 167.
23 ibid. p. 169.
24 McDonald, letter to the author, 28 June 2003.
25 Horner, *Crisis of Command*, p. 280.
26 The fact that Potts often gave lectures/talks about the campaign is verified by Lieutenant-General Sir Donald Dunstan, who at that time was a recent Duntroon graduate then serving with the

27th Militia Battalion in Darwin. Dunstan, interview with the author, 28 December 1997.

27 Confirmed by Bill Edgar, Potts' biographer. Tel. con. 26 June 2003. Confirmed by Potts' daughter, who vividly remembers the Paull visit to Kojonup. Her only doubt was whether the visit lasted two or three weeks. Tel. con. May 2003.

28 Paull, *Retreat from Kokoda*, p. viii.

29 ibid. p. vii.

30 National Library of Australia. The Wilmot Papers, MS 8436 Series 2, Box 12.

31 The names, in order, and the military positions of each are taken straight from the *Age* letter to the editor of 8 August 1958.

32 Hetherington, *Blamey: Controversial Soldier*, p. 263.

33 Carlyon, *I Remember Blamey*, p. 111.

34 McCarthy, *South-West Pacific Area—First Year*, pp. 334–5.

35 McCarthy, *South-West Pacific Area—First Year*, p. 591.

BIBLIOGRAPHY

OFFICIAL RECORDS

AUSTRALIAN ARCHIVES

Advisory War Council Minutes Files, A2684

NATIONAL LIBRARY OF AUSTRALIA

Vasey Papers, MS 3782

AUSTRALIAN WAR MEMORIAL

Advanced Land Headquarters, Weekly Intelligence Summaries AWM 54 423/11/63

Advanced Land Headquarters G Branch August 1942 AWM 52 1/2/1

ATIS SWPA Current Japanese Translations, AWM 55 3/1

Berryman Papers, Lieutenant-General Sir F.H. AWM PR 84/370

Blamey Papers, Field Marshal Sir Thomas, AWM DRL 6643

Captured Documents—JAP Expeditionary Force Orders for Attack on Milne Bay 20 August 1942, AWM 54 779/3/77

Clowes Papers, Major-General C.A., AWM DRL 4143

Field, Brigadier John, File—Diary, Letters, Articles AWM MSS 785

Headquarters I Australian Corps, Weekly Intelligence Summaries AWM 54 423/11/132

Headquarters 7 Division, War Diary 1/5/14

Headquarters 11 Division, G.S. Branch AWM 52 1/5/25 August 1942

Headquarters 7th Australian Infantry Brigade—the May–October Diaries 1942 AWM 52 8/2/7

Headquarters 18th Australian Infantry Brigade—the July–December War Diaries 1942 and January 1943, AWM 52 8/2/18 appendices (separate files) were also examined
Headquarters 21st Australian Infantry Brigade—August–December 1942 AWM 52 8/2/21
Headquarters Command Milne Force August–December 1942 AWM 52 10/2/15
Interrogation of Prisoners of War Captured in Milne Bay Area . . . AWM 54 779/3/77
Medical Condition of New Guinea Force & Report ADMS Milne Force AWM 54 481/12/234
Messages Between Milne Force and New Guinea Force—Operations August–October 1942 AWM 54 579/7/9
Parry-Okeden Papers, Lieutenant-Colonel AWM PR 00321
Report By Comd Milne Force On Operation Between 25 Aug 42 and 7 Sep 42, AWM 54 579/7/17
Report into Operations 21st Brigade—Owen Stanley Campaign
Rowell Papers, Lieutenant-General Sir Sydney, AWM DRL 6763
Signals Milne Force AWM 54 7/26/1 June–September 1942
2/9th Australian Infantry Battalion Unit Diary, AWM 52 8/3/9 July 1942–January 1943
2/10th Australian Infantry Battalion Unit Diary, AWM 52 8/3/10 July 1942–January 1943
2/12th Australian Infantry Battalion Unit Diary, AWM 52 8/3/12 July 1942–January 1943
2/14th Australian Infantry Battalion Unit Diary, AWM 52 8/3/14 August–December 1942
2/16th Australian Infantry Battalion Unit Diary, AWM 52 8/3/16 August–December 1942
2/27th Australian Infantry Battalion Unit Diary, AWM 52 8/3/27 August–December 1942
9th Australian Infantry Battalion Unit Diary, June–October 1942
25th Australian Infantry Battalion Unit Diary, June–October 1942
39th Australian Infantry Battalion Unit Diary, March–December 1942
49th Australian Infantry Battalion Unit Diary, April–December 1942
53rd Australian Infantry Battalion Unit Diary, April–December 1942
55/53rd Australian Infantry Battalion Unit Diary, April–December 1942
61st Australian Infantry Battalion Unit Diary, June–October 1942

STATE LIBRARY OF SOUTH AUSTRALIA

THE MORTLOCK LIBRARY

The Times Handy Atlas, Bartholomew, Selfridge & Co Ltd 1935, S 912 c

Everyman's Library, Ernest Rhys (edit), No date, S 912.5 B287

The Adelaide History Grade VII Oldham, W., SA Education Department 1930, Z942

A Course of Study for Central Schools (Boys), Education Department of South Australia, 1939

CORRESPONDENCE: DIARIES, PRIVATE PAPERS, QUESTIONNAIRES, LETTERS, TAPES

Abernethy, Lieutenant T.J., 25th Battalion and 7 Brigade HQ, letter from Brisbane, 27 March 1995

Andrews, Sergeant C., 49th Battalion, March 1986

Andrews, the late Lieutenant J.P., 2/10th Battalion, letter from Scarness, Queensland, 17 August, 7 October 1992

Angus, Private D.E., 2/16th Battalion, August 1987

Avery, the late Lieutenant A., 2/14th Battalion, 2 July 1987

Barnet, Corporal E.H., 2/6th Armoured Regiment, taped questionnaire reply from New South Wales, 16 May 1995

Barry, Private J., 36th Battalion, Sydney, received 20 February 2003

Barry, Private K., 55/53rd Battalion, 10 June 1987

Bisset, Captain S.Y., 2/14th Battalion, 28 June 1987

Bloomfield, Private C., 2/26th Battalion, letter, March 1993

Bowden, Lieutenant L.F., 2/12th Battalion, taped questionnaire reply from Kangaroo Island, South Australia, 1 February 1996

Butler, Sergeant N.J., 36th Battalion, 16 February 2003

Byrnes, Private J., 61st Battalion, taped questionnaire reply from Queensland, 1993

Campbell, Captain K.C., 61st Battalion, letter from Brisbane, 16 March 1995

Chilton, Brigadier Sir Frederick, Milne Force HQ, letter from Sydney, 18 July 1994

Clarke, the late Captain D.S., 2/12th Battalion, taped questionnaire from Sydney, 29 September 1995

Clemens, Private R.O., 2/14th Battalion, letter, 3 July 1987

Clerehan, Dr Brian, Military Historian, letters from 2/10th officers to him were lent to the author, 28 March 1993

Company Commanders' Reports 2/10th Battalion for Milne Bay KB Mission battle, copies most kindly given to the author by the late Captain A. Kumnick, 2/10th Battalion, May 1992

Connolly, Private R.A., 61st Battalion, taped questionnaire, Queensland 1993

Cranston, Warrant-Officer 2 F.H., 49th Battalion, March 1986

Deoberitz, Captain A.A., 49th Battalion, July 1986

Dolly, Sergeant A.P., 9th Battalion, letter from Brisbane, 23 August 1993

Donnelly, Captain V.J., 2/9th Battalion, taped questionnaire from Whitfield Queensland, 12 May 1995

Dunlop, Sergeant W.R., 53rd Battalion, March 1987

Edwards, Lieutenant C.E., 2/27th Battalion, July 1987

Ellenden, Corporal A.P.J., 61st Battalion, questionnaire from Brisbane, August 1994

Evans, the late Sergeant A.A., 2/10th Battalion, taped questionnaire from Melbourne, 31 July 1995

Evans, Private M.J., 53rd Battalion, March 1987

Fielding, Corporal H.W., 2/14th Battalion, 20 July 1987

Fitzpatrick, Corporal R.F., 2/9th Battalion, questionnaire from Goolwa, South Australia, 5 February 1996

Ganderton, Trooper C.E., 2/6th Armoured Regiment, questionnaire from Sydney, 8 May 1995

Gardner, Corporal A., 2/12th Battalion, questionnaires from Brisbane 10 May, 16 August 1995

Garland, Lieutenant A.G., 39th Battalion, March 1993

Gerke, Lieutenant J., 2/16th Battalion, 10 July 1987

Glavin, Warrant-Officer 1 J., 2/14th Battalion, 6 July 1987, March 1993

Greenwood, Private N.W., 49th Battalion, March 1987

Gresham, Lieutenant E.N., 55/53rd Battalion, April 1986

Gwillim, the late Major J.E., 2/14th Battalion, 6 July 1987

Hanson, Brigadier A.G., 2/1st Field Regiment, April 1993

Harlen, Captain A., 7th Brigade Signals, manuscript from Brisbane, June 1994

Harris, Private R.L., 53rd Battalion, 17 August 1989

Hearman, the late Major J., 2/16th Battalion, 23 April 1989, April 1993

Helmore, the late Padre J., 2/10th Battalion, copy of his diary most kindly given to the author by his son Donald from Kew, Victoria, August 1992

Hocking, Lance-Corporal J.A., 2/16th Battalion, August 1987
Honner, the late Lieutenant-Colonel R., 39th Battalion, October 1988
Hope, Private P.D., 2/12th Battalion, questionnaire from Newtown Tasmania, 27 November 1995
Irwin, Sergeant K.J., 53rd Battalion, 20 March 1989
Ison, Sergeant L., 55/53rd Battalion, April 1987
Jackson, Private J.K., 36th Battalion, 17 February 2003
Jeffrey, Private J.N., 2/14th Battalion, 8 August 1987
Jeffrey, Private W., 2/14th Battalion, 31 July 1987
Jolly, Lance-Corporal J.N., 2/14th Battalion, 21 July 1987
Katekar, the late Major H.J., 2/27th Battalion, August 1987
Kemp, Warrant-Officer 2 R.A., 49th Battalion, August 1987
Kienzle, the late Captain H.T., ANGAU, December 1986
Lambert, Sergeant A.M., 36th Battalion, questionnaire from Marsfield New South Wales, 17 February 2003
Lang, Sergeant E.K., 2/14th Battalion, 29 July 1987
Latimore, Staff-Sergeant V.C., 2/9th Battalion, questionnaire from Maryborough, Queensland, 13 February 1995
Lockie, Staff-Sergeant W.J., 49th Battalion, July 1987
Lorimer, Private G., 61st Battalion, questionnaire from Brisbane, 26 August 1993
Lynch, Sergeant F.R., 2/12th Battalion, taped questionnaire from Turkey Beach, Queensland, 13 June 1995
Lynn, Corporal R., 2/6th Armoured Regiment, questionnaire from Glen Innes, New South Wales, 4 May 1995
McCready, Captain S.P., 2/9th Battalion, questionnaire from Brisbane, 20 February 1995
McCulloch, Corporal C., 61st Battalion, questionnaire from Brisbane, 23 August 1993
McDermant, Sergeant D.A., 49th Battalion, April 1987
Mahoney, the late Major J.C., Brigade Major 7th Brigade, letter from Brisbane, 6 September 1993
Mallyon, the late Lieutenant A.R., 2/10th Battalion, letters to his father most kindly lent to the author
Manol, the late Sergeant J., 39th Battalion, March 1993
Meredith, Corporal C.C., 53rd Battalion, letter March 1987
Millett, Sergeant F.H., 2/12th Battalion, questionnaire from Brisbane, 17 May 1995
Morris, Corporal A.H., 2/14th Battalion, 1 June 1989
Morris, Sergeant C.J., 2/9th Battalion, taped questionnaire from Brisbane, 4 May 1995
Newman, Private R.D., 2/16th Battalion, 30 July 1987

Parbury, Lieutenant-Colonel C.B., questionnaire from Tenterfield, New South Wales, 25 May 1995

Pascoe, Private R., 55th Battalion, 14 April 1987

Paterson, Major J.S., 61st Battalion, questionnaire from Melbourne, 24 February 1995

Peters, Lieutenant W.A.A., 49th Battalion, August 1987

Pollard, the late Major L.J., 2/10th Battalion, May 1992, personal diary December 1940–November 1945

Pulling, Trooper K., 2/6th Armoured Regiment, questionnaire from New South Wales, 28 June 1995

Quilty, Captain H., 2/9th Battalion, questionnaire from Sydney, 7 April 1995

Randell, Sergeant E.J., 2/9th Battalion, questionnaire from Sarina, Queensland, 4 January 1995

Roberts, Lance-Corporal J.H., 2/14th Battalion, 21 July 1987

Robinson, Corporal G.B., 2/10th Battalion, questionnaire from Gorokan, New South Wales, 7 February 1996

Rodgers, Colonel R.F., 2/12th Battalion, questionnaires from Sydney, 21 August, 9 December 1995

Rolleston, Corporal F.J., 2/9th Battalion, questionnaire from Queensland, 16 March 1995

Rosewarne, the late Sergeant P., 2/6th Armoured Regiment, questionnaire from Queensland, 13 June 1995

Russell, Captain N.H., 2/9th Battalion, questionnaire from Brisbane, 31 July 1995

Sandaver, Private R., 2/9th Battalion, letter from MacKay, Queensland, 16 May 1995

Schmedje, the late Lieutenant-Colonel T.J., 2/10th Battalion, letter from Canberra, 20 February 1995

Scott, Lieutenant J., 2/16th Battalion, letter from Perth to Lieutenant-Colonel Ralph Honner; copy most kindly given to the author November 1992

Sheldon, Lieutenant E.F., 2/14th Battalion, July 1987

Sly, Sergeant S.A., 55/53rd Battalion, April 1987

Spencer, the late Sergeant W.B., 2/9th Battalion, letter from Adelaide, 2 June 1996

Spratford, Sergeant J.W., 2/16th Battalion, August 1987

Stephen, Sergeant A., 49th Battalion, March 1987

Sublet, Lieutenant-Colonel F.H., 2/16th Battalion, questionnaire from Perth, 20 July 1987

Suthers, Captain A.G., 2/12th Battalion, letter from Sydney, 15 February 1996

Thomas, Corporal J.L., 2/6th Armoured Regiment, questionnaire from Mangerton, New South Wales, 7 April 1995

Thomas, Lieutenant V.F., 2/9th Battalion, questionnaire from Queensland, March 1995

Thompson, Captain R.N., 2/14th Battalion, questionnaire from Mannum, July 1987, letter, April 1993

Thomson, Lieutenant Corporal L.J., 2/6th Armoured Regiment, questionnaire from Connells Point, New South Wales, 27 March 1995

Woodward, Corporal R.F., 2/14th Battalion, July 1987

Walker, Private W., 2/14th Battalion, July 1987

Warbrick, Lieutenant D.M., 49th Battalion, 10 March 1987

Watson, Sergeant R., 2/14th Battalion, July 1987

Widdows, the late Able Seaman R., diary kept during service with HMAS *Arunta,* copy most kindly given to the author by Mr Widdows July 1992

Wilson, Sergeant J.A., 2/6th Armoured Regiment, questionnaire from Queensland, 4 May 1995

Wilson, the late J.D., 61st Battalion, questionnaire from Queensland, 31 July 1993

Wood, Trooper J.S., 2/6th Armoured Regiment, questionnaire from Leeton, New South Wales, 4 May 1995

Wood, Corporal L.W., 49th Battalion, March 1987

Worthington, the late Captain N.A., 2/9th Battalion, letter from Adelaide, 21, 29 January 1996

Wotten, Chaplain R.A.W., 2/12th Battalion, questionnaire from Blue Bay, New South Wales, 10 May 1995

INTERVIEWS

Acreman, Lieutenant K.A., 101 Tank Attack Regiment 4 Battery, Brisbane, 3 October 1992

Allanson, Private W.G.B., 2/10th Battalion, Adelaide, 4 March 1993

Andrews, the late Lieutenant J.P., 2/10th Battalion, Hervey Bay, Queensland, 2, 3, 4 January 1994

Armitage, Private L., 39th Battalion, Melbourne, 8 June 1986

Ashton, Private A.G., 2/27th Battalion, Adelaide, 26 November 1986

Atkinson, Private G., 2/27th Battalion, Adelaide, 17 March 1993

Bailey, Private J.H., 2/10th Battalion, Adelaide, 2 September 1995

Baldwin, Sergeant R., 2/27th Battalion, Adelaide, 16 March 1993

Bamberry, Private W.T., 25th Battalion, Toowoomba, Queensland, 6 January 1994

Barker, Private G.E., 9th Battalion, Brisbane, 2 October 1992

Barry, Private K., 55/53rd Battalion, Sydney, 13 November 1988
Beard, Sergeant E.W.H., 9th Battalion, Brisbane, 2 October 1992
Beattie, Lieutenant E.K., 2/9th Battalion, Brisbane, 16 January 1995
Bennetts, Private L.A., 2/10th Battalion, Adelaide, 20 May 1995
Bidstrup, the late Major M.L., 39th Battalion, Adelaide, 9 November 1985, 7 January, 14 January, 13 March, 11 June, 25 August, 13 November 1986, 1 March 1989
Black, Private P.R., 2/10th Battalion, Adelaide, 18 May 1995
Bowden, the late P.L., 2/10th Battalion, Adelaide, 25 January 1993, 7 March 1994, 18 May 1995
Bradford, Corporal E.B., 61st Battalion, Brisbane, 1 October 1992
Breakey, the late Private J., 2/27th Battalion, Adelaide, 8 April 1989
Brown, the late Wing Commander B.E., 75 Squadron, Sydney, 1 April 1993
Brown, the late Brigadier M.J., 2/10th Battalion, Brisbane, 4 October 1992, 8 January 1994
Bruce, Private J., 61st Battalion, Brisbane, 1 October 1992
Budden, the late Lieutenant F., 55/53rd Battalion, Sydney, 31 August 1986
Burfein, Private G.F., 61st Battalion, Brisbane, 1 October 1992
Burns, Sergeant J.H., 2/27th Battalion, Adelaide, September 1988
Cameron, The Honourable C., former MHR, Adelaide, 9 August 1988
Campbell, Captain K.C., 61st Battalion, Brisbane, 4 October 1992
Capper, Sergeant J.H., 9th Battalion, Brisbane, 2 October 1992, 8 January 1994
Charnstram, Private R.L., 2/10th Battalion, Adelaide, 3 March 1993
Chilton, Brigadier Sir F.O., Sydney, 17 May 1992
Clarke, the late Corporal J.R., 2/10th Battalion, Adelaide, 17 June 1992
Clerehan, Doctor B., Military Historian, Melbourne, 4 January 1993, 28 March 1993
Constantis, Private J.L., 2/10th Battalion, Adelaide, 19 June 1992, 9 September 1995
Coombe, Private J.L., 2/10th Battalion, Adelaide, 19 June 1992, 9 September 1995
Cooper, the late Lieutenant-Colonel G.D.T., 2/27th Battalion, Adelaide, 19 September 1986, 13 August 1988, 4 April 1989, 10 March 1993
Crawford, Flight-Sergeant R.W., 75 Squadron, Sydney, 1 April 1993
Crowley, the late Private K., 39th Battalion, Melbourne, 8 June 1986
Cummings, Lieutenant-Colonel C.J., 2/9th Battalion, interview by Baker and Knight, kindly lent to the author

Dalby, the late Captain H., 39th Battalion, Adelaide, 6 March, 24 April, 27 July, 6 October 1986, 23 March 1993
Davey, Lieutenant K.J., 2/10th Battalion, Adelaide, 4 September 1995
Deane-Butcher, the late W., Squadron Medical Officer, 75 Squadron, Sydney, 1 April 1993
Dixon, the late Sergeant H.T., 2/9th Battalion, Adelaide, 6 November 1994
Dougherty, the late Major-General Sir I.N., Sydney, 12 November 1988
Drake, Private N.S.W., 2/10th Battalion, Adelaide, 20 May 1995
Dunstan, Lieutenant-General Sir Donald, Adelaide, 28 December 1997
Edwardes, Sergeant G.E., 2/10th Battalion, Adelaide, 10 January 1993
Edwardes, Lieutenant I.C., 2/10th Battalion, Adelaide, 6 May 1992
Edwards, Lieutenant C.E., 2/27th Battalion, Adelaide, 24 November 1986, 8 March 1993
Elliot, Lieutenant A., 2/9th Battalion, Brisbane, 13 October 1994
Ellis, the late Corporal J., 2/10th Battalion, Adelaide, 9 September 1992, 6 May 1995
Eylward, Private D.R., 2/10th Battalion, Adelaide, 5 March 1994
Eylward, Private K.J., 2/10th Battalion, Adelaide, 9 March 1993
Fee, the late Sergeant R.C., 2/10th Battalion, Adelaide, 12 May 1992, 6 May 1995
Fotheringham, the late Major J.D., 49th Battalion, Adelaide, 17 July 1986
Fountain, Lance-Corporal J.F. (Jim), 2/9th Battalion, Brisbane, 10 October 1994
Fountain, Private W.D. (William), 2/9th Battalion, Brisbane, 11 October 1994
Garland, Lieutenant A.G., 39th Battalion, Melbourne, 7 June 1986
George, Private E., 61st Battalion, Brisbane, 1 October 1992
George, Corporal N., 2/27th Battalion, Adelaide, 7 December 1986
Gilbert, Private M.N., 2/27th Battalion, Adelaide, 26 November 1986
Gillespie, Lieutenant W.R., 49th Battalion, Adelaide, October 1986
Goldsmith, the late D.K., 2/26th Battalion, Adelaide, 25 May 1987
Graham, Lance-Corporal B.D., 2/9th Battalion, Brisbane, 16 January 1995
Gray, Private F., 2/10th Battalion, Adelaide, 7 March 1994, 18 May 1995
Gummow, Sergeant A.A., 2/10th Battalion, Adelaide, 15 February 1993, 7 March 1994

Hackett, Corporal P.K., 7th Brigade Signals, Brisbane, 7 January 1994
Hall, Sergeant K.L., 2/9th Battalion, Brisbane, 16 January 1995
Hansen, Sergeant V., 2/9th Battalion, Brisbane, 10 October 1994
Hardie, the late J.L., 39th Battalion, Melbourne, 27 March 1993
Harlen, Captain A., 7th Brigade Signals, Brisbane, 2 October 1992
Hartnett, Sergeant T.J., 2/10th Battalion, Adelaide, 15 February 1993
Hastings, Corporal R.M., 2/27th Battalion, Mount Gambier, South Australia, 24 March 1993
Hildred, Private R., 61st Battalion, Toowoomba, Queensland, 6 January 1994
Hill, Private A., 25th Battalion, Toowoomba, Queensland, 6 January 1994
Hilton, Private J.A., 25th Battalion, Toowoomba, Queensland, 6 January 1994
Hines, Corporal L.H., 2/19th Battalion, Brisbane, 16 January 1995
Hinz, the late Private A.B., 2/9th Battalion, Brisbane, 12 October 1994
Hobbs, Private J., 2/27th Battalion, Adelaide, 9 March 1993
Honner, the late Lieutenant-Colonel R., 39th Battalion, Sydney, 1 September 1986, 11 November 1988
Hook, Lance-Corporal D.W., 61st Battalion, Brisbane, 2 October 1992
Hornick, Lance-Corporal K.A.J., 61st Battalion, Brisbane, 1 October 1992
Hoy, Sergeant C., 61st Battalion, Brisbane, 3 October 1992
Hynes, Gunner J.J.D., 2/1st Field Regiment, Sydney, 30 March 1993
Isaachsen, Lieutenant-Colonel O.C., 36th Battalion, Adelaide, June 1989, 22 March 1995
Jennings, Private J.C., 2/10th Battalion, Adelaide, 4 March 1993
Johns, Lieutenant R., 2/27th Battalion, Adelaide, 15 March 1993
Johnston, E., 7th Brigade Signals, Brisbane, 2 October 1992
Jorgensen, Lance-Corporal E.N., 25th Battalion, Toowoomba, Queensland, 6 January 1994
Katekar, the late Major H.J., 2/27th Battalion, Adelaide, 13 August, 30 September 1988, 4 April 1989, 10 March 1993
Keane, Private D., 2/27th Battalion, Adelaide, 24 November 1986
Kelly, Lieutenant H.H., 39th Battalion, Melbourne, 29 March 1993
Kingston, Private W.L., 2/10th Battalion, Adelaide, 9 February 1993
Kirkmoe, Private J.P., 2/10th Battalion, Adelaide, 4 March 1993
Leamey, Corporal A.M., 2/27th Battalion, Mount Gambier, South Australia, 24 March 1993
Lee, Lieutenant-Colonel Sir A.J., 2/27th Battalion, Adelaide, 13 July 1988

Lethbridge, the late Lieutenant S.D., 2/10th Battalion, Victor Harbour, South Australia, 15 June 1992

Little, Private E.A., 2/27th Battalion, Adelaide, 25 November 1986

Lovell, the late Lieutenant-Colonel D.J.H., 55/53rd Battalion, Adelaide, April 1988

Lovell, Private G.W., 2/10th Battalion, Adelaide, 8 May 1992

McClean, Major D.I.H., 39th Battalion, Melbourne, 7 June 1986, 29 March 1993

McCosker, Sergeant H.F., 9th Battalion, Brisbane, 8 January 1994

McCready, Lieutenant S.P., 2/9th Battalion, Brisbane, 17 January 1995

McFarlane, Private D., 61st Battalion, Brisbane, 1 October 1992

McGee, Private W.L., 2/10th Battalion, Adelaide, 15 February 1993

MacKenzie, Sergeant J.R., 61st Battalion, Brisbane, 3 October 1992

McLaughlan, Private J.F., 25th Battalion Toowoomba, Queensland, 6 January 1994

Magarey, the late Major Sir J.R., 2/6th Field Ambulance, Adelaide, 10 June 1987

Mallyon, the late Lieutenant A.R., 2/10th Battalion, Adelaide, 9 May 1992

Manol, the late Sergeant J., 39th Battalion, Melbourne, 7 June 1986

Masters, Flight-Lieutenant P.A., 75 Squadron, Adelaide, 11 March 1992

Moore, Lieutenant A.W., 39th Battalion, Melbourne, 27 March 1993

Moore, Sergeant J., 2/10th Battalion, Adelaide, 30 December 1994, 18 May 1995

Moroney, Lance-Corporal W.M., 2/10th Battalion, Adelaide, 10 September 1995

Morris, Sergeant C.J., 2/9th Battalion, Brisbane, 17 January 1995

Mortensen, E.L., 7th Brigade Signals, Brisbane, 2 October 1992, 7 January 1994

Mortimore, Lieutenant H.E., 39th Battalion, Melbourne, 7 June 1986, 28 March 1993

Murdoch, the late Lieutenant-Colonel, 2/16th Battalion, 21st Brigade HQ, Adelaide, 25 February 1988

Murphy, Private P., 2/9th Battalion, Brisbane, 10 October 1994

Neate, the late Sergeant W.M., 2/10th Battalion, Adelaide, 18 February 1993, 6 September 1995

Newcomb, the late Sergeant J., 61st Battalion, Brisbane, 3 October 1992

Nichols, Private C.R., 2/9th Battalion, Brisbane, 16 January 1995

O'Brien, the late Warrant-Officer 2 J.F.P., 2/10th Battalion, Seymour, Victoria, 8 August 1992

O'Brien, Corporal P.B., 2/10th Battalion, Adelaide, 9 February 1993
O'Connor, Private B.J., 2/27th Battalion, Mount Gambier, 24 March 1993
O'Donnell, Sergeant T., 61st Battalion, Brisbane, 1 October 1992
Pank, Squadron Leader D.L., 75, 76 Squadrons, Adelaide, 16 March 1992
Pannell, Lance-Corporal E.G., 2/27th Battalion, Mount Gambier, South Australia, 24 March 1993
Peek, Major E.G.F., 2/9th Battalion, Brisbane, 17 January 1995
Pender, Lance-Corporal P., 61st Battalion, Brisbane, 3 October 1992
Peterson, Sergeant L., 2/10th Battalion, Adelaide, 9 February 1993
Pettet, Pilot-Officer J.H.S., 75 Squadron, Sydney, 1 April 1993
Pollard, the late Major L.G., 2/10th Battalion, Adelaide, 11 May 1992
Price, Corporal R.J., 2/10th Battalion, Adelaide, 4 November 1995
Radford, Lieutenant D.P., 9th Battalion, Brisbane, 8 January 1994
Rickards, Sergeant D., 2/9th Battalion, Brisbane, 16 January 1995
Rosenberg, Corporal P., 2/10th Battalion, Adelaide, 4 August 1992
Rosengren, the late Sergeant R.S., 39th Battalion, Melbourne, 8 June 1986
Royce, Private W.F., 7th Brigade Signals, Brisbane, 2 October 1992, 7 January 1994
Russell, E.A., 7th Brigade Signals, Brisbane, 2 October 1992
Sanderson, Private R.S., 2/10th Battalion, Adelaide, 14 May 1992
Saunders, the late Lieutenant-Colonel D.F., 2/10th Battalion, LO 18th Brigade HQ, 7th Division HQ, Adelaide, 19 February 1993
Schindler, Lieutenant A., 25th Battalion, Brisbane, 7 January 1994
Schmedje, the late Lieutenant-Colonel T.J., 2/10th Battalion, Canberra, 16 May, 8 October 1992
Seddon, the late Captain R.W., 2/10th Battalion, Melbourne, 4 January 1993
Seekamp, the late A.H., 39th Battalion, Adelaide, 24 April 1986
Sellers, Private R.I., 2/10th Battalion, Adelaide, 22 June 1992
Sherwin, Lieutenant A.B., 2/27th Battalion, Adelaide, 24 June 1986, 8 March 1993
Simonson, Captain D.J., 39th Battalion, Adelaide, 3 July 1988
Sims, Brigadier C.A.W., 2/27th Battalion, Adelaide, 24 August 1987, 26 September 1988, 4 April 1989
Slade, Private L.G., 2/10th Battalion, Adelaide, 28 March 1994
Spencer, the late Sergeant W.B., 2/9th Battalion, Adelaide, 31 October 1994

Staatz, Sergeant A.I., 7th Brigade Signals, Brisbane, 2 October 1992, 7 January 1994
Stack, Private A.W., 2/9th Battalion, Brisbane, 13 October 1994
Stephen, Private R.K., 2/10th Battalion, Adelaide, 2 September 1995
Stephens, Private J., 55/53rd Battalion, Sydney, 31 August 1986, 13 November 1988
Stewart, Sergeant R.D., 61st Battalion, Brisbane, 1 October 1992
Strong, Private C.E., 25th Battalion, Toowoomba, Queensland, 6 January 1994
Sublet, Lieutenant-Colonel F.H., 2/26th Battalion, Adelaide, 6 August 1988
Summers, Corporal D.H., 61st Battalion, Brisbane, 1 October 1992
Suthers, Captain A.G., 2/12th Battalion, Sydney, 8 October 1994
Symington, the late Major N.M., 39th Battalion, Adelaide 15 July 1987
Tabe, the late Warrant-Officer 1 L.E., 2/10th Battalion, Adelaide, 11 June 1992, 9 September 1995
Thomas, Corporal J.R.S., 2/10th Battalion, Angaston, South Australia, 20 March 1994
Thomson, Warrant-Officer 2 A., 2/27th Battalion, Adelaide, 8 December 1986, 8 April 1989
Thornton, Private H.E., 2/9th Battalion, Brisbane, 16 January 1995
Thredgold, the late Sergeant L.J. 'Pee Wee', 2/27th Battalion, Adelaide, 7 December 1986
Thredgold, Sergeant R.T. 'Roy', 2/27th Battalion, Adelaide, 8 April 1989
Todd, Private H.A.G., 2/10th Battalion, Adelaide, 5 March 1994, 2 September 1995
Treschman, Private A.A. 'Bert', 2/12th Battalion, Brisbane, 3 October 1992
Verco, the late Major G.W., 2/10th Battalion, Adelaide, 13 May 1992
Walker, the late Private M., 2/10th Battalion, Mount Barker, South Australia, 8 September 1993
Walpole, Private G., 2/9th Battalion, Brisbane, 10 October 1994
Ward, Private A.N., 2/27th Battalion, Adelaide, 8 December 1986, 8 April 1989, 8 March 1993
Warren, Warrant-Officer 2 R.H., 2/10th Battalion, Renmark, South Australia, 15 July 1993
Watson, Flight-Officer B.D., 75 Squadron, Sydney, 1 April 1993
Watts, Private J., 61st Battalion, Brisbane, 1 October 1992
Wells, Sergeant B.E., 2/9th Battalion, Brisbane, 12 October 1994
Whybird, Lance-Corporal J., 61st Battalion, Brisbane 3 October 1992

Wilkins, Private C., 55/53rd Battalion, Sydney, 13 November 1988
Williams, the late Private A., 2/24th Battalion, Adelaide, 3 July 1986
Williams, Private C.J., 2/27th Battalion, Adelaide, 26 November 1986
Williamson, T.A., 7th Brigade Signals, Brisbane, 2 October 1992, 7 January 1994
Willing, Private M.R., 2/10th Battalion, Adelaide, 14 January 1993
Williss, Corporal G., 2/27th Battalion, Adelaide, 25 November 1986
Wilson, the late Private J., 61st Battalion, Brisbane, 3 October 1992
Wilson, Lieutenant J.D., 61st Battalion, Brisbane, 5 January 1994
Winen, Sergeant L.G., 2/10th Battalion, Adelaide, 5 May, 25 May 1992, 2 September 1995
Wockner, Sergeant H.W., 2/9th Battalion, Brisbane, 16 January 1995
Wood, Sergeant A.J., 2/10th Battalion, Renmark, South Australia, 15 July 1993
Worthington, the late Captain N.A., 2/9th Battalion, Adelaide, 4 August 1993, 24 January 1995
Worton, Sergeant N.S., 61st Battalion, Brisbane 1995
Wright, Sergeant C., 61st Battalion, Brisbane, 1 October 1992

BOOKS

Allchin, F. *Purple and Blue: The History of the 2/10th Battalion AIF*, Adelaide, the 2/10th Ex-Servicemen's Association 1960
Austin, V. *To Kokoda and Beyond: The Story of the 39th Battalion 1941–43*, Melbourne, Melbourne University Press, 1988
Baker, C. and Knight G. *Milne Bay 1942*, Sydney, Baker-Knight Pub., 1991
Barrett, John. *We Were There: Australian Soldiers of World War II tell their stories*, Sydney, Viking, 1987
Bleakley, Jack. *The Eavesdroppers*, Canberra, Australian Government Publishing Services, 1992
Brigg, Stan & Les. *The 36th Australian Infantry Battalion, 1939–45*, Sydney, 36th Battalion Association, 1967
Brune, P. *Gona's Gone! The Battle for the Beach-head 1942*, Sydney, Allen & Unwin, 1994
—— *The Spell Broken: Exploding the myth of Japanese invincibility*, Sydney, Allen & Unwin, 1997
—— *Those Ragged Bloody Heroes: From the Kokoda Trail to Gona Beach 1942*, Sydney, Allen & Unwin, 1991
—— *We Band of Brothers: A biography of Ralph Honner, soldier and statesman*, Sydney, Allen & Unwin, 2000

Budden, F. *That Mob: The Story of the 55/53rd Australian Infantry Battalion AIF*, Sydney, 1973

Burns, J. *The Brown and Blue Diamond at War*, Adelaide, 2/27th Ex-Servicemen's Association, 1960

Carlyon, N.D. *I Remember Blamey*, Melbourne, Macmillan, 1980

Churchill, Winston, S. *The Second World War: Volume IV, The Hinge of Fate*, London, Cassell, 1951

Connolly, Bob & Anderson, Robin. *First Contact*, New York, Viking, 1987

Cranston, *Always Faithful: The history of the 49th Battalion*, Brisbane, Boolarong, 1983

Day, David. *Reluctant Nation: Australia and the Allied defeat of Japan 1942–45*, Melbourne, Oxford University Press, 1992

—— *The Great Betrayal: Britain, Australia and the onset of the Pacific War 1939–42*, Melbourne, Oxford University Press, 1988

Deane-Butcher, W. *Fighter Squadron Doctor: 75 Squadron R.A.A.F. New Guinea 1942*, Sydney, self-published, 1989

Dornan, Peter. *The Silent Men: Syria to Kokoda and on to Gona*, Sydney, Allen & Unwin, 1999

Drea, Edward J. *MacArthur's Ultra: Codebreaking and the war against Japan, 1942–1945*, Lawrence, Kansas, University Press of Kansas, 1992

Edgar, Bill. *Warrior of Kokoda: A biography of Brigadier Arnold Potts*, Sydney, Allen & Unwin, 1999

Eichelberger, R.L. *Jungle Road to Tokyo*, London, Odhams, 1951

Fearnside, G.H. and Clift, K. *Dougherty: A great man among men*, Sydney, Alpha, 1979

Feldt, E. *The Coast Watchers*, Melbourne, Oxford University Press, 1946

Gill, G.H. *Royal Australian Navy, 1939–42*, Canberra, Australian War Memorial, 1958

Gillison, D. *Royal Australian Air Force 1939–42*, Canberra, Australian War Memorial, 1962

Graeme-Evans, A.L. *Of Storms and Rainbows: The story of the men of the 2/12th Battalion AIF*, vol. 2, Hobart, 2/12th Battalion Association, 1991

Greenwood, Gordon. *Australia: A social and political history*, Sydney, Angus and Robertson, 1977

Hall, T. *New Guinea 1942–44*, Sydney, Methuen, 1981

Hammel, E. *Guadalcanal, Starvation Island*, New York, Crown, 1987

Hart, B.H. Liddell. *Thoughts on War*, London, Faber & Faber, 1943

Hartley, F.J. *Sananda Interlude*, Melbourne, The Book Depot, 1949

Hasluck, P. *The Government and the People 1939–41*, Canberra, Australian War Memorial, 1952

Hayward, E.V. *Six Years in Support Official history of 2/1st Australian Field Regiment*, Sydney, Angus and Robertson, 1959
Henderson, J. *Onward Boy Soldiers: The Battle for Milne Bay, 1942*, Perth, University of Western Australia Press, 1992
Hetherington, J. *Blamey: Controversial Soldier*, Canberra, Australian War Memorial 1973
Honner, R. 'The 39th at Isurava', *Australian Army Journal*, July 1967
—— 'This is the 39th', *The Bulletin*, 3 August 1995
Hopkins, Major-General R.N.L. *Australian Armour: A History of The Royal Australian Armoured Corps 1927–1972*, Canberra, the Australian War Memorial and the Australian Government Publishing Service, 1978
Horner, David. *Blamey: Commander-in-Chief*, Sydney, Allen & Unwin, 1998
—— (ed.), *The Commanders: Australian military leadership in the twentieth century*, Sydney, George Allen & Unwin, 1984
—— *Crisis of Command: Australian generalship and the Japanese threat, 1941–1943*, Canberra, Australian War Memorial 1978
—— *General Vasey's War*, Melbourne, Melbourne University Press, 1992
—— *High Command: Australia's struggle for an independent war strategy 1939–1945*, Sydney, Allen & Unwin, 1992
—— *Inside the War Cabinet*, Sydney, Allen & Unwin, 1996
Knightley, Phillip. *Australia: A biography of a nation*, London, Jonathan Cape, 2000
Leary, William M. *We Shall Return!: MacArthur's commanders and the defeat of Japan 1942–1945*, Lexington, the University of Kentucky, 1988
Lewin, R. *The Other Ultra*, London, Hutchinson, 1982
Lewis, D.C. 'The Plantation Dream: Developing British New Guinea and Papua 1884–1942', *Journal of Pacific History*, in Canberra, 1996
Lindsay, Patrick. *The Spirit of Kokoda: Then and Now*, Melbourne: Hardie Grant Books, 2002
Long, G. *Greece, Crete and Syria*, Canberra, Australian War Memorial, 1953
——*MacArthur: as Military Commander*, Sydney, Angus and Robertson, 1969
—— *The Six Years' War*, Canberra, Australian War Memorial, 1953
—— *To Benghazi*, Canberra, Australian War Memorial, 1953
MacArthur, Douglas. *Reminiscences*, New York, McGraw-Hill, 1964
McAulay, Lex. *Blood and Iron*, Melbourne, Hutchinson, 1991
McCarthy, D. *South-West Pacific Area—First Year*, Canberra, Australian War Memorial, 1959

McDonald, Neil. *War Cameraman: The story of Damien Parer*, Melbourne, Lothian, 1994

McDonald, Neil and Brune, Peter. *200 Shots: Damien Parer, George Silk and the Australians at war in New Guinea*, Sydney, Allen & Unwin, 1998

Manchester, W. *American Caesar, Douglas MacArthur 1880–1964*, Boston, Little, Brown and Company,1978

Maughan, *Tobruk and Alamein*, Canberra, Australian War Memorial, 1966

Mayo, Lida. *Bloody Buna*, New York, Doubleday, 1974

Milner, S. *Victory in Papua*, Washington, Office of the Chief of Military History, Department of the Army, 1957

Monash, General Sir John. *The Australian Victories in France in 1918*, Melbourne, Lothian, 1923

O'Brien, John. *Guns and Gunners: The story of the 2/5th Australian Field Regiment In World War I*, Sydney, Angus and Robertson, 1950

Paull, R.A. *Retreat from Kokoda*, Melbourne, Heinemann, 1958

Perret, Geoffrey. *Old Soldiers Never Die: The life of Douglas MacArthur*, New York, Random House, 1996

Robertson, J. and McCarthy, J. *Australian War Strategy, 1939–1945: A documentary history*, St Lucia, University of Queensland Press, 1985

Robinson, Bruce. *Record of Service*, Melbourne, Macmillan, 1944

Rogers, E.S. *New Guinea: Big Man Island*, Toronto, the Royal Ontario Museum, 1970

Rolleston, Frank. *Not a Conquering Hero*, Eton, Queensland, self-published, 1984

Rowell, S.F. *Full Circle*, Melbourne, Melbourne University Press, 1974

Rowley, C.D. *The New Guinea Villager*, Melbourne, F.W. Cheshire, 1965

Russell, W.B. *The History of the Second Fourteenth Battalion*, Sydney, Angus and Robertson, 1948

Scott, G. *The Knights of Kokoda*, Sydney, Horwitz, 1963

Slessor, Kenneth. *Poems by Kenneth Slessor*, Sydney, Angus and Robertson, 1957

Slim, Sir William. *Defeat into Victory*, London, Cassell, 1956

Souter, Gavin. *New Guinea: The last unknown*, Sydney, Angus and Robertson, 1963

Spencer, Bill. *In the Footsteps of Ghosts: With the 2/9th Battalion in the African desert and the jungles of the Pacific*, Sydney, Allen & Unwin, 1999

Steward, H.D. *Recollections of a Regimental Medical Officer*, Melbourne, Melbourne University Press, 1981

Taylor, Lance. *Snake Road: A guide to the history, people and places of the Sogeri District*, Port Moresby, Sogeri Publication, 1992

Uren, M. *A Thousand Men at War*, Melbourne, Heinemann, 1959

Waiko, John Dademo. *A Short History of Papua New Guinea*, Melbourne, Oxford University Press, 1993

Walker, Allan. S. *Clinical Problems of War*, Canberra, Australian War Memorial, 1952

—— *The Island Campaigns*, Canberra, Australian War Memorial, 1957

West, F.J. *Hubert Murray: The Australian pro-consul*, Melbourne: Oxford University Press, 1968

Wigmore, Lionel. *The Japanese Thrust*, Canberra, Australian War Memorial, 1957

THESIS

Brune, Peter. *The Australian Infantry at Milne Bay and the 18th Brigade at Buna-Sanananda 1942–43*, PhD Thesis, Flinders University, South Australia, 1998

NEWSPAPERS, MAGAZINES

The *Advertiser*

The *Age*

The *Melbourne Herald*

The *Sydney Morning Herald*

Smith's Weekly

FILM AND VIDEO

MacArthur (Part One—Destiny), (also Part Two—I Shall Return) written, produced and directed by Austin Holt, directed and co-produced by Sarah Holt

INDEX

Scope of index
This is an index of personal and place names and book titles only. A range of page numbers (e.g. 89–92) indicates that the subject is *mentioned* on each of those consecutive pages. It does not mean that the subject is the only topic discussed on those pages.